America
Past and Present

BRIEF SEVENTH EDITION

1 2 3

A
B
C
D
E
F
G

CANADA

N

45°

Olympia
Seattle
Tacoma
Spokane
WASHINGTON
Columbia R.
COASTAL RANGES
Portland
Salem
OREGON

40°

CALIFORNIA
Sacramento
San Francisco
Stockton
SIERRA
Fresno
NEVADA
Bakersfield
Los Angeles
San Diego

35°

Carson City
NEVADA
Las Vegas

30°

PACIFIC
OCEAN

120°

Boise
IDAHO
Snake R.

Helena
MONTANA
Billings

ROCKY

WYOMING

MOUNTAINS

Great
Salt Lake
Salt Lake
City
UTAH
Colorado R.

Cheyenne

Denver
COLORADO
Colorado Springs
Pueblo

ARIZONA
Phoenix Mesa
Tucson

Albuquerque
Santa Fe
NEW
MEXICO
Rio Grande
El Paso

NORTH DAKOTA
Bismarck Fargo

SOUTH DAKOTA
Pierre
Sioux Fa
Missouri R.

Missouri R.

NEBRASKA
Linco

KANSAS

Arkansas R.

Amarillo
Lubbock
Fort Wort
Red R.

OKLAH

TEXAS

Aust

Rio Grande
Sar

MEXICO

F

RUSSIA
ARCTIC OCEAN
Bering Strait
ALASKA
Yukon R.
CANADA
160°
Anchorage
60°
Bering
Sea
Gulf of Alaska
Kodiak Island
Juneau
Aleutian Islands
160° 140°

0 200 400 mi
0 200 400 km

160°
Kauai
Oahu Honolulu
PACIFIC
Molokai Maui
Lanai
OCEAN
20°
HAWAII
Hawaii

0 50 100 mi
0 50 100 km

G

1 2 3 4

America
Past and Present

BRIEF SEVENTH EDITION
VOLUME I: TO 1877

ROBERT A. DIVINE
University of Texas

T. H. BREEN
Northwestern University

GEORGE M. FREDRICKSON
Stanford University

R. HAL WILLIAMS
Southern Methodist University

ARIELA J. GROSS
University of Southern California

H. W. BRANDS
University of Texas

RANDY ROBERTS
Purdue University

PEARSON
Longman

New York   San Francisco   Boston
London   Toronto   Sydney   Tokyo   Singapore   Madrid
Mexico City   Munich   Paris   Cape Town   Hong Kong   Montreal

Executive Editor: Michael Boezi
Development Editor: Karen Helfrich
Executive Marketing Manager: Sue Westmoreland
Supplements Editor: Brian Belardi
Production Manager: Ellen MacElree
Project Coordination, Text Design, and Electronic Page Makeup: Elm Street Publishing Services, Inc.
Senior Cover Design Manager: Nancy Danahy
Cover Designer: Susan Koski Zucker
Cover and Frontispiece Images: Cover Inset: SuperStock, Inc. Large Photo: © Connie Ricca/CORBIS. All Rights
    Reserved. Frontispiece photo: The Granger Collection.
Art Studio: Maps.com and Burmar Technical Corporation
Photo Research: Julie Tesser
Senior Manufacturing Buyer: Dennis J. Para
Printer and Binder: Quebecor World/Dubuque
Cover Printer: Phoenix Color Corps.

For permission to use copyrighted material, grateful acknowledgment is made to the copyright holders on
pp. C-1–C-2, which are hereby made part of this copyright page.

Library of Congress Cataloging-in-Publication Data

America past and present / Robert A. Divine . . . [et al.].—Brief 7th ed.
    p. cm.
  Includes bibliographical references and index.
  ISBN 0-321-42180-9
    1. United States—History—Textbooks.   I. Divine, Robert A.

E178.1.A4894 2008
973—dc22
                                                                    2006050944

ISBN 0-321-42180-9 (Complete Brief Edition)
ISBN 0-321-42181-7 (Volume I)
ISBN 0-321-42182-5 (Volume II)

6 7 8 9 10—QWV—09

Brief Contents

Detailed Contents

Maps

Charts, Figures, and Tables

Features

Preface

America Past and Present, Brief Seventh Edition, is derived from the full-length America Past and Present, Eighth Edition. The Brief Seventh Edition shares the goal of its parent text: to present a clear, relevant, and balanced history of the United States as an unfolding story of national development, from the days of the earliest inhabitants to the present. The goal of the abridgement is to produce a condensation true to the original in all its dimensions—a miniaturized replica or *bonsai*, as it were—retaining the style and tone, and the interpretations, with their nuances and subtleties intact. This Brief Seventh Edition contains about two-thirds of the text of the full-length book, more than one-half of the maps, charts, and figures, and a commensurate proportion of the illustration program.

Presenting American history as the story of a nation in flux, America Past and Present, Brief Seventh Edition, goes beyond recounting the major events that have helped to shape the nation—the wars fought, the presidents elected, the treaties signed. The impact of change on human lives adds a vital dimension to the understanding of history. How did the American Revolution affect the lives of ordinary citizens? What was it like for both blacks and whites to live in a plantation society? How did the shift from an agrarian to an industrial economy affect men and women alike? What impact did technology, in the form of the automobile and the computer, have on patterns of life in the twentieth century? As the narrative explores answers to these and other questions, it blends the excitement and drama of the American experience with insights about the social, political, economic, and cultural issues that underlie it.

America Past and Present, Brief Seventh Edition, espouses no particular ideology or point of view; instead the text encourages readers to explore the American past and reach their own conclusions about its significance in their lives. And yet the text does not avoid examining controversial issues but seeks to offer balanced and reasoned judgments on such morally charged subjects as the nature of slavery and the use of nuclear weapons. Although history may rarely repeat itself, the story of the American past is relevant to the problems and dilemmas facing the American nation and the American people today.

TEXT REVISIONS

The principal revisions in America Past and Present, Brief Seventh Edition, have been undertaken with the goals of clarifying the prose and sharpening the analysis, taking account of new scholarship, and offering new perspectives. As in previous editions, the roles that women and minority groups have played in the nation's development merit particular attention. These people appear not as passive witnesses to the historical narrative but as active participants in its evolution. New and expanded material throughout the chapters includes the following:

- Chapter 3, expanded discussion of mercantilism and free markets in the seventeenth century.

- Chapter 5, new opening vignette highlighting the personal sacrifices of one family in the Revolutionary fight for liberty.

- Chapter 7, new discussion of George Washington's mastery of symbolic political power and bringing the new government to the people.

- Chapter 9, expanded discussion of Native American societies before the Indian Removal, emphasizing the cultural transformation of Southeastern Indians under pressure of contact from white settlers.

- Chapter 11, augmented discussion of paternalism and racial theories used as justification for slavery.

- Chapter 12, expanded discussions of marriage in the American middle class and experiences of childhood across class and ethnic lines in the mid-nineteenth century.

- Chapters 31 through 33 have been revised, restructured, and condensed into two chapters: Chapter 31, "To a New Conservatism, 1969–1988," and Chapter 32, "To the Twenty-first Century, 1989–2006." Although some material in the previous edition's final three chapters has been carefully trimmed to make these chapters more manageable, we have also updated content and added new sections. These enhancements include discussions of the new environmentalism of the oil shock 1970s and challenges of the new century, including the continued war in Iraq, renewed culture wars, immigration issues, and concerns about

American quality of life, particularly employment and health care. Chapter 32 begins with a new opening vignette about George H. W. Bush, the first Persian Gulf War, and the initiation of a new foreign policy in the post–Cold War era.

STRUCTURE AND FEATURES

The structure and features of *America Past and Present,* Brief Seventh Edition, are intended to stimulate student interest and to reinforce learning. Each chapter begins with a vignette that introduces the chapter themes and previews topics to be discussed. The chapter chronology includes key events covered in the chapter. The recommended readings and suggested Web sites at the end of each chapter are sources students can consult for further information on many topics. Key terms, highlighted in boldface type in the chapter text, are defined in context and in a running glossary in the text margins.

Eight essays entitled "We Americans" appear in the text, each focusing on some aspect of diversity or multiculturalism in America. Some of the "We Americans" essays explore the roles different ethnic groups have played in shaping the nation; others examine change and constancy in the American population and national ethos. The eight "We Americans" essays are:

- "Learning to Live with Diversity in the Eighteenth Century: What Is an American?" (Chapter 4)
- "Counting the People: The Federal Census of 1790" (Chapter 7)
- "Women of Southern Households" (Chapter 11)
- "The Irish in Boston, 1845–1865" (Chapter 13)
- "Hispanic America After 1848: A Case Study in Majority Rule" (Chapter 14)
- "Blacks in Blue: The Buffalo Soldiers in the West" (Chapter 17)
- "Ellis Island: Isle of Hope, Isle of Tears" (Chapter 19)
- "Unintended Consequences: The Second Great Migration" (Chapter 30)

Each "We Americans" essay now includes new "Questions for Discussion" to spark class discussion or to prompt writing assignments.

A second feature in *America Past and Present,* Brief Seventh Edition, is "A Look at the Past." These representations of material culture artifacts show students some of the variety of materials that historians use to learn about and interpret the past. Captions with the photographs include critical thinking questions that encourage students to reflect on the historical purpose and significance of the object pictured.

A new feature in this edition is "Past and Present." Each of these eight brief essays explores connections between a past event, phenomenon, or trend and a similar or related event or phenomenon in a later period. These features explore contrasts as well as similarities. The "Past and Present" essays are:

- "Politics of Fear: From the Wars of Empire to the Cold War" (Chapter 4)
- "Revolutionary Communication" (Chapter 5)
- "Evangelical Religion in Politics" (Chapter 12)
- "Anti-Immigrant Movements" (Chapter 14)
- "Connecting the World: From the Transcontinental Railroad to the World Wide Web" (Chapter 18)
- "From John D. Rockefeller to Bill Gates: Philanthropy in American Life" (Chapter 23)
- "Challenging Social Security" (Chapter 26)
- "War Strategy: Korea and Iraq" (Chapter 28)

SUPPLEMENTS FOR QUALIFIED COLLEGE ADOPTERS

Instructor Supplements

MyHistoryLab

MyHistoryLab provides students with an online package complete with the entire comprehensive electronic textbook and numerous study aids. With several hundred primary sources, many of which are assignable and  link to a gradebook, pre- and post-tests that result in an individualized study plan, and map activities with gradable quizzes, the site offers students a unique, interactive experience that brings history to life. The comprehensive site also includes original videos, images and audio clips, as well as a History Bookshelf with fifty of the most commonly assigned history books and a History Toolkit with tutorials and helpful links.

Delivered in CourseCompass™, BlackBoard™, or WebCT™, as well as in a non-course-management Web site version, MyHistoryLab is easy to use and flexible. MyHistoryLab is organized according to the table of contents of this textbook. With the course management version, instructors can create a further customized product by adding their own syllabus, content, and assignments, or they can use the materials as presented and download our comprehensive test bank.

Please see www.myhistorylab.com to learn more, or to see a demo.

Instructor's Resource Manual

Created for the full version of *America Past and Present*, this resource manual is appropriate for the Brief Seventh Edition as well. Prepared by James Walsh of Central Connecticut State University, each chapter of this resource manual contains chapter outlines, interpretative essays, anecdotes and references to biographical or primary sources, and a comprehensive summary of the text. ISBN: 0-321-48540-8.

Test Bank

This test bank contains notations indicating questions that are particularly relevant to the Brief Seventh Edition. Prepared by Denise Wright of the University of Georgia, the test bank contains more than 1200 multiple-choice, true/false, matching, and completion questions. ISBN: 0-321-21721-7.

TestGen-EQ Computerized Testing System

This flexible, easy-to-master computerized test bank on a dual-platform CD includes all of the items in the printed test bank and allows instructors to select specific questions, edit existing questions, and add their own items to create exams. Tests can be printed in several different fonts and formats and can include figures such as graphs and tables. ISBN: 0-321-48675-7.

History Digital Media Archive CD-ROM

The Digital Media Archive CD-ROM contains electronic images and interactive and static maps, along with media elements such as video. These media assets are fully customizable and ready for classroom presentation or easy downloading into your PowerPoint™ presentations or any other presentation software. ISBN: 0-321-14976-9.

Digital Media Archive, Updated Second Edition

Now on two CD-ROMs and with added content, this Digital Media Archive is an encyclopedic collection that contains dozens of narrated vignettes and videos as well as hundreds of photos and illustrations ready for use in your own PowerPoint™ presentations, course Web sites, or on-line courses. Available to qualified college adopters when bundled. ISBN 0-321-18694-X.

The American History Study Site

Students can take advantage of this online resource that supports the American history survey course. The site includes practice tests, Web links, and flash cards that cover the scope of topics covered in a typical world history classroom. Available for no additional cost at www.longmanamericanhistory.com.

PowerPoint™ Presentations

These presentations contain an average of fifteen PowerPoint™ slides for each chapter. These slides may include key points and terms for a lecture on the chapter as well as four-color slides of all maps, graphs, and charts within a particular chapter. The presentations are available for download at www.ablongman.com/irc.

Comprehensive American History Transparency Set

This collection includes more than 200 four-color American history map transparencies on subjects ranging from the first Native Americans to the end of the Cold War, covering wars, social trends, elections, immigration, and demographics. The transparencies are available for download at www.ablongman.com/irc.

Text-specific Transparency Set

Created for the full version of *America Past and Present*, this transparency set is appropriate for the Brief Seventh Edition as well. The transparencies are available for download at www.ablongman.com/irc.

For Students

MyHistoryLab

MyHistoryLab provides students with an online package complete with the entire comprehensive electronic textbook, numerous study aids, primary sources, and chapter exams. With several hundred primary sources, maps, images, videos, and  audio clips, many of which link to a gradebook, and pre- and post-tests that result in an individualized study plan, the site offers students a unique, interactive experience that brings history to life. The comprehensive site also includes a History Bookshelf with fifty of the most commonly assigned history books and a History Toolkit with tutorials and helpful links. Available for purchase at www.myhistorylab.com, or packaged with your textbook.

Study Guide and Practice Tests

Prepared by Thomas F. Jorsch of Ferris State University, each volume of the study guide begins with an introductory essay, "Skills for Studying and Learning History." Each chapter contains a summary; learning objectives; identification list; map exercises; glossary; multiple-choice, completion, and essay questions; and critical thinking exercises involving primary sources. Volume One: ISBN: 0-205-52177-0; Volume Two: ISBN: 0-205-52178-9.

VangoNotes

Study on the go with Vango Notes. Just download chapter reviews from your text and listen to them on any mp3 player. Now wherever you are—whatever you're doing—you can study by listening to the following for each chapter of your textbook:

- **Big Ideas:** Your "need to know" for each chapter

- **Practice Test:** A gut check for the Big Ideas—tells you if you need to keep studying
- **Key Terms:** Audio "flash-cards" to help you review key concepts and terms

- **Rapid Review:** A quick drill session—use it right before your test.

VangoNotes are flexible; download all the material directly to your mp3 player, or only the chapters you need. And they're efficient. Use them in your car, at the gym, walking to class, wherever. So get yours today. And get studying. Find out more, or download a chapter at www.VangoNotes.com.

Longman American History Atlas

A four-color reference tool and visual guide to American history that includes almost one hundred maps and covers the full scope of history. This Atlas is $3.00 when bundled with college adoptions. ISBN: 0-321-00486-8.

Mapping American History, **Third Edition**

This two-volume workbook, written by Sharon Bollinger of El Paso Community College, presents the basic geography of the United States and helps students place the history of the United States into spatial perspective. Available at no additional cost to qualified college adopters when bundled. Volume I: ISBN: 0-321-47559-3; Volume II: ISBN: 0-321-47560-7.

Research Navigator Guide

This guidebook includes exercises and tips on how to use the Internet to further your study of American history. It also includes an access code for Research Navigator™—the easiest way for students to start a research assignment or research paper. Research Navigator™ is composed of three exclusive databases of credible and reliable source material including EBSCO's ContentSelect™ Academic Journal Database, New York Times Search by Subject Archive, and "Best of the Web" Link Library. This comprehensive site also includes a detailed help section. ISBN: 0-205-40838-9.

A Short Guide to Writing About History, **Sixth Edition**

Richard Marius, Harvard University; Melvin E. Page, Eastern Tennessee University. This engaging and practical text helps students get beyond merely compiling dates and facts; it teaches them how to incorporate their own ideas into their papers and to tell a story about history that interests them and their peers. Covering both brief essays and the documented resource paper, the text explores the writing and researching processes, different modes of historical writing including argument, and concludes with guidelines for improving style. ISBN: 0-321-43536-2.

Study Card for American History

Colorful, affordable, and packed with useful information, Longman's Study Cards make studying easier, more efficient, and more enjoyable. Course information is distilled down to the basics, helping you quickly master the fundamentals, review a subject for understanding, or prepare for an exam. Because they're laminated for durability, you can keep these Study Cards for years to come and pull them out whenever you need a quick review. ISBN: 0-321-29232-4.

Additional Readers

Longman offers a variety of options for reading beyond the textbook, from primary and secondary sources to biographies and Penguin titles. All of these options can be packaged with the textbook at a discount to students. Here are a few Longman titles. For a complete listing of Longman readers, please go to www.ablongman.com/history.

Voices of **America Past and Present**

This two-volume collection of primary sources includes both classic and lesser-known documents describing the rich mosaic of American life from the pre-contact era to the present day. The sources, both public and private documents—ranging from letters, diary excerpts, stories, and novels, to speeches, court cases, and government reports—tell the story of American history in the words of those who lived it. Available at no additional cost to qualified college adopters when bundled. Volume I: 0-321-41161-7; Volume II: 0-321-39601-4.

Library of American Biography Series

Each of these interpretive biographies focuses on a figure whose actions and ideas significantly influenced the course of American history and national life. At the same time, each biography relates the life of its subjects to the broader theme and developments of the times. Brief and inexpensive, they are ideal for any U.S. history course. Volumes include Edmund S. Morgan, *The Puritan Dilemma: The Story of John Winthrop;* Charles W. Akers, *Abigail Adams: A Revolutionary*

American Woman; Harold C. Livesay, *Andrew Carnegie and the Rise of Big Business;* Randolph B. Campbell, *Sam Houston and the American Southwest;* Walter L. Hixson, *Charles Lindbergh: Lone Eagle;* Jack N. Rakove, *James Madison and the Creation of the American Republic;* Sam W. Haynes, *James K. Polk and the Expansionist Impulse;* and J. William T. Youngs, *Eleanor Roosevelt: A Personal and Public Life.* New additions to the series include Allan M. Winkler, *Franklin D. Roosevelt and the Making of Modern America,* Dan La Botz, *César Chávez and la Causa,* and Jules Tygiel, *Ronald Reagan and the Triumph of American Conservatism,* Second Edition.

Please see www.ablongman.com/html/lab for a complete listing.

Penguin Books

The partnership between Penguin USA and Longman Publishers offers your students a discount on many Penguin titles when they are bundled with any Longman survey text. Please see www.ablongman.com/penguin for a complete listing of titles. Available titles include the following:

Horatio Alger, Jr., *Ragged Dick*

Horatio Alger, Jr., *Struggling Upward*

Louis Auchincloss, *Woodrow Wilson*

Edward Bellamy, *Looking Backward*

Roy Blount, Jr., *Robert E. Lee*

Clayborne Carson (Editor), *Eyes on the Prize Civil Rights Reader*

Willa Cather, *My Antonia*

Willa Cather, *O Pioneers!*

Ina Chang, *A Separate Battle*

Abraham Chapman (Editor), *Black Voices*

Charles W. Chesnutt, *The Marrow of Tradition*

George Dawson, *Life Is So Good*

Alexis De Tocqueville, *Democracy in America*

Frederick Douglass, *My Bondage and My Freedom*

Frederick Douglass, *Narrative of the Life of Frederick Douglass*

W. E. B. DuBois, *Souls of Black Folk*

William Fletcher, *Rebel Private: Front and Rear*

Benjamin Franklin, *Ben Franklin: The Autobiography and Other Writings*

Nelson George, *The Death of Rhythm and Blues*

William Golding, *Lord of the Flies*

Al Gore, *Earth in the Balance*

Woody Guthrie, *Bound for Glory*

Joel Chandler Harris (Editor), *Nights with Uncle Remus*

Nathanial Hawthorne, *The Scarlet Letter*

Gordon Hunter (Editor), *Immigrant Voices*

Harriet Jacobs, *Incidents in the Life of a Slave Girl*

Thomas Jefferson, *Notes on the State of Virginia*

James Weldon Johnson, *The Autobiography of an Ex-Colored Man*

Alvin M. Josephy, *The Patriot Chiefs*

Jack Kerouac, *On the Road*

Ralph Ketcham, *The Anti-Federalist Papers and the Constitutional Convention Debates*

Martin Luther King, Jr., *Why We Can't Wait*

Julius Lester, *From Slave Ship to Freedom Road*

Ellen Levine, *Freedom's Children*

David Lewis, *The Portable Harlem Renaissance Reader*

Sinclair Lewis, *Babbitt*

Brian Macarthur, *The Penguin Book of Twentieth-Century Speeches*

James McBride, *The Color of Water*

Joe McGinniss, *The Selling of the President*

Herman Melville, *Moby-Dick*

John Stuart Mill, *On Liberty*

Arthur Miller, *Death of A Salesman*

Toni Morrison, *The Bluest Eye*

George Orwell, *1984*

George Orwell, *Animal Farm*

Samuel K. Padover, *Jefferson*

Thomas Paine, *Common Sense*

Dorothy Parker, *The Portable Dorothy Parker*

Rosa Parks, *Rosa Parks: My Story*

William L. Riordan, *Plunkitt of Tammany Hall*

Randall Robinson, *The Debt*

Upton Sinclair, *The Jungle*

John Steinbeck, *The Grapes of Wrath*

John Steinbeck, *Of Mice & Men*

John Steinbeck, *The Pear*

Harriet Beecher Stowe, *Uncle Tom's Cabin*

Sojourner Truth, *The Narrative of Sojourner Truth*

Mark Twain, *The Adventures of Huckleberry Finn*

Various, *Against Slavery*

Various, *The Classic Slave Narratives*

Various, *Colonial American Travel Narratives*

Various, *The Federalist Papers*

Rebecca Walker, *Black, White, and Jewish: Autobiography of a Shifting Self*

Booker T. Washington, *Up From Slavery*

Phyllis Wheatley, *Complete Writings*

August Wilson, *Fences*

August Wilson, *Joe Turner's Come & Gone*

Hamet L. Wilson, *Our Nig*

Acknowledgments

We extend special thanks to Professor Jeanne Whitney of Salisbury State University for her contribution in selecting images for several of the "Look at the Past" illustrations in a previous edition and writing the informative and thought-provoking captions to accompany them. We also express our gratitude to the following reviewers who gave generously of their time and knowledge to provide thoughtful evaluations and suggestions for revision of the full-length edition:

Samantha Barbas, *Chapman University*
James Baumgardner, *Carson-Newman College*
Joseph E. Bisson, *San Joaquin Delta College*
Cynthia Carter, *Florida Community College at Jacksonville*
Katherine Chavigny, *Sweet Briar College*
Cole Dawson, *Warner Pacific College*
James Denham, *Florida Southern College*
Kathleen Feely, *University of Redlands*
Jennifer Fry, *King's College*
Paul B. Hatley, *Rogers State University*
Sarah Heat, *Texas A&M University–Corpus Christi*
Ben Johnson, *Southern Arkansas University*
Carol Keller, *San Antonio College*
Elizabeth Kuebler-Wolf, *Indiana University-Purdue University, Fort Wayne*
Rick Murray, *College of the Canyons*
Carrie Pritchett, *Northeast Texas Community College*
Thomas S. Reid, *Valencia Community College*
Mark Schmellor, *Binghamton University*
C. Edward Skeen, *University of Memphis*
Ronald Spiller, *Edinboro University of Pennsylvania*
Pat Thompson, *University of Texas, San Antonio*
Stephen Tootle, *University of Northern Colorado*
Stephen Warren, *Augustana College*
Stephen Webre, *Louisiana Tech University*

Gisela R. Ables, *Houston Community College*
James Barringer, *Hillsborough Community College*
Albert Berger, *University of North Dakota*
Vincent F. Bonelli, *Bronx Community College*
John P. Boubel, *Bethany Lutheran College*
John Braeman, *University of Nebraska*
Susan Meyer Butler, *Cerritos College*
William R. Cario, *Concordia University*
Simon Cordery, *Monmouth College*
Sandra McGee Deutsch, *University of Texas, El Paso*
Alan L. Golden, *Lock Haven University*
Gregory L. Goodwin, *Bakersfield College*
James Graham, *Carl Sandburg College*
Robert Hilderbrand, *University of South Dakota*
Howard Jablon, *Purdue University, North Central*
Chana Kai, *Indiana University*
Ted Kallman, *San Joaquin Delta College*
Lawrence F. Kohl, *University of Alabama*
Armand S. LaPorin, *State University College*
Margaret Lowe, *Bridgewater State College*
Jonathan Lurie, *Rutgers University*
James E. McMillan, *New Mexico State University*
Manuel F. Medrano, *University of Texas, Brownsville*
Douglas C. Oliver, *Skyline College*
Marguerite Renner, *Glendale Community College*
John Ricks, *Middle Georgia College*
Rob Schorman, *Miami University–Middletown*
Megan Seaholm, *University of Texas*
Charles J. Shindo, *Louisiana State University*
William P. Short, Jr., *Cecil Community College*
Sheila Skemp, *University of Mississippi*
Grant W. Smart, *Salt Lake Community College*
Kay C. Starnes, *University of North Carolina, Charlotte*
Roger Tate, *Somerset Community College*
Jason Tetzloff, *Defiance College*
Kenneth Townsend, *Coastal Carolina University*
Dean Wolfe, *Kingwood College*

THE AUTHORS

We also acknowledge with gratitude the contributions of reviewers of previous editions of this text. Their suggestions, too, have helped shape this book.

About the Authors

ROBERT A. DIVINE

Robert A. Divine, George W. Littlefield Professor Emeritus in American History at the University of Texas at Austin, received his Ph.D. from Yale University in 1954. A specialist in American diplomatic history, he taught from 1954 to 1996 at the University of Texas, where he was honored by both the student association and the graduate school for teaching excellence. His extensive published work includes *The Illusion of Neutrality* (1962); *Second Chance: The Triumph of Internationalism in America During World War II* (1967); and *Blowing on the Wind* (1978). His most recent work is *Perpetual War for Perpetual Peace* (2000), a comparative analysis of twentieth-century American wars. He is also the author of *Eisenhower and the Cold War* (1981) and editor of three volumes of essays on the presidency of Lyndon Johnson. His book *The* Sputnik *Challenge* (1993) won the Eugene E. Emme Astronautical Literature Award for 1993. He has been a fellow at the Center for Advanced Study in the Behavioral Sciences and has given the Albert Shaw Lectures in Diplomatic History at Johns Hopkins University.

T. H. BREEN

T. H. Breen, William Smith Mason Professor of American History at Northwestern University, received his Ph.D. from Yale University in 1968. He has taught at Northwestern since 1970. Breen's major books include *The Character of the Good Ruler: A Study of Puritan Political Ideas in New England* (1974); *Puritans and Adventurers: Change and Persistence in Early America* (1980); *Tobacco Culture: The Mentality of the Great Tidewater Planters on the Eve of Revolution* (1985); and, with Stephen Innes of the University of Virginia, *"Myne Owne Ground": Race and Freedom on Virginia's Eastern Shore* (1980). His *Imagining the Past* (1989) won the 1990 Historic Preservation Book Award. His most recent book is *Marketplace of Revolution: How Consumer Politics Shaped American Independence* (2004). In addition to receiving several awards for outstanding teaching at Northwestern, Breen has been the recipient of research grants from the American Council of Learned Societies, the Guggenheim Foundation, the Institute for Advanced Study (Princeton), the National Humanities Center, and the Huntington Library. He has served as the Fowler Hamilton Fellow at Christ Church, Oxford University (1987–1988), the Pitt Professor of American History and Institutions, Cambridge University (1990–1991), and the Harmsworth Professor of American History at Oxford University (2000–2001), and was a recipient of the Humboldt Prize (Germany). He is currently completing a book tentatively entitled, *America's Insurgency: The People's Revolution, 1774–1776.*

GEORGE M. FREDRICKSON

George M. Fredrickson is Edgar E. Robinson Professor Emeritus of United States History at Stanford University. He is the author or editor of several books, including *The Inner Civil War* (1965), *The Black Image in the White Mind* (1971), and *White Supremacy: A Comparative Study in American and South African History* (1981), which won both the Ralph Waldo Emerson Award from Phi Beta Kappa and the Merle Curti Award from the Organization of American Historians. His most recent books are *Black Liberation: A Comparative History of Black Ideologies in the United States and South Africa* (1995), *The Comparative Imagination: Racism, Nationalism, and Social Movements* (1997), and *Racism: A Short History* (2002). He received his A.B. and Ph.D. from Harvard and has been the recipient of a Guggenheim Fellowship, two National Endowment for the Humanities senior fellowships, and a fellowship from the Center for Advanced Studies in the Behavioral Sciences. Before coming to Stanford in 1984, he taught at Northwestern. He has also served as Fulbright lecturer in American History at Moscow University and as the Harmsworth Professor of American History at Oxford. He served as president of the Organization of American Historians in 1997–1998.

R. HAL WILLIAMS

R. Hal Williams is professor of history at Southern Methodist University. He received his A.B. from Princeton University in 1963 and his Ph.D. from Yale University in 1968. His books include *The Democratic Party and California Politics, 1880–1896* (1973), *Years of Decision: American Politics in the 1890s* (1978), and *The Manhattan Project: A Documentary Introduction to the Atomic Age* (1990). A specialist in American political history, he taught at Yale University from 1968 to 1975 and came to SMU in 1975 as chair of the Department of History. From 1980 to 1988, he served as dean of Dedman College, the school of humanities and sciences, at SMU, where he is currently dean of Research and Graduate Studies. In 1980, he was a visiting professor at University College, Oxford University. Williams has received grants from the American Philosophical Society and the National Endowment for the Humanities, and has served on the Texas Committee for the Humanities. He is currently working on a study of the presidential election of 1896 and a biography of James G. Blaine, the late-nineteenth-century speaker of the House, secretary of state, and Republican presidential candidate.

H. W. BRANDS

H. W. Brands is the Dickson Allen Anderson Centennial Professor of History at the University of Texas at Austin. He is the author of numerous works of history and international affairs, including *The Devil We Knew: Americans and the Cold War* (1993), *Into the Labyrinth: The United States and the Middle East* (1994), *The Reckless Decade: America in the 1890s* (1995), *TR: The Last Romantic* (a biography of Theodore Roosevelt) (1997), *What America Owes the World: The Struggle for the Soul of Foreign Policy* (1998), *The First American: The Life and Times of Benjamin Franklin* (2000), *The Strange Death of American Liberalism* (2001), *The Age of Gold: The California Gold Rush and the New American Dream* (2002), *Woodrow Wilson* (2003), and *Andrew Jackson* (2005). His writing has received critical and popular acclaim; *The First American* was a finalist for the Pulitzer Prize and a national best-seller. He lectures frequently across North America and in Europe. His essays and reviews have appeared in the *New York Times,* the *Wall Street Journal,* the *Washington Post,* the *Los Angeles Times,* and *Atlantic Monthly.* He is a regular guest on radio and television, and has participated in several historical documentary films.

ARIELA J. GROSS

Ariela J. Gross is professor of law and history at the University of Southern California. She received her B.A. from Harvard University, her J.D. from Stanford Law School, and her Ph.D. from Stanford University. She is the author of *Double Character: Slavery and Mastery in the Antebellum Southern Courtroom* (2000) and numerous law review articles and book chapters, including "'Caucasian Cloak': Mexican Americans and the Politics of Whiteness in the Twentieth-Century Southwest" in *Georgetown Law Journal* (2006). Her current work in progress, *What Blood Won't Tell: Racial Identity on Trial in America,* to be published by Farrar, Straus & Giroux, is supported by fellowships from the Guggenheim Foundation, the National Endowment for the Humanities, and the American Council for Learned Societies.

RANDY ROBERTS

Randy Roberts earned his Ph.D. from Louisiana State University. His areas of special interest include modern U.S. history and the history of sports and films in America. He is a faculty member at Purdue University where he has won the Murphy Award for outstanding teaching, the Teacher of the Year Award, and the Society of Professional Journalists Teacher of the Year Award. The books he has authored or co-authored include *Jack Dempsey: The Manassa Mauler* (1979, expanded ed., 1984), *Papa Jack: Jack Johnson and the Era of White Hopes* (1983), *Heavy Justice: The State of Indiana vs. Michael G. Tyson* (1994), *My Lai: A Brief History with Documents* (1998), *John Wayne: American* (1995), *Where the Domino Fell: America in Vietnam, 1945–1990* (1990, rev. ed., 1996), *Winning Is the Only Thing: Sports in America Since 1945* (1989), *Pittsburg Sports: Stories from the Steel City* (2000), and *A Line in the Sand: The Alamo in Blood and Memory* (2001). He edited *The Rock, The Curse, and The Hub: A Random History of Boston Sports* (2005). Roberts serves as co-editor of the Sports and Society series, University of Illinois Press, and is on the editorial board of the *Journal of Sports History.*

America
Past and Present

Chapter 1

New World Encounters

Clash of Cultures:
Interpreting Murder in Early Maryland

New World conquest sparked unexpected, often embarrassing contests over the alleged superiority of European culture. Not surprisingly, the colonizers insisted they brought the benefits of civilization to the primitive and savage peoples of North America. Native Americans never shared that perspective, voicing a strong preference for their own values and institutions. In early seventeenth-century Maryland the struggle over cultural superiority turned dramatically on how best to punish the crime of murder, an issue about which both Native Americans and Europeans had firm opinions.

The actual events that occurred at Captain William Claiborne's trading post in 1635 may never be known. Surviving records indicate that several young Native American males identified as Wicomess Indians apparently traveled to Claiborne's on business, but to their great annoyance, they found the proprietor entertaining Susquehannock Indians, their most hated enemies. The situation deteriorated rapidly after the Susquehannock men ridiculed the Wicomess youths. Unwilling to endure public humiliation, the Wicomess group later ambushed the Susquehannock men, killing five, and then returned to the trading post where they murdered three Englishmen.

Wicomess leaders realized immediately that something had to be done. They dispatched a trusted messenger to inform the governor of Maryland that they intended "to offer satisfaction for the harm . . . done to the English." The murder of the Susquehannock Indians was another matter, best addressed by the Native Americans themselves. The governor praised the Wicomess for coming forward, announcing that "I expect that those men, who have done this outrage, should be delivered unto me, to do with them as I shall think fit." The Wicomess spokesman was dumbfounded. The governor surely did not understand basic Native American legal procedure. "It is the matter amongst us Indians, that if any such like accident happens," he explained, "we do redeem the life of a man that is so slain with 100 Arms length of *Roanoke* (which is a sort of Beads that they make, and use for money.)" The governor's demand for prisoners seemed doubly impertinent, "since you [English settlers] are here strangers, and coming into our Country, you should rather conform your selves to the Customs of our Country, than impose yours upon us." At this point the governor hastily ended the conversation, perhaps uncomfortably aware that if the legal tables had been turned and the murders had been committed in England, he would be the one loudly defending "the Customs of our Country."

Europeans sailing in the wake of Admiral Christopher Columbus constructed a narrative of superiority that survived long after the Wicomess had been dispersed—a fate that befell them in the late seventeenth century. The story recounted first in Europe and then in the United States depicted heroic adventurers, missionaries, and soldiers sharing Western civilization with the peoples of the New World and opening a vast virgin land to economic development. The familiar tale celebrated material progress, the inevitable spread of European values, and the taming of frontiers.

That narrative of events no longer provides an adequate explanation for European conquest and settlement. It is not so much wrong as partisan, incomplete, and even offensive. History recounted from the perspective of the victors inevitably silences the voices of the victims, the peoples who, in the victors' view, foolishly resisted economic and technological progress. Heroic tales of the advance of Western values only serve to deflect modern attention away from the rich cultural and racial diversity that characterized North American societies. More disturbing, traditional tales of European conquest also obscure the sufferings of the millions of Native Americans, as well as huge numbers of Africans sold as slaves in the New World.

By placing these complex, often unsettling, experiences within an interpretive framework of *creative adaptations*—rather than of *exploration* or *settlement*—progress is made in recapturing the full human dimensions of conquest and resistance. While the New World often witnessed tragic violence and systematic betrayal, it allowed ordinary people of three different races and many different ethnic identities opportunities to shape their own lives as best they could within diverse, often hostile environments. It should be remembered that neither Native Americans nor Africans were passive victims of European exploitation. Within their own families and communities they made choices, sometimes rebelling, sometimes accommodating, but always trying to make sense in terms of their own cultures of what they were experiencing. Of course, that was precisely what the Wicomess messenger tried to tell the governor of Maryland.

NATIVE AMERICAN HISTORIES BEFORE CONQUEST

The peopling of North America did not begin with Columbus's arrival in 1492. Although Spanish invaders proclaimed the discovery of a "New World," they really brought into contact three worlds—Europe, Africa, and America—that in the fifteenth century were already old. Indeed, the first migrants reached the North American continent some fifteen to twenty thousand years ago.

Environmental conditions played a major role in this story. Twenty thousand years ago, the earth's climate was considerably colder than it is today. Huge glaciers, often more than a mile thick, extended as far south as the present states of Illinois and Ohio and covered broad sections of western Canada. Much of the world's moisture was transformed into ice, and the oceans dropped hundreds of feet below their current levels. The receding waters created a land bridge connecting Asia and North America, a region now submerged beneath the Bering Sea that modern archaeologists have named Beringia.

Even at the height of the last ice age, much of the far North remained free of glaciers. Small bands of spear-throwing Paleo-Indians pursued giant mammals— woolly mammoths and mastodons, for example—across Beringia. Because these migrations took place over a long period of time and involved small, independent bands of highly nomadic people, the Paleo-Indians never developed a common identity. Each group focused on its own immediate survival, adjusting to the opportunities presented by various microenvironments.

The Environmental Challenge: Food, Climate, and Culture

Some twelve thousand years ago global warming substantially reduced the glaciers, allowing nomadic hunters to pour into the heart of North America. Within just a few thousand years, Native Americans had reached the southern tip of South America. Blessed with a seemingly inexhaustible supply of meat, the early migrants experienced rapid population growth. Archaeologists have discovered that this sudden expansion of human population coincided with the loss of scores of large mammals. Some archaeologists have suggested that the Paleo-Indian hunters bear responsibility for the mass extinction of so many animals. It is more probable that climatic warming put the large animals under severe stress, and the early humans simply contributed to an ecological process over which they had little control.

The Indian peoples adjusted to the changing environmental conditions. Dispersing across the North American continent, they found new food sources, such as smaller mammals, fish, nuts, and berries. About five thousand years ago, they discovered how to cultivate certain plants. The peoples living in the Southwest acquired cultivation skills long before the bands living along the Atlantic coast as knowledge of maize (corn), squash, and beans spread north from central Mexico. The shift to basic crops—a transformation that is sometimes termed the **Agricultural Revolution**—profoundly altered Native American societies. Freed from the insecurity of an existence based solely on hunting and gathering, Native Americans began settling in permanent villages. They also began to produce ceramics, a valuable technology for the storage of grain. As the food supply increased, the Native American population greatly expanded, especially in the Southwest and in the Mississippi Valley.

Agricultural Revolution The gradual shift from hunting and gathering to cultivating basic food crops that occurred worldwide from 7000 to 9000 years ago.

Mysterious Disappearances

Several magnificent sites in North America provide powerful testimony to the cultural and social achievements of native peoples before European conquest. One of the more impressive is Chaco Canyon on the San Juan River in present-day New Mexico. The massive pueblo was the center of Anasazi culture, serving both political and religious functions, and it is estimated that its complex structures may have housed as many as fifteen thousand people. The Anasazi sustained their agriculture through a huge, technologically sophisticated network of irrigation canals that carried water long distances. They also constructed a transportation system connecting Chaco Canyon by road to more than seventy outlying villages.

Equally impressive urban centers developed throughout the Ohio and Mississippi Valleys. In present-day Ohio, the Adena and Hopewell peoples—names assigned by archaeologists to distinguish differences in material culture—built large ceremonial mounds, where they buried the families of local elites. Around A.D. 1000, the groups gave way to the Mississippian culture, a loose collection of communities along the Mississippi River from Louisiana to Illinois that shared similar technologies and beliefs. Cahokia, a huge fortification and ceremonial site in Illinois that originally rose high above the

A Look at the Past

Effigy Jar

Clay effigy jars reveal the complexity of Mississippian culture. Members of the culture built large earthen temple mounds, practiced elaborate burials, and made clay jars depicting the faces of respected dead members. ✴ What do these customs, particularly the effigy jars, reveal about the Mississippian attitude toward death?

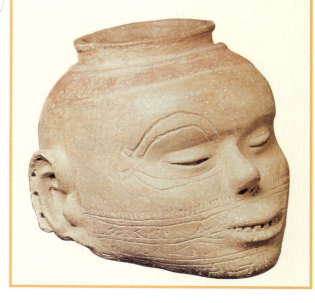

river and supported a population of almost twenty thousand, represented the greatest achievement of the Mississippian peoples.

Recent research reveals that Native American peoples did not isolate themselves in their own communities. Over the millennia they developed different cultural and social practices, and more than three hundred separate languages had evolved in North America before European conquest. Members of different groups traded goods over extremely long distances. Burial mounds in the Ohio Valley, for example, have yielded obsidian from western Wyoming, shells from Florida, mica quarried in North Carolina and Tennessee, and copper from near Lake Superior.

Yet however advanced the Native American cultures of the southwest and Mississippi Valley may have been, both cultures disappeared rather mysteriously just before the arrival of the Europeans. No one knows what caused the disappearances. Some scholars have suggested that climatic changes and continuing population growth affected food supplies; others insist that chronic warfare destabilized the social order. Still others argue that diseases carried to the New World by the first European adventurers ravaged the cultures. No matter what the explanation, modern commentators agree that the breakdown of Mississippian culture caused smaller bands to disperse, construct new identities, and establish different political structures. These were the peoples who encountered the first European arrivals along the Atlantic Coast.

Aztec Dominance

The stability resulting from the Agricultural Revolution allowed the Indians of Mexico and Central America to structure their societies in more complex ways. Like the Incas who lived in what is now Peru, the Mayan and Toltec peoples of Central Mexico built vast cities, formed government bureaucracies that dominated large tributary populations, and developed hieroglyphic writing as well as an accurate solar calendar.

Not long before Columbus began his voyage across the Atlantic, the Aztec, an aggressive, warlike people, swept through the Valley of Mexico, conquering the great cities of their enemies. Aztec warriors ruled by force, reducing defeated rivals to tributary status. In 1519, the Aztec's main ceremonial center, Tenochtitlán, contained as many as 250,000 people as compared with only 50,000 in Seville, the port from which the early Spaniards had sailed. Elaborate human sacrifice associated with Huitzilopochtli, the Aztec sun god, horrified Europeans, who apparently did not find the savagery of their own civilization so objectionable. The Aztec ritual killings were connected to the agricultural cycle, and the Indians believed the blood of their victims possessed extraordinary fertility powers.

Eastern Woodland Cultures

Indians living in the northeast region along the Atlantic coast, who numbered less than a million at the time of conquest, generally supplemented farming with seasonal hunting and gathering. Most belonged to what ethnographers term the Eastern Woodland cultures. Small bands formed villages during the warm summer months. The women cultivated maize and other crops while the men hunted and fished. During the winter, difficulties associated with feeding so many people forced the communities to disperse. Each family lived off the land as best it could.

Seventeenth-century English settlers were most likely to have encountered the Algonquian-speaking peoples who occupied much of the territory along the Atlantic Coast from North Carolina to Maine. Included in this large linguistic group were the Powhatan of Tidewater Virginia, the Narragansett of Rhode Island, and the Abenaki of northern New England.

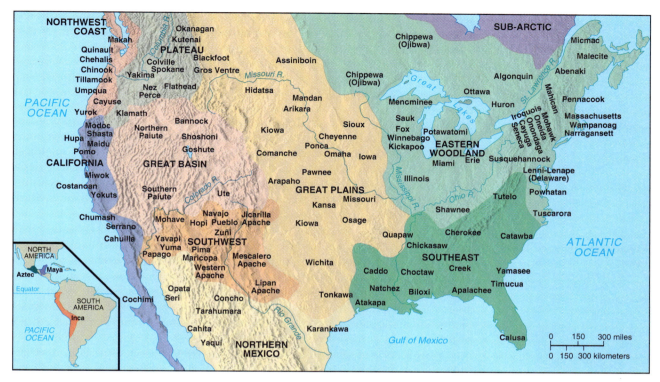

THE FIRST AMERICANS: LOCATION OF MAJOR INDIAN GROUPS AND CULTURE AREAS IN THE 1600s   *Native Americans had complex social structures and religious systems and a well-developed agricultural technology when they came into initial contact with Europeans.* ■

Despite common linguistic roots, the scattered Algonquian communities would have found communication extremely difficult because they had developed very different dialects. Furthermore, linguistic ties had little effect on Indian politics. Algonquian groups who lived in different regions, exploited different resources, and spoke different dialects did not develop strong ties of mutual identity. When their own interests were involved, they were more than willing to ally themselves with Europeans against other Algonquian speakers. Divisions among Indian groups would in time facilitate European conquest.

However divided the Indians of eastern North America may have been, they shared many cultural values and assumptions. Most Native Americans, for example, defined their place in society through kinship. Such personal bonds determined the character of economic and political relations. The farming bands living in areas eventually claimed by England were often matrilineal, which meant in effect that women owned the planting fields and houses, maintained tribal customs, and had a role in tribal government. The native communities of Canada and the northern Great Lakes were more likely to be patrilineal. In these groups, men owned the hunting grounds that the family needed to survive.

Eastern Woodland communities organized diplomacy, trade, and war around reciprocal relationships that impressed Europeans as being remarkably democratic. Chains of native authority were loosely structured. Native leaders were accomplished public speakers because persuasive rhetoric was often their only effective source of power. It required considerable oratorical skill for an Indian leader to persuade independent-minded warriors to support a certain policy.

Before the arrival of the Europeans, Indian wars were seldom very lethal. Fatalities, when they did occur, sparked cycles of revenge. Young warriors attacked neighboring bands largely to exact revenge for a previous insult or the death of a relative, or to secure captives. Some captives were tortured to death; others were adopted into the community as replacements for fallen relatives.

A WORLD TRANSFORMED

The arrival of Europeans on the North American continent profoundly altered Native American cultures. Indian villages located on the Atlantic Coast came under severe pressure almost immediately; inland groups had more time to adjust. Wherever they lived, however, Indians discovered that conquest strained traditional ways of life, and as daily patterns of experience changed almost beyond recognition, native peoples had to devise new ways to survive in physical and social environments that eroded tradition.

Cultural change was not the only effect of Native Americans' contact with Europeans. The ecological transformation, known as the **Columbian Exchange,** profoundly affected both groups of people. Some aspects of the exchange were beneficial. Europeans introduced into the Americas new plants—bananas, oranges, and sugar, for example—and animals—pigs, sheep, cattle, and especially horses—that altered the diet, economy, and way of life for the native peoples. Native American plants and foods, such as maize, squash, tomatoes, and potatoes, proved equally transforming in Europe.

Other aspects of the Columbian Exchange were far more destructive, especially for Native Americans. The most immediate biological consequence of contact between Europeans and Indians was the transfer of disease. Native Americans lacked natural immunity to many common European diseases and when exposed to influenza, typhus, measles, and especially smallpox, they died by the millions.

Columbian Exchange The exchange of plants, animals, culture, and diseases between Europe and the Americas from first contact throughout the era of exploration.

Cultural Negotiations

Native Americans were not passive victims of forces beyond their control. So long as they remained healthy, they held their own in the early exchanges, and although they eagerly accepted certain trade goods, they generally resisted other aspects of European cultures. The earliest recorded contacts between Indians and explorers suggest curiosity and surprise rather than hostility. A Southeastern Indian who encountered Hernando de Soto in 1540 expressed awe (at least that is what a Spanish witness recorded): "The things that seldom happen bring astonishment. Think, then, what must be the effect on me and mine, the sight of you and your people, whom we have at no time seen . . . things so altogether new, as to strike awe and terror to our hearts."

What Indians desired most was peaceful trade. The earliest French explorers reported that natives waved from shore, urging the Europeans to exchange metal items for beaver skins. In fact, the Indians did not perceive themselves at a disadvantage in these dealings. They could readily see the technological advantage of guns over bows and arrows. Metal knives made daily tasks much easier. To acquire such goods they traded pelts, which to them seemed in abundant supply. "The English have no sense," one Indian informed a French priest. "They give us twenty knives like this for one Beaver skin."

Trading sessions along the eastern frontier were really cultural seminars. The Europeans tried to make sense out of Indian cultures, and although they may have called the natives "savages," they quickly discovered that the Indians drove hard bargains. They demanded gifts; they set the time and place of trade. Indians used the occasions to study the newcomers. They formed opinions about the Europeans, some flattering, some less so, but they never concluded from their observations that Indian culture was inferior to that of the colonizers.

For Europeans, communicating with the Indians was always an ordeal. The invaders reported having gained deep insight into Native American cultures through sign languages. How much accurate information explorers and traders took from these crude improvised exchanges is a matter of conjecture. In the absence of meaningful conversation, Europeans often concluded that the Indians held them in high regard, perhaps seeing the newcomers as gods. Sometimes the adventurers did not even try to communicate, assuming from superficial observation— as did the sixteenth-century explorer Giovanni da Verrazzano— "that they have no religion, and that they live in absolute freedom, and that everything they do proceeds from Ignorance."

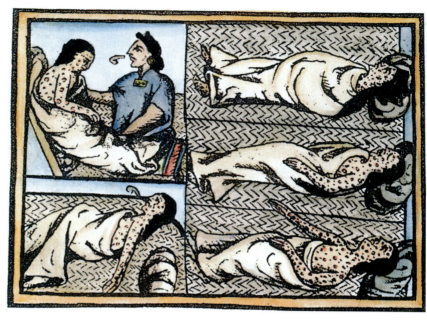

■ As Native Americans were exposed to common Old World diseases, particularly smallpox, they died by the millions. ■

Ethnocentric Europeans tried repeatedly to "civilize" the Indians. In practice that meant persuading natives to dress like the colonists, attend white schools, live in permanent structures, and, most important, accept Christianity. The Indians listened more or less patiently, but in the end they usually rejected European values. Although some Indians accepted Christianity, most paid it lip service or found it irrelevant to their needs. As one Huron told a French priest, "It would be useless for me to repent having sinned, seeing that I never have sinned."

Among some Indian groups, gender figured prominently in a person's willingness to convert to Christianity. Native men who traded pelts for European goods had more frequent contact with Europeans, and they proved more receptive to the arguments of missionaries. But native women jealously guarded traditional culture, a system that often sanctioned polygamy—a husband having several wives—and gave women substantial authority over the distribution of food within the village. French Jesuit missionaries insisted on monogamous marriages, an institution based on Christian values but that made little sense in Indian societies where constant warfare against the Europeans killed off large numbers of young males and increasingly left native women without sufficient marriage partners.

Even matrimony seldom eroded the Indians' attachment to their own customs. When Native Americans and Europeans married, the European partner usually chose to live among the Indians. Impatient settlers who regarded the Indians simply as an obstruction to progress sometimes developed more coercive methods, such as enslavement, to achieve cultural conversion. Again, from the European perspective, the results were disappointing. Indian slaves ran away or died. In either case, they did not become European.

Threats to Survival: Trade and Disease

Over time, cooperative encounters between Native Americans and Europeans became less frequent. The Europeans found it almost impossible to understand the Indians' relation to the land and other natural resources. English planters cleared the forests and fenced the fields and, in the process, radically altered the ecological systems on which the Indians depended. The European system of land use inevitably reduced the supply of deer and other animals essential to traditional native cultures.

Trade, too, came to threaten Native Americans' survival. The Indians welcomed European commerce, but like so many consumers throughout recorded history, they discovered that the objects they most desired led them into debt. To pay for the goods, the Indians hunted more aggressively and so further reduced the population of fur-bearing animals.

Commerce affected Indian survival in other ways. After several disastrous wars—the Yamasee War in South Carolina in 1715, for example—the natives learned that demonstrations of force usually resulted in the suspension of normal trade, on which the Indians had grown quite dependent for guns and ammunition, among other things.

It was disease, however, that ultimately brought disaster to many North American tribes. European adventurers exposed Indians to bacteria and viruses to which they had no natural immunity. Smallpox, measles, and influenza decimated the Native American population. Other diseases such as alcoholism took a terrible toll.

Within a generation of initial contact with Europeans, the Carib, who gave the Caribbean its name, were virtually extinct. The Algonquian communities of New England experienced appalling rates of death. Historical demographers now estimate that some tribes suffered a 90 to 95 percent population loss within the first century of European contact. The population of the Arawak of Santo Domingo, for example, dropped from about 3,770,000 in 1496 to only 125 in 1570. The death of so many Indians decreased the supply of indigenous laborers, whom the Europeans needed to work the mines and cultivate staple crops such as sugar and tobacco. The decimation of native populations may have persuaded colonists throughout the New World to seek a substitute labor force in Africa. Indeed, the enslavement of blacks has been described as an effort by Europeans to "repopulate" the New World.

Some native peoples, such as the Iroquois, who lived a long way from the coast and thus had more time to adjust to the challenge, withstood the crisis better than did those who immediately confronted the Europeans. Refugee Indians from the hardest hit eastern communities were absorbed into healthier western groups. However horrific the crisis may have been, it demonstrated how much the environment—a source of opportunity as well as devastation—shaped human encounters throughout the New World.

WEST AFRICA: ANCIENT AND COMPLEX SOCIETIES

During the era of the European slave trade, a number of myths about sub-Saharan Africa were propagated. Europeans maintained that the sub-Saharan Africans lived simple, isolated lives. Indeed, some scholars still depict the vast region stretching from the Senegal River south to modern Angola as a single cultural unit, as if at one time all the men and women living there had shared a common set of political, religious, and social values.

Such was not the case. Sub-Saharan West Africa was rich in political, religious, and cultural diversity. Centuries earlier, the Muslim religion had slowly spread into black Africa, and although many West Africans resisted the Islamic faith, it was widely accepted in the Senegal Valley. The Muslim traders from North Africa and the Middle East who introduced their religion to West Africans also established sophisticated trade networks that linked the villagers of Senegambia with the urban centers of northwestern Africa—Tangier, Algiers, Tunis, and Tripoli. Great camel caravans regularly crossed the Sahara carrying trade goods, which were exchanged for gold and slaves.

West Africans spoke many languages and organized themselves into diverse political systems. As in Europe, kingdoms rose and fell, and when the first European traders arrived, Mali, Benin, and Kongo were among the major states. Other Africans lived in stateless societies organized along lineage structures. But whatever the form of government, men and women found their primary social identity within well-defined lineage groups, which consisted of persons claiming descent from a common ancestor. In these lineage groups, the clan elders made the important economic and social decisions, from who should receive land to who might take a wife. These communities were usually self-sufficient, producing both food and trade goods.

The first Europeans to reach the West African coast by sail were the Portuguese. In the fifteenth century, they journeyed to Africa in search of gold and slaves. Africans were willing partners in the commerce but insisted that Europeans respect their trade regulations. They required the Europeans to pay tolls and other fees and restricted the foreign traders to conducting their business in small forts or castles located at the mouths of the major rivers. Local merchants acquired slaves and gold in the interior and transported them to the coast, where they were exchanged for European goods. Strong African armies and deadly diseases prevented Europeans from moving into the interior regions of Africa.

Even before Europeans colonized the New World, the Portuguese were purchasing almost a thousand slaves a year on the West African coast and sending them to Portuguese and Spanish island plantations across the Atlantic. Current estimates are that approximately 10.7 million Africans were taken to the New World as slaves. The slave trade was so extensive that during every year between 1650 and 1831, more Africans than Europeans relocated to the Americas. As one historian noted, "In terms of immigration alone . . . America was an extension of Africa rather than Europe until late in the nineteenth century."

■ *Artists in West Africa depicted the European traders who arrived in search of gold and slaves. This sixteenth-century Benin bronze relief sculpture portrays two Portuguese men.* ■

■ *Local African rulers allowed European traders to build compounds along the West African coast. Constructed to expedite the slave trade, each of these so-called slave factories served a different European interest. Cape Coast Castle, which changed hands several times as rival nations fought for its control, became one of the largest slave-trading posts in the world after the British captured and reinforced it in 1665.* ■

EUROPE ON THE EVE OF CONQUEST

In ancient times, points west had an almost mythical appeal among people living along the shores of the Mediterranean Sea. Classical writers speculated about the fate of the legendary Atlantis, a great civilization that had mysteriously sunk beneath the ocean waves. In the fifth century A.D., an intrepid Irish monk, Saint Brendan, reported finding enchanted islands far out in the Atlantic where he also met a talking whale. Such stories aroused curiosity but proved difficult to verify.

About A.D. 1000, Scandinavian seafarers known as Norsemen or Vikings actually established settlements in the New World. In the year 984, a band of Vikings led by Eric the Red sailed west from Iceland to a large island in the North Atlantic, which Eric inappropriately named Greenland in an effort to attract colonists to the icebound region. A few years later, Eric's son, Leif, pushed even farther west to northern Newfoundland. Poor communications, hostile natives, and political upheavals at home, however, made maintenance of these distant outposts impossible. The Vikings' adventures were not widely known; when Columbus set out on his great voyage in 1492, he was most likely unaware of these earlier exploits.

Building New Nation-States

The Viking achievement went unnoticed partly because other Europeans were not prepared to sponsor transatlantic exploration and settlement. Medieval kingdoms were loosely organized, and for several centuries, fierce provincial loyalties, widespread ignorance of classical learning, and dreadful plagues such as the Black Death discouraged people from thinking about the world beyond their villages.

In the fifteenth century, these conditions began to change. The expansion of commerce, a more imaginative outlook fostered by the European cultural awakening and humanistic movement known as the **Renaissance,** and population growth after 1450 contributed to the exploration impulse. Land became more expensive, and landowners prospered. Demands from wealthy landlords for such luxury goods as spices and jewels, obtainable only in distant ports, introduced powerful new incentives for exploration and trade.

Renaissance A cultural awakening that began in Italy and spread throughout Europe in the fifteenth and sixteenth centuries.

This period also witnessed the victory of the "new monarchs" over feudal nobles; political authority was centralized. The changes came slowly—and in numerous areas, violently—but wherever they occurred, the results altered traditional political relationships between the nobility and the crown, between the citizen and the state. The new rulers recruited national armies and paid for them with national taxes. These rulers could be despotic, but they usually restored a measure of peace to communities tired of chronic feudal war.

The story was the same throughout most of western Europe. Henry VII in England, Louis XI in France, and Ferdinand of Aragon and Isabella of Castile in Spain forged strong nations from weak kingdoms. If these political changes had not occurred, the major European countries could not possibly have generated the financial and military resources necessary for worldwide exploration. Indeed, the formation of aggressive nation-states prepared the way for the later wars of empire.

During this period, naval innovators revolutionized ship design and technology. Before the fifteenth century, the ships that plied the Mediterranean were clumsy and slow. But by the time Columbus sailed from Spain, they were faster, more maneuverable, and less expensive to operate. Most important of all was a new type of rigging developed by the Arabs, the lateen sail, which allowed large ships to sail into the wind, permitting transatlantic travel and difficult maneuvers along the rocky, uncharted coasts of North America. By the end of the fifteenth century, seafarers set sail with a new sense of confidence.

The final prerequisite to exploration was knowledge. The rediscovery of classical texts and maps in the humanistic Renaissance of the fifteenth century helped stimulate fresh investigation of the globe. And because of the invention of the printing press in the 1430s, this new knowledge could spread across Europe. The printing press opened the European mind to exciting possibilities that had only been dimly perceived when the Vikings sailed the North Atlantic.

IMAGINING A NEW WORLD

In the early fifteenth century, Spain was politically divided, its people were poor, and its harbors were second-rate. There was little to indicate that this land would take the lead in conquering the New World. But in the early sixteenth century, Spain came alive. The union of Ferdinand and Isabella sparked a drive for political consolidation that, owing to the monarchs' militant Catholicism, took on the characteristics of a religious crusade. The new monarchs waged a victorious war against the Muslim states in southern Spain, which ended in 1492 when Granada, the last Muslim stronghold, fell. Out of this volatile political and social environment came the **conquistadores,** explorers eager for personal glory and material gain, uncompromising in matters of religion, and unswerving in their loyalty to the crown. These were the men who first carried European culture to the New World.

conquistadores Sixteenth-century Spanish adventurers, often of noble birth, who subdued the Native Americans and created the Spanish empire in the New World.

Myths and Reality

If it had not been for Christopher Columbus (Cristoforo Colombo), Spain might never have gained an American empire. Born in Genoa, Italy, in 1451 of humble parentage, Columbus devoured classical learning and became obsessed with the idea of sailing west across the Atlantic Ocean to reach Cathay, as China was then known. In 1484, he presented his plan to the king of Portugal, who was also interested in a route to Cathay. But the Portuguese were more interested in the route that went around the tip of Africa. After a polite audience, Columbus was refused support.

Undaunted by rejection, Columbus petitioned Isabella and Ferdinand for financial backing. They initially were no more interested in his grand design than the Portuguese had been. But fear of Portugal's growing power, as well as Columbus's confident talk of wealth and empire, led the new monarchs to reassess his scheme. Finally, the two sovereigns provided the supremely self-assured navigator with three ships, named *Niña, Pinta,* and *Santa Maria.* The indomitable admiral set sail for Cathay in August 1492, the year of Spain's unification.

Educated Europeans in the fifteenth century knew without question that the world was round. The question was size, not shape. Columbus estimated the distance to the mainland of Asia to be about 3000 nautical miles, a voyage that his small ships would have had no difficulty completing. The actual distance is 10,600 nautical miles, however, and had he not bumped into the New World along the way, he and his crew would have run out of food and water long before they reached China.

After stopping in the Canary Islands for ship repairs and supplies, Columbus crossed the Atlantic in thirty-three days, landing on an island in the Bahamas. He searched for the fabled cities of Asia, never considering that he had come upon a landmass completely unknown in Europe. Since his mathematical calculations had been correct, it didn't occur to him that he had come upon a new world, where he met friendly, though startled, Native Americans, whom he called Indians.

Three more times Columbus returned to the New World in search of fabled Asian riches. He died in 1506, a frustrated but wealthy entrepreneur, unaware that he had reached a previously unknown continent. The final blow came in December 1500 when an ambitious falsifier, Amerigo Vespucci, published a sensational travel account that convinced German mapmakers that he had beaten Columbus to the New World. By the time the deception was discovered, *America* had gained general acceptance throughout Europe as the name for the newly discovered continent.

The Conquistadores: Faith and Greed

Treaty of Tordesillas Treaty negotiated by the pope in 1494 to resolve competing land claims of Spain and Portugal in the New World. It divided the world along a north-south line in the middle of the Atlantic Ocean, granting to Spain all lands west of the line and to Portugal lands east of the line.

Under the **Treaty of Tordesillas** (1494), Spain and Portugal divided the New World between themselves. Portugal got Brazil, and Spain laid claim to all the remaining territories. Spain's good fortune unleashed a horde of conquistadores on the Caribbean. They came not as colonists but as fortune hunters seeking instant wealth, preferably gold, and they were not squeamish about the means they used to obtain it. The primary casualties of their greed were the Native Americans. In less than two decades, the tribes that had inhabited the Caribbean islands had been exterminated, victims of exploitation and disease.

Around then, rumors of fabulous wealth in Mexico began to lure the conquistadores from the islands Columbus had found to the mainland. On November 18, 1518, Hernán Cortés, a minor government functionary in Cuba, and a small army set sail for Mexico. There Cortés soon demonstrated that he was a leader of extraordinary ability, a person of intellect and vision who managed to rise above the goals of his avaricious followers.

His adversary was the legendary Aztec emperor Montezuma. It was a duel of powerful personalities. After burning his ships to cut off his army from a possible retreat, Cortés led his band of six hundred followers across difficult mountain trails toward the Valley of Mexico. The sound of gunfire and the sight of armor-clad horses, both unknown to Native Americans, frightened them. Added to the technological advantages was a potent psychological factor. At first Montezuma thought that the Spaniards were gods, representatives of the fearful plumed serpent, Quetzalcoatl. By the time the Aztec ruler realized his error, it was too late to save his empire.

From Plunder to Settlement

Cortés's victory in Mexico, coupled with other Spanish conquests, notably in Peru, transformed the mother country into the wealthiest nation in Europe. But the Spanish crown soon faced new difficulties. The conquistadores had to be brought under royal authority. Adventurers like Cortés were stubbornly independent, quick to take offense, and thousands of miles from the seat of government. One solution was the *encomienda* system. Conquistadores were rewarded with local villages and control over native labor. They also had the responsibility of protecting the Indians, who suffered terribly under this cruelly exploitative system of labor tribute. The system did make the colonizers very dependent on the king, however, for it was he who legitimized their title. As one historian noted, the system transformed "a frontier of plunder into a frontier of settlement."

encomienda An exploitative labor system designed by Spanish rulers to reward conquistadores in the New World by granting them local villages and control over native labor.

Bureaucrats dispatched directly from Spain soon replaced the aging conquistadores. Unlike the governing system that later existed in England's mainland American colonies, Spain's rulers maintained tight control over their American possessions through their government officials. After 1535, a viceroy, a nobleman appointed to oversee the king's colonial interests, ruled the people of New Spain. Working independently of the viceroy, an *audiencia,* the supreme judicial body, brought a measure of justice to the Indians and Spaniards and made certain that the viceroys did not slight their responsibilities to the king. Finally, the Council of the Indies in Spain handled colonial business. Although cumbersome and slow, somehow the rigidly controlled system worked.

The Spanish also brought Catholicism to the New World. The Dominicans and Franciscans, the two largest religious orders, established Indian missions throughout New Spain, and some barefoot friars protected the Native Americans from the worst forms of exploitation. One courageous Dominican, Fra Bartolomé de Las Casas, even published an eloquent defense of Indian rights, *Historia de las Indias,* that among other things questioned the European conquest of the New World. The

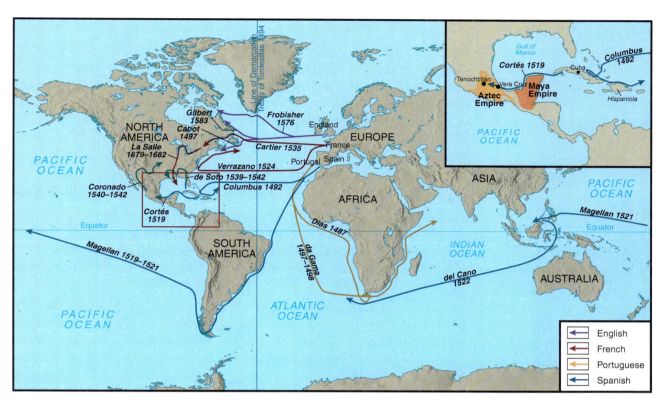

VOYAGES OF EXPLORATION   *The routes of the major voyages in the Age of Exploration.*
The great explorers and navigators established land claims for the European nations. ■

book led to reforms designed to bring greater "love and moderation" to Spanish-Indian relations.

About 750,000 people migrated to the New World from Spain. Most of the colonists were impoverished, single males in their late twenties in search of economic opportunities. They generally came from the poorest agricultural regions of southern Spain. Since few Spanish women migrated, especially in the sixteenth century, the men often married Indians and, later, blacks, unions that produced offspring known, respectively, as *mestizos* and *mulattoes*. The frequency of interracial marriage created a society of more fluid racial categories than there were in the English colonies, where the sex ratio of the settlers was more balanced and the racially mixed population comparatively small.

The lure of gold drew Spanish conquistadores to the unexplored lands to the north of Mexico. Between 1539 and 1541, Hernando de Soto trekked across the Southeast from Florida to the Mississippi River looking for gold and glory, and at about the same time, Francisco Vásquez de Coronado set out from New Spain in search of the fabled Seven Cities of Cíbola. Neither conquistador found what he was searching for. In the seventeenth century, when Juan de Oñate established outposts in the Southwest, the Spanish came into open conflict with Native Americans in that region. In 1680, the Indians drove the invaders completely out of the territory. Thereafter, the Spanish decided to maintain only a token presence in present-day Texas and New Mexico in order to discourage French encroachment on Spanish lands. For the same reason, the Spanish colony of St. Augustine was established in Florida in 1565. Spanish authorities showed little interest in California, a land of poor Indians and even poorer natural resources. Had it not been for the work of a handful of priests, Spain would have had little claim to California.

Even so, Spain claimed far more of the New World than it could possibly manage. After the era of the conquistadores, Spain's rulers regarded the American colonies primarily as a source of precious metal, and between 1500 and 1650 an estimated 200 tons of gold and 16,000 tons of silver were shipped back to the Spanish treasury in Madrid. The resulting inflation hurt the common people in Spain and prevented the growth of Spanish industry. Unimaginative leadership and debilitating wars hastened the Spanish decline. As one insightful observer declared in 1603, "The New World conquered by you has conquered you in its turn." Nonetheless, Spain's great cultural contribution to the American people is still very much alive today.

FRENCH EXPLORATION AND SETTLEMENT

French interest in the New World developed more slowly. In 1534, Jacques Cartier first sailed to the New World in search of a northwest passage to China. At first he was depressed by the rocky, barren coast of Newfoundland. He grumbled, "I am rather inclined to believe that this is the land God gave to Cain." But the discovery of a large, promising waterway raised Cartier's spirits. He reconnoitered the Gulf of St. Lawrence, traveling up the river as far as Montreal, but he did not discover a northwest passage, nor did he find gold or other precious metals. After several voyages to Canada, Cartier became discouraged by the harsh winters and meager findings; he returned home for good in 1542. Not until seventy-five years later did the brilliant navigator Samuel de Champlain rediscover the region for France. He founded Quebec in 1608.

In Canada, the French developed an economy based primarily on the fur trade, a commerce that required close cooperation with the Native Americans. They also explored the heart of the continent. In 1673, Père Jacques Marquette journeyed down the Mississippi River, and nine years later, Sieur de La Salle traveled all the way to the Gulf of Mexico. In the early eighteenth century, the French established small settlements in Louisiana, the most important being New Orleans.

Although the French controlled the region along the Mississippi and its tributaries, their dream of a vast American empire suffered from several serious flaws. From the first, the king remained largely indifferent to colonial affairs. An even greater problem was the nature of the land and climate. Few rural peasants or urban artisans wanted to venture to the inhospitable northern country, and throughout the colonial period, New France was underpopulated. By the first quarter of the eighteenth century, the English settlements had outstripped their French neighbors in population as well as in volume of trade.

THE ENGLISH NEW WORLD

The earliest English visit to North America remains something of a mystery. Fishermen working out of the western English ports may have landed in Nova Scotia and Newfoundland as early as the 1480s. John Cabot (Giovanni Caboto), a Venetian sea captain, completed the first recorded transatlantic voyage by an English vessel in 1497. Henry VII had rejected Columbus's enter-

■ *This seventeenth-century woodcut depicts Samuel de Champlain's fortified camp at Quebec on the St. Lawrence River. Champlain founded Quebec for France in 1608.* ■

prise for the Indies, but the first Tudor monarch apparently experienced a change of heart after hearing of Spain's success.

Like other explorers of that time, Cabot believed that he could find a northwest passage to Asia. He doggedly searched the northern waters for a likely opening, but a direct route to Cathay eluded him. Cabot died during a second attempt in 1498. Although Sebastian Cabot continued his father's explorations in the Hudson Bay region in 1508–1509, English interest in the New World waned. For the next three-quarters of a century, the English people were preoccupied with more pressing domestic and religious concerns. The Cabot voyages did, however, establish an English claim to American territory.

Religious Turmoil and Reformation in Europe

The reign of Henry VII was plagued by domestic troubles. England possessed no standing army, a small, weak navy, and many strong and independent local magnates. During the sixteenth century, however, the next Tudor king, Henry VIII, and his daughter, Elizabeth I, developed a strong central government and transformed England into a Protestant nation. These changes propelled England into a central role in European affairs and were crucial to the creation of England's North American empire.

The Protestantism that eventually stimulated colonization was definitely not of English origin. In 1517, a relatively obscure German monk, Martin Luther, publicly challenged certain tenets and practices of Roman Catholicism, and within a few years, the religious unity of Europe was forever shattered. Luther's message was straightforward. God spoke through the Bible, Luther maintained, not through the pope or priests. Pilgrimages, fasts, alms, indulgences—none of these traditional acts could ensure salvation. Luther's radical ideas spread rapidly across northern Germany and Scandinavia.

Other Protestant reformers soon spoke out against Catholicism. The most important of these was John Calvin, a lawyer turned theologian, who lived in the Swiss city of Geneva. Calvin stressed God's omnipotence over human affairs. The Lord, he maintained, chose some persons for "election," the gift of salvation, while condemning others to eternal damnation. Human beings were powerless to alter this decision by their individual actions.

Common sense suggests that such a bleak doctrine might lead to fatalism or hedonism. After all, why not enjoy worldly pleasures if they have no effect on God's judgment? But common sense would be wrong. Indeed, the Calvinists constantly were busy searching for signs that they had received God's gift of grace. The uncertainty of their eternal state proved a powerful psychological spur, for as long as people did not know whether they were scheduled for heaven or hell, they worked diligently to demonstrate that they possessed at least the seeds of grace. This doctrine of predestination became the distinguishing mark of Calvin's followers throughout northern Europe. In the seventeenth century, they were known in France as Huguenots and in England and America as Puritans.

Popular anticlericalism was the basis for the **Protestant Reformation** in England. Although they observed traditional Catholic ritual, the English people had long resented paying monies to a distant pope. Early in the sixteenth century, opposition to the clergy grew increasingly vocal. Cardinal Thomas Wolsey, the most powerful prelate in England, flaunted his immense wealth and became a symbol of spiritual corruption. Parish priests were ridiculed for their ignorance and greed. Anticlericalism did not run as deep in England as in Germany, but by the late 1520s, the Roman Catholic clergy had strained the allegiance of the great mass of the population. Ordinary men and women throughout the kingdom were ready to leave the institutional church.

Protestant Reformation
Sixteenth-century religious movement to reform and challenge the spiritual authority of the Roman Catholic Church, associated with figures such as Martin Luther and John Calvin.

The catalyst for the Reformation in England was Henry VIII's desire to end his marriage to Catherine of Aragon, daughter of the king of Spain. Their union in 1509 had produced a daughter, Mary, but no son. The need for a male heir obsessed Henry. He and his counselors assumed that a female ruler could not maintain domestic peace and that England would fall once again into civil war. Henry petitioned Pope Clement VII for a divorce. Unwilling to tolerate the public humiliation of Catherine, Spain forced the pope to procrastinate. In 1527, time ran out. Henry fell in love with Anne Boleyn, who later bore him a daughter, Elizabeth. The king divorced Catherine without papal consent.

The final break with Rome came swiftly. Between 1529 and 1536, the king, acting through Parliament, severed all ties with the pope, seized church lands, and dissolved many of the monasteries. In March 1534, the Act of Supremacy boldly named Henry VIII "supreme head of the Church of England." Land formerly owned by the Catholic Church passed quickly into private hands, and property holders acquired a vested interest in Protestantism. In 1539, William Tyndale and Miles Coverdale issued an English edition of the Bible, which made it possible for the common people to read the Scriptures in their own language rather than Catholicism's Latin. The separation was complete.

When Henry died in 1547, his young son Edward VI came to the throne. But Edward was a sickly child. Militant Protestants took advantage of the political uncertainty to introduce Calvinism into England. In breaking with the papacy, Henry had shown little enthusiasm for theological change; most Catholic ceremonies remained. But opponents now insisted that the Church of England remove every trace of its Catholic origins. Edward died in 1553, and these ambitious efforts came to a sudden halt. Henry's eldest daughter, Mary I, ascended the throne. Fiercely loyal to the Catholic faith, she vowed to return England to the pope. Hundreds of Protestants were executed; others scurried off to Geneva and Frankfurt, where they absorbed the radical Calvinist doctrines. When Mary died in 1558 and was succeeded by Elizabeth I, these "Marian exiles" returned, more eager than ever to purge the Tudor church of Catholicism. Mary had inadvertently advanced the cause of Calvinism by creating so many Protestant martyrs. The Marian exiles now controlled the Elizabethan church, which remained fundamentally Calvinist until the end of the sixteenth century.

The Protestant Queen

Elizabeth was a woman of extraordinary talent. She governed England from 1558 to 1603, an intellectually exciting period during which some of her subjects took the first halting steps toward colonizing the New World.

Elizabeth's most urgent duty was to end the religious turmoil that had divided the country for a generation. She had no desire to restore Catholicism. After all, the pope openly referred to her as a woman of illegitimate birth. Nor did she want to recreate the church exactly as it had been in the final years of her father's reign. Rather, Elizabeth established a unique church, near-Catholic in ceremony but Protestant in doctrine. The examples of Edward and Mary had demonstrated that neither radical change nor widespread persecution gained a monarch lasting popularity.

Elizabeth still faced serious religious challenges. Catholicism and Protestantism were warring faiths; each was an ideology, a body of deeply held beliefs that influenced the way that average men and women interpreted the experiences of everyday life. The confrontation between Protestantism and Catholicism affected Elizabeth's entire reign.

Militant Calvinists urged her to drop all Catholic rituals, and fervent Catholics wanted her to return to the Roman church. Pope Pius V excommunicated her in 1570. Spain, the most intensely Catholic state in Europe, vowed to restore England to the "true" faith, and the Catholic terrorists plotted to overthrow the Tudor monarchy.

Religion, War, and Nationalism

English Protestantism and English nationalism slowly merged. A loyal English subject in the late sixteenth century loved the monarch, supported the Church of England, and hated Catholics, especially those who happened to live in Spain. Elizabeth's subjects adored their Virgin Queen, and they applauded when her famed "Sea Dogs"—dashing naval commanders such as Sir Francis Drake and Sir John Hawkins—seized Spanish treasure ships in American waters. The English naval raids were little more than piracy, but they passed for grand victories. With each engagement, each threat, each plot, English nationalism took deeper root. By the 1570s, the English people were driven by powerful ideological forces similar to those that had moved the subjects of Isabella and Ferdinand almost a century earlier.

In the mid-1580s, Philip II of Spain constructed a mighty fleet carrying thousands of Spain's finest infantry. The Armada was built to cross the English Channel and destroy the Protestant queen. When one of Philip's lieutenants viewed the Armada at Lisbon in May 1588, he described it as *la felicissima armada,* the invincible fleet. The king believed that with the support of England's oppressed Catholics, Spanish troops would sweep Elizabeth from power.

It was a grand scheme; it was an even grander failure. In 1588, a smaller, more maneuverable English navy dispersed the Armada and revealed Spain's vulnerability. Philip's hopes for a Catholic England lay wrecked along the rocky coasts of Scotland and Ireland. Elizabeth's subjects remained loyal throughout the crisis. Inspired by success in the Channel, bolder personalities dreamed of acquiring riches and planting colonies across the North Atlantic. Spain's American monopoly had been broken.

REHEARSAL IN IRELAND FOR AMERICAN COLONIZATION

England's first colony was Ireland. On that island, enterprising Englishmen first learned to subdue a foreign population and seize its lands. Ireland's one million inhabitants were scattered mainly along the coast, and there were few villages. To the English, the Irish seemed wild and barbaric. They were also fiercely independent. The English dominated a small region around Dublin, but much of Ireland remained in the hands of Gaelic-speaking Catholics who presumably lived beyond the reach of civilization.

During the 1560s and 1570s, the English decided that money could be made in Ireland, despite the hostility of the Irish. English colonists moved in and forced the Irish either into tenancy or off the land altogether. Semimilitary colonies were planted in Ulster and Munster.

Colonization brought about severe cultural strains. The English settlers, however humble their own origins, felt superior to the Irish. After all, the English had championed the Protestant religion, constructed a complex market economy, and created a powerful nation-state. To the English, the Irish appeared lazy, lawless, superstitious, and often stupid. Even educated representatives of the two cultures found communication virtually impossible. English colonists, for example, criticized Ireland's pastoral farming methods. It seemed perversely wasteful for the Irish to be forever moving about because this practice retarded the development of towns. Sir John Davies, a leading English colonist, declared that if the Irish were left to themselves, they would "never . . . build houses, make townships or villages or manure or improve the land *as it ought to be.*" Such wastefulness became the standard English justification for seizing more land. No matter what the Irish did, they could never be sufficiently English to please their new masters.

English ethnocentrism was relatively benign so long as the Irish accepted subservient roles. But they rebelled frequently, and English condescension turned quickly to violence. Resistance smacked of disrespect, and for the good of the Irish and the safety of the English, it had to be crushed. Sir Humphrey Gilbert was especially brutal. A talented man who wrote treatises on geography, Gilbert explored the coast of North America and entertained Queen Elizabeth with witty conversation. But as military governor in Ireland, he tolerated no opposition.

In 1569, when the Irish rose up in Munster, he executed everyone he could catch, "man, woman, and child." He cut off the heads of many enemy soldiers killed in battle, and in the words of one contemporary, Gilbert laid his macabre trophies "on the ground by each side of the way leading into his tent, so that none should come into his tent for any cause but commonly he must pass through a lane of heads." Instead of bringing peace and security, such behavior generated a hatred so deep that it continues to this day.

The Irish experiments served as models for later English colonies in the New World, shaping the English view of America and its people. English adventurers in the New World compared Native Americans to the "wild" Irish. This ethnocentrism was a central element in the transfer of English culture to America. The English, like the Spanish and the French, did not perceive America in objective terms. They had already constructed an image of America, and the people and objects that greeted them on the other side of the Atlantic were forced into Old World categories, some of them Irish.

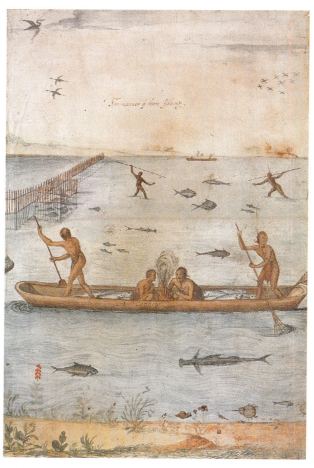

■ John White depicts several fishing techniques practiced by the Algonquian Indians of the modern Carolinas. Riders in the canoe use dip nets and multipronged spears. In the background, Indians stab at fish with long spears. At left, a weir traps fish by taking advantage of the river current's natural force. ■

AN UNPROMISING BEGINNING: MYSTERY AT ROANOKE

By the 1570s, England was ready to challenge Spain and reap the profits of Asia and America. Only dimly aware of Cabot's voyages and with very limited colonization experience in Ireland, the English adventurers made almost every mistake that one could possibly imagine between 1575 and 1600. They did, however, acquire valuable information about winds and currents, supplies, and finance that laid the foundation for later, more successful ventures.

Sir Walter Ralegh's experience provided all English colonizers with a sobering example of the difficulties that awaited them in America. In 1584, he dispatched two captains to the coast of present-day North Carolina to claim land granted to him by Elizabeth. The men returned with glowing reports about the fertility of the soil. Diplomatically, Ralegh renamed this marvelous region Virginia, in honor of his patron, the Virgin Queen.

Ralegh's enterprise seemed ill-fated from the start. Though encouraged by Elizabeth, he received no financial backing from the crown, and despite careful planning, everything went wrong. In 1585, Sir Richard Grenville transported a group of men to Roanoke Island, but the colonists did not arrive in Virginia until nearly autumn. The settlement was also poorly located, and even experienced navigators found it dangerous to reach. Finally, Grenville alienated the local Indians when he senselessly destroyed an entire Indian village in retaliation for the theft of a silver cup.

Grenville hurried back to England in the autumn of 1585, leaving the colonists to fend for themselves. They performed quite well. But when an expected shipment of supplies failed to arrive on time, the colonists grew dis-

Chronology

30,000–20,000 B.C.	Settlers cross the Bering Strait land bridge into North America
2000–1500 B.C.	Agricultural Revolution transforms Native American life
A.D. 1001	Norsemen establish a small settlement in Vinland (Newfoundland)
1438	Printing method using movable type is invented
1492	Marriage of Isabella and Ferdinand leads to the unification of Spain
1492	Columbus lands at San Salvador
1497	Cabot leads first English exploration of North America
1502	Montezuma becomes emperor of the Aztec
1506	Columbus dies in Spain after four voyages to America
1517	Martin Luther's protests set off the Reformation in Germany
1521	Cortés achieves victory over the Aztec at Tenochtitlan
1529–1536	Henry VIII provokes the English Reformation
1534	Cartier claims Canada for France
1536	Calvin's *Institutes* is published
1540	Coronado explores the North American Southwest for Spain
1558	Elizabeth becomes queen of England
1583	Sir Humphrey Gilbert dies
1585	First Roanoke settlement is established on the coast of North Carolina
1588	Spanish Armada is defeated by the English
1603	Elizabeth I dies
1608	Champlain founds Quebec
1682	La Salle travels the length of the Mississippi River

contented. In the spring of 1586, Sir Francis Drake unexpectedly landed at Roanoke, and the colonists impulsively decided to return home with him.

In 1587, Ralegh launched a second colony. The new settlement was more representative, containing men, women, and even children. The settlers feasted on Roanoke's fish and game and bountiful harvests of corn and pumpkin. Yet within weeks after arriving, the leader of the settlement, John White, returned to England at the colonists' urging to obtain additional food and clothing and to recruit new immigrants.

Once again, Ralegh's luck turned sour. War with Spain pressed every available ship into military service. When rescuers eventually reached the island in 1590, they found the village deserted. The fate of the "lost" colonists remains a mystery. The best guess is that they were absorbed by neighboring groups of natives, some from as far as the southern shore of the James River.

CONCLUSION: PROPAGANDA FOR EMPIRE

Richard Hakluyt, a supremely industrious man, never saw America. Nevertheless, his vision of the New World powerfully shaped public opinion. He interviewed captains and sailors and carefully collected their travel stories in a massive book titled *The Principall Navigations, Voyages, and Discoveries of the English Nation* (1589).

Although each tale appeared to be a straightforward narrative, Hakluyt edited each piece to drive home the book's central point: England needed American colonies. English settlers, he argued, would provide the mother country with critical natural resources, and in the process they would grow rich themselves.

Hakluyt's enthusiasm for the spread of English trade throughout the world may have blinded him to the aspirations of other peoples who actually inhabited those distant lands. He continued to collect testimony from adventurers and sailors who claimed to have visited Asia and America. In a popular new edition of his work published between 1598 and 1600 and titled *Voyages,* he catalogued in great detail the commercial opportunities awaiting ambitious English colonizers. His entrepreneurial perspective obscured other aspects of the English Conquest, which within only a short amount of time would transform the face of the New World. He paid little attention, for example, to the rich cultural diversity of the Native Americans; he said not a word about the pain of the Africans who traveled to North and South America as slaves. Instead, he and other polemicists for the English colonization led the ordinary men and women who crossed the Atlantic to expect nothing less than a paradise on earth. By encouraging such unreal expectations, Hakluyt persuaded European settlers that the New World was theirs for the taking, a self-serving view that invited ecological disaster and human suffering.

KEY TERMS

Agricultural Revolution, p. 3

Columbian Exchange, p. 6

Renaissance, p. 10

conquistadores, p. 11

Treaty of Tordesillas, p. 12

encomienda, p. 12

Protestant Reformation, p. 15

RECOMMENDED READING

The histories of three different peoples coming together for the first time in the New World has sparked innovative scholarship. Many interdisciplinary works explore diverse patterns of cultural adaptation. Some of the best titles bring fresh insights to the Native Americans' response to radical environmental and social change. Among these are Charles C. Mann, *1491: New Revelations of The Americas Before Columbus* (2005); James H. Merrell, *The Indians' New World: Catawbas and Their Neighbors From European Contact Through the Era of Removal* (1989); and James F. Brooks, *Captives and Cousins: Slavery, Kinship and Community in the Southwest Borderlands* (2002). Other broad-ranging volumes examine how early European invaders imagined the New World and how they translated what they thought they had seen into a familiar and unthreatening language: Stephen Greenblatt, *Marvelous Possessions: The Wonder of the New World* (1991), and Anthony Pagden, *European Encounters with the New World: From Renaissance to Romanticism* (1992). The impact of the environment—a major theme of this chapter—is the topic of three pioneering investigations: A. W. Crosby, *The Columbian Voyages, The Columbian Exchange, and Their Historians* (1987); William Cronon, *Changes in the Land: Indians, Colonists, and the Ecology of New England* (1983); and Shepard Krech III, *The Ecological Indian: Myth and History* (1999). The best overview of the European response to the Conquest is John H. Elliott, *The Old World and New, 1492–1650* (1970). For the Irish experience one should consult Nicholas Canny, *Making Ireland British 1580–1650* (2001). Two outstanding interpretations of the English Reformation are Ethan H. Shagan, *Popular Politics and the English Reformation* (2003) and Eamon Duffy, *The Stripping of the Altars: Traditional Religion in England 1400–1580* (1992). Books that offer boldly original interpretations of the conquest are Kirkpatrick Sale, *The Conquest of Paradise: Christopher Columbus and the Columbian Legacy* (1990); and Kathleen M. Brown, *Good Wives, Nasty Wenches, and Anxious Patriarchs: Gender, Race, and Power in Colonial Virginia* (1996).

SUGGESTED WEB SITES

Vikings in the New World

emuseum.mnus.edu/prehistory/vikings/vikhome.html

This site explores the history of some of the earliest European visitors to America.

Sir Francis Drake

www.mcn.org/2/oseeler/drake.htm

This comprehensive site covers much of Drake's life and voyages.

Ancient Mesoamerican Civilizations

www.angelfire.com/ca/humanorigins/index.html

Kevin L. Callahan of the University of Minnesota Department of Anthropology maintains this page regarding Mesoamerican civilizations with well-organized essays and photos.

National Museum of the American Indian

www.si.edu/nmai

The Smithsonian Institution maintains this site, providing information about the museum, which is dedicated to everything about Native Americans.

1492: An Ongoing Voyage

www.loc.gov/exhibits/1492

An exhibit of the Library of Congress, Washington, D.C., with brief essays and images about early civilizations and contact in the Americas.

The Computerized Information Retrieval System on Columbus and the Age of Discovery

muweb.millersville.edu/~columbus/

The History Department and Academic Computing Services of Millersville University of Pennsylvania provide this text retrieval system containing more than one thousand text articles from various magazines, journals, newspapers, speeches, official calendars, and other sources relating to various encounter themes.

Cahokia Mounds

www.cahokiamounds.com

The Cahokia Mounds State Historical Site gives information about a fascinating pre-Columbian culture in North America.

Mexican Pre-Columbian History

www.mexonline.com/precolum.htm

This site "provides information on the Aztecs, Maya, Mexica, Olmecs, Toltec, Zapotecs, and other Pre-European cultures, as well as information on museums, archeology, language and education."

White Oak Fur Post

www.whiteoak.org/

This site documents an eighteenth-century fur trading post among the Indians in what would become Minnesota.

La Salle's Shipwreck Project

www.thc.state.tx.us/belle/lasbelle.html

Texas Historical Commission site about this archaeological dig to recover the ship of one of America's famous early explorers.

The Discoverer's Web

www.win.tue.nl/cs/fm/engels/discovery/

Andre Engels maintains this most complete collection of information on the various efforts at exploration.

Chapter 2

Conflicting Visions: England's Seventeenth-Century Colonies

Profit and Piety: Competing Blueprints for English Settlement

In the spring of 1644, John Winthrop, governor of Massachusetts Bay, learned that Native Americans had overrun the scattered tobacco plantations of Virginia, killing as many as five hundred colonists. Winthrop never thought much of the Chesapeake settlements. He regarded the people who had migrated to that part of America as grossly materialistic, and because Virginia had recently expelled several Puritan ministers, Winthrop decided that the hostilities were God's way of punishing the tobacco planters for their worldliness. He gave the Virginians neither help nor sympathy.

In 1675, Native Americans declared all-out war against the New Englanders, and reports of the destruction of Puritan communities were soon circulating in Virginia. Sir William Berkeley, Virginia's royal governor, was not displeased by the news of New England's adversity. He and his friends held the Puritans in contempt. Indeed, the New Englanders reminded them of the religious fanatics who had provoked civil war in the mother country and who, in 1649, had executed Charles I. In reasoning that echoed Winthrop's, Berkeley concluded that the Native American attacks were God's revenge on the Puritans. He, in turn, declined to send the New Englanders the necessary supplies or sympathy.

Unity and nationalism were not part of Winthrop's and Berkeley's America. English colonization in the seventeenth century did not spring from a desire to build a centralized empire in the New World similar to that of Spain or France. Instead, the English Crown awarded colonial charters to a wide variety of people including merchants, religious idealists, and aristocratic adventurers, all of whom established separate and profoundly different colonies.

BREAKING AWAY

Changes in the mother country occurring throughout the period of settlement help explain the diversity of English colonization. Far-reaching economic, political, and religious transformations swept seventeenth-century England. Many people left the villages where they were born in search of fresh opportunities. Thousands traveled to London, by 1600 a city of several hundred thousand inhabitants. A large number of English settlers migrated to Ireland; lucrative employment and religious freedom attracted others to Holland. Others set out for more exotic destinations. The most adventurous individuals went to the New World—to Caribbean islands such as Barbados or to the mainland colonies.

Various reasons drew the colonists across the Atlantic. The quest for a purer form of worship motivated many, while the dream of owning land attracted others. And a few came to escape bad marriages, jail terms, and poverty. But whatever their reasons for crossing the ocean, English men and women who emigrated to America in the seventeenth century left a mother country wracked by recurrent and often violent political and religious controversies. During the 1620s, the Stuart monarchs—James I (ruled 1603–1625) and his son Charles I (1625–1649)—fought constantly with the elected members of Parliament. In 1640, the conflict escalated into a bloody civil war between the king and supporters of Parliament. Finally, in 1649, the victorious parliamentarians beheaded Charles, and for almost a decade Oliver Cromwell, a brilliant general and religious reformer, governed England as Lord Protector.

The unrest did not end with the death of Charles I. After Cromwell's death, the Stuarts were restored to the throne (1660). But through the reigns of Charles II (1660–1685) and James II (1685–1688), the political turmoil continued. When the authoritarian James openly favored his fellow Catholics, the nation rose up in the so-called **Glorious Revolution** (1688), sent him into permanent exile, and placed his staunchly Protestant daughter, Mary, and son-in-law, William, on the throne.

Political turmoil, religious persecution, and economic insecurity determined the flow of emigration. Men and women thought more seriously about living in the New World at such times. Ever-changing conditions in England help explain the diversity of American settlement.

Regardless of when they came, the colonists carried with them a bundle of ideas, beliefs, and assumptions that shaped the way they viewed their new environment. The New World tested and sometimes transformed their values but never destroyed them. The different subcultures that emerged in America were determined largely by the interaction between these values and such physical elements as climate, crops, and soil. The Chesapeake, the New England Colonies, the Middle Colonies, and the Carolinas formed distinct regional identities that persisted long after the first settlers had passed from the scene.

Glorious Revolution
Replacement of James II by William and Mary as English monarchs in 1688, marking the beginning of constitutional monarchy in Britain. American colonists celebrated this moment as a victory for the rule of law over despotism.

THE CHESAPEAKE: THE LURE OF WEALTH

The Roanoke debacle raised questions about America's promise, but with the aid of visionaries such as Richard Hakluyt, the dream persisted. Writers insisted that there were profits to be made in the New World. In addition, goods from America would supply England with raw materials that it would otherwise be forced to purchase from European rivals—Holland, France, and Spain. The three motives of making money, helping England, and annoying Catholic Spain constituted a powerful incentive. Shortly after James I ascended the throne, the settlers were given an opportunity to test their theories in the Chesapeake colonies of Virginia and Maryland.

Entrepreneurs in Virginia

Money had been an early obstacle to colonization. The **joint-stock company** removed the barrier. A business organization in which scores of people could invest without fear of bankruptcy, it proved very successful. A person could purchase a share of stock at a stated price and at the end of several years could anticipate recovering the initial investment plus a portion of whatever profits the company had made. Within a very short time, some of the enterprises were able to amass large amounts of capital, enough to finance a new colony. Virginia was the first such venture.

On April 10, 1606, James I issued a charter authorizing the London Company under the dynamic leadership of Sir Thomas Smythe to establish plantations in Virginia. Although the boundaries mentioned in the charter were vague, the

joint-stock company Business enterprise that enabled investors to pool money for commercial trading activity and funding for sustaining colonies.

Susquehannock

MARYLAND   Lenni-Lenape
(Delaware)

Conoy

Severn
R.

Potomac R.

Nanticoke

Rappahannock R.

St. Mary's City

Chesapeake Bay

Delaware Bay

Powhatan

James R.

Parnunkey

Jamestown

ATLANTIC
OCEAN

Nottoway

VIRGINIA

Tutelo

Tuscarora

Pamlico

0   50   100 miles

0   50   100 kilometers

CHESAPEAKE COLONIES, 1640   *The many deep rivers that flowed into the Chesapeake Bay provided scattered English planters with a convenient transportation system, linking them directly to European markets.* ∎

London Company promptly renamed itself the Virginia Company and set out to find the treasure that Hakluyt had promised. In December 1606, under the command of Captain John Smith, the *Susan Constant,* the *Godspeed,* and the *Discovery,* with 104 men and boys aboard, sailed for America. The land the voyagers found was lush and well watered, with "faire meadowes and goodly tall trees."

They soon found something else—death and dissension. The low-lying ground on which they set up their base was 30 miles up the James River on a marshy peninsula they named Jamestown. It proved to be a disease-ridden death trap; even the drinking water was contaminated with salt. However, a peninsula was easier to defend, and they feared a surprise attack more than sickness.

Almost instantly, the colonists began quarreling. Tales of beaches strewn with rubies and diamonds had lured them to Virginia. Once there, instead of cooperating for the common good—guarding the palisade or farming—each individual pursued personal interests. Meanwhile, disease, hostile Indians, and then starvation ravaged the hapless settlers.

Had it not been for Captain John Smith, Virginia might have gone the way of Roanoke. Smith told tales of fighting the Turks and being saved from certain death by various beautiful women, claims that modern historians have largely verified. In Virginia, Smith brought order out of anarchy. He traded with the Indians for food, mapped the Chesapeake Bay, and was even rescued from execution by a precocious Indian princess, Pocahontas. After seizing control of the ruling council in 1608, he instituted a tough military discipline, forcing the lazy to work and breathing life back into the dying colony.

Leaders of the Virginia Company in London soon recognized the need to reform the entire enterprise. A new charter in 1609 granted the company the right to make all commercial and political decisions affecting the colonists. Moreover, in an effort to obtain scarce capital, the original partners opened the joint-stock company to the general public. The company sponsored a spirited publicity campaign; pamphlets and sermons extolled the colony's potential and exhorted patriotic English citizens to invest in the enterprise.

This burst of energy came to nothing. Bad luck and poor planning plagued the Virginia Company. A ship carrying settlers and supplies went aground in the Caribbean; the governor, Lord De La Warr, postponed his departure for America; and Captain Smith suffered a debilitating accident and had to return to England. As a result, between 1609 and 1611, the remaining settlers lacked capable leadership. Food supplies grew short. The terrible winter of 1609–1610—termed the "starving time"—drove a few desperate colonists to cannibalism. Smith reported that one crazed settler killed, salted, and ate parts of his wife before the murder was discovered. Many people lost their will to live.

Governor De La Warr finally arrived in June 1610. He and the deputy governors who succeeded him ruled by martial law. Men and women marched to work by the beat of the drum. These extreme measures saved the colony, but Virginia did not flourish. In 1616, the year profits were to be distributed to shareholders, the

A Look at the Past

Armor

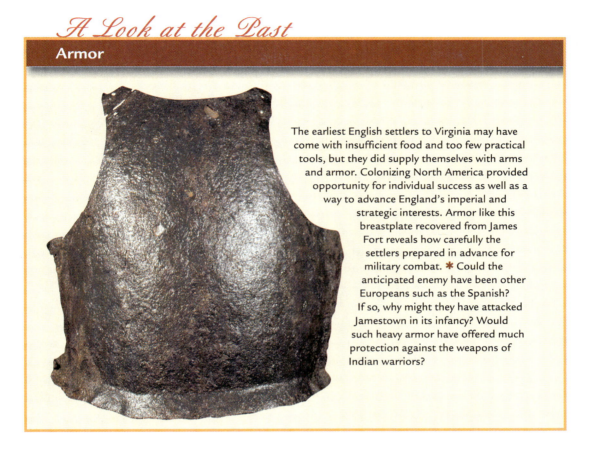

The earliest English settlers to Virginia may have come with insufficient food and too few practical tools, but they did supply themselves with arms and armor. Colonizing North America provided opportunity for individual success as well as a way to advance England's imperial and strategic interests. Armor like this breastplate recovered from James Fort reveals how carefully the settlers prepared in advance for military combat. ✳ Could the anticipated enemy have been other Europeans such as the Spanish? If so, why might they have attacked Jamestown in its infancy? Would such heavy armor have offered much protection against the weapons of Indian warriors?

company hovered near bankruptcy, with only a vast expanse of unsurveyed land 3000 miles from London to show for all its efforts.

"Stinking Weed"

The solution to Virginia's problems grew in the vacant lots of Jamestown. Only Indians cultivated tobacco—for religious purposes—until John Rolfe realized that this local weed might be a valuable export crop. Rolfe, who married Pocahontas, developed a milder tobacco leaf that greatly appealed to European smokers.

Virginians suddenly possessed a means to make money. Tobacco was easy to grow, and settlers who had avoided work now threw themselves into its production with single-minded diligence. James I initially considered smoking immoral and unhealthy; he changed his mind as the duties he collected on tobacco imports mounted.

The Virginia Company in 1618 launched one last effort to transform Virginia into a profitable enterprise, promising a series of reforms, including relaxation of martial law and establishment of a representative assembly called the **House of Burgesses.** Sir Edwin Sandys (pronounced Sands), a gifted entrepreneur, led the faction of stockholders who pumped life into the faltering organization, encouraging private investors to develop their own estates in Virginia. Sandys even introduced a new method for distributing land. Colonists who paid their own way to Virginia were guaranteed a **headright,** a 50-acre lot for which they paid only a small annual rent. Additional headrights were granted to the adventurers for each servant that they brought to the colony. This procedure enabled planters to build up huge estates with dependent labor, a land system that persisted long after the company's collapse. Headrights were awarded not to the newly freed servant, but to the great

House of Burgesses An elective representative assembly in colonial Virginia. It was the first example of representative government in the English colonies.

headright System of land distribution through which settlers were granted a 50-acre plot of land from the colonial government for each servant or dependent they transported to the New World. The system encouraged the recruitment of a large servile labor force.

indentured servants
Individuals who contracted to serve a master for a set number of years in exchange for the cost of boat transport to America. Indentured servitude was the dominant form of labor in the Chesapeake colonies before slavery.

planters who had borne the cost of the servant's transportation to the New World and paid for food and clothing during the indenture. And even though **indentured servants** were promised their own land at the moment of freedom, they were most often cheated, becoming members of a growing, disaffected landless class in seventeenth-century Virginia.

Sandys had only just begun. He also urged the settlers to diversify their economy. He envisioned colonists busily producing iron and tar, silk and glass, sugar and cotton, as well as tobacco. To finance such a huge project, Sandys relied on a lottery. The final element in the grand scheme was people. Sandys sent thousands of hopeful settlers to Virginia, newcomers swept up by the same hopes as the original colonists of 1607.

Time of Reckoning

Between 1619 and 1622, colonists arrived in Virginia in record numbers. Most of the 3570 individuals who emigrated to the colony during those years were single males in their teens or early twenties. Most of them came as indentured servants. In exchange for transportation across the Atlantic, they agreed to serve a master for a stated number of years. The younger the servant, the longer he or she was expected to serve. In return, the master promised to give the laborers proper care and, at the conclusion of their contracts, to provide them with tools and clothes according to "the custom of the country."

Since the Virginia masters needed strong servants able to do heavy field work, young males were preferred. Thus the gender ratio in Virginia was dramatically skewed. In the early decades, men outnumbered women by as much as six to one. Even if a man lived to the end of his indenture, he could not realistically expect to start a family of his own. Moreover, servants were often treated harshly. They were sold, traded, even gambled away in games of chance. It does not require much imagination to see that a society that tolerated such an exploitative labor system might later embrace slavery.

Most Virginians did not live long enough to worry about marrying and starting a family. Between 1618 and 1622, perhaps three out of every four persons in Virginia died. Contagious diseases killed the most. Salt poisoning also took a toll. And on Good Friday, March 22, 1622, the local Indians slew 347 settlers in a well-coordinated surprise attack. Those who survived must have lived with a sense of impermanence and a desire to escape Virginia with a little money before they, too, met an early death.

On both sides of the Atlantic, people wondered who should be blamed for the debacle. The burden of responsibility lay with the Virginia Company. Neither food nor shelter awaited the settlers when they arrived in Virginia. Weakened by the long sea voyage, the malnourished colonists quickly succumbed to contagious diseases.

Officials in Virginia also shared the guilt. Their greed caused them to overlook both the common good and the public defenses. Jamestown took on the characteristics of a boom town. Unrestrained self-advancement was the dominant feature of this highly individualistic, competitive society.

In 1624, King James took charge, dissolving the bankrupt enterprise and finally transforming Virginia into a royal colony. He appointed a governor and a council but made no provision for the continuation of

■ *This tobacco label advertises Virginia's valuable export— tobacco. Despite King James's initial attitude toward the "stinking weed," once the government saw that tobacco made a profit, it dropped its moral criticism of the American crop.* ■

Virginia's representative assembly. Even without the king's authorization, however, the House of Burgesses gathered annually, and in 1639, James's successor, Charles I, belatedly recognized its existence.

Charles had no choice. The colonists who served on the council or in the assembly were strong-willed, ambitious men. Having survived privation, disease, and Native American attacks, they were single-mindedly determined to get rich and had no intention of surrendering their control over local affairs. Governors who opposed the council did so at considerable personal risk. Nor was Charles, encountering his own problems at home, much disposed to intervene. In 1634, the assembly divided the colony into eight counties, each of which was governed by a justice of the peace. The "county court"—as these officers were called—remained the center of Virginia's social, political, and commercial life long after the American Revolution.

The changes in government had little impact on the character of daily life in Virginia. The isolated tobacco plantations that dotted Virginia's many navigable rivers were the focus of the settlers' lives. This dispersed pattern of settlement retarded the development of institutions such as schools and churches. And for more than a century, Jamestown was the only place that could reasonably be called a town.

Maryland: A Troubled Refuge for Catholics

Maryland's roots lay not in a wild scramble for wealth but in a nobleman's desire to create a sanctuary for England's persecuted Catholics. The driving force behind the settlement of Maryland was Sir George Calvert, later known as Lord Baltimore. Well educated, charming, ambitious, and from an excellent family, he became a favorite of James I. Although for a time he kept his religious beliefs private, he showed great interest in the progress of Virginia and New England. By the late 1620s, after publicly declaring himself a Catholic, Calvert longed to establish a colony of his own.

On June 30, 1632, Charles I granted George Calvert's son, Cecilius, a charter for a colony to be located on the Chesapeake Bay, north of Virginia. George died while the negotiations were in progress, but his vision shaped the character of the new settlement, named "Mariland, in honor of the Queene." For his part, Charles wanted to halt the southward spread of Dutch influence from New Netherland and regarded Baltimore's project as a cheap and convenient way to do so.

The charter itself is an odd document, part medieval and part modern. Lord Baltimore held absolute authority over the colonists. He was as powerful in his colony as a lord on a feudal estate. As proprietor, Baltimore owned the land outright, but he subdivided it into manors where landed aristocrats could establish their own courts of law. The more land a person owned, the more privileges that person enjoyed in the government.

Embedded in this feudal scheme was a concept that broke boldly with the past. Unlike the European leaders of his day, Baltimore championed religious freedom for all people who accepted the divinity of Christ. Even though Maryland's early settlers—Catholics as well as Protestants—occasionally persecuted each other, Baltimore's commitment to toleration never flagged.

In 1634, the first of Maryland's immigrants landed at St. Mary's, near the mouth of the Potomac River. As noted, Maryland attracted both Catholics and Protestants, and for a brief period, the two groups seemed capable of living in peace. Unlike the Virginia settlers, these early colonists were not threatened by starvation, and they maintained friendly relations with the local Indians.

Lord Baltimore's feudal system never took root in Chesapeake soil. People simply refused to play the social roles that he had assigned. Most important, the elected assembly, which first met in 1635, insisted on exercising traditional parliamentary privileges that eventually undermined Baltimore's authority. With each passing year, the proprietor's absolute control over the men and women of Maryland progressively weakened.

Despite Lord Baltimore's efforts to establish liberty of conscience, Maryland's gravest problems grew out of the colonists' religious intolerance. Aggressive Jesuits frightened Protestants, who in turn tried to unseat the proprietor on the grounds that he and his chief advisers were Catholic. In fact, Baltimore's experiment led to chronic instability during the first thirty years after settlement. Violence, not toleration, resulted from his efforts to put freedom of conscience into practice.

In this troubled sanctuary, planters cultivated tobacco on dispersed riverfront plantations. No towns developed. The tobacco culture permeated every aspect of society. A steady stream of indentured servants supplied the plantations with dependent laborers until they were replaced, at the end of the seventeenth century, by slaves. Both Maryland and Virginia were peopled by settlers occupied primarily by their own personal concerns.

REFORMING ENGLAND IN AMERICA

Legend surrounds the Pilgrims. These brave refugees crossed the cold Atlantic in search of religious liberty, signed a democratic compact aboard the *Mayflower,* landed at Plymouth Rock, and gave us our Thanksgiving Day. As with most mythic accounts, this one contains only a core of truth.

The Pilgrims were not crusaders who set out to change the world. They were humble English farmers from Scrooby Manor. They believed that the Church of England retained too many traces of its Catholic origin, that its very rituals compromised God's true believers. And so, in the early years of the reign of James I, the Scrooby congregation formally left the state church. Like others who followed this logic, they were called Separatists. Because English statute required citizens to attend established Church of England services, the Scrooby Separatists moved to Holland in 1608–1609 rather than compromise their souls.

The Netherlands provided the Separatists with a good home—too good. They feared that their distinct identity was threatened, that their children were becoming Dutch. By 1617, a portion of the Scrooby congregation vowed to sail to America. A group of English investors who were only marginally interested in Separatism underwrote their trip. In 1620, they sailed for Virginia aboard the *Mayflower.*

Hardship soon shattered the voyagers' optimism. Because of an error in navigation, the Pilgrims landed not in Virginia but in New England, where their land patent from the Virginia Company had no validity. Without a patent, the colonists possessed no authorization to form a civil government, a serious matter, in that some of the sailors who were not Pilgrims threatened mutiny. To preserve the struggling community from anarchy, forty-one men signed an agreement to "covenant and combine our selves together into a civil body politick."

Mayflower Compact
Agreement among the Pilgrims aboard the Mayflower in 1620 to create a civil government at Plymouth Colony.

Unfortunately, this **Mayflower Compact,** as the voluntary agreement was called, could not ward off disease and hunger. During the first months at Plymouth, death claimed approximately half of the 102 people who had initially set out from England. Moreover, debts contracted in the mother country severely burdened the new colony. Through strength of will and self-sacrifice, their elected leader, William Bradford, persuaded frightened men and women that they could survive in America.

Bradford had a lot of help. Almost anyone who has heard of the Plymouth Colony knows of Squanto, a Patuxt Indian who welcomed the first Pilgrims in excellent English. In 1614, unscrupulous adventurers had kidnapped Squanto and sold him in Spain as a slave. Somehow this resourceful man escaped bondage, making his way to London, where a group of merchants who owned land in Newfoundland taught him to speak English. They apparently hoped that he would deliver moving public testimonials about the desirability of moving to the New World. In any case, Squanto returned to the Plymouth area just before the Pilgrims arrived. Squanto joined Massasoit, a local Native American leader, in teaching the Pilgrims much about hunting and agriculture, a debt that Bradford freely acknowledged. Although evidence for the so-called First Thanksgiving is extremely sketchy, it is certain that without Native American support the Europeans would have starved.

The Pilgrims never became very prosperous, but they did build a humble farm community and practice their Separatist beliefs. Although they experimented with commercial fishing and the fur trade, most families relied on mixed husbandry, raising grain and livestock. Never a populous colony, in 1691, Plymouth was absorbed into its thriving, larger neighbor, Massachusetts Bay.

"The Great Migration"

During the seventeenth century, Puritan zeal transformed the face of England and America. The popular image of a **Puritan**—a carping critic who condemned liquor and sex, dressed in drab clothes, and minded the neighbors' business—is based on a fundamental misunderstanding of the actual nature of Puritanism. Puritans were radical reformers committed to far-reaching institutional change, not Victorian-type prudes. Not only did they found several American colonies, but they also sparked the English civil war and the bold new thinking about popular representation that accompanied it.

The Puritan movement came out of the Protestant Reformation. It accepted the notion that an omnipotent God predestined some people to salvation and damned others throughout eternity (see Chapter 1). Puritans constantly monitored themselves for signs of grace, hints that God had in fact placed them among his "elect." And their attempt to live as if they *were* saved—that is, according to the Scriptures—became the driving engine for reform on this earth.

They saw their duty clearly: to eradicate unscriptural elements and practices from the Church of England; to campaign vigorously against the sins of sexual license and drunkenness; and to inveigh against alliances with papist (Catholic) states. Puritans were more combative than the Pilgrims had been. They wanted to purify the English Church from within, and Separatism held little appeal for them.

From the Puritan perspective, the early Stuarts, James I and Charles I, seemed unconcerned about the spiritual state of the nation. The monarchs, Puritans believed, courted Catholic alliances and showed no interest in purifying the Church of England. As long as Parliament met, Puritan voters in the various boroughs and counties throughout the nation elected men sympathetic to their point of view. These outspoken representatives criticized royal policies. And because of their defiance, Charles decided in 1629 to rule England without Parliament. Four years later, he named as archbishop of Canterbury the Puritans' most conspicuous clerical opponent, William Laud. The last doors of reform slammed shut; the corruption remained.

John Winthrop, the future governor of Massachusetts Bay, was caught up in these events. A man of modest wealth and education, he believed that God would punish England, although he was confident that the Lord would provide shelter somewhere for his Puritan flock. Other Puritans, some wealthier and better connected than Winthrop, reached similar conclusions about England's future. They turned their attention to the possibility of establishing a colony in America. On March 4, 1629, their Massachusetts Bay Company obtained a charter directly from the king.

The king may have believed that Massachusetts Bay would be simply another commercial venture, but Winthrop and his associates knew better. In the Cambridge Agreement (August 1629), they pledged to emigrate, knowing that their charter allowed the company to hold meetings wherever the stockholders desired,

Puritan Member of a reformed Protestant sect in Europe and America that insisted on removing all vestiges of Catholicism from popular religious practice.

even in America. And if they were in America, the king could not easily interfere in their affairs.

"A City on a Hill"

The Winthrop fleet departed England in March 1630. By the end of the year, almost two thousand people had arrived in Massachusetts Bay, and before the Great Migration concluded in the early 1640s, almost sixteen thousand men and women would arrive in the new Puritan colony.

Unlike the early immigrants to Virginia and Maryland, they moved to Massachusetts Bay as nuclear families: fathers, mothers, and their dependent children. This guaranteed a more balanced gender ratio than in the Chesapeake colonies. Most significantly, these colonists thrived. In fact, their life expectancy compares favorably to that of modern Americans. This remarkable phenomenon alleviated the emotional shock of long-distance migration.

Their common sense of purpose provided another source of strength and stability. God, they insisted, had formed a special covenant with them. On his part, the Lord expected them to live according to Scripture, to reform the church—in other words, to create a "city on a hill" that would stand as a beacon of righteousness for the rest of the Christian world. If everyone kept the covenant, the colonists could expect peace and prosperity. They had no doubt that they would transform their religious vision into a social reality.

They arrived in Massachusetts Bay without a precise plan for their church, other than that they refused to separate formally from the Church of England. Reform, not separation, was their mission. Gradually, they came to accept a form of church government known as Congregationalism. Under this system, each congregation was independent of outside interference. The people (known as "saints") *were* the church. They pledged as a body to uphold God's law. In Congregational churches, full members—men and women who testified that they were among the Lord's elect—selected a minister, punished errant members, and determined matters of theology. This loose structure held together for more than a century.

In creating a civil government, the Bay Colony faced a particularly difficult challenge. Its charter allowed the investors in a joint-stock company to set up a business organization. When the settlers arrived in America, however, company leaders—men like Winthrop—moved quickly to transform the commercial structure into a colonial government. In 1631, they expanded the franchise to include all adult males who had become members of a Congregational church. During the 1630s, at least 40 percent of the adult male population could vote in elections—a percentage far above the standards in England. These "freemen" elected their own governor, magistrates, local representatives, and even military officers.

Two popular misconceptions about the government should be dispelled. It was neither a democracy nor a theocracy. Magistrates ruled in the name of the electorate but believed that their responsibilities as rulers were to God. And Congregational ministers possessed no formal political authority; they could not even hold civil office.

NEW ENGLAND COLONIES, 1650 *The early settlers quickly carved up New England. New Haven briefly flourished as a separate colony before being taken over by Connecticut in 1662. Long Island later became part of New York; Plymouth was absorbed into Massachusetts, and in 1677 New Hampshire became a separate colony.* ■

Unlike in Virginia, the town, rather than the county, became the center of public life in the Bay Colony. Groups of men and women voluntarily covenanted together to live by certain rules. They constructed their communities around a meetinghouse where church services and town meetings were held. Each townsman received land sufficient to build a house and to support a family. The house lots were clustered around the meetinghouse; the fields were located on the village perimeter. Land was free, but villagers were obliged to contribute to the minister's salary, to pay local and colony taxes, and to serve in the town militia.

The Challenge of Religious Dissent

The settlers of Massachusetts Bay managed to live in peace. When differences arose, as they often did, the courts settled matters. People believed in a rule of law, as was illustrated in 1648 when the colonial legislature drew up the *Laws and Liberties,* the first alphabetized code of law printed in English. This code clearly stated the colonists' rights and responsibilities as citizens of the commonwealth. It engendered public trust in government and discouraged magistrates from the arbitrary exercise of authority.

The most serious challenges to Puritan orthodoxy in Massachusetts Bay came from two remarkable individuals. The first, Roger Williams, arrived in 1631. He was well liked and immediately attracted a body of loyal followers. But he preached extreme Separatism. Moreover, he questioned the validity of the colony's charter, since the king had not first purchased the land from the Indians. Williams also insisted that the civil rulers of Massachusetts had no business punishing settlers for their religious beliefs. The magistrates believed that Williams threatened the social and religious foundation of the colony, and in 1636, they banished him. Williams then bought a tract of land from the Narragansett Indians and founded the Providence settlement in Rhode Island.

The magistrates of the Bay Colony rightly concluded that Anne Hutchinson posed an even greater threat to the peace of the commonwealth. Intelligent and outspoken, she questioned the authority and theology of some of the most respected

■ *One early Puritan meetinghouse was the Old Ship Meetinghouse in Hingham, Massachusetts. Its name derives from its interior design, which resembles the hull of a ship. The oldest wooden church in the United States, it could accommodate about seven hundred people, nearly the entire population of seventeenth-century Hingham. Members of the congregation would have sat on backless wooden benches in the unheated building, listening to the preacher address them, not from an altar but from an undecorated square speaking box.* ■

antinomianism Religious belief rejecting traditional moral law as unnecessary for Christians who possess saving grace and affirming that an individual could experience divine revelation and salvation without the assistance of formally trained clergy.

ministers of the colony. As justification for her own views, known as **antinomianism,** she cited divine inspiration, rather than the Bible or the clergy. In other words, Hutchinson's teachings could not be tested by Scripture, a position that Puritan leaders regarded as dangerously subjective. Without clear, external standards, one person's truth was as valid as that of anyone else's, and from Winthrop's perspective, Hutchinson's teachings invited civil and religious anarchy. But her challenge to authority was not simply theological. As a woman, her aggressive speech sparked a deeply misogynist response from the colony's male leaders.

When she described some of the leading ministers as unconverted men, the General Court intervened. Hutchinson was cross-examined for two days in 1637, but she knew Scripture too well to be easily tripped up. Then she made a slip that led to her undoing. She stated that what she knew of God came "by an immediate revelation." She had heard a voice. This "heretical" declaration fulfilled the worst fears of the colony's rulers, and they were relieved to exile Hutchinson and her followers to Rhode Island.

Mobility and Division

Massachusetts Bay spawned four new colonies, three of which survived to the American Revolution. New Hampshire became a separate colony in 1677, although its population grew slowly, and for much of the colonial period it remained economically dependent on Massachusetts.

Far more people were drawn to the fertile lands of the Connecticut River Valley. Populated by settlers from the Bay Colony under the ministry of Thomas Hooker, the valley took on the religious and cultural characteristics of Massachusetts. In 1639, representatives from the Connecticut towns drafted the Fundamental Orders, a blueprint for civil government; in 1662, Charles II awarded the colony a charter of its own. That same year, Connecticut absorbed the New Haven colony, a struggling Puritan settlement on Long Island Sound.

Rhode Island experienced a wholly different history. From the beginning, it drew people of a highly independent turn of mind. One Dutch visitor uncharitably characterized it as "the receptacle of all sorts of riff-raff people." However, the colony's broad toleration attracted many men and women who held unorthodox religious beliefs.

Toleration, however, did not mean cooperation. Villagers fought over land and schemed with outside speculators to divide the tiny colony into even smaller pieces. Even a royal charter obtained in 1663 did not calm the political turmoil. For most of the seventeenth century, colonywide government existed in name only. But despite all the bickering, Rhode Island's population grew, and the colony's commerce flourished.

CULTURAL DIVERSITY IN THE MIDDLE COLONIES

New York, New Jersey, Pennsylvania, and Delaware were founded for quite different reasons. William Penn, for example, envisioned a Quaker sanctuary; the duke of York worried chiefly about his own income. Despite the founders' intentions, however, some common characteristics emerged. Each colony developed a strikingly heterogeneous population of men and women of different ethnic and religious backgrounds. This cultural diversity became a major influence on the economic, political, and ecclesiastical institutions of the Middle Colonies and foreshadowed later American society.

Anglo-Dutch Rivalry on the Hudson

By the early decades of the seventeenth century, the Dutch had established themselves as Europe's most aggressive traders. Holland's merchant fleet was second to none, trading in Asia, Africa, and America. While searching for the elusive Northwest Passage in 1609, Henry Hudson, an English explorer employed by a Dutch company, sailed up the river that bears his name and claimed the area for Holland. Hudson's sponsors, the Dutch West India Company, established two permanent settlements, Fort Orange (Albany) and New Amsterdam (New York City) in the colony of New Netherland.

The first Dutch settlers in New Netherland were not actually colonists. Rather they were salaried employees of the company, who were expected to spend most of their time gathering animal fur pelts. They received no land for their efforts. Needless to say, this arrangement attracted relatively few Dutch immigrants.

Although the colony's population was small, only 270 in 1628, it contained an extraordinary ethnic mix. By the 1640s, Finns, Germans, and Swedes lived there, along with a sizable community of free blacks. Another contribution to the cacophony of languages was added by New England Puritans who moved to New Netherland to stake out farms on Long Island.

The company sent a succession of directors-general to oversee and govern. Without exception, these men were temperamentally unsuited to govern an American colony. They were autocratic, corrupt, and, above all, inept. The Long Island Puritans complained bitterly about the absence of any sort of representative government, and none of the colonists felt much loyalty to the trading company.

In August 1664, the Dutch lost their tenuous hold on New Netherland. The English Crown, eager to score an easy victory over a commercial rival, dispatched a fleet of warships to New Amsterdam (renamed New York City). No real fighting was needed. Although the last director-general, Peter Stuyvesant (1647–1664), urged resistance, the settlers decided otherwise. They accepted the Articles of Capitulation, a generous agreement that allowed Dutch nationals to remain in the province and to retain their property.

Charles II had already granted his brother, James, the duke of York, a charter for the newly captured territory and much else besides. He became absolute proprietor of Maine, Nantucket, Martha's Vineyard, and land extending from the Connecticut River to Delaware Bay. The duke was no more receptive to the idea of a representative government than the Dutch trading company had been; to appease the complaining colonists, the governor, Colonel Richard Nicolls, drew up a legal code known as the Duke's Laws. It guaranteed religious toleration and created local governments.

There was no provision, however, for an elected assembly. Nor was there much harmony in the colony. The Dutch, for example, continued to speak their own language, worship in their own churches (as Dutch Reformed Calvinists), and eye their English neighbors with suspicion. In fact, the colony seemed little different from what it had been under the Dutch West India Company: a loose collection of independent communities ruled by an ineffectual central government.

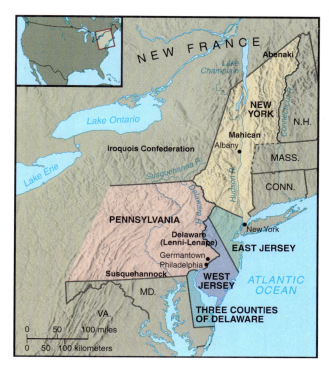

MIDDLE COLONIES, 1685   *Until the Revolution, the Iroquois blocked European expansion into western New York. East Jersey and West Jersey initially attracted English and Irish Quakers, who soon were joined by thousands of Protestant Irish and Germans.* ■

Confusion in New Jersey

Only three months after receiving a charter for New York, the duke made a terrible mistake—something this stubborn, humorless man was quite prone to do. He awarded the land situated between the Hudson and Delaware rivers to two courtiers, John, Lord Berkeley, and Sir George Carteret. This colony was named New Jersey in honor of Carteret's birthplace, the isle of Jersey in the English Channel.

The duke's impulsive act bred confusion. Before learning of James's decision, the governor of New York allowed migrants from New England to take up farms west of the Hudson River, promising them an opportunity to establish an elected assembly and liberty of conscience in exchange for the payment of a small annual quitrent to the duke. Berkeley and Carteret recruited colonists on similar terms. The new proprietors assumed, of course, that they would receive the rent money.

The result was chaos. Legally, only James could set up a colonial government or authorize an assembly. But knowledge of the law failed to quiet the controversy, and through it all, the duke showed not the slightest interest in the peace and welfare of the people of New Jersey.

Matters were further complicated in 1674 when Berkeley tired of the venture and sold his proprietary rights to a group of surprisingly quarrelsome Quakers. The colony was legally divided into East and West Jersey, but neither half prospered. When the West Jersey proprietors went bankrupt in 1702, the Crown mercifully re-united the two Jerseys into a single royal colony.

In 1700, the population of New Jersey amounted to approximately fourteen thousand. Its residents lived on scattered, often isolated farms; villages of more than a few hundred people were rare. And as in New York, the ethnic and religious diversity of the settlers was striking. Yet the colonists of New Jersey somehow managed to live together peaceably.

QUAKERS IN AMERICA

Quakers Members of a radical religious group, formally known as the Society of Friends, that rejected formal theology and stressed each person's "Inner Light," a spiritual guide to righteousness.

Quakers founded Pennsylvania. This radical religious group, formally known as the Society of Friends, gained its informal name from the English civil authorities' disparaging observation that its members "tremble at the word of the Lord." George Fox (1624–1691) was the tireless spokesman of the Society of Friends. He preached that every man and woman possessed a powerful, consoling "Inner Light." This was a wonderfully liberating message, especially for persons of lower-class origin. Gone was the stigma of original sin; discarded was the notion of eternal predestination. Everyone could be saved.

Quakers practiced humility. They wore simple clothes and employed old-fashioned terms of address that set them apart from their neighbors. They were also pacifists. According to Fox, all persons were equal in the sight of the Lord, a belief that annoyed people of rank and achievement. Moreover, they refused to keep their thoughts to themselves, spreading the light throughout England, Ireland, and America. Harassment, imprisonment, and even execution failed to curtail their activities. In fact, such measures proved counterproductive, for persecution only inspired the Quakers to redouble their efforts.

William Penn lived according to the Inner Light, a commitment that led eventually to the founding of Pennsylvania. He was a complex man: an athletic person interested in intellectual pursuits, a visionary capable of making pragmatic decisions, and an aristocrat whose religious beliefs involved him with the lower classes. Penn's religious commitment irritated his father, who hoped William would become a favorite at the Stuart court. Instead, Penn was expelled from Oxford University for holding unorthodox religious views, moved to the forefront of the Quaker movement, and even spent two years in an English jail for his beliefs.

Precisely when Penn's thoughts turned to America is not known, but in 1681, he negotiated one of the most impressive deals in the history of American real estate. Charles II awarded Penn a charter making him the sole proprietor of a vast area called Pennsylvania (literally, "Penn's woods"), a name that embarrassed the modest Quaker. The next year, Penn purchased from the duke of York the so-called

Three Lower Counties that eventually became Delaware. This astute move guaranteed that Pennsylvania would have open access to the Atlantic and determined even before Philadelphia had been established that it would become a great commercial center.

Penn lost no time in launching his Holy Experiment. His plan blended traditional notions about the privileges of a landed aristocracy with daring concepts of personal liberty. Penn guaranteed that the settlers would enjoy, among other things, liberty of conscience, freedom from persecution, no taxation without representation, and due process of law. He believed that both rich and poor had to have a voice in political affairs; neither should be able to overrule the legitimate interests of the other class. In his Frame of Government (1682), he envisioned a governor appointed by the proprietor, a provisional council responsible for initiating legislation, and an assembly that could accept or reject the bills presented to it. Penn apparently thought that the council would be filled by the colony's richest landholders and that the assembly would be peopled by the smaller landowners. It was a fanciful, clumsy structure, and the entire edifice crumbled ultimately under its own weight.

Penn promoted his colony aggressively throughout England, Ireland, and Germany. The response was overwhelming. People poured into Philadelphia and the surrounding area. Most of the early settlers were Quakers—Irish, Welsh, and English. But men and women from other lands soon joined the Quaker surge toward Penn's woods. One newcomer called the vessel that brought him to Philadelphia a "Noah's ark" of nationalities and religions.

Penn himself emigrated to America in 1682. His stay, however, was unexpectedly short and unhappy. The council and assembly fought over the right to initiate legislation. Wealthy Quaker merchants dominated the council, and rural settlers unconcerned about the Holy Experiment controlled the assembly. Many colonists refused to pay quitrents, and the Baltimore family claimed that much of

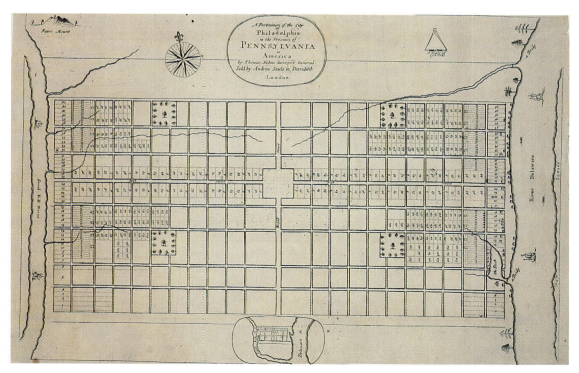

■ *William Penn's plan for Philadelphia shows the city laid out where the Scool Kill (Schuylkill) and Delaware rivers parallel each other. Four of the five public squares were intended to be parks while the fifth (at the center) was designated for public buildings. Today it is the site of Philadelphia's city hall.* ■

Pennsylvania actually lay in Maryland. In 1684, to defend his charter against Baltimore's attack, Penn returned to London.

Penn did not see his colony again until 1699. By that time, the settlement had changed considerably. Although it had prospered, a contentious quality pervaded its politics. Even the Quakers split into hostile factions. As the seventeenth century closed, few colonists still shared the founder's desire to create a godly, paternalistic society.

In 1701, legal challenges in England again forced Penn to depart for the mother country. Just before he sailed, Penn signed the Charter of Liberties, a new framework of government that established a unicameral, or one-house, legislature (the only one in colonial America) and gave the representatives the right to initiate legislation. The charter also provided for the political separation of the Three Lower Counties (Delaware) from Pennsylvania, something people living in the area had demanded for years. This hastily drafted document served as Pennsylvania's constitution until the American Revolution.

His experience in America must have depressed Penn, now old and sick. In England, Penn was imprisoned for debts incurred by dishonest colonial agents, and in 1718, Pennsylvania's founder died a broken man.

PLANTING THE CAROLINAS

In some ways, Carolina society seemed very similar to the one that had developed in Virginia and Maryland. In both areas, white planters forced unfree laborers to produce staple crops for a world market. But such superficial similarities masked substantial regional differences. In fact, "the South"—certainly the fabled solid South of the early nineteenth century—did not exist during the colonial period. The Carolinas, joined at a much later date by Georgia, stood apart from their Chesapeake neighbors.

Carolina owed its establishment to the restoration of the Stuarts to the English throne. Court favorites who had followed the Stuarts into exile during the civil war demanded tangible rewards for their loyalty. New York and New Jersey were obvious plums. So, too, was Carolina. On March 24, 1663, King Charles II granted Sir John Colleton and seven other courtiers a charter to the vast territory between Virginia and Florida and running west "as far as the South Seas."

Unlike so many Englishmen before them, the eight proprietors did not think of America in terms of instant wealth. Their plan involved luring settlers from established American colonies by means of an attractive land policy and such other incentives as a representative assembly, liberty of conscience, and a liberal headright system. In exchange for their privileges, they demanded only a small annual quitrent.

After dividing their grant into three distinct jurisdictions—Albemarle, Cape Fear, and Port Royal—proprietors waited for the money to roll in; to their dismay, no one seemed particularly interested in moving to the Carolina frontier. Plans for the settlement of Cape Fear and Port Royal fell through, and the majority of the surviving proprietors gave up on Carolina.

Anthony Ashley Cooper, later known as the earl of Shaftesbury, was an exception. In 1669, he persuaded the remaining proprietors to invest their own capital in the colony. He then dispatched more than three hundred English colonists to Carolina. After a rough voyage that saw one ship destroyed by Atlantic gales, the settlers arrived at the Ashley River. Later the colony's administrative center, Charles Town (it did not become Charleston until 1783), was established at the junction of the Ashley and Cooper Rivers.

Cooper also wanted to bring order to the new society. With assistance from John Locke, the famous English philosopher (1632–1704), Cooper devised the Fundamental Constitutions of Carolina. His goal was to create a landed aristocracy that governed the colony through the Council of Nobles, a body designed to adminis-

ENGLAND'S PRINCIPAL MAINLAND COLONIES

Name	Original Purpose	Date of Founding	Principal Founder	Major Export	Estimated Population ca. 1700
Virginia	Commercial venture	1607	Captain John Smith	Tobacco	64,560
New Amsterdam (New York)	Commercial venture	1613 (made English colony, 1664)	Peter Stuyvesant, Duke of York	Furs, grain	19,107
Plymouth	Refuge for English Separatists	1620 (absorbed by Massachusetts, 1691)	William Bradford	Grain	Included with Massachusetts
New Hampshire	Commercial venture	1623	John Mason	Wood, naval stores	4,958
Massachusetts	Refuge for English Puritans	1628	John Winthrop	Grain, wood	55,941
Maryland	Refuge for English Catholics	1634	Lord Baltimore (George Calvert)	Tobacco	34,100
Connecticut	Expansion of Massachusetts	1635	Thomas Hooker	Grain	25,970
Rhode Island	Refuge for dissenters from Massachusetts	1636	Roger Williams	Grain	5,894
New Sweden (Delaware)	Commercial venture	1638 (included in Penn grant, 1681; given separate assembly, 1703)	Peter Minuit, William Penn	Grain	2,470
North Carolina	Commercial venture	1663	Anthony Ashley Cooper	Wood, naval stores, tobacco	10,720
South Carolina	Commercial venture	1663	Anthony Ashley Cooper	Naval stores, rice, indigo	5,720
New Jersey	Consolidation of new English territory, Quaker settlement	1664	Sir George Carteret	Grain	14,010
Pennsylvania	Refuge for English Quakers	1681	William Penn	Grain	18,950
Georgia	Discourage Spanish expansion; charity	1733	James Oglethorpe	Rice, wood, naval stores	5,200 (in 1750)

Sources: U.S. Bureau of the Census, *Historical Statistics of the United States: Colonial Times to 1970,* Washington, D.C., 1975; John J. McCusker and Russell R. Menard, *The Economy of British America, 1607–1789,* Chapel Hill, 1985.

ter justice, oversee civil affairs, and initiate legislation. A parliament in which smaller landowners had a voice could accept or reject bills drafted by the council. The very poor were excluded from political activity altogether. Cooper's plans for a "balance of government" between aristocracy and democracy, however, never conformed to the realities of Carolina society, and his Council of Nobles remained a paper dream.

Before 1680, almost half the men and women who settled in the Port Royal area came from Barbados. This small Caribbean island, which produced an annual fortune in sugar, depended on slave labor. By the third quarter of the seventeenth century, Barbados had become overpopulated, and Barbadians looked to Carolina for relief. These migrants, many of whom were quite wealthy, traveled to Carolina both as individuals and as family groups. Some brought slave gangs with them. The Barbadians carved out plantations on the tributaries of the Cooper River and established themselves immediately as the colony's most powerful political faction. The society they created was closer to the slave-based plantation society they left than to any of the other English colonies.

Much of the planters' time was taken up with the search for a profitable crop. They experimented with a number of plants—tobacco, cotton, silk, and grapes. The most successful items in the early years turned out to be beef, cattle, furs, and naval stores (especially tar, used to maintain ocean vessels). It was not until the 1690s that the planters came to appreciate fully the value of rice, but once they had done so, it quickly became the colony's main staple.

Proprietary Carolina was in a constant political uproar. Barbadian settlers resisted the proprietors' policies, and the proprietors appointed a series of utterly incompetent governors. By the end of the century, the lower houses of assembly had assumed the right to initiate legislation. In 1719, the colonists overthrew the last proprietary government, and in 1729, the king created separate royal governments in North and South Carolina.

THE FOUNDING OF GEORGIA

The early history of Georgia was strikingly different from that of Britain's other mainland colonies. Its settlement was really an act of aggression against Spain, a country that had as good a claim to the area as the English did. During the eighteenth century, the two nations were often at war (see Chapter 4), and South Carolinians worried that the Spaniards moving up from bases in Florida would occupy the disputed territory between Florida and the Carolina grant.

The colony owed its existence primarily to James Oglethorpe, a British general and member of Parliament who believed that he could thwart Spanish designs on the area south of Charles Town while providing a fresh start for London's debtors. Although Oglethorpe envisioned Georgia as an asylum as well as a garrison, the military aspects of his proposal were especially appealing to the leaders of the British government. In 1732, the king granted Oglethorpe and a board of trustees a charter for a new colony. The trustees living in the mother country were given complete control over Georgia politics, a condition the settlers soon found intolerable.

At first, the colony did not fare very well. Few English debtors showed any desire to move there, and the trustees provided little incentive for emigration. No settler could amass more than 500 acres of land. Moreover, land could be passed only to an eldest son, and if a planter died without a son, the holding reverted to Oglethorpe and the trustees. Slavery and rum were prohibited.

The settlers wanted more—slaves, a voice in local government, unrestricted land ownership. Oglethorpe met their demands with angry rebuffs. Eventually, however, Oglethorpe lost interest in his colonial experiment, and the trustees were then forced to compromise their principles. In 1738, they eliminated all restrictions on the amount of land a person could own and allowed women to inherit land. Slaves came next, then rum. In 1751, the trustees gave up on what had become a hard-drinking, slave-holding plantation society and returned Georgia to the king. That same year, the king authorized an assembly. But even with these social and political changes, Georgia attracted very few new settlers.

THE CAROLINAS AND GEORGIA   *Caribbean sugar planters migrated to the Goose Creek area where, with knowledge supplied by African slaves, they eventually mastered rice cultivation. Poor harbors in North Carolina retarded the spread of European settlement in that region.* ■

Chronology

1607	First English settlers arrive at Jamestown
1608–1609	Scrooby Congregation (Pilgrims) leaves England for Holland
1609–1611	"Starving time" in Virginia threatens survival of the colonists
1619	Virginia assembly, called House of Burgesses, meets for the first time ■ First slaves sold at Jamestown
1620	Pilgrims sign the Mayflower Compact
1622	Surprise attack by local Indians devastates Virginia
1624	Dutch investors create permanent settlements along the Hudson River ■ James I, king of England, dissolves the Virginia Company
1625	Charles I ascends the English throne
1630	John Winthrop transfers Massachusetts Bay charter to New England
1634	Colony of Maryland is founded
1638	Anne Hutchinson is exiled to Rhode Island
1639	Connecticut towns accept Fundamental Orders
1649	Charles I is executed during the English civil war
1660	Stuarts are restored to the English throne
1663	Rhode Island obtains royal charter ■ Proprietors receive charter for Carolina
1664	English soldiers conquer New Netherland
1677	New Hampshire becomes a royal colony
1681	William Penn granted patent for his Holy Experiment

CONCLUSION: LIVING WITH DIVERSITY

The seventeenth-century English colonies had little in common beyond their allegiance to the king. A contemporary visitor could find along the Atlantic Coast a spectrum of settlements, from the almost feudal hierarchy of Carolina to the visionary paternalism of Pennsylvania to the Puritan commonwealth of Massachusetts Bay. The diversity of English colonization needs to be emphasized precisely because it is so easy to overlook. Even though the colonists eventually banded together and fought for independence and established a federal government, persistent differences separated New Englanders from Virginians, Pennsylvanians from Carolinians.

KEY TERMS

Glorious Revolution, p. 23	headright, p. 25	Puritan, p. 29
joint-stock company, p. 23	indentured servants, p. 26	antinomianism, p. 32
House of Burgesses, p. 25	Mayflower Compact, p. 28	Quakers, p. 34

RECOMMENDED READING

The literature of seventeenth-century English settlement in North America is immense. To comprehend better the diversity of American colonial experience, it is wise to start with the society from which the settlers migrated. A good introduction to England's participation in an Atlantic World is Nicholas Canny, ed., *The Oxford History of the British Empire, vol. 1, The Origins of Empire: English Overseas Enterprise from the Beginning to the Close of the Seventeenth Century* (1998). The best single work on Puritanism remains Perry Miller, *The New England Mind: From Colony to*

Province (1956). David D. Hall explores popular religious practice in New England in *Worlds of Wonder, Days of Judgment: Popular Religious Belief in Early New England* (1989). Also valuable is Michael P. Winship, *Making Heretics: Militant Protestantism and Free Grace in Massachusetts, 1636–1641* (2002). Original studies of the founding of Virginia are Edmund S. Morgan, *American Slavery, American Freedom: The Ordeal of Colonial Virginia* (1975); Kathleen M. Brown, *Good Wives, Nasty Wenches, and Anxious Patriarchs: Gender, Race, and Power in Colonial Virginia* (1996); and James Horn, *A Land as God Made It: Jamestown and the Birth of America* (2005). T. H. Breen compares the development of seventeenth-century New England and the Chesapeake in *Puritans and Adventurers: Change and Persistence in Early America* (1980). The forces that drove migration to the New World during this period are the subject of David Cressy's *Coming Over: Migration and Communication Between England and New England in the Seventeenth Century* (1987) and James Horn's *Adapting to a New World: English Society in the Seventeenth-Century Chesapeake* (1994). On the experience of captives during the wars against the French and Native Americans, see James Axtell, *The Invasion Within: The Conquest of Cultures in Colonial North America* (1985), and Evan Haefeli and Kevin Sweeney, *Captors and Captives* (2003). Useful investigations of the founding of New York and Pennsylvania are Gary B. Nash, *Quakers and Politics: Pennsylvania 1681–1726* (1968); Richard S. Dunn and Mary Maples Dunn, eds., *The World of William Penn* (1986); and Russell Shorto, *The Island at the Center of the World* (2004).

SUGGESTED WEB SITES

The Plymouth Colony Archive Project at the University of Virginia
etext.virginia.edu/users/deetz
This site contains comprehensive and fairly extensive information about late seventeenth-century Plymouth Colony.

Jamestown Rediscovery
www.apva.org
This site, mounted by the Association for the Preservation of Virginia Antiquity, has excellent material on archaeological excavations at Jamestown.

Lost Worlds: Georgia Before Oglethorpe
www.lostworlds.org/ga_before_oglethorpe.html
This resources guide informs the viewer about Native American Georgia in the seventeenth century.

William Penn, Visionary Proprietor
xroads.virginia.edu/~CAP/PENN/pnhome.html
William Penn had an interesting life, and this site is a good introduction to the man and some of his achievements.

Chapter 3

Putting Down Roots: Opportunity and Oppression in Colonial Society

Families in an Atlantic Empire

The Witherspoon family moved from Great Britain to the South Carolina back-country early in the eighteenth century. Their son, Robert, who was only a small child when his family moved to America, later produced an exceptional and candid account of their pioneer life. On arrival in South Carolina, the Witherspoons experienced a wave of despondency. Where they expected to find a fine-timbered house and the comforts of England, they discovered acres of wilderness and "a very mean dirt house." For many years, the Witherspoons feared that they would be killed by Indians, become lost in the woods, or be bitten by snakes.

The Witherspoons managed to survive the early difficult years on the Black River. Although the Carolina backcountry did not look very much like the world they had left behind, Robert's father remained optimistic about the future. He assured his family that soon the trees would be cut down and the land would be populated by neighbors.

Robert Witherspoon's account serves as a reminder that early American history was created by families and not, as some commentators would have people believe, by individuals. Neither the peopling of the Atlantic frontier, the cutting down of the forests, nor the creation of communities was part of what would be considered state policy today. Families determined much of the character of the American colonies. It was within this primary social unit that most colonists earned their livelihoods, educated their children, defined gender roles, sustained religious traditions, and nursed each other in sickness.

Early colonial families did not exist in isolation. They were part of larger societies. The characteristics of the first English settlements in the New World varied substantially (see Chapter 2), and these initial differences grew stronger during the seventeenth century as each region responded to different environmental conditions and developed its own traditions. The characteristics of the local societies reflected their supply of labor, abundance of land, and commercial ties with European markets.

By 1660, the regional differences had nearly undermined any possibility of a unified English empire in America. During the reign of King Charles II, however, a trend toward cultural convergence began. Such unifying forces as a common language and a common religion began to overcome the economic and cultural differences and pull the English colonists together. Parliament took advantage of this trend and began to establish a uniform set of rules for the expanding American empire. The process was slow and uneven, often sparking violent colonial resistance. By the end of the seventeenth century, England had made significant progress toward transforming New World provinces into an empire that produced

Outline

Sources of Stability: New England Family Values in the Seventeenth Century

The Challenge of the Chesapeake Environment

Race and Freedom in British America

Rise of a Commercial Empire

Colonial Factions Spark Political Revolt, 1676–1691

Conclusion: Local Aspirations Within an Atlantic Empire

raw materials and purchased manufactured goods. If a person was black and enslaved, however, he or she was more apt to experience oppression rather than opportunity in British America.

SOURCES OF STABILITY: NEW ENGLAND FAMILY VALUES IN THE SEVENTEENTH CENTURY

Seventeenth-century New Englanders successfully replicated in America a traditional social order they had known in England. The transfer of a familiar way of life to the New World seemed less difficult for these Puritan migrants than it did for the many English men and women who settled in the Chesapeake colonies. Their contrasting experiences, fundamental to an understanding of the development of both cultures, can be explained, at least in part, by the extraordinary strength and resilience of New England families.

Tradition and a New Social Order

Early New Englanders believed that God ordained the family for human benefit. It was essential to the maintenance of social order, since outside the family, men and women succumbed to carnal temptation. Such people had no one to sustain them, no one to remind them of Scripture. And just as Scripture taught obedience to the Lord, the godly seventeenth-century family required obedience to the patriarch at its head.

Familial experience exercised a powerful influence on early New England life. Mature adults who migrated to America within nuclear families preserved local English customs more fully than did the youths who traveled to other parts of the continent as single men and women. Not only did traveling with one's family help reduce the shock of migration, but it also ensured that the ratio between men and women would be fairly well balanced. Persons who had not already married in England could expect to form nuclear families of their own.

The Great Migration of the 1630s and early 1640s brought approximately twenty thousand persons to New England. The English civil war reduced this flood to a trickle, but by the end of the century, the population of New England had reached almost 120,000, an amazing increase considering the small number of original immigrants. Historians have long searched for the reason. Men and women in New England married no earlier than they did in England: for a first marriage, men's average age was in the mid-twenties; women wed in their early twenties. Nor were Puritan families unusually large by the standards of the period.

The reason turned out to be longevity. Put simply, people who, under normal conditions, would have died in contemporary Europe survived in New England. Indeed, the life expectancy of seventeenth-century settlers was not very different from that of Americans today. Males who survived infancy could expect to see their seventieth birthday. The figures for women were only slightly lower. No one is sure why they lived longer, but pure drinking water, a cool climate that retarded the spread of fatal contagious disease, and a dispersed population promoted general good health.

Longer life altered family relations. New England may have been one of the first societies in recorded history in which a person could reasonably anticipate knowing his or her grandchildren. The traditions of particular families and communities therefore remained alive, literally, in the memories of the colony's oldest citizens.

Commonwealth of Families

The life cycle of the family in New England began with marriage. Young men and women generally selected their own partners, usually a neighbor. Prospective brides were expected to possess a dowry worth approximately one-half what the bridegroom brought to the union. The overwhelming majority of the region's population married, for in New England, the single life was not only physically difficult but also morally suspect.

The household was primarily a place of work—very demanding work. The primary goal, of course, was to clear enough land to feed the family. But a family also needed a surplus crop to pay for items that could not be manufactured at home—metal tools, for example. The belief that early American farmers were self-sufficient is a misconception.

During the seventeenth century, men and women generally lived in the communities of their parents and grandparents. Towns, in fact, were collections of families, not individuals. Over time, the families intermarried, so that the community became an elaborate kinship network. In many towns, the original founders dominated local politics and economic affairs for several generations. Not surprisingly, newcomers who were not absorbed into the family system tended to move away from the village with greater frequency than the sons and daughters of the established lineage groups.

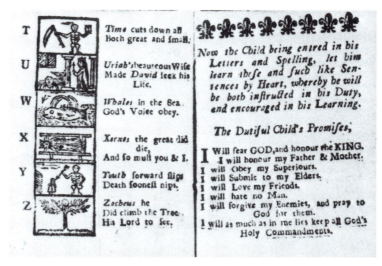

■ *New England parents took seriously their responsibility for the spiritual welfare of their children. To seek the word of God, young people had to learn to read.* The New England Primer, *shown here, was their primary vehicle.* ■

Congregational churches were also built on a family foundation. During the earliest years of settlement, the churches accepted persons who could demonstrate that they were among God's "elect." But when the sons and daughters of the elect failed to experience saving grace, a synod in 1662 adopted the so-called Half-Way Covenant. The compromise allowed the grandchildren of persons in full communion to be baptized even though their own parents could not demonstrate conversion. Obsession with family meant that by the end of the century, Congregational churches often failed to meet the religious needs of New Englanders who were not members of the select families.

Colonists regarded education as primarily a family responsibility. The ability to read was considered essential for learning the principles of Christianity. For this reason, the Massachusetts legislature ordered towns containing at least fifty families to open elementary schools supported by local taxes. Larger towns supported more advanced grammar schools, which taught a basic knowledge of Latin. After 1638, young men could attend Harvard College, the first institution of higher learning founded in England's mainland colonies.

This family-based education system worked. A majority of the region's adult males could read and write, an accomplishment not achieved in the Chesapeake colonies for another century. The literacy rate for women was somewhat lower, but by the standards of the period, it was still impressive.

Women's Lives in Puritan New England

The status of women in colonial New England was complex. Although subordinate to men by law and custom, their productive labor was essential to the survival of most households. They cooked, washed, made clothes, milked cows, gardened, and raised poultry. Sometimes, by selling surplus food, wives achieved some economic independence. Women also joined churches in greater numbers than men did, and it is possible that their involvement in these institutions encouraged them to express their ideas.

In both political and legal matters, society sharply curtailed the rights of colonial women. According to common law practice, a wife exercised no control over property. And since a divorce was extremely difficult to obtain, a woman married to a cruel or irresponsible spouse had little recourse but to run away or accept the unhappy situation.

Yet most women were neither prosperous entrepreneurs nor abject slaves. Like men, they generally accepted the roles that they thought God had ordained. Although Puritan couples worried that the affection they felt for a husband or a wife might turn their thoughts away from God's perfect love, this was a danger they were willing to risk.

Social Hierarchy in New England

During the seventeenth century, the New England colonies attracted neither noblemen nor paupers, an incomplete social structure by contemporary European standards. The lack of very wealthy, titled persons was particularly troublesome. According to the prevailing hierarchical view of the structure of society, well-placed individuals were *natural rulers,* people intended by God to exercise political authority over the rank and file. Migration forced the colonists, however, to choose their rulers from men of more modest status, ignoring the "ordinariness of their persons."

The colonists gradually sorted themselves out into distinct social groupings. To become part of the ruling elite, it helped to possess at least moderate wealth and education; it was also expected that leaders would belong to a Congregational church and defend religious orthodoxy. The Winthrops, Dudleys, and Pynchons fulfilled these expectations, and in public affairs they assumed dominant roles. They took their responsibility quite seriously and certainly did not look kindly on anyone who spoke of their "ordinariness."

The problem was that while most New Englanders accepted a hierarchical view of society, they disagreed over their assigned places. Both Massachusetts Bay and Connecticut enacted sumptuary laws—statutes that restricted the wearing of fine apparel to the wealthy and prominent—designed to curb the pretensions of lower-status individuals. By the end of the century, the character of the ruling class in New England had changed, and personal piety figured less importantly in social ranking than family background and a large estate.

Most northern colonists were yeomen (independent farmers), few of whom became rich and even fewer of whom fell hopelessly into debt. Possession of land gave agrarian families a sense of independence from external authority, but during the seventeenth century, this independence was balanced by an equally strong feeling of local identity. Not until the late eighteenth century, when a large number of New Englanders left their familial villages in search of new land, did many northern yeomen place personal material ambition above traditional community bonds.

It was not unusual for northern colonists to work as servants among their neighbors at some point in their lives. New Englanders recruited few servants from the Old World. Their forms of agriculture, which mixed cereal with dairy farming, made employment of large gangs of dependent workers uneconomical. New England servants more resembled apprentices than anything else, and servitude was more a vocational training program than an exploitative system. This was vastly different from the institutions that developed in the Southern Colonies.

By the end of the seventeenth century, the New England Puritans had developed a compelling story about their own history in the New World. The founders had been extraordinarily godly men and women, and in a heroic effort to establish a purer form of religion, pious families had passed "over the vast ocean into this vast and howling wilderness." Although the children and grandchildren of the first generation sometimes questioned their own ability to please the Lord, they recognized the mission to the New World as a success.

A Look at the Past

Freake Portraits

Bright colors, lace, embroidery, and other lavish details on the clothing John and Elizabeth Freake wore for their portraits, painted by an unknown artist in the 1670s, refute the notion that Puritans wore only somber clothes. The Freakes's attire also reveals attitudes about children and gender roles. Elizabeth is holding her son, dressed in a gown as both male and female babies were at the time. Note how similar their gowns are; her son's is nearly a miniaturized version of Elizabeth's. ✱ If babies wore miniaturized adult clothing, what does that suggest about the lives of children? Was childhood a distinctive developmental stage to be relished?

THE CHALLENGE OF THE CHESAPEAKE ENVIRONMENT

An entirely different regional society developed in England's Chesapeake colonies, Virginia and Maryland. Although the two areas were founded at roughly the same time by Protestant Englishmen, the regions were worlds apart in terms of environmental conditions, labor systems, and agrarian economies. The most important reason for the distinctiveness of these early southern plantation societies, however, turned out to be the Chesapeake's death rate, a frighteningly high mortality that tore at the very fabric of family life.

Family Life at Risk

Unlike the New England settlers, the men and women who migrated to the Chesapeake region did not move in family units. Nor were most entirely free when they arrived. Between 70 and 85 percent of the white colonists who went to Virginia and Maryland during the seventeenth century owed four or five years' labor in exchange for the cost of passage to America. Most of these indentured servants were men, and although more women made the voyage after 1640, the gender ratio in the Chesapeake was never as balanced as it had been in early Massachusetts.

Most immigrants to the Chesapeake region died soon after arriving. Malaria and other diseases took a frightful toll, and drinking water contaminated with salt killed many colonists living in low-lying areas. Life expectancy for Chesapeake males was about 43, some ten to twenty years less than for men born in New England! For women, life expectancy was even shorter. A full 25 percent of all children died in infancy. Another 25 percent did not see their twentieth birthday. The survivors were often weak or ill, unable to perform hard physical labor.

These demographic conditions retarded normal population increase. Young women who might have become wives and mothers could not do so until they had completed their terms of servitude. They thus lost several reproductive years, and in a society in which so many children died in infancy, late marriages greatly restricted family size. Moreover, the unbalanced gender ratio meant that many men could not find wives. Without a constant flow of immigrants, the population of Virginia and Maryland would have actually declined.

High mortality compressed the family cycle into a few short years. Marriages were extremely fragile, and one partner usually died within seven years. Not only did children not meet grandparents, but they also often did not even know their own parents. Widows and widowers quickly remarried, and children frequently grew up with persons to whom they had no blood relation. People had to adjust to the impermanence of family life and to cope with a high degree of personal insecurity.

The unbalanced gender ratio in the Chesapeake may have provided women with the means to improve their social status. Because of the uneven numbers, women could be confident of finding husbands, regardless of their abilities, attractiveness, or moral character. Despite liberation from some traditional restraints, however, women as servants were still vulnerable to sexual exploitation by their masters. Moreover, childbearing was extremely dangerous; women in the Chesapeake usually died twenty years earlier than their New England counterparts.

The Structure of Planter Society

Tobacco cultivation formed the basis of the Chesapeake economy. Although anyone with a few acres of cleared land could grow leaves for export, cultivation of the Chesapeake staple did not produce a society of individuals roughly similar in wealth and status. To the contrary, it generated inequality. The amassing of a large fortune involved the control of a large labor force. More workers in the fields meant larger harvests and, of course, larger profits. Since free persons showed no interest in toiling away in another man's fields of tobacco, not even for wages, wealthy planters relied on laborers who were not free as well as on slaves. The social structure that developed in the seventeenth-century Chesapeake reflected a wild, often unscrupulous scramble to bring men and women of three races—black, white, and Indian—into various degrees of independence.

Great planters dominated Chesapeake society. The group was small and, during the early decades of the seventeenth century, constantly changing. Not until the 1650s did the family names of those who would become famous eighteenth-century gentry appear on the records. These ambitious men arrived in America with capital. They invested immediately in laborers, and one way or another, they obtained huge tracts of the best tobacco-growing land. Though not aristocrats, but rather the younger sons of English merchants and artisans, they soon acquired political and social power. Over time, these gentry families—including the Burwells, Byrds, Carters, and Masons—intermarried so extensively that they created a vast network of cousins. During the eighteenth century, it was not uncommon to find a half dozen men with the same surname sitting simultaneously in the Virginia House of Burgesses.

Freemen formed the largest class in Chesapeake society. Most came as indentured servants, unlike New England's yeomen farmers, and by sheer good fortune managed to stay alive to the end of their contracts. When their period of indenture was over, many freemen lived on the edge of poverty, although a few lived better than they might have in England.

Below the freemen came indentured servants. Membership in this group was not demeaning; after all, servitude was a temporary status. But servitude in the Chesapeake colonies was not the benign institution it was in New England. Great planters took on servants to grow tobacco, and they were not overly concerned with the well-being of the laborers. The unhappy servants regarded their servitude as a form of slavery, while the planters worried that discontented servants and impoverished freemen would rebel at the slightest provocation. Later events would justify these fears.

Social mobility changed during the seventeenth century. Before the 1680s, movement into the planter elite by newcomers who possessed capital was relatively easy. After the 1680s, however, life expectancy rates improved in the Chesapeake colonies, and the sons of great planters replaced their fathers in powerful government positions. The key to success was possession of slaves. Planters who owned more slaves could grow more tobacco and thus purchase additional laborers. Over time, the rich not only became richer, but they also formed a distinct ruling elite that newcomers found increasingly difficult to enter.

Opportunities for advancement also decreased for the region's freemen. As the gentry consolidated its hold on political and economic institutions, ordinary people discovered that it was much harder to rise in Chesapeake society. Men and women with more ambitious dreams headed for Pennsylvania, North Carolina, and western Virginia.

■ This painting, Henry Darnall III as a Child *(ca. 1710), by the German émigré painter Justus Engelhardt Kuhn depicts the son of a wealthy planter family in Maryland armed with a bow and arrow. To the left, an African American slave holds a dead bird. This is the earliest known depiction of an African American in a colonial painting. The formal architecture and gardens in the background suggest an idealized European landscape and a connection to the European culture that some members of the colonial gentry imagined for themselves.* ■

Social institutions that figured importantly in the New Englanders' daily lives were either weak or nonexistent in the Chesapeake, partly due to the high infant mortality rates. There was little incentive to build elementary schools, for example, since only half the children would reach adulthood. The development of higher education languished, similarly, and the great planters sent their sons to English or Scottish schools through much of the colonial period.

Tobacco also inhibited the growth of towns in this region. Owners of isolated plantations along the riverbanks traded directly with English merchants and had little need for local markets. People met sporadically at scattered churches, courthouses, and taverns. Seventeenth-century Virginia could not boast of even one printing press.

RACE AND FREEDOM IN BRITISH AMERICA

Many people who landed in the colonies had no desire to come to the New World; they were brought from Africa as slaves to cultivate rice, sugar, and tobacco. As the Native Americans were exterminated and the supply of white indentured servants dried up, white planters demanded ever more African laborers.

Roots of Slavery

Between the sixteenth and nineteenth centuries, slave traders carried almost eleven million blacks from Africa to the New World, mainly to Brazil and the Caribbean. Only a small part of this commerce involved British North America. Young black males predominated in the human cargo; the planters preferred this group for the hard physical labor of the plantations. In many early slave communities, black men outnumbered women by a ratio of two to one.

English colonists did not hesitate to enslave black people; the decision to import African slaves to the British colonies was based primarily on economic considerations. But English masters never justified the practice purely in terms of planter profits. They associated blacks in Africa with heathen religion, barbarous behavior, sexual promiscuity—in fact, with evil itself. From such a perspective, the enslavement of African men and women seemed unobjectionable. Planters avowed that loss of freedom was a small price for the civilizing benefits of conversion to Christianity.

Africans first landed in Virginia in 1619. For the next fifty years, their status remained unclear. English settlers classified some black laborers as slaves for life, others as indentured servants. A few blacks purchased their freedom. Several seventeenth-century Africans even became successful Virginia planters.

One reason that Virginia lawmakers tolerated such confusion was that the black population remained very small. Planters wanted more African slaves, but during this period, slave traders sold their cargoes on Barbados or the other sugar islands of the West Indies, where they fetched a higher price than Virginians could afford. In fact, before 1680, most blacks who reached England's colonies on the North American mainland came from Barbados or through New Netherland rather than directly from Africa.

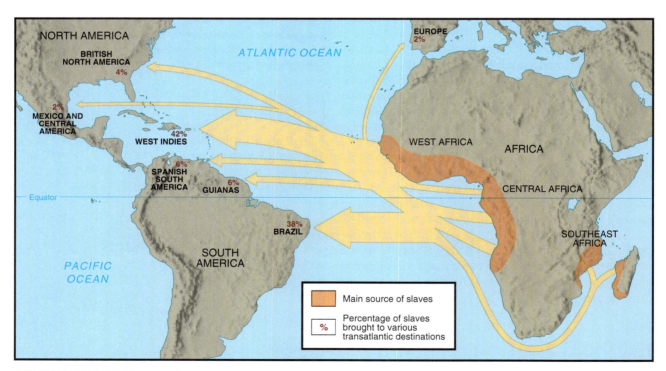

ORIGINS AND DESTINATIONS OF AFRICAN SLAVES, 1619–1760 *Although many African slaves were transported to Britain's North American colonies, far more slaves were sold in the Caribbean sugar colonies and Brazil, where because of horrific health conditions, the death rate far exceeded that of the British mainland colonies.* ■

By the end of the seventeenth century, the status of Virginia's black people was no longer in doubt. They were slaves for life, as were their children after them. Slavery was unequivocally based on skin color alone. This transformation reflected an increase in the supply of Africans to British North America. After 1672, the Royal African Company undertook to meet the colonial planters' rising demands for black laborers, and during the eighteenth century, many American merchants entered the lucrative trade.

The expanding black population apparently frightened white colonists, and lawmakers drew up ever stricter slave codes. The white planter could deal with his black property as he alone saw fit, and one extraordinary Virginia statute excused a master who killed a slave on the grounds that no rational person would purposely "destroy his own estate." Furthermore, children born to a slave woman became slaves regardless of the father's race. Nor did conversion to Christianity free blacks from bondage. Unlike the Spanish colonies, where persons of lighter color enjoyed greater privileges in society, in the English colonies, racial mixing was not tolerated, and mulattoes received the same treatment as pure Africans.

Constructing African American Identities

The slave experience varied substantially from colony to colony. The size and density of the slave population determined in large measure how successfully blacks could maintain a separate cultural identity. On isolated rice plantations in South Carolina, where during the eighteenth century 60 percent of the population was black, African Americans developed creoles, languages that blended English with words from African tongues. Slaves on these large plantations were also able to establish elaborate and enduring kinship networks that may have helped reduce the more dehumanizing aspects of bondage.

Blacks made up a smaller percentage of the population in New England and the Middle Colonies (less than 10 percent) and even in Virginia (40 percent). Most slaves in the Northern Colonies worked as domestics and lived in their masters' homes. Close contact with whites made it more difficult to preserve and reaffirm an African heritage and identity.

In eighteenth-century Virginia, native-born blacks had learned to cope with whites on a daily basis. They looked with disdain on slaves who had just arrived

■ Old Plantation, *a watercolor by an unknown artist (about 1800), shows that African customs survived plantation slavery. The man and women in the center dance (possibly to celebrate a wedding) to the music of drum and banjo. Instruments, turbans, and scarves reflect a distinctive African American culture in the New World.* ■

from Africa. Blacks as well as whites pressed these "outlandish" newcomers to accept elements of English culture, especially to speak the English language.

Despite their wrenching experiences, black slaves did establish cultural traditions that involved an imaginative reshaping of African and European customs into something that was neither African nor European; it was African American. For example, slaves embraced Christianity but transformed it into an expression of religious feeling in which an African element remained vibrant.

During the early decades of the eighteenth century, blacks living in England's mainland colonies began to experience reproductive success as live births exceeded deaths. This demographic milestone was not reached in the Caribbean or South American colonies until a much later date. Historians surmise that North American blacks enjoyed a healthier climate and a better diet than other New World slaves.

But longer lives did not make them any less slaves. Nor did it prevent slave protests, including organized revolt. The most serious slave rebellion of the colonial period was the Stono Uprising, which took place in September 1739. One hundred and fifty South Carolina blacks rose up and murdered several whites. They marched toward Florida and the promise of freedom, but the local militia overtook and crushed the revolt. Such rebellions were rare; in fact, the level of interracial violence in colonial North America was quite low. But the fear of slave rebellions was pervasive, prompting whites to take drastic defensive measures.

RISE OF A COMMERCIAL EMPIRE

Just as the status of slaves changed during the seventeenth century, so did the status of white colonists. Until the middle of the seventeenth century, English political leaders largely ignored the American colonists. After the restoration of Charles II to the throne in 1660, however, intervention replaced indifference. The Crown, Parliament, and the mercantile interests decided that the colonies should be brought more tightly under the control of the mother country. Regulatory policies that evolved during this period formed a framework for empire that survived with only minor adjustments until 1765.

Response to Economic Competition

mercantilism An economic theory that shaped imperial policy throughout the colonial period, mercantilism was built on the assumption that the world's wealth was a fixed supply. In order to increase its wealth, a nation needed to export more goods than it imported. Favorable trade and protective economic policies, as well as new colonial possessions rich in raw materials, were important in achieving this balance.

By the 1660s, the dominant commercial powers of Europe adopted economic principles that later critics would term **mercantilism.** Proponents of this position argued that since trading nations were engaged in a fierce competition for the world's resources—mostly for raw materials transported from dependent colonies—one nation's commerical success translated directly into a loss for its rivals. It seemed logical, therefore, that England would want to protect its own markets from France or Holland. Later advocates of free trade, such as the famous eighteenth-century Scottish economist Adam Smith, claimed that mercantilism actually worked against the nation's true economic interests. Smith insisted that an open competition among merchants would stimulate trade and raise everyone's standard of living. But for seventeenth-century planners free markets made no sense. They argued that trade tightly regulated by the central government represented the only way to increase the nation's wealth at the expense of competitors.

Smith's specific term, however, is misleading. "Mercantilist system" as administered by the policymakers of the late seventeenth century was not nearly as well thought out or organized as Smith suggested. Rather, it represented a series of individual responses to the needs of several powerful interest groups.

Each group looked to colonial commerce to solve a different problem. Charles wanted money to pay his enormous debts. English merchants were eager to exclude Dutch rivals from lucrative American markets, but without government assistance, they could not compete successfully with the Dutch merchant marine. Parliament wanted to strengthen England's navy, and the expansion of the domestic shipbuilding industry was a fine starting place. And almost everyone agreed with the mercantilist view that the mother country should establish a more favorable balance of trade—that is, increase exports, decrease imports, and grow richer at the expense of other European states. Together, these ideas provided a blueprint for England's first empire, a complex set of regulations that shaped the character of Anglo-American cultural and economic relations until the American Revolution.

Regulating Colonial Trade

In 1660, Parliament passed the first Navigation Act, the most important piece of imperial legislation drafted before the American Revolution. Colonists from Maine to South Carolina paid close attention to the act, which stated (1) that no ship could trade in the colonies unless it had been constructed in either England or America and carried a crew that was at least 75 percent English, and (2) that certain **enumerated goods** of great value that were not produced in England—tobacco, sugar, cotton, indigo, dye, wool, ginger—could be transported from the colonies *only* to an English or colonial port. Early in the next century, Parliament added rice, molasses, wood resins, tars, and turpentines to the enumerated list.

The Navigation Act of 1660 was masterfully conceived. It encouraged the development of domestic shipbuilding, prohibited European rivals from obtaining enumerated goods anywhere except in England, and provided the Crown with added revenue. Parliament supplemented the act in 1663 with the second Navigation Act, known as the Staple Act, that closed off nearly all direct trade between European nations and the American colonies. With a few noted exceptions, nothing could be imported into America unless it had first been transshipped through the mother country, a process that greatly added to the price paid by colonial consumers.

During the 1660s, Virginians showed little enthusiasm for the new imperial regulation. Not only did the collection of customs on tobacco greatly reduce profits, but with the exclusion of the Dutch as the middlemen in American commerce, tobacco planters had to sell their crops to English merchants at artificially low prices. Virginia's loss (£100,000 in import duties collected for the Crown by 1670) was Charles II's gain. At first, New England merchants ignored or cleverly circumvented the commercial restrictions. The crafty traders picked up cargoes of enumerated goods such as sugar or tobacco, sailed to another colonial port (thereby technically fulfilling the letter of the law), and then made directly for Holland or France. Along the way, they paid no customs duties.

To plug this loophole, Parliament passed another Navigation Act in 1673. This statute established a plantation duty to be collected at the various colonial ports. New Englanders could no longer escape paying customs fees. And in 1675, as part of the new imperial firmness, the Privy Council formed a powerful subcommittee, the Lords of Trade, whose members monitored colonial affairs.

Despite the legal reforms, serious obstacles impeded the execution of imperial policy. The customs service did not have enough effective agents in American ports to enforce the **Navigation Acts** fully, and imperial officials of various independent agencies often worked at cross-purposes.

Parliament passed the last major piece of imperial legislation in 1696. Among other things, the statute tightened enforcement procedures, putting pressure specifically on the colonial governors to keep England's competitors out of American ports. The Navigation Act of 1696 also expanded the American customs service and for the first time set up vice-admiralty courts in the colonies. This decision particularly rankled the colonists. Established to settle disputes that occurred at sea, vice-admiralty courts required neither juries nor oral cross-examination, both traditional elements of common law. On the eve of the American Revolution, a sudden expansion of the admiralty system raised a storm of protest.

The year 1696 witnessed one other significant change in the imperial system. William III replaced the ineffective Lords of Trade with a body of policy advisers

enumerated goods Certain essential raw materials produced in the North American colonies, such as tobacco, sugar, and rice, specified in the Navigation Acts, which stipulated that these goods could be shipped only to England or its colonies.

Navigation Acts A series of commercial restrictions passed by Parliament intended to regulate colonial commerce in such a way as to favor England's accumulation of wealth.

that came to be known as the Board of Trade. This group was expected to monitor colonial affairs closely, and for several decades, at least, it energetically carried out its responsibilities.

The members of Parliament believed that these reforms would belatedly compel the colonists to accept the Navigation Acts, and in large measure they were correct. By 1700, American goods transshipped through the mother country accounted for a quarter of *all* English exports, an indication that the colonists found it profitable to obey the commercial regulations. In fact, during the eighteenth century, smuggling from Europe to America dried up almost completely.

The Navigation Acts of the seventeenth century also shaped the colonists' material culture. Over time, Americans grew increasingly accustomed to purchasing British goods; they established close ties with specific merchant houses in London, Bristol, or Glasgow. Thus it is not surprising that by the mid-eighteenth century, the colonists preferred the manufactures of the mother country over those of England's commercial rivals. In other words, the Navigation Acts affected the development of consumer habits throughout the empire, and it is not an exaggeration to suggest that this regulatory system was in large part responsible for the Anglicization of eighteenth-century American culture (see Chapter 4).

COLONIAL FACTIONS SPARK POLITICAL REVOLT, 1676–1691

The Navigation Acts created an illusion of unity; the imperial statutes superimposed a system of commercial regulations on all the colonies. But within each society, men and women struggled to bring order out of disorder, to establish stable ruling elites, to defuse ethnic and racial tensions, and to cope with population pressures that imperial planners only dimly understood. During the final decades of the seventeenth century, these efforts sometimes sparked revolt between factions of the local gentry, usually the "outs" versus the "ins," for political power.

Civil War in Virginia: Bacon's Rebellion

Virginia was the first colony to experience this political unrest. After 1660, the Virginia economy suffered a prolonged depression. Returns from tobacco had not been good for some time, and the Navigation Acts reduced profits even further. Into this unhappy environment came thousands of ambitious indentured servants.

The reality bore little relation to their dreams. A hurricane destroyed one entire tobacco crop, and in 1667, Dutch warships captured the tobacco fleet just as it was about to sail for England. Indentured servants complained about lack of food and clothing. No wonder that Virginia's governor, Sir William Berkeley, despaired of ever ruling "a People where six parts of seven at least are Poor, Endebted, Discontented and Armed." In 1670, he and the House of Burgesses disfranchised all landless freemen, persons they regarded as troublemakers, but the threat of social violence remained.

Enter Nathaniel Bacon. This ambitious young man arrived in Virginia in 1674. He came from a respectable English family and set himself immediately as a substantial planter. But he wanted more. Bacon envied the government patronage monopolized by Berkeley's cronies, a group known locally as the Green Spring faction. When Bacon attempted to obtain a license to engage in the fur trade, he was rebuffed. This lucrative commerce was reserved for the governor's friends. If Bacon had been willing to wait, he would probably have been accepted into the ruling clique, but as subsequent events would demonstrate, Bacon was not a man of patience.

In 1675, Indian attacks on outlying plantations thrust Bacon suddenly into the center of Virginia politics. Virginians expected the governor to send an army to retaliate. Instead, Berkeley called for the construction of a line of defensive forts.

Settlers suspected that the governor was simply trying to protect his own fur interests and was rewarding his friends with contracts to build useless forts.

In response, Bacon boldly offered to lead a volunteer army against the Indians at no cost to the hard-pressed Virginia taxpayers. All he demanded was an official commission from Berkeley giving him military command. The governor steadfastly refused.

What followed, known as **Bacon's Rebellion,** would have been comic had not so many people died. Bacon thundered against the governor's treachery; Berkeley labeled Bacon a traitor. Bacon led several campaigns against the Indians, failing to kill any enemies but managing to massacre some friendly Indians. Bacon also burned Jamestown to the ground, forcing Berkeley to flee to the colony's eastern shore. Charles II sent troops to aid the governor, but by the time they arrived, Berkeley had gained full control of the colony's government. In October 1676, Bacon died after a brief illness, and his band of rebels dispersed within a few months.

Order was soon restored, and in 1677, the crown recalled the embittered Berkeley. The governors who followed were unusually greedy, and the local gentry formed a united front against them.

Bacon's Rebellion An armed rebellion in Virginia (1675–1676) led by Nathaniel Bacon against the colony's royal governor, Sir William Berkeley. Although some of his followers called for an end of special privilege in government, Bacon was chiefly interested in gaining a larger share of the lucrative Indian trade.

The Glorious Revolution in the Bay Colony

During John Winthrop's lifetime, the settlers of Massachusetts developed an inflated sense of their independence from the mother country. After the Restoration in 1660, however, the Crown put an end to that illusion. Royal officials demanded full compliance with the Navigation Acts, which were constant reminders of New England's colonial status. The growth of commerce attracted new merchants who were there to make money and were restive under the Puritan strictures. These developments divided Bay Colony leaders. A few Puritan ministers and magistrates regarded compromise with England as treason, a breaking of the Lord's covenant. Other spokesmen recognized the changing political realities within the empire and urged a more moderate course.

In 1675, the Indians dealt the New Englanders a terrible setback. Metacomet, a Wampanoag chief whom the whites called King Philip, declared war against the colonists; he was joined by the powerful Narragansett Indians. In little more than a year of fighting, the Indians destroyed scores of frontier villages, killed hundreds of colonists, and disrupted the entire regional economy. "In proportion to population, King Philip's War inflicted greater casualties upon the people than any other war in our history," wrote historian Douglas Leach.

Another shock followed. In 1684, the Court of Chancery, sitting in London and acting under a petition from King James II, annulled the charter of the Massachusetts Bay Company. The decision forced even the most stubborn Puritans to recognize that they were part of an empire run by people who did not share their particular religious vision.

In the place of representative governments, James II created the Dominion of New England. In various stages from 1686 to 1689, it incorporated Massachusetts, Connecticut, Rhode Island, Plymouth, New York, New Jersey, and New Hampshire under a single appointed royal governor. For this demanding position, James

■ *Metacomet, the Wampanoag chief known to the English colonists as King Philip, led Native Americans in a major war designed to remove the Europeans from New England.* ■

selected Sir Edmund Andros (pronounced Andrews), a military veteran of tyranni-cal temperament. He quickly abolished elective assemblies and town meetings and enforced the Navigation Acts so rigorously that he brought about a commercial de-pression. His high-handed methods alienated almost all the colonists.

Early in 1689, news of the Glorious Revolution reached Boston. The English people had deposed James II, an absolutist monarch who openly espoused Catholicism. His Protestant daughter, Mary, and her husband, William of Orange, ascended the throne as joint monarchs in James's place. William and Mary had ac-cepted a "bill of rights" that set out the constitutional rights of their subjects. Almost immediately, the Bay colonists overthrew the hated Andros regime and jailed the governor. No one came to Andros's defense.

However united they were, the Bay colonists could not take the newly crowned monarchs' support for granted. But thanks largely to the tireless lobbying of Increase Mather, a Congregational minister and father of Cotton Mather, who pleaded the colonists' case in London, King William abandoned the Dominion of New England and in 1691 conferred a new royal charter on Massachusetts. This document provided for a crown-appointed governor and a franchise based on property ownership rather than church membership. On the local level, town gov-ernment remained much as it had been in Winthrop's time.

Terror of Witchcraft

During these politically troubled times, excessively fearful men and women living in Salem Village, a small, struggling farming community, created panic in Massachusetts Bay. In late 1691, during a very cold winter, several adolescent girls began to behave in strange ways. They cried for no apparent reason; they twitched on the ground. The girls attributed their suffering to the work of witches. The arrest of several alleged witches did not relieve the girls' "fits," and other arrests followed. At least one person confessed, providing a frightening description of the devil as "a thing all over hairy, all the face hairy, and a long nose." By the end of the summer, a specially convened court had hanged nineteen individuals; another was pressed to death. Several more suspects died in jail awaiting trial.

Then suddenly, the storm was over. Led by Increase Mather, a group of promi-nent Congregational ministers urged leniency and restraint. Especially troubling to the clergymen was the court's decision to accept **spectral evidence,** reports of dreams and visions in which the accused appeared as the devil's agent. The colonial government accepted the minister's advice and convened a new court, which promptly acquitted, pardoned, or released the remaining suspects.

No one knows exactly what sparked the terror in Salem Village. The community had a history of discord, and during the 1680s, the people split into angry factions over the choice of a minister. Jealousy and bitterness apparently festered to the point that adolescent girls who would normally have been disciplined were allowed to in-cite judicial murder. As often happens in incidents like this one, the accusers later came to their senses and apologized for the cruel suffering that they had inflicted.

The Glorious Revolution in New York and Maryland

When news of the Glorious Revolution reached New York City in May 1689, Jacob Leisler, a German immigrant with mercantile ties to the older Dutch elite, raised a group of militiamen and seized a local fort in the name of William and Mary. For a short time, he controlled the city. But English newcomers and powerful Anglo-Dutch families who had recently risen to prominence opposed the older Dutch group to which he was allied, and Leisler was never able to construct a secure polit-ical base.

In 1691, a new royal governor, Henry Sloughter, arrived in New York and or-dered Leisler to surrender his authority. Leisler hesitated; he may have feared the

spectral evidence In the Salem witch trials, the court allowed re-ports of dreams and visions in which the accused appeared as the devil's agent to be introduced as testimony. The accused had no de-fense against this kind of evidence. When the judges later disallowed this testimony, the executions for witchcraft ended.

Chronology

1619	First blacks arrive in Virginia
1638	Harvard College is established
1660	Charles II is restored to the English throne ■ First Navigation Act is passed by Parliament
1663	Second Navigation (Staple) Act is passed
1673	Plantation duty is imposed to close loopholes in commercial regulations
1675	King Philip's War devastates New England
1676	Bacon's Rebellion threatens Governor Berkeley's government in Virginia
1684	Charter of Massachusetts Bay Company is revoked
1685	Duke of York becomes James II
1686	Dominion of New England is established
1688	James II is driven into exile during the Glorious Revolution
1689	Rebellions break out in Massachusetts, New York, and Maryland
1691	Jacob Leisler is executed
1692	Salem Village is wracked by witch trials
1696	Parliament establishes the Board of Trade
1739	Stono Uprising of South Carolina slaves terrifies white planters

vengeance of rival factions. The pause cost Leisler his life. He was declared a rebel, promptly tried, and executed in grisly fashion. Four years later, Parliament officially pardoned him, but the decision came a bit late. The bitter political factionalism that engendered this unfortunate episode plagued New York throughout the next century.

Tensions in Maryland between Protestants and Catholics ran high during the last third of the seventeenth century. When news of James's overthrow reached Maryland early in 1689, pent-up antiproprietary and anti-Catholic sentiment exploded. John Coode, a member of the assembly and an outspoken Protestant, formed a group called the Protestant Association, which forced the governor appointed by Lord Baltimore to resign.

The Protestant Association petitioned the newly crowned Protestant monarchs to transform Maryland into a royal colony, alleging many wrongs suffered at the hands of the Catholic-dominated upper house. William complied, sending a royal governor in 1691. The new assembly then proclaimed the Church of England as the established religion and excluded Catholics from public office. Baltimore lost control of the colony's government. In 1715, however, the fourth Lord Baltimore, who had been raised a member of the Church of England, regained full proprietorship from the Crown. Maryland remained in the hands of the Calvert family until 1776.

CONCLUSION: LOCAL ASPIRATIONS WITHIN AN ATLANTIC EMPIRE

"It is no little Blessing of God," Cotton Mather announced proudly in 1700, "that we are part of the *English* nation." A half century earlier, John Winthrop would not have spoken these words, at least not with such enthusiasm. The two men were products of different political cultures. It was not so much that the character of Massachusetts society had changed. In fact, the Puritan families of 1700 were much like those of the founding generation. Rather, the difference was in England's attitude toward the colonies. Rulers living more than three thousand miles away now made political and economic demands that Mather's contemporaries could not ignore.

The creation of a new imperial system did not, however, erase profound sectional differences. By 1700, for example, the Chesapeake colonies were more, not less, committed to the cultivation of tobacco and slave labor. Although the separate regions were being pulled slowly into England's commercial orbit, they did not have much to do with each other. The elements that sparked a powerful sense of nationalism among colonists dispersed over a huge territory would not be evident for a very long time. It would be a mistake, therefore, to anticipate the coming of the American Revolution.

KEY TERMS

mercantilism, p. 50

enumerated goods, p. 51

Navigation Acts, p. 51

Bacon's Rebellion, p. 53

spectral evidence, p. 54

RECOMMENDED READING

The most innovative research of chapters covered in this chapter explores the history of New World slavery during the period before the American Revolution. Much of this literature is boldly interdisciplinary, providing not only a fresh comparative interpretation of the creation and development of African American cultures in the New World, but also splendid insight into how imaginative scholars reconstruct the pasts of peoples who for a very long time have been denied a voice in mainstream histories. Among the more impressive contributions are Ira Berlin, *Many Thousands Gone: The First Two Centuries of Slavery in North America* (2000); Philip Morgan, *Slave Counterpoint: Black Culture in the Eighteenth-Century Chesapeake and Lowcountry* (1998); and Robin Blackburn, *The Making of New World Slavery, 1492–1800* (1997). A pioneering work of high quality is Winthrop D. Jordan, *White Over Black: American Attitudes Toward the Negro, 1550–1812* (1968). S. Max Edelson provides an original interpretation of the development of the southern slave plantation in *Plantation Enterprise in Colonial*

South Carolina (2006). The world of Anthony Johnson, a free black planter in early Virginia, is reconstructed in T. H. Breen and Stephen Innes, *"Myne Owne Ground": Race and Freedom on Virginia's Eastern Shore, 1640–1676* (rev. ed., 2004). The most recent account of the Salem witch trials can be found in Mary Beth Norton, *In the Devil's Snare: The Salem Witchcraft Crisis of 1692* (2002). Richard Godbeer provides a solid account of the Puritans' intimate lives in *Sexual Revolution in Early America* (2002), but one should also consult Laurel T. Ulrich, *Good Wives: Image and Reality in the Lives of Women in Northern New England, 1650–1750* (1982), and a path-breaking essay by Lois G. Carr and Lorena Walsh, "The Planter's Wife: The Experience of White Women in Seventeenth-Century Maryland," *William and Mary Quarterly*, 3rd ser., 34 (1977): 542–571. A provocative discussion of cultural tensions within the British Empire can be found in Linda Colley, *Captives: The Story of Britain's Pursuit of Empire and How its Soldiers and Civilians Were Held Captive by the Dream of Global Supremacy, 1600–1850* (2002).

SUGGESTED WEB SITES

DPLS Archive: Slave Movement During the Eighteenth and Nineteenth Centuries (Wisconsin)
dpls.dacc.wisc.edu/slavedata/index.html
This site explores the slave ships and the slave trade that carried thousands of Africans to the New World.

Excerpts from Slave Narratives
www.vgskole.net/prosjekt/slavrute/primary.htm
The seventeenth- through nineteenth-century accounts of slavery in this site speak volumes about the many impacts of slavery.

Salem Witch Trials: Documentary Archive and Transcription Project
etext.virginia.edu/salem/witchcraft/
Extensive archive of the 1692 trials and life in late seventeenth-century Massachusetts.

Salem Witchcraft Trials (1692)
www.law.umkc.edu/faculty/projects/ftrials/salem/salem.htm
Images, chronology, court and official documents by Dr. Doug Linder at University of Missouri–Kansas City Law School.

Colonial Documents
www.yale.edu/lawweb/avalon/18th.htm
The key documents of the Colonial era are reproduced here, as are some of the important documents from earlier and later time periods in American history.

Chapter 4

Experience of Empire: Eighteenth-Century America

Constructing an Anglo-American Identity: The Journal of William Byrd

William Byrd II (1674–1744) was a type of English American that would not have been encountered during the earliest years of settlement. This successful Tidewater planter was a product of a new, more cosmopolitan environment, as much at home in London as in his native Virginia. In 1728, at the height of his political influence in Williamsburg, the capital of colonial Virginia, Byrd accepted a commission to help survey a disputed boundary between North Carolina and Virginia. During his long journey into the distant back country, Byrd kept a detailed journal, a satiric, often bawdy chronicle of daily events.

On his trip into the wilderness, Byrd met many different people. No sooner had he departed a familiar world of tobacco plantations than he came across a self-styled hermit, an Englishman who apparently preferred the freedom of the woods to the constraints of society. As the boundary commissioners pushed farther into the back country, they encountered more highly independent men and women of European descent, small frontier families that Byrd regarded as living no better than savages. He attributed their uncivilized behavior to a diet of too much pork. The pork, he thought, made them "extremely hoggish in their Temper, & many of them seem to Grunt rather than Speak in their ordinary conversation." The wilderness journey also brought Byrd's party of surveyors into regular contact with Native American tribes.

Byrd's journal invites readers to perceive the rapidly developing eighteenth-century back country from a fresh perspective. It was not a vast empty territory awaiting the arrival of European settlers. Maps often sustain this erroneous impression. They depict cities and towns, farms and plantations clustered along the Atlantic Coast; they suggest a "line of settlement" steadily pushing outward into a huge blank area with no mark of civilization. The people Byrd met on his journey into the back country would not have understood such maps. After all, the empty space on the maps was their home. They experienced the frontier as populous zones of many cultures stretching from the English and French settlements in the north all the way to the Spanish borderlands in the far southwest.

The point is not to discount the significance of the older Atlantic settlements. During the eighteenth century, Britain's thirteen colonies underwent a profound transformation. The population in the colonies grew at unprecedented rates. German and Scots-Irish immigrants arrived in huge numbers. So, too, did African slaves. Wherever they lived, colonial Americans of this period found they were not as isolated from each other as they had been during most of the seventeenth century. Indeed, after 1690, men and women expanded their cultural horizons, becoming part of a larger Anglo-American empire. The change was striking. Colonists whose

Outline

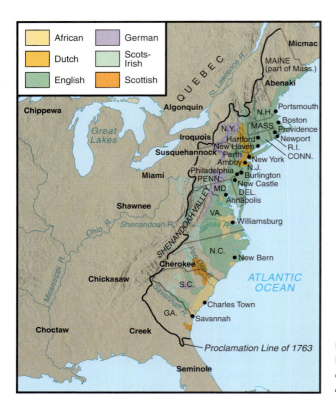

DISTRIBUTION OF EUROPEAN AND AFRICAN IMMIGRANTS IN THE THIRTEEN COLONIES *A flood of non-English immigrants swept the British colonies between 1700 and 1775.* ∎

parents or grandparents had come to the New World to confront a "howling wilderness" now purchased imported European manufactures, read English journals, participated in imperial wars, and sought favors from a growing number of resident royal officials. No one could escape the influence of Britain. The cultural, economic, and political links connecting the colonists to the imperial center in London grew stronger with time.

This surprising development raises a difficult question for the modern historian. If the eighteenth-century colonists were so powerfully attracted to Great Britain, why did they ever declare independence? The answer may well be that as the colonists became more British, they inevitably became more American as well. This development helps explain the appearance after midcentury of a genuine nationalist sentiment. Political, commercial, and military links that brought the colonists into more frequent contact with Great Britain also made them more aware of other colonists. It was within an expanding, prosperous empire that they first began seriously to consider what it meant to be American.

GROWTH AND DIVERSITY

The phenomenal growth of British America during the eighteenth century amazed Benjamin Franklin, one of the first persons to bring scientific rigor to the study of demography. The population of the English colonies doubled approximately every twenty-five years, and if the expansion continued at such an extraordinary rate, according to calculations Franklin made in 1751, in another century more Englishmen would live in America than in England.

Few societies in recorded history have expanded so rapidly, and if the growth rate had not dropped substantially during the nineteenth and twentieth centuries, the current population of the United States would stand at more than one billion people. Natural reproduction was responsible for most of the growth. More families bore children who in turn lived long enough to have children of their own. Because of this sudden expansion, the population of the late colonial period was strikingly young.

Not only was the total population increasing at a very rapid rate, it also was becoming more dispersed and heterogeneous. Each year witnessed the arrival of thousands of non-English Europeans, most of whom soon moved to the **back country** of Pennsylvania and the southern colonies in the hope of obtaining their own land and setting up as independent farmers. Although they planned to follow customs they had known in Europe, they found the challenge of surviving on the British frontier more demanding than they had anticipated. They plunged into a complex, fluid, often violent society that included large numbers of Native Americans and African Americans as well as other Europeans.

back country In the eighteenth century, the edge of settlement extending from western Pennsylvania to Georgia. This region formed the second frontier as settlers moved westward from the Atlantic coast into the nation's interior.

Scots-Irish and Germans

Non-English colonists poured into American ports throughout the eighteenth century, creating rich ethnic diversity in areas originally settled by Anglo-Saxons. The largest group of newcomers was the Scots-Irish. The experiences of these people in Britain influenced not only their decision to move to the New World but also their behavior once they arrived. During the seventeenth century, English rulers thought they could thoroughly dominate Catholic Ireland by transporting thousands of lowland Scottish Presbyterians to the northern region of that war-torn country. The plan failed, and after a short time, many of the Scots-Irish elected to emigrate to America, where they hoped to find the freedom and prosperity that had been denied them in Ireland. Often entire Presbyterian congregations followed charismatic ministers to the New World, intent on replicating a distinctive, fiercely independent culture on the frontier. It is estimated that about 150,000 Scots-Irish migrated to the colonies before the American Revolution.

Most Scots-Irish immigrants landed initially in Philadelphia, but they soon moved west and carved out farms on Pennsylvania's western frontier. The colony's proprietors welcomed the influx of new settlers, for it seemed they would form an ideal barrier between the Indians and the older, coastal communities. The Penn family soon had second thoughts, however. The Scots-Irish settled wherever they found unoccupied land, regardless of who owned it, and challenged the established order.

A second large body of non-English settlers, more than 100,000 people, came from the upper Rhine Valley, the German Palatinate. Some of the migrants belonged to small pietistic Protestant sects, and they came to America in search of religious toleration. Most Germans, however, sought the peace and good lands of the colonies. The German migrants—mistakenly called Pennsylvania Dutch because the English confused *Deutsch* (German) with *Dutch* (from Holland)—began reaching Philadelphia in large numbers after 1717, and by 1766, persons of German stock accounted for more than one-third of Pennsylvania's total population. Even their most vocal detractors admitted that the Germans were the best farmers in the colony.

■ *This folk art painting from the cover of a clothes box depicts a well-dressed German American farmer. The stock around the farmer's neck, his coat, and walking stick indicate that he enjoyed a middling to high status.* ■

Ethnic differences in Pennsylvania bred disputes. The Scots-Irish as well as the Germans preferred to live with people of their own background, and they sometimes fought to keep members of the other nationality out of their areas. The English were suspicious of both groups. Indeed, many Pennsylvanians shared Franklin's opinion that the Germans posed a threat to the primacy of the English language and government in that colony.

Such prejudice may have persuaded members of both groups to search for new homes. After 1730, Germans and Scots-Irish pushed southward from western Pennsylvania into the Shenandoah Valley, thousands of them settling in the back country of Virginia and the Carolinas. The Germans usually remained wherever they found unclaimed fertile land. By contrast, the Scots-Irish often moved two or three times. But wherever the newcomers settled, they often found themselves living beyond the effective authority of the various colonial governments. These conditions heightened the importance of religious institutions within the small ethnic communities. Although the original stimulus for coming to America may have been a desire for economic independence and prosperity, back country families—especially the Scots-Irish—flocked to evangelical Protestant preachers, to Presbyterian and later to Baptist and Methodist ministers who not only fulfilled the settlers' spiritual needs but also gave these scattered back country communities a pronounced moral character that survived long after the colonial period.

Convict Settlers

Since the story of European migration tends to be upbeat—men and women engaged in a largely successful quest for a better material life—it often is forgotten that British courts compelled many people to come to America. Indeed, the African slaves were not the only large group of people coerced into moving to the New World. In 1718, Parliament passed the Transportation Act, allowing judges in England, Scotland, and Ireland to send convicted felons to the American colonies. Between 1718 and 1775, the courts shipped approximately fifty thousand convicts across the Atlantic, with the majority seemingly having committed only minor crimes against property. Although transported convicts—almost 75 percent of whom were young males—escaped the hangman, they found life difficult in the colonies. Sold primarily in the Chesapeake colonies as indentured servants, they faced an uncertain future, and few prospered.

Although Americans contracted with the convict servants, they expressed fear that the men and women would create a dangerous criminal class. In one irate essay, Benjamin Franklin asked his readers to consider just how the colonists might repay the leaders of Great Britain for shipping so many felons to America. He suggested that rattlesnakes, distributed liberally in the gardens throughout England, might be the appropriate gift. The Revolution forced the British courts to redirect the flow of convicts to another part of the world; an indirect result of American independence was the founding of Australia by transported felons.

Native Americans: Strategies for Survival

In some histories of the colonial period, Native Americans make only a brief appearance, usually during the earliest years of conquest and settlement. After initial contact with the first European invaders, the Indians seem mysteriously to disappear from the central narrative of colonization, and it is not until the nineteenth century that they turn up again, this time to wage a last desperate battle against the encroachment of white society.

This obviously inadequate account slights one of the richest chapters of Native American history. To be sure, during much of the seventeenth century, various Indian groups that contested the English settlers for control of coastal lands suffered terribly, sometimes from war but more often from the spread of contagious diseases such as smallpox. The two races found it very difficult to live in close proximity. But the Indians managed to survive. By the eighteenth century, the site of the most intense and creative contact between the races had shifted to the huge territory between the Appalachian Mountains and the Mississippi River, where several hundred thousand Native Americans made their homes.

Many Indians had only recently migrated to the area. Some moved to escape confrontation with European invaders; others were refugees of lost wars. These survivors joined with other Indians to establish new multiethnic communities. In this respect, the Native American villages may not have seemed all that different from the mixed European settlements of the back country.

Stronger groups of Indians such as the Creek, Choctaw, Chickasaw, Cherokee, and Shawnee generally welcomed the refugees. Strangers were formally adopted to take the places of family members killed in battle or overcome by sickness, and it should be appreciated that many seemingly traditional Indian villages of the eighteenth century actually represented innovative responses to rapidly shifting external conditions.

The concept of a *middle ground* helps us comprehend more fully how eighteenth-century Indians held their own in the back country beyond the Appalachian Mountains. The Native Americans never intended to isolate themselves completely from European contact. They relied on white traders, French as well as English, to provide essential metal goods and weapons. The goal of the Indian confederacies rather was to maintain a strong independent voice in these commercial exchanges, playing the French off against the British whenever possible. So long as the confederacies had sufficient military strength, they compelled everyone who came to negotiate in the middle ground to give them proper respect. It would be incorrect, therefore, to characterize their relations with the Europeans as a stark choice between total war or abject surrender. Native Americans took advantage of rivals when possible; they compromised when necessary. It is best to imagine the Indians' middle ground as an open, dynamic process of creative interaction.

The survival of the middle ground depended ultimately on factors over which the Native Americans had little control. Imperial competition between France and Britain enhanced the Indians' bargaining position, but after the British defeated the French in 1763, the Indians no longer received the same solicitous attention as they had in earlier times. Keeping old allies happy seemed to the British a needless expense. Moreover, contagious disease continued to take a fearful toll. In the southern back country between 1685 and 1790, the Indian population dropped an astounding 72 percent. In the Ohio Valley, the numbers suggest similar rates of decline. In fact, there is some evidence that British military officers consciously practiced germ warfare against the Native Americans, giving them blankets contaminated by smallpox. By the time the United States took control of this region, the middle ground itself had become a casualty of history.

SPANISH BORDERLANDS OF THE EIGHTEENTH CENTURY

In many traditional histories of North America, the Spanish make only a brief appearance, usually as fifteenth-century conquistadores. But as soon as they have conquered Mexico, they are dropped from the story as if they had no serious part to play in the ongoing development of the continent. This is, of course, a skewed perspective that masks the roots of ethnic diversity in this country. The Spanish empire did not disappear. Indeed, it continued to shape the character of borderlands societies well into the eighteenth century. As anyone who visits the modern American Southwest quickly discovers, Spanish administrators and priests—not to

■ *Baroque-style eighteenth-century Spanish mission at San Xavier del Bac in present-day Arizona. Catholic missions dotted the frontier of northern New Spain from Florida to California.* ■

mention ordinary settlers—left a lasting imprint on the cultural landscape of the United States.

Turbulence on the Northern Frontier

Spanish settlers established no communities north of the Rio Grande until late in the sixteenth century. The local Pueblo tribes resisted the invasion of colonists, soldiers, and missionaries, and in a major rebellion in 1680, the native peoples drove the whites completely out of New Mexico. Not until 1692 were the Spanish able to reconquer this fiercely contested area. By then, Native American hostility, coupled with the settlers' failure to find precious metal, had cooled Spain's enthusiasm for the northern frontier.

Concern over French encroachment in the Southeast led Spain to colonize St. Augustine in Florida in 1565. Although this enterprise never flourished, it claims attention as the first permanent European settlement established in what would become the United States, predating the founding of Jamestown and Plymouth by several decades. Pedro Menéndez de Avilés brought some fifteen hundred soldiers and settlers to St. Augustine, where they constructed an impressive fort, but the colony failed to attract additional Spanish migrants.

California never figured prominently in Spain's plans for the New World. Early explorers reported finding only impoverished Indians living along the Pacific Coast. Adventurers saw no natural resources worth mentioning, and since the area proved extremely difficult to reach from Mexico City, California received little attention. Fear that the Russians might seize the entire region belatedly sparked Spanish activity, however, and after 1769, two indomitable servants of empire, Fra Junípero Serra and Don Gaspar de Portolá, organized permanent missions and presidios (forts) at San Diego, Santa Barbara, Monterey, and San Francisco.

Peoples of the Spanish Borderlands

In sharp contrast to the English frontier settlements of the eighteenth century, the Spanish outposts in North America grew very slowly. A few Catholic priests and imperial administrators traveled to the northern provinces, but the danger of Indian attack and the harsh physical environment discouraged ordinary colonists. The European migrants were overwhelmingly male, most of them soldiers in the pay of the empire. Although some colonists came directly from Spain, most had been born in other Spanish colonies such as Minorca, the Canaries, or New Spain, and because European women rarely appeared on the frontier, Spanish males formed relationships with Indian women, fathering large numbers of mestizos, children of mixed race.

As in other European frontiers of the eighteenth century, encounters with Spanish soldiers, priests, and traders altered Native American cultures. The experience here was markedly different from that of the whites and Indians in the British back country. The Spanish exploited Native American labor, reducing entire Indian villages to servitude. Many Indians moved to the Spanish towns, and although they lived in close proximity to the Europeans—something rare in British America—

THE SPANISH BORDERLANDS, CA. 1770   *In the late eighteenth century, Spain's North American empire stretched across what is now the southern United States from Florida through Texas and New Mexico to California.* ■

they were consigned to the lowest social class, objects of European contempt. However much their material conditions changed, the Indians of the Southwest resisted strenuous efforts to convert them to Catholicism. The Pueblo Indians maintained their own religious forms—often at great personal risk—and they sometimes murdered priests who became too intrusive.

The Spanish empire never had the resources necessary to secure the northern frontier fully. It would be misleading, however, to stress the fragility of Spanish colonization. The urban design and public architecture of many southwestern cities still reflect the vision of the early Spanish settlers, and to a large extent, the old borderlands remain Spanish-speaking to this day.

THE IMPACT OF EUROPEAN IDEAS ON AMERICAN CULTURE

The character of the older, more established British colonies changed almost as quickly as that of the back country. The rapid growth of an urban cosmopolitan culture impressed eighteenth-century commentators, and even though most Americans still lived on scattered farms, they had begun to participate aggressively in an exciting consumer marketplace that expanded their imaginative horizons.

Provincial Cities

Despite the rate of population growth, few eighteenth-century Americans lived in cities. Boston, Newport, New York, Philadelphia, and Charles Town—the five largest cities—contained only about 5 percent of the colonial population. In 1775, none held more than forty thousand persons. The explanation for the dearth of city dwellers can be found in the highly specialized nature of colonial commerce. Port towns served as intermediary trade and shipping centers in which bulk cargoes were broken up for inland distribution; they did not support large-scale manufacturing. Moreover, men who worked for wages in Europe usually became farmers in America.

Yet American cities profoundly affected colonial culture, for it was in the cities that the English influence was most pronounced. Wealthy merchants and lawyers tried to emulate the culture of the mother country. They went to the theater, attended concerts, and dressed in the high fashion of London society. The architectural splendor was especially noticeable. Homes of enduring beauty, modeled on English country houses, were constructed during the reign of Britain's early Hanoverian kings. Since all these kings were named George, the term *Georgian* was applied to this style of architecture.

Their owners filled the houses with fine furniture. Each city patronized certain skilled craftsmen, but the artisans of Philadelphia were known for producing magnificent copies of the works of Thomas Chippendale, Great Britain's most renowned furniture designer. These developments gave American cities an elegance they had not possessed in the previous century.

Enlightenment: American Style

European historians often refer to the eighteenth century as the Age of Reason. During this period, a body of new ideas, collectively called the **Enlightenment,** altered the way that educated Europeans thought about God, nature, and society. Enlightenment philosophers replaced the concept of original sin with a far more optimistic view of human nature. A benevolent God, they argued, having set the universe in motion, gave human beings the power of reason to enable them to comprehend the orderly workings of his creation. Everything, even human society, operated according to these mechanical laws. It was the duty of men and women, therefore, to make certain that institutions such as church and state conformed to self-evident natural laws. Through the use of reason, they asserted, human suffering could be eliminated and perfection achieved.

The American Enlightenment was a rather tame affair compared to its European counterpart. Colonists welcomed the advent of experimental science but stoutly defended the tenets of traditional Christianity. Americans emphasized the search for useful knowledge, ideas, and inventions. What mattered was practical experimentation, and the Enlightenment spawned scores of earnest scientific tinkers, people who dutifully recorded changes in temperature, the appearance of strange plants or animals, and the particulars of astronomical phenomena.

The greatest of all these American experimenters was Benjamin Franklin (1706–1790). As a young man working in his brother's Boston print shop, he discovered a copy of a new British journal, the *Spectator*. It was like a breath of fresh air to a boy growing up in Puritan New England. In August 1721, he and his brother founded the *New-England Courant*, a weekly newspaper that satirized Boston's political and religious leaders in the manner of the contemporary British press. Proper Bostonians were not prepared for such a critical journal, and in 1723, Franklin left Massachusetts in search of a less antagonistic intellectual environment.

He settled in Philadelphia. There he devoted himself to the pursuit of useful knowledge. Franklin never denied the existence of God. Rather he pushed the Lord aside, making room for the free exercise of reason. A naturally curious man, he was constantly experimenting and broadening his understanding of science, always with some practical end in mind. The lightning rod and a marvelously efficient stove are only two of Franklin's important contributions to material progress through human ingenuity.

Franklin energetically promoted the spread of Enlightenment ideas. In Philadelphia, he formed "a club for mutual Improvement, which we call'd the Junto" and a library association to discuss literature, philosophy, and science. The members of these groups communicated with Americans living in other colonies,

Enlightenment Philosophical and intellectual movement that began in Europe during the eighteenth century. It stressed the application of reason to solve social and scientific problems.

providing them not only with the latest information from Europe but also with models for their own clubs and associations. Such efforts broadened the intellectual horizons of many colonists, especially city dwellers.

Economic Transformation

The colonial economy kept pace with the stunning growth in population. Per capita income never fell behind the population explosion. An abundance of land and the extensive growth of agriculture accounted for this economic success. Each year, more Americans produced more tobacco, wheat, and rice—just to cite the major export crops—and by this means, they maintained a high level of individual prosperity without developing an industrial base.

Half of the American goods produced for export went to Great Britain. The Navigation Acts (see Chapter 3) were still in effect, and enumerated items such as tobacco and furs had to be landed first at a British port. Over the years, specific

A Look at the Past

Westover

By the mid-eighteenth century a native-born elite class took shape in Virginia and other colonies. Many constructed houses to signify their status and power. Few houses were as grand as Westover in Virginia, probably built by William Byrd III around 1750, but all "great houses" impressed visitors with their size and level of interior decorations. Such houses required vast sums of money as well as knowledge of the latest European styles to construct, maintain, and furnish. The funds needed to maintain these estates often came from the production of export crops such as tobacco and rice, crops cultivated by an unfree black labor force. ✻ How do you think the typical Virginian, who lived in a one-room house, reacted to houses such as this one? What did the difference between great houses like Westover and the typical one-room house suggest about eighteenth-century Virginia society? How did building large, elaborate, and fashionable houses contribute to cementing gentry power?

legislation brought white pine trees, molasses, hats, and iron under imperial control as England regulated colonial trade to its advantage.

The statutes might have created tensions between the colonists and the mother country had they been rigorously enforced. Crown officials, however, generally ignored the new laws. But even without the Navigation Acts, a majority of colonial exports would have been sold on the English markets. The emerging consumer society in Great Britain was beginning to create a generation that possessed enough income to purchase American goods, especially sugar and tobacco. This rising demand was the major market force shaping the colonial economy.

Roughly one-fourth of all American exports went to the West Indies. Colonial ships carrying food sailed for the Caribbean and returned immediately to the Middle Colonies or New England with cargoes of molasses, sugar, and rum. "Triangular trade," crossing first to the west coast of Africa, was insignificant. In addition, the West Indies played a vital role in preserving American credit. Without this source of income, colonists would not have been able to pay for the manufactured items that they purchased in the mother country. The cost of goods imported from Great Britain normally exceeded the revenues collected on American exports to the mother country. To cover this small but recurrent deficit, colonial merchants relied on profits made in the West Indies.

Birth of a Consumer Society

After midcentury, however, the balance of trade turned dramatically against the colonists. Americans began buying more English goods than their parents and grandparents had done. Between 1740 and 1770, English exports to the American colonies increased by an astounding 360 percent.

In part, this shift reflected the increased production of British industries. Because of technological advancements in manufacturing, Great Britain was able to produce certain goods more efficiently and more cheaply than the colonists could. Americans started to buy as never before; Staffordshire china and imported cloth replaced crude earthenware and rough homespun. In this manner, British industrialization undercut American handicrafts and folk art.

To help Americans purchase manufactured goods, British merchants offered generous credit. For many people, the temptation to acquire English finery blinded them to hard economic realities. Colonists deferred settlement by agreeing to pay interest on their debts, and by 1760, the total indebtedness had reached £2 million. Colonial governments could delay the balance-of-payments crisis for a time by issuing paper money, but the problem was not resolved.

The eighteenth century brought a substantial increase in intercoastal trade. Southern planters sent tobacco and rice to New England and the Middle Colonies, where these staples were exchanged for meat and wheat as well as for goods imported from Great Britain. By 1760, approximately 30 percent of the colonists' total tonnage capacity was involved in this extensive "coastwise" commerce. In addition, American colonists carried on a substantial amount of commerce over the rough, back country highway known as the Great Wagon Road, which stretched 735 miles along the Blue Ridge Mountains from Pennsylvania to South Carolina. The long, gracefully designed Conestoga wagon was vital to this overland trade.

The shifting patterns of trade had an immense effect on the development of an American culture. First, the flood of British imports eroded local and regional identities. Deep sectional differences remained, of course, but Americans from New Hampshire to Georgia were increasingly drawn into a sophisticated economic network centered in London.

Second, the expanding coastwise and overland trade brought colonists of different backgrounds into more frequent contact, exchanging ideas and experience as well as tobacco and wheat. New journals and newspapers appeared. Americans were kept abreast of the latest news in the colonies as well as in London. Americans were expanding their horizons, and slowly, sometimes painfully, a distinct culture was emerging.

REVIVAL: THE APPEAL OF EVANGELICAL RELIGION

A sudden, spontaneous series of Protestant revivals known as the **Great Awakening** had a far greater impact than the Enlightenment on the lives of the common people. This unprecedented evangelical outpouring caused men and women to rethink basic assumptions about society, church, and state. In our own time, we have witnessed the forces of religious revival in different regions of the world. It is no exaggeration to claim that a similar revolution took place in mid-eighteenth-century America.

Great Awakening Widespread evangelical religious revival movement of the mid-1700s. The movement divided congregations and weakened the authority of established churches in the colonies.

The Great Awakening

Only with hindsight does the Great Awakening seem a unified religious movement. Revivals occurred in different places at different times. The first signs of a spiritual awakening appeared in New England during the late 1730s. The intensity of the event varied from region to region. Revivals were most important in Massachusetts, Connecticut, Rhode Island, Pennsylvania, New Jersey, and, in the 1750s and 1760s, Virginia. No single religious denomination or sect monopolized the Awakening; mainly Congregationalist churches were affected in New England, but elsewhere revivals involved Presbyterians, Methodists, and Baptists.

The evangelism of the Great Awakening infused a new sense of vitality into religions that had lost their fervor. People in New England complained that Congregational ministers seemed obsessed with dull, scholastic matters; their sermons no longer touched the heart. And in the Southern Colonies, there were simply not enough ordained ministers to tend to the religious needs of the population.

The Great Awakening began unexpectedly in Northampton, a small farm community in western Massachusetts, sparked by the preaching of Jonathan Edwards, the local Congregationalist minister. With fervent zeal, Edwards reminded the members of his flock that their fate had been determined for all eternity by an omnipotent God. He thought his fellow ministers had grown soft and were preaching easy salvation. Edwards disabused his congregation of that false comfort. With calm self-assurance, he described in vivid detail the torments of the damned, those whom God had not elected to receive divine grace.

Why this uncompromising Calvinist message set off religious revivals during the late 1730s is not known. Whatever the explanation for the sudden popular response to Edwards's preaching, young people began flocking to church. They experienced a searing conversion, a sense of "new birth" and utter dependence on God. The excitement spread, and evangelical ministers concluded that God must be preparing Americans, his chosen people, for the millennium, the time when Christ would rule on Earth.

The Voice of Popular Religion

The best-known figure of the Great Awakening was George Whitefield, a young, inspiring preacher from England who toured the colonies from Georgia to New Hampshire. He was an extraordinary public speaker who cast a spell over the throngs who came to see and hear him.

Whitefield's audience came from all groups of American society, rich and poor, young and old, rural and urban. Though Whitefield described himself as a Calvinist, he welcomed all Protestants, and he spoke from any pulpit that was available. "Don't tell me you are a Baptist, an Independent, a Presbyterian, a dissenter," he thundered. "Tell me you are a Christian, that is all I want."

American-born **itinerant preachers** followed Whitefield's example. The most famous was Gilbert Tennent, a Presbyterian of Scots-Irish background who had been educated in the Middle Colonies. He and other revivalists of like mind traveled from town to town, colony to colony, challenging local clergymen who seemed hostile to evangelical religion. Many ministers remained suspicious of the itinerants and their methods. Some complaints may have amounted to little more than jealousy. Others raised serious questions: How could the revivalists be certain that God had sparked the Great Awakening? And how could the revivalists be certain that the "dangers of enthusiasm" would not lead them astray? During the 1740s and 1750s, many congregations split between defenders of the new emotional preaching, the New Lights, and those who regarded the entire movement as dangerous nonsense, the Old Lights.

itinerant preachers Traveling revivalist ministers of the Great Awakening movement. These charismatic preachers spread revivalism throughout America.

Although Tennent did not condone the excesses of the Great Awakening, his direct attacks on formal learning invited the crude anti-intellectualism of such deranged revivalists as James Davenport. Davenport preached under the light of smoky torches; he danced and stripped, shrieked and laughed. He also urged people to burn books written by anyone who had not experienced the "new light."

To focus on occasional anti-intellectual outbursts is to obscure the positive ways in which this vast revival changed American society. First, the New Lights founded several important centers of higher education. They wanted to train young men who would carry on the good works of Edwards, Whitefield, and Tennent. Princeton (1747), Brown (1764), Rutgers (1766), and Dartmouth (1769) were all colleges founded by revivalist leaders.

Second, the Great Awakening encouraged men and women who had been taught to remain silent before traditional figures of authority to take an active role in their own salvation. They could no longer rely on ministers or institutions. The individual alone stood before God. This emphasis on personal religious choices shattered the old harmony that existed among Protestant sects and in its place introduced a boisterous, often bitterly fought competition.

With religious contention, however, came an awareness of a larger community, a union of fellow believers that extended beyond the boundaries of town and colony. In fact, evangelical religion was one of several forces at work during the mid-eighteenth century that brought scattered colonists into contact with one another for the first time. In this sense, the Great Awakening was a "national" event long before a nation actually existed.

People who had been touched by the Great Awakening saw America as "an instrument of Providence." With God's help, social and political progress was achievable, and from this perspective, of course, the New Lights did not sound much different from the mildly rationalist American spokesmen of the Enlightenment. Both groups prepared the way for the development of a revolutionary mentality in colonial America.

■ *The fervor of the Great Awakening was intensified by the eloquence of itinerant preachers such as George Whitefield, the most popular evangelical of the mid-eighteenth century.* ■

CLASH OF POLITICAL CULTURES

The political history of this period illuminates a growing tension within the empire. Americans of all regions repeatedly stated their desire to replicate British political institutions. Parliament, they claimed, provided a model for the American assemblies. They revered the English constitution. According to its defenders, the balanced constitution of Great Britain protected life, liberty, and property better than any other contemporary government. However, the more colonists studied British political theory and practice—in other words, the more they attempted to become British—the more aware they became of major differences. By trying to copy Great Britain, they unwittingly discovered something about being American.

The Theory and the Reality of British Politics

The English constitution incorporated three distinct parts: the monarch, the House of Lords, and the House of Commons. Thus, in theory, the government represented the socioeconomic interests of the king, the nobility, and the common people. Acting alone, each body would run to excess, even tyranny, but operating within a mixed system, each automatically checked the others' ambitions, for the common good.

The reality of daily political life, however, bore little relation to theory. The three elements of the constitution did not, in fact, represent distinct socioeconomic groups. Men elected to the House of Commons often came from the same social background as those who served in the House of Lords. All represented the interests of Britain's landed elite. Moreover, there was no attempt to maintain strict constitutional separation. The king exerted considerable influence, for example, in the House of Commons.

The claim that the members of the House of Commons represented all the people of England also seemed farfetched. In 1715, only about 20 percent of English adult males had the right to vote, and there was no standard size for electoral districts. Some representatives to Parliament were chosen by several thousand voters, others by only a handful of electors.

Before 1760, few people in England spoke out against these constitutional abuses. The main exception was a group of radical publicists whom historians have labeled the "Commonwealthmen." These writers decried the corruption of political life, warning that the nation that compromised its civic virtue deserved to lose its liberty and property. The most famous Commonwealthmen were John Trenchard and Thomas Gordon, who penned a series of essays titled *Cato's Letters* between 1720 and 1723. They warned the nation to be vigilant against tyranny by England's rulers.

But however shrilly these writers protested, however many newspaper articles they published, the Commonwealthmen won little support for their potential reforms. Englishmen were not willing to tamper with a system of government that had so recently survived a civil war and a Glorious Revolution. Americans, however, took Trenchard and Gordon to heart.

The Awkward Realities of Colonial Government

The colonists assumed—perhaps naively—that their governments were modeled on the balanced constitution of Great Britain. They argued that within their political systems, the governor corresponded to the king, the governor's council to the House of Lords, and the colonial assemblies to the House of Commons. As the colonists discovered, however, English theories about the mixed constitution were no more relevant in America than they were in the mother country.

By midcentury, royal governors appointed by the Crown ruled a majority of the mainland colonies. Many of the appointees were career army officers who through luck, charm, or family connection had gained the ear of someone close to the king. These patronage posts did not generate income sufficient to interest the most powerful or talented personalities of the period, but they did draw middle-level bureaucrats who were ambitious or desperate (or both).

Before departing for the New World, royal governors received an elaborate set of instructions drafted by the Board of Trade. The document dealt with almost every aspect of colonial life—political, economic, and religious—and no one knew for certain that these orders even possessed the force of law.

About the governors' powers, however, there was no doubt; they were enormous. In fact, royal governors could do certain things in America that a king could not do in eighteenth-century England. Among these were the right to veto legislation and to dismiss judges. The governors also served as commanders in chief in each province.

Royal governors were advised by a council, usually a body of about twelve wealthy colonists selected by the Board of Trade in London on the recommendation of the governor. By the eighteenth century, however, the council had lost most of its power. This body was certainly no House of Lords.

Nor were the colonial assemblies much like the House of Commons. A far greater proportion of men could vote in America than in Britain. In most colonies, adult white males who owned a small amount of land could vote in countywide elections. Although participation in government was not high, and most colonists were content to let gentry represent them in the assemblies, the potential for throwing the rascals out was always present.

Representatives of the People

Members of the assemblies were convinced that they had a special obligation to preserve colonial liberties. Any attack on the legislature was perceived as an assault on the rights of Americans. So aggressive were these bodies in seizing privileges, determining procedures, and controlling money bills that some historians refer to the political developments of eighteenth-century America as "the rise of the assemblies."

This political system seemed designed to generate hostility. There was simply no reason for the colonial legislature to cooperate with appointed royal governors. A few governors managed briefly to create in America a political culture of patronage akin to what they knew in England. But usually such efforts clashed with the colonists' perceptions of politics. They truly believed in the purity of the balanced constitution, and attempts to revert to a patronage system were met by loud protests in language that seemed to be directly lifted from the pages of *Cato's Letters*.

The major source of shared political information was the weekly journal, a new and vigorous institution in American life. In New York and Massachusetts especially, weekly newspapers urged readers to preserve civic virtue and to exercise extreme vigilance against the spread of privileged power. Through such journals, a pattern of political rhetoric that in Britain had gained only marginal respectability became after 1765 America's normal form of political discourse.

The rise of the assemblies shaped American culture in other, subtler ways. Over the course of the century, the language of the law became increasingly Anglicized. Varying local legal practices that had been widespread during the seventeenth century became standardized. Indeed, by 1750, there was little difference between the colonial legal system and that of the mother country. Not surprisingly, a number of men who served in colonial assemblies were lawyers or others who had received legal training. When Americans from different regions met, they discovered that they shared a commitment to the preservation of the English common law.

But if eighteenth-century political developments drew the colonists closer to the mother country, they also brought Americans a greater awareness of one another. As their horizons widened, they learned that they operated within the same general imperial system and that they shared similar problems. Like the revivalists and merchants—people who crossed old boundaries—colonial legislators laid the foundation for a broader cultural identity.

FIGHTING BRITAIN'S WARS IN AMERICA

The scope and style of warfare in the colonies changed radically during the eighteenth century. Local conflicts with the Indians, such as King Philip's War (1675–1676) in New England, gave way to hostilities that originated on the other side of the Atlantic, in rivalries between Great Britain and France over geopolitical considerations and commercial ambitions. The external threat to security forced people in different colonies to devise unprecedented measures of military and political cooperation.

On paper, at least, the British settlements enjoyed military superiority. Nonetheless, for most of the first half of the eighteenth century, their advantage proved more apparent than real. While the British settlements possessed a larger and more prosperous population than the French—1,200,000 to 75,000—they were divided into separate governments that sometimes seemed more suspicious of each other than of the French. When war came, French officers and Indian allies exploited these jealousies with considerable skill. Moreover, the small population of New France was concentrated along the St. Lawrence, and it could easily mass the forces needed to defend Montreal and Quebec.

King William's and Queen Anne's Wars

Colonial involvement in imperial war began in 1689, when England's new king, William III, declared war on France's Louis XIV. Europeans called this struggle the War of the League of Augsburg, but to the Americans, it was simply King William's War. Canadians raided the northern frontiers of New York and New England, and although they made no territorial gains, they caused considerable suffering among the civilian population of Massachusetts and New York.

The war ended with the Treaty of Ryswick (1697), but the colonists were drawn almost immediately into a new conflict, Queen Anne's War, a dynastic conflict known in Europe as the War of the Spanish Succession (1702–1713). Colonists in South Carolina as well as New England battled against the French and their Indian allies. The bloody combat along the American frontier was formally terminated in 1713 when Great Britain and France signed the Treaty of Utrecht. European concerns were paramount in the peace negotiations. Although two decades of fighting had taken a fearful toll in North America, neither France nor the English colonists had much to show for their sacrifice.

When George I, the first Hanoverian king of Great Britain, replaced Queen Anne in 1714, parliamentary leaders were determined to preserve peace. But on the American frontier, hostilities continued. At stake was the entire West, including the Mississippi Valley. English colonists believed that the French planned to "encircle" them, to confine them to a narrow strip of land along the Atlantic Coast. As evidence, they pointed to the French forts that had been constructed through the heart of America. On their part, the French suspected that their rivals intended to seize all of North America. They noted that land speculators and Indian traders were pushing aggressively into territory claimed by France. And so the two sides lined up their Indian allies and made ready for war.

King George's War and Its Aftermath

In 1743, the Americans were dragged once again into the imperial conflict. During King George's War (1743–1748), known in Europe as the War of the Austrian Succession, the colonists scored a magnificent victory over the French. In June 1745,

NORTH AMERICA, 1750

By 1750, the French had established a chain of settlements southward through the heart of the continent from Quebec to New Orleans. The English saw this development as a threat to their own seaboard colonies, which were expanding westward. ■

an army of New England troops under the command of William Pepperrell captured Louisbourg, a gigantic fortress on Cape Breton Island guarding the approaches to the Gulf of St. Lawrence and Quebec. The Americans, however, were in for a shock. When the war ended with the signing of the Treaty of Aix-la-Chapelle in 1748, the British government handed Louisbourg back to the French in exchange for concessions elsewhere. New Englanders saw this as an insult, one they did not soon forget.

By the conclusion of King George's War, the goals of the conflict had clearly changed. Americans no longer aimed simply at protecting their territory from attack. They now wanted to gain complete control over the West, a region obviously rich in economic opportunity. Vast tracts of land and lucrative trade with the Indians awaited ambitious colonists.

The French were not prepared to surrender an inch. But time was running against them. Not only were the English colonies growing more populous, but they also possessed a seemingly inexhaustible supply of manufactured goods to trade with the Indians. The French decided in the early 1750s, therefore, to seize the Ohio Valley before their rivals could do so. They established forts throughout the region, the most formidable being Fort Duquesne, located at the strategic fork in the Ohio River near the modern city of Pittsburgh.

Although France and England had not officially declared war, British officials advised the governor of Virginia to "repel force by force." The Virginians, who had their eyes on the Ohio Valley, needed no encouragement. In 1754, several militia companies, under the command of a promising young officer named George

Past and Present

Politics of Fear: From the Wars of Empire to the Cold War

The study of history suggests ways to understand the character of similar events separated by long periods of time. Knowledge of the past certainly serves to illuminate more recent occurrences. The reverse is also true. A deeper appreciation of events that have directly shaped our own lives or those of family members can reveal dimensions of historical experience that might otherwise remain obscure. We might consider, for example, the Cold War, which ended in 1991. That great struggle between the world's superpowers—the United States and the Soviet Union—invites us to take a fresh look at the eighteenth-century wars of empire that mobilized the British people against France.

The experience of living through the Cold War runs deep in modern political memory. After emerging victorious from World War II, the United States and the Soviet Union found themselves locked in a bitter rivalry that threatened to trigger nuclear destruction of the entire planet. At stake in this contest were not only national ambitions, but also incompatible ideologies—capitalism and communism—that amplified popular suspicion and animosity. Americans feared that as agents of world communism, the leaders of the Soviet Union planned the destruction of the free market as well as individual liberty. Indeed, Americans became convinced, especially during the McCarthy "Red Scare" Era of the early 1950s, that the Soviet Union had organized an insidious conspiracy that reached into the State Department and Pentagon and compromised the interests of the United States. Playing on the fear of ordinary citizens, Senator Joseph McCarthy accused famous writers, filmmakers, and musicians of being Soviet spies and Communists intent on helping the enemy. Wars waged in far-off countries such as Vietnam aimed to halt the spread of communism, and a growing anxiety over imagined Soviet aggression served to heighten among the American people a sense of the United States having a special mission as defender of democracy and capitalism.

During the eighteenth century, similar tensions divided the British Empire from its chief rival, France. Although it is hard now to imagine these two modern allies as bitter enemies, we must remember that they were once locked in a contest to control European politics and the economic resources flowing from colonies throughout the world. For Americans living along the frontier of empire—especially in northern New England and western Pennsylvania—fear of raids by French and Indian forces became a condition of everyday life. What provides a parallel to the Cold War was the colonists' firm belief that French territorial ambitions were driven by a destructive ideology that aimed to undermine the freedom and prosperity of the subjects of Great Britain. The threat came not from communism, but rather, from Catholicism, the religion espoused by the government of France.

Intense hostility to Catholicism had a long history in England dating back to the reign of Queen Elizabeth and the Gun Powder Plot in 1605, when a group of Catholics attempted to blow up Parliament. Over time, anti-Catholicism and animosity toward France merged powerfully in British public opinion. As historian Linda Colley explained, recurrent wars with France "ensured that the vision so many Britons cherished of their own history became fused in an extraordinary way with their current experience. To many of them, it seemed that the old popish enemy was still at the gates."

Like the anti-Soviet propaganda that flooded the United States during the 1950s, reports of a conspiracy of French Catholics spread through the British Empire, fueling anger and suspicion, and transforming warfare against the French and Indians into a patriotic crusade. American ministers took up the cause. In a strident sermon the Reverent John Burt claimed that French policy was "the Offspring of the *Scarlet Whore, that Mother of Harlots,* who is justly *the Abomination of the Earth.*" Other colonists called France an "Antichristian Power," and one advised that "the art of War becomes a Part of our Religion."

Comparisons across time suggest that when nationalist ideologies take root in public opinion they can generate a determination to preserve all that is valuable in one's culture. But as the experiences of the Cold War and the eighteenth-century wars of empire reveal, patriotism focused on an external enemy and fueled by fear of conspiracy can also create intolerance and an excuse for violence against innocent people who find themselves caught up in the rhetoric of hate.

Washington, constructed Fort Necessity not far from Fort Duquesne. The plan failed. French and Indian troops overran the badly exposed outpost (July 3, 1754). Among other things, this humiliating setback revealed that a single colony could not defeat the French.

Albany Congress and Braddock's Defeat

Benjamin Franklin, for one, understood the necessity for intercolonial cooperation. When British officials invited representatives from Virginia and Maryland, as well as the northern colonies, to Albany (June 1754) to discuss relations with the Iroquois, Franklin used the occasion to present a bold blueprint for colonial union.

His so-called **Albany Plan** envisioned the formation of a Grand Council, made up of elected delegates from the various colonies, to oversee matters of common defense, western expansion, and Indian affairs. Most daring of all, he wanted to give the council the power of taxation.

First reaction to the Albany Plan was enthusiastic, but ultimately neither the separate colonial assemblies nor Parliament approved the plan. The assemblies were jealous of their fiscal authority, whereas the English thought the scheme undermined the Crown's power in the colony.

Even though there was still no formal declaration of war, the British resolved to destroy Fort Duquesne, and to that end, in 1755 they dispatched units of the regular army to the Ohio Valley under the command of Major General Edward Braddock. A poor leader who inspired no respect, on July 9, Braddock led his force of British "redcoats" and colonists into one of the worst defeats in British military history. The French and Indians opened fire as Braddock's forces were wading across the Monongahela River, about 8 miles from Fort Duquesne. Enraged, Braddock ordered a senseless counterattack. In the end, nearly 70 percent of Braddock's troops were either killed or wounded, and Braddock himself was dead. The French remained in firm control of the Ohio Valley.

Seven Years' War

Britain's imperial war effort had hit rock bottom. No one in England or America seemed to possess the leadership necessary to drive the French from the Mississippi Valley. Still, on May 18, 1756, Great Britain declared war on France, a conflict called the French and Indian War in America and the **Seven Years' War** in Europe.

William Pitt, the most powerful minister in the cabinet of George II, finally provided Great Britain with what it needed most, a forceful leader. Arrogant and conceited, Pitt nevertheless offered a bold, new imperial policy. Rather than fight great battles in Europe, where France had the advantage, Pitt decided that the critical theater of the war would be North America, where Britain and France were struggling for control of colonial markets and raw materials. His goal was clear: to expel the French from the continent, however great the cost.

To effect this ambitious scheme, Pitt took personal command of the army and navy. He mapped out strategy; he promoted promising young officers over the heads of their superiors. He convinced Parliament to pour millions of pounds into his imperial efforts, thus creating an enormous national debt that would soon haunt both Britain and its colonies.

To direct the grand campaign, Pitt selected two relatively obscure colonels, Jeffrey Amherst and James Wolfe. It was a masterful choice that soon proved sound. Forces under their direction captured Louisbourg on July 26, 1758, effectively severing the Canadians' main supply line with France. Time was now on the side of the British. Two poor harvests, in 1756 and 1757, and a population too small to meet the military demands of the accelerated conflict led to a desperate situation for the French empire in North America. Frontier forts began to fall; Fort Duquesne was abandoned in 1758. French and Indian troops retreated to Quebec and Montreal, surrendering key outposts at Ticonderoga, Crown Point, and Niagara as they withdrew.

■ *Native Americans often depended on trade goods supplied by the British and sometimes adopted British dress. Here, the Mohawk chief Theyanoguin, called King Hendrick by the British, wears a cloak he received from Queen Anne during a visit to London in 1710. During the Seven Years' War, Theyanoguin mobilized Mohawk support for the British.* ■

A Century of Conflict: Major Wars, 1689–1763

Dates	European Name	American Name	Major Allies	Issues	Major American Battle	Treaty
1689–1697	War of the League of Augsburg	King William's War	Britain, Holland, Spain, their colonies, and Native American allies against France, its colonies, and Native American allies	Opposition to French bid for control of Europe	New England troops assault Quebec under Sir William Phips (1690)	Treaty of Ryswick (1697)
1702–1713	War of the Spanish Succession	Queen Anne's War	Britain, Holland, their colonies, and Native American allies against France, Spain, their colonies, and Native American allies	Austria and France hold rival claims to Spanish throne	Attack on Deerfield (1704)	Treaty of Utrecht (1713)
1743–1748	War of the Austrian Succession (War of Jenkin's Ear)	King George's War	Britain, its colonies, and Native American allies, and Austria against France, Spain, their Native American allies, and Prussia	Struggle among Britain, Spain, and France for control of New World territory; among France, Prussia, and Austria for control of central Europe	New England forces capture of Louisbourg under William Pepperrell (1745)	Treaty of Aix-la-Chapelle (1748)
1756–1763	Seven Years' War	French and Indian War	Britain, its colonies, and Native American allies against France, its colonies, and Native American allies	Struggle among Britain, Spain, and France for worldwide control of colonial markets and raw materials	British and Continental forces capture Quebec under Major General James Wolfe (1759)	Peace of Paris (1763)

The climax to a century of war came dramatically in September 1759. Wolfe, now a major general, assaulted Quebec, held by a brilliant French commander, the marquis de Montcalm. The remarkable campaign saw Wolfe's men scale a cliff under the cover of darkness and launch a successful surprise attack at dawn on September 13, 1759. Both Wolfe and Montcalm were mortally wounded. When an aide informed Wolfe that the French had been routed, he sighed, "Now, God be praised, I will die in peace." One year later, Amherst accepted the final surrender of the French army at Montreal.

The Peace of Paris, signed on February 10, 1763, almost fulfilled Pitt's grandiose dreams. Great Britain took possession of an empire that stretched around the globe. After a century-long struggle, the French had been driven from America, retaining only their sugar islands in the Caribbean. The treaty gave Britain title to Canada, Florida, and all the land east of the Mississippi River. The colonists were overjoyed. It was a time of good feelings and imperial pride.

The Seven Years' War made a deep impression on American society. The military struggle had forced the colonists to cooperate on an unprecedented scale. It also drew them into closer contact with the mother country. They became aware of being part of a great empire, but in the very process of waging war, they acquired a more intimate sense of an America that lay beyond the plantation and the village. Moreover, the war trained a corps of American officers, people such as George Washington, who learned from firsthand experience that the British were not invincible.

British officials later accused the Americans of ingratitude. The English charged that they had sent troops and provided funds to liberate the colonists from the threat of French attack, but the Americans had refused to shoulder their fair share of the costs. The British used this argument to justify parliamentary taxation in America. In fact, the Americans had been slow in providing men and materials needed to fight the French, but in the end, they did contribute to the defense of the

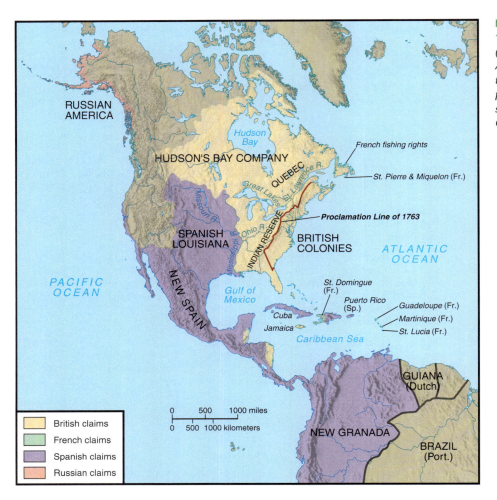

The Peace of Paris (1763) redrew the map of North America. Great Britain received all the French holdings except for a few islands in the Atlantic and some sugar-producing islands in the Caribbean. ■

empire. The colonies supplied almost twenty thousand soldiers and spent well over £2 million. Americans believed they had played a vital role.

CONCLUSION: RULE BRITANNIA?

James Thomson, an Englishman, understood the hold of empire on the popular imagination of the eighteenth century. In 1740, he composed words that British patriots have sung proudly ever since:

> Rule Britannia, rule the waves
> Britons never will be slaves

Colonial Americans of British background joined the chorus. By midcentury, they took their political and cultural cues from Great Britain. They fought its wars, purchased its consumer goods, flocked to hear its evangelical preachers, and read its many publications. Without question, the empire provided the colonists with a compelling source of identity.

An editor justified the establishment of New Hampshire's first newspaper in precisely these terms. "By this Means," the publisher observed, "the spirited *Englishman*, the mountainous *Welshman*, the brave *Scotchman*, and *Irishman*, and the loyal *American*, may be firmly united and mutually RESOLVED to guard the glorious Throne of BRITANNIA . . . as *British Brothers*, in defending the Common Cause." Even new immigrants, the Germans, Scots-Irish, and Africans, who felt no

Chronology

1689	William and Mary accede to the English throne
1702	Anne becomes queen of England
1706	Benjamin Franklin is born
1714	George I of Hanover becomes monarch of Great Britain
1727	George II accedes to the British throne
1732	Colony of Georgia is established ■ George Washington is born
1734–1736	First expression of the Great Awakening appears at Northampton, Massachusetts
1740	George Whitefield electrifies his listeners at Boston
1745	Colonial troops capture Louisbourg
1754	Albany Congress meets
1755	Braddock is defeated by the French and Indians in western Pennsylvania
1756	French and Indian War (Seven Years' War) is formally declared
1759	British are victorious at Quebec ■ Wolfe and Montcalm are killed in battle
1760	George III becomes king of Great Britain
1763	Peace of Paris ending French and Indian War is signed

political loyalty to Great Britain or affinity for British ways, had to assimilate to some degree to the dominant English culture of the colonies.

Americans hailed Britannia. In 1763, they were the victors, the conquerors of the back country. In their moment of glory the colonists assumed that Britain's rulers saw the Americans as "brothers," as equal partners in the business of empire. Only slowly would they realize that the British had a different perception. For them, "American" was a way of saying "not quite English."

KEY TERMS

back country, p. 59

Enlightenment, p. 64

Great Awakening, p. 67

itinerant preachers, p. 68

Albany Plan, p. 74

Seven Years' War, p. 74

RECOMMENDED READING

The central theme of this chapter has been the re-integration of the American colonies into an increasingly powerful and prosperous British Empire. A good introduction to the imperial dimension of eighteenth-century experience is P. J. Marshall, ed., *The Oxford History of the British Empire, vol. 2, The Eighteenth Century* (1998). In *Britons: Forging the Nation, 1707–1837* (1992), Linda Colley provides an excellent discussion of the aggressive spirit of the British nationalism that the Americans came to celebrate. The arrival of new ethnic groups is examined in Eric Hinderaker and Peter C. Mancall, *At the Edge of Empire: The Backcountry in British North America* (2003); Patrick Griffin, *The People with No Name: Ulster's Presbyterians in a British Atlantic World, 1688–1763* (2001); and Bernard Bailyn and Philip D. Morgan, eds.,

Strangers Within the Realm: Cultural Margins of the First British Empire (1991). Richard White has transformed how we think about Native American resistance during this period in *The Middle Ground: Indians, Empires, and Republics in the Great Lakes Region* (1991). Two other fine books explore the Indians' response to the expanding European empires: Timothy Shannon, *Indians and Colonists at the Crossroads of Empire: The Albany Congress of 1754* (2000) and Gregory Evans Dowd, *War Under Heaven: Pontiac, The Indian Nations and the British Empire* (2002). The complex story of Spanish colonization of the Southwest is told masterfully in David J. Weber, *The Spanish Frontier in North America* (1992). Fred Anderson offers the most complete treatment of war and empire in *Crucible of War: The Seven Years' War and the Fate of*

Empire in British North America, 1754–1766 (2000). A splendid examination of Benjamin Franklin as a colonial voice of the Enlightenment is Joyce Chaplin, *The First Scientific American: Benjamin Franklin and the Pursuit of Genius* (2006). The extraordinary impact of evangelical religion on colonial life is addressed in Mark A. Noll, *America's God: From Jonathan Edwards to Abraham Lincoln* (2002); Frank Lambert, *"Pedlar of Divinity": George Whitefield and the Transatlantic Revivals, 1734–1770* (1994); and Timothy D. Hall, *Contested Boundaries: Itinerancy and the Reshaping of the Colonial Religious World* (1994). The cultural concerns of a rising Anglicized colonial middle class are analyzed in David S. Shields, *Civil Tongues and Polite Letters in British America* (1997).

SUGGESTED WEB SITES

History Buff's—American History Library
www.historybuff.com/library
Brief journalistic essays on newspaper coverage of sixteenth- to eighteenth-century American history.

Benjamin Franklin Documentary History Web Site
www.english.udel.edu/lemay/franklin/
University of Delaware professor J. A. Leo Lemay tells the story of Franklin's varied life in seven parts on this intriguing site.

Jonathan Edwards
www.jonathanedwards.com/
Speeches by this famous preacher of the Great Awakening are on this site.

Religion and the Founding of the American Republic
lcweb.loc.gov/exhibits/religion/religion.html
This Library of Congress site is an on-line exhibit about religion and the creation of the United States.

Smithsonian Institution: You Be the Historian
www.americanhistory.si.edu/hohr/springer
Part of the Smithsonian's on-line museum, this exhibit enables students to examine artifacts from the home of New Castle, Delaware, residents Thomas and Elizabeth Springer and interpret the lives of a late eighteenth-century American family.

National Museum of the American Indian
www.si.edu/nmai
The Smithsonian Institution maintains this site, providing information about the museum. The museum is dedicated to everything about Native Americans.

The French and Indian War
web.syr.edu/~laroux/
This site is about French soldiers who came to New France between 1755 and 1760 to fight in the French and Indian War.

DoHistory, Harvard University Film Study Center
www.dohistory.org/
Focusing on the life of Martha Ballard, a late eighteenth-century New England woman, this site employs selections from her diary, excerpts from a book and film of her life, and other primary documents to enable students to conduct their own historical investigation.

We Americans

Learning to Live with Diversity in the Eighteenth Century
What Is an American?

Americans have had a hard time dealing with difference. It is only recently that some commentators have begun to describe social diversity as a positive good. For most of our history, attempts to define national identity have inevitably excluded members of minority groups or newcomers whose language and culture were not English. Over the past two centuries those in authority have devised various strategies for accommodating ethnic and racial diversity, some more successful than others, but all of them at any moment are as likely to produce anger and violence as mutual understanding. These explosive issues first sparked public debate during the eighteenth century, long before Americans advocated independence.

The sudden arrival of thousands of men and women born in Ireland and Germany worried colonial leaders who assumed that being British meant that a person spoke English and accepted the basic traditions of English law and politics. Problems related to ethnic diversity seemed most pressing in the Middle Colonies such as Pennsylvania, for after the 1720s poor people from the German Palatinate and the area around Belfast, Ireland, flocked to America in search of economic opportunity. James Logan, the provincial secretary of Pennsylvania, sounded the alarm, warning those of English stock of the "foreigners" who threatened to transform the local culture. Because of the number of Germans entering the colony, Logan argued, "these colonies will in time be lost to the Crown." The Scots-Irish were even more menacing. These Protestant migrants who fled the north of Ireland to escape chronic poverty appeared intent on making "themselves Proprietors of the Province."

It might have been predicted that English colonists would have welcomed so many able workers, people who could pay taxes and defend the frontiers. But such was not the case. Benjamin Franklin, often depicted as the voice of reason, almost panicked when he contemplated the growing diversity. Why, he demanded, should the Germans be allowed "to swarm into our Settlements, and by herding together establish their Language and Manners to the Exclusion of ours? Why should Pennsylvania, founded by the English, become a Colony of *Aliens?*" In fact, Franklin predicted that "Instead of their Learning our Language, we must learn theirs, or live as in a foreign Country." As in so many cultural confrontations of this sort, the representatives of the dominant group defined difference as a contest in which one either won or lost. Accommodation had little appeal for those so anxious to preserve the purity of their own heritage.

The question for people such as Franklin was how best to make the Germans and the Scots-Irish more like the English. It was thought that education might save the day. After all, the "foreigners" could be taught to accept a common set of values that obviously served as the foundation for society. Pennsylvania leaders contended that these standards rested ultimately on "the noble Privilege or Birth-Right of an *English Subject.*" As anyone could see, English identity meant developing a deep respect for the law, property, and institutions originally erected by migrants from England and their descendants. During the years of heaviest immigration, those who claimed to speak for the cultural mainstream extolled the "sober and prudent conduct of the ancient Settlers and their Successors," in other words, those who understood that "the Rights and Privileges of this Colony, [rested] on the true basis of English *Liberty and Property.*" Some enthusiasts even encouraged the colonial legislature to pass laws for the encouragement of "Virtue, Sobriety, and Industry . . . [to] prevent an English Plantation from Being turned into a Colony of Aliens."

The key to preserving social order in the face of growing diversity was Anglicization, a process of transforming Germans and Scots-Irish into people who at least seemed English. Success was just a matter of time. Strange languages, customs, and beliefs could be made to disappear under a veneer of Englishness. Thomas Penn, whose family actually owned Pennsylvania, predicted that the Germans would "certainly by degrees loose their attachment to their Language, and become English, and as they acquire property I dare prophecy will become good Subjects." Indeed, so confident was his brother John of the ability of the Germans to acculturate that he concluded "we ought by no Means to Debar their coming over," because "when settled these [people] will Esteem themselves Pennsylvanians." To accomplish this goal, "Foreigners imported, should not be allowed to settle in large separate Districts . . . because for many

Generations they may continue, as it were, a separate People in Language, Modes of Religion, Customs and Manners." The newcomers, therefore, were best "intermixed with the *British* settlers." But one had to be on guard. By "distinguishing themselves" from the dominant culture the members of these groups showed contempt for English traditions. After all, asked a colonial official, "How far is it consistent with the Peace, Honour or Security of an English Government that they, who . . . have had the utmost Protection, should upon Occasions, be thus nationally distinguished?"

All the advice apparently fell on deaf ears. The migrants failed to measure up to English standards, and differences came to be seen as rejection and hostility. To the chagrin of fully Anglicized Pennsylvanians, the German settlers could not be "restrained" from forming tight-knit ethnic communities. They refused to abandon the culture they had known in Europe. Moreover, they did not intermarry with those from other groups, established newspapers in their own language, and set up German-speaking schools. The Scots-Irish raised even more hackles. Although they had demonstrated their loyalty to the British crown in the Old World, they seemed in the New to "have

little Honesty and less Sense." An unruly people, they squatted on lands owned by the Penn family or by Native Americans. What is more, they showed no desire to mix with neighbors of different ethnicity. The Scots-Irish held that "no strangers should be admitted to settle within [their] Bounds," and instead of taking their legal disputes to the province's official courts—as any proper Englishman would do—they relied on church elders. To make matters worse for critics such as Franklin, they often reacted to minor insults with violence and were "generally rough" with the Indians. When some Scots-Irish murdered twenty Native Americans in 1763, Franklin called them "Christian white savages," while another colonial official dubbed them "the very scum of mankind."

As has been so often the case with cultural tensions of this sort, the various participants gradually reached an accommodation, often perhaps without even realizing how much they had adjusted to changing conditions. The "foreigners" did not in fact destroy Pennsylvania. Indeed, political leaders who identified themselves as English were soon soliciting the votes of the migrant population, and over time, it became clear that the colony's prosperity in the Atlantic World owed a lot to

hardworking aliens. And on the eve of revolution, some Americans had come to realize that diversity was not all that objectionable. As one patriot who called himself "A Son of Liberty" observed in 1768, "It is true that the first emigrations were from *England;* but upon the whole, more settlers have come from *Ireland, Germany,* and other parts of *Europe,* than from *England.*"

Questions for Discussion

* Why did the English settlers have such a hard time accepting ethnic diversity in the New World?
* How would you contrast the experiences of the German and Scots-Irish migrants in British America?
* Did gradual accommodation of British culture and institutions represent a defeat for the Germans and Scots-Irish? Why or why not?

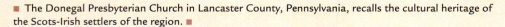

■ The Donegal Presbyterian Church in Lancaster County, Pennsylvania, recalls the cultural heritage of the Scots-Irish settlers of the region. ■

Chapter 5

The American Revolution: From Elite Protest to Popular Revolt, 1763–1783

Rethinking the Meaning of Equality

Even as the British army poured into Boston and demanded complete obedience to king and Parliament, few Americans welcomed the possibility of revolutionary violence. For many colonial families, it would have been easier, certainly safer, to accede to imperial demands for taxes enacted without their representation. But they did not do so.

For the Pattens, the time of reckoning arrived in the spring of 1775. Matthew Patten had been born in Ulster, a Protestant Irishman. With Scots-Irish relatives and friends, he migrated to New Hampshire, where they founded a farming settlement known as Bedford. In time, distant political decisions shattered the peace of Bedford, and the Pattens found themselves drawn into a war not of their own making. They were compelled to sacrifice the security of everyday life for liberty.

On April 20, 1775, accounts of Lexington and Concord reached Bedford. Matthew's son John marched with neighbors in support of the Massachusetts soldiers. The departure was tense. The entire family helped John prepare. The demands of war had only just begun, however. In late 1775, John volunteered for an American march on British Canada. On the long trek over impossible terrain, the boy died. He was twenty-four years old.

The initial stimulus for rebellion came from the gentry—from the rich and well-born. They pronounced their unhappiness in public statements and in speeches before elected assemblies. However, they soon lost control as the revolutionary movement generated a momentum of its own. As relations with the mother country deteriorated, the traditional leaders of colonial society were forced to invite the common folk to join the protest—as rioters, as petitioners, and finally as soldiers. What had started as a squabble among the gentry had been transformed into a mass movement, and once the common people had become involved in shaping the nation's destiny, they could never again be excluded.

The American Revolution involved a massive military commitment. If ordinary militiamen such as John Patten had not been willing to stand up to seasoned British troops, to face the terror of the bayonet charge, independence would have remained a dream of intellectuals. Proportionate to the population, a greater percentage of Americans died in military service during the Revolution than in any war in American history, with the exception of the Civil War. Liberty to them was more than an abstraction studied by political theorists, and those Americans who risked death and survived the ordeal saw new meaning in the concept of equality as well.

Outline

Structure of Colonial Society

Eroding the Bonds of Empire

Steps Toward Independence

Fighting for Independence

The Loyalist Dilemma

Winning the Peace

Conclusion: Preserving Independence

STRUCTURE OF COLONIAL SOCIETY

Only with hindsight can one see the coming of the American Revolution. The lives of most free colonists were filled with economic and political expectations. It was a period of optimism. The population continued to grow, and the standard of living continued to improve. To be sure, wealth was not evenly distributed. The southern colonies were richer than the northern colonies. But even the poorest colonists benefited from the rising standard of living. Economic and political discontent was out of step with the tempo of the age.

No one consciously set out in 1763 to achieve independence. The bonds of loyalty that had cemented the British Empire dissolved slowly. At several points, the British rulers and American colonists could have compromised. Their failure to do so was the result of thousands of separate decisions, errors, and misunderstandings. The Revolution was, in fact, a complex series of events, full of unexpected turns, extraordinary creativity, and great personal sacrifice.

Breakdown of Political Trust

Ultimate responsibility for preserving the empire fell to George III, whose reign began in 1760. He was only twenty-two years old and poorly educated, the product of a sheltered and loveless upbringing. He displayed little understanding of the larger implications of government policy, and many people who knew him considered him dull-witted. Unfortunately, the king could not be ignored, and during a difficult period that demanded imagination, generosity, and wisdom, George muddled along as best he could.

Unlike the preceding Georges, George III decided to play an aggressive role in government. He selected as his chief minister the earl of Bute, a Scot whose only qualification for office appeared to be his friendship with the young king and the young king's mother. The **Whigs,** a political faction that dominated Parliament, believed that George was attempting to turn back the clock to the time before the Glorious Revolution; in other words, attempting to reestablish a monarchy free from traditional constitutional restraints. George did not, in fact, harbor such arbitrary ambitions, but his actions threw customary political practices into doubt.

In 1763, Bute left office. What followed was a seven-year period of confusion during which ministers came and went, often for no other reason than George's personal dislike. Because of this chronic instability, subministers, the minor bureaucrats who directed routine colonial affairs, did not know what was expected of them. In the absence of a long-range policy, the ministers showed more concern for their own future than for coping with the problems of empire building.

The king does not bear the sole responsibility for England's loss of empire in the American colonies. The members of Parliament, the men who actually drafted the statutes that drove a wedge between the colonies and the mother country, failed to respond creatively to the challenge of events. They clung doggedly to the principle of **parliamentary sovereignty,** and when Americans questioned whether that legislative body in London should govern colonial affairs, parliamentary spokesmen provided no constructive basis for compromise. They refused to see a middle ground between the preeminent authority of Parliament and complete American independence.

Parliament's attitude was in part a result of ignorance. Few men active in English government had visited America. For those who attempted to follow colonial affairs, accurate information proved extremely difficult to obtain. One could not expect to receive an answer from America to a specific question in less than three months. As a result of the lag in communication between England and America, rumors sometimes passed for true accounts, and misunderstanding influenced the formulation of colonial policy.

Whigs In the mid-eighteenth century, the Whigs were a political faction that dominated Parliament. Generally they were opposed to royal influence in government and wanted to increase the control and influence of Parliament. Later they were associated with parliamentary reform.

parliamentary sovereignty Principle that emphasized the power of Parliament to govern colonial affairs as the preeminent authority.

But failure of communication alone was not to blame for the widening gap between the colonies and England. Even when complete information was available, the two sides were often unable to understand each other's positions. The central element in this Anglo-American debate was a concept known as parliamentary sovereignty. The English ruling classes viewed the role of Parliament from a historical perspective that most colonists never shared. They insisted that Parliament was the dominant element within the constitution. Indeed, this elective body protected rights and property from an arbitrary monarch. During the reign of the Stuarts, especially under Charles I (r. 1625–1649), the authority of Parliament had been challenged, and it was not until the Glorious Revolution of 1688 that the English Crown formally recognized Parliament's supreme authority in matters such as taxation.

Such a constitutional position did not leave much room for compromise. Most members of Parliament took a hard line on this issue. The notion of dividing or sharing sovereignty simply made no sense to the English ruling class. As Thomas Hutchinson, royal governor of Massachusetts, explained, no middle ground existed "between the supreme authority of

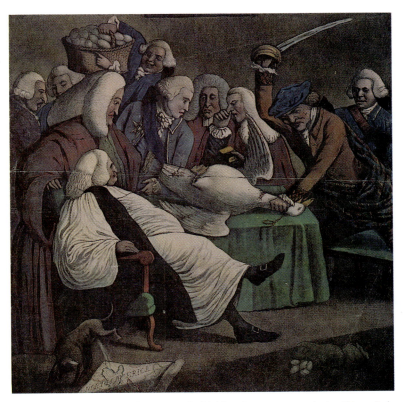

■ Cartoons became a popular means of criticizing the government during this period. Here, King George III watches as the kilted Lord Bute slaughters the goose America. A cabinet member holds a basket of golden eggs at the rear. At front left, a dog relieves itself on a map of North America. ■

Parliament and the total dependence of the colonies." The logic of this argument seemed self-evident to the British. In fact, parliamentary leaders could never quite understand why the colonists were so difficult to persuade.

No Taxation Without Representation: The American Perspective

At the conclusion of the Seven Years' War (French and Indian War), it seemed inconceivable that the colonists would challenge the supremacy of Parliament. But the crisis in imperial relations that soon developed impelled the Americans first to define and then to defend principles that were rooted deeply in the colonial political culture.

For more than a century, the colonists' ideas about their role within the British empire had remained a vague, untested bundle of assumptions about personal liberties, property rights, and representative institutions. But by 1763, certain fundamental beliefs had become clear. Americans accepted the authority of representative local assemblies to tax their constituents, but to declare that the House of Commons in London enjoyed the same right made no sense to them. Moreover, the colonists rejected the distinction that the British officials sometimes made between taxes imposed directly on a person's estate and taxes on trade that could be passed on to consumers. Americans firmly believed that a tax was a tax by whatever name and that Parliament had no right to collect taxes on the American side of the Atlantic, especially since no Americans sat in Parliament.

Loyalists Throughout the conflict with Great Britain, many colonists sided with the king and Parliament. Also called Tories, these people feared that American liberty might promote social anarchy.

Political thought in the colonies contained a strong moral component, one that British rulers and American **Loyalists** (people who sided with the king during the Revolution) never fully understood. The origins of this perspective on civil government are difficult to pinpoint, but certainly the moral fervor of the Great Awakening and the reformist writings of the Commonwealthmen played a part (see Chapter 4). Whatever the intellectual sources may have been, colonists viewed *power* as extremely dangerous, unless it was countered by *virtue*.

Insistence on civic virtue—sacrifice of self-interest to the public good—became the dominant theme of revolutionary political writing. American pamphleteers shared the outlook of those who regarded bad government not as human error but as sin. They saw a host of external threats and plots—arbitrary taxation, standing armies, bishops sent over by the Church of England—all designed to crush American liberty. Popular writers seldom took a dispassionate, legalistic approach in their analysis of Anglo-American relations. They described events in conspiratorial terms, using language charged with emotion.

Colonial newspapers spread these ideas through a large, dispersed population. A majority of adult white males—a great majority in the northern colonies—were literate, and the number of journals in the country increased dramatically during the revolutionary period. The newspaper united the colonies, informing each colony about the political activities in the others, and provided the rhetoric that successfully roused ordinary folk to take up arms against Britain.

ERODING THE BONDS OF EMPIRE

Following the Seven Years' War, more than seven thousand British troops, members of the regular army, remained in North America. Their alleged purpose was to provide a buffer between Indians and frontiersmen and to preserve order in the newly conquered territories of Florida and Quebec. But not one person in the British government actually made the decision to keep an army in the colonies. The army was not recalled simply because of bureaucratic confusion and inertia.

The war had saddled Britain with a national debt so huge that more than one-half of the annual budget went to interest payments. Maintaining a peacetime army so far from the mother country fueled the budgetary crisis. The growing financial burden weighed heavily on restive English taxpayers and sent the government leaders scurrying in search of new sources of revenue.

For their part, colonists doubted the value of this very expensive army. First, the British troops did not maintain peace effectively. This was demonstrated in 1763 when Ottawa Chief Pontiac, who had been allied with the French and hated the British, organized a general uprising along the western frontier. His warriors easily slipped by the redcoats and slew several thousand settlers. In fact, relations between whites and Indians deteriorated. Unable to play the British off against the French, the Indians suffered terribly from the imperial reorganization. Second, the colonists resented the Proclamation of 1763, which attempted unsuccessfully to restrain Americans from moving onto Indian lands west of the Appalachian Mountains, and they identified the hated policy with the British troops who guarded the frontier.

The task of reducing England's debt fell to George Grenville, the somewhat unimaginative chancellor of the exchequer who replaced Bute in 1763 as the king's first minister. Grenville decided that the colonists would have to contribute to the maintenance of the army. The first bill he steered through Parliament was the Revenue Act of 1764, known as the Sugar Act.

This legislation placed a new burden on the Navigation Acts, which had governed the flow of colonial commerce for almost a century (see Chapter 3). Their primary purpose was not to raise money but to force Americans to trade with the mother country. The Sugar Act, by contrast, was specifically designed to generate revenue. It imposed new import duties on sugar, coffee, wines, and other imports; instituted tougher customs collection methods; and expanded the jurisdiction of the vice-admiralty courts. The act also included provisions aimed at curbing colonial smuggling of molasses and bribery of customs officials.

American reaction came swiftly. James Otis, a fiery orator from Massachusetts, exclaimed that the legislation deprived Americans of "the rights of assessing their own taxes." Petitions of protest involved no violence, but to Grenville and persons of his temperament, even petitions smacked of ingratitude. After all, they reasoned, had not the mother country saved the Americans from the French? But Grenville's perspective overlooked the contribution of colonial staples such as rice and tobacco to the prosperity of the mother country. Moreover, American markets helped sustain British industry (see Chapter 4). The colonists saw no justification for Grenville's aggressive new policy now that the military emergency had passed.

Popular Protest

Even before the Sugar Act had gone into effect, Grenville put the final touches on a second revenue measure, the Stamp Act. Although a few members of Parliament warned that the Americans would bitterly resent the act, the majority of the House of Commons supported the legislation. Specifically, the Stamp Act required printed documents—such as newspapers, legal contracts, and marriage licenses—to bear revenue stamps purchased from royal stamp distributors. The act was to go into effect November 1, 1765.

Word of the Stamp Act reached America by May, and the colonial reaction against it was swift. In Virginia's House of Burgesses, eloquent young Patrick Henry introduced five resolutions protesting the act. He timed his move carefully. It was late in the session; many of the more conservative burgesses had already departed for their plantations. Even then, Henry's resolves declaring that Virginians had the right to tax themselves as they alone saw fit passed by narrow margins.

The Virginia Resolves might have remained a local matter had it not been for the colonial press. Newspapers throughout America printed Henry's resolutions. The newspaper accounts, however, were not always accurate. Some accounts said that all five of Henry's resolutions had passed when in fact the fifth resolution, which announced that Britain's actions were "illegal, unconstitutional, and unjust," had been stricken from the legislative record. Several newspapers even printed two resolutions that Henry had not dared to introduce. The result of this misunderstanding, of course, was that the Virginians appeared to have taken an extremely radical position on the issue of the supremacy of Parliament, one that other Americans now trumpeted before their own assemblies.

Not to be outdone by Virginia, the Massachusetts assembly in June proposed a general meeting to protest Grenville's policy. Nine colonies sent representatives to the **Stamp Act Congress,** which convened in New York City in October 1765. The delegates drafted petitions to the king and Parliament that restated the colonists' belief "that no taxes should be imposed on them, but with their own consent, given personally, or by their representatives." There was no mention of independence or disloyalty to the Crown.

Stamp Act Congress Meeting of colonial delegates in New York City in October 1765 to protest the Stamp Act, a law passed by Parliament to raise revenue in America. The delegates drafted petitions denouncing the Stamp Act and other taxes imposed on Americans without colonial consent.

Resistance to the Stamp Act soon moved from assembly petitions to mass protests in the streets. In Boston, a mob calling itself the Sons of Liberty burned the local stamp distributor in effigy. The violent outbursts frightened colonial leaders; yet the evidence suggests that they encouraged the lower classes to intimidate royal officials. After 1765, it was impossible for either royal governors or patriot leaders to take for granted the support of ordinary men and women.

By November 1, 1765, stamp distributors in almost every American port had publicly resigned, and without distributors, the hated revenue stamps could not be sold. The Sons of Liberty convinced colonial merchants to boycott British goods.

A Look at the Past

Stamp Act Teapot

Colonists could celebrate the repeal of the hated Stamp Act by purchasing goods decorated like this teapot. Because no manufacturers of fine ceramics existed in British America, the teapot came from England. As this piece indicates, English manufacturers readily produced goods suited to colonial tastes. British merchants and manufacturers had good reason to celebrate the repeal of the Stamp Act as it meant that colonists resumed purchasing English goods. ✳ What does this teapot suggest about the economic and cultural connections between England and the colonies? Why would some individuals in England regard imperial actions as unfavorably as some colonists did?

What most Americans did not yet know—communication with the mother country took months—was that in July, Grenville had fallen from power. His replacement as first lord of the treasury, Lord Rockingham, envisioned a prosperous empire founded on an expanding commerce, with local government under the gentle guidance of Parliament. Grenville, now simply a member of Parliament, urged a tough policy toward America, but important men, such as William Pitt, defended the colonists' position. Finally, Rockingham called for the repeal of the Stamp Act. On March 18, 1766, the act was repealed.

Repeal failed to restore imperial harmony. Lest its retreat on the Stamp Act be interpreted as weakness, the House of Commons passed the Declaratory Act (March 1766), a shrill defense of parliamentary supremacy over the Americans "in all cases whatsoever." The colonists' insistence on no taxation without representation failed to impress British rulers. Clearly, if America thought it won the Stamp Act battle, Parliament was announcing that it fully expected to win the war.

In America, too, attitudes hardened. Respect for imperial officeholders as well as Parliament had diminished. Suddenly, royal governors, customs collectors, and military personnel appeared alien, as if their interests were not those of the people over whom they exercised authority. Indeed, it is testimony to the Americans' lingering loyalty to the British crown and constitution that rebellion did not occur in 1765.

Fueling the Crisis

Rockingham's ministry soon gave way to a government headed once again by William Pitt, now the earl of Chatham. The aging Pitt suffered horribly from gout, and during his long absences from London, Charles Townshend, his chancellor of the exchequer, made important political decisions. Townshend's mouth often outran his mind, and in January 1767, he pleased the House of Commons by announcing that he knew a way to obtain revenue from the Americans.

His plan turned out to be a grab bag of duties on American imports of paper, glass, paint, and tea, collectively known as the Townshend Revenue Acts (June 1767). To collect these duties, he created the American Board of Customs Commissioners, a body based in Boston and supported by reorganized vice-admiralty courts in port cities.

Americans were no more willing to pay Townshend's duties than they had been to buy Grenville's stamps. In major ports, the Sons of Liberty organized boycotts of British goods. Imported finery came to symbolize England's political corruption. Americans prided themselves on wearing homespun clothes as a badge of simplicity and virtue. Women were ardent supporters of the boycott, holding public spinning bees to produce more homespun.

On February 11, 1768, the Massachusetts House of Representatives drafted a circular letter, a provocative appeal that it sent directly to the other colonial assemblies. The letter requested suggestions on how best to thwart the Townshend Acts. Although the letter was mild, Lord Hillsborough, England's secretary for American affairs, took offense. He called the letter a "seditious paper" and ordered the Massachusetts representatives to rescind it; the legislators refused.

Suddenly, the circular letter became a cause célèbre. When the royal governor of Massachusetts dissolved the House of Representatives, the other colonies demonstrated their support of the Bay Colony by taking up the circular letter in their assemblies. Hillsborough promptly dissolved more colonial legislatures. Parliament's challenge had brought about the very results it most wanted to avoid: a basis for intercolonial communication and a growing sense among the colonists of the righteousness of their position.

Fatal Show of Force

In October 1768, British rulers made another critical mistake. The issue was the army. In part to intimidate colonial troublemakers, the ministry stationed four thousand regular troops around Boston. The armed strangers camped on Boston Commons, sometimes shouting obscenities at citizens passing the site. To make relations worse, the redcoats, ill-treated and underpaid, competed in their spare time for jobs with local dockworkers and artisans.

When citizens questioned why the army had been sent to a peaceful city, pamphleteers claimed that the soldiers in Boston were simply another phase of a conspiracy originally conceived by the earl of Bute to oppress Americans, to take away their liberties, and to collect illegal revenues. Grenville, Hillsborough, and Townshend were all, supposedly, part of the plot. To Americans raised on the political theories of the Commonwealthmen, the pattern of tyranny seemed obvious.

Colonists had no difficulty interpreting the violence that erupted in Boston on March 5, 1770. In the gathering dusk of that afternoon, young boys and street toughs used rocks and snowballs to bombard a small isolated patrol outside the offices of the hated customs commissioners in King Street. The details of the incident are obscure, but it appears that as the mob grew and became more threatening, the troops panicked and fired, leaving five Americans dead.

Pamphleteers promptly labeled the incident a "massacre," its victims cast as martyrs. To the propagandists, what actually happened during the **Boston Massacre** mattered little. Their job was to inflame emotions; they performed their work well. Confronted with such an intense reaction and with the possibility of massive armed resistance, Crown officials wisely moved the army to an island in Boston harbor.

At this critical moment, the king's new first minister restored a measure of tranquillity. Lord North, congenial, well meaning, but not very talented, was appointed the first minister in 1770, and for the next twelve years—indeed, throughout most of the American crisis—he managed to retain his office. His secret formula seems to have been an ability to get along with George III and to build an effective majority in Parliament.

One of North's first recommendations to Parliament was the repeal of the ill-conceived Townshend duties. Not only had the duties enraged Americans, but they

Boston Massacre A violent confrontation between British troops and a Boston mob on March 5, 1770. Five citizens were killed when the troops fired into the crowd. The incident inflamed anti-British sentiment in Massachusetts.

■ *Outrage over the Boston Massacre was fanned by propaganda, such as this etching by Paul Revere, which showed British redcoats firing on ordinary citizens. In subsequent editions of the print, the blood spurting from the dying Americans became more conspicuous.* ■

also hurt British manufacturers by encouraging Americans to develop their own industries. Parliament responded by dropping all the duties, with the exception of the tax on tea. But Parliament still maintained that it held total supremacy over the colonies. For a time, Americans drew back from the precipice of confrontation, frightened by the events of the past two years.

Collapse of the Old Order, 1770–1773

For a brief moment, the American colonists and British officials put aside their recent animosities. Merchants returned to familiar patterns of trade, and American indebtedness grew. Even in Massachusetts, the people decided that they could accept their new royal governor, an American, Thomas Hutchinson.

But appearances were deceiving. The bonds of imperial loyalty remained fragile, and even as Lord North attempted to win the colonists' trust, Crown officials in America created new strains. Customs commissioners abused their powers of search and seizure and in the process lined their own pockets. Any failure to abide by the Navigation Acts, no matter how minor, could bring confiscation of ship and cargo.

The commissioners were not only corrupt but also foolish. They harassed the wealthy and powerful as well as the common folk. The commissioners' actions drove members of the colonial ruling class, men such as John Hancock of Boston, into opposition to the king's government. Eventually, the commissioners' greed brought the colonists closer together.

Samuel Adams (1722–1803) refused to accept the notion that the repeal of the Townshend duties had secured American liberty. During the early 1770s, while colonial leaders turned to other matters, Adams kept the cause alive with a drumfire of publicity. He never allowed the people of Boston to forget the many real and alleged wrongs perpetrated by the Crown. Adams was a genuine revolutionary, seemingly obsessed with the need to preserve civic virtue and moral values in the conduct of public affairs. With each new attempt by Parliament to assert its supremacy over the colonists, more and more Bostonians listened to what Adams had to say. By 1772, Adams had attracted broad support for the formation of a **committee of correspondence** to communicate grievances to villagers throughout Massachusetts. People in other colonies soon copied his idea and established intercolonial committees as well. It was a brilliant stroke; Adams developed a structure of political cooperation completely independent of royal government.

committee of correspondence
Vast communication network formed in Massachusetts and other colonies to communicate grievances and provide colonists with evidence of British oppression.

The Final Provocation: The Boston Tea Party

In May 1773, Parliament resumed its old tricks. It passed the Tea Act, a strange piece of legislation that Parliament thought the colonists would welcome. The statute was designed to save the floundering East India Company, not to raise revenue. It allowed the company to ship tea directly to America, thereby eliminating the colonial middlemen and permitting Americans to purchase tea at bargain rates. The plan, however, was flawed. First, since the Townshend duty on tea remained in effect, the new arrangement seemed to be a devious way to win popular support for Parliament's right to tax the colonists without representation. Second, the act threatened to undercut tea smugglers and the powerful mercantile groups operating in Boston.

Americans soon registered their protest. Boston took the most dramatic stand. Although colonists in Philadelphia and New York City turned back tea ships before they could unload, in Boston, Governor Hutchinson would not permit the vessels to return to England. Local patriots would not let them unload. So the ships sat in Boston harbor crammed with tea until the night of December 16, 1773, when a group of men in Indian garb boarded the ships and pitched 340 chests of tea worth £10,000 into the water.

When news of the "Tea Party" reached London in January 1774, the North ministry was stunned. The people of Boston had treated parliamentary supremacy with utter contempt, and British rulers saw no humor whatsoever in the destruction of private property by subjects of the Crown dressed in costume. To quell such rebelliousness, Parliament passed a series of laws called the **Coercive Acts.** (In America, they were referred to as the Intolerable Acts.) The legislation (1) closed the port of Boston until the city fully compensated the East India Company for the lost tea; (2) restructured the Massachusetts government by transforming the upper house from an elective to an appointed body and restricting the number of legal town meetings to one a year; (3) allowed the royal governor to transfer British officials arrested for offenses committed in the line of duty to England or Canada, where there was little likelihood they would be convicted; and (4) authorized the army to quarter troops wherever they were needed, even if this required the compulsory requisition of uninhabited private buildings. George III enthusiastically supported the tough policy; he appointed General Thomas Gage to serve as the colony's new royal governor.

Coercive Acts Also known as the Intolerable Acts, the four pieces of legislation passed by Parliament in 1774 in response to the Boston Tea Party that were meant to punish the colonies.

The sweeping series of laws confirmed the colonists' worst fears. The vindictiveness of the acts strengthened the influence of men such as Samuel Adams and undermined the influence of colonial moderates. In Parliament, a saddened Edmund Burke, one of America's few remaining friends, warned his countrymen that the acts could lead to war.

In the midst of this constitutional crisis, Parliament announced plans to establish a new civil government for the Canadian province of Quebec. The Quebec Act (June 22, 1774)

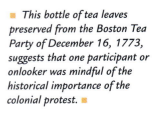

■ *This bottle of tea leaves preserved from the Boston Tea Party of December 16, 1773, suggests that one participant or onlooker was mindful of the historical importance of the colonial protest.* ■

also extended the province's boundaries all the way south to the Ohio River and west to the Mississippi. The act made no provision for an elective assembly, but it granted French-speaking Roman Catholics religious and political rights and a large voice in local affairs. These measures were seen by Americans as a denial of *their* rights to settle and trade in this fast-developing region.

Americans everywhere rallied to Massachusetts's defense. Few persons advocated independence, but they could not remain passive while Boston was destroyed. They sent food and money and, during the autumn of 1774, reflected more deeply than ever on what it meant to be a colonist in the British empire. And the more they reflected, the more they objected to the idea of the sovereignty of Parliament.

STEPS TOWARD INDEPENDENCE

First Continental Congress
Meeting of delegates from twelve colonies in Philadelphia in 1774. The Congress denied Parliament's authority to legislate for the colonies, condemned British actions toward the colonies, created the Continental Association, and endorsed a call to take up arms.

Samuel Adams had prepared Americans for this moment. Something had to be done. But what? The committees of correspondence endorsed a call for a continental congress, a gathering of fifty-five elected delegates from twelve colonies (Georgia sent none but agreed to support the action taken). The **First Continental Congress** convened in Philadelphia on September 5, 1774, and included such respected leaders as John Adams, Samuel Adams, Patrick Henry, Richard Henry Lee, and George Washington.

But the delegates were strangers to one another. They knew little about the customs and values, geography, and economy of Britain's other American provinces. Differences of opinion soon surfaced. Delegates from the middle colonies wanted to proceed with caution, but before they knew what had happened, Samuel Adams maneuvered these moderates into a position far more radical than they found comfortable. Boston's master politician engineered congressional commendation of the Suffolk Resolves, a bold statement drawn up in Suffolk County, Massachusetts, that encouraged Americans to resist the Coercive Acts forcibly.

The tone of the meeting was set. The more radical delegates carried the day. They agreed to form an "association" to halt all commerce with the mother country until Parliament repealed the Intolerable Acts. They also agreed to meet in the coming year. Meanwhile, in London, George III told his confidants, "Blows must decide whether [New England governments] are to be subject to this country or independent."

Shots Heard Around the World

Before Congress reconvened, "blows" fell at Lexington and Concord, two small farm villages in eastern Massachusetts. On the evening of April 18, 1775, General Gage dispatched troops from Boston to seize rebel supplies. Paul Revere, a renowned silversmith and active patriot, with the help of William Dawes and Samuel Prescott, warned the colonists that the redcoats were coming. The militia of Lexington, a collection of ill-trained farmers, decided to stand on the village green the following morning, April 19, as the British soldiers passed on the road to Concord. No one planned to fight, but in a moment of confusion someone (probably a colonist) fired; the redcoats discharged a volley, and eight Americans lay dead.

Word of the incident spread rapidly. "Minutemen," special companies of Massachusetts militia prepared to respond instantly to military emergencies, went into action. The redcoats found nothing of significance in Concord and turned back to Boston. The long march back became a rout; the minutemen swarmed all over the redcoats. On June 17, colonial militiamen again held their own against seasoned troops at the battle of Bunker Hill (actually Breed's Hill). The British finally captured the hill, but after this costly "victory" in which he lost 40 percent of his troops, Gage took the American militiamen more seriously.

Past and Present

Revolutionary Communication

Over the entire course of American history, visionaries have greeted every advance in the speed and ease of mass communication as an opportunity for broadening the base of political participation. The telegraph, telephone, and television all seemed to possess the potential to promote the exchange of ideas and grievances among ordinary men and women. In more recent times, effusive rhetoric about communications technology has accompanied the spread of computers and growing availability of the Internet. The argument seems to be that new, almost instantaneous access to information allows Americans to challenge traditional authority. Without doubt, by bringing obscure records and reports before the general public, the Internet makes it more difficult for officials in government and corporations to hide activities that might harm the common good.

Although colonial Americans had nothing to compare with blogging or visiting on-line chat rooms, they used print technology in revolutionary ways that transformed the character of politics. Indeed, it would not be an exaggeration to state that without newspapers the Americans would have found waging war against Great Britain impossible. Like the modern entrepreneurs who advertise on the Internet, publishers on the eve of independence knew that dull products do not sell. The shrill opinion pieces that appeared in the weekly journals hammered away at the alleged dishonesty, corruption, and despotism of the British government. One piece entitled "The Crisis" that ran in many American newspapers during the late spring of 1775, for example, came close to advocating regicide, in other words, killing George III as a means to free Americans from tyranny. The newspapers circulated widely; they were read and discussed in taverns and coffeehouses.

Perhaps even more significant, the newspapers of the revolutionary period encouraged what we might call interactive communications. People not only read the news of the day, but they also responded to it, often in highly critical pieces of their own. And when small communities throughout the colonies voted to support non-importation or to resist parliamentary authority, they sent word of their decisions to the nearest newspapers with instructions that their actions should be shared with other Americans. In this way the journals stimulated a sense of political trust, for even if one did not personally know anyone in a distant town or colony, one learned from these journals that strangers were prepared to join in common cause against the British. Whether the blogs and chat rooms of our own time will spark a similar sustained political debate is impossible to predict, but whatever occurs, it seems certain that a free and open exchange of news and analysis is essential to broad participation in the political process.

Beginning "The World Over Again"

Members of the **Second Continental Congress** gathered in Philadelphia in May 1775. They faced an awesome responsibility. British government in the mainland colonies had almost ceased to function, Americans were fighting redcoats, and the country desperately needed strong central leadership. Congress provided that leadership. The delegates formed a Continental Army, appointed George Washington its commander, purchased military supplies, and, to pay for them, issued paper money. But they refused to take the final step—independence.

Indecision drove John Adams nearly mad with frustration. He and other like-minded delegates ranted against their timid colleagues. Haste, however, would have been a terrible mistake, for many Americans were not convinced that independence was either necessary or desirable. If Congress had moved too quickly, it might have faced charges of extremism and thereby lost mass support for its cause.

The British government appeared intent on transforming colonial moderates into angry rebels. In December 1775, Parliament passed the Prohibitory Act, declaring war on American commerce. The British navy blockaded colonial ports and seized American ships on the high seas. Lord North also hired German mercenaries to put down the rebellion. And in America, royal governors such as Lord Dunmore further undermined the possibility of reconciliation by urging Virginia's slaves to take up arms against their masters.

Thomas Paine (1737–1809) pushed the colonists even closer to independence. In January 1776, Paine, a recent arrival from England, published a pamphlet titled **Common Sense.** In this powerful democratic manifesto, Paine urged

Second Continental Congress This meeting took place in Philadelphia in May 1775, in the midst of rapidly unfolding military events. It organized the Continental Army and commissioned George Washington to lead it, then began requisitioning men and supplies for the war effort.

Common Sense Revolutionary tract written by Thomas Paine in January 1776. It called for independence and the establishment of a republican government in America.

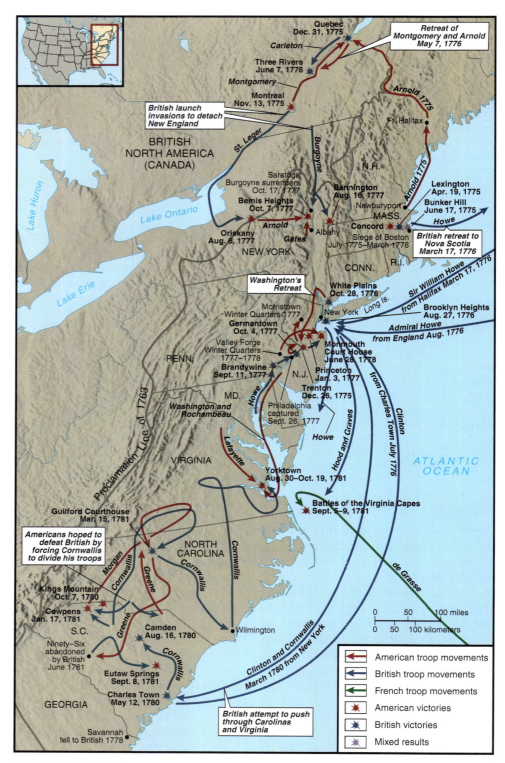

THE AMERICAN REVOLUTION, 1775–1781 *The War for Independence ranged over a huge area. Battles were fought in the colonies, north and south, on the western frontier, and along the Gulf of Mexico. The major battles of the first years of the war, from the spontaneous rising at Concord in 1775 to Washington's well-coordinated attack on Trenton in December 1776, were fought in the northern colonies. In the middle theater of war, Burgoyne's attempt in 1777 to cut off New England from the rest of the colonies failed when his army was defeated at Saratoga. Action in the final years of the war, from the battles at Camden, Kings Mountain, Cowpens, and Guilford Courthouse to the final victory at Yorktown, occurred in the southern theater of war.* ■

the colonists to resist "tyranny and false systems of government." The essay became an instant best-seller. More than 120,000 copies were sold in the first three months after publication. *Common Sense* systematically stripped kingship of historical and theological justification. Contrary to traditional English belief, Paine said, monarchs could and did commit many wrongs. George III was simply a "royal brute" who by his arbitrary behavior had surrendered his claim to the colonists' obedience.

Paine's greatest contribution to the revolutionary cause was persuading ordinary folk to sever their ties with Great Britain. "Europe, and not England," he exclaimed, "is the parent country of America. This new world hath been the asylum for the persecuted lovers of civil and religious liberty from *every part* of Europe." The time had come for the colonists to form an independent republic. "We have it in our power," Paine wrote in one of his most moving statements, "to begin the world over again. . . . The birthday of a new world is at hand."

On July 2, 1776, after a long and tedious debate, Congress finally voted for independence. The motion passed: twelve states for, none against. Thomas Jefferson, a young Virginia lawyer and planter who enjoyed a reputation as a graceful writer, drafted a formal declaration that was accepted two days later with only minor alterations. Much of the Declaration of Independence consisted of a list of specific grievances against George III and his government. But the document's enduring fame rests on statements of principle that are tested anew in each generation of Americans: that "all men are created equal"; that they are endowed with certain rights, among which are "life, liberty, and the pursuit of happiness"; and that governments are formed to protect these rights.

FIGHTING FOR INDEPENDENCE

Only fools and visionaries expressed optimism about America's prospects of winning independence in 1776. The Americans had taken on a formidable military power whose population was perhaps four times greater than their own. Britain also possessed a strong industrial base, a well-trained regular army supplemented by thousands of hired German (Hessian) troops, and a navy that dominated the world's oceans. Many British officers had battlefield experience. They already knew what the Americans would slowly learn—that waging war requires great discipline, money, and sacrifice.

The British government entered the conflict fully confident that it could beat the Americans. Lord North and his colleagues regarded the war as a police action. They anticipated that a mere show of armed force would intimidate the upstart colonists. Humble the rebels in Boston, they reasoned, and Americans will abandon independence like rats fleeing a burning ship.

As later events demonstrated, of course, Britain had become involved in an impossible military situation, somewhat analogous to that in which the United States found itself in Vietnam. Three separate elements neutralized advantages held by the larger power over its adversary. First, the British had to transport men and supplies across the Atlantic, a logistic challenge of unprecedented complexity. Second, America was too vast to be conquered by conventional military methods. Redcoats might gain control over the major port cities, but as long as the Continental Army remained intact, the rebellion continued. And third, British strategies never appreciated the depth of the Americans' commitment to a political ideology. European troops before the French Revolution served because they were paid or because they were professional soldiers but not because they hoped to advance a set of constitutional principles. Americans were different. Although some joined the army for the bounty money or to escape unhappy families or because they were drafted, a remarkable number of American troops were committed to republican ideals.

Building a Professional Army

During the earliest months of rebellion, American soldiers—especially those of New England—suffered no lack of confidence. Indeed, they interpreted their engagements at Concord and Bunker Hill as evidence that brave, yeoman farmers could lick British regulars on any battlefield. George Washington spent the first years of the war disabusing the colonists of this foolishness. As he had learned during the French and Indian War, military success depended on careful planning, endless drill, and tough discipline.

Washington insisted on organizing a regular, well-trained field army. He rejected the idea of waging a guerrilla war. He recognized that the Continental Army served not only as a fighting force but also as a symbol of the republican cause. Its very existence would sustain American hopes, and so long as the army survived, American agents could plausibly solicit foreign aid. This thinking shaped Washington's cautious wartime strategy; he studiously avoided any "general actions" in which the Continental Army might be destroyed.

If the commander in chief was correct about the army, however, he failed to comprehend the political importance of local militias. These scattered, almost amateur military units seldom altered the outcome of a battle, but they did maintain control over large areas of the country not directly affected by the British army. Throughout the war, they compelled men and women who would rather have remained neutral to support the American effort actively. Without the local militias' political coercion, Washington's task would have been considerably more difficult.

For the half million African American colonists, most of them slaves, the fight for independence took on special poignancy. After all, they wanted to achieve personal as well as political freedom, and many African Americans supported those who seemed most likely to deliver them from bondage. It is estimated that some five thousand African Americans took up arms to fight against the British. In 1778, the legislature of Rhode Island voted to free any slave who volunteered to serve, since, according to the lawmakers, history taught that "the wisest, the freest, and bravest nations . . . liberated their slaves, and enlisted them as soldiers to fight in defence of their country." In the South, especially in Georgia and South Carolina, more than ten thousand African Americans supported the British, and after the patriots had won the war, most of these men and women left the United States, relocating to Nova Scotia, Florida, and Jamaica, with some eventually resettling in Africa.

Testing the Popular Will

After the embarrassing losses in Massachusetts, the king appointed General Sir William Howe to replace the ill-fated Gage. British rulers now understood that a simple police action would not be sufficient to crush the American rebellion. Howe promptly evacuated Boston—an untenable strategic position—and on July 3, 1776, his forces stormed Staten Island in New York harbor. From this central position, he hoped to cut off New Englanders from the rest of America.

When Washington learned that the British were digging in at New York, he transferred many of his inexperienced soldiers to Long Island, where they suffered a serious defeat (August 26, 1776). Howe drove the Continental Army across the Hudson River into New Jersey, but he failed to annihilate Washington's entire army. Nevertheless, the Americans were on the run, and in the fall of 1776, contemporaries predicted that the rebels would soon capitulate.

His swift victories in New York and New Jersey persuaded General Howe that few Americans enthusiastically supported independence. He issued a general pardon, therefore, to anyone who would swear allegiance to George III. More than three thousand Americans responded to Howe's peaceful overtures. However, the pardon plan eventually failed, partly because Howe's soldiers and officers regarded loyal Americans as inferior provincials, an attitude that did little to promote good relations, and partly because the rebel militias often retaliated against Americans who had deserted the patriots' cause.

In December 1776, Washington's bedraggled forces retreated across the Delaware River into Pennsylvania. American prospects appeared bleaker than at any other time during the war. "These are the times that try men's souls," Tom Paine wrote in a pamphlet titled *American Crisis.* "The summer soldier and the sunshine patriot will, in this crisis, shrink from the service of their country, but he that stands it *now* deserves . . . love and thanks of man and woman." Before winter, Washington determined to attempt one last desperate stroke.

Howe played into Washington's hands. The British army was strung out across New Jersey. On the night of December 25, Continental soldiers slipped over the ice-covered Delaware River and at Trenton took nine hundred sleeping Hessian mercenaries by complete surprise. Cheered by success, Washington returned a second time to Trenton, but on this occasion a large British force headed by Lord Cornwallis trapped the Americans. Washington secretly, by night, marched his little army around Cornwallis's left flank. On January 3, 1777, the Americans surprised a British garrison at Princeton. Having regained their confidence, Washington's forces then went into winter quarters. The British, fearful of losing any more outposts, consolidated their troops, thus leaving much of the state in the hands of the patriot militias.

Victory in a Year of Defeat

In 1777, England's chief military strategist, Lord George Germain, still perceived the war in conventional European terms. He believed that England could achieve a complete victory by crushing Washington's army in a major battle. Unfortunately, the Continental forces proved extremely elusive, and while one British army vainly tried to corner Washington in Pennsylvania, another was forced to surrender in the forests of upstate New York.

■ Defeat of the British at the Battle of Princeton, *oil painting by William Mercer, ca. 1786–1790. The painting shows George Washington (left, on horseback) directing cannon fire with his sword. Often risking his own life, Washington led the American troops into battle. The artist's father was mortally wounded in the battle.* ■

In the summer of 1777, General John Burgoyne marched south from Canada determined to clear the Hudson Valley of rebel resistance. He intended to join Howe's army, which was to come up to Albany, thereby cutting New England off from the other states. Burgoyne moved slowly, weighed down by a German band, thirty carts filled with the general's liquor and belongings, and two thousand dependents and camp followers. The campaign was a disaster. American military units cut the enemy force apart in the deep woods north of Albany and overwhelmed Burgoyne's German mercenaries at Bennington. After it became clear that Howe could provide no relief, the haughty Burgoyne was forced to surrender 5800 men to the American General Horatio Gates at Saratoga (October 17).

General Howe could provide no support to Burgoyne because about the time Burgoyne left Canada, Howe unexpectedly decided to move his main army from New York City to Philadelphia, trying to devise a way to destroy Washington's forces. The British troops sailed to the head of the Chesapeake Bay and then marched north to Philadelphia. Washington's troops obstructed the enemy's progress, but they could not stop the British from entering the city on September 26, 1777.

Lest these defeats discourage Congress and the American people, Washington attempted one last battle before the onset of winter. In a curious engagement at Germantown (October 4), beset by bad luck and confusion, the Americans launched a major counterattack on a fog-covered battlefield, but just at the moment when success seemed assured, the Americans broke off the fight. The discouraged Continental Army dug in for the winter at Valley Forge, 20 miles outside of Philadelphia, where camp diseases took 2500 American lives.

The French Alliance

Even before the Americans declared their independence, agents of the government of Louis XVI began to explore ways to aid the colonists, not so much because the French monarchy favored the republican cause but because it hoped to avenge its defeat in the Seven Years' War and lessen the power of Britain. During the early months of the Revolution, the French covertly sent tons of essential military supplies to the Americans but refused to recognize American independence or sign an outright military alliance with the rebels. The international stakes were too great for the king openly to back a cause that had little chance of success.

The American victory at Saratoga convinced the French that the rebels had formidable forces and were serious in their resolve. Meanwhile, in Paris, American representative Benjamin Franklin hinted that Congress might accept a recently tendered British peace overture. Hence, if the French wanted the war to continue and if they really wanted to strike at their old rival, they formally had to recognize the independence of the United States.

The stratagem paid off handsomely. On February 6, 1778, the French presented American representatives with two separate treaties. The first, called the Treaty of Amity and Commerce, established commercial relations between France and the United States. It tacitly accepted the existence of a new, independent republic. The Treaty of Alliance was even more generous. In the event that France and England went to war (they did so on June 14), the French agreed to reject any peace initiative until Britain recognized American independence. The Americans pledged that they would not sign a separate peace with Britain without first informing their new ally. Amazingly, France made no claim to Canada or any territory east of the Mississippi River.

French intervention instantly transformed British military strategy. What had been a colonial rebellion suddenly became a world conflict, a continuation of the great wars for empire of the late seventeenth century (see Chapter 4). Scarce military resources, especially newer fighting ships, had to be diverted from the

American theater to guard the English Channel. England realized that the French navy posed a serious challenge to the overextended British fleet.

The Final Campaign

British General Henry Clinton replaced Howe, who resigned after the battle of Saratoga. As a subordinate officer, Clinton was imaginative, but as commander of British forces in America, his resolute self-confidence suddenly dissolved. Perhaps he feared failure. Whatever the explanation for his vacillation, Clinton's record in America was little better than Howe's or Gage's.

Military strategists calculated that Britain's last chance of winning the war lay in the southern colonies, a region largely untouched in the early years of fighting. They believed that with proper support and encouragement, the Loyalists in Georgia and South Carolina would take up arms for the Crown. The southern strategy devised by Germain and Clinton in 1779 turned the war into a bitter guerrilla conflict, and during the last months of battle, British officers worried that their search for an easy victory had inadvertently opened a Pandora's box of uncontrollable partisan furies.

The southern campaign opened in the spring of 1780. Savannah had already fallen, and Clinton reckoned that if the British could take Charles Town, they would be able to control the entire South. Clinton and his second in command, General Cornwallis, gradually encircled the city, and on May 12, the six-thousand-man American army in Charles Town surrendered.

The defeat took Congress by surprise, and without making the proper preparations, it dispatched a second army to South Carolina under Horatio Gates, the hero of Saratoga. He, too, failed. At Camden, Cornwallis outmaneuvered the raw American recruits (August 16). Gates galloped from the scene and did not stop until he reached Hillsboro, North Carolina, 200 miles away.

Even at this early stage of the southern campaign, the savagery of partisan warfare had become evident. Loyalist raiders plundered or occasionally killed neighbors against whom they harbored ancient grudges. Men who supported independence or who had merely fallen victim to the Loyalist guerrillas bided their time. On October 7 at Kings Mountain, North Carolina, they struck back against a force of Loyalists and British regulars who had strayed too far from base. This was the most vicious fighting of the Revolution; the Americans gave no quarter.

Cornwallis, badly confused and poorly supported, proceeded to squander his strength, senselessly chasing American forces across the Carolinas in the winter and early spring of 1781. When he did engage a freshly formed army under the command of Nathanael Greene, the most capable general on Washington's staff, Cornwallis was outmaneuvered and outfought at Cowpens and Guilford Courthouse. His army's strength sapped, Cornwallis pushed north into Virginia, planning apparently to establish a base of operations on the coast.

He selected Yorktown, a sleepy tobacco market located on a peninsula bounded by the York and James Rivers. Washington watched the maneuvers closely. The canny Virginia planter knew the territory intimately, and he sensed that Cornwallis had made a serious blunder. When Washington learned that the French fleet could attain temporary dominance in the Chesapeake Bay, he rushed south from New Jersey. With him marched thousands of well-trained French troops commanded by Comte de Rochambeau; they were joined along the way by a sizable contingent of forces led by the marquis de Lafayette. All the pieces fell into place. The French admiral, Comte de Grasse, cut Cornwallis off from the sea, while Washington and his lieutenants encircled the British on the land. On October 19, 1781, Cornwallis surrendered his entire army of six thousand men. The Continental Army had completed its mission; the task of securing independence now rested in the hands of American diplomats.

THE LOYALIST DILEMMA

The war lasted longer than anyone had predicted in 1776. The nation had won its independence, but its people had paid a terrible price. Indeed, a great many men and women decided that no matter how much they had loved living in America, they could not accept the new government.

No one knows for certain how many Americans supported the Crown during the Revolution. But more than 100,000 men and women permanently left America. Although a number of these exiles had served as British officeholders, they came from all ranks and sections of society—farmers, merchants, tradesmen. The wealthier exiles went to London and begged for pensions from the king. Others relocated to Canada or the West Indies.

The Loyalists, or Tories, were caught in a difficult squeeze. The British did not trust them; they were, after all, Americans. Nor could they trust the British, who, after urgently soliciting their support, left them exposed to rebel retaliation. In England, the exiles found themselves treated as second-class citizens. Embittered and unwanted in America, they often found themselves just as embittered and unwanted in London.

Americans who actively supported independence saw these people as traitors. According to one patriot, "A Tory is a thing whose head is in England, its body in America, and its neck ought to be stretched." In many states, revolutionary governments confiscated Loyalist property. Some Loyalists were beaten, and a few were

LOYALIST STRONGHOLDS *The highest concentrations of Loyalists were in the colonies of New York, North Carolina, South Carolina, and Georgia, especially in the areas around port cities such as New York City, Wilmington, Charleston, and Savannah.* ■

even executed. Long after the victorious Americans turned their attentions to the business of building a new republic, Loyalists remembered a comfortable, ordered world that had been lost forever at Yorktown. Theirs was a sad, often lonely fate.

WINNING THE PEACE

Congress appointed a skilled delegation to negotiate a peace treaty: Benjamin Franklin, John Adams, and John Jay. According to their official instructions, they were to insist only on the recognition of the independence of the United States. On other issues, Congress ordered its delegates to defer to the counsel of the French government.

But in Paris there were grave problems. The French had formed a military alliance with Spain, and French officials announced that they could not consider the details of an American settlement until after the Spanish had recaptured Gibraltar from the British. The prospects for a Spanish victory were not good. More than anything, the American representatives feared that some European intrigue might cost the United States its independence.

While the three American delegates publicly paid their respects to French officials, they secretly entered into negotiations with an English agent. These actions—in violation of the men's instructions—did not fool the French for a moment. French spies reported what transpired at these meetings, and though the French could have protested the American breach of faith, they did not do so.

CHRONICLE OF COLONIAL–BRITISH TENSION

Legislation	Date	Provisions	Colonial Reaction
Sugar Act	April 5, 1764	Revised duties on sugar, coffee, tea, wine, other imports; expanded jurisdiction of vice-admiralty courts	Several assemblies protest taxation for revenue
Stamp Act	March 22, 1765; repealed March 18, 1766	Printed documents (deeds, newspapers, marriage licenses, etc.) issued only on special stamped paper purchased from stamp distributors	Riots in cities; collectors forced to resign; Stamp Act Congress (October 1765)
Quartering Act	May 1765	Colonists must supply British troops with housing, other items (candles, firewood, etc.)	Protest in assemblies; New York Assembly punished for failure to comply, 1767
Declaratory Act	March 18, 1766	Parliament declares its sovereignty over the colonies "in all cases whatsoever"	Ignored in celebration over repeal of the Stamp Act
Townshend Revenue Acts	June 26, 29, July 2, 1767; all repealed—except duty on tea, March 1770	New duties on glass, lead, paper, paints, tea; customs collections tightened in America	Nonimportation of British goods; assemblies protest; newspapers attack British policy
Tea Act	May 10, 1773	Parliament gives East India Company right to sell tea directly to Americans; some duties on tea reduced	Protests against favoritism shown to monopolistic company; tea destroyed in Boston (December 16, 1773)
Coercive Acts (Intolerable Acts)	March–June 1774	Closes port of Boston; restructures Massachusetts government; restricts town meetings; troops quartered in Boston; British officials accused of crimes sent to England or Canada for trial	Boycott of British goods; First Continental Congress convenes (September 1774)
Prohibitory Act	December 22, 1775	Declares British intention to coerce Americans into submission; embargo on American goods; American ships seized	Drives Continental Congress closer to decision for independence

Chronology

1763	Peace of Paris ends the Seven Years' War (February)
1764	Parliament passes the Sugar Act to collect American revenue (April)
1765	Stamp Act receives support of the House of Commons (March) ▪ Stamp Act Congress meets in New York City (October)
1766	Stamp Act is repealed the same day as the Declaratory Act becomes law (March 18)
1767	Townshend Revenue Acts stir American anger (June–July)
1768	Massachusetts assembly refuses to rescind circular letter (February)
1770	British troops "massacre" Boston civilians (March) ▪ Parliament repeals all Townshend duties except the duty on tea (March)
1772	Samuel Adams forms committee of correspondence (October–November)
1773	Lord North's government passes the Tea Act (May) ▪ Bostonians hold the Tea Party (December)
1774	Parliament punishes Boston with the Coercive Acts (March–June) ▪ First Continental Congress convenes (September)
1775	Patriots take a stand at Lexington and Concord (April) ▪ Second Continental Congress gathers (May) ▪ Americans hold their own at Bunker Hill (June)
1776	Congress votes for independence; Declaration of Independence is signed (July) ▪ British defeat Washington off Long Island (August) ▪ Americans score a victory at Trenton (December)
1777	General Burgoyne surrenders at Saratoga (October)
1778	French treaties recognize independence of the United States (February)
1780	British take Charles Town (May), later renamed Charleston
1781	Washington forces Cornwallis to surrender at Yorktown (October)
1783	Peace treaty is signed (September) ▪ British evacuate New York City (November)

The negotiators drove a remarkable bargain. The preliminary agreement, signed on September 3, 1783, not only guaranteed the independence of the United States but also transferred all the territory east of the Mississippi River—except Florida, which remained under Spanish sovereignty—to the new republic. The treaty established generous boundaries on the north and south and gave the Americans important fishing rights in the North Atlantic. In exchange, Congress promised to help British merchants collect debts contracted before the Revolution and to compensate Loyalists whose land had been confiscated by the various state governments. The preliminary treaty did not take effect until after the French reached their own agreement with Great Britain, thus formally honoring the Franco-American alliance. It is hard to imagine how Franklin, Adams, and Jay could have negotiated a more favorable conclusion to the war. In the fall of 1783, the last redcoats sailed from New York City, ending 176 years of colonial rule.

CONCLUSION: PRESERVING INDEPENDENCE

The American people had waged war against the most powerful nation in Europe and emerged victorious. The treaty marked the conclusion of a colonial rebellion, but it remained for the men and women who had resisted taxation without representation to work out the full implications of republicanism. What would be the scope of the new government? What powers would be delegated to the people, the states, the federal authorities? How far would the wealthy, well-born leaders of the rebellion be willing to extend political, social, and economic rights? The war was over, but the drama of the American Revolution was still unfolding.

KEY TERMS

Whigs, p. 82

parliamentary sovereignty, p. 82

Loyalists, p. 84

Stamp Act Congress, p. 85

Boston Massacre, p. 87

committee of correspondence, p. 89

Coercive Acts, p. 89

First Continental Congress, p. 90

Second Continental Congress, p. 91

Common Sense, p. 91

RECOMMENDED READING

Several books have had a profound impact on how historians think about the ideas that energized the Revolution. In a moving narrative account, Edmund S. Morgan and Helen M. Morgan explore how Americans interpreted the first great imperial controversy: *The Stamp Act Crisis: Prologue to Revolution* (1953). In his classic study, *The Ideological Origins of the American Revolution* (1967), Bernard Bailyn maps an ideology of power that informed colonial protest. In *Marketplace of Revolution: How Consumer Politics Shaped American Independence* (2004), T. H. Breen attempts to integrate more fully the experiences of ordinary men and women into the analysis of popular mobilization. Alfred F. Young demonstrates that it is possible to write about revolution from the perspective of working class colonists in *The Shoemaker and the Tea Party: Memory and the American Revolution* (2000). Works that focus productively on popular mobilization in specific colonies include Rhys Isaac, *The Transformation of Virginia, 1740–1790* (1983); Robert A. Gross, *The Minutemen and Their World* (1976); Woody Holton, *Forced Founders: Indians, Debtors,*

Slaves and the Making of the American Revolution in Virginia (1999); and T. H. Breen, *Tobacco Culture: The Mentality of the Great Tidewater Planters on the Eve of Revolution* (1985). The tragedy that visited the Native Americans is examined in Colin C. Calloway, *American Revolution in Indian Country: Crisis and Diversity in Native American Communities* (1995), and Gregory Evans Dowd, *War Under Heaven: Pontiac, The Indian Nations and the British Empire* (2002). A useful study of the aspirations and disappointments of American women during this period is Linda Kerber, *Women of the Republic: Intellect and Ideology in Revolutionary America* (1980). Charles Royster investigates the changing attitudes of the American people about the Continental Army in *A Revolutionary People at War: The Continental Army and American Character, 1775–1783* (1979). Also valuable is John W. Shy, *A People Numerous and Armed: Reflections on the Military Struggle for American Independence,* rev. ed. (1990). Sidney Kaplan, *The Black Presence in the Era of the American Revolution* (1973), documents the hopes of African Americans during a period of radical political change.

SUGGESTED WEB SITES

Canada History
www.civilization.ca/indexe.asp
Canada and the United States shared a colonial past but developed differently in the long run. This site is a part of the virtual museum of the Canadian Museum of Civilization Corporation.

Georgia's Rare Map Collection
scarlett.libs.uga.edu/darchive/hargrett/maps/colamer.html
scarlett.libs.uga.edu/darchive/hargrett/maps/revamer.html
These two sites contain maps for Colonial and Revolutionary America.

Maryland Loyalism and the American Revolution
users.erols.com/candidus/index.htm
This look at Maryland's Loyalists promotes the author's book, but it has good information about an underappreciated phenomenon, including Loyalist songs and poems.

The American Revolution
revolution.h-net.msu.edu/
This site accompanies the PBS *Revolution* series with essays and resource links.

Chapter 6

The Republican Experiment

A New Moral Order

In 1788, Lewis Hallam and John Henry petitioned the General Assembly of Pennsylvania to open a theater. Although a 1786 state law banned the performance of stage plays and other "disorderly sports," many Philadelphia leaders favored the request to hold "dramatic representation" in their city. A committee appointed to study the issue concluded that a theater would contribute to "the general refinement of manners and the polish of society." Some supporters even argued that the sooner the United States had a professional theater the sooner the young republic would escape the "foreign yoke" of British culture.

The Quakers of Philadelphia dismissed such claims out of hand. They warned such "seminaries of lewdness and irreligion" would quickly undermine "the virtue of the people." They pointed out that "no sooner is a playhouse opened than it becomes surrounded with . . . brothels." Since Philadelphia was already suffering from a "stagnation of commerce [and] a scarcity of money"—unmistakable signs of God's displeasure—it seemed to them unwise to risk divine punishment by encouraging new "hot-beds of vice."

Such rhetoric did not sit well with other citizens who interpreted the revolutionary experience from an entirely different perspective. At issue, they insisted, was not popular morality, but state censorship. If the government silenced the stage, then "the same authority . . . may, with equal justice, dictate the shape and texture of our dress, or the modes and ceremonies of our worship." Depriving those who wanted to see plays of an opportunity to do so, they argued, "will abridge the natural right of every freeman, to dispose of his time and money, according to his own tastes and dispositions."

Throughout post–Revolutionary America apparently trivial matters such as the opening of a new playhouse provoked passionate public debate. These divisions were symptomatic of a new, uncertain political culture struggling to find the proper balance between public morality and private freedom. During the long fight against Great Britain, Americans had defended individual rights. The problem was that the same people also believed that a republic that compromised its virtue could not long preserve liberty and independence. During the 1780s Americans understood their responsibility not only to each other, but also to history. They worried, however, that they might not successfully meet the challenge.

DEFINING REPUBLICAN CULTURE

Today, the term *republican* no longer possesses the evocative power it did for most eighteenth-century Americans. For them, it defined an entire political culture. After all, they had done something that no other people had achieved for a very long time. They founded a national government without a monarch or aristocracy; in other words, a genuine republic. Making the new system work was a daunting task. Those Americans who read deeply in ancient and renaissance history knew that most republics had failed, often within a few years, only to be replaced by tyrants who cared not at all what ordinary people thought about the public good. To preserve their republic from such a fate, victorious revolutionaries such as Samuel Adams recast fundamental political values. For them, **republicanism** represented more than a particular form of government. It was a way of life, a core ideology, an uncompromising commitment to liberty and equality.

Adams and his contemporaries certainly believed that creating a new nation-state involved more than simply winning independence from Great Britain. More than did any other form of government, they insisted, a republic demanded an exceptionally high degree of public morality. If American citizens substituted "luxury, prodigality, and profligacy" for "prudence, virtue, and economy," then their revolution surely would have been in vain. Maintaining popular virtue was crucial to success. An innocent stage play, therefore, set off alarm bells. Such "foolish gratifications" seemed to compromise republican goals.

White Americans came out of the Revolution with an almost euphoric sense of the nation's special destiny. This expansive outlook, encountered among so many ordinary men and women, owed much to the spread of Protestant evangelicalism. However skeptical Jefferson and Franklin may have been about revealed religion, the great mass of American people subscribed to an almost utopian vision of the country's future. To this new republic, God had promised progress and prosperity. The signs were visible for everyone.

Such experience did not translate easily or smoothly into the creation of a strong central government. Modern Americans tend to take for granted the acceptance of the Constitution. Its merits seem self-evident largely because it has survived for two centuries. But in the early 1780s, no one could have predicted that the Constitution as we know it would have been written, much less ratified. It was equally possible that the Americans would have supported a weak confederation or perhaps allowed the various states and regions to go their separate ways.

In this uncertain political atmosphere, Americans divided sharply over the relative importance of *liberty* and *order*. The revolutionary experience had called into question the legitimacy of any form of special privilege. A legislative leader in Pennsylvania put the point bluntly: "No man has a greater claim of special privilege for his $100,000 than I have for my $5." The man who passionately defended social equality for those of varying economic status, however, may still have resisted the extension of civil rights to women or blacks. Nevertheless, liberty was contagious, and Americans of all backgrounds began to make new demands on society and government. For them, the Revolution had suggested radical alternatives, and in many forums throughout the nation—especially in the elected state assemblies—they insisted on being heard.

In certain quarters, the celebration of liberty met with mixed response. Some Americans—often the very men who had resisted British tyranny—worried that the citizens of the new nation were caught up in a wild, destructive scramble for material wealth. Democratic excesses seemed to threaten order, to endanger the rights of property. Surely a republic could not long survive unless its citizens showed greater self-control. For people concerned about the loss of order, the state assemblies appeared to be the greatest source of instability. Popularly elected

republicanism Concept that ultimate political authority is vested in the citizens of the nation. The character of republican government was dependent on the civic virtue of its citizens to preserve the nation from corruption and moral decay.

representatives lacked what men of property defined as real civic virtue, an ability to work for the common good rather than their private interests.

Working out the tensions between order and liberty, between property and equality, generated an outpouring of political genius. At other times in American history, persons of extraordinary talent have been drawn to theology, commerce, or science, but during the 1780s, the country's intellectual leaders—Thomas Jefferson, James Madison, Alexander Hamilton, and John Adams, among others—focused their creative energies on the problem of how republicans ought to govern themselves.

LIVING IN THE SHADOW OF REVOLUTION

If America's revolution seems less radical than that of other nations, particularly France, it may be because eighteenth-century Americans had fewer entrenched barriers to overcome in the first place. Indeed, the American Revolution confirmed many rights that colonial Americans had long enjoyed—broad suffrage, religious toleration, freedom of movement. Although the Revolution did not bring about massive changes in American society, it did raise issues of immense importance for the later history of the United States. Republican spokesmen, such as Samuel Adams and Thomas Jefferson, insisted that equality, however narrowly defined, was an essential element of republican government. Even though they failed to institute universal manhood suffrage, abolish slavery, or apply equality to women, they vigorously articulated a set of assumptions about people's rights and liberties that challenged future generations of Americans to make good on the promise of the Revolution.

Social and Political Reform

Following the war, Americans aggressively ferreted out and, with republican fervor, denounced any traces of aristocratic pretense. As colonists, they had long resented the claims of certain Englishmen to special privilege simply because of noble birth. A society based on artificial status was contrary to republican principles.

The appearance of equality was as important as its actual achievement. In fact, the distribution of wealth in postwar America was more uneven than it had been a few decades earlier. Yet Americans attempted to root out the notion of a privileged class. States abolished laws of primogeniture and entail, which in colonial times allowed a landholder to pass his entire estate to his eldest son or to declare that his property could never be divided, sold, or given away. Although America had never been affected greatly by such customs, their abolition was an important symbolic blow against the idea of a landed aristocracy.

Republican ferment also encouraged many states to lower property requirements for voting. After the revolutionary experience, such a step seemed logical. The concept of a representative government was well accepted in America. These reforms, however, did not significantly expand the American electorate. Long before the Revolution, an overwhelming percentage of free males had owned enough land to vote, and few leaders at that time were willing to entertain the idea of universal manhood suffrage.

The most important changes in voting patterns were the result of western migration. As Americans moved to the frontier, they received full political representation in their state legislatures, and because new districts tended to be poorer than established coastal settlements, their inhabitants selected representatives who seemed less cultured and less well trained than those sent by eastern voters. Moreover, western delegates resented traveling so far to attend legislative meetings, and they lobbied successfully to transfer state capitals to more convenient locations.

After independence, Americans also reexamined the relationship between church and state. Republican spokesmen such as Thomas Jefferson argued in favor of the disestablishment of state churches. They insisted that rulers had no right to interfere with the free expression of an individual's religious beliefs. Nor did they believe that churches should be supported with taxpayers' monies. Massachusetts and Connecticut did not alter the status of their Congregational churches, but most of the southern states did disestablish the Anglican Church. Americans championed religious toleration, though few favored irreligion or secularism.

African Americans in the New Republic

Revolutionary fervor forced Americans to confront the most appalling contradiction to republican principles—slavery. During the 1780s, abolitionist sentiment spread. Both in private and in public, people began to criticize slavery in other than religious language. No doubt, the double standard of their own political rhetoric embarrassed many white Americans. They hotly demanded liberation from British enslavement at the same time that they held several hundred thousand blacks in bondage.

By keeping the issue of slavery before the public through writing and petitioning, African Americans powerfully undermined arguments advanced in favor of human bondage. They demanded freedom, reminding white lawmakers that African American men and women had the same natural right to liberty as did other Americans. In 1779, for example, a group of African Americans asked the members of the Connecticut assembly "whether it is consistent with the present Claims, of the United States, to hold so many Thousands, of the Race of Adam, our Common Father, in perpetual Slavery."

The scientific accomplishments of Benjamin Banneker (1731–1806), Maryland's African American astronomer and mathematician, and the international fame of Phillis Wheatley (1753–1784), Boston's celebrated "African muse," made it increasingly difficult for white Americans to maintain credibly that African Americans could not hold their own in a free society. Wheatley's poems went through many editions, and after reading her work, the French philosopher Voltaire rebuked a friend who had claimed "there never would be Negro poets." Banneker, like Wheatley, enjoyed a well-deserved reputation, in his case for contributions as a scientist. After receiving a copy of an almanac that Banneker had published in Philadelphia, Thomas Jefferson concluded "that nature has given to our black brethren, talents equal to those of the other colors of men."

In the northern states, where there was no economic justification for slavery, white laborers resented having to compete in the workplace against slaves. This economic situation, combined with the acknowledgment of the double standard represented by slavery, contributed to the establishment of antislavery societies, groups that included such prominent figures as Alexander Hamilton, John Jay, and Benjamin Franklin. By 1792, antislavery societies meeting from Virginia to Massachusetts put slaveholders on the intellectual defensive for the first time in American history.

In several states north of Virginia, the attack on slavery took a number of different forms. The Vermont constitution of 1777 specifically prohibited slavery. In 1780, the Pennsylvania legislature abolished the practice. Other states followed suit. By 1800, slavery was well on the road to extinction in the North.

These developments did not mean that white people accepted blacks as equals. In the very states that outlawed slavery, African Americans still faced systematic discrimination. Free blacks were generally excluded from voting, juries, and militia duty—rights and responsibilities usually associated with full citizenship. They rarely enjoyed access to education, and in cities such as Philadelphia and New York, where African Americans went to look for work, they ended up living in segregated wards or neighborhoods. Even in the churches—institutions that had often spoken out against slavery—free African Americans were denied equal standing with white worshipers. Humiliations of this sort persuaded African Americans to form their own churches. In Philadelphia, Richard Allen, a former slave, founded the Bethel Church for Negro Methodists (1793) and later organized the African Methodist Episcopal Church (1814), an institution of great cultural as well as religious significance for nineteenth-century American blacks.

Even in the South, where African Americans made up a large percentage of the population, slavery disturbed thoughtful white republicans. Some planters simply freed their slaves, and by 1790, the number of free blacks living in Virginia was 12,766. By 1800, the figure had reached 30,750. Most southern slaveholders rejected this course of action. Perhaps more significant, however, is the fact that no southern leader during the era of republican experimentation defended slavery as a positive good. Such overtly racist rhetoric did not become part of the public discourse until the nineteenth century.

Despite promising starts in that direction, the southern states did not abolish slavery. The economic incentives to maintain a servile labor force, especially after the invention of the cotton gin in 1793 and the opening up of the Alabama and Mississippi frontier, overwhelmed the initial abolitionist impulse. An opportunity to translate the principles of the American Revolution into social practice had been lost, at least temporarily.

The Challenge of Women's Rights

The revolutionary experience accelerated changes in how ordinary people viewed the family. At the beginning of the eighteenth century, fathers claimed absolute authority over other members of their families simply on the grounds that they were fathers. At the time of the American Revolution, however, few seriously accepted the notion that fathers—be they tyrannical kings or heads of ordinary families—enjoyed unlimited powers over women and children. Indeed, people in England as well as America increasingly described the family in terms of love and companionship. Instead of duties, they spoke of affection. This transformation in the way men and women viewed relations of power within the family was most evident in the popular novels of the period. Americans devoured *Pamela* and *Clarissa*, stories by the English writer Samuel Richardson about women who were the innocent victims of unreformed males, usually deceitful lovers and unforgiving fathers.

In this changing intellectual environment, American women began making new demands not only on their husbands but also on republican institutions. Abigail Adams, one of the generation's most articulate women, instructed her husband, John, as he set off for the opening of the Continental Congress: "I desire you would Remember the Ladies, and be more generous and favourable to them than your ancestors. Do not put such unlimited power into the hands of the Husbands." John responded in a condescending manner. The "Ladies" would have to wait until the country achieved independence.

In fact, women justified their assertiveness largely on the basis of political ideology. If survival of republics really depended on the virtue of their citizens, they argued, then it was the special responsibility of women as mothers to nurture the right values in their children and as wives to instruct their husbands in proper behavior.

Ill-educated women could not possibly fulfill these high expectations. They required education that was at least comparable to what men received. Scores of female academies were established during this period to meet what many Americans, men as well as women, now regarded as a pressing social need. The schools may have received widespread encouragement precisely because they did not radically alter traditional gender roles. After all, the educated republican woman of the late eighteenth century did not pursue a career; she returned to the home, where she followed a familiar routine as wife and mother.

During this period, women petitioned for divorce on new grounds. One case is particularly instructive concerning changing attitudes toward women and the family. In 1784, John Backus, an undistinguished Massachusetts silversmith, was hauled before a local court and asked why he beat his wife. He responded that "it was Partly owing to his Education for his father treated his mother in the same manner." The difference was that Backus's wife refused to tolerate such abuse, and she sued successfully for divorce. Studies of divorce patterns in Connecticut and Pennsylvania show that after 1773 women divorced on about the same terms as men.

The war itself presented some women with fresh opportunities. In 1780, Ester DeBerdt Reed founded a large volunteer women's organization in Philadelphia—the first of its kind in the United States—that raised more than $300,000 for Washington's army. Other women ran family farms and businesses while their husbands fought the British. And in 1790, the New Jersey legislature explicitly allowed women who owned property to vote.

Despite these scattered gains, republican society still defined women's roles exclusively in terms of mother, wife, and homemaker. Other pursuits seemed unnatural, even threatening, and it is perhaps not surprising, therefore, that in 1807, New Jersey lawmakers—angry over a close election in which women voters may have determined the result—repealed woman suffrage in the interests of "safety, quiet, and good order and dignity of the state."

■ *Questions of equality in the new republic extended to the rights of women. In this illustration, which appeared as the frontispiece in the 1792 issue of* The Lady's Magazine and Repository of Entertaining Knowledge, *the "Genius of the Ladies Magazine" and the "Genius of Emulation" (holding in her hand a laurel crown) present to Liberty a petition for the rights of woman.* ■

THE STATES: EXPERIMENTS IN REPUBLICANISM

In May 1776, the Second Continental Congress urged the states to adopt constitutions. Rhode Island and Connecticut already had republican governments by virtue of their unique charters, and the rest of the new states soon complied. Several constitutions were frankly experimental, and some states later rewrote documents that had been drafted in the first flush of independence. But if these early constitutions were provisional, they nevertheless provided the framers of the federal Constitution of 1787 with valuable insights into the strengths and weaknesses of government based on the will of the people.

Blueprints for State Government

Despite disagreements over details, Americans who wrote the various state constitutions shared certain political assumptions. First, they insisted on preparing *written* documents. As colonists, they had lived under royal charters, documents that described the workings of local government in detail, and they felt comfortable with the contractual language of legal documents.

However logical the decision to produce written documents may have seemed to the Americans, it represented a major break with English practice. Political philosophers in the mother country had long boasted of Britain's unwritten constitution, a collection of judicial reports and parliamentary statutes. Yet this highly vaunted system had not protected the colonists from oppression. It is understandable, then, why, after declaring independence, Americans demanded that their state constitutions explicitly define the rights of the people as well as the powers of their rulers. They desired more from public officials than simply assurances of good faith.

The authors of the state constitutions believed that men and women possessed certain **natural rights** over which government exercised no control whatsoever. So that future rulers—potential tyrants—would know the exact limits of their authority, these fundamental rights were carefully spelled out.

Eight state constitutions contained specific declarations of rights. In general, they affirmed three fundamental freedoms: of religion, of speech, and of the press. They protected citizens from unlawful searches and seizures; they upheld trial by jury. Ultimately, the best expression of this impulse is contained in the famed Bill of Rights, the first ten amendments to the federal Constitution.

In almost every state, delegates to constitutional conventions drastically reduced the power of the governor. He was allowed to make almost no political appointments, and while the state legislators closely monitored his activities, he possessed no veto over their decisions (Massachusetts being the lone exception). Most early constitutions lodged nearly all effective power in the legislature. In fact, the writers of the state constitutions were so fearful of the concentration of power in the hands of one person that they failed to recognize that governors, like the representatives, were servants of a free people.

The legislature dominated early state government. Some states even questioned the need for a senate or upper house, and Pennsylvania and Georgia instituted a unicameral, or one-house, system. Many Americans believed that the lower house could handle all the state's problems. The two-house form survived the Revolution largely because it was familiar and because some persons had already begun to suspect that certain checks on the popular will, however arbitrary they might appear, were necessary to preserve minority rights.

natural rights Fundamental rights over which the government could exercise no control. An uncompromising belief in such rights energized the popular demand for a formal bill of rights in 1791.

Power to the People

Perhaps the most significant state constitution was the one adopted by the people of Massachusetts because they hit upon a remarkable political innovation. Their state constitution was drafted by a specifically elected convention of delegates, not ordinary officeholders.

John Adams served as the chief architect of the governmental framework of the state. It included a house and a senate, a popularly elected governor who possessed a veto over legislative bills, and property qualifications for officeholders as well as voters. The most striking aspect of the 1780 constitution, however, was its opening sentence: "We . . . the people of Massachusetts . . . agree upon, ordain, and establish . . . " This powerful vocabulary would be echoed in the federal Constitution.

The state constitutions ushered a different type of person into public office. When one Virginian surveyed the newly elected House of Burgesses in 1776, he discovered that it was "composed of men not quite so well dressed, not so politely educated, nor so highly born as some Assemblies I have formerly seen." They were indeed the people's people, representative republicans. Whether this new breed of representative would be virtuous enough to safeguard the fledgling republic remained a hotly debated question.

STUMBLING TOWARD A NEW NATIONAL GOVERNMENT

When the Second Continental Congress convened in 1775, the delegates found themselves waging war in the name of a country that did not yet exist. As the military crisis deepened, Congress gradually—though often reluctantly—assumed greater authority over national affairs, but everyone agreed that such narrowly conceived measures were a poor substitute for a legally constituted government. The separate states could not possibly deal with the range of issues that now confronted the American people. Indeed, if independence meant anything in a world of sovereign nations, it implied the creation of a central authority capable of conducting war, borrowing money, regulating trade, and negotiating treaties.

Articles of Confederation

The first attempt to produce a framework for national government failed miserably. Congress appointed a committee headed by John Dickinson, a lawyer who had written an important revolutionary pamphlet titled *Letters from a Farmer in Pennsylvania.* Dickinson's plan for creating a strong central government shocked the delegates, who had assumed that the constitution would authorize a loose confederation of states.

Dickinson's plan called for equal state representation in Congress. This upset states such as Virginia and Massachusetts that were more populous than others and fueled tensions between large and small states. Also unsettling was Dickinson's recommendation that taxes be paid to Congress on the basis of a state's total population, black as well as white, a formula that angered Southerners.

Not unexpectedly, the draft that Congress finally approved in November 1777 bore little resemblance to Dickinson's original plan. The **Articles of Confederation** jealously guarded the sovereignty of the states. The delegates who drafted this framework shared a general republican conviction that power—especially power so far removed from the people—was inherently dangerous and that the only way to preserve liberty was to place as many constraints as possible on federal authority.

They succeeded marvelously; Congress created a government that many people regarded as powerless. The Articles provided for a single legislative body, consisting of representatives selected annually by the state legislatures. Each state possessed a single vote in Congress. There was no independent executive and, of course, no veto over legislative decisions. The Articles also denied Congress the power of taxation, a serious oversight in time of war. The national government could obtain funds only by asking the states for contributions, called requisitions. If a state failed to cooperate—and many did—Congress limped along without financial support. Amendments to this constitution required unanimous assent by all thirteen states. The authors of the new system apparently expected a powerless national government to handle foreign relations, military matters, Native American affairs, and interstate disputes. They most emphatically did not award Congress ownership of the lands west of the Appalachian Mountains.

Articles of Confederation Ratified in 1781, this document was the United States' first constitution, providing a framework for national government. The articles sharply limited central authority by denying the national government any taxation or coercive powers.

Western Land: Key to the First Constitution

Once the new constitution had been sent to the states for ratification, the major bone of contention became the disposition of the vast, unsurveyed territory west of the Appalachians that everyone hoped the British would soon surrender. Although the region was claimed by the various states, most of it actually belonged to the Native Americans. In a series of land grabs that federal negotiators called treaties, the United States government took the land comprising much of modern Ohio, Indiana, Illinois, and Kentucky. Since the Indians had put their faith in the British during the war, they could do little to resist the humiliating treaty agreements at Fort McIntosh (1785), Fort Stanwix (1784), and Fort Finney (1786).

Some states, such as Virginia and Georgia, claimed land all the way from the Atlantic Ocean to the elusive "South Sea" by virtue of royal charters. People who lived in those states not blessed with vague or ambiguous royal charters seemed to be in danger of being permanently cut off from the anticipated bounty. In protest, the "landless" states stubbornly refused to ratify the Articles of Confederation. All states had sacrificed during the Revolution, they reasoned, and so all states should profit from the fruits of victory—in this case, from the sale of western lands. Marylanders were particularly vociferous, fearing depopulation by settlers in search of cheap farmland.

The states resolved this bitter controversy in 1781 as much by accident as by design. Virginia, a landed state, realized the problems inherent in the situation. If the state were to extend beyond the mountains, poor transportation links would make

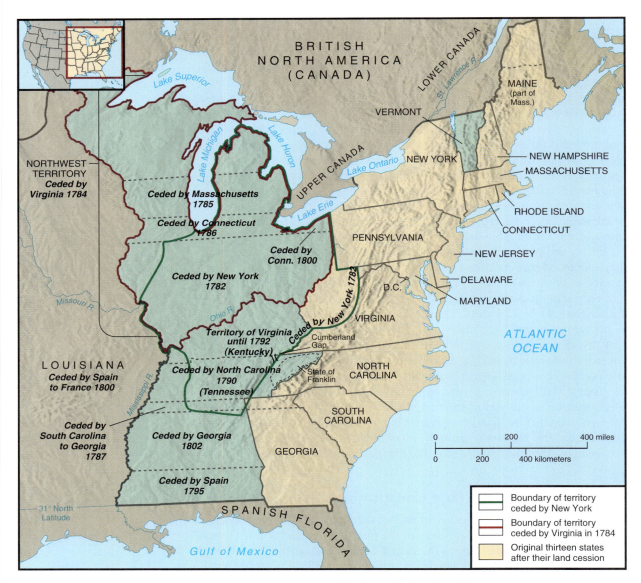

WESTERN LAND CLAIMS CEDED BY THE STATES   *After the Revolution, the major issue facing the Continental Congress under the Articles of Confederation was mediating conflicting states' claims to rich western land. By 1802, the states had ceded all rights to the federal government.* ■

it difficult or even impossible to govern such a large territory effectively from Richmond. The western settlers might even come to regard Virginia as a colonial power insensitive to their needs. Virginia therefore opted to cede its western land claims to Congress, and the other landed states soon followed suit. These transfers established an important principle, for after 1781 there was no question that the West belonged not to the states but to the United States.

No one greeted ratification of the Articles with jubilation. Americans were still fully occupied with winning independence. In 1781, the new government began setting up a bureaucracy. It created the Departments of War, Foreign Affairs, and Finance. By far the most influential presence within the Confederation government was Robert Morris (1734–1806), a freewheeling Philadelphia merchant who was appointed the first superintendent of finance. His decisions provoked controversy. Contemporaries who feared the development of a strong national government identified Morris with efforts to undermine the authority of the states and to seize the power of taxation; at least one congressional critic labeled him a "pecuniary dictator."

Northwest Ordinance: The Confederation's Major Achievement

Whatever the weaknesses of Congress, it scored one impressive triumph. Congressional action brought order to western settlement, especially in the Northwest Territory, and incorporated frontier Americans into an expanded federal system.

In 1781, however, the prospects for success did not seem promising. For years, colonial authorities had ignored people who migrated far inland, sending neither money nor soldiers to protect them from Indian attack. Tensions between the seaboard colonies and the frontier regions had occasionally flared into violence. With thousands of men and women, most of them squatters, pouring across the Appalachian Mountains, Congress had to act quickly to avoid the past errors of royal and colonial authorities.

The initial attempt to deal with this explosive problem came in 1784. Jefferson, then serving as a member of Congress, drafted an ordinance that became a basis for later, more enduring legislation. He recommended carving ten new states out of the western lands located north of the Ohio River. He specified that each new state establish a republican form of government. When the population of a territory

LAND ORDINANCE OF 1785

Grid pattern of a township
36 sections of 640 acres (1 square mile each)

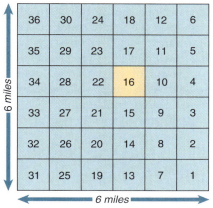

6 miles

6 miles

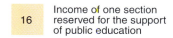

16   Income of one section reserved for the support of public education

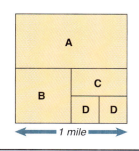

1 mile

A Half-section   320 acres
B Quarter-section   160 acres
C Half-quarter section   80 acres
D Quarter-quarter section   40 acres

equaled that of the smallest state already in the Confederation, the region could apply for full statehood. In the meantime, free adult males could participate in local government, a democratic guarantee that frightened several of Jefferson's more conservative colleagues.

The impoverished Congress was eager to sell off the western territory as quickly as possible. After all, the frontier represented a source of income that did not depend on the unreliable generosity of the states. A second ordinance, passed in 1785 and called the Land Ordinance, established an orderly process for laying out new townships and marketing public lands. After surveying and subdividing various regions, the government planned to auction off its holdings in 640-acre (1-square-mile) sections at prices of not less than $1 an acre, payable in coin only. Section 16 was set aside for the support of public education, and four other sections were held for the government.

Public response disappointed Congress. Surveying the lands took far longer than anticipated, and few persons possessed enough hard currency to make even the minimum purchase of 640 acres. Finally, a solution to the problem came from Manasseh Cutler, a land speculator and congressional lobbyist. He and his companions offered to purchase more than 6 million unsurveyed acres of land located in present-day southeastern Ohio by persuading Congress to accept at full face value government loan certificates that had been issued to soldiers during the Revolution. The speculators could pick up these certificates on the open market for as little as 10 percent of their face value. Like so many other get-rich-quick schemes, however, this one failed to produce the anticipated millions.

Congress also had reservations about frontier democracy. In the 1780s, the West seemed to be filling up with people who, by eastern standards, were uncultured. The attitude was as old as the frontier itself. Indeed, seventeenth-century Englishmen had felt the same way regarding the earliest Virginians. The belief that the westerners were lawless, however, persisted, and even a sober observer like Washington insisted that the West crawled with "banditti." The Ordinance of 1784 placed the government of the territories in the hands of people about whom congressmen and speculators had second thoughts.

Northwest Ordinance
Legislation that formulated plans for governments in America's northwestern territories, defined a procedure for the territories' admission to the Union as states, and prohibited slavery north of the Ohio River.

These various currents shaped the Ordinance of 1787, one of the final acts passed under the Confederation. This bill, also called the **Northwest Ordinance,** provided a new structure for government of the Northwest Territory. The plan authorized the creation of between three and five territories, each to be ruled by a governor, a secretary, and three judges appointed by Congress. When the population reached five thousand, voters who owned property could elect an assembly, but the decisions were subject to the governor's absolute veto. Once sixty thousand persons resided in a territory, they could write a constitution and petition for full statehood. Although the procedures represented a retreat from Jefferson's original proposal, the Ordinance of 1787 contained several significant features. A bill of rights guaranteed the settlers trial by jury, freedom of religion, and due process of law. In addition, the act outlawed slavery, a prohibition that freed the future states of Ohio, Indiana, Illinois, Michigan, and Wisconsin from the curse of human bondage.

By contrast, the growing settlements south of the Ohio River seemed chaotic. Between 1775 and 1784, for example, the population of what was to become Kentucky jumped from around one hundred to thirty thousand. In this and other southwestern regions, land speculators were an ever-present problem. By 1796, the entire region south of the Ohio River had been transformed into a crazy quilt of claims and counterclaims that generated lawsuits for many years thereafter.

STRENGTHENING FEDERAL AUTHORITY

Throughout the country, Americans became increasingly critical of the Articles of Confederation. Complaints varied from region to region and from person to person, but most disappointment reflected economic frustration. Americans had assumed that peace would restore prosperity. When such was not the case, they searched the political horizon for a reason.

The Nationalist Critique

Renewed trade with Great Britain on a large scale undermined the stability of the American economy. Specie (coins) flowed eastward across the Atlantic, leaving the United States desperately short of hard currency. When British merchants called in their debts, thriftless American buyers often fell into bankruptcy. Critics also pointed to the government's inability to regulate trade. Southerners in particular resisted any such attempts. They protested that any controls on the export of tobacco, rice, and cotton smacked of the Navigation Acts.

To blame the Confederation alone for the economic depression would be unfair. Nevertheless, during the 1780s, many people agreed that a stronger government could somehow have softened the blow. In their rush to acquire imported luxuries, Americans seemed to have deserted republican principles, and a weak Congress was helpless to restore national virtue.

The country's chronic fiscal instability increased public anxiety. During the war, Congress printed more than $200 million in paper currency, but because of an extraordinarily high rate of inflation, the rate of exchange for Continental bills soon declined to a fraction of their face value. In 1781, Congress turned to the states for help, asking them to retire the worthless money. Instead, several states not only recirculated the Continental bills but also issued worthless currency of their own.

A heavy burden of state and national debt compounded the general sense of economic crisis. Revolutionary soldiers had yet to be paid, and the government owed money to domestic and foreign creditors. The pressure to pay the debts grew, but Congress was unable to respond. Since Congress was prohibited from taxing the American people, it required little imagination to see that the Confederation would soon default on its legal obligations unless something was done quickly.

A Look at the Past

Continental Paper Money

Fighting the American Revolution cost a lot of money. The new government of the United States simply did not have sufficient gold and silver—called specie—to pay the troops and buy weapons. Pressed on all sides by creditors, the fledgling government issued huge quantities of paper money, such as these bills issued from the colony of New Jersey in 1776 and the Continental Congress in 1778. The flood of Continental currency sparked massive inflation, as nearly worthless money chased a finite supply of consumer goods. ✱ Considering the threat of economic stability, should the Continental Congress have printed so much paper money? Did it have other realistic alternatives? What sorts of people in this society were most harmed by hyperinflation?

nationalists Group of leaders who favored replacing the Articles of Confederation with a stronger national government.

In response, an aggressive group of men announced that they knew how to save the Confederation. The **nationalists**—led by Alexander Hamilton, James Madison, and Robert Morris—called for major constitutional reforms, the chief of which was an amendment allowing Congress to collect a 5 percent tax on imported goods. Revenues generated by the proposed Impost of 1781 would be used by the Confederation to reduce the national debt. Twelve states accepted the impost, but Rhode Island resolutely refused to cooperate. One negative vote on this proposed constitutional change was enough to kill the taxing plan; amending the Articles required unanimous consent.

The nationalists sparked fierce opposition. Many Americans were apprehensive of their plans. The nationalists, for their part, regarded their opponents as economically naive and argued that a country with the potential of the United States required a complex, centralized fiscal system. But for all their pretensions to realism, the nationalists of the early 1780s were politically inept. They underestimated the depth of republican fears, and in their rush to strengthen the Articles, they overplayed their hand.

A group of extreme nationalists even appealed to the army for support. To this day, no one knows the full story of the Newburgh Conspiracy of 1783. Officers of the Continental army stationed at Newburgh, New York, worried that Congress would disband them without funding their pensions and began to lobby intensively for relief. The officers' initial efforts were harmless enough, but frustrated nationalists such as Morris and Hamilton decided that if the army exerted sufficient pressure on the government, perhaps even threatened a military takeover, stubborn Americans might be compelled to amend the Articles.

The conspirators failed to take George Washington's integrity into account. In a surprise visit, he confronted the officers directly at Newburgh. So great was his personal influence that a few words from him ended any chance of rebellion. Washington, indeed, deserves credit for preserving civilian rule in this country. He refused to consider any scheme that contemplated using the army as a political instrument.

In April 1783, Congress proposed a second impost, but it, too, failed to win unanimous ratification. Even a personal appeal by Washington could not save the amendment. With this defeat, nationalists gave up on the Confederation. Morris retired from government, and Madison returned to Virginia utterly depressed by what he had witnessed.

Diplomatic Humiliation

In foreign affairs, Congress endured further embarrassment. American negotiators had promised Great Britain that its citizens could collect debts contracted before the Revolution. The states, however, dragged their heels, and several even passed laws obstructing the settlement of legitimate prewar claims. Congress was powerless to force compliance. The British responded to this apparent provocation by refusing to evacuate troops from posts located in the Northwest Territory. A strong central government would have driven the redcoats out, but without adequate funds, the weak Congress was powerless to act.

Congress's postrevolutionary dealings with Spain were equally humiliating. That nation refused to accept the southern boundary of the United States established by the Treaty of Paris. Spanish agents schemed with southern Indian tribes to resist American expansion, and on July 21, 1784, Spain added a further insult by closing the lower Mississippi River to citizens of the United States. This last event devastated western farmers, who needed unrestricted use of the Mississippi to send their crops to the world's markets. Without the river, the economic development of the entire Ohio Valley was in jeopardy.

In 1786, a Spanish official, Don Diego de Gardoqui, opened talks with John Jay, a New Yorker appointed by Congress to obtain rights to navigation on the

Mississippi. Jay soon discovered that Gardoqui would not compromise, but he pressed on, attempting to win concessions that would have commercially linked the United States to Spain and benefited northern traders while forgoing free navigation of the Mississippi for twenty-five years. When Congress learned of Jay's plans, it wisely terminated the negotiations with Spain.

By the mid-1780s, Congress had squandered whatever respect it may once have enjoyed. It met irregularly, and some states did not even bother to send delegates. The nation lacked a permanent capital, and Congress thus drifted from Philadelphia to Princeton to Annapolis to New York City, prompting one humorist to suggest that the government purchase an air balloon to allow members of Congress to "float along from one end of the continent to the other" and "suddenly pop down into any of the states they please."

"HAVE WE FOUGHT FOR THIS?"

Thoughtful Americans, especially those who had provided leadership during the Revolution, agreed that something had to be done. By 1785, the country seemed to be drifting; the buoyant optimism that had sustained revolutionary patriots had dissolved into pessimism and doubt. Washington was soon asking his countrymen exactly why they had fought the Revolution.

A Crisis Mentality

The country's problems could be traced in part to the republicans' own ideology. More than anything else, they feared the concentration of power in the hands of unscrupulous rulers. They therefore created governments—national and state—with weak chief executives and strong assemblies. However, too many of the people who manned the state assemblies and Congress were not up to the task. The result was a government of excessive individualism where legitimate minority rights took a backseat to the desires of the majority.

Facing economic chaos, many states blithely churned out worthless currency, while others passed laws impeding the collection of debts. In Rhode Island, the situation became absurd. State legislators made it illegal for merchants to reject Rhode Island money even though everyone knew it had no value. As Americans tried to interpret these experiences within a republican framework, they were checked by the most widely accepted political wisdom of the age. Baron de Montesquieu (1689–1755), a French political philosopher of immense international reputation, declared flatly that a republican government could not flourish in a large territory. For such a government to function properly, the people had to be able to keep a close eye on their representatives. Americans treated Montesquieu's theories as self-evident truths, and they were thus nervous about tampering with the sovereignty of the states.

James Madison rejected Montesquieu's argument and in so doing helped Americans think of republican government in exciting new ways. This soft-spoken, rather unprepossessing Virginian was the most brilliant American political thinker of his generation. Based on his reading of the Scottish philosopher David Hume and others, Madison became convinced that Americans need not fear a greatly expanded republic. In fact, he believed that a republican form of government would work better in a large country than in a small one. In small states such as Rhode Island, for example, legislative majorities tyrannized the propertied minority. In a large republic, these injustices could be avoided. With so many people scattered over a huge area, no one faction would be able to form an effective majority, and one powerful interest would be checked by some other equally powerful interest.

Madison did not, however, advocate a modern "interest group" model of political behavior. Rather he thought that the competing selfish factions would neutralize each other, leaving the business of governing the republic to the ablest, most virtuous persons that the nation could produce. In other words, the government Madison envisioned would be based on the will of the people and yet detached from their narrowly based demands. This thinking formed the foundation of Madison's most famous political essay, *The Federalist* No. 10.

A concerted movement to overhaul the Articles of Confederation developed in the mid-1780s. The Massachusetts legislature asked Congress to call a convention for the purpose of revising the entire constitution. Nothing came of the suggestion until 1786, when Madison and his friends persuaded the Virginia assembly to recommend a convention to explore the creation of a unified system of "commercial regulation." Congress supported the idea. However, only five states sent delegates to the Annapolis convention. Rather than try to conduct any business, the Annapolis delegates advised Congress to hold a second meeting in Philadelphia to consider constitutional changes. Congress authorized a grand convention to gather in May 1787.

Events played into Madison's hands. Soon after the Annapolis meeting, an uprising known as **Shays's Rebellion,** involving several thousand impoverished farmers, shattered the peace of western Massachusetts. The farmers complained of high taxes, of high interest rates, and of a state government insensitive to their economic problems. In 1786, Daniel Shays, a veteran of the battle of Bunker Hill, and his armed neighbors closed a county courthouse where creditors were suing to foreclose farm mortgages. His band then marched to Springfield, site of a federal arsenal, but the state militia soon put down the rebellion.

> **Shays's Rebellion** Armed insurrection of farmers in western Massachusetts led by Daniel Shays, a veteran of the Continental Army. Intended to prevent state courts from foreclosing on debtors unable to pay their taxes, the rebellion was put down by the state militia. Nationalists used the event to justify the calling of a constitutional convention to strengthen the national government.

Nationalists throughout the United States overreacted to news of Shays's Rebellion. From their perspective, the incident symbolized the breakdown of law and order that they had long predicted. Even more important, the event persuaded persons who might otherwise have ignored the Philadelphia meeting to participate in drafting a new constitution.

The Philadelphia Convention

In the spring of 1787, fifty-five men representing twelve states traveled to Philadelphia. Only Rhode Island refused to take part in the proceedings. The delegates were practical men: lawyers, merchants, and planters, many of whom had fought in the Revolution and served in the Congress of the Confederation. The majority were in their thirties and forties. The gathering included George Washington, James Madison, George Mason, Robert Morris, John Dickinson, Benjamin Franklin, and Alexander Hamilton. Absent were John Adams and Thomas Jefferson, who were conducting diplomacy in Europe; Patrick Henry stayed home in Virginia because he "smelled a rat."

As soon as the convention opened on May 25, the delegates made several procedural decisions of utmost importance. First, they ruled that their discussions would be kept absolutely secret. This determination allowed delegates to speak their minds freely without fear of criticism from people who had not actually witnessed the debates. The delegates also decided to vote by state, but to avoid the kinds of problems that had plagued the Confederation, they ruled that key proposals needed the support of only a majority instead of the nine states required in the Articles.

> **Virginia Plan** Offered by James Madison and the Virginia delegation at the Constitutional Convention, this proposal called for a new government with a strong executive office and two houses of Congress, each with representation proportional to a state's population.

Inventing a Federal Republic

Madison understood that whoever sets the agenda controls the meeting. Even before the delegates had arrived, he drew up a framework for a new federal system known as the **Virginia Plan.** He wisely persuaded Edmund Randolph, Virginia's popular governor, to present this scheme to the convention on May 29. In his plan,

Madison advocated a strong central government, one that could override the short-sighted local legislatures.

The Virginia Plan envisioned a national legislature consisting of two houses, one elected directly by the people, the other chosen by the first house from nominations made by the state assemblies. Representation in both houses was proportional to the state's population. The Virginia Plan provided for an executive elected by Congress. To the surprise of the states' rights supporters, the entire package carried easily, and the convention found itself discussing the details of "a *national* Government . . . consisting of a *supreme* Legislature, Executive, and Judiciary."

On June 15, William Paterson, a New Jersey lawyer, presented a counterproposal. The **New Jersey Plan** preserved the fundamental spirit of the Articles of Confederation, including the retention of a unicameral legislature. Paterson argued that his revisions, though more modest than Madison's plan, would have greater appeal for the American people. The delegates listened politely to his plan, which would have given Congress extensive new powers to tax and regulate trade, and then they soundly rejected it on June 19.

Rejection of the New Jersey Plan, however, did not clear the way for a final vote. Delegates from small states feared that Madison's plan would hurt their states. These men maintained that unless each state possessed an equal vote in Congress, the small states would find themselves at the mercy of their larger neighbors. Countering this claim, delegates from the large states argued that it was absurd to assert that Rhode Island, with only 68,000 people, should have the same voice in Congress as Virginia's 747,000 inhabitants.

New Jersey Plan Proposal of the New Jersey delegation at the Constitutional Convention that called for a strong government with one house of Congress in which all states would have equal representation.

Compromise Saves the Convention

The mood of the convention was tense. Hard work and frustration, coupled with Philadelphia's sweltering summer heat, frayed nerves. Although some members predicted that the meeting would accomplish nothing of significance, the gathering did not break up; the delegates desperately wanted to produce a constitution. On July 2, a "grand committee" of one person from each state was elected by the convention to resolve persistent differences between the large and small states.

The grand committee did just that. It recommended that the states be equally represented in the upper house of Congress and proportionately by population in the lower house. Only the lower house could initiate money bills. The committee also decided that one member of the lower house should be selected for every forty thousand inhabitants of a state, and for this purpose, a slave was to be counted as three-fifths of a freeman. This compromise overcame the impasse between large and small states.

On July 26, the convention formed a "committee of detail," a group that prepared a rough draft of the Constitution. When its work was done, the delegates debated each article. The task required the better part of a month.

During the sessions, the members of the convention concluded that the president, as they now called the executive, should be selected by an electoral college, a body of prominent men in each state chosen by local voters. The number of electoral votes held by each state equaled its number of representatives and senators. Whoever received the second-largest number of votes in the electoral college automatically became vice president. In the event that no person received a majority of the votes, the election would be decided by the lower house—the House of Representatives—with each state casting a single vote.

Delegates also armed the chief executive with a veto power over legislation as well as the right to nominate judges. Both privileges would have been unthinkable a decade earlier, but the state experiences revealed the importance of having an independent executive to maintain a balanced system of republican government. The

Philadelphia convention thus telescoped into four months the process of constitutional education that had taken more than four years to learn at the state level.

Compromising with Slavery

During the final days of August, two new issues suddenly disrupted the convention. One was a harbinger of the great sectional crisis of the nineteenth century. Many northern representatives detested the slave trade and wanted to end it immediately. In order to win southern support for the Constitution, however, the northern delegates promised that the legislature would not interfere with the slave trade until 1808 (see Chapter 8).

The second issue was the absence in the Constitution of a bill of rights. Such declarations had been included in most state constitutions. Virginians such as George Mason insisted that the states and their citizens needed explicit protection from possible excesses by the federal government. Though many delegates sympathized with Mason's appeal, they insisted that the proposed constitution provided sufficient security for individual rights. During the hard battle over ratification, the delegates to the convention may have regretted passing over the issue so lightly.

The delegates adopted an ingenious procedure for ratification. Instead of submitting the Constitution to the various state legislatures, all of which had a vested interest in maintaining the status quo, they called for the election of thirteen state conventions especially chosen to review the new federal government. Moreover, the Constitution would take effect after the assent of only nine states. There was no danger, therefore, that the proposed system would fail simply because a single state such as Rhode Island withheld approval.

The convention asked Gouveneur Morris, a delegate from Pennsylvania noted for his urbanity, to make final stylistic changes in the wording of the Constitution. Since the wording of the working draft spoke of the collection of states forming a new government, a strong possibility existed that several New England states would

■ *Although the words* slave *and* slavery *do not appear in the U.S. Constitution, debate over slavery and the slave trade resulted in a compromise in which both institutions persisted in the new Republic. Not everyone was pleased with the compromise. The Library Company of Philadelphia commissioned this painting* Liberty Displaying the Arts and Sciences *(1792) by Samuel Jennings. The broken chain at the feet of the goddess Liberty is meant to demonstrate her opposition to slavery.* ■

reject the document. Morris's brilliant phrase, "We, the People of the United States," eliminated this difficulty. The new nation was a republic of people, not of states.

On September 17, thirty-nine men signed the Constitution. A few members of the convention, like Mason, could not support the document. Others had already gone home. Out of the three months of heat and effort, a new form of government had emerged.

WHOSE CONSTITUTION? STRUGGLE FOR RATIFICATION

Supporters of the Constitution recognized that ratification would not be easy. After all, the convention had been authorized only to revise the Articles. Instead it produced a radical new plan that fundamentally altered relations between the states and the central government. The delegates dispatched a copy of the document to the Congress of Confederation, which in turn referred it to the separate states. The fight for ratification had begun.

Federalists and Antifederalists

Proponents of the Constitution enjoyed great advantages over the unorganized opposition. In the contest for ratification, however, they took no chances. Their most astute move was the adoption of the label **Federalists,** a term that cleverly suggested that they stood for a confederation of states rather than for the creation of a supreme national authority. In fact, they envisioned the creation of a strong centralized national government capable of fielding a formidable army. Critics of the Constitution—who tended to be somewhat poorer, less urban, and less well educated than their opponents—cried foul, but there was little they could do. They were stuck with the name **Antifederalists,** an awkward term that made their cause seem a rejection of the very notion of a federation of the states.

The Federalists recruited the most prominent public figures of the day. In every state convention, speakers favoring the Constitution were more polished, better educated, and more fully prepared than their opponents. In New York, the campaign to win ratification sparked publication of *The Federalist,* a remarkable series of essays written by Madison, Hamilton, and Jay during the fall and winter of 1787–1788. The nation's newspapers threw themselves overwhelmingly behind the new government. Few journals even bothered to carry Antifederalist writings. Nor were the Federalists above using threats and even strong-arm tactics. They were determined to win. A nation was at stake.

With so many factors working against them, the Antifederalists still came very near victory. Voting was exceptionally close in three large states: Massachusetts, New York, and Virginia. Apparently those who resisted ratification were not so far removed from the political mainstream as has sometimes been suggested by scholars who dismiss the Antifederalists as "narrow-minded local politicians."

The Antifederalists spoke in the language of the Commonwealthmen (see Chapter 4). Like the extreme republicans who wrote the first state constitutions, the Antifederalists were deeply suspicious of political power. During the debates over ratification, they warned that public officials, however selected, would be constantly scheming to expand their authority. It seemed obvious to these critics of the Constitution that the larger the republic, the greater the opportunity for political corruption. Local voters could not possibly know what their representatives in a distant capital were doing. Antifederalists possessed a narrow view of representation. They argued that elected officials should reflect the character of their constituents as closely as possible. They feared that in large congressional districts, representatives would lose touch with the people, and the wealthy would win the

Federalists Supporters of the Constitution who advocated its ratification.

Antifederalists Critics of the Constitution who expressed concern that it seemed to possess no specific provision for the protection of natural and civil rights.

The Federalist A series of essays penned by Alexander Hamilton, James Madison, and John Jay that explained and defended the stronger national government created by the Constitutional Convention of 1787.

REVOLUTION OR REFORM?
THE ARTICLES OF CONFEDERATION AND THE CONSTITUTION COMPARED

Political Challenge	Articles of Confederation	Constitution
Mode of ratification or amendment	Require confirmation by every state legislature	Requires confirmation by three-fourths of state conventions or legislatures
Number of houses in legislature	One	Two
Mode of representation	Two to seven delegates represent each state; each state holds only one vote in Congress	Two senators represent each state in upper house; each senator holds one vote. One representative to lower house represents every 30,000 people (in 1788) in a state; each representative holds one vote
Mode of election and term of office	Delegates appointed annually by state legislatures	Senators chosen by state legislatures for six-year term (direct election after 1913); representatives chosen by vote of citizens for two-year term
Executive	No separate executive: delegates annually elect one of their number as president, who possesses no veto, no power to appoint officers or to conduct policy. Administrative functions of government theoretically carried out by Committee of States, practically by various single-headed departments	Separate executive branch: president elected by electoral college to four-year term; granted veto, power to conduct policy and to appoint ambassadors, judges, and officers of executive departments established by legislation
Judiciary	Most adjudication left to state and local courts; Congress is final court of appeal in disputes between states	Separate branch consisting of Supreme Court and inferior courts established by Congress to enforce federal law
Taxation	States alone can levy taxes; Congress funds the Common Treasury by making requisitions for state contributions	Federal government granted powers of taxation
Regulation of commerce	Congress regulates foreign commerce by treaty but holds no check on conflicting state regulations	Congress regulates foreign commerce by treaty; all state regulations must obtain congressional consent

elections. Older on the average than their opponents, they recalled how aristocrats in Britain had abused their power.

Federalist speakers mocked their opponents' limited perspective. The Constitution deserved general support precisely because it ensured that future Americans would be represented by "natural aristocrats," individuals possessing greater insights, skills, and training than the average citizen. These talented leaders, Federalists insisted, could discern the interests of the entire population. They were not tied to the selfish needs of local communities. The first ten amendments to the Constitution are the major legacy of the Antifederalist argument. The absence of a bill of rights troubled many people. In almost every state convention, opponents of the Constitution pointed to the need for greater protection of individual liberties and rights that people presumably possessed naturally, such as freedom of religion and the right to a jury trial. To counter this complaint, Federalists pledged to present a bill of rights to Congress as soon as the Constitution was ratified.

The Constitution drew support from many different types of people. In fact, historians have been unable to discover sharp correlations between wealth and occupation on the one hand and attitudes toward the proposed system of government on the other. In general, Federalists lived in more commercialized areas than their opponents did. Men involved in commerce—artisans as well as merchants—tended to vote for ratification, while farmers only marginally involved in commercial agriculture frequently voted Antifederalist.

Despite passionate pleas from Patrick Henry and other Antifederalists, most of the state conventions quickly adopted the Constitution. Although the battle was

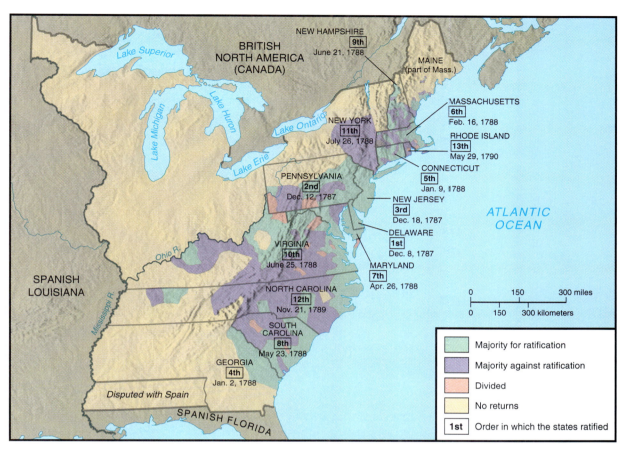

RATIFICATION OF THE CONSTITUTION *Advocates of the new Constitution called themselves Federalists, and those who opposed its ratification were known as Antifederalists.* ∎

close in several states, and although it took almost three years for Rhode Island to ratify, all the states eventually ratified the Constitution. And once the ratification process was over, Americans soon closed ranks behind the new government.

Adding the Bill of Rights

The first ten amendments to the Constitution are the major legacy of the Antifederalist argument. In almost every state convention, opponents of the Constitution pointed to the need for greater protection of individual liberties, rights that people presumably had possessed in a state of nature and that protected the minority from the majority. The list of fundamental rights varied from state to state, but most Antifederalists demanded specific guarantees for jury trial and freedom of religion. They wanted prohibitions against cruel and unusual punishments. There was also considerable, though not universal, support for freedom of speech and freedom of the press.

Madison and others regarded the proposals with little enthusiasm. But after the adoption of the Constitution had been assured, Madison moderated his stand. If nothing else, passage of a bill of rights would appease able men such as George Mason and Edmund Randolph, who might otherwise remain alienated from the new federal system.

The crucial consideration was caution. A number of people throughout the nation advocated calling a second constitutional convention, one that would take Antifederalist criticism into account. Madison wanted to avoid such a meeting, and

Chronology

1776	Second Continental Congress authorizes colonies to create republican governments ■ Eight states draft new constitutions; two others already enjoy republican government by virtue of former colonial charters
1777	Congress accepts Articles of Confederation after long debate
1780	Massachusetts ratifies state constitution
1781	States ratify Articles of Confederation following settlements of Virginia's western land claims ■ British army surrenders at Yorktown
1782	States fail to ratify proposed impost tax
1783	Newburgh Conspiracy thwarted ■ Treaty of Peace signed with Great Britain
1785	Land Ordinance for Northwest Territory passed by Congress
1786	Jay-Gardoqui negotiations over Mississippi navigation anger southern states ■ Annapolis Convention suggests second meeting to revise the Articles of Confederation ■ Shays's Rebellion frightens American leaders
1787	Constitutional Convention convenes in Philadelphia ■ Northwest Ordinance passed by Congress; restructures territorial government
1787–1788	Federal Constitution is ratified by all states except North Carolina and Rhode Island
1791	Bill of Rights (first ten amendments of the Constitution) ratified by states

he feared that some members of the first Congress might use a bill of rights as an excuse to revise the entire Constitution or to promote a second convention.

Madison carefully reviewed the state recommendations as well as the various declarations of rights that had appeared in the early state constitutions, and on June 8, 1789, he placed before the House of Representatives a set of amendments designed to protect individual rights from government interference. Madison told the members of Congress that the greatest dangers to popular liberties came from "the majority [operating] against the minority." A committee compressed and revised his original ideas into twelve amendments, ten of which were ratified and became known collectively as the **Bill of Rights.**

Bill of Rights The first ten amendments to the U.S. Constitution, adopted in 1791 to preserve the rights and liberties of individuals.

The Bill of Rights protects the freedoms of assembly, speech, religion, and the press; guarantees speedy trial by an impartial jury; preserves the people's right to bear arms; and prohibits unreasonable searches. Other amendments deal with legal procedure. Only the Tenth Amendment addresses the states' relation to the federal system. This crucial article, designed to calm Antifederalists' fears, specifies that all "powers not delegated to the United States by the Constitution, nor prohibited by it to the States, are reserved to the States respectively, or to the people."

On September 25, 1789, the Bill of Rights passed both houses of Congress, and by December 15, 1791, these amendments had been ratified by more than the requisite three-fourths of the states. Madison was justly proud of his achievement. He had effectively secured individual rights without undermining the Constitution.

CONCLUSION: SUCCESS DEPENDS ON THE PEOPLE

By 1789, one phase of American political experimentation had come to an end. During these exciting years, the people gradually, often haltingly, learned that in a republican society, they themselves were sovereign. They could no longer blame the failure of government on inept monarchs or greedy aristocrats. They bore a great responsibility. Americans had demanded a government of the people only to discover during the late 1780s that in some situations the people cannot be trusted with power, that majorities can tyrannize minorities, that the best government can abuse individual rights. They had the good sense, therefore, to establish an effective system of checks and balances that protected the people from themselves.

The country's prospects seemed brighter. Benjamin Franklin captured the national mood during the final moments of the constitutional convention. As the delegates came forward to sign the document, he observed that there was a sun carved on the back of Washington's chair. "I have . . . often in the course of the session . . . looked at the sun behind the President without being able to tell whether it was rising or setting: but now at length I have the happiness to know that it is a rising and not a setting sun."

KEY TERMS

republicanism, p. 103

natural rights, p. 108

Articles of Confederation, p. 109

Northwest Ordinance, p. 112

nationalists, p. 114

Shays's Rebellion, p. 116

Virginia Plan, p. 116

New Jersey Plan, p. 117

Federalists, p. 119

Antifederalists, p. 119

The Federalist, p. 119

Bill of Rights, p. 122

RECOMMENDED READING

The best way to comprehend the major issues debated at the Philadelphia Convention and then later at the separate state ratifying conventions is to examine the key documents of the period. One could do no better than reading James Madison, *Journal of the Federal Constitution* (reprinted in many modern editions), our only detailed account of what actually occurred during the closed debates in Philadelphia. A good introduction to the contest between the Federalists and Antifederalists over ratification is Bernard Bailyn, ed., *The Debate on the Constitution: Federalist and Antifederalist Speeches, Articles, and Letters During the Struggle Over Ratification* (1993). Gordon S. Wood analyzes late-eighteenth-century republican political thought in *The Creation of the American Republic, 1776–1787* (1969). Three recent titles interpret the complex political experience of the 1780s: Jack N. Rakove, *Original Meanings: Politics and Ideas in the Making of the Constitution* (1996); Peter Onuf, *Statehood and Union: A History of the Northwest Ordinance* (1987); and Max M. Edling, *A Revolution in Favor of Government: Origins of the U.S. Constitution and the Making*

of the American State (2003). For a thoughtful investigation of the many different meanings of "republicanism," see Richard Beeman et al., eds., *Beyond Confederation: Origins of the Constitution and American National Identity* (1987) and Daniel T. Rodgers, "Republicanism: The Career of a Concept," *Journal of American History,* vol. 79 (June 1992), 1–38. On the expectations of African Americans and women during this period, see the final sections of Winthrop Jordan, *White Over Black: American Attitudes Toward the Negro, 1550–1812* (1968); T. H. Breen, "Making History: The Force of Public Opinion and the Last Years of Slavery in Revolutionary Massachusetts," in Ronald Hoffman et al., eds., *Through a Glass Darkly: Reflections on Personal Identity in Early America* (1997), 67–95; and Ronald Hoffman and Peter J. Albert, eds., *Women in the Age of the American Revolution* (1990). The Newburgh Conspiracy is explored in Richard H. Kohn, *Eagle and Sword: The Federalists and the Creation of the Military Establishment in America, 1783–1802* (1975). On Shays's Rebellion, see Robert A. Gross, ed., *In Debt to Shays: The Bicentennial of an Agrarian Rebellion* (1993).

SUGGESTED WEB SITES

The Leslie Brock Center for the Study of Colonial Currency
etext.lib.virginia.edu/users/brock
This site includes both useful primary and secondary documents on early American currency.

Northwest Territory Alliance
www.nwta.com/main.html
This Revolutionary Era reenactment organization site contains several links and is an interesting look at historical reenactment.

Independence Hall National Historical Park
www.nps.gov/inde/visit.html
This site includes images and historical accounts of Independence Hall and other Philadelphia buildings closely associated with the nation's founding.

Biographies of the Founding Fathers
www.colonialhall.com/
This site provides interesting information about the men who signed the Declaration of Independence and includes a trivia section.

The Federalist Papers

www.law.emory.edu/FEDERAL/federalist/

A collection of the most important Federalist Papers, a series of documents designed to convince people to support the new Constitution and the Federal party.

The Constitution and the Amendments

www.law.emory.edu/FEDERAL/usconst.html

A searchable site to the Constitution, especially useful for its information about the Bill of Rights and other constitutional amendments.

Documents from the Continental Congress and the Constitutional Convention, 1774–1789

memory.loc.gov/ammem/bdsds/bdsdhome.html

The Continental Congress Broadside Collection (253 titles) and the Constitutional Convention Broadside Collection (21 titles) contain 274 documents relating to the work of Congress and the drafting and ratification of the Constitution.

Chapter 7

Democracy and Dissent: The Violence of Party Politics, 1788–1800

Partisan Passions

While presiding over the first meeting of the United States Senate in 1789, Vice President John Adams raised a pressing procedural question: How should the senators address George Washington, the newly elected president? Adams insisted that Washington deserved an impressive title, a designation that would lend dignity and weight to his office. Adams recommended "His Highness, the President of the United States, and Protector of their Liberties," but some senators favored "His Elective Majesty" or "His Excellency."

Washington and many other people regarded the entire debate as ridiculous. Madison believed that such a discussion befit European aristocrats more than American republicans. When the senators learned that their efforts embarrassed Washington, they dropped the topic. The leader of the new Republic would be called President of the United States. One wag, however, dubbed the portly Adams "His Rotundity."

The comic-opera quality of the debate about Washington's title should not obscure the participants' seriousness. During the 1790s, decisions about the use of power, about actual governmental policies and positions, had the potential to set a lasting precedent and thus to reinforce or imperil the Revolution itself. But the question of how best to put widely shared republican principles into practice divided Americans. Pressured by Great Britain and France, and unsure about how to transform their country into an economically strong and commercially viable nation, Americans advanced different solutions. Public figures increasingly gravitated to Alexander Hamilton or Thomas Jefferson, the two most powerful personalities of the decade, and before Washington retired from the presidency, these loose political affiliations had hardened into open party identification, either Federalist or Republican, a development that no one in 1787 had anticipated or desired.

POWER OF PUBLIC OPINION

Although no one welcomed them, political parties gradually took shape during this period. Neither the Jeffersonians nor the Federalists—as the two major groups were called—doubted that the United States would one day become a great commercial power. They differed, however, on how best to manage the transition from an agrarian household economy to an international system of trade and industry. The Federalists encouraged rapid integration of the United States into a world economy, but however enthusiastic they were about capitalism, they did not trust the people or local government to do the job effectively. A modern economy, they insisted, required strong national institutions that would be directed by a social elite that understood the financial challenge and that would work in the best interests of the people.

Such claims frightened persons who came to identify themselves as Jeffersonians. Strong financial institutions, they thought, had corrupted the government of Great Britain from which they had just separated themselves. They searched for alternative ways to accommodate the needs of commerce and industry. Unlike the Federalists, the Jeffersonians put their faith in the people, defined for the most part politically as white yeoman farmers. The Jeffersonians insisted that ordinary entrepreneurs, if they could be freed from intrusive government regulations, could be trusted to resist greed and crass materialism and to sustain the virtue of the republic.

During the 1790s, former allies were surprised to discover themselves at odds over such basic political issues. One person—Hamilton, for example—would stake out a position. Another, such as Jefferson or Madison, would respond, perhaps speaking a little more extravagantly than a specific issue demanded, goaded by the rhetorical nature of public debate. The first in turn would rebut passionately the new position. By the middle of the decade, this dialectic had almost spun out of control, taking the young republic to the brink of political violence.

Leaders of every persuasion had to learn to live with "public opinion." The revolutionary gentry had invited the people to participate in government, but the gentlemen assumed that ordinary voters would automatically defer to their social betters. Instead, the Founders discovered they had created a rough-and-tumble political culture, a robust public sphere of cheap newspapers and street demonstrations. The newly empowered "public" followed the great debates of the period through articles they read in hundreds of highly partisan journals and magazines.

Just as television did in the twentieth century, print journalism opened politics to a large audience that previously might have been indifferent to the activities of elected officials. By the time John Adams left the presidency in 1800, he had learned this lesson well. The ordinary workers and farmers of the United States, feisty individuals who thought they were as good as anyone else and who were not afraid to let their political opinions be known, were not likely to let their president become an "Elective Majesty."

PRINCIPLE AND PRAGMATISM: ESTABLISHING A NEW GOVERNMENT

In 1788, George Washington enjoyed great popularity throughout the nation. In America's first presidential election, he received the unanimous support of the electoral college, an achievement that no subsequent president has duplicated. John Adams was elected vice president.

Washington owed much of his success as the nation's first president to an instinctive feeling for the symbolic possibilities of political power. Although he possessed only modest speaking abilities and never matched the intellectual brilliance of some contemporaries, Washington sensed that he had come to embody the hopes and fears of the new republic, and thus, without ever quite articulating the attributes necessary to achieve charisma—an instinctive ability that some leaders have to merge their own personality with the abstract goals of the government—he carefully monitored his official behavior. Washington knew that if he did not convincingly demonstrate the existence of a strong republic, people who championed the sovereignty of the individual states would attempt to weaken federal authority before it was ever properly established.

No example better illustrates Washington's mastery of symbolic power than his grand trips in 1789 and 1791. Accompanied by only a secretary and a few servants, he journeyed from the present state of Maine to Georgia. Along the way, ordinary men and women flocked to see the president and to celebrate the new political order. His sacrifice—the roads were terrible and the food worse—visibly brought the new federal government to the people. In Boston, organizers honored Washington with a huge arch on which they inscribed on one side, "To the Man who united all hearts," and on the other, "To Columbia's favorite Son." Civic leaders in Charleston, South Carolina, outdid themselves. They arranged to have Washington taken over the water to the city "in a 12 oared barge rowed by 12 American Captains of Ships, most elegantly dressed. There were a great number of other Boats with Gentlemen and ladies in them; and two Boats with Music; all of whom attended me across." It all worked as Washington planned. By celebrating a visit by the president of the United States, the people also recognized the power and unity of the new nation.

The first Congress quickly established executive departments. Each department was headed by a secretary nominated by the president and serving at the president's pleasure. For the Departments of War, State, and the Treasury, Washington nominated Henry Knox, Thomas Jefferson, and Alexander Hamilton, respectively. Edmund Randolph served as part-time attorney general, a position that ranked slightly lower in prestige than the head of a department. As head of the Treasury, which oversaw the collection of customs and other federal taxes, Hamilton could anticipate having several thousand political patronage jobs to dispense.

To modern Americans accustomed to a huge federal bureaucracy, the size of Washington's government seems amazingly small. Jefferson, for example, ran the entire State Department with a staff of two chief clerks, two assistants, and a part-time translator. The situation in most other departments was similar. Overworked clerks scribbled madly just to keep up with the press of correspondence. Considering the workloads of men such as Jefferson, Hamilton, and Adams, it is no wonder that the president had difficulty persuading able people to accept positions in the new government.

Congress also provided for a federal court system. The Judiciary Act of 1789 created a Supreme Court staffed by a chief justice and five associate justices. In addition, the statute set up thirteen district courts authorized to review the decisions of the state courts. John Jay, a leading figure in New York politics, agreed to serve as chief justice, but since federal judges in the 1790s were expected to travel hundreds of miles over terrible roads to attend sessions of the inferior courts, few persons of outstanding talent and training joined Jay on the federal bench.

Remembering the financial insecurity of the old Confederation government, the newly elected congressmen passed the tariff of 1789, a tax of approximately 5 percent on imports. The act generated considerable revenue, but it also sparked controversy. Southern planters, who relied heavily on European imports, claimed the tariff discriminated against their interests in favor of those of northern merchants. These battle lines would form again and again in the years to come.

A Look at the Past

Eagle Decoration

Following the American Revolution, patriotic symbols and themes became common in decorative arts. Eagles, a traditional symbol of strength, enjoyed special popularity. English manufacturers printed eagles on ceramics and textiles. Women embroidered eagles and appliquéd them onto quilts and coverlets like the one pictured here. Such objects reflected pride in a new, untested nation. ✱ Why would consumers want patriotic emblems on their fine fabrics and furniture? Could the popularity of patriotic symbols reveal something besides pride?

CONFLICTING VISIONS: JEFFERSON AND HAMILTON

Washington's first cabinet included two extraordinary personalities, Alexander Hamilton and Thomas Jefferson. Both had served the country with distinction during the Revolution, were recognized by contemporaries as men of special genius as well as high ambition, and brought to public office a powerful vision of how the American people could achieve greatness. The story of their opposing views during the decade of the 1790s provides insight into the birth and development of political parties. It also reveals how a common political ideology, republicanism, could be interpreted in two vastly different ways, turning former friends into bitter adversaries. Indeed, the falling out of Hamilton and Jefferson reflected deep and potentially explosive political divisions within American society.

Hamilton was a brilliant, dynamic young lawyer who had distinguished himself as Washington's aide-de-camp during the Revolution. Born in the West Indies, the child of an adulterous relationship, Hamilton employed charm, courage, and intellect to fulfill his inexhaustible ambition. He strove not for wealth but for reputation. Men and women who fell under his spell found him almost irresistible, but to enemies, Hamilton appeared a dark, calculating, even evil genius. He advocated a strong central government and refused to be bound by the strict wording of the Constitution. He loved America, but he admired English culture, and during the 1790s, he advocated closer commercial and diplomatic ties with Britain.

Jefferson possessed a profoundly different temperament. More reflective, he shone less brightly in society than Hamilton did. He thirsted not for power or wealth but for an opportunity to advance the democratic principles that he had stated so eloquently in the Declaration of Independence. He became secretary of state just after returning from Paris, where he had witnessed the first exhilarating moments of the French Revolution. He believed that republicanism would everywhere replace absolute monarchy and aristocratic privilege. His European experiences biased Jefferson in favor of France over Great Britain when the two nations clashed.

Both Hamilton and Jefferson insisted that they were working for the creation of a strong, prosperous republic. Rather than seeing them as spokesmen for competing ideologies, Hamilton and Jefferson should be viewed as different kinds of republicans who during the 1790s attempted as best they could to cope with unprecedented political challenges.

The two men did seriously disagree on precisely how the United States should fulfill its destiny. As head of the Treasury Department, Hamilton urged his fellow citizens to think in terms of bold commercial development, of farms and factories embedded within a complex financial network that would reduce the nation's reliance on foreign trade. Because Great Britain had already established an elaborate system of banking and credit, the secretary looked to that country for economic models that might be reproduced on this side of the Atlantic.

Hamilton's pessimistic view of human nature caused him to fear democratic excess. Anarchy, not monarchy, was his nightmare. The best hope for the survival of the republic, Hamilton believed, lay with the country's monied classes. If the wealthiest people could be persuaded that their economic self-interest could be advanced by the central government, they would strengthen it and, by so doing, bring a greater measure of prosperity to the common people. From Hamilton's perspective, there was no conflict between private greed and public good; one was the source of the other.

In almost every detail, Jefferson challenged Hamilton's analysis. The secretary of state assumed that the strength of the American economy lay not in its industrial potential but in its agricultural productivity. He recognized the necessity of change, and because he thought that persons who worked the soil were more responsible citizens than those who labored in factories for wages, he encouraged the nation's farmers to participate in an expanding international market.

Unlike Hamilton, Jefferson expressed faith in the ability of the American people to shape policy. He had a boundless optimism in the judgment of the common folk. He instinctively trusted the people, feared that uncontrolled government power might destroy their liberties, and insisted that public officials follow the letter of the Constitution. The greatest threat to the young republic, he argued, came from the corrupt activities of pseudo aristocrats, persons who placed the protection of property and civil order above the preservation of liberty. Under no circumstances did he want to mortgage the nation's future—through the creation of a large national debt—to the selfish interests of bankers, manufacturers, and financial speculators.

HAMILTON'S PLAN FOR PROSPERITY AND SECURITY

The unsettled state of the nation's finances presented a staggering challenge to the new government. Congress turned to Hamilton for a policy, and he eagerly accepted the assignment. He read deeply in abstruse economic literature, but the reports he wrote bore the unmistakable stamp of his own creative genius. The secretary synthesized a vast amount of information into an economic blueprint so complex and so innovative that even his allies were slightly baffled. Certainly, Washington never fully grasped the subtleties of Hamilton's plan.

The secretary presented his *Report on the Public Credit* to Congress on January 14, 1790. His research revealed that the nation's outstanding debt stood at approximately $54 million. This sum represented various foreign and domestic obligations that the United States government had incurred during the Revolutionary War. But that was not all. The states still owed creditors approximately $25 million. During the 1780s, Americans desperate for cash had been forced to sell government loan certificates to speculators at greatly discounted prices, and it was estimated that approximately $40 million of the nation's debt was owed to twenty thousand people, only 20 percent of whom were the original creditors.

Funding and Assumption

Hamilton's report contained two major recommendations covering the areas of funding and assumption. First, under his plan, the United States promised to fund its foreign and domestic obligations at full face value. Current holders of loan certificates, whoever they were and no matter how they obtained the documents, could exchange the old certificates for new government bonds bearing a moderate rate of interest. Second, the secretary urged the federal government to assume responsibility for paying the remaining state debts.

Hamilton reasoned that his credit system would accomplish several desirable goals. It would significantly reduce the power of the individual states to shape national economic policy, something Hamilton regarded as essential in maintaining a strong federal government. Moreover, the creation of a fully funded national debt signaled to investors throughout the world that the United States was now solvent, that its bonds represented a good risk. Hamilton hoped that American investment capital would remain in America, providing a source of money for commercial and industrial growth, rather than flow to Europe. In short, Hamilton invited the country's wealthiest citizens to invest in the future of the United States.

To Hamilton's great surprise, his friend Madison attacked the funding scheme in the House of Representatives. He, too, wanted the United States to pay its debts, but he was more concerned with the original buyers of the certificates than with the speculators who had purchased them from the hard-pressed patriots. However, far too many records had been lost since the Revolution for the Treasury Department to be able to identify all the original holders. In the end, Congress sided with Hamilton's more practical position.

Assumption unleashed even greater criticism. Hamilton's program seemed designed to reward states that had not paid their debts. In addition, the secretary's opponents in Congress became suspicious that assumption was only a ploy to increase the power and wealth of Hamilton's immediate friends. On April 12, 1790, a rebellious House, led by Madison, defeated assumption.

The victory was short-lived. Hamilton and congressional supporters resorted to legislative horse trading to revive his foundering program. In exchange for locating the new federal capital on the Potomac River, a move that would stimulate the depressed economy of northern Virginia, several key congressmen who shared Madison's political philosophy changed their votes on assumption. In August, Washington signed assumption and funding into law. The first element of Hamilton's design was now securely in place.

Interpreting the Constitution: The Bank Controversy

The persistent Hamilton submitted his second report to Congress in January 1791. He proposed that the United States government charter a national bank. This privately owned institution would be funded in part by the federal government. The **Bank of the United States** not only would serve as the main depository of the United States government but also would issue currency acceptable in payment of federal taxes. Because of that guarantee, the money would maintain its value while in circulation.

Bank of the United States
National bank proposed by Secretary of the Treasury Alexander Hamilton and established in 1791. It served as a central depository for the U.S. government and had the authority to issue currency.

Madison and others in Congress immediately raised a howl of protest. They feared that banks might "perpetuate a large monied interest" in America. And what about the Constitution? That document said nothing specifically about chartering financial corporations, and they warned that if Hamilton and his supporters were allowed to stretch fundamental law on this occasion, they could not be held back in the future. On this issue, Hamilton stubbornly refused to compromise.

The intense controversy involving his closest advisers worried the president. Even though the bank bill passed Congress (February 8), Washington seriously considered vetoing the legislation on constitutional grounds. Before doing so, however, he requested written opinions from the members of his cabinet. Jefferson's rambling attack on the bank was wholly predictable; Hamilton's defense was masterful. He boldly articulated a doctrine of *implied powers*—that the "necessary and proper" clause of the Constitution (Article I, Section 8) gave Congress more power than it specified. Neither Madison nor Jefferson had anticipated this interpretation of the Constitution. Hamilton's so-called loose construction carried the day, and on February 25, 1791, Washington signed the bank act into law.

Hamilton triumphed in Congress, but the general public regarded his actions with growing fear and hostility. Many persons associated huge national debts and privileged banks with the decay of public virtue. They believed that Hamilton was intent on turning the future of America over to corrupt speculators. To backcountry farmers, making money without actually engaging in physical labor appeared immoral, unrepublican, and un-American. When the greed of a former Treasury Department official led to several serious bankruptcies in 1792, people began to listen more closely to what Madison, Jefferson, and their associates were saying about growing corruption in high places.

Setback for Hamilton

In his third major report, *Report on Manufactures,* submitted to Congress in December 1791, Hamilton revealed the final details of his grand design for the economic future of the United States. The lengthy document suggested ways by which the federal government might stimulate manufacturing and thus free itself from dependence on European imports. What was needed was direct government intervention. Hamilton argued that protective tariffs and special industrial bounties would greatly accelerate the growth of a balanced economy, and with proper planning, the United States would soon hold its own with England and France.

In Congress, the battle lines were clearly drawn. Hamilton's opponents ignored his economic arguments and instead engaged him on moral and political grounds. Madison took a states' rights position and railed against the dangers of "consolidation," a process that threatened to concentrate all power in the federal government, leaving the states defenseless. Jefferson argued that the development of manufacturing entailed urbanization, and cities bred every sort of vice. Other southern congressmen saw tariffs and bounties as vehicles for enriching Hamilton's northern friends at the planters' expense. The recommendations in the *Report on Manufactures* were soundly defeated in the House of Representatives.

Washington detested political squabbling. In August 1792, he begged Hamilton and Jefferson to rise above their differences. The appeal came too late. Hamilton's reports eroded the goodwill of 1788, and by the conclusion of Washington's term, neither secretary trusted the other's judgment. Their sparring had produced congressional factions, but as yet no real parties with permanent organizations that engaged in campaigning had come into existence.

CHARGES OF TREASON: THE BATTLE OVER FOREIGN AFFAIRS

During Washington's second presidential term (1793–1797), war in Europe dramatically thrust foreign affairs into the forefront of American life. Officials who had disagreed over Hamilton's economic policies now were divided by the fighting between France and Britain. Bitter feelings, inflamed emotions, and accusations of treason were common. This poisonous atmosphere spawned the formation of formal political organizations—the Federalists and the Republicans. The clash between the groups developed over how best to preserve the new republic. The Republicans advocated states' rights, strict interpretation of the Constitution, friendship with France, and vigilance against "the avaricious, monopolizing Spirit of Commerce and Commercial Man." The Federalists urged a strong national government, central economic planning, closer ties with Great Britain, and maintenance of public order, even if that meant calling out federal troops.

The Peril of Neutrality

Great Britain treated the United States with arrogance. Contrary to the instructions of the Treaty of 1783, British troops continued to occupy military posts in the Northwest Territory. Moreover, even though 75 percent of American imports came from Great Britain, that country refused to grant the United States full commercial reciprocity.

France presented a very different challenge. In the spring of 1789, the **French Revolution** began, and Louis XVI was dethroned. The men who seized power were militant republicans, ideologues eager to liberate all Europe from feudal institutions. Once the French Revolution was set in motion, however, the leaders lost control. Constitutional reform turned into bloody purges, and one radical group, the Jacobins, guillotined thousands of people during the so-called Reign of Terror (October 1793–July 1794). These horrific events left Americans confused. While those who shared Jefferson's views celebrated the spread of republicanism, those who sided with Hamilton condemned French expansionism and political excess.

French Revolution A social and political revolution in France (1789–1799) that toppled the monarchy.

In the face of growing international tension, neutrality seemed the most prudent course for the United States. But the policy was easier for a weak country to proclaim than to defend. In February 1793, France declared war on Great Britain, and both countries immediately challenged the official American position on shipping: "free ships make free goods," meaning that belligerents should not interfere with the shipping of neutral carriers. To make matters worse, no one was certain whether the Franco-American treaties of 1778 (see Chapter 5) legally bound the United States to support its old ally against Great Britain.

Both Hamilton and Jefferson wanted to avoid war. Jefferson believed that if Great Britain refused to honor America's neutrality and observe neutral shipping rights—in other words, if the Royal Navy seized American sailors—then the United States should award France special trade advantages. Hamilton thought Jefferson's scheme insane. He pointed out that Britain possessed the largest navy in the world and was not likely to be coerced by American threats. The United States, he advised, should appease the former mother country, even if that meant swallowing national pride.

A newly appointed French minister to the United States, Edmond Genêt, precipitated the first major diplomatic crisis. This incompetent young man arrived in Charleston, South Carolina, in April 1793. He found considerable popular enthusiasm for the French Revolution, and heartened by this reception, he authorized privately owned American vessels to seize British ships in the name of France. Such actions clearly violated United States neutrality and invited British retaliation. When government officials warned Genêt to desist, he threatened to take his appeal directly to the American people, who presumably loved France more than the Washington administration did.

The confrontation particularly embarrassed Jefferson, the most outspoken pro-French member of the cabinet. He condemned Genêt's imprudent actions. Washington did not wait to determine if the treaties of 1778 were still in force. Even before he had formally received the French minister, the president issued a proclamation of neutrality (April 22).

Jay's Treaty Sparks Domestic Unrest

Great Britain failed to take advantage of Genêt's insolence. Instead, it pushed the United States to the brink of war. British forts on U.S. soil in the Northwest Territory remained a constant source of tension. In June 1793, a new element was added. The London government closed French ports to neutral shipping, and in November, its navy captured several hundred American vessels trading in the French West Indies. Outraged members of Congress, especially those who identified with Jefferson and Madison, demanded retaliation, an embargo, a stoppage of debt payment, even war.

Before the rhetoric produced violence, Washington made one final effort to preserve peace. In May 1794, he sent Chief Justice John Jay to London to negotiate a formidable list of grievances. Jay's major objectives were removal of the British forts on U.S. territory, payment for ships taken in the West Indies, improved commercial relations, and acceptance of the American definition of neutral rights.

Jay's mission had little chance of success, partly because Hamilton had secretly informed British officials that the United States would compromise on most issues. Jay did persuade the British to abandon their frontier posts and to allow small American ships to trade in the British West Indies, but they rejected out of hand the United States' position on neutral rights. The British would continue to search American vessels on the high seas for contraband and to seize sailors suspected of being British citizens. Moreover, there would be no compensation for the ships seized in 1793 until the Americans paid British merchants for debts contracted before the Revolution. And to the particular annoyance of Southerners, not a word was said about the slaves that the British army had carried off at the conclusion of the war. Jay may have salvaged the peace, but only by betraying the national interest.

News of **Jay's Treaty** produced an angry outcry in the nation's capital. Even Washington was apprehensive. He submitted the document to the Senate without recommending ratification. After an extremely bitter debate, the upper house, controlled by Federalists, narrowly accepted a revised version of the treaty (June 1795).

The details of the Jay agreement soon leaked to the press. Throughout the country, Jay was burned in effigy. Southerners made known that they would not pay prewar debts to British merchants. And when news of the treaty reached the House of Representatives, a storm of protest broke out. Followers of Jefferson—now calling themselves Republicans—thought they could stop Jay's Treaty in Congress by withholding funds for its implementation.

But the president still had a trump card to play. He raised the possibility that the House was really contemplating his impeachment. Such an action was, of course, unthinkable, and public support quickly swung toward Washington and the Federalists, as the followers of Hamilton were now known. Jay's Treaty was saved, but the division between the two parties was beyond repair.

By the time that Jay's Treaty became law (June 14, 1795), the two giants of Washington's first cabinet had retired. Late in 1793, Jefferson returned to his Virginia plantation, Monticello, where despite his separation from day-to-day political affairs, he remained the chief spokesman for the Republican party. His rival, Hamilton, left the Treasury in January 1795 to return to private life in New York City. He maintained close ties with important Federalist officials, however, and even more than Jefferson, Hamilton concerned himself with the details of party organization.

> **Jay's Treaty** Controversial treaty with Britain negotiated by Chief Justice John Jay in 1794 to settle American grievances and avert war. Though the British agreed to surrender forts on U.S. territory, the treaty failed to realize key diplomatic goals and provoked a storm of protest in America.

Pushing the Native Americans Aside

Before Great Britain finally withdrew its troops from the western forts in 1796, its military officers encouraged local tribes to attack settlers and traders from the United States. The Indians won several impressive victories over federal troops in the area that would become western Ohio and Indiana. But the tribes were actually more vulnerable than they realized, for when they met up with the United States army under the command of General Anthony Wayne, they received no support from their British allies. At the battle of Fallen Timbers (August 20, 1794), Wayne's forces crushed Indian resistance in the Northwest Territory, and the tribes were compelled to sign the Treaty of Greenville, formally ceding to the United States government much of the land that became Ohio.

Shrewd negotiations mixed with pure luck helped secure the nation's southwestern frontier. For complex reasons having to do with the state of European diplomacy, Spanish officials in 1795 encouraged the United States' representative in Madrid to discuss navigation on the Mississippi River. Before this initiative, the Spanish government had not only closed the river to American commerce but also incited the Indians of the region to harass U.S. settlers (see Chapter 6). Relations between the two countries would probably have deteriorated further had the United States not signed Jay's Treaty. The Spanish assumed—quite erroneously—that Great Britain and the United States had formed an alliance to strip Spain of its North American possessions.

■ *At the Treaty of Greenville in 1795, negotiators shared this calumet, or peace pipe, a spiritually symbolic act for Native Americans. This superficial recognition of the legitimacy of Native American cultures barely disguised the Indians' crushing loss of sovereignty.* ■

To avoid the imagined disaster, officials in Madrid offered the American envoy, Thomas Pinckney, extraordinary concessions: the opening of the Mississippi, the right to deposit goods in New Orleans without paying duties, a secure southern boundary on the 31st parallel, and a promise to stay out of Indian affairs. An amazed Pinckney signed the Treaty of San Lorenzo (also called Pinckney's Treaty) on October 27, 1795, and in March, the Senate ratified the document without a single dissenting vote.

POPULAR POLITICAL CULTURE

Ratification of Jay's Treaty generated intense political strife during Washington's administration. It divided Americans along party lines at a time when parties were viewed as subversive. Party conflict also suggested that Americans had lost the sense of common purpose that had united them during the Revolution. Politicians agreed that opposition smacked of disloyalty and therefore should be eliminated by any means, fair or foul. But who should eliminate whom? That was the question that occupied both Federalists and Republicans.

More than any other single element, newspapers transformed the political culture of the United States. Americans were voracious readers, and they were well supplied with newspapers. Most of the journals were fiercely partisan. Rumor and opinion were presented as fact, and public officials were regularly dragged through

CONQUEST OF THE WEST *Withdrawal of the British, defeat of Native Americans, and negotiations with Spain secured the nation's frontiers.* ■

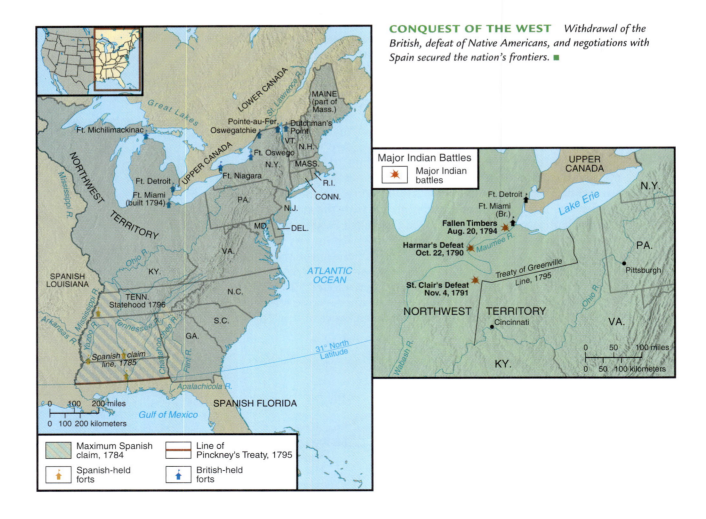

the rhetorical mud. Jefferson, for example, was accused of cowardice, and Hamilton was vilified as an adulterer.

Even poets and essayists were caught up in the political fray. The better writers often produced party propaganda. American writers sometimes complained that the culture of the young republic was too materialistic, too unappreciative of the subtler forms of art then popular in Europe. But it was clear that poets who ignored patriotism and politics simply did not sell well in the United States.

The decade also witnessed the birth of political clubs. Modeled on the political debating societies that sprang up in France during the early years of the French Revolution, the clubs emphasized political indoctrination. By 1794, at least twenty-four clubs were holding regular meetings. Along with newspapers, they provided the common people with highly partisan political information.

Whiskey Rebellion: Charges of Republican Conspiracy

Political tensions became explosive in 1794. The Federalists convinced themselves that the Republicans were actually prepared to employ violence against the U.S. government. Though the charge was without foundation, it took on plausibility in the context of growing party strife.

The crisis developed when a group of farmers living in western Pennsylvania protested a federal excise tax on distilled whiskey that Congress had originally passed in 1791. These men did not relish paying any taxes, but this tax struck them as particularly unfair. They made a good deal of money distilling their grain into whiskey, but the excise could seriously reduce the profits.

Largely because the Republican governor of Pennsylvania refused to suppress the angry farmers, Washington and other leading Federalists assumed that the insurrection represented a direct political challenge. The president called out fifteen thousand militiamen, and accompanied by Hamilton, he marched against the rebels. The expedition was an embarrassing fiasco. The distillers disappeared, and, predictably enough, no one living in the Pittsburgh region seemed to know where the troublemakers had gone. Two supposed rebels were convicted of high crimes against the United States, one reportedly a "simpleton" and the other insane. Washington eventually pardoned both men. As peace returned to the frontier, Republicans gained much electoral support from voters whom Federalists had alienated.

In the national political forum, however, the **Whiskey Rebellion** had just begun. Washington blamed the "Republican" clubs for promoting civil unrest. Jefferson labeled the entire episode a Hamiltonian device to create an army for the purpose of intimidating Republicans. How else could one explain the administration's gross overreaction to a few disgruntled farmers? The response of both parties reveals a pervasive fear of some secret, evil design to destroy the republic. The clubs and newspapers fanned these anxieties, convincing many government officials that the First Amendment should not be interpreted as protecting political dissent.

Whiskey Rebellion Protests in 1794 by western Pennsylvania farmers resisting payment of a federal tax on whiskey. The uprising was forcibly suppressed when President George Washington called an army of 15,000 troops to the area, where they encountered almost no resistance.

Washington's Farewell

In September 1796, Washington published his famed **Farewell Address,** formally declaring his intention to retire from the presidency. Written largely by Hamilton, drawing on a draft by Madison, it sought to advance the Federalist cause in the forthcoming election. By waiting until September to announce his retirement, Washington denied the Republicans valuable time to organize an effective campaign. There was an element of irony in this initiative. Washington had always maintained that he stood above party lines. Though he may have done so in the early years of his presidency, events such as the signing of Jay's Treaty and the suppression of the Whiskey Rebellion transformed him in the eyes of many Americans into a spokesman solely for Hamilton's Federalist party.

Farewell Address In this 1796 speech, President George Washington announced his intention not to seek a third term in office. He also stressed federalist interests and warned the American people to avoid political factions and foreign entanglements that could sacrifice U.S. security.

In the address, Washington issued two warnings. First, he warned his country against all political factions. Second, he counseled the United States to avoid making any permanent alliances with distant nations that had no real interest in promoting American security. If few Americans paid attention to the first part of his message, the second part guided foreign relations for many years and became the credo of later American isolationists.

THE ADAMS PRESIDENCY

The election of 1796 took place in an atmosphere of mutual distrust. Jefferson, candidate of the Republicans, believed he was running against American representatives of the British aristocracy. The Federalists were convinced that their Republican opponents wanted to hand the government over to French radicals. By modern standards, the structures of both parties and the campaign methods employed were still primitive.

During the campaign, the Federalists sowed the seeds of their eventual destruction. Party stalwarts agreed that John Adams should run against Jefferson. Hamilton, however, could not leave well enough alone. From his law office in New York City, he schemed to deprive Adams of the presidency. He apparently feared that an independent-minded Adams would be difficult to manipulate. He was correct.

Hamilton exploited an awkward feature of the electoral college. In accordance with the Constitution, each elector cast two ballots, and the person who gained the most votes became president. The runner-up, regardless of party affiliation, served as vice president. Ordinarily, the Federalist electors would have cast one vote for Adams and one for Thomas Pinckney, the party's choice for vice president. Everyone hoped, of course, that there would be no tie. Hamilton secretly urged southern Federalists to support Pinckney with their first vote, which meant throwing away an elector's second vote. The strategy backfired when New Englanders loyal to Adams heard of Hamilton's maneuvering. They dropped Pinckney, and when the votes were counted, Adams had 71, Jefferson 68, and Pinckney 59. Hamilton's treachery not only angered the new president but also heightened tensions within the Federalist party.

Adams assumed the presidency under intolerable conditions. He found himself saddled with the members of Washington's old cabinet, who regularly consulted with Hamilton behind Adams's back. But to have dismissed them summarily would have called Washington's judgment into question, and Adams was not prepared publicly to take that risk. Adams also had to work with a Republican vice president. Adams hoped that he and Jefferson could cooperate, but partisan pressures soon overwhelmed the president's good intentions. After a short time, Adams stopped consulting Jefferson.

The XYZ Affair and Domestic Politics

Foreign affairs immediately occupied Adams's full attention. The French government regarded Jay's Treaty as an affront. By allowing Great Britain to define the condition for neutrality, the United States had in effect sided with that nation against the interest of France.

Relations between the two countries steadily deteriorated. The French dismissed Charles Cotesworth Pinckney, the United States' representative in Paris, and the French minister in Philadelphia openly supported Jefferson for president in 1796. In 1797, French privateers began seizing American ships. During this period, neither country bothered to declare war, and for that reason the hostilities came to be known as the Quasi-War.

Hamilton and his friends welcomed the popular outpouring of anti-French sentiment. They counseled the president to prepare for all-out war, hoping that war

would purge the United States of French influence. Adams was not persuaded to escalate the conflict. Instead he sent a three-member commission—Charles Pinckney, John Marshall, and Elbridge Gerry—to Paris in a final attempt to remove the sources of antagonism. They were instructed to obtain compensation for the ships seized by French privateers as well as release from the treaties of 1778. In exchange, the commission offered France the same commercial privileges granted to Great Britain in Jay's Treaty.

The commission was shocked by the outrageous treatment it received in France. Instead of dealing directly with Talleyrand, the French minister of foreign relations, they met with obscure intermediaries who reported that Talleyrand would not open negotiations unless he was given $250,000. In addition, the French government expected a "loan" of millions of dollars. The Americans refused to play the insulting game.

The event set off a domestic political explosion. When Adams presented the commission's official correspondence before Congress—the names of Talleyrand's lackeys were disguised as X, Y, and Z—the Federalists burst out with a war cry. At last, because of the **XYZ Affair,** they would be able to even old scores with the Republicans. So tense was the atmosphere that old friendships between Federalists and Republicans were shattered. As Jefferson wrote to an old colleague: "Men who have been intimate all their lives, cross the streets to avoid meeting, and turn their heads another way, lest they should be obliged to touch their hats."

XYZ Affair A diplomatic incident in which American peace commissioners sent to France by President John Adams in 1797 were insulted with bribe demands from their French counterparts, dubbed X, Y, and Z in American newspapers. The incident heightened war fever against France.

Crushing Political Dissent

In the spring of 1798, the followers of Hamilton—called High Federalists—assumed that it was just a matter of time until Adams asked Congress for a formal declaration of war. In the meantime, they pushed for a general rearmament, new fighting ships, additional harbor fortifications, and a greatly expanded U.S. army. About the need for land forces, Adams remained understandably skeptical. He saw no likelihood of a French invasion.

The president missed the political point. The army the Federalists wanted was intended not to thwart French aggression but to stifle internal opposition. Indeed, militant Federalists used the XYZ Affair as the occasion to institute what Jefferson termed the "reign of witches." Jefferson was right; the threat to Republicans was real.

During the summer of 1798, a provisional army gradually came into existence. George Washington agreed to lead the troops, but he would do so only on condition that Adams appoint Hamilton as second in command. Although Adams did not want to promote Hamilton to the command over others who outranked him and were more agreeable, he was not about to refuse Washington's request.

The chief of the High Federalists threw himself into the task of recruiting and supplying the troops. No detail escaped his attention. Only loyal Federalists received a commission—even Adams's son-in-law was denied a post—as Hamilton put the finishing touches on his plan to restore domestic order. The mood of the nation grew tense, and many politicians predicted that a civil war would soon erupt.

Hamilton should not have treated Adams with such open contempt. After all, without presidential cooperation, Hamilton could not fulfill his grand military ambitions. Whenever pressing questions concerning the army arose, Adams was nowhere to be found. He delayed Hamilton at every step, making it quite clear that his first love was the navy. In May 1798, the president even persuaded Congress to establish the Navy Department. Moreover, Adams steadfastly refused to ask Congress for a formal declaration of war. As the weeks passed, the American people increasingly regarded the idle army as an expensive extravagance.

Silencing Political Opposition: The Alien and Sedition Acts

Alien and Sedition Acts
Collective name given to four laws passed in 1798 designed to suppress criticism of the federal government and to curb liberties of foreigners living in the United States.

The Federalists did not rely solely on the army to crush political dissent. During the summer of 1798, the party's majority in Congress passed a group of bills known collectively as the **Alien and Sedition Acts.** The legislation authorized the use of federal courts and the powers of the presidency to silence the Republicans. The acts were born of fear and vindictiveness, and in their efforts to punish the followers of Jefferson, the Federalists created the nation's first major crisis over civil liberties.

Congress drew up three separate Alien Acts. The first, the Alien Enemies Law, vested the president with extraordinary wartime powers. On his own authority, he could detain or deport foreigners who behaved in a manner he thought suspicious. Due to the fact that Adams refused to ask for a declaration of war, this legislation never went into effect. The second act, the Alien Law, empowered the president to expel any foreigner from the United States simply by executive decree. Though Adams did not attempt to enforce the act, the mere threat of arrest caused some Frenchmen to flee the country. The third act, the Naturalization Law, was the most flagrantly political of the group. The act established a fourteen-year probationary period before foreigners could apply for full U.S. citizenship. This act was designed to limit the "hordes of wild Irishmen" and other immigrants who voted Republican.

The Sedition Law struck at the heart of free political exchange. It defined criticism of the U.S. government as criminal libel; citizens found guilty by a jury were subject to fines and imprisonment. Republicans were justly worried that the Sedition Law undermined rights guaranteed by the First Amendment. As far as the Federalists were concerned, if their opposition could be silenced, they were willing to restrict freedom of speech.

Americans living in widely scattered regions of the country soon witnessed political repression firsthand. District courts staffed by Federalist appointees indicted seventeen people for criticizing the government. The most celebrated trial occurred in Vermont. A Republican congressman, Matthew Lyon, who was running for re-election, publicly accused the Adams administration of mishandling the Quasi-War. Lyon, an Irish immigrant, had earlier angered Federalists by spitting in the eye of a Federalist congressman during a heated exchange. Now a Federalist court was pleased to have the opportunity to convict him of libel. But Lyon enjoyed the last laugh. While he served his term in jail, his constituents reelected him to Congress.

As this and other cases demonstrated, the federal courts had become political tools. Although the fumbling efforts at enforcement of the Sedition Law did not silence opposition—indeed, they sparked even greater criticism and created martyrs—the actions of the administration persuaded Republicans that the survival of free government was at stake.

Kentucky and Virginia Resolutions

By the fall of 1798, Jefferson and Madison were convinced that the Federalists envisioned the creation of a police state. Some extreme Republicans such as John Taylor of Virginia recommended secession from the Union; others advocated armed resistance. But Jefferson wisely counseled against such extreme strategies. Instead he turned to the state legislatures for help.

As the crisis deepened, Jefferson and Madison drafted separate protests known, respectively, as the **Kentucky and Virginia Resolutions.** Both statements vigorously defended the right of individual state assemblies to interpret the constitutionality of federal law. Jefferson wrote the Kentucky Resolutions in November 1798, and in an outburst of partisan anger, he flirted with a doctrine as dangerous to the survival of the United States as anything advanced by Hamilton and his High Federalist friends.

In the Kentucky Resolutions, Jefferson described the federal union as a compact. The states transferred certain explicit powers to the national government, but in his opinion, they retained full authority over all matters not specifically mentioned in the Constitution. Jefferson rejected Hamilton's broad interpretation of the "general welfare" clause. He believed that individual states had the right to nullify any law that was not specifically within the charter of the Constitution. Carried to an extreme, Jefferson's logic could have led to the breakup of the federal government. Although Madison agreed that the Alien and Sedition Acts were unconstitutional, his Virginia Resolutions were more moderate than Jefferson's Kentucky Resolutions.

The Kentucky and Virginia Resolutions must be viewed in proper historical context. They were not intended as statements of abstract principles and most certainly not as a justification for southern secession. They were pure political party propaganda. Jefferson and Madison were simply reminding American voters during a period of severe domestic tension that the Republicans offered a clear alternative to Federalist rule.

In the early years of the republic, political dissent sometimes escalated to physical violence. This fistfight took place on the floor of Congress, February 15, 1798. The combatants are Republican Matthew Lyon and Federalist Roger Griswold.

Kentucky and Virginia Resolutions Statements penned by Thomas Jefferson and James Madison to mobilize opposition to the Alien and Sedition Acts, which they argued were unconstitutional. Jefferson's statement (the Kentucky Resolutions) suggested that states should have the right to declare null and void congressional acts they deemed unconstitutional. Madison produced a more temperate resolution, but most Americans rejected such an extreme defense of states' rights.

Adams's Finest Hour

In February 1799, President Adams belatedly declared his independence from the Hamiltonian wing of the Federalist party. Throughout the confrontation with France, Adams had shown little enthusiasm for war, and after the XYZ Affair, the French changed their tune. Talleyrand now sent word that he was ready to negotiate in good faith. The High Federalists ridiculed this report, but Adams decided to accept the peace initiative. In February, he asked the Senate to confirm William Vans Murray as the United States' representative to France.

In November 1799, Murray and several other negotiators arrived in France. By then, Napoleon Bonaparte had come to power, but he cooperated with the Americans. Together, they drew up an agreement known as the Convention of Mortefontaine. The French refused to compensate the Americans for vessels taken during the Quasi-War, but they did declare the treaties of 1778 null and void. Moreover, the convention removed annoying French restrictions on United States commerce. Not only had Adams avoided war, but he had also created an atmosphere of mutual trust that paved the way for the purchase of the Louisiana Territory. The negotiations brought Adams personal satisfaction, but they cost him reelection.

THE PEACEFUL REVOLUTION: THE ELECTION OF 1800

On the eve of the election of 1800, the Federalists were fatally divided between the followers of both Adams and Hamilton. Once again, the former secretary of the treasury attempted to rig the voting in the electoral college so that the party's vice presidential candidate, Charles Cotesworth Pinckney, would receive more ballots than Adams did. Again the conspiracy backfired, and the Republicans carried the election.

A Look at the Past

Washington Mourning Art

The death of George Washington on December 14, 1799, was followed by an outpouring of collective mourning expressed in poetry, music, art, and memorial items, both mass produced and made by hand. Portrait miniatures of Washington were especially popular and allowed people to pay their respects in an intimate way, wearing a small icon of the nation's first president around their necks or pinned to their lapels. Women with skills in needlepoint also made elaborate scenes of mourners at Washington's tomb, surrounded by weeping willows and angels. This engraving from c. 1801 by artist Thomas Clarke shows a weeping man and woman and the figure of Columbia with her arm raised visiting George Washington's tomb, which is decorated with a portrait of Washington and the epitaph "There is rest in Heaven." At the bottom of the engraving there is an inscription "Sacred to the Memory of the Illustrious G. Washington." ✳ Why do you think Washington's death triggered such widespread expressions of grief? How do you think public rituals and the production of memorial items commemorating Washington's death might have affected how people viewed the process of mourning the loss of other national figures or members of their own families? Have you seen more recent examples of mourning art? If so, who is being commemorated?

Chronology

1787	Constitution of the United States signed (September)
1789	George Washington inaugurated (April) ■ Louis XVI of France calls meeting of the Estates General (May)
1790	Congress approves Hamilton's plan for funding and assumption (July)
1791	Bank of the United States is chartered (February) ■ Hamilton's *Report on Manufactures* is rejected by Congress (December)
1793	France's revolutionary government announces a "war of all people against all kings" (February) ■ Genêt affair strains relations with France (April) ■ Washington issues Proclamation of Neutrality (April) ■ Spread of "democratic" clubs alarms Federalists ■ Jefferson resigns as secretary of state (December)
1794	Whiskey Rebellion is put down by the United States Army (July–November) ■ General Anthony Wayne defeats Indians at the battle of Fallen Timbers (August)
1795	Hamilton resigns as secretary of the treasury (January) ■ Jay's Treaty divides the nation (June) ■ Pinckney's Treaty with Spain is a welcome surprise (October)
1796	Washington publishes his Farewell Address (September) ■ John Adams is elected president (December)
1797	XYZ Affair poisons U.S. relations with France (October)
1798	Quasi-War with France begins ■ Congress passes the Alien and Sedition Acts (June, July) ■ Provisional army is formed ■ Kentucky and Virginia Resolutions protest the Alien and Sedition Acts (November, December)
1799	George Washington dies (December)
1800	Convention of Mortefontaine is signed with France, ending the Quasi-War (September)
1801	House of Representatives elects Thomas Jefferson president (February)

But to everyone's surprise, the election was not resolved in the electoral college. When the ballots were counted, Jefferson and his running mate, Aaron Burr, had tied. This accident—a Republican elector should have thrown away his second vote—sent the selection of the next president to the House of Representatives, a body still controlled by members of the Federalist party.

As the House began its work on February 27, 1801, excitement ran high. Each state delegation cast a single vote, with nine votes needed to be elected. The drama dragged on for days. To add to the confusion, the ambitious Burr refused to withdraw. Finally, leading Federalists decided that Jefferson, whatever his faults, would make a more responsible president than the shifty Burr. On the thirty-sixth ballot, Jefferson was elected. The Twelfth Amendment, ratified in 1804, saved the American people from repeating this potentially dangerous turn of events. Henceforth, the electoral college cast separate ballots for president and vice president.

During the final days of his presidency, Adams appointed as many Federalists as possible to the federal bench. Jefferson protested the hasty manner in which these "midnight judges" were selected. One of them, John Marshall, became chief justice of the United States, a post he held with distinction for thirty-four years. But behind the last-minute flurry of activity lay bitterness and disappointment. On the morning of Jefferson's inauguration, Adams slipped away from the capital—now located in Washington—unnoticed and unappreciated.

In the address that Adams missed, Jefferson attempted to quiet partisan fears. "We are all Republicans; we are all Federalists," he declared. He did not mean that there were no longer any party differences, only that all politicians shared a deep commitment to a federal union based on republican ideals. Indeed, the president interpreted the election of 1800 as a fulfillment of the principles of 1776.

CONCLUSION: DANGER OF POLITICAL EXTREMISM

From a broader historical perspective, the election of 1800 seems noteworthy for what did not occur. There were no riots in the streets, no attempted coup by military officers, no secession from the Union, nothing except the peaceful transfer of government from the leaders of one political party to those of the opposition.

Americans had weathered the Alien and Sedition Acts, the meddling by predatory foreign powers in domestic affairs, the shrilly partisan rhetoric of hack journalists, and now, at the start of a new century, they were impressed with their own achievement. As one woman who attended Jefferson's inauguration noted, "The changes of administration which in every government and in every age have most generally been epochs of confusion, villainy and bloodshed, in this our happy country take place without any species of distraction, or disorder." But as she well understood—indeed, as modern Americans must constantly relearn—extremism in the name of partisan political truth can easily unravel the delicate fabric of representative democracy and leave the republic at the mercy of those who would manipulate the public for private benefit.

KEY TERMS

Bank of the United States, p. 130

French Revolution, p. 131

Jay's Treaty, p. 133

Whiskey Rebellion, p. 135

Farewell Address, p. 135

XYZ Affair, p. 137

Alien and Sedition Acts, p. 138

Kentucky and Virginia Resolutions, p. 139

RECOMMENDED READING

The sudden development of deeply partisan politics on the national level dominated public life during the 1790s. Several recent accounts capture the sense of anger and disappointment that informed the political culture: Joanne B. Freeman, *Affairs of Honor: National Politics in the New Republic* (2001) and Joseph J. Ellis, *Founding Brothers: The Revolutionary Generation* (2000). Joyce Appleby provides useful insights into the ideological tensions that divided former allies in *Liberalism and Republicanism in the Historical Imagination* (1992). Jack N. Rakove offers a fine short introduction to James Madison's political thought in *James Madison and the Creation of the American Republic* (1990). An excellent discussion of the conflicting economic visions put forward by Hamilton and Jefferson can be found in Drew McCoy, *The Elusive Republic: The Political Economy in Jeffersonian America* (1980). Anyone curious about the controversial rise of political parties should consult Richard Hofstadter, *The Idea of a Party System: The Rise of Legitimate Opposition in the United States, 1780–1840* (1997) and

Stanley Elkins and Eric McKitrick, *The Age of Federalism: The Early Republic* (1993). One can obtain many useful and readable biographies of the dominant leaders of the period. Two more analytic studies are Peter Onuf, ed., *Jeffersonian Legacies* (1993) and Paul K. Longmore, *The Invention of George Washington* (1999). How Americans constructed a convincing sense of national identity is examined in David Waldstreicher, *In the Midst of Perpetual Fetes: The Making of American Nationalism, 1776–1820* (1997). Two regional studies suggest how republican values worked themselves out among ordinary people: Alan Taylor, *Liberty Men and Great Proprietors: The Revolutionary Settlement of the Maine Frontier, 1760–1820* (1990) and Andrew Cayton, *Frontier Republic: Ideology and Politics in Ohio Country, 1780–1825* (1986). Conor Cruise O'Brien helps explain why foreign affairs, especially with the leaders of the French Revolution, disrupted domestic politics: *The Long Affair: Thomas Jefferson and the French Revolution, 1785–1800* (1996).

Suggested Web Sites

Temple of Liberty—Building the Capitol for a New Nation
www.lcweb.loc.gov/exhibits/us.capitol/s0.html
Compiled from holdings in the Library of Congress, this site contains detailed information on the design and early construction of the Capitol building in Washington, D.C.

U.S. Electoral College
www.nara.gov/fedreg/elctcoll/index.html
This National Archives and Records Administration site explains how the electoral college works.

George Washington Papers
www.virginia.edu/gwpapers/
Information on the publishing project, with selected documents, essays, and an index of the published volumes.

George Washington's Mount Vernon
www.mountvernon.org/
Pictures and documents of Mount Vernon, the home of the first president, George Washington.

George Washington Papers at the Library of Congress, 1741–1799
memory.loc.gov/ammem/gwhtml/gwhome.html
This site is described as follows: "The complete George Washington Papers from the Manuscript Division at the Library of Congress consists of approximately 65,000 documents. This is the largest collection of original Washington documents in the world."

Archiving Early America
earlyamerica.com/
Old newspapers are excellent windows into the issues of the past. This site includes the Keigwin and Matthews collection of historic newspapers.

John Adams
www.ipl.org/div/potus/jadams.html
This Internet Public Library page contains biographical information about the second president, his inaugural address, and links to more information.

Counting the People
The Federal Census of 1790

Modern Americans have more or less come to take the federal census for granted. During the early days of the new national government, however, no one had much experience in counting the people. The various imperial administrators who ruled before the Revolution had only a very rough sense of how many men and women lived in Great Britain's mainland colonies, and population estimates advanced by able mathematicians such as Benjamin Franklin amounted to little more than informed speculation. But the creation of a representative republic, one that boldly claimed to reflect the will of "We the People of the United States," demanded much greater precision.

As they struggled to organize a new federal government, the delegates to the Constitutional Convention had to figure out how to apportion "representation and direct taxation" among the states. The ineffectual Articles of Confederation provided no practical solution for determining either, stipulating simply that each state—regardless of size—have a single vote in Congress. Moreover, during the 1780s the states had the responsibility of levying and collecting federal taxes, leading their assemblies to try any connivance to lighten the local tax burden.

The framers of the Constitution solved both problems by basing taxation and representation on a state's population. "It is of great importance," James Madison argued, "that the State should feel as little bias as possible to swell or reduce the amount of their numbers." Madison believed that "were their share of representation alone to be governed by this rule, they would have an interest in exaggerating their inhabitants. Were the rule to decide their share of taxation alone, a

contrary temptation would prevail." In article 1, section 2, the Constitution called for the federal government to conduct a census every ten years. In counting the people, the framers considered white inhabitants as "whole numbers." Indians, who were neither taxed nor represented, would be "excluded" from the count. Slaves, referred to as "all other persons," were neither fully people nor wholly property and were counted as three-fifths of the white population in determining a state's representation in Congress.

The First Congress faced the challenge of putting the admittedly racist principles into practice. Madison lobbied for a schedule that would "embrace some other objects besides the bare enumeration of the inhabitants." The House of Representatives passed an enumeration bill that empowered the federal government to distinguish white males over sixteen years of age from those younger, heads of households from dependents, slaves from free citizens, and men from women. Madison also proposed tallying the occupations of the people so that Congress "might proceed to make property provisions for the agricultural, commercial, and manufacturing interests." Senators modified the bill, voting for an enumeration act that did not require inhabitants to list their occupations. Asking for too many details about personal matters, some suggested, "might excite some disagreeable ideas in the minds of the people," leading to charges "that the Government was too particular, in order to learn their ability to bear the burden of direct or other taxes." After more than two centuries, suspicion about the use of private data still agitates many Americans, who see the

census as potentially compromising their right of privacy.

The first official count began on August 2, 1790. President George Washington appointed Thomas Jefferson, his secretary of state, to administer the census and to oversee the federal marshals who would carry it out. Marshals hired a total of 650 enumerators, each to survey a distinct district or county and to report the findings within nine months. Beyond this charge, they received few instructions. The government agreed to pay enumerators who canvassed cities and towns $1 for every 300 inhabitants they listed. In rural areas, where travel proved difficult and the people scattered, census takers received $1 for every 150 entries they registered.

In some areas of the country, the census progressed smoothly. Boston's enumerator began his work on August 2 and within three weeks had counted each of the city's 18,000 inhabitants. Virginia's federal marshal, Edward Carrington, anticipated similar results as his assistants began their work. "There exists throughout every part of the Country," he declared, "so favorable a disposition upon this subject that I am confident the business will be done with greater accuracy than any person at first expected." Simple entries hastened the process. In the South, for example, enumerators listed slaves as "Peter negro (Chas. Wells property)," and free African Americans as "Ruth Free negro." As returns accumulated, Jefferson exclaimed "The census has made considerable progress." Based on early estimates, "our numbers," he insisted, "will be between 4 and 5 millions." Larger totals were seen as an indication of the nation's commercial prospects and military strength.

Optimism about the first census was short-lived. Assistants faced considerable challenges in reaching a reliable count. In Maine—then still part of Massachusetts—"natural obstacles of woods, hills" as well as "the want of roads" slowed enumerators. "Where the habitations are as scattered as they are in Kentucky," one Congressman warned, marshals "would be obliged to hire a man on purpose to travel over a tract of land of 160 or 170 miles." With uncertain boundaries, poor transportation, and a mobile citizenry, census takers made mistakes. In some regions, they counted inhabitants two or three times. In others, not at all.

Enumerators also encountered men and women who rejected the entire notion of counting the people. A failure to cooperate with the census could result in a $20 fine. Nonetheless, as Washington complained, "the religious scruples of some, would not allow them to give their lists." A number of New Yorkers, who remembered an epidemic that followed an earlier colonial census, refused to participate in 1790 because of "the Sin of David." According to the Old Testament, King David had incurred God's wrath by ordering a head count of the nation of Israel. Although Carrington encountered similar beliefs in Virginia, especially among "old people," he found a way to alleviate the problem. "The assistants, who are truly respectable characters," he argued, "will be able to come at the Numbers in a variety of ways," including interrogating neighbors. Suspicion of federal authority also thwarted an accurate count. Washington believed that a widespread "fear" that the census "was intended as

the foundation of a tax" encouraged inhabitants "to conceal" the truth. A North Carolina enumerator, "after Riding horses almost to Death," could not complete his circuit. No citizen, he found, "that understands will have anything to do with it." In South Carolina, where the census dragged on for eighteen months, the government brought charges against a number of frontier settlers who refused to provide information.

As the final numbers arrived, federal officials could hardly conceal their disappointment. They wanted to demonstrate to European nations the power of the United States, but as Washington conceded, "we shall hardly reach four millions." The final tally of 3,929,214, including 700,000 enslaved African Americans, confirmed the president's fears. Jefferson issued

copies to his ministers abroad with two sets of numbers, an actual count in black ink, another in red reflecting his estimate of a more accurate number. Yet for a cost of $44,377.28 the census proved a bargain. After the count of 1790, Congress increased the number of representatives in the House from 65 to 105 and gained a more certain idea of a proper apportionment of taxation. The count also brought legitimacy to the struggling young government. "The authenticated number," Washington declared, "is far greater . . . than has ever been allowed in Europe, and will have no small influence in enabling them to form a more just opinion of our present and growing importance than has yet been entertained there."

Questions for Discussion

* What information did the 1790 census enumerators gather? Why did they not collect information on occupations?
* Why do you think federal officials wanted to distinguish white males over sixteen years of age from younger white males?
* How has the role of the census changed as the nation expanded? What kind of information does the census gather today?

This Liverpool Ware jug records the results of the nation's first census in 1790. Symbols of prosperity surround the census figures, even though the results disappointed many people who hoped the final count would show a population of more than four million people. ■

Chapter 8

Republican Ascendancy: The Jeffersonian Vision

Limits of Equality

British visitors often disliked Jeffersonian society. Wherever they traveled in the young republic, they met ill-mannered people inspired with a ruling passion for liberty and equality. Charles William Janson, an Englishman who lived in the United States for thirteen years, was particularly upset by the lack of deference in American society. He remembered one woman who worked for an acquaintance of his and who refused to acknowledge that any person was her master. She told Janson: "I'd have you know, *man,* that I am no *sarvant* [sic]; none but *negers* [sic] are *sarvants*."

This was the authentic voice of Jeffersonian republicanism—self-confident, assertive, blatantly racist, and having no intention of being relegated to low social status. The maid believed that she was her employer's equal. She may even have fostered dreams of having employees of her own some day. After all, for the men and women who believed in the vision that Jefferson and other Republicans offered, America was a land of boundless opportunity.

Yet the limits of the Jeffersonian vision were obvious even to contemporaries. The people who spoke most nobly about equality often owned slaves. Little had changed since the Revolution. African Americans, who represented one-fifth of the population of the United States, were totally excluded from the new opportunities opening up in the cities and the West. Indeed, the maid in the incident just described insisted—with no apparent sense of inconsistency—that her position was superior to that of blacks, who were brought involuntarily to lifelong servitude.

It is not surprising that in this highly charged racial climate leaders of the Federalist Party accused the Republicans, especially those who lived in the South, of hypocrisy. The race issue simply would not go away. Beneath the political maneuvering over the acquisition of the Louisiana Territory and of the War of 1812 lay fundamental disagreement about the spread of slavery to the western territories.

In other areas, the Jeffersonians did not fulfill even their own high expectations. As members of the opposition party during the presidency of John Adams, they insisted on a strict interpretation of the Constitution, peaceful foreign relations, and a reduction of the role of the federal government in the lives of the average citizen. But following the election of 1800, Jefferson and his supporters discovered that unanticipated pressures, foreign and domestic, forced them to moderate these goals. Before he retired from public office, Jefferson interpreted the Constitution in a way that permitted the government to purchase the Louisiana Territory when the opportunity arose; he regulated the national economy with a rigor that would have made Alexander Hamilton blush; and he led the country to the brink of war. Some Americans praised the president's pragmatism; others felt betrayed.

REGIONAL IDENTITIES IN A NEW REPUBLIC

During the early decades of the nineteenth century, the population of the United States experienced substantial growth, more the result of natural reproduction than immigration. The 1810 census counted 7,240,000 Americans, a jump of almost 2 million in just ten years. Of this total, approximately 20 percent were blacks. It was a young population. The largest single group in the society was children, boys and girls who were born after Washington's administration and who came of age at a time when the nation's boundaries were rapidly expanding.

Even as Americans defended the rights of individual states, they were forming strong regional identifications. In commerce and politics they perceived themselves as representatives of distinct subcultures, as Southerners, New Englanders, or Westerners. Pride and defensiveness mingled together to produce sectional identities, which in time became stronger than even state loyalties.

This shifting focus of attention resulted not only from an awareness of shared economic interests but also from a sensitivity to outside attacks on slavery. Long before Jefferson died in 1826, Southerners raised the specter of secession and showed how fragile national unity was.

Westward the Course of Empire

The most striking changes occurred in the West. Before the end of the American Revolution, only Indian traders and a few hardy settlers had ventured across the Appalachians. After 1790, however, a flood of people poured west to stake out farms on the rich soil. Pittsburgh and Cincinnati, both strategically located on the Ohio River, became important commercial ports. Congress rapidly formed new territories and admitted new states. Wherever they located, Westerners depended on water transportation. Riverboats represented the cheapest and fastest way to get crops to market. The Mississippi River was the crucial commercial link for the entire region.

Families who moved west attempted to transplant familiar Eastern customs to the frontier. In some areas such as the Western Reserve, a narrow strip of land along Lake Erie in northern Ohio, the influence of New England remained strong. In general, however, a creative mixing of peoples of different backgrounds in a strange environment generated distinctive folkways. They developed their own heroic figures and prided themselves on their toughness, ambition, and self-confidence. Restless and excited by the challenges and opportunities of the frontier, these settlers thought little about packing up their belongings and moving farther west.

Only one obstacle barred the way—Indians. Native Americans still lived in the greater Ohio valley, and they insisted that they owned the land. The tragedy was that the Indians, many of them dependent on trade with whites and ravaged by disease and alcohol, lacked unity. Small groups allegedly representing the interests of an entire tribe sold off huge pieces of land, often for whiskey or trinkets.

These fraudulent transactions disgusted the brilliant Shawnee leaders, Tecumseh, and his brother, Tenskwatawa (known as the Prophet). These men desperately tried to revitalize tribal culture, encouraging Indians to avoid contact with whites, to resist alcohol, and to hold on to their land. The frontiersmen saw Tecumseh as a threat to progress, and during the War of 1812, they shattered the Indians' dream of a cultural renaissance. American settlers pushing west swept away the Indian barrier.

Well-meaning Jeffersonians did not intend to exterminate the Indians. The president talked about creating a vast reservation beyond the Mississippi River. He planned to turn the Indians into yeoman farmers. But even the most enlightened thinkers of the day did not believe that the Indians possessed a culture worth preserving.

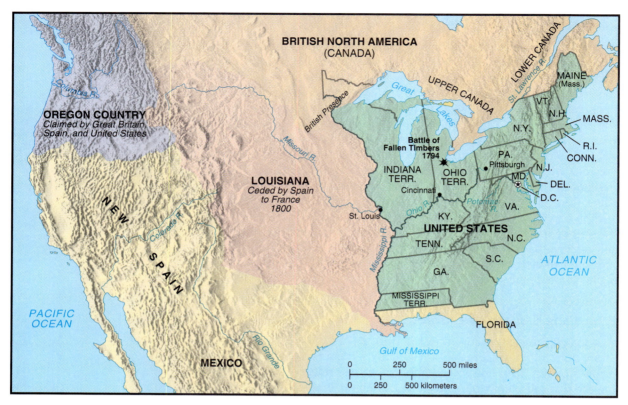

NORTH AMERICA IN 1800   *In the 1790s, diplomatic agreements with Britain and Spain and defeat of the Native Americans at the battle of Fallen Timbers opened the way to U.S. settlement of the land beyond the Appalachian Mountains.* ■

Commercial Life in the Cities

Before 1820, the prosperity of the United States depended primarily on its agriculture and trade. Jeffersonian America was by no stretch of the imagination an industrial economy. Except for the cotton gin, important mechanical and chemical inventions did not appear for another generation. Southerners concentrated on staple crops—tobacco, rice, and cotton. In the North, people generally raised livestock and cereal crops. Regardless of location, however, the nation's farmers, who represented 84 percent of the population, followed a backbreaking work routine that did not differ substantially from that of their parents and grandparents. Probably the major innovation of this period was the agricultural fair, which was first introduced in the hope of improving animal breeding.

The merchant marine represented an equally important element in America's preindustrial economy. At the turn of the century, ships flying the Stars and Stripes transported a large share of the world's trade. Merchants in Boston, New York, and Philadelphia received handsome profits from this commerce. Their vessels provided essential links between European countries and their Caribbean colonies. This trade, along with the export of domestic staples, especially cotton, generated great fortunes. Unfortunately, the boom did not last. The success of the "carrying trade" depended in large measure on friendly relations between the United States and the major European powers. When England and France began seizing American ships—as both did after 1805—national prosperity suffered.

The cities of Jeffersonian America functioned chiefly as depots for international trade. Only about 7 percent of the nation's population lived in urban centers, which were densely inhabited, and most of these people owed their livelihoods either directly or indirectly to the carrying trade. Shipbuilders, stevedores, and artisans, as well as merchants, contributed to the shipping business. As the merchant families grew wealthy, their demand for luxury items drew a group of master craftsmen whose beautiful and intricate pieces—such as New England clocks—were perhaps the highest artistic achievement of the period.

American cities had only a marginal economic influence on the nation's vast hinterland. Because of the high cost of land transportation, urban merchants seldom purchased goods for export—flour and meat, for example—from more than 150 miles away. The separation between rural and urban Americans was far more pronounced during Jefferson's presidency than it was after the development of canals and railroads a few decades later.

The booming carrying trade may have in effect retarded the industrialization of the United States. The lure of large profits drew investment capital—a scarce resource in a developing society—into commerce. By contrast, manufacturing seemed too risky.

Industry was not entirely forgotten, however. Samuel Slater, an English-born designer of textile machinery, did establish several cotton-spinning mills in New England, but before the 1820s, these plants employed only a small number of workers. Another farsighted inventor, Robert Fulton, sailed the first American steamship up the Hudson River in 1807. In time, this marvelous innovation opened new markets for domestic manufacturers, especially in the West.

JEFFERSON AS PRESIDENT

The District of Columbia seemed an appropriate capital for a Republican president. At the time of Jefferson's first inauguration, Washington was still an isolated rural village. Jefferson fit comfortably into Washington society. He despised formal ceremony and sometimes shocked foreign dignitaries by meeting them in his slippers or a threadbare jacket. Reading and reflection were his primary escapes from official duties.

The president was a poor public speaker. He wisely refused to deliver annual addresses before Congress. In personal conversation, however, Jefferson exuded considerable charm. His dinner parties were major social events, and in this forum, Jefferson regaled politicians with his knowledge of literature, philosophy, and science.

Notwithstanding his commitment to the life of the mind, Jefferson was a politician to the core. He ran for the presidency in order to achieve specific goals: reduction of the size and cost of federal government, repeal of Federalist legislation such as the Alien Acts, and the maintenance of international peace. Jefferson realized that he required the full cooperation of congressional Republicans, some of whom were fiercely independent men. To accomplish his program, Jefferson developed friendships, wrote memoranda, and held intimate meetings with key Republicans. In two terms as president, Jefferson never had to veto a single act of Congress.

Jefferson carefully selected the members of his cabinet. During Washington's administration, he had witnessed—even provoked—severe infighting; as president, he nominated only men who enthusiastically supported his programs. James Madison became secretary of state, and Albert Gallatin, a Swiss-born financier who understood the complexities of the federal budget, accepted Jefferson's appointment as secretary of the treasury. Henry Dearborn, Levi Lincoln, and Robert Smith, all loyal to Jefferson, filled the other cabinet posts.

Jeffersonian Reforms

A top priority of the new government was cutting the national debt. Throughout American history, presidents have advocated such reductions, but into the twenty-first century, few have achieved them. Jefferson succeeded. Both he and Gallatin associated debt with Alexander Hamilton's Federalist financial programs, measures they considered harmful to republicanism. Jefferson claimed that legislators elected by the current generation did not have the right to mortgage the future of unborn Americans.

Jefferson also wanted to diminish the activities of the federal government. He urged Congress to repeal all direct taxes. Gallatin linked federal income to the carrying trade. He calculated that the entire cost of national government could be borne by customs receipts. The only problem with Gallatin's plan was that it depended on peaceful international relations, a factor that was not predictable.

To help pay the debt inherited from the Adams administration, Jefferson ordered substantial cuts in the national budget. He closed several embassies in Europe, slashed military spending, and during his first term reduced the size of the army by 50 percent. In addition, he retired a majority of the navy's warships, a move he claimed promoted peace.

More than just budgetary considerations prompted Jefferson's military reductions. A product of the revolutionary experience, he was deeply suspicious of standing armies. In the event of foreign attack, he reasoned, the militia would rise in defense of the republic. To ensure that the citizen soldiers would receive professional leadership in battle, Jefferson created the Army Corps of Engineers and the military academy at West Point in 1802.

Political patronage greatly annoyed the new president. Although he controlled several hundred jobs, he refused to dismiss all the Federalists. To transform federal hiring into an undisciplined spoils system, especially at the highest levels of the federal bureaucracy, struck Jefferson as shortsighted. Moderate Federalists might be converted to the Republican party, and in any case, there was a good chance that they possessed the expertise needed to run the government.

Jefferson's political moderation helped hasten the demise of the Federalist party. But the Federalists also contributed to their own decline. The party's organization was loose, and Federalist leaders refused to adopt the popular forms of campaigning that the Republicans had developed so successfully during the late 1790s. The mere prospect of flattering the common people was odious enough to drive some Federalists into political retirement.

Many of them also sensed that national expansion worked against their interests. Western states inevitably seemed to send Republican representatives to Washington. By 1805, the Federalists retained only Delaware and a few states in New England.

Faced with the imminent death of their party, younger Federalists belatedly attempted to pump life into their organization. They experimented with popular election techniques, tightened party organization, held nominating conventions, and campaigned energetically for office. But the results of these activities were disappointing. Even the younger Federalists thought it was demeaning to appeal to voters.

The Louisiana Purchase

When Jefferson first took office, he was confident that Louisiana and Florida would eventually become part of the United States. He hoped to persuade the notoriously weak Spanish rulers to sell the territory, but failing in this, he was prepared to threaten forcible occupation.

In May 1801, however, prospects for the easy or inevitable acquisition of Louisiana suddenly darkened. Jefferson learned that Spain had secretly transferred title of the entire region to France. To make matters worse, the French ruler, Napoleon Bonaparte, seemed intent on reestablishing an empire in North America. Napoleon dispatched a large army to put down a rebellion in France's sugar-rich Caribbean colony, Santo Domingo. From that island stronghold in the

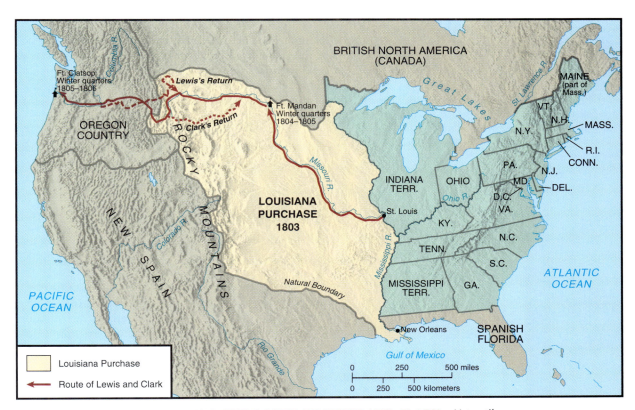

THE LOUISIANA PURCHASE AND THE ROUTE OF LEWIS AND CLARK   *Not until Lewis and Clark had explored the Far West did citizens of the United States realize just how much territory Jefferson had acquired through the Louisiana Purchase.* ■

West Indies, French troops could seize New Orleans and close the Mississippi River to American trade.

A sense of crisis enveloped Washington. Tensions increased when the Spanish officials who still governed New Orleans announced the closing of that port to American commerce (October 1802). Jefferson and his advisers assumed that the Spanish had acted on orders from France, but despite this serious provocation, the president preferred negotiations to war. In January 1803, he asked James Monroe, a loyal Republican from Virginia, to join the American minister, Robert Livingston, in Paris. The president instructed the two men to explore the possibility of purchasing the city of New Orleans. If Livingston and Monroe failed, Jefferson realized that he would be forced to turn to Great Britain for military assistance.

By the time Monroe joined Livingston in France, Napoleon's army in Santo Domingo had succumbed to tropical disease, and he had lost interest in establishing an American empire. Knowing nothing of these developments, the American diplomats were taken by surprise when they were offered the entire Louisiana Territory for only $15 million. At one stroke, the Americans doubled the size of the United States, although the boundaries were vague.

The American people responded enthusiastically to news of the treaty that formalized the **Louisiana Purchase** (May 1803). Jefferson, of course, was relieved that the nation had avoided war with France, but he worried that the agreement might be unconstitutional. The president pointed out that the Constitution did not specifically authorize the acquisition of vast new territories and the incorporation of thousands of foreign citizens. To escape this apparent legal dilemma, Jefferson proposed an amendment to the Constitution, but Napoleon's impatience for money convinced the president to forgo the amendment and act quickly.

Louisiana Purchase U.S. acquisition of the Louisiana Territory from France in 1803 for $15 million. The purchase secured American control of the Mississippi River and doubled the size of the nation.

A Look at the Past

Buffalo Robe

Lewis and Clark collected Native American artifacts, including this Mandan buffalo robe. They sent the robe to Jefferson following a winter spent with the Mandan Indians. ✳ Why do you think the Mandan gave Lewis and Clark a robe that depicted a recent battle with their traditional enemy, the Sioux? Why did Lewis and Clark send the robe to Jefferson?

Lewis and Clark expedition
Overland expedition to the Pacific coast (1804–1806) led by Meriwether Lewis and William Clark. Commissioned by President Thomas Jefferson, the exploration of the Far West brought back a wealth of scientific data about the country and its resources.

Barbary War In response to constant attacks on trading vessels by pirates from the North African Barbary states, in 1801 President Thomas Jefferson sent a naval squadron to resolve the problem through military force. After failing to achieve most of its military objectives, the administration signed an 1805 treaty ending the war.

Jefferson's fears about the incorporation of the new territory were not unwarranted. The Spanish and French people who lived in the region were unfamiliar with America's customs, government, and laws. Jefferson frankly questioned whether these people would be loyal to the United States. He therefore recommended to Congress a transitional government consisting entirely of appointed officials. Some congressmen attacked the bill as antirepublican because it imposed taxes on the citizens of Louisiana without their consent. By a narrow margin the bill passed.

The Lewis and Clark Expedition

In the midst of the Louisiana controversy, Jefferson dispatched a secret message to Congress requesting $2,500 for the exploration of the Far West. How closely this decision was connected to the Paris negotiations is not clear. The president asked his talented private secretary, Meriwether Lewis, to discover whether the Missouri River offered a direct and practical "water communication across this continent for the purposes of commerce." Jefferson also regarded the expedition as a wonderful opportunity to collect precise data about flora and fauna. While preparing for this great adventure, Lewis's second in command, William Clark, assumed such a prominent role that the effort became known as the **Lewis and Clark expedition.** The effort owed much of its success to a young Shoshoni woman known as Sacagawea. Setting out from St. Louis in May 1804, the exploring party reached the Pacific Ocean in November 1805. The group returned safely the following September. The results of this expedition not only fulfilled Jefferson's scientific expectations but also reaffirmed his faith in the future economic prosperity of the United States.

Conflict with the Barbary States

During this period, Jefferson dealt with another problem. For several decades, the North African states of Morocco, Algiers, Tripoli, and Tunis—the Barbary states—had preyed on commercial shipping. Most European nations paid these pirates tribute, hoping in this way to protect merchants trading in the Mediterranean. In 1801, Jefferson responded to a demand for more tribute by dispatching a small fleet to the Barbary Coast to, as one commander commented, negotiate "through the mouth of a cannon." In the fighting that followed, Tripoli captured the U.S. frigate *Philadelphia,* and Jefferson had to pay $60,000 for the safe return of the crew.

The **Barbary War** dragged on for four years. By 1805, the United States' vigorous naval blockade helped end the war. One diplomat observed that the war demonstrated to Europe the proper way to negotiate with pirates.

Jefferson concluded his term on a wave of popularity. He had maintained the peace, reduced taxes, and expanded the boundaries of the United States. He overwhelmed Federalist Charles Cotesworth Pinckney in the election of 1804. So far, Jefferson's "revolution" had been successful.

JEFFERSON'S CRITICS

At the moment of Jefferson's greatest electoral victory, a perceptive person might have seen signs of serious division within the Republican party and within the country. The president's heavy-handed attempts to reform the federal courts stirred deep animosities. Republicans had begun sniping at other Republicans, and one leading member of the party, Aaron Burr, became involved in a bizarre plot to separate the West from the rest of the nation. Congressional debates over the future of the slave trade revealed the existence of powerful sectional loyalties and profound disagreement on the issue.

Attack on the Judges

Jefferson's controversy with the federal bench commenced the moment he became president. The Federalists, realizing that they would soon lose control over the executive branch, passed the Judiciary Act of 1801, which expanded the federal court system. Through his "midnight" appointments, Adams filled the posts with loyal Federalists. Jefferson opposed the attempt by Federalists to maintain their political control. Even more infuriating was Adams's appointment of John Marshall as the new chief justice. Marshall was one of the few men in the country who could hold his own against Jefferson.

In January 1802, Jefferson's congressional allies called for repeal of the Judiciary Act. Although they avoided the political issues, no one doubted that their attack was politically motivated. But the Constitution held that judges could be removed only when they were found guilty of high crimes and misdemeanors. By repealing the Judiciary Act, Congress would in effect be dismissing judges without a trial, a clear violation of their constitutional rights. Unimpressed by this argument, in March, Congress voted for repeal.

While Congress debated the Judiciary Act, another controversy suddenly erupted. One of Adams's midnight appointees, William Marbury, complained that the new administration would not give him his commission for the office of justice of the peace for the District of Columbia. He sought redress before the Supreme Court, demanding that the federal justices compel James Madison, the secretary of state, to deliver the necessary papers. In his celebrated ***Marbury v. Madison*** decision (February 1803), Marshall berated the secretary of state for withholding Marbury's commission. Nevertheless, he concluded that the Supreme Court did not possess jurisdiction over such matters. Poor Marbury was out of luck. The Republicans proclaimed victory. However, they failed to examine the logic of Marshall's decision. He had ruled that part of the earlier judiciary act on which Marbury based his appeal, the one Congress passed in 1789, was unconstitutional. Thus *Marbury* v. *Madison* set an important precedent for judicial review of federal statutes.

Neither Marbury's defeat nor repeal of the Judiciary Act placated extreme Republicans. They insisted that federal judges should be made more responsible to the will of the people. One solution, short of electing federal judges, was impeachment. Early in 1803, John Pickering, an incompetent judge from New Hampshire, presented the Republicans with a curious test case. This Federalist appointee suffered from alcoholism as well as insanity. However, Pickering had not committed any high crimes against the federal government. Ignoring such legal niceties, Jefferson's allies in the Senate impeached Pickering (March 1804), and he was removed from the bench.

Jefferson had his sights set on bigger game even before Pickering's impeachment. In the spring of 1803, he accused Samuel Chase, a justice of the Supreme Court, of delivering a treasonous speech. Republican congressmen took the hint,

Marbury v. *Madison* In this 1803 landmark decision, the Supreme Court first asserted the power of judicial review by declaring an act of Congress, the Judiciary Act of 1789, unconstitutional.

agreeing that Chase, who had frequently attacked Republican policies, had committed an indictable offense.

At this stage, some members of Congress expressed uneasiness. The charges drawn up against the judge were purely political. No one denied that Chase had been indiscreet, accusing Republicans of threatening "peace and order, freedom and property." But his attack on the Jefferson administration hardly seemed criminal. It was clear that if the Senate convicted Chase, every member of the Supreme Court, including Marshall, might also be dismissed.

Chase's impeachment trial before the Senate was one of the most dramatic events in American legal history. Aaron Burr, the vice president, organized the proceeding, and he redecorated the Senate chamber for the event. In this luxurious setting, Chase and his lawyers conducted a masterful defense. By contrast, John Randolph, the congressman who served as chief prosecutor, behaved in an erratic manner, betraying repeatedly his ignorance of relevant points of law. On March 1, 1805, the Senate acquitted the justice of all charges. This trial, too, set a valuable precedent: even though most Republican senators personally disliked the arrogant Chase, they refused to expand the constitutional definition of impeachable offenses.

Politics of Desperation

The collapse of the Federalists on the national level encouraged dissension within the Republican party. Extremists in Congress insisted on monopolizing the president's ear, and when he listened to political moderates, they rebelled. During Jefferson's second term, these critics, labeled "Tertium Quids" ("third sorts," at neither extreme), argued that the president's policies, foreign and domestic, sacrificed virtue for pragmatism. Their chief spokesmen were two members from Virginia, John Randolph and John Taylor. They both despised commercial capitalism and urged Americans to return to a simple agrarian way of life.

The Yazoo controversy raised the Quids from political obscurity. A complex legal battle began in 1795 when a thoroughly corrupt Georgia assembly sold 35 million acres of western land, known as the Yazoo claims, to private companies at bargain prices. It soon became apparent that every member of the legislature had been bribed, and in 1796, state lawmakers rescinded the entire agreement. Unfortunately, some land had already changed hands. Jefferson inherited the entire mess when he became president. The special commission he appointed to look into the matter recommended that Congress set aside 5 million acres for buyers who had unwittingly purchased land from the discredited companies.

Randolph immediately cried foul. Such a compromise, however well-meaning, condoned fraud. Republican virtue hung in the balance. Finally, the Marshall Supreme Court ruled in *Fletcher* v. *Peck* (1810) that legislative fraud did not impair private contracts and that the Georgia assembly of 1796 did not have the authority to take away lands already sold to innocent buyers. This important case upheld the Supreme Court's authority to rule on the constitutionality of state laws.

Murder and Conspiracy: The Curious Career of Aaron Burr

Vice President Aaron Burr created far more serious difficulties for the president. The two men had never been close, and Burr's refusal to bow out during the election of 1800 further strained the relationship. During Jefferson's first term, the ambitious Burr played a distinctly minor role in shaping policy.

In the spring of 1804, Burr decided to run for the governorship of New York. Although he was a Republican, he curried the favor of High Federalists who were plotting the secession of New England and New York from the Union. Alexander Hamilton frustrated Burr's efforts, however, when he described the Republican as "a dangerous man . . . who ought not to be trusted with the reins of government."

Burr blamed Hamilton for his subsequent defeat and challenged his tormentor to a duel. On July 11, 1804, at Weehawken, New Jersey, the vice president shot and killed the former secretary of the treasury. Both New York and New Jersey indicted Burr for murder. His political career lay in shambles.

In his final weeks as vice president, Burr hatched a scheme so audacious that the people with whom he dealt could not decide whether he was a genius or a madman. Although he told different stories to different men, he evidently planned a filibustering campaign against a Spanish colony, perhaps Mexico, and he envisioned separating the western states and territories from the Union. The persuasive Burr convinced a handful of politicians and adventurers to follow him. Even James Wilkinson, commander of the U.S. Army in the Mississippi Valley, joined Burr.

Late in the summer of 1806, Burr put his ill-defined plan into action. It ended almost before it started. Wilkinson had a change of heart and denounced Burr to Jefferson. This started a general stampede, as conspirators rushed pell-mell to save their own skins. Federal authorities arrested Burr in February 1807 and took him to Richmond to stand trial for treason. Even before a jury had been called, Jefferson announced publicly that Burr's guilt was beyond question.

Jefferson spoke prematurely. The trial judge was John Marshall, who insisted on a narrow constitutional definition of treason. He refused to hear testimony regarding Burr's supposed intentions and demanded two witnesses to each overt act of treason.

Burr, of course, had been too clever to leave this sort of evidence. While Jefferson complained bitterly about the miscarriage of justice, the jurors declared on September 1, 1807, that the defendant was "not proved guilty by any evidence submitted to us." Although Marshall had acted in an undeniably partisan manner, his actions inadvertently helped protect the civil rights of all Americans. If the chief justice had admitted circumstantial evidence into the Richmond courtroom, if he had listened to rumor and hearsay, he would have made it much easier for later presidents to use trumped-up conspiracy charges to silence legitimate political opposition.

The Slave Trade

Slavery sparked angry debate at the Constitutional Convention of 1787. If delegates from the northern states had refused to compromise on this issue, Southerners would not have supported the new government. At the convention, the South agreed that after 1808, Congress *might consider* banning the importation of slaves into the United States. In return, the North agreed to count a slave as three-fifths of a free white male, which increased southern representatives in Congress and accounted for Jefferson's 1800 presidential victory.

In an annual message sent to Congress in December 1806, Jefferson urged the representatives to prepare legislation outlawing the slave trade. During the early months of 1807, congressmen debated various ways of ending the embarrassing commerce. Although northern representatives generally favored a strong bill, southern congressmen responded with threats and ridicule. They explained to their northern colleagues that no one in the South regarded slavery as evil. It appeared naive, therefore, to expect local planters to enforce a ban on the slave trade or to inform federal agents when they spotted a smuggler.

The bill that Jefferson finally signed in March 1807 probably pleased no one. The law prohibited the importation of slaves into the United States after the new year. Whenever customs officials captured a smuggler, the slaves were turned over to state authorities and disposed of according to local custom. Southerners did not cooperate, and for many years African slaves continued to pour into southern ports. Undoubtedly Great Britain, which outlawed the slave trade in 1807, was the greatest single force in limiting the number of African slaves shipped to the United States. Ships of the Royal Navy took British—and in this case, American—laws seriously.

Arise! Arise! and weep no more dry up your tears, we shall part no more. Come rose we go to Tennessee, that happy Shore. To old virginia never — never — return.

■ *Although the external slave trade was officially outlawed in 1808, the commerce in humans persisted. An estimated 250,000 African slaves were brought illicitly to the United States between 1808 and 1860. The internal slave trade continued as well. Folk artist Lewis Miller sketched this slave coffle marching from Virginia to new owners in Tennessee under the watchful eyes of mounted white overseers.* ■

EMBARRASSMENTS OVERSEAS

During Jefferson's second term (1805–1809), the United States found itself in the midst of a world at war. A brief peace in Europe ended abruptly in 1803, and the two military giants of the age, France and Great Britain, fought for supremacy on land and sea. It was a total war, an ideological war, a type of war unknown in the eighteenth century. Britain was the master of the seas, but France held supremacy on land.

During the early stages of the war, the United States profited from European adversity. As "neutral carriers," the American ships transported goods to any port in the world where they could find a buyer, and American merchants grew wealthy serving Britain and France.

Napoleon's successes on the battlefield, however, quickly strained Britain's economic resources. In response, Britain tightened its control over the seas. British warships seized American vessels engaged in trade beneficial to France, and British captains stepped up impressment of sailors on ships flying the United States flag. Then in 1806, the British government issued a series of trade regulations known as Orders in Council. These proclamations forbade neutral commerce with the European Continent and threatened with seizure any ship that violated the orders. The declarations created what were in effect "paper blockades," for even the powerful British navy could not monitor the activities of every continental port.

Napoleon responded to Britain's commercial regulations with his own paper blockade, called the Continental System. In the Berlin Decree of November 1806 and the Milan Decree of December 1807, he announced the closing of all continental ports to British trade and decreed that neutral vessels carrying British goods were subject to seizure. Since French armies occupied most of the territory between Spain and Germany, the decrees cut the British out of a large market. Americans were caught between two conflicting systems. To please one power was to displease the other.

The unhappy turn of international events baffled Jefferson. He had assumed that civilized countries would respect neutral rights; justice obliged them to do so. Appeals to reason, however, made little impression on states at war. Jefferson tried to negotiate with Britain, but the agreement that resulted was unacceptable to the president.

The United States soon suffered an even greater humiliation. A ship of the Royal Navy, the *Leopard,* sailing off the coast of Virginia, commanded an American warship to submit to a search for deserters (June 21, 1807). When the captain of the *Chesapeake* refused to cooperate, the *Leopard* opened fire, killing three men and wounding eighteen. The attack clearly violated the sovereignty of the United States. The American people demanded revenge.

Despite the pressure of public opinion, Jefferson played for time. He recognized that the United States was unprepared for war against a powerful nation such as Great Britain. The president worried that an expensive conflict with Great Britain would quickly undo the fiscal reforms of his first term. For Jefferson, war entailed deaths, debts, and taxes, none of which he particularly relished.

Embargo Divides the Nation

Jefferson found what he regarded as a satisfactory way to deal with European predators with a policy he called "peaceable coercion." If Britain and France refused to respect the rights of neutral carriers, then the United States would keep its ships at home. Not only would this action protect them from seizure, but it would also deprive the European powers of much-needed American goods, especially food. Jefferson predicted that a total embargo of American commerce would soon force Britain and France to negotiate with the United States in good faith. Congress passed the **Embargo Act** on December 22, 1807.

Peaceable coercion turned into a Jeffersonian nightmare. Americans objected strenuously to the legislation, and Jefferson had to push through a series of acts to force compliance. By the middle of 1808, Jefferson and Gallatin were involved in the regulation of the smallest details of American economic life. The federal government supervised the coastal trade and regulated the overland trade with Canada. When violations still occurred, Congress gave customs collectors the right to seize a vessel merely on suspicion of wrongdoing. Jefferson's eagerness to pursue a reasonable foreign policy blinded him to the fact that he and a Republican Congress would have to establish a police state to make it work.

Northerners hated the embargo and regularly engaged in smuggling. Persons living near Lake Champlain in upper New York State simply ignored the regulations, and they roughed up collectors who interfered with the Canadian trade. Jefferson was so determined to stop the illegal activity that he even urged the governor of New York to call out the militia. In a decision that George III might have applauded, Jefferson dispatched federal troops to overawe the citizens of New York.

New Englanders regarded the embargo as lunacy. Merchants preferred to take their chances on the high seas. Sailors and artisans were thrown out of work. The popular press maintained a constant howl of protest. One writer observed that embargo in reverse spelled "O grab me!" Opposition to the embargo caused a brief revival of the Federalist party in New England, and a few extremists suggested the possibility of state assemblies' nullifying federal laws.

By 1809, the bankruptcy of Jefferson's foreign policy was obvious. The embargo never seriously damaged the British economy. Napoleon liked the embargo because it seemed to harm Great Britain more than it did France. Finally, Republicans in Congress panicked and repealed the embargo a few days before James Madison's

Embargo Act In response to a British attack on an American warship off the coast of Virginia, this 1807 law prohibited foreign commerce.

■ *The Ograbme* (embargo *spelled backward) snapping turtle, created by cartoonist Alexander Anderson, is shown here biting an American tobacco smuggler who is breaking the embargo.* ■

inauguration. Relations between the United States and the great European powers were much worse in 1809 than they had been in 1805.

A New Administration Goes to War

Madison followed his good friend Jefferson into the White House. As president, Madison suffered from several personal and political handicaps. Although his intellectual abilities were great, he lacked the qualities necessary for effective leadership. His critics argued that his modest and unassuming manner indicated a weak and vacillating character.

During the election of 1808, Randolph and the Quids tried unsuccessfully to persuade James Monroe to challenge Madison's candidacy. Jefferson favored his old friend Madison. In the end, a caucus of Republican congressmen gave the official nod to Madison, the first time in American history that such a congressional group controlled a presidential nomination. Although Madison won the presidency, the Federalists made impressive gains in the House of Representatives. Madison compounded his difficulties by appointing cabinet members who actively opposed his policies.

The new president inherited Jefferson's foreign policy problems. Neither Britain nor France showed the slightest interest in respecting American neutral rights. Madison's solution was to implement the weak and clumsy Non-Intercourse Act (March 1, 1809), which Congress passed at the same time it repealed the embargo. The new bill authorized the resumption of trade between the United States and all nations of the world *except* Britain and France. Either of these countries could restore full commercial relations simply by promising to observe the rights of neutral carriers.

The British immediately took advantage of the offer. Their minister to the United States, David M. Erskine, informed Madison that the British government had modified its position on a number of sensitive commercial issues. Encouraged by these talks, Madison announced that trade with Great Britain could resume on June 10, 1809. Unfortunately, Erskine had not conferred with his superiors, who rejected the agreement out of hand. While an embarrassed Madison fumed in Washington, the Royal Navy seized the American ships that had already put to sea.

Britain's apparent betrayal led the artless Madison straight into a French trap. In May 1810, Congress passed Macon's Bill Number Two. In a complete reversal of strategy, this poorly drafted legislation reestablished trade with *both* England and France. It also contained a curious carrot-and-stick provision. As soon as either of these European states repealed restrictions on neutral shipping, the U.S. government promised to halt all commerce with the other.

Napoleon spotted a rare opportunity. He announced that he would respect American neutral rights. Again, Madison acted impulsively, announcing that unless Britain repealed the Orders in Council by November, the United States would cut off all commercial relations. Only later did Madison learn that Napoleon had no intentions of living up to his side of the bargain. But humiliated by the Erskine experience, Madison decided to ignore French provocations and to pretend that the emperor was behaving in an honest manner.

Events unrelated to international commerce fueled anti-British sentiment in the newly settled parts of the United States. Westerners believed—incorrectly, as it turned out—that British agents operating out of Canada had persuaded Tecumseh's warriors to resist the spread of American settlement. General William Henry Harrison, governor of the Indian Territory, marched an army to the edge of a large Shawnee village at the mouth of Tippecanoe Creek near the banks of the Wabash River. On the morning of November 7, 1811, the American troops bested the Indians at the battle of Tippecanoe. The incident forced Tecumseh to seek British military assistance, something he probably would not have done had Harrison left him alone.

Fumbling Toward Conflict

In 1811, the anti-British mood of Congress intensified. A group of militant representatives, some of them elected to Congress for the first time in the election of 1810, announced that they would no longer tolerate national humiliation. These aggressive nationalists, many from the South and West, have sometimes been labeled the **War Hawks.** Men such as Henry Clay and John C. Calhoun spoke about honor and pride, as if foreign relations were some sort of duel between gentlemen. Although Republicans themselves, the War Hawks repudiated Jefferson's policy of peaceful coercion.

Madison surrendered to the War Hawks. On June 1, 1812, he sent Congress a message requesting a declaration of war against Great Britain. The timing of his action was peculiar. Over the preceding months, tensions between the two countries had relaxed, and the British government was suspending the Orders in Council.

However inadequately Madison communicated his goals, he was able to enforce a plan. His major aim was to force the British to respect American maritime rights, especially in Caribbean waters. The president's problem was to figure out how a nation as small and as militarily weak as the United States could bring effective pressure on Great Britain. The answer—at least Madison's answer—seemed to be Canada. This colony supplied Britain's Caribbean possessions with much-needed foodstuffs. The president therefore reasoned that by threatening to seize Canada, the Americans might compel the British to make concessions on maritime issues. It was this logic that Secretary of State James Monroe had in mind when he explained in June 1812 that "it might be necessary to invade Canada, not as an object of the war, but as a means to bring it to a satisfactory conclusion."

Even contemporaries expressed confusion about the causes of the War of 1812. Madison's formal message to Congress listed Great Britain's violation of maritime rights, impressment of American seamen, and provocation of Indians. The War Hawks wanted war for other reasons. Some probably hoped to conquer Canada. For others, the whole affair may have truly been a matter of national pride. Surprisingly, New Englanders, in whose commercial interests the war would supposedly be waged, ridiculed such chauvinism. Although Congress voted for war, the nation was clearly divided about the need to fight Britain. Madison's slim victory over De Witt Clinton, nominated by a faction of antiwar Republicans, in the election of 1812 indicated this split in America.

THE STRANGE WAR OF 1812

Optimism among the War Hawks ran high. However, they failed to appreciate how unprepared the country was for war, and they also refused to mobilize needed resources. The House rejected proposals for direct taxes and authorized naval appropriations only with the greatest reluctance. They did not seem to understand that a weak, highly decentralized government—the one that Jeffersonians championed—was incapable of waging an expensive war against the world's greatest sea power.

New Englanders refused to cooperate with the war effort. Throughout the **War of 1812,** they carried on a lucrative, though illegal, commerce with the enemy. The British government apparently believed that the New England states might negotiate a separate peace, and during the first year of the war, the Royal Navy did not bother to blockade the major northern ports.

American military operations focused initially on the western forts, but the battles in the region demonstrated that the militia, no matter how enthusiastic, was no match for well-trained European veterans. American forces surrendered Detroit and Michilimackinac to the enemy, and poorly coordinated marches on Niagara and Montreal accomplished nothing. On the sea, the United States did much better.

War Hawks Congressional leaders who, in 1811 and 1812, called for war against Britain to defend the national honor and force Britain to respect America's maritime rights.

War of 1812 War between Britain and the United States. U.S. justifications for war included British violations of American maritime rights, impressment of seamen, provocation of the Indians, and defense of national honor.

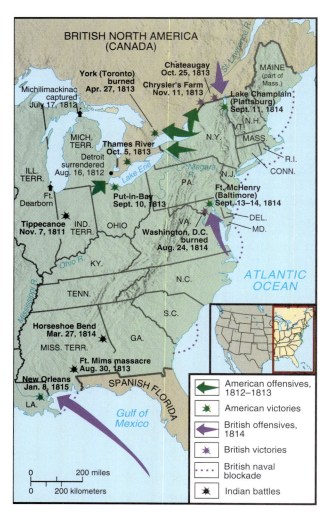

THE WAR OF 1812 *Major battles of the War of 1812 brought few lasting gains to either the British or the Americans.* ■

In August, Captain Isaac Hull's *Constitution* defeated HMS *Guerrière* in a fierce battle, and American privateers destroyed or captured a number of British merchantmen. These victories, however, indicate that Britain was more concerned with Napoleon than the United States. As soon as peace returned to Europe in the spring of 1814, Britain redeployed its fleet and easily blockaded the tiny U.S. Navy.

The campaigns of 1813 revealed that conquering Canada would be more difficult than the War Hawks ever imagined. Both sides in this war recognized that whoever controlled the Great Lakes controlled the West. On Lake Erie, the Americans won the race for naval superiority. Oliver Hazard Perry won an important naval battle at Put-in-Bay, and General Harrison overran an army of British troops and Indian warriors at the battle of Thames River. During this engagement, Tecumseh was killed. On the other fronts, however, the war went badly for the Americans.

In 1814, the British took the offensive. Following their victory over Napoleon, British strategists planned to increase pressure on three separate American fronts: the Canadian frontier, Chesapeake coastal settlements, and New Orleans. In the Canadian theater, the British suffered a setback. The American victory off Plattsburg on Lake Champlain accelerated peace negotiations, for after news of the battle reached London, the British government concluded that major land operations along the Canadian border were futile.

Throughout the year, British warships harassed the Chesapeake coast. To their surprise, the British found the region almost totally undefended, and on August 24, 1814, a small force of British marines burned the nation's capital, a victory more symbolic than strategic. Encouraged by their easy success, the British launched a full-scale attack on Baltimore (September 14). To everyone's surprise, the fort guarding the harbor held out against a heavy bombardment, and the British gave up the operation. The survival of Fort McHenry inspired Francis Scott Key to write "The Star-Spangled Banner."

The battle of New Orleans should never have occurred: it took place after the diplomats in Europe had concluded their peace negotiations. But General Edward Pakenham, the commander of the British forces, was not aware of the negotiations, and on January 8, 1815, he foolishly ordered a frontal attack against General Andrew Jackson's well-defended positions. In a matter of hours, the entire British force had been destroyed. The victory not only transformed Jackson into a national folk hero but also provided the people of the United States with a much needed source of pride. Even in military terms, the battle was significant, for if the British had managed to occupy New Orleans, they would have been difficult to dislodge regardless of the specific provisions of the peace treaty.

Hartford Convention: The Demise of the Federalists

In the fall of 1814, a group of leading New England politicians, most of them moderate Federalists, gathered in Hartford to discuss relations between the people of their region and the federal government. The **Hartford Convention** delegates were

Hartford Convention An assembly of New England federalists who met in Hartford, Connecticut, in December 1814 to protest Madison's foreign policy in the War of 1812, which had undermined commercial interests in the North. They proposed amending the Constitution to prevent future presidents from declaring war without a two-thirds majority in Congress.

angered and hurt by the Madison administration's seeming insensitivity to the economic interests of the New England states.

The men who met at Hartford on December 15 did not advocate secession from the Union. Although people living in other sections of the country cried treason, the convention delegates only recommended changes in the Constitution. Frustrated by the three-fifths clause that gave southern slaveholders a disproportionately large voice in the House, delegates proposed that congressional representation should be calculated on the basis of the number of white males living in a state. The convention also wanted to limit each president to a single term in office, a

A Look at the Past

"We Owe Allegiance to No Crown"

Patriotic symbols abound in this print by John Archibald Woodside, Jr. Carrying a liberty cap on a pole, Miss Liberty crowns an American sailor with a laurel wreath, signifying that American liberty is victorious. The sentiment expressed visually and emphatically, "We Owe Allegiance to No Crown," seems appropriate for the revolutionary era, but in fact this print dates much later, to the early nineteenth century, when the War of 1812 sparked nationalism. ✳ What does this print suggest about American confidence at that time? Does it raise questions about United States–British relations following the American Revolution?

Chronology

1801	Thomas Jefferson is elected president ■ Adams makes "midnight" appointments of federal judges (March)
1802	Judiciary Act is repealed (March)
1803	Chief Justice John Marshall rules on *Marbury* v. *Madison,* setting precedent for judicial review (February) ■ Louisiana Purchase is concluded with France (May)
1804–1806	Lewis and Clark explore the Northwest
1804	Aaron Burr kills Alexander Hamilton in a duel (July) ■ Jefferson is elected to a second term (November)
1805	Justice Samuel Chase is acquitted by the Senate (March)
1807	American warship *Chesapeake* is fired on by the British *Leopard* (June) ■ Burr is tried for conspiracy (August–September) ■ Embargo Act is passed (December)
1808	Slave trade is ended (January) ■ Madison is elected president (November)
1809	Embargo is repealed; Non-Intercourse Act is passed (March)
1810	Macon's Bill Number Two reestablishes trade with Britain and France (May)
1811	Harrison defeats Indians at Tippecanoe (November)
1812	War is declared against Great Britain (June) ■ Madison is elected to a second term, defeating De Witt Clinton of New York (November)
1813	Perry destroys the British fleet at Put-in-Bay (September) ■ Harrison wins again at Thames River (October)
1814	Jackson crushes Creek Indians at Horseshoe Bend (March) ■ British burn Washington, D.C. (August) ■ Americans turn back the British at Plattsburg (September) ■ Hartford Convention meets to recommend constitutional changes (December) ■ Treaty of Ghent ends War of 1812 (December)
1815	Jackson routs the British at New Orleans (January)

reform that New Englanders hoped might end Virginia's monopoly of the executive mansion. Finally, to protect their region from what they saw as the tyranny of southern Republicans, the delegates insisted that a two-thirds majority should be necessary before Congress could declare war, pass commercial regulations, or admit new states to the Union.

The convention's recommendations arrived in Washington at the same time as news of the battle of New Orleans. Republican leaders in Congress accused the hapless New Englanders of disloyalty, and people throughout the country were persuaded that a group of wild secessionists had attempted to destroy the Union. The Hartford Convention accelerated the demise of the Federalist party.

Treaty of Ghent Ends the War

In August 1814, the United States dispatched a distinguished negotiating team to Ghent, a Belgian city where the Americans opened talks with their British counterparts. During the early weeks of discussion, the British made impossible demands. They insisted on territorial concessions from the United States, the right to navigate the Mississippi River, and the creation of a large Indian buffer state in the Northwest Territory. The Americans listened to the presentation, more or less politely, and then rejected the entire package. In turn, they lectured their British counterparts about maritime rights and impressments.

Fatigue finally broke the diplomatic deadlock. The British government realized that no amount of military force could significantly alter the outcome of hostilities in the United States. Weary negotiators signed the Treaty of Ghent on Christmas Eve in 1814. The document dealt with virtually none of the topics contained in Madison's original war message. Neither side surrendered territory; Great Britain refused even to discuss the topic of impressment. In fact, the treaty was simply an agreement to stop fighting. The Senate apparently concluded that stalemate was preferable to continued conflict and ratified the treaty 35 to 0.

Most Americans thought the War of 1812 an important success. Even though the country's military accomplishments had been unimpressive, the people of the United States had been swept up in a contagion of nationalism. For many Americans, this "second war of independence" reaffirmed their faith in themselves and the revolutionary experience.

Conclusion: Republican Legacy

A remarkable coincidence occurred on July 4, 1826, the fiftieth anniversary of the Declaration of Independence. On that day, Thomas Jefferson died at Monticello. His last words were, "Is it the Fourth?" On the same day several hundred miles to the north, John Adams also passed his last day on earth. His mind was on his old friend and sometime adversary, and during his final moments, Adams found comfort in the assurance that "Thomas Jefferson still survives." The political battles that occupied both men during their presidencies had already passed into history and were largely forgotten. But the spirit of the Declaration of Independence survived, and Jefferson's vision of a society in which "all men are created equal" challenged later Americans to make good on the promise of 1776.

Key Terms

Louisiana Purchase, p. 151

Lewis and Clark expedition, p. 152

Barbary War, p. 152

Marbury v. *Madison,* p. 153

Embargo Act, p. 157

War Hawks, p. 159

War of 1812, p. 159

Hartford Convention, p. 160

Recommended Reading

A challenge for historians of this period is explaining how Thomas Jefferson and his followers managed to reconcile Republican theories of government with the practical responsibilities of the presidency. The fullest account of his administration can be found in Merrill D. Peterson, *Thomas Jefferson and the New Nation: A Biography* (1970). Three more recent books examine Jefferson's complex character as well as the impact of Republican policies on the larger society: Peter S. Onuf, *Jeffersonian America* (2001); Joseph J. Ellis, *American Sphinx: The Character of Thomas Jefferson* (1997); and James Horn, et al., eds., *The Revolution of 1800: Democracy, Race, and the New Republic* (2002). The tensions that made this political culture so explosive are treated in Roger Sharp, *American Politics in the Early Republic: The New Nation in Crisis* (1993) and Bernard A. Weisberger, *America Afire: Jefferson, Adams, and the Revolutionary Election of 1800* (2000). The controversies over how best to interpret the

Constitution and the politics of the Supreme Court are explored in Jean Edward Smith, *John Marshall: Definer of a Nation* (1996). Also valuable for understanding difficult legal issues are Richard E. Ellis, *The Jeffersonian Crisis: Courts and Politics in the Young Republic* (1971); Leonard W. Levy, *Emergence of a Free Press* (1985); and Morton J. Horowitz, *The Transformation of American Law, 1780–1860* (1977). The Louisiana Purchase is the subject of Alexander DeConde, *The Affair of Louisiana* (1976). On the Lewis and Clark Expedition, see James P. Ronda, *Lewis and Clark Among the Indians* (1984) and Donald Jackson, *Thomas Jefferson and the Stony Mountains: Exploring the West from Monticello* (1981). Several fine studies chronicle the politics of slavery and Jefferson's own problems with freeing African Americans; Henry Wiencek tells how Washington confronted the problem in *An Imperfect God: George Washington, His Slaves, and the Creation of America* (2003). On foreign relations, see

Peter S. Onuf, ed., *America and the World: Diplomacy, Politics, and War* (1991); J. C. A. Stagg, *Mr. Madison's War: Politics, Diplomacy, and Warfare in the Early American Republic* (1983); James E. Lewis, Jr., *The American Union and the Problem of Neighborhood: The United States and the Collapse of the Spanish Empire, 1783–1829* (1998); and Franklin

Lambert, *The Barbary Wars: American Independence in the Atlantic World* (2005). Two splendid works demonstrate how Evangelical Protestantism shaped early nineteenth-century public culture: Nathan O. Hatch, *The Democratization of American Christianity* (1989) and Mark A. Noll, *America's God: From Jonathan Edwards to Abraham Lincoln* (2002).

SUGGESTED WEB SITES

Thomas Jefferson
www.pbs.org/jefferson/
A companion site to the Public Broadcasting Service series on Jefferson, especially important because it contains a fine collection of other people's views of Jefferson.

White House Historical Association
www.whitehousehistory.org/
This site contains a timeline of the history of the White House and several interesting photos and links.

Thomas Jefferson Digital Archive at the University of Virginia
etext.virginia.edu/jefferson/
Mr. Jefferson's University—the University of Virginia—houses this site with numerous on-line resources about Jefferson and his times, including electronic versions of texts by Jefferson, a page of selected quotations, and a comprehensive annotated bibliography of works on Jefferson from 1826 to 1997.

Lewis and Clark: The Maps of Exploration 1507–1814
www.lib.virginia.edu/speccol/exhibits/lewisclark/home.html
Maps and charts reveal knowledge and conceptions about the known and the unknown. This site includes a number of eighteenth-century maps.

PBS Online—Lewis and Clark
www.pbs.org/lewisandclark/
This is a companion site to Ken Burns's documentary on Lewis and Clark containing a timeline of the expedition, a collection of related links, a bibliography, and more than eight hundred minutes of unedited, full-length RealPlayer interviews with seven experts featured in the film.

The War of 1812
members.tripod/com/~war1812/index.html
In-depth and varied information about the War of 1812.

Chapter 9

Nation Building and Nationalism

A Revolutionary War Hero Revisits America in 1824

When the Marquis de Lafayette returned to the United States in 1824, he marveled at how the country had changed in the more than forty years since he had served with George Washington. The country had grown remarkably, and steam-powered boats now united the various western outposts. Everywhere Lafayette was greeted with patriotic oratory celebrating the liberty, prosperity, and progress of the new nation. Always the diplomat, Lafayette told Americans what they wanted to hear. He hailed the "immense improvements" and "admirable communications" that he had witnessed and declared himself deeply moved by "all the grandeur and prosperity of these happy United States, which, at the same time they nobly seem the complete assertion of American independence, reflect on every part of the world the light of a far superior political civilization."

There were good reasons why Americans made Lafayette's return visit the occasion for patriotic celebration and reaffirmation. Free from foreign threats, America was growing rapidly in population, size, and wealth. Its republican form of government was apparently working well. In his first inaugural address, James Monroe had anticipated Lafayette's observations. It was a speech full of national self-satisfaction. "No country was ever happier with respect to its domain," Monroe said. As for the government itself, it was so near to perfection that "in respect to it we have no essential improvements to make."

Beneath the optimism and self-confidence, however, there were undercurrents of doubt and anxiety about the future. Almost all the Founders were dead. Could their example of republican virtue and self-sacrifice be maintained in an increasingly prosperous and materialistic society? Many Americans feared the answer. And what about the place of slavery in a "perfect" democratic republic? Lafayette himself wondered why the United States had not yet extended freedom and equality to the slaves.

But the peace following the War of 1812 did open the way for a great surge of nation building. Transportation improvements created new markets, and advances in the processing of raw materials led to the first stirrings of industrialization. Political leadership provided little active direction for the process of growth and expansion, but an active judiciary took up part of the slack in a series of decisions that served to promote economic development and assert the priority of national over state and local interests. To guarantee the peace and security essential for internal progress, statesmen proclaimed a foreign policy designed to insulate America from external involvements. A new nation of great potential wealth and power was emerging.

EXPANSION AND MIGRATION

The new peaceful relations with Great Britain in 1815 allowed the American people to shift their attention from Europe and the Atlantic to the vast lands of North America that lay before them. Two treaties negotiated with Great Britain dealt with northern borders. The Rush-Bagot Agreement (1817) limited U.S. and British naval forces on the Great Lakes and Lake Champlain and guaranteed that the British would never try to invade the United States from Canada and that the United States would never try to take Canada from the British. The Anglo-American Convention of 1818 set the border between the lands of the Louisiana Purchase and Canada at the 49th parallel and provided for joint U.S. and British occupation of Oregon.

Between the Appalachians and the Mississippi, settlement already had begun, especially in the new states of Ohio, Kentucky, and Tennessee. In the lower Mississippi Valley, the former French colony of Louisiana had been admitted as a state in 1812, and a thriving settlement existed around Natchez in the Mississippi Territory. Elsewhere in the trans-Appalachian west, white settlement was sparse and much land remained in Indian hands. U.S. citizens, eager to expand into lands held by Indian nations as well as by Spain, used diplomacy, military action, force, and fraud to "open" lands for U.S. settlement and westward migration.

Extending the Boundaries

The first goal of postwar expansionists was to obtain Florida from Spain. The Spanish claimed possession of land extending along the Gulf Coast to the Mississippi, but in 1812, the United States had annexed the area between the Mississippi and Perdido Rivers in what became Alabama. The remainder, known as East Florida, became the prime object of territorial ambition for President James Monroe and his energetic secretary of state, John Quincy Adams. Spanish claims west and east of the Mississippi blocked Adams's grand design for continental expansion.

General Andrew Jackson provided Adams with an opportunity to acquire the land. In 1816, United States troops touched off a conflict when they went into East Florida in pursuit of hostile Seminole Indians and the fugitive slaves that they were harboring. In April and May 1818, Jackson exceeded his official orders and occupied East Florida. This operation became known as the First Seminole War. In addition, Jackson court-martialed and executed two British subjects whom he accused of being enemy agents. Although his actions were widely criticized by government officials, no disciplinary action was taken.

Secretary Adams informed the Spanish government that the United States had acted in self-defense and that further conflict could be avoided only if East Florida was ceded to the United States. Weakened by Latin American revolutions and liberation movements, Spain was in no position to resist American bullying. Spanish minister Luis de Onís acceded. In addition to relinquishing Florida, de Onís agreed to a dividing line between Spanish and American territory that ran all the way to the Pacific, thus giving up Spain's claim to Pacific coastal areas north of California and opening a path for future American expansion. These understandings were formalized in the **Adams-Onís Treaty** (1819), also known as the Transcontinental Treaty. Great Britain and Russia still had competing claims to the Pacific Northwest, but the United States was now poised to acquire some frontage on a second ocean. Secretary Adams described the agreement on a definite boundary to the Pacific as "forming a great epoch in our history."

Interest in exploitation of the Far West continued to grow between 1810 and 1830. In 1811, a New York merchant, John Jacob Astor, founded the fur-trading post of Astoria at the mouth of the Columbia River in the Oregon country. In the 1820s and 1830s, fur traders operating out of St. Louis worked their way up the Missouri to the northern Rockies and beyond. First they limited themselves to trading for

Adams-Onís Treaty Signed by Secretary of State John Quincy Adams and Spanish minister Luis de Onís in 1819, this treaty allowed for American annexation of Florida.

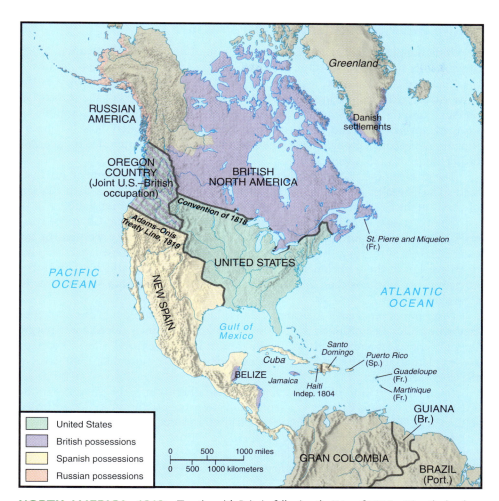

NORTH AMERICA, 1819   *Treaties with Britain following the War of 1812 setting the border between the United States and Canada (British North America) made this border the longest unfortified boundary line in the world.* ■

furs with the Indians, but eventually the "mountain men" went after game on their own and sold the furs to agents of the Rocky Mountain Fur Company at an annual meeting or "rendezvous."

These colorful characters, who included such legendary figures as Jedediah Smith, Jim Bridger, Kit Carson, and Jim Beckwourth, accomplished prodigious feats of survival under harsh natural conditions. Although they actually depleted the animal resources on which the Indians depended, the mountain men projected an image of being part of their environment rather than destroyers of it. To later generations, they typified a romantic ideal of lonely self-reliance in harmony with unspoiled nature.

The reports of military expeditions provided better information about the Far West than the tales of the mountain men, most of whom were illiterate. The most notable of the postwar expeditions was mounted by Major Stephen S. Long in 1819–1820. Long mapped some of the rivers of the Great Plains and endorsed the somewhat misleading view that the plains beyond the Missouri were a "great American desert" unfit for cultivation or settlement. The real focus of attention between 1815 and the 1840s, therefore, was the nearer West, the rich agricultural lands between the Appalachians and the Mississippi that were inhabited by numerous Indian tribes.

Native American Societies Under Pressure

Five Indian nations, with a combined population of nearly 60,000, occupied much of what later became Mississippi, Alabama, Georgia, and Florida. These nations—the Cherokee, Chickasaw, Choctaw, Creek, and Seminole—became known as the "Five Civilized Tribes" because by 1815 they had adopted many of the features of the surrounding white Southern society: an agricultural economy, a republican form of government, and the institution of slavery. No matter how "civilized" Indians had become, though, most white Americans were not interested in incorporating them into U.S. society.

The five nations varied in their responses to white encroachment on their lands. The Cherokee adopted a strategy of accommodation to increase their chances of survival; the Creek and Seminole, by contrast, took up arms in resistance.

The Cherokee were the largest of the five nations. Traditional Cherokee society had combined hunting by men and subsistence farming by women. In the early nineteenth century, the shift to a more agrarian, market-based economy led to an erosion of the traditional matrilineal kinship system, in which a person belonged to his mother's clan, and also helped introduce American-style slavery to Cherokee society.

Discrimination against Africans in all five nations grew under pressure of contact with whites. Beginning in the 1820s, the Cherokee Council passed laws limiting the rights of slaves and free blacks. By the time of Indian Removal, a few Cherokees owned plantations with hundreds of slaves, and there were more than 1500 slaves in the Cherokee Nation.

In an effort to head off encroachments by southern states, the Cherokee in the 1820s tried to centralize power in a republican government. This process culminated in the 1827 adoption of a formal written constitution based on the U.S. Constitution.

At the same time, a renaissance of Cherokee culture was spurred by Sequoyah's invention of a written Cherokee language in 1821–1822. While the alphabet was complex and the system lacked punctuation, "Sequoyan" provided the Cherokee a new means of self-expression and a reinvigorated sense of Cherokee identity. The first American Indian newspaper, the *Cherokee Phoenix,* was published in Sequoyan in 1828.

The Seminole Nation, the smallest of the five nations, presents perhaps the starkest cultural contrast to the Cherokee, both because the Seminole reacted to pressure from white settlers with armed resistance rather than accommodation, and because their multicultural history gave them a very different relationship to slavery.

The Seminole Nation in Florida formed after the European conquest of America, an amalgam of many different peoples with roots in Africa as well as other parts of the New World. Disparate groups of Creeks migrating from Georgia and Alabama in the wake of war and disease mingled with the remnants of native Floridians to form the new tribe known as the Seminole. At the same time, Spain had granted asylum to runaway African American slaves from the Carolinas, who created "maroon communities" in Florida, striking up alliances with the Seminole Indians to ward off slave catchers. African Americans and Native Americans intermingled, and by the late eighteenth century, some African Americans were already known as "Seminole Negroes" or "estelusti."

Although the Seminole adopted African slavery at some point in the first decades of the nineteenth century,

■ *Sequoyah's invention of the Cherokee alphabet enabled thousands of Cherokee to read and write primers and newspapers published in their own language.* ■

it was very different from slavery as it existed among whites, or even among the Cherokee and Creek. Seminole "slaves" lived in separate towns, planted and cultivated fields in common, owned large herds of livestock, and paid their "owners" only an annual tribute, similar to that paid by Seminole towns to the *micco* or chief.

During the 1820s and 1830s, the estelusti and the Seminoles were allies in a series of wars against the Americans although their alliance came under increasing strain. During the 1830s, the estelusti played a major role in the Second Seminole War, fought in resistance to Indian Removal from 1835 to 1842.

The federal government used a combination of deception, bribery, and threats to induce the five nations to give up their land; sometimes a few individuals were persuaded to sign treaties, with the government purporting that the few represented the entire tribe. When federal action did not yield results fast enough to suit southern whites who coveted Indian land for mining, speculation, and cotton production, state governments began to act on their own, proclaiming state jurisdiction over lands still allotted by federal treaty to Indians within the state's borders. The stage was thus set for the forced removal of the five civilized tribes to the trans-Mississippi West during the administration of Andrew Jackson.

Farther north, in the Ohio Valley and the Northwest Territory, Native Americans had already suffered military defeat in the conflict between Britain and the United States. Consigned by treaty to reservations outside the main lines of white advance, most of the tribes were eventually forced west of the Mississippi.

In 1831–1832, a faction of the confederated Sac and Fox Indians under Chief Black Hawk attempted to reoccupy lands east of the Mississippi previously ceded by another tribal faction. Federal troops and Illinois state militia routed the Indians. It was the last stand of the woodland Indians of the Midwest.

Uprooting the once populous Indian communities of the Old Northwest was part of a national program for removing Indians of the eastern part of the country to an area beyond the Mississippi. Not everyone agreed with Thomas Jefferson's belief that Indians, unlike blacks, had the natural ability to adopt white ways and become useful citizens of the republic. People living on the frontier who coveted Indian land and risked violent retaliation for trying to take it, were more likely to think of Native Americans as irredeemable savages, or even as vermin to be exterminated if necessary. Whites also believed that Indians impeded "progress." Furthermore, Indians held land communally and not in private parcels; white settlers regarded this practice as an insuperable obstacle to economic development. During the Monroe era, it became clear that white settlers wanted the removal of all Indians. Andrew Jackson presided over a shift to a far more aggressive Indian removal policy.

Settlement to the Mississippi

While the Indians were being driven beyond the Mississippi, settlers poured into the agricultural heartland of the United States. This movement was the most dramatic and significant phase of the great westward expansion of population and settlement that began in the early colonial period and lasted until the 1880s. In 1810, only about one-seventh of the American population lived beyond the Appalachians; by 1840, more than one-third did. Eight new states were added to the Union during this period. The government took care of Indian removal, but the settlers faced the difficult task of gaining a livelihood from the land.

Much of the vast acreage opened up by the western movement passed through the hands of land speculators before it reached those of the farmers and planters. After a financial panic in 1819 brought ruin to many who had purchased tracts on credit, the minimum price was lowered from $2.00 to $1.25 an acre, but full payment was required in cash. This change favored wealthy speculators, who bought land in massive quantities.

■ *View of the Great Treaty Held at Prairie du Chien (1825). Representatives of eight Native American tribes met with government agents at Prairie du Chien, Wisconsin, in 1825 to define the boundaries of their respective land claims. The United States claimed the right to make "an amicable and final adjustment" of the claims. Within twenty-five years, most of the tribes present at Prairie du Chien had ceded their land to the U.S. government.* ■

Eventually, most of the land did find its way into the hands of actual cultivators. In some areas, squatters arrived before the official survey and formed claims associations that policed land auctions to prevent "outsiders" from bidding up the price and buying their farms out from under them. Squatters also insisted that they had the right to buy the land that they had already improved at the minimum price, a program called "preemption." In 1841, Congress formally acknowledged the right to farm on public lands with assurance of a *future* preemption right.

Settlers who arrived after speculators had secured title had to deal with land barons. Fortunately for the settlers, most speculators operated on credit and were forced to obtain a quick return on their investment. They did this by selling land at a profit to settlers who had some capital and by arranging finance plans for tenants who did not. Thus the family farm or owner-operated plantation quickly became the typical unit of western agriculture.

Since debt was common in the West, most farmers found it necessary to do more than simply raise enough food to subsist; they had to produce something for market. Most of the earliest settlement was along rivers, which provided cheap transportation. But even in more remote areas, farmers managed to get their corn, wheat, cotton, or cured meat to market. To meet the needs of the farmers, local marketing centers quickly sprang up, usually at river junctions. Cities emerged seemingly overnight, and they in turn accelerated regional development.

The People and Culture of the Frontier

Most of the hundreds of thousands of settlers who populated the West were farmers from the seaboard states. They migrated for all sorts of reasons, but prominent among them were overpopulation, rising land prices, and declining fertility of the soil in the older regions. Most moved as family units and tried to recreate their former way of life as soon as possible. Women were often reluctant to migrate in the first place, and when they arrived in new areas, they strove valiantly to recapture the comfort and stability that they had left behind.

New Englanders carried with them their churches, schools, notions of community uplift, and Puritan ideals of hard work and self-denial. Similarly, settlers from Virginia and the Carolinas retained their devotion to family honor, personal independence, and ideas of white supremacy. In the West, differences between the North and South soon emerged.

In general, the pioneers sought out the kind of terrain and soil with which they were already familiar. People from the eastern uplands favored the hill country of the West. Piedmont and tidewater farmers and planters usually made for the lower and flatter areas. Both groups avoided the fertile but unfamiliar prairies. Rather than being the bold and deliberate innovators of myth, the typical agricultural pioneers were deeply averse to changing their traditional habits.

Yet some adjustments were necessary simply to survive under frontier conditions. Initially, at least, an isolated homestead required a high degree of self-sufficiency. The settlers built their own homes and raised their own crops; they made their own clothes and manufactured their own household necessities, such as soap and candles.

But this picture of frontier self-reliance is not the whole story. Most settlers in fact found it extremely difficult to accomplish all the tasks using only family labor. A more common practice was the sharing of work by a number of pioneer families. Assembling the neighbors to raise a house, harvest wheat, or sew quilts helped turn collective work into rare festive occasions. The jug was passed, and various contests sped the work along. Sharing the work was a creative response to the shortage of labor that also provided a source for communal solidarity. These events probably tell us more about the "spirit of the frontier" than the conventional image of the pioneer as a lonely individualist.

Restlessness and geographic mobility also characterized many of the settlers. The wandering of young Abraham Lincoln's family from Kentucky to Indiana and finally to Illinois between 1816 and 1830 was fairly typical. Improved land could be sold at a profit and the proceeds used to buy new acreage beyond the horizon where the soil was reportedly richer. Hence few early-nineteenth-century American farmers developed the kind of attachment to the land that is often associated with rural populations in other parts of the world.

A REVOLUTION IN TRANSPORTATION

It took more than the spread of settlement to bring prosperity to new areas and ensure that they would identify with older regions or with the country as a whole. Along the eastern seaboard, land transportation was so primitive that in 1813 it took seventy-five days for one wagon of goods drawn by four horses to make a trip of 1000 miles, and traveling west over the mountains meant months on the trail.

After the War of 1812, political leaders realized that national security, economic progress, and political unity were all more or less dependent on binding the nation together through a greatly improved transportation network. Accordingly, President Monroe called for a federally supported program of "internal improvements" in 1815. In the ensuing decades, the nationalist's vision of a transportation revolution was realized to a considerable extent, although the direct role of the federal government turned out to be less important than anticipated.

Roads and Steamboats

Americans who wanted to get from place to place rapidly and cheaply needed new and improved roads. The first great federal transportation project was the building between 1811 and 1818 of the National Road between Cumberland, Maryland, on the Potomac, and Wheeling, Virginia, on the Ohio. This impressive, gravel-surfaced toll road was subsequently extended and reached Vandalia, Illinois, in 1838. Soon state governments promoted the building of other "turnpikes," as these privately owned toll roads chartered by the states were called. By about 1825, thousands of miles of turnpikes crisscrossed southern New England, upstate New York, much of Pennsylvania, and northern New Jersey.

But the toll roads benefited travelers more than they did transporters of bulky freight. The latter usually found that total expenses—toll plus the cost and maintenance of heavy wagons and great teams of horses—were too high to guarantee a satisfactory profit from haulage. Hence traffic was less than anticipated, and investors were disappointed with returns. In the final analysis, turnpikes failed to link up the settled seaboard areas with the new West. What was desperately needed was a form of transportation that could inexpensively haul freight over long distances.

The fact that the United States had a great natural transportation system in its river network was one of the most significant reasons for the country's rapid economic development. The Ohio-Mississippi system in particular provided ready access to the rich agricultural areas of the interior and a natural outlet for their products. By 1815, flatboats loaded with wheat, flour, salt pork, and cotton were floating toward New Orleans. Even after the coming of the steamboat, flatboats continued to carry a major share of the downriver trade.

But the flatboat trade was necessarily a one-way traffic. A farmer from Ohio or Illinois, or someone hired to do the job, could float down to New Orleans easily enough, but there was generally no way to get back except by walking overland through rough country. Until the problem of upriver navigation was solved, the Ohio and Mississippi could not carry the manufactured goods that farmers desired in exchange for their crops.

Fortunately, a solution was readily at hand—the use of steam power for river transportation. Inventor Robert Fulton improved on an idea that many men had toyed with for years. In 1807, he successfully propelled the *Clermont* 150 miles up the Hudson River. The first steamboat launched in the West was the *New Orleans*, which made the trip from Pittsburgh to New Orleans in 1811–1812. The steamboat revolutionized the commerce of the West. By 1820, sixty-nine steamboats with a total capacity of 13,890 tons were plying western waters.

Steam transport reduced costs, increased the speed of moving goods and people, and allowed two-way commerce on the Mississippi and Ohio Rivers. The steamboat quickly captured the American imagination. The great paddle wheelers became luxurious floating hotels, the natural habitats of gamblers and confidence men. But the boats also had a lamentable safety record, frequently running aground, colliding, or blowing up. As a result of such accidents, the federal government began in 1838 to regulate steamboats and monitor their construction and operation. This legislation stands as the only instance in the pre–Civil War period of direct federal regulation of domestic transportation.

The Canal Boom

A transportation system based solely on rivers and roads had one enormous gap—it did not provide an economical way to ship western farm produce directly east to the growing urban market of the seaboard states. The solution offered by the politicians and merchants of the Middle Atlantic and midwestern states was to build a system of canals to link seaboard cities directly to the Great Lakes, the Ohio, and ultimately the Mississippi.

The best natural location for a canal between a river flowing into the Atlantic and one of the Great Lakes was between Albany and Buffalo, a relatively flat stretch of more than 350 miles. When the New York legislature approved the bold

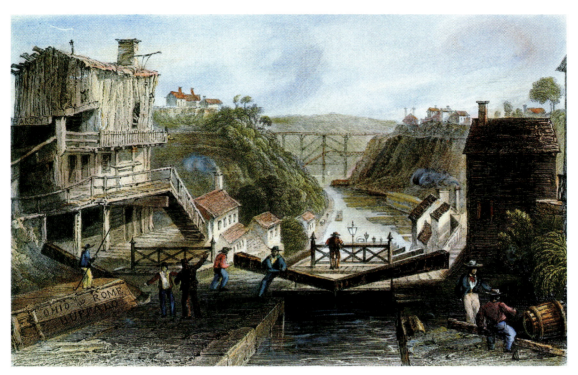

■ *Illustration of a lock on the Erie Canal at Lockport, New York, 1838. The successful canal facilitated trade by linking the Great Lakes regions to the eastern seaports.* ■

project in 1817, no more than about 100 miles of canal existed in the entire United States. Credit for the enterprise belongs to New York's governor, De Witt Clinton, who convinced the state legislature that the project could be successfully financed by issuing bonds. In 1825, the completed canal was opened, to great public acclaim.

Some 364 miles long, 40 feet wide, and 4 feet deep, and containing 84 locks, the Erie Canal was the most spectacular engineering achievement of the young republic. Furthermore, it was a great economic success. It reduced the cost of moving goods from Buffalo to Albany to one-twelfth the previous rate. Easterners and Westerners could now buy each other's goods at sharply reduced prices. The canal also helped make New York City the unchallenged commercial capital of the nation.

The great success of the Erie Canal inspired other states to extend public credit for canal building. During the 1830s and 1840s, Pennsylvania, Ohio, and Illinois embarked on ambitious canal construction projects, from Philadelphia to Pittsburgh, from the Ohio River to Cleveland, and from Chicago to the Illinois River and the Mississippi.

The canal boom ended when it became apparent in the 1830s and 1840s that most of these waterways were unprofitable. State credit had been overextended, and the panic and depression of the late 1830s and early 1840s forced retrenchment. Moreover, by this time, railroads were beginning to compete successfully for the same traffic, and a new phase in the transportation revolution was beginning.

But canals should not be written off as economic failures that contributed little to the improvement of transportation. Some of them continued to be important arteries up to the time of the Civil War and even beyond. Furthermore, the failure of many of the canals was due solely to their inability to yield an adequate return on the money invested in them. The problem of financing tells little or nothing about their public usefulness. Had the canals been thought of as providing a service rather than yielding a profit—in the manner of modern interstate highways—they might have maintained a high reputation for serving the economic interests of the nation. As it was, they contributed enormously to creating vital economic ties between the agricultural West and the industrializing Northeast.

EMERGENCE OF A MARKET ECONOMY

The desire to reduce the costs and increase the speed of shipping heavy freight over great distances laid the groundwork for a new economic system. With the advent of steamboats and canals, western farmers could inexpensively ship their crops both to the Northeast and New Orleans. This improved transport led to an increase in farm income and provided a stimulus for commercial agriculture.

The Beginning of Commercial Agriculture

At the beginning of the nineteenth century, the typical farming household consumed most of what it produced and sold only a small surplus in nearby markets. Most manufactured articles were produced at home. Easier and cheaper access to distant markets effected a decisive change in this pattern. Between 1800 and 1840, agricultural output increased remarkably. The rise in productivity was partly due to technological advances. Iron or steel plows proved better than wooden ones, the grain cradle replaced the scythe, and better varieties of crops, grasses, and livestock were introduced. But the availability of good land and a revolution in marketing were the most important spurs to profitable commercial farming. Transportation facilities made distant markets available and plugged farmers into a commercial network that provided credit and relieved them of the need to do their own selling.

The emerging exchange network encouraged movement away from diversified farming toward a regional concentration on staple crops. Wheat was the main cash crop in the North, and the center of its cultivation moved westward as soil depletion, pests, and plant disease lowered yields in older regions. On the rocky hillsides of New England, sheep raising was displacing the mixed farming of an earlier era. But the prime example of successful staple production in this era was the rise of the cotton kingdom in the South.

A number of factors made the South the world's greatest producer of cotton. First was the great demand generated by the rise of textile manufacturing in England and, to a lesser extent, in New England. Second was the effect of the cotton gin in processing. Invented by Eli Whitney in 1793, this simple device cut the labor costs involved in cleaning short-staple cotton. Third was the availability of good land in the Southeast. Similar to the movement of the center of wheat cultivation in the North, the center of cotton growing moved steadily westward from South Carolina and Georgia, primarily, toward the fertile plantation areas of Alabama, Mississippi, and Louisiana.

A fourth factor—the existence of slavery, which provided a flexible system of forced labor—permitted operations on a scale impossible for the family labor system

A Look at the Past

Merino Sheep

Increasing commercialism and industrialism affected both urban and rural dwellers during the early nineteenth century. Farmers could choose to participate in the changing economy in several ways. Supplying factories with raw materials and workers with food numbered among their options. Successful agriculture required farmers to alter their strategies. Some farmers intensified production, experimented with scientific methods, increased their herd sizes, and imported improved livestock breeds such as these very woolly merino sheep. Importing livestock, breeding improved varieties, and increasing production required money. ✷ What kind of a risk did a farmer take by enthusiastically producing for factories? What do the changes farmers made reveal about economic attitudes?

of the agricultural North. Finally, the cotton economy benefited from the South's splendid natural transportation system, its great network of navigable rivers. The South had less need than other agricultural regions for artificial "internal improvements" such as canals and roads. Planters could simply establish themselves on or near a river and ship their crops to market via natural waterways.

Commerce and Banking

As regions specialized in the growing of commercial crops, a new system of marketing emerged. During an early or pioneer stage in many areas, farmers did their marketing personally. With the growth of country towns, local merchants took over the crop near the source, bartering clothing and other manufactured goods for produce. These intermediaries shipped the farmers' crops to larger local markets such as Pittsburgh, Cincinnati, and St. Louis. Cotton growers in the South were more likely to deal directly with factors (agents) in the port cities from which their crop was exported. But even in the South, intermediaries existed in inland towns such as Macon, Nashville, and Shreveport.

The extension of credit was a crucial element in the whole system. Farmers borrowed from local merchants, who received an advance of their own when they consigned the crop to a commission house or factor. The commission agents relied on credit from merchants or manufacturers at the ultimate destination, which might be Liverpool or New York City. The need for credit encouraged the growth of money and banking.

Before the revolutions in transportation and marketing, small-scale local economies could survive to a considerable extent on barter. But long-distance transactions involving credit and deferred payment required money and lots of it. Although the Constitution authorized only the federal government to issue money, in the early to mid-nineteenth century, the government printed no paper money and produced gold and silver coins in such inappreciable quantities that it utterly failed to meet the expanding economy's requirement for a circulating currency.

Private or state banking institutions filled the void by issuing banknotes, promises to redeem their paper in *specie*—gold or silver—at the bearer's request. The demand for money and credit during the economic boom after 1815 led to a vast increase in the number of state banks—from 88 to 208 in two years. The resulting flood of state banknotes caused this form of currency to depreciate well below its face value and threatened a runaway inflation. In an effort to stabilize the currency, Congress established a second Bank of the United States in 1816.

The Bank was expected to serve as a check on the state banks by forcing them to resume specie payments. But it did not perform this task well in its early years. In fact, its own free-lending policies contributed to an overextension of credit that led to financial panic and depression in 1819. As a result, hostility to banks became a prominent feature of American politics.

Early Industrialism

The growth of the market economy also created new opportunities for industrialists. In 1815, most manufacturing in the United States was still carried on in households, in the workshops of skilled artisans, or in small mills. The factory form of production, in which supervised workers operated or tended machines under one roof, was rare. Even in the American textile industry, most of the spinning of thread and weaving, cutting, and sewing of cloth was still done in the home.

Most of the clothing worn by Americans was made entirely by female family members. But a growing proportion was produced for market, rather than direct home consumption. Under the "putting-out system" of manufacturing, merchant capitalists provided raw material to people in their own homes, picked up the finished or semifinished products, paid the workers, and took charge of distribution. The putting-out system was centered in the Northeast, and besides textiles, such items as shoes and hats were made in this manner.

Articles that required greater skill were made primarily by artisans working in small shops in towns. But in the decades after 1815, the merchants who purchased from these workers gained greater control over production. Shops expanded in size, masters tended to become entrepreneurs rather than working artisans, and journeymen often became wage earners rather than aspiring masters. At the same time, the growing market for low-priced goods led to a stress on speed, quantity, and standardization of the methods of production.

A fully developed factory system emerged first in textile manufacturing. The establishment of the first cotton mills that used the power loom as well as spinning machinery—thereby making it possible to turn fiber into cloth in a single factory—resulted from the efforts of a trio of Boston merchants, Francis Cabot Lowell, Nathan Appleton, and Patrick Tracy Jackson.

As the Boston Manufacturing Company, the associates began their operation in Waltham, Massachusetts, in 1813. Their phenomenal success led to the erection of larger and even more profitable mills. The mill at nearby Lowell became a great showplace for early American industrialization. Its large and seemingly contented workforce of unmarried women residing in supervised dormitories, its unprecedented scale of operation, its successful mechanization of almost every stage of production—all captured the American middle-class imagination in the 1820s and 1830s. But in the late 1830s and 1840s conditions in the mills changed for the worse as the owners began to require more work for lower pay, and some of the "mill girls" became militant labor activists. Other mills using similar methods sprang up throughout New England, and the region became the first important manufacturing area in the United States.

The shift away from the putting-out system to factory production changed the course of capitalistic activity in the region. Before the 1820s, New England merchants concentrated mainly on international trade. A major source of capital was the lucrative China trade carried on by fast, well-built New England vessels. When the success of Waltham and Lowell became clear, many merchants shifted their capital away from oceanic trade and into manufacturing. Politically, this change meant that representatives from New England no longer advocated a low tariff that favored exporters over importers. They now became leading proponents of a high duty rate designed to protect manufacturers from foreign competition.

The development of other "infant industries" in the wake of the War of 1812 was less dramatic and would not come to fruition until the 1840s and 1850s. But the first stirrings of an iron industry and a small arms industry were felt during this period. And although most manufacturing was centered in the Northeast, the West also made modest industrial progress as the number and size of facilities such as gristmills, slaughterhouses, and tanneries increased. Distilleries in Kentucky and Ohio were particularly active.

It should not be assumed, however, that America had already experienced an industrial

■ *Lowell, Massachusetts, became America's model industrial town in the first half of the nineteenth century. Textile mills sprang up throughout Lowell in the 1820s and 1830s, employing thousands of workers, mostly women. In this photograph from c. 1848, a woman is shown working at a loom.* ■

revolution by 1840. Most of the nation's labor force was still employed in agriculture; fewer than one of every ten workers was directly involved in factory production. The revolution that did occur during these years was essentially one of distribution rather than production. The growth of a market economy of national scope was the principal economic development of this period. And it was one that had vast repercussions for all aspects of American life.

For those who benefited from it most directly, the market economy provided firm evidence of progress and improvement. But many of those who suffered from its periodic panics and depressions were receptive to politicians and reformers who attacked corporations and "the money power."

THE POLITICS OF NATION BUILDING AFTER THE WAR OF 1812

Geographic expansion, economic growth, and the changes in American life that accompanied them were bound in the long run to generate political controversy. Federal and state policies meant to encourage or control growth and expansion did not benefit farmers, merchants, manufacturers, and laborers equally. Conflicts inevitably arose. Northerners, Southerners, and Westerners were affected in different ways, too. But the temporary lack of a party system meant that politicians did not have to band together and offer the voters a choice of programs and ideologies. A myth of national harmony prevailed, culminating in the **Era of Good Feelings** during James Monroe's two terms as president.

Behind the facade, individuals and groups fought for advantage, as always, but without the public accountability and need for broad popular approval that a party system would have required. As a result, popular interest in national politics fell to a low ebb.

The absence of party discipline and programs did not completely immobilize the federal government. The president took important initiatives in foreign policy, Congress legislated on matters of national concern, and the Supreme Court made far-reaching decisions. The common theme of the public policies that emerged between the War of 1812 and the Age of Jackson was an awakening nationalism—a sense of American pride and purpose that reflected the events of the period.

Era of Good Feelings A descriptive term for the era of President James Monroe, who served two terms from 1817–1823. During Monroe's administration, partisan conflict abated and bold federal initiatives suggested increased nationalism.

The Republicans in Power

By the end of the War of 1812, the Federalist party was no longer a significant force in national politics, although the Republicans had adopted some of their rivals' policies. Retreating from their original philosophy of states' rights and limited government, Republican party leaders now openly embraced a national bank, a protective tariff for industry, and a program of federally financed internal improvements.

In Congress, Henry Clay of Kentucky took the lead in advocating that the government take action to promote economic development. The keystone of what Clay called the **American system** was a high protective tariff to stimulate industrial growth and provide a "home market" for the farmers of the West, making the nation economically self-sufficient and free from a dangerous dependence on Europe.

In 1816, Congress took the first step toward Clay's goal by passing a tariff that raised import duties an average of 20 percent. The tariff was passed to protect American industry from British competition and received patriotic support in all sections of the country. Americans viewed the act as a move toward economic independence, a necessity to protect political independence.

Later the same year, Congress voted to establish the second Bank of the United States. Organized much like the first Bank, it was a mixed public-private institution. The Bank served the government by providing a depository for its funds, an outlet for marketing its securities, and a source of redeemable banknotes that could be used

American system A national economic strategy championed by Kentucky Senator Henry Clay, the American system stressed high tariffs and internal improvements.

for the payment of taxes or the purchase of public lands. State banking interests and strict constructionists opposed the bank bill, but the majority of Congress found it a necessary and proper means for promoting financial stability and meeting the federal government's constitutional responsibility to raise money from taxation and loans.

Legislation dealing with internal improvements made less headway. Except for the National Road, the federal government undertook no major transportation projects during the Madison and Monroe administrations. Both presidents believed that internal improvements were desirable but that a constitutional amendment was required before federal monies could legally be used for the building of roads and canals within individual states. Both men vetoed internal improvement bills. Consequently, public aid for the building of roads and canals continued to come almost exclusively from state and local governments.

Monroe as President

Like Jefferson before him, President Madison chose his own successor in 1816. James Monroe thus became the third successive Virginian to occupy the White House for two full terms. Experienced but stolid and unimaginative, he lacked the intellectual depth and agility of his predecessors, but he was reliable, dignified, and high-principled.

The keynote of Monroe's presidency was national harmony, which meant that he went out of his way to avoid controversy. Indeed, one newspaper writer announced that party strife was a thing of the past and that an "era of good feelings" had begun. The principal aim of Monroe's administrations was to see that the good feelings persisted. He wanted to end all sectional and economic differences and assert American power and influence on the world stage. His choice of a cabinet was well calculated to serve these purposes. His secretary of state, John Quincy Adams, was not only a diplomat of great experience and skill but also a New Englander. If recent precedent was to be followed, he would succeed Monroe as president and thus end the "Virginia dynasty." As secretary of war, Monroe chose John C. Calhoun, a leading Southerner who was at this time a fervent nationalist. To accommodate the old-line states' rights wing of the party, he appointed William C. Crawford of Georgia as secretary of the treasury.

The first challenge to Monroe's hopes for domestic peace and prosperity was the Panic of 1819, an economic depression that ended the postwar boom. Congress acted by passing debt relief legislation, but Monroe himself had no program to relieve the crisis. He was able to remain above the fray and persuade the American public that he was in no way responsible for the state of the economy, nor was he in a position to do anything about it. Unlike a modern president, Monroe could retain his full popularity during hard times.

Monroe prized national harmony even more than economic prosperity. But during his first administration, a bitter controversy developed between the North and the South over the admission of Missouri to the Union. Once again, Monroe remained above the battle and suffered little damage to his own prestige. It was left entirely to Congress to deal with the nation's most serious domestic political crisis between the War of 1812 and the late 1840s.

The Missouri Compromise

In 1817, the Missouri territorial assembly applied for statehood. It was clear that Missouri expected to be admitted to the Union as a slave state. Since Missouri was the first state other than Louisiana to be carved out of the Louisiana Purchase, the resolution of the status of slaves there would have implications for the rest of the trans-Mississippi West.

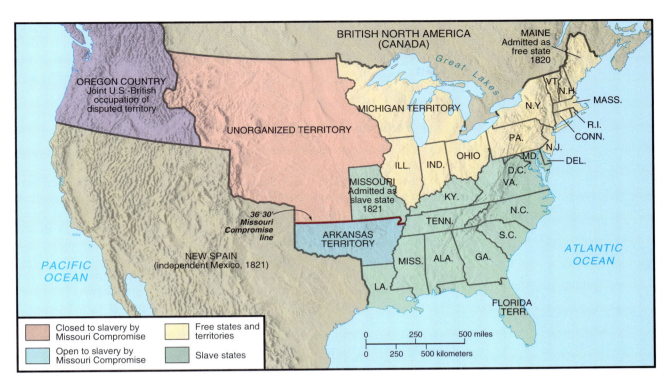

THE MISSOURI COMPROMISE, 1820–1821   *The Missouri Compromise kept the balance of power in the Senate by admitting Missouri as a slave state and Maine as a free state. The agreement temporarily settled the argument over slavery in the territories.* ■

When the question came before Congress in early 1819, submerged sectional fears and anxieties came bubbling to the surface. Many Northerners resented southern control of the presidency and the three-fifths clause of the Constitution. Southerners feared for the future of what they regarded as a necessary balance of power between the sections. Up until 1819, strict equality had been maintained by alternately admitting slave and free states. Because the North had a decisive majority in the House of Representatives, the South saw its equal vote in the Senate as essential to preserving the balance.

In February 1819, Congressman James Tallmadge of New York introduced an amendment to the statehood bill banning further introduction of slaves into Missouri and providing for the gradual emancipation of those already there. The amendment was approved by the House but voted down by the Senate. The issue remained unresolved until a new Congress convened in December 1819. In the meantime, the measure elicited hot debate. Southern senators saw the Tallmadge amendment as an attack on the principle of equality between the states—a northern ploy to upset the balance of power. They also were concerned about the future of African American slavery and the white racial privilege that went with it.

A separate statehood petition from the people of Maine suggested a way out of the impasse. In February 1820, the Senate passed the **Missouri Compromise,** voting to couple the admission of Missouri as a slave state with the admission of Maine as a free state. A further amendment was also passed prohibiting slavery in the rest of the Louisiana Purchase north of the southern border of Missouri, or above the latitude of 36°30′. The Senate's compromise then went back to the House where Henry Clay, who broke the proposal into three separate bills, adroitly maneuvered it through to narrow victory.

A major sectional crisis had been resolved. But the Missouri affair had ominous overtones for the future of North-South relations. Thomas Jefferson described the

Missouri Compromise A sectional compromise in Congress in 1820 that admitted Missouri to the Union as a slave state and Maine as a free state. It also banned slavery in the remainder of the Louisiana Purchase territory above the latitude of 36°30′.

controversy as "a fire bell in the night," threatening the peace of the Union. Clearly, the subject of slavery or its extension aroused deep sectional feeling. Emotional rhetoric about morality and fundamental rights issued from both sides. If the United States were to acquire any new territories in which the status of slavery had to be determined by Congress, renewed sectional strife would be inevitable.

Postwar Nationalism and the Supreme Court

While the Monroe administration was proclaiming national harmony and congressional leaders were struggling to reconcile sectional differences, the Supreme Court was making a more substantial and enduring contribution to the growth of nationalism and a strong federal government, thanks to Chief Justice John Marshall. A Virginian, a Federalist, and a devoted disciple of George Washington, Marshall served as chief justice from 1801 to 1835, and during that entire period, he dominated the Court as no other chief justice has ever done.

As the author of most of the major opinions issued by the Supreme Court during its formative period, Marshall gave shape to the Constitution and clarified the crucial role of the Court in the American system of government. He placed the protection of individual liberty, especially the right to acquire property, above the attainment of political, social, and economic equality. Ultimately he was a nationalist, believing that the strength, security, and happiness of the American people depended mainly on economic growth and the creation of new wealth. As he saw it, the Constitution existed to provide the political ground rules for a society of industrious and productive individuals who could enrich themselves while adding to the strength of the nation as a whole.

The role of the Supreme Court, in Marshall's view, was to interpret and enforce the ground rules, especially against the efforts of state legislatures to interfere with the constitutionally protected rights of individuals or combinations of individuals to acquire property through productive activity. The Court also permitted the federal government to assume broad powers so that it could fulfill its constitutional responsibility to promote the general welfare by encouraging economic development and national prosperity.

In a series of major decisions between 1819 and 1824, the Marshall Court enhanced the power of the judicial branch and used the contract clause of the Constitution (which prohibited a state from passing a law "impairing the obligations of contacts") to limit the power of state legislatures. It also strengthened the federal government by sanctioning a broad or loose construction of its constitutional powers and by clearly affirming its supremacy over the states.

In ***Dartmouth College* v. *Woodward*** (1819), the Marshall Court made the far-reaching determination that any charter granted by a state to a private corporation was fully protected by the contract clause. In practical terms, the Court's ruling in the Dartmouth case meant that the kinds of business enterprises then being incorporated by state governments—such as turnpike or canal companies and textile manufacturing firms—could hold on indefinitely to any privileges or favors that had been granted in their original charters. The decision therefore increased the power and independence of business corporations by weakening the ability of the states to regulate them or withdraw their privileges.

About a month after the Dartmouth ruling, in March 1819, the Marshall Court handed down its most important decision. In ***McCulloch* v. *Maryland*,** the Court ruled that a Maryland tax on the Bank of the United States was unconstitutional. The two main issues were whether Congress had the right to establish a national bank and whether a state had the power to tax or regulate an agency or institution created by Congress.

In response to the first question, Marshall set forth his doctrine of "implied powers"—that the federal government could assume powers that helped it fulfill

Dartmouth College v. *Woodward* Ruling in 1819, the Supreme Court decided that the Constitution protected charters given to corporations by states.

McCulloch v. *Maryland* Ruling on this banking case in 1819, the Supreme Court propped up the idea of "implied powers," meaning the Constitution could be broadly interpreted. This pivotal ruling also asserted the supremacy of federal power over state power.

the "great object" for which it had been founded. Marshall thus struck a blow for "loose construction" of the Constitution. In answer to the second question, Marshall held that if a state had the power to tax a federal agency, it would also have the power to destroy it. Shot through the decision was the belief that the American people "did not design to make this government dependent on the states." In the continuing debate between states' righters and nationalists, the Marshall Court came down firmly on the side of the nationalists.

In *Gibbons v. Ogden* (1824), a steamboat monopoly granted by the state of New York was challenged by a competing ferry service. The Supreme Court declared the New York grant unconstitutional in a move that further broadened the power of the federal government at the expense of the states by bolstering the right of Congress to regulate interstate commerce. At the same time, the Court encouraged the growth of a national market economy. The actions of the Supreme Court provide the clearest example of the main nationalistic trends of the postwar period—the acknowledgment of the federal government's major role in promoting the growth of a powerful and prosperous America and the rise of a nationwide capitalistic economy.

Gibbons v. Ogden In this 1824 case, the Supreme Court affirmed and expanded the power of the federal government to regulate interstate commerce.

Nationalism in Foreign Policy: The Monroe Doctrine

The new spirit of nationalism was also reflected in foreign affairs. The main diplomatic challenge Monroe faced after his reelection in 1820 was how to respond to the successful revolt of most of Spain's Latin American colonies after the Napoleonic wars. Henry Clay and many other Americans favored immediate recognition of the new republics, believing that their neighbors to the south were simply following the example of the United States in its own struggle for independence.

Before 1822, the administration struck a policy of neutrality. But Congress clamored for recognition. Starting in 1822, Monroe reversed his position, and during the next four years, the United States officially recognized Mexico, Colombia, Chile, Argentina, Brazil, the Federation of Central American States, and Peru.

Recognizing the republics put the United States on a possible collision course with the major European powers. In 1822, Austria, Prussia, Russia, and France met in Verona and formed the Grand Alliance, a reactionary union committed to rolling back the tides of liberalism, self-government, and national self-determination that had arisen during the French Revolution and its Napoleonic aftermath. Although the Grand Alliance did not undertake direct intervention in Latin America, it did give France the green light to invade Spain and, if so disposed, to reconquer the empire. Both Great Britain and the United States were alarmed by this prospect.

American policymakers were particularly troubled by Czar Alexander I, who was attempting to extend Russian claims on the Pacific Coast of North America south to the 51st parallel—into the Oregon country that the United States wanted for itself. The Russian threat weighed heavily on the mind of Secretary of State Adams as he formulated foreign policy during Monroe's second term.

The threat from the Grand Alliance compelled America to move closer to Great Britain, which for trading reasons favored independent Latin American countries. In August 1823, the British foreign secretary, George Canning, suggested to the U.S. minister to Great Britain the possibility of joint Anglo-American action against the designs of the Alliance. Monroe, as well as former Presidents Jefferson and Madison, welcomed the suggestion and favored open cooperation with the British.

Secretary of State Adams, however, favored a different approach. He believed that the national interest would best be served by avoiding all entanglement in European politics while at the same time discouraging European intervention in the Americas. In addition, political ambition motivated Adams, and he did not want to be labeled pro-British. He therefore advocated unilateral action by the United States rather than some kind of joint declaration with the British.

Chronology

1813	Boston Manufacturing Company founds cotton mill at Waltham, Massachusetts
1815	War of 1812 ends
1816	James Monroe is elected president
1819	Supreme Court hands down far-reaching decisions in the Dartmouth College case and in *McCulloch* v. *Maryland* ■ Adams-Onís Treaty cedes Spanish territory to the United States ■ Financial panic is followed by a depression lasting until 1823
1820	Missouri Compromise resolves the nation's first sectional crisis ■ Monroe is reelected president unanimously
1823	Monroe Doctrine is proclaimed
1824	Lafayette revisits the United States ■ Supreme Court decides *Gibbons* v. *Ogden* ■ John Quincy Adams elected president
1825	Erie Canal is completed; Canal Era begins

Monroe Doctrine A key foreign policy made by President James Monroe in 1823, it declared the western hemisphere off-limits to new European colonization; in return, the United States promised not to meddle in European affairs.

In the end, Adams managed to swing Monroe around to his viewpoint. In his annual message to Congress on December 2, 1823, Monroe included a far-reaching statement on foreign policy that was actually written primarily by Adams, who did become president in 1824. What came to be known as the **Monroe Doctrine** solemnly declared that the United States opposed any further colonization in the Americas or any effort by European nations to extend their political systems outside of their own hemisphere. In return, the United States pledged not to involve itself in the internal affairs of Europe or to take part in European wars.

Although the Monroe Doctrine made little impression on the great powers of Europe at the time it was proclaimed, it signified the rise of a new sense of independence and self-confidence in American attitudes toward the Old World. The Doctrine also reflected the inward-looking nationalism that had arisen after the War of 1812.

CONCLUSION: THE END OF THE ERA OF GOOD FEELINGS

The Era of Good Feelings turned out to be a passing phase and something of an illusion. The idea that an elite group of nonpartisan statesmen could define common purposes and harmonize competing elements—the concept of leadership embodied in Monroe and Adams—would no longer be viable in the more contentious and democratic America of the Jacksonian era. Increasingly, the power of the "common man" and sectionalism would shape national debates and policy.

KEY TERMS

Adams-Onís Treaty, p. 166

Era of Good Feelings, p. 177

American system, p. 177

Missouri Compromise, p. 179

Dartmouth College v. *Woodward*, p. 180

McCulloch v. *Maryland*, p. 180

Gibbons v. *Ogden*, p. 181

Monroe Doctrine, p. 182

RECOMMENDED READING

The standard surveys of the period between the War of 1812 and the age of Jackson are two works by George Dangerfield: *The Era of Good Feelings* (1952) and *Awakening of American Nationalism, 1815–1828* (1965); but see also the early chapters of Charles Sellers, *The Market Revolution: Jacksonian America, 1815–1846* (1991). For a positive account of the venturesome, entrepreneurial spirit of the age, see Joyce Appleby, *Inheriting the Revolution: The First Generations of Americans* (2000). On westward expansion, see John Mack Faragher, *Women and Men on the Overland Trail* (1979); Stephen Aron, *How the West Was Lost: The Transformation of Kentucky from Daniel Boone to Henry Clay* (1996); and Richard White, *It's Your Misfortune and None of My Own* (1992). On Native American life in the antebellum Southeast, see William G. McLoughlin, *Cherokee Renascence in the New Republic* (1986), and Theda Perdue, *Slavery and the Evolution of Cherokee Society, 1540–1866* (1979).

Outstanding studies of economic transformation and the rise of a market economy are George R. Taylor, *The Transportation Revolution, 1815–1860* (1951); Paul W. Gates, *The Farmer's Age: Agriculture, 1815–1860* (1960); Stuart Bruchey, *Enterprise: The Dynamic Economy of a Free People* (1990); and Douglas C. North, *The Economic Growth of the United States, 1790–1860* (1961). Early manufacturing is described in David J. Jeremy, *Transatlantic Industrial Revolution* (1981) and Robert F. Dalzell, *The Boston Associates and the World They Made* (1987). On early mill workers, see Thomas Dublin, *Women at Work: The Transformation of Work and Community in Lowell, Massachusetts, 1826–1860* (1979).

On the Marshall Court and legal change in this era, see Morton Horwitz, *The Tansformation of American Law, 1780–1865* (1977), and G. Edward White, *The Marshall Court and Cultural Change, 1815–1835* (1991). Samuel F. Bemis, *John Quincy Adams and the Foundations of American Policy* (1949) provides the classic account of the statesmanship that led to the Monroe Doctrine. But see also Ernest May, *The Making of the Monroe Doctrine* (1976), for a persuasive interpretation of how the doctrine originated.

SUGGESTED WEB SITES

The Era of the Mountain Men
www.xmission.com/~drudy/amm.html
Private letters can speak volumes about the concerns and environment of the writers and recipients. Letters from early settlers west of the Mississippi River are offered on this site.

Pioneering the Upper Midwest
memory.loc.gov/ammem/umhtml/umhome.html
This collection of firsthand accounts and memoirs vividly depicts life on the Midwestern frontier.

Prairietown, Indiana
www.connerprairie.org/explore/prairietown.html
This fictional model of a town and its inhabitants on the early frontier says much about America's movement westward and the everyday lives of Americans.

The Seminole Tribe of Florida
www.seminoletribe.com/
Before he was president, Andrew Jackson began a war against the Seminole Indians. This site presents information on their history and culture.

Erie Canal On-line
www.syracuse.com/features/eriecanal
This site, built around the diary of a fourteen-year-old girl who traveled from Amsterdam to Syracuse, New York, in the early nineteenth century, explores the construction and importance of the Erie Canal.

Whole Cloth: Discovering Science and Technology through American Textile History
www.si.edu/lemelson/centerpieces/wholecloth/
The Jerome and Dorothy Lemelson Center for the Study of Invention and Innovation/Society for the History of Technology put together this site which includes excellent activities and sources concerning early American manufacturing and industry.

Road Through the Wilderness: The Making of the National Road
www.connerprairie.org/historyonline/ntlroad.html
The National Road was a hot political topic in the early republic and was part of the beginning of the development of America's infrastructure. This on-line essay by historian Timothy Crumrin discusses the making of the National Road.

Chapter 10

The Triumph of White Men's Democracy

Democratic Space: The New Hotels

During the 1820s and 1830s, the United States became a more democratic country for at least some of its population. The emerging spirit of popular democracy found expression in a new institution—the large hotel with several stories and hundreds of rooms. When he arrived in Washington to prepare for his administration, President-elect Andrew Jackson stayed in the recently opened National Hotel, only one of several large "first class" hotels that opened immediately before or during his presidency.

The hotel boom responded to the increasing tendency of Americans in the 1820s and 1830s to move about the country. It was to service the rising tides of travelers, transients, and new arrivals that entrepreneurs erected these large places of accommodation, which provided lodging, food, and drink on a large scale in the center of many cities. A prototype was the Boston Exchange Hotel, with its eight stories and three hundred rooms.

The "democratic" mingling of the social classes in these new hotels often caused foreigners to view them as "a true reflection of American society." Their very existence showed that people were on the move geographically and socially. Among their patrons were traveling salesmen, ambitious young men seeking to establish themselves in a new city, and restless pursuers of economic opportunities who were not yet ready to put down roots.

Hotel managers shocked European visitors by failing to enforce traditional social distinctions among their clientele. Under the "American plan," guests were required to pay for their meals, and everyone, regardless of class, ate at a common table. With two crucial exceptions—unescorted women and people of color—almost anyone who could pay enjoyed the kind of personal service previously available only to a privileged class.

The hotel culture revealed some of the limitations of the era's democratic ideals and aspirations. Blacks and women were excluded or discriminated against, just as they were denied suffrage at a time when it was being extended to all white males. The genuinely poor simply could not afford to patronize the hotels and were consigned to squalid rooming houses. If the social equality *within* the hotel reflected a decline in traditional rigid class lines, the broad gulf between potential patrons and those who could not pay the rates signaled the growth of inequality based squarely on wealth rather than inherited status.

The hotel life also reflected the emergence of democratic politics. Professional politicians of a new breed, pursuing the votes of a mass electorate, spent much of their time in hotels as they traveled about. Those elected to Congress or a state legislature often lodged and conducted political transactions in hotels.

The hotel can thus be seen as a fitting symbol for the democratic spirit of the age, one that shows its shortcomings as well as its strengths. The new democracy was first of all political, involving the extension of suffrage to virtually all white males and the rise of modern political parties appealing to a mass electorate. It was also social in that it undermined the habit of deferring to people because of their birth or ancestry and offered a greater expectation that individuals born in relatively humble circumstances could climb the ladder of success. But the ideals of equal citizenship and opportunity did not extend across the lines of race and gender, which actually hardened to some degree during this period.

DEMOCRACY IN THEORY AND PRACTICE

Historians have often viewed Andrew Jackson's coming to power—his election in 1828 and the boisterous "people's inauguration" that followed—as the critical moment when a democratic spirit took possession of American culture and public life. But that oversimplifies a very complex movement. The rise of Jackson took place in an atmosphere of ferment and a changing climate of opinion that turned America in a more democratic direction.

During the 1820s and 1830s, the term *democracy* first became generally accepted as a way of describing how American institutions were supposed to work. The Founders had defined democracy as direct rule by the masses of the people; most of them rejected that approach to government because it was at odds with their conception of a well-balanced republic led by a "natural aristocracy." For champions of popular government in the Jacksonian period, however, the people were truly sovereign and could do no wrong. "The voice of the people is the voice of God" was their clearest expression of principle.

Besides evoking this heightened sense of "popular sovereignty," the democratic impulse seemed to stimulate a process of social leveling. Early Americans had usually assumed that the rich and well-born should be treated with special respect and recognized as natural leaders of the community and guardians of its culture and values. By the 1830s, the disappearance of inherited social ranks and clearly defined aristocracies or privilege groups struck European visitors as the most radical feature of democracy in America. The spirit of deference was dying in America.

"Self-made men" of lowly origins could now rise more readily to positions of power and influence. Exclusiveness and aristocratic pretension were now likely to provoke popular hostility or scorn. But economic equality, in the sense of an equitable sharing of wealth, was not part of the agenda of mainstream Jacksonianism. The watchword was equality of *opportunity*, not equality of rewards. Historians now generally agree that economic inequality was actually increasing during this period of political and social democratization.

Democracy and Society

Although some inequalities persisted or even grew during the age of democracy, they did so in the face of a growing belief that equality was the governing principle of American society. What this meant in practice was that no one could expect special privileges because of family connections. The popular hero was the self-made man who had climbed the ladder of success through his own efforts without forgetting his origin.

Except for southern slaveholders, wealthy Americans could not depend on a distinctive social class for domestic service. Instead of keeping "servants," they hired "help"—household workers who sometimes insisted on sharing meals with their employers. No true American was willing to be considered a member of a servant class, and those engaged in domestic work considered it a temporary stopgap.

Except as a euphemistic substitute for the word *slave,* the term *servant* virtually disappeared from the American vocabulary.

Another sign of equality was the decline of distinctive modes of dress for the upper and lower classes. The elaborate periwigs and knee breeches worn by eighteenth-century gentlemen gave way to short hair and pantaloons, a style that was adopted by men of all social classes. Those with a good eye for detail might detect subtle differences in taste or in the quality of materials, but the casual observer could easily conclude that all Americans belonged to a single social class.

Of course, Americans were not all of one social class. In fact, inequality based on control of productive resources was increasing during the Jacksonian period. The rise of industrialization was creating a permanent class of landless, low-paid wage earners in America's cities. In rural areas, there was a significant division between successful commercial farmers or planters and those who subsisted on marginal land. Nevertheless, European observers commented on the fact that all white males were equal before the law and at the polls.

Furthermore, traditional forms of privilege and elitism were indeed under strong attack, as evidenced by changes in the organization and status of the learned professions. State legislatures abolished the licensing requirements for physicians previously administered by local medical societies. As a result, practitioners of unorthodox modes of healing were permitted to compete freely with established medical doctors. The legal profession was similarly opened up to far more people. The result was not always beneficial.

For the clergy, "popular sovereignty" meant that they were increasingly under the thumb of the laity. Ministers had ceased to command respect merely because of their office, and to succeed in their calling, they were forced to develop a more popular and emotional style of preaching. Preachers, as much as politicians, prospered by pleasing the public.

In this atmosphere of democratic leveling, the popular press came to play an increasingly important role as a source of information and opinion. Written and read by common folk, hundreds of newspapers and magazines ushered the mass of white Americans into the political arena. New political views—which in a previous generation might have been silenced by those in power—could now find an audience. Reformers of all kinds could easily publicize their causes, and the press became the venue for the great national debates on issues such as the government's role in banking and the status of slavery in new states and territories. As a profession, journalism was open to anyone who was literate and believed they had something to say. The editors of newspapers with a large circulation were the most influential opinion makers of the age.

Democratic Culture

The democratic spirit also found expression in the rise of new forms of literature and art directed at a mass audience. The intentions of individual artists and writers varied considerably. Some sought success by pandering to popular taste in defiance of traditional standards of high culture. Others tried to capture the spirit of the age by portraying the everyday life of ordinary Americans rather than the traditional subjects of "aristocratic" art. A notable few hoped to use literature and art as a way of improving popular taste and instilling deeper moral and spiritual values. But all of them were aware that their audience was the broad citizenry of a democratic nation rather than a refined elite.

The romantic movement in literature, which came to the fore in the early nineteenth century in both Europe and America, valued strong feeling and mystical intuition over the calm rationality and appeal to common experience that had prevailed in the writing of the eighteenth century. Romanticism was not necessarily connected with democracy; in Europe, it sometimes went along with a reaffirma-

A Look at the Past

Portrait of Andrew Jackson

Andrew Jackson's presidency ushered in a more democratic era and his fashionable clothing reflects that spirit. By the early nineteenth century, plain, dark fabrics had become common for men's suits. No longer did wealthy men flaunt their financial success by wearing sumptuous, richly colored fabrics trimmed with gold and lace. As decent-quality, manufactured textiles became more available and cheaper and ready-made clothing started to become available, fabric quality and fit became less likely to indicate expense. In short, distinctions in men's clothing lessened. The change from the elaborate and body-conscious fashions of the eighteenth century to the modest and somber styles of the nineteenth century suggests that other changes were under way in the culture as well. ✳ How do Jackson's clothes suggest an egalitarian society? Why did American men abandon elaborate, body-conscious fashions and adopt somber, concealing suits? In addition to becoming more democratic, in what other ways was the United States changing in the early nineteenth century and how did changes in men's fashion reflect those changes?

tion of feudalism and the right of a superior few to rule over the masses. In the American setting, however, romanticism often appealed to the feelings and intuitions of ordinary people: the innate love of goodness, truth, and beauty that all people were thought to possess. Writers in search of popularity and economic success, however, often deserted the high plane of romantic art for crass sentimentalism—a willingness to pull out all emotional stops to thrill readers or bring tears to their eyes.

A mass market for popular literature was made possible by a rise in literacy and a revolution in the technology of printing. An increase in potential readers and a decrease in publishing costs led to a flood of lurid and sentimental novels, some of which became the first American best-sellers. Many of the new sentimental novels were written by and for women. Some female authors implicitly protested against their situation by portraying men in general as tyrannical, unreliable, or cruel and the women, whom these men made miserable, as resourceful individualists capable of making their own way. But the standard happy endings sustained the convention that a woman on her own was an unnatural thing, for a virtuous and protective man always turned up and saved the heroine from a truly independent life.

In the theater, melodrama became the dominant genre, involving the inevitable trio of beleaguered heroine, mustachioed villain, and a hero who arrives in the nick of time. Another favorite was the patriotic comedy in which the rustic Yankee foiled the foppish European aristocrat. Men and women of all classes went

■ *William Sidney Mount,* Rustic Dance After a Sleigh Ride, *1830. Mount's portrayals of country people folk dancing, gambling, playing music, or horse trading were pieces that appealed strongly to contemporaries. Art historians have found much to praise in his use of architecture, particularly that of the common barn, to achieve striking compositional effects.* ■

to the theater, and those in the cheap seats often openly voiced their displeasure with an actor or a play.

The spirit of popular sovereignty expressed itself less dramatically in the visual arts, but its influence was nonetheless felt. Beginning in the 1830s, painters turned from portraying great events and famous people to depicting scenes from everyday life. Democratic genre painting captured the lives of plain folk with both skill and understanding. Popular recreation and electioneering activity were common motifs.

Architecture and sculpture reflected the democratic spirit in another mode; they were viewed as civic art forms meant to extol the achievements of the republic. In the 1820s and 1830s, the classical Greek style, with its columned facades, was favored for banks, hotels, and private dwellings as well as for public buildings. Similarly, sculpture was intended strictly for public admiration or inspiration, and its principal subjects were the heroes of the republic.

Serious exponents of a higher culture and a more refined sensibility sought to reach the new public in the hope of elevating its taste or uplifting its morals. The "Brahmin poets" of New England—Henry Wadsworth Longfellow, James Russell Lowell, and Oliver Wendell Holmes—offered lofty sentiments to a receptive middle class; Ralph Waldo Emerson carried his philosophy of spiritual self-reliance to lyceums and lecture halls across the country; and great novelists such as Nathaniel Hawthorne and Herman Melville experimented with the popular romantic genres. But the ironic and pessimistic view of life that permeated the fiction of these two authors clashed with the optimism of the age, and their work failed to gain a large readership.

The ideal of art for art's sake was utterly alien to the instructional spirit of mid-nineteenth-century American culture. The responsibility of the artist in a democratic society, it was generally assumed, was to contribute to the general welfare by encouraging virtue and proper sentiments. Only Edgar Allan Poe seemed to fit the European image of the romantic genius rebelling against middle-class pieties. The most original of the antebellum poets, Walt Whitman, sought to be a direct mouthpiece for the rising democratic spirit, but his abandonment of traditional verse forms and his freedom in dealing with the sexual side of human nature left him isolated and unappreciated during his most creative years.

The Democratic Ferment

The supremacy of democracy was most obvious in the new politics of universal white manhood suffrage and mass political parties. By the 1820s, most states had removed the last remaining barriers to voting participation by all white males. This change was not as radical or controversial as it would be later in nineteenth-century Europe; ownership of land was so common in the United States that a general suffrage did not mean men without property became a voting majority.

Accompanying this broadening of the electorate was a rise in the proportion of public officials who were elected rather than appointed. More and more judges, as well as legislative and executive officeholders, were chosen by the people. As a result, a new style of politicking developed, emphasizing dramatic speeches that played to the voters' fears and concerns.

Skillful and farsighted politicians such as Martin Van Buren in New York began in the 1820s to build stable statewide political organizations out of what had been loosely organized factions of the Jeffersonian party. Earlier politicians had regarded parties as a threat to republican virtue and had embraced them only as a temporary expedient. But in Van Buren's opinion, regular parties were an effective check on the temptation to abuse power, a tendency deeply planted in the human heart. The major breakthrough in American political thought during the 1820s and 1830s was the idea of a "loyal opposition," ready to capitalize politically on the mistakes or excesses of the "ins" without denying their right to act in the same way when the "ins" became the "outs."

Changes in the method of nominating and electing a president fostered the growth of a two-party system on the national level. By 1828, presidential electors were chosen by popular vote rather than by state legislatures in all but two of the twenty-four states. The need to mobilize grassroots support behind particular candidates required some form of national organization. When national nominating conventions made their appearance in 1831, the choice of candidates became a matter for representative party assemblies rather than congressional caucuses or ad hoc political alliances. These democratic practices generated far more widespread interest in politics. Between 1824 and 1840, the percentage of eligible voters who cast their ballot in presidential elections tripled.

Economic questions dominated the political controversies of the 1820s and 1830s. The Panic of 1819 and the subsequent depression heightened popular interest in government economic policy. Americans advanced several solutions for keeping the economy healthy. Some, especially small farmers, favored a return to a simpler and more "honest" economy without banks, paper money, and the easy credit that encouraged speculation. Others, particularly emerging entrepreneurs, saw salvation in government aid and protection for venture capital. Politicians and eventually political parties responded to these conflicting views.

The party disputes that arose over corporations, tariffs, banks, and internal improvements involved more than the direct economic concerns of particular interest groups. They were viewed in the context of republican fears of conspiracy against American liberty and equality. Charges of corruption and impending tyranny were common.

The notion that the American experiment was a fragile one, constantly threatened by power-hungry conspirators, eventually took two principal forms. For Jacksonians, it was "the money power" that endangered the survival of republicanism; for their opponents, it was men like Jackson himself, alleged "rabble-rousers" who duped the electorate into ratifying high-handed and tyrannical action contrary to the true interests of the nation.

A Voice from the People!

Great Meeting in the Park!!

■ *Working men's parties of the late 1820s and 1830s sought to protect and defend workers and to improve working conditions. This poster called for workers to unite in protest over the conviction of union shoemakers for conspiracy.* ■

An object of increasing concern for both sides was the role of the federal government. National Republicans and later the Whigs believed that government should take active steps to foster economic growth; Jacksonians only wanted to eliminate "special privileges." How best to guarantee equality of opportunity—whether by active governmental promotion of commerce and industry or by strict laissez-faire policies—was a hotly debated issue of the period.

For one group of dissenters, democracy took on a more radical meaning. Leaders of the workingmen's parties and trade unions condemned the growing gap between the rich and the poor resulting from early industrialization and the growth of the market economy. Society, in their view, was divided between "producers"—laborers, artisans, farmers, and small business owners who ran their own enterprises—and nonproducing "parasites"—bankers, speculators, and merchant capitalists. Their aim was to give the producers greater control over the fruits of their labor. They advocated such things as abolition of inheritance and a redistribution of land, as well as educational reforms, a ten-hour workday, abolition of imprisonment for debt, and a currency system based exclusively on hard money so that workers could no longer be paid in depreciated banknotes.

Northern abolitionists and early proponents of women's rights made another kind of effort to extend the meaning and scope of democracy. Radical men and women advocated immediate emancipation for slaves and equal rights for blacks and women. But Jacksonian America was too permeated with racism and male chauvinism to listen to such reformers. In some ways, the civil and political status of both blacks and women deteriorated during this "age of the common man" (see Chapter 12).

JACKSON AND THE POLITICS OF DEMOCRACY

The public figure who came to symbolize the triumph of democracy was Andrew Jackson, although he came out a loser in the presidential election of 1824. His victory four years later, his actions as president, and the great political party that formed around him refashioned national politics in a more democratic mold. No wonder historians have called the spirit of the age **Jacksonian Democracy.**

The Election of 1824 and John Quincy Adams's Administration

Jacksonian Democracy A historian's term for the political culture of white male citizens in the 1820s and 1830s. It celebrated the "self-made man" and rejected the idea that leaders should be drawn from the intellectual and economic elite. Andrew Jackson, the first "people's president," exemplified the spirit of the age.

The election of 1824 was one of the most complicated and controversial in American history. As Monroe's second term ended, the ruling Republican party was in disarray and could not agree on who should succeed to the presidency. The party's congressional caucus chose William Crawford of Georgia, an old-line Jeffersonian. But a majority of congressmen showed their disapproval of this outmoded method of nominating candidates by refusing to attend the caucus. Soon John Quincy Adams, Henry Clay, John C. Calhoun, and Andrew Jackson had their hats in the ring.

Initially Jackson was not given much of a chance. He was a military hero, not a national politician, and few party leaders believed that wartime victories were enough to catapult him into the White House. But after testing the waters, Calhoun withdrew and chose instead to run for vice president. Then Crawford suffered a debilitating stroke that weakened his chances. These events made Jackson the favorite in the South. He also found favor among those in the North and West who were disenchanted with the economic nationalism of Clay and Adams.

In the election, Jackson won a plurality of the electoral votes. But since he lacked the necessary majority, the contest was thrown into the House of Representatives, where the legislators were to choose from the three top candidates. Adams emerged victorious over Jackson and Crawford. Clay, who had just missed making the final three, provided the winning margin by persuading his supporters to vote for Adams. When Adams proceeded to appoint Clay as his secretary of state, the Jacksonians charged that a "corrupt bargain" had deprived their favorite of the presidency. Even though the charges were unproven, Adams assumed office under a cloud of suspicion.

Although he was a man of integrity and vision, Adams was an inept politician. He refused to bow to the public antipathy toward nationalistic programs and called for an expansion of governmental activity. Congress, however, had no intention of following Adams's lead.

The new Congress that was elected in 1826 was clearly under the control of men hostile to the administration and favorable to the presidential aspirations of Andrew Jackson. The main business before Congress was the tariff issue. Pressure for greater protection came not only from manufacturers but also from many farmers. The cotton-growing South—the only section where tariffs of all kinds were unpopular—was already safely in the general's camp. To gain popularity in the other sections, Jackson tacitly lent his support to the tariff of 1828. This **tariff of abominations** was a congressional grab bag that contained substantial across-the-board increases in duties—gifts for all sections save the South. It was not, however, simply a ploy to get Jackson elected; it was in fact an early example of how special interest groups can achieve their goals in democratic politics through the process of legislative bargaining known as logrolling.

tariff of abominations An 1828 protective tariff, or tax on imports, motivated by special interest groups. It resulted in a substantial increase in duties that angered many southern free traders.

Jackson Comes to Power

The campaign of 1828 actually began early in the Adams administration. Resurrecting the corrupt-bargain charge, Jackson's supporters began to organize on the state and local levels. So successful were their efforts that influential state and regional leaders who had supported other candidates in 1824 now rallied behind Jackson to create a formidable coalition.

The most significant of these leaders were Vice President Calhoun, who now spoke for the militant states' rights sentiment of the South; Senator Martin Van Buren, who dominated New York politics through the political machine known as the Albany Regency; and two Kentucky editors, Francis P. Blair and Amos Kendall, who worked to mobilize opposition to Henry Clay and his "American system" in the West. These men and their followers laid the foundation for the first modern American political party, the Democrats. And from this time on, national parties existed primarily to engage in a contest for the presidency. Without this great prize, there would have been little incentive to create national organizations out of the parties and factions developing in the states.

The election of 1828 saw the birth of a new era of mass democracy. Jackson's supporters made widespread use of such electioneering techniques as huge public rallies, torchlight parades, and lavish barbecues or picnics paid for by the candidate's organization. Personalities and mudslinging dominated the campaign, which reached its low point when Adams's supporters accused Jackson's wife, Rachel, of bigamy and adultery and Jackson's associates charged that Adams's wife was born out of wedlock.

What gave the Jacksonians the edge was their success in portraying their candidate as an authentic man of the people, despite his substantial fortune in land and slaves. They emphasized Jackson's backwoods upbringing, military record, and common sense unclouded by a fancy education. Adams, according to Democratic propagandists, was the exact opposite—an overeducated aristocrat, more at home in the salon and the study than among the plain people. Anti-intellectualism was a potent force, and Adams never really had a chance.

The result had the appearance of a landslide for Old Hickory. But the verdict of the people was not as decisive as the returns might suggest. Although Jackson had piled up massive majorities in some of the slave states, the voters elsewhere divided fairly evenly. Furthermore, it was not clear what kind of a mandate he had won. Most of the politicians in his camp favored states' rights and limited government as against the nationalism of Adams and Clay, but the general himself had never taken a clear public stand on such issues as banks, tariffs, and internal improvements. His victory was more a triumph of image and personality than the popular endorsement of a particular set of programs.

Jackson turned out to be one of the most forceful and domineering of American presidents. His most striking character traits were an indomitable will, an intolerance of opposition, and a prickly pride that would not permit him to forgive or forget an insult or a supposed act of betrayal. His violent temper had led him to fight a number of duels, and as a soldier his critics claimed he was guilty of using excessive force. His frontier background and military experiences had made him tough and resourceful but had also deprived him of the flexibility normally associated with successful politicians. Yet he generally got what he wanted.

Jackson's presidency began with his open endorsement of rotation of officeholders, or what his critics called the "spoils system." Although he did not actually depart radically from his predecessors in the degree to which he removed federal officeholders and replaced them with his supporters, he was the first president to defend the practice as a legitimate application of democratic doctrine. He contended that the duties of public officers were simple and that any man of intelligence could readily fill the positions.

Jackson also established a new kind of relationship with his cabinet. Cabinet members became less important than they had been in previous administrations. Old Hickory regarded himself as "the direct representative of the people" and his cabinet as an interchangeable set of administrators whose sole function was to carry out the will of the chief executive. He used his cabinet members more for consultation than for policymaking, and he diluted their influence even further by relying heavily on the advice of an unofficial and confidential set of advisers known as his Kitchen Cabinet.

Midway in his first administration, Jackson completely reorganized his cabinet. The apparent cause of this upheaval was the Peggy Eaton affair. Peggy O'Neale Eaton, the daughter of a Washington tavern owner, married Secretary of War John Eaton in 1829. Because of gossip about her moral character, the wives of other cabinet members refused to receive her socially. Jackson became her champion. Eventually all but one of his cabinet members resigned over the incident, and Jackson formed a fresh cabinet. Perhaps the most important consequence of the affair was that Martin Van Buren, although he resigned with the rest, also supported Peggy Eaton and therefore won Jackson's favor.

Indian Removal

The first major policy question before the Jackson administration concerned the fate of Native Americans. Jackson had long favored removing eastern Indians to lands beyond the Mississippi. His support of removal was no different from the policy of previous administrations. The only real issue was how rapidly and thoroughly the process should be carried out and by what means. At the time of Jackson's election, some states were clamoring for quick action.

Georgia, Alabama, and Mississippi extended their state laws over the Cherokee, moves that defied provisions of the Constitution giving the federal government exclusive jurisdiction over Indian affairs and also violated specific treaties. Jackson, however, endorsed the state actions. His own attitude was that Indians were children when they did the whites' bidding, and savage beasts when they resisted. In his December 1829 message to Congress, he advocated a new and more coercive removal policy. Denying Cherokee autonomy, he asserted the primacy of states' rights over Indian rights and called for the speedy and thorough removal of all eastern Indians to designated areas beyond the Mississippi.

Early in 1830, the president's congressional supporters introduced a bill to implement the policy. The ensuing debate was vigorous and heated, but senators and House members from the South and the western border states pushed the bill through. Jackson then moved quickly to conclude the necessary treaties, using the threat of unilateral government action to bludgeon the tribes into submission. In 1832, he condoned Georgia's defiance of a Supreme Court decision (*Worcester v. Georgia*) that denied the right of a state to extend its jurisdiction over tribal lands. The fate of the eastern Indians was sealed.

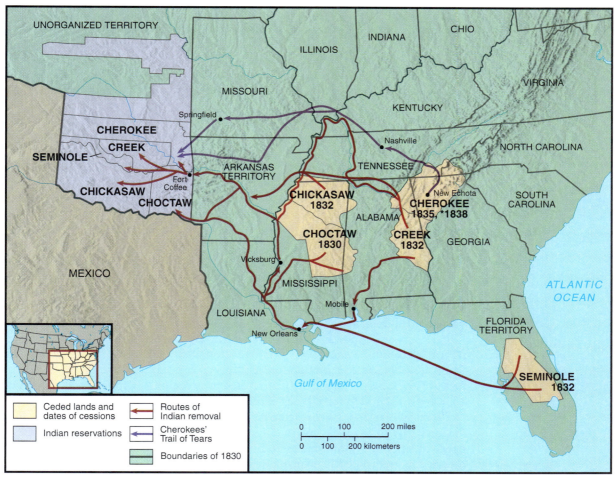

* Treaty signed in 1835 by minority factions forced removal in 1838.

INDIAN REMOVAL   *Because so many Native Americans, uprooted from their lands in the East, died on the forced march to Oklahoma, the route they followed became known as the Trail of Tears.* ■

The members of a stubbornly resisting majority faction of the Cherokee held out until 1838 when military pressure forced them to march to Oklahoma. The trek, known as the **Trail of Tears,** was made under such harsh conditions that almost a quarter of the Indians died on the way. Nothing more than a ruthless land grab, the Cherokee removal exposed the prejudiced and greedy side of Jacksonian democracy.

The Nullification Crisis

Trail of Tears In the winter of 1838–1839, the Cherokee were forced to evacuate their lands in Georgia and travel under military guard to present-day Oklahoma. Due to exposure and disease, roughly one-quarter of the 16,000 forced migrants died en route.

During the 1820s, Southerners became increasingly fearful of federal encroachment on the rights of the states. Behind this concern, in South Carolina at least, was a strengthened commitment to the preservation of slavery and a resulting anxiety about possible uses of federal power to strike at that peculiar institution. Hoping to keep the explosive slavery issue out of the political limelight, South Carolinians seized on another genuine grievance, the protective tariff, as the issue on which to take their stand in favor of state veto power over federal actions that they viewed as contrary to their interests. As a staple-producing and -exporting region, the South was hurt by any tariff that increased the prices for manufactured goods and threatened to undermine foreign markets by inciting counterprotection.

nullification The supposed right of any state to declare a federal law inoperative within its boundaries. In 1832, South Carolina created a firestorm when it attempted to nullify the federal tariff.

Vice President John C. Calhoun emerged as the leader of the states' rights insurgency in South Carolina. After the passage of the tariff of abominations in 1828, the state legislature declared the new duties unconstitutional and endorsed a lengthy disquisition—written anonymously by Calhoun—that affirmed **nullification,** or the right of an individual state to set aside federal law. Calhoun and South Carolina believed that Jackson would defend their position. They saw room for hope in the president's position on Georgia's de facto nullification of federal treaties upholding Indian tribal rights and his veto of a major internal improvement bill, the Maysville Road in Kentucky, based on a strict interpretation of the Constitution.

In the meantime, a bitter personal feud developed between Jackson and Calhoun. As Calhoun lost favor with Jackson because of his position on the Eaton affair, it became clear that Van Buren would be Jackson's designated successor. The personal breach between Jackson and Calhoun colored and intensified their confrontation over the nullification and tariff issues.

But there were also differences of principle. Although generally a defender of states' rights and strict construction of the Constitution, Jackson opposed the theory of nullification as a threat to the survival of the Union. The differences between Jackson and Calhoun came into the open at the Jefferson Day dinner in 1830, when Jackson offered the toast "Our Union: It must be preserved"—to which Calhoun responded: "The Union: next to Liberty most dear. May we always remember that it can only be preserved by distributing equally [its] benefits and the burdens."

In 1830 and 1831, the movement against the tariff gained strength in South Carolina. Calhoun resigned as vice president and openly took the lead. In 1832, Congress passed a new tariff that lowered the rates slightly but retained the principle of protection. Supporters of nullification then succeeded in persuading the South Carolina state legislature to call a special convention. When the convention met in November 1832, the members voted overwhelmingly to nullify the tariffs of 1828 and 1832 and to forbid the collection of customs duties within the state.

Jackson reacted with characteristic decisiveness. He asked Congress to vote him the authority to use the army to enforce the tariff. At the same time, he sought to pacify the nullifiers somewhat by recommending a lower tariff. Congress responded by enacting the Force Bill, which gave the president the military powers he sought, and the compromise tariff of 1833. Faced with the combination of force and compromise, South Carolina eventually rescinded the nullification ordinance. But to clearly demonstrate that they had not conceded their constitutional position, the convention delegates concluded their deliberations by nullifying the Force Bill.

The nullification crisis revealed that South Carolinians would not tolerate any federal action that seemed contrary to their interests or raised doubts about the institution of slavery. The nullifiers' principle of state sovereignty implied the right of secession as well as the right to declare laws of Congress null and void. Although in many ways Jackson was a pro-slavery president, some farsighted southern loyalists were alarmed by the Unionist doctrines the president propounded in his proclamation against nullification. More strongly than any previous president, he had asserted that the federal government was supreme over the states and that the Union was indivisible. What was more, he had justified the use of force against states that denied federal authority.

THE BANK WAR AND THE SECOND PARTY SYSTEM

Jackson's most important and controversial use of executive power was his successful attack on the Bank of the United States. The so-called **Bank War** revealed some of the deepest concerns of Jackson and his supporters and expressed their concept of democracy in a dramatic way. It also aroused intense opposition to the president and his policies, an opposition that crystallized in a new national party known as the Whigs. The destruction of the Bank and the economic disruption that followed brought to the forefront the issue of the government's relationship to the nation's financial system. Differences on this question helped sustain the new two-party system and provided the stuff of political controversy during the administration of Jackson's handpicked successor, Martin Van Buren.

Bank War Between 1832–1836, Andrew Jackson used his presidential power to fight and ultimately destroy the second Bank of the United States.

Biddle, the Bank Veto, and the Election of 1832

The Bank of the United States had long been embroiled in public controversy. The South and West openly blamed it for the Panic of 1819 and the depression that followed. But after Nicholas Biddle took over the Bank's presidency in 1823, it regained public confidence. Cultured and able, Biddle probably understood the mysteries of banking and currency better than any other American of his generation. But he was arrogant and vain, as sure of his own judgment as Jackson himself.

Old-line Jeffersonians had always opposed the Bank on the grounds that its establishment was unconstitutional and it placed too much power in the hands of a small, privileged group. Its influence on the national economy was tremendous, and because of this, it was a convenient scapegoat for anything that went wrong with the economy. In an era of rising democracy, the most obvious and telling objection to the Bank was simply that it possessed great power and privilege without being under popular control.

Jackson came into office with strong reservations about banking and paper money in general. He also harbored suspicions that branches of the Bank of the United States had illicitly used their influence on behalf of his opponent in the presidential election. In his annual messages in 1829 and 1830, he called on Congress to begin discussing ways of reducing the Bank's power.

Biddle began to worry about the fate of the Bank's charter when it came up for renewal in 1836. At the same time, Jackson's Kitchen Cabinet advised him that an attack on the Bank would provide a good party issue for the election of 1832. Biddle then made a fateful blunder. He determined to seek recharter by Congress in 1832, four years ahead of schedule. Senator Henry Clay, leader of the anti-administration forces on Capitol Hill, encouraged the move because he was convinced that Jackson had chosen the unpopular side of the issue. The bill to recharter, therefore, was introduced in the House and Senate in early 1832. It passed Congress with ease.

The next move was Jackson's, and he made the most of the opportunity. He vetoed the bill and defended his action with ringing statements of principle. The Bank was unconstitutional, he said, and even worse, because it was a monopoly, it violated the fundamental rights of the people in a democratic society. Jackson

■ *Aided by Van Buren (center), Jackson wields his veto rod against the Bank of the United States, whose heads represent the directors of the state branches. Bank president Nicholas Biddle is wearing the top hat.* ■

believed that the government should guarantee equality of opportunity, not grant privileges that provided special interests with exclusive advantages.

Jackson thus called on the common people to join him in fighting the "monster" corporation. His veto message was the first to go beyond strictly constitutional arguments to deal directly with social and economic issues. Congressional attempts to override the veto failed, and Jackson resolved to take the entire issue to the people in the upcoming presidential election, which he viewed as a referendum to decide whether he or the Bank would prevail.

The 1832 election pitted Jackson against Henry Clay, standard-bearer of the National Republicans. The Bank recharter was the major issue. In the end, Jackson won a great personal triumph, garnering 219 electoral votes to 49 for Clay. As far as Old Hickory was concerned, he had his mandate.

Killing the Bank

Not content with preventing the Bank from getting a new charter, the victorious Jackson now resolved to attack it directly by removing federal deposits from Biddle's vaults. Jackson told Van Buren, "the bank . . . is trying to kill me, but I will kill it." Old Hickory regarded Biddle's opposition during the presidential race as a personal attack, part of a devious plot to destroy the president's reputation and deny him the popular approval that he deserved. As always, Jackson believed his opponents were not merely wrong but evil besides and deserved to be destroyed. Furthermore, he viewed the election result as his popular mandate to go after the Bank.

To remove the deposits from the Bank, Jackson had to overcome strong resistance in his own cabinet. When one secretary of the treasury refused to support the policy, he was shifted to another cabinet post. When a second balked at carrying out removal, he was replaced by Roger B. Taney, a Jackson loyalist and dedicated opponent of the Bank. Beginning in late September 1833, Taney ceased depositing government money in the Bank and began to withdraw the funds already there. The funds were then ill-advisedly placed in selected state banks. Opponents charged that the banks had been chosen for political rather than fiscal reasons and dubbed them Jackson's "pet banks." Since Congress refused to approve administration proposals to regulate the credit policies of these banks, Jackson's efforts to shift to a hard-money economy were quickly nullified by the use the state banks made of the new deposits. They extended credit more recklessly than before and increased the amount of paper money in circulation.

The Bank counterattacked by calling in outstanding loans and instituting a policy of credit contraction that helped bring on an economic recession. Biddle hoped to win support for recharter by demonstrating that weakening the Bank's position would be disastrous for the economy. But all he showed, at least to the president's supporters, was that they had been right all along about the Bank's excessive power. They blamed the economic distress on Biddle, and the Bank never did regain its charter.

Even more serious than the conflict over the Bank was the strong opposition to Jackson's fiscal policies that developed in Congress. Led by Henry Clay, the Senate approved a motion of censure against Jackson, charging him with exceeding his constitutional authority in removing the deposits. Jacksonians in the House were able to block such action, but the president was further humiliated when the Senate refused to confirm Taney as secretary of the treasury. Anti-Jacksonians were gaining strength.

The Emergence of the Whigs

The coalition that passed the censure resolution in the Senate provided the nucleus for a new national party, the **Whigs.** The leadership of the new party and a majority of its support came from National Republicans and ex-Federalists. But the Whigs also picked up critical backing from southern proponents of states' rights who had been upset by Jackson's stand on nullification and now saw an unconstitutional abuse of power in his withdrawal of federal deposits from the Bank of the United States. The Whig label was chosen because of its associations with both English and American Revolutionary opposition to royal power and prerogatives; its rallying cry was "executive usurpation" by the tyrannical designs of "King Andrew."

The Whigs also gradually absorbed the Anti-Masonic party, a surprisingly strong northeastern political movement that exploited traditional American fears of secret societies and conspiracies. They also appealed successfully to the moral concerns of the northern middle class under the sway of an emerging evangelical Protestantism. Anti-Masons detested Jacksonianism mainly because it stood for a toleration of diverse lifestyles. They believed that the government should restrict such "sinful" behavior as drinking, gambling, and breaking the Sabbath.

As the election of 1836 approached, the government's fiscal policies also provoked a localized rebellion among the urban, working-class elements of the Democratic coalition. This group favored a strict hard-money policy and condemned Jackson's transfer of federal deposits to the state banks as inflationary. Because they wanted working people to be paid in specie rather than inflated banknotes, the "Loco-Focos"—named for the matches they used for illumination when their opponents turned off the gaslights at a party meeting—went beyond opposition to the Bank of the United States and attacked state banks as well. Seeing no basis for cooperation with the Whigs, they established the independent Equal Rights party and nominated a separate state ticket in 1836.

Jackson himself had hard-money sentiments and probably regarded the "pet banks" solution as a temporary expedient. Nonetheless, in early 1836, he surrendered to congressional pressure and signed legislation allocating surplus federal revenues to the deposit banks, increasing their numbers and weakening federal controls over them. The result was runaway inflation, wild land speculation, and irresponsible printing of paper money. Reacting somewhat belatedly to the speculative mania he had helped create, Jackson pricked the bubble on July 11, 1836. He issued

Whigs Members of the Whig party, which coalesced around opposition to Andrew Jackson. The name derived from the British Whigs, who opposed the king in the late seventeenth century. In general, the Whig party supported federal power and internal improvements but not territorial expansion. The party collapsed in the 1850s.

specie circular In 1836, President Andrew Jackson issued this executive order that required purchasers of public land to pay in "specie," gold or silver coin, rather than paper money.

his **specie circular** stipulating that after August 15, only gold and silver would be accepted in payment for public lands. This action served to curb inflation and land speculation but did so in such a sudden and drastic way that it helped precipitate the financial panic of 1837.

The Rise and Fall of Van Buren

As his successor, Jackson chose Martin Van Buren, a master of practical politics. The Democratic National Convention of 1835 unanimously confirmed Jackson's choice. Van Buren promised to "tread generally in the footsteps of General Jackson."

The newly created Whig party, reflecting the diversity of its constituency, was unable to decide on a single standard-bearer and chose instead to run three regional candidates—Daniel Webster in the East, William Henry Harrison in the Old Northwest, and Hugh Lawson White in the South. The Whigs hoped to deprive Van Buren of enough electoral votes to throw the election into the House of Representatives, where one of the Whigs might stand a chance.

The strategy proved unsuccessful. Van Buren won a clear victory. But the election foreshadowed future trouble for the Democrats, particularly in the South. There the Whigs ran virtually even. The emergence of a two-party system in the previously solid South resulted from two factors: opposition to some of Jackson's policies and the image of Van Buren as an unreliable Yankee politician.

Panic of 1837 A financial depression that lasted until the 1840s.

The main business of Van Buren's administration was to straighten out the financial disorder resulting from the destruction of the Bank of the United States and the issuing of Jackson's specie circular. Van Buren took office in the face of a catastrophic depression. The **Panic of 1837** was not exclusively, or even primarily, the result of government policies. It was in fact international in scope and reflected some complex changes in the world economy that were beyond the control of American policymakers.

But the Whigs were quick to blame the state of the economy on Jacksonian finance, and the administration had to make a politically effective response. Since Van Buren and his party were committed to a policy of laissez-faire on the federal level, there was little or nothing they could do to relieve economic distress through subsidies or relief measures. But the president could at least try to salvage the federal funds deposited in shaky state banks and devise a new system of public finance that would not contribute to future panics by fueling speculation and credit expansion.

Van Buren's solution was to establish a public depository for government funds with no connections whatsoever to commercial banking. His proposal for an "independent subtreasury" aroused intense opposition from the congressional Whigs, and it was not until 1840 that it was enacted into law. In the meantime, the economy had temporarily revived in 1838, only to sink again into a deeper depression the following year.

Van Buren's chances for reelection in 1840 were undoubtedly hurt by the state of the economy. But the principal reason for his defeat was that he lacked Jackson's charisma and was thus unable to overcome the extremely effective campaign mounted by the Whigs. The Whig party of 1840 was well organized on a grassroots level, and it found its own Jackson in William Henry Harrison, a military hero of advanced age, who was associated in the public mind with the battle of Tippecanoe and the winning of the West. To balance the ticket and increase its appeal in the South, they chose John Tyler of Virginia, a converted states' rights Democrat, to be Harrison's running mate.

Using the slogan "Tippecanoe and Tyler, Too," the Whigs pulled out all stops in their bid for the White House. Imitating the Jacksonian propaganda against Adams in 1828, they portrayed Van Buren as a luxury-loving aristocrat and compared him with their own homespun candidate. The Democrats tried but were unable to pro-

A Look at the Past

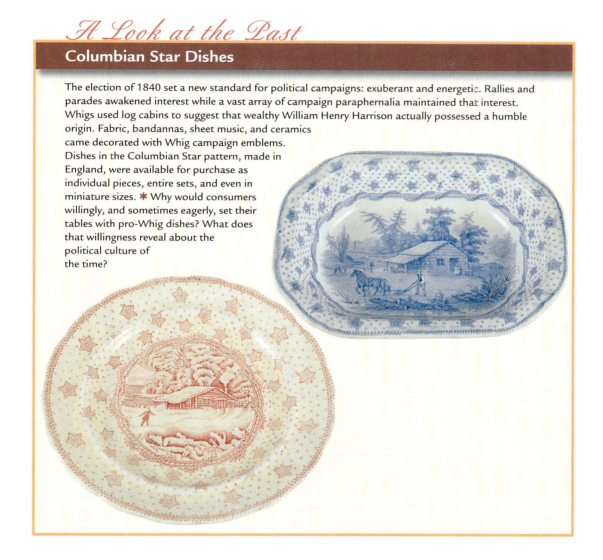

Columbian Star Dishes

The election of 1840 set a new standard for political campaigns: exuberant and energetic. Rallies and parades awakened interest while a vast array of campaign paraphernalia maintained that interest. Whigs used log cabins to suggest that wealthy William Henry Harrison actually possessed a humble origin. Fabric, bandannas, sheet music, and ceramics came decorated with Whig campaign emblems. Dishes in the Columbian Star pattern, made in England, were available for purchase as individual pieces, entire sets, and even in miniature sizes. ✳ Why would consumers willingly, and sometimes eagerly, set their tables with pro-Whig dishes? What does that willingness reveal about the political culture of the time?

ject Van Buren as a man of the people. Harrison won, and the Whigs gained control of both houses of Congress.

Contrary to what most historians used to believe, personalities and hoopla did not decide the election of 1840. The economy was in dire straits, and the Whigs, unlike the Democrats, had a program that seemed to offer hope for a solution—the latest version of Henry Clay's American System. Whigs proposed to revive the Bank of the United States in order to restore fiscal stability, raise tariffs to protect manufacturers and manufacturing jobs, and distribute federal revenues to the states for internal improvements that would stimulate commerce and employment. Whig victories in the state and local elections of 1840, many of which preceded the presidential vote, strongly suggest that voters were responding to the party and its program, not merely to the man who headed the ticket and to the Whigs' newfound skill at entertaining the electorate.

HEYDAY OF THE SECOND PARTY SYSTEM

America's **second party system** came of age in the election of 1840. The rivalry of Democrats and Whigs made the two-party pattern an enduring feature of the electoral politics in the United States. During the 1840s, the two national parties

second party system A historian's term for the national two-party rivalry between Democrats and Whigs. The second party system began in the 1830s and ended in the 1850s with the demise of the Whig party and the rise of the Republican party.

competed on fairly equal terms for the support of the electorate. Allegiance to one party or the other became an important source of personal identity for many Americans and increased their interest and participation in politics.

In addition to drama and entertainment, the parties offered the voters a real choice of programs and ideologies. Whigs stood for a "positive liberal state," in which the government had the right and duty to subsidize or protect enterprises that could contribute to general prosperity and economic growth. Democrats advocated a "negative liberal state," in which the government would keep its hands off the economy.

Conflict over economic issues helped determine each party's base of support. In the Whig camp were many industrialists and merchants, plus a large proportion of farmers and planters who had adapted successfully to the market economy. Democrats appealed mainly to small farmers, workers, declining gentry, and emerging entrepreneurs who were excluded from the established commercial groups that stood to benefit most from Whig programs. But issues such as the tariff could further complicate this pattern; workers in protected industries often voted Whig, while importers normally voted for the Democrats and freer trade.

Economic interest was not the only factor behind the choice of parties. Lifestyles and ethnic or religious identities strongly affected party loyalties during this period. In the northern states, one way to tell the typical Whig from the typical Democrat was to see where each went on Sunday. Anyone at an evangelical Protestant church was likely to be a Whig. A person who belonged to a ritualized church—Catholic, Lutheran, or Episcopalian—or did not go to church at all was probably a Democrat.

■ County Election *by George Caleb Bingham portrays the variety of activities that occurred on election day. Some men cast their ballots, while others exchange their views or enjoy refreshments. Note the absence of women in the scene.* ■

Chronology

1824	House of Representatives elects John Quincy Adams president
1828	Congress passes the Tariff of Abominations ■ Jackson is elected president over John Quincy Adams
1830	Jackson vetoes the Maysville Road bill ■ Congress passes the Indian Removal Act
1831	Jackson reorganizes his cabinet ■ First national nominating conventions meet
1832	Jackson vetoes the bill rechartering the Bank of the United States ■ Jackson is reelected, defeating Henry Clay (National Republican candidate)
1832–1833	Crisis erupts over South Carolina's attempt to nullify the tariff of 1832
1833	Jackson removes federal deposits from the Bank of the United States
1834	Whig party comes into existence
1836	Jackson issues his specie circular ■ Martin Van Buren is elected president
1837	Financial panic occurs, followed by depression lasting until 1843
1840	Congress passes the Independent Subtreasury Bill ■ Harrison (Whig) defeats Van Buren (Democrat) for the presidency

The Democrats were the favored party of immigrants, Catholics, freethinkers, backwoods farmers, and persons of all classes who enjoyed traditional amusements condemned by the new breed of moral reformers. One thing that all the groups had in common was a desire to be left alone, with freedom to think and behave as they liked. The Whigs welcomed the market economy but wanted to restrain the individualism and disorder it created by enforcing cultural and moral values derived from the Puritan tradition. Most of those who sought to be "their brothers' keepers" were Whigs.

Nevertheless, party conflict in Congress continued to center on national economic policy. Whigs stood firm for a loose construction of the Constitution and for positive federal guidance and support for business and economic development. The Democrats persisted in their defense of strict construction, states' rights, and laissez-faire. Debates over tariffs, banking, and internal improvements remained vital and vigorous during the 1840s.

True believers in both parties saw a deep ideological or moral meaning in the clash over economic issues. The Democrats were the party of individualism and personal liberty. For them, the role of government was to remove obstacles to individual rights, which could mean the right to rise economically, the right to drink hard liquor, or the right to be unorthodox in religion. Democrats were ambivalent about the rise of the market economy because of the ways it threatened individual independence. The Whigs, by contrast, were the party of orderly progress under the guidance of an enlightened elite. They believed that the propertied, the well-educated, and the pious were responsible for guiding the masses toward the common good. Believing that a market economy would benefit everyone in the long run, they had no qualms about the rise of commercial and industrial capitalism.

Each, in a sense, reflected one side of a broader democratic impulse. This Jacksonian legacy was a stress on individual freedom and ethnic or cultural tolerance (except for blacks). The Whigs perceived that in a republic, strong government could serve the general interest and further the spirit of national unity.

CONCLUSION: TOCQUEVILLE'S WISDOM

The French traveler Alexis de Tocqueville, author of the most influential account ever written of the emergence of American democracy, visited the United States in 1831. He found much to praise in America, from the country's genius for local self-government to the participation of ordinary citizens in the affairs of their communities. But Tocqueville was also acutely aware of the limitations of American democracy. He knew that the kind of democracy white men were practicing in the Jacksonian era did not include women. He also believed that the nullification crisis foreshadowed the destruction of the Union and predicted that the problem of slavery would lead eventually to civil war and racial conflict. He noted the power of white supremacy, providing an unforgettable firsthand description of the sufferings of an Indian community in the course of forced migration to the West as well as a graphic account of the way free blacks were segregated and driven from the polls in northern cities. His belief that problems associated with slavery would endanger the Union was keenly prophetic.

KEY TERMS

Jacksonian Democracy, p. 190

tariff of abominations, p. 191

Trail of Tears, p. 194

nullification, p. 194

Bank War, p. 195

Whigs, p. 197

specie circular, p. 198

Panic of 1837, p. 198

second party system, p. 199

RECOMMENDED READING

Arthur M. Schlesinger, Jr., *The Age of Jackson* (1945), sees Jacksonian democracy as a progressive protest against big business and stresses the participation of urban workers. Marvin Meyers, *The Jacksonian Persuasion: Politics and Belief* (1960), argues that Jacksonians appealed to nostalgia for an older America—"an idealized ancestral way" they believed was threatened by commercialization. Lee Benson, *The Concept of Jacksonian Democracy: New York as a Test Case* (1964), finds an ethnocultural basis for democratic allegiance. A sharply critical view of Jacksonian leadership—one that stresses opportunism, greed, and demagoguery—can be found in Edward Pessen, *Jacksonian America: Society, Personality, and Politics,* rev. ed. (1979). An excellent survey of Jacksonian politics is Harry L. Watson, *Liberty and Power* (1990), which stresses the crisis of "republicanism" at a time of "market revolution." Daniel Feller, *Jacksonian Promise: America, 1815–1840* (1995), focuses on the optimism that marked all sides of the political conflict and points to the similarities between the political parties. Development of the view that Jacksonianism was a negative reaction to the rise of market capitalism can be found in Charles Sellers, *The Market Revolution* (1991).

The classic study of the new party system is Richard P. McCormick, *The Second Party System: Party Formation in the Jacksonian Era* (1966). See also Glenn C. Altschuler and Herbert Bluman, *Rude Republic: Americans and Their Politics in the Nineteenth Century* (2000). On who the anti-Jacksonians were, what they stood for, and what they accomplished, see Michael Holt's magisterial, *The Rise and Fall of the American Whig Party* (1999). James C. Curtis, *Andrew Jackson and the Search for Vindication* (1976), provides a good introduction to Jackson's career and personality. On Jackson's popular image, see John William Ward, *Andrew Jackson: Symbol for an Age* (1955). His Indian removal policy is the subject of Anthony F. C. Wallace, *The Long Bitter Trail: Andrew Jackson and the Indians* (1993). On the other towering political figures of the period, see Merrill D. Peterson, *The Great Triumvirate: Webster, Clay, and Calhoun* (1987). The culture of the period is well surveyed in Russel B. Nye, *Society and Culture in America, 1830–1860* (1960). Alexis de Tocqueville, *Democracy in America,* 2 vols. (1945), is a foreign visitor's wise and insightful analysis of American life in the 1830s.

On the role of race in the formation of political parties and social divisions during this period, see David Roediger, *The Wages of Whiteness: Race and the Making of the American Working Class* (1991); Jean H. Baker, *Affairs of Party: The Political Culture of Northern Democrats in the Mid-Nineteenth Century* (1983); and Alexander Saxton, *The Rise and Fall of the White Republic: Class, Politics, and Mass Culture in Nineteenth-Century America* (1990).

SUGGESTED WEB SITES

Indian Affairs: Laws and Treaties, compiled and edited by Charles J. Kappler (1904)
digital.library.okstate.edu/kappler
This digitized text at Oklahoma State University includes pre-removal treaties with the Five Civilized Tribes and other tribes.

Medicine of Jacksonian America
www.connerprairie.org/historyonline/jmed.html
Survival was far from certain in the Jacksonian Era. This site discusses some of the reasons and some of the possible cures of the times.

The University of Pennsylvania in 1830
www.archives.upenn.edu/histy/features/1830/
This virtual tour shows a fairly typical campus and what student life was like at one of the larger universities in the Antebellum Era.

Nineteenth-Century Scientific American On-Line
www.history.rochester.edu/ScientificAmerican/
Magazines and journals are windows through which we can view society. This site provides on-line editions of one of the more interesting nineteenth-century journals.

National Museum of the American Indian
www.si.edu/nmai
The Smithsonian Institution maintains this site, providing information about the museum, which is dedicated to the history and culture of Native Americans.

The Alexis de Tocqueville Tour: Exploring Democracy in America
www.tocqueville.org/
Text, images, and teaching suggestions are a part of this companion site to C-SPAN's programming on de Tocqueville.

Chapter *11*

Slaves and Masters

Nat Turner's Rebellion: A Turning Point in the Slave South

On August 22, 1831, the worst nightmare of southern slaveholders became reality. A group of slaves in Southampton County, Virginia, rose in open and bloody rebellion. Their leader was Nat Turner, a preacher and prophet who believed God had given him a sign that the time was ripe to strike for freedom. When white forces dispersed the rampaging slaves forty-eight hours later, Turner's band had killed nearly sixty whites. The rebels were then rounded up and executed, along with dozens of other slaves who were vaguely suspected of complicity. Turner was the last to be captured, and he went to the gallows unrepentant, convinced he had acted in accordance with God's will.

Southern whites were determined to prevent another such uprising. Their anxiety and resolve were strengthened by the fact that 1831 also saw the emergence of a more militant northern abolitionism. Nat Turner and William Lloyd Garrison were viewed as two prongs of a revolutionary attack on the southern way of life. Afraid that abolitionist agitation might set about another revolt, southern whites launched a massive campaign to quarantine the slaves from possible exposure to antislavery ideas and attitudes.

A series of new laws severely restricted the rights of slaves to move about, assemble without white supervision, or learn to read and write. Other laws prevented white dissenters from publicly criticizing or even questioning the institution of slavery. The South rapidly became a closed society with a closed mind. Proslavery agitators sought to create a mood of crisis and danger requiring absolute unity and single-mindedness among the white population. This embattled attitude lay behind the growth of a more militant sectionalism and inspired threats to secede from the Union if security for slaveholding seemed to require it.

The campaign for repression after the Nat Turner rebellion apparently achieved its original aim. Turner's revolt was the last mass slave uprising. Slave resistance, however, did not end; it simply took less dangerous forms. Slaves sought or perfected other methods of asserting their humanity and maintaining their self-esteem. This heroic effort to endure slavery without surrendering to it gave rise to a resilient African American culture.

This culture combined unique family arrangements, religious ideas of liberation, and creative responses to the oppression of servitude. Among white Southerners, the need to police and control this huge population of enslaved people influenced every aspect of daily life and produced an increasingly isolated, divided, and insecure society. While long-standing racial prejudice contributed to the divided society, the determination of whites to preserve the institution of slavery derived in large part from the important role slavery played in the southern economy.

Outline

The Divided Society of the Old South

The World of Southern Blacks

White Society in the Antebellum South

Slavery and the Southern Economy

Conclusion: Worlds in Conflict

WE AMERICANS
Women of Southern Households

204

THE DIVIDED SOCIETY OF THE OLD SOUTH

Slavery would not have lasted as long as it did—and Southerners would not have reacted so strongly to real or imagined threats to its survival—if an influential class of whites had not had a vital and growing economic interest in this form of human exploitation. Since the early colonial period, forced labor had been considered essential to the South's plantation economy. In the period between the 1790s and the Civil War, plantation agriculture expanded enormously, and so did dependence on slave labor.

The fact that all whites were free and most blacks were slaves created a sharp cleavage between the races in Southern society. Yet the overwhelming importance of race gives an impression of a basic equality within the "master race" that some would say is an illusion. The truth may lie somewhere in between. In the language of sociologists, inequality in the **Old South** was determined in two ways: by class (differences in status resulting from unequal access to wealth and productive resources) and by caste (inherited advantages or disadvantages associated with racial ancestry). Awareness of both systems of social ranking is necessary for an understanding of southern society.

White society was divided by class and by region; both were important for determining a white Southerner's relationship to the institution of slavery. More than any other factor, the ownership of slaves determined gradations of social prestige and influence among whites. The large planters were the dominant class, and nonslaveholders were of lower social rank. Planters (defined as those who owned twenty or more slaves) tended to live in the plantation areas of the "Cotton Belt" stretching from Georgia across Alabama, Mississippi, Louisiana, and Texas, as well as lowcountry South Carolina. In upcountry and frontier areas lived yeoman farmers who owned no or just a few slaves.

In 1860, only one-quarter of all white Southerners belonged to families owning slaves. Even in the Cotton Belt, slaveholders were a minority of whites on the eve of the Civil War. Planters were the minority of a minority, just 4 percent of the total white population of the South in 1860. Three-fourths of all whites owned no slaves at all. Thus, Southern society was dominated by a planter class that was a numerical and geographically isolated minority; inequalities of class became divisions of region as well.

There were also divisions within black society. Most African Americans in the South were slaves, but a small number, about 6 percent, were free. Even free blacks faced increasing restrictions on their rights during the antebellum era. Among slaves, the great majority lived on plantations and worked in agriculture, but a small number worked either in industrial jobs or in a variety of tasks in urban settings. Even on plantations, there were some differences in status and experience between field hands and servants who worked in the house or in skilled jobs such as carpentry or blacksmithing. Yet because all blacks, even those who were free, suffered under the yoke of racial prejudice and legal inequality, these diverse experiences did not translate into the kind of class divisions that caused rifts within white Southern society. Rather, most blacks shared the goal of ending slavery.

Old South The term refers to the slave-holding states between 1830 and 1860, when slave labor and cotton production dominated the economies of the southern states. This period is also known as the antebellum era.

THE WORLD OF SOUTHERN BLACKS

African Americans of the early to mid-nineteenth century experienced slavery on plantations; the majority of slaves lived on units owned by planters who had twenty or more slaves. The masters of these agrarian communities sought to ensure their personal safety and the profitability of their enterprises by using all the means—physical and psychological—at their command to make slaves docile and obedient. Through word and deed, they tried to convince the slaves that whites were superior and had a right to rule over blacks. As increasing numbers of slaves were converted to Christianity and attended white-supervised services, they were forced to hear, over and over again, that God had commanded slaves to serve and obey their masters.

Despite these pressures, most African Americans managed to retain an inner sense of their own worth and dignity. When conditions were right, they openly asserted their desire for freedom and equality and showed their disdain for white claims that slavery was a "positive good." Although slave culture did not normally provoke violent resistance to the slaveholders' regime, the inner world that slaves made for themselves gave them the spiritual strength to thwart the masters' efforts to take over their hearts and minds. After emancipation, this resilient cultural heritage would combine with the tradition of open protest created by rebellious slaves and free black abolitionists to inspire and sustain new struggles for equality.

Slaves' Daily Life and Labor

Slaves' daily life varied enormously depending on the region in which they lived and the type of plantation or farm on which they worked. On large plantations in the Cotton Belt, most slaves worked in "gangs" under an overseer. White overseers, sometimes helped by black "drivers," enforced a workday from sunup to sundown, six days a week. Cotton cultivation required year-round labor, so there was never a slack season under "King Cotton." Enslaved women and children were expected to work in the fields as well, often bringing babies and young children to the fields where they could be cared for by older children, and nursed by their mothers during brief breaks. Some older children worked in "trash gangs," doing lighter tasks such as weeding and yard cleaning.

Not all slaves in agriculture worked in gangs. In the low country of South Carolina and Georgia, slaves who cultivated rice worked under a task system that gave them more control over the pace of labor. With less supervision, many were able to complete their tasks within an eight-hour day. Likewise, slaves who lived on small farms often worked side by side with their masters rather than in large groups of slaves. Such intimacy, however, did not necessarily mean a leveling of power relationships, and despite masters' efforts to control the pace of work, even under the gang system, slaves resisted working on "clock" time, enforcing customary rights to take breaks and especially to take Sunday off completely.

While about three-quarters of slaves were field workers, slaves performed many other kinds of labor. They dug ditches, built houses, worked on boats and in mills (often hired out by their masters for a year at a time), and labored as house servants, cooking, cleaning, and gardening. Some slaves also worked within the slave community as preachers, caretakers of children, and healers, especially women. While white masters sometimes treated domestic workers or other personal servants as having a special status, it would be a mistake to assume that their ranking system was shared by slaves. What evidence we have suggests that those with highest status within slave communities were preachers and healers, people whose special skills and knowledge directly benefited their communities.

A small number of slaves, about 5 percent, worked in industry in the South, including mills, iron works, and railroad construction. Slaves in cities took on a wider

■ *Although cotton cultivation required constant attention, many of the tasks involved were relatively simple. Thus on a plantation the majority of slaves, including women and children, were field hands who performed the same tasks. Here, a slave family stands behind baskets of picked cotton in a Georgia cotton field.* ■

range of jobs than plantation slaves—as porters, waiters, cooks, and skilled laborers in tradesmen's shops—and in general enjoyed more autonomy. Some urban slaves even lived apart from their masters and hired out their own time, returning a portion of their wages to their owners.

In addition to the work they did for their masters in the fields or in other jobs, most slaves kept gardens or small farm plots for themselves to supplement their daily food rations. They also fished, hunted and trapped animals. Many slaves also worked "overtime" for their own masters on Sundays or holidays in exchange for money or goods, or hired out their overtime hours to others. This underground economy suggests slaves' overpowering desire to provide for their families, sometimes even raising enough funds to purchase their freedom.

Slave Families, Kinship, and Community

More than any other, the African American family was the institution that prevented slavery from becoming utterly demoralizing. Contrary to what historians and sociologists used to believe, slaves had a strong and abiding sense of family and kinship. But the nature of the families or households that predominated on particular plantations or farms varied according to local circumstances. On large plantations with relatively stable slave populations, a substantial majority of slave children lived in two-parent households, and many marriages lasted for as long as twenty to thirty years. They were more often broken up by the death or sale of one of the partners than by voluntary dissolution of the union. Close bonds united mothers, fathers, and children, and parents shared child-rearing responsibilities (within the limits allowed by the masters). Marital fidelity was encouraged by masters who believed that stable unions produced more offspring and by Christian churches that viewed adultery and divorce as sinful.

But in areas where most slaves lived on farms or small plantations, and especially in areas of the upper South where the trading and hiring out of slaves was frequent, a different pattern seems to have prevailed. Under these circumstances, slaves frequently had spouses who resided on other plantations or farms, often some distance away, and ties between husbands and wives were looser and more fragile. The result was that female-headed families were the norm, and responsibility for child rearing was vested in mothers, assisted in most cases by female relatives and friends. Mother-centered families with weak conjugal ties were a natural response to the infrequent presence of fathers and to the prospect of their being moved or sold beyond visiting distance. Where the breakup of unions by sale or relocation could be expected at any time, it did not pay to invest all of one's emotions in a conjugal relationship. But whether the basic family form was nuclear or matrifocal (female-headed), the ties that it created were infinitely precious to its members. Masters acquired great leverage over the behavior of slaves by invoking the threat of family breakup through sale to enforce discipline.

The terrible anguish that usually accompanied the breakup of families through sale showed the depth of kinship feelings. After emancipation, thousands of freed slaves wandered about looking for spouses, children, or parents from whom they had been forcibly separated years before.

Feelings of kinship and mutual obligation extended beyond the nuclear family. Grandparents, uncles, aunts, and even cousins were often known to slaves through direct contact or family lore. Nor were kinship ties limited to blood relations. When families were broken up by sale, individual members who found themselves on plantations far from home were likely to be assimilated into new kinship networks. Orphans or children without responsible parents were quickly absorbed without prejudice into new families.

Studies of the slave family reveal that kinship provided a model for personal relationships and the basis for a sense of community. Elderly slaves were addressed

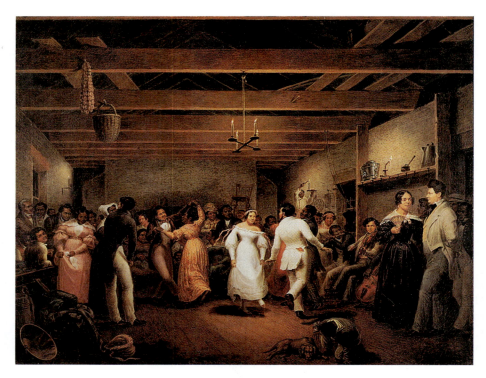

■ *On large plantations, slave men and women formed stable monogamous unions that often lasted until the couple was broken up by the death or sale of one of the partners. This painting by Christian Mayr portrays a slave wedding celebrated in White Sulphur Springs, Virginia, in 1838. The wedding couple wears white attire.* ■

as "uncle" and "aunty," and younger slaves commonly called each other "brother" or "sister." Slave culture was a family culture, and this was one of its greatest sources of strength and cohesion. The kinship network also provided a vehicle for the transmission of African American folk traditions from one generation to the next. Together with slave religion, kinship gave African Americans some sense that they were members of a community, not just a collection of individuals victimized by oppression.

African American Religion

From the realm of culture and fundamental beliefs, African Americans drew the strength to hold their heads high and look beyond their immediate condition. Religion was the cornerstone of this emerging African American culture. Black Christianity was far from a mere imitation of white religious forms and beliefs. This distinctive variant of evangelical Protestantism incorporated elements of African religion and stressed those portions of the Bible that spoke to the aspirations of an enslaved people thirsting for freedom.

Most slaves did not encounter Christianity in a church setting. There were a few independent black churches in the antebellum South, which mainly served free blacks and some urban slaves with indulgent masters. These included a variety of autonomous Baptist groups as well as Southern branches of the highly successful **African Methodist Episcopal (AME) Church,** a national denomination founded in 1816 by the Reverend Richard Allen of Philadelphia. But the mass of blacks did not have access to the independent churches.

Plantation slaves who were exposed to Christianity either attended the neighboring white churches or worshiped at home. On large estates, masters or white missionaries often conducted Sunday services. But white-sanctioned religious activity was only a superficial part of the slaves' spiritual life. The true slave religion was practiced at night, often secretly, and was led by black preachers.

This covert slave religion was a highly emotional affair that featured singing, shouting, and dancing. In some ways, the atmosphere resembled a backwoods re-

African Methodist Episcopal (AME) Church Richard Allen founded the African Methodist Episcopal Church in 1816 as the first independent black-run Protestant church in the United States. The AME Church was active in the promotion of abolition and the founding of educational institutions for free blacks.

vival meeting. But much of what went on was actually an adaptation of African religious beliefs and customs. The chanting mode of preaching—with the congregation responding at regular intervals—and the expression of religious feelings through rhythmic movements, especially the counterclockwise movement known as the ring shout, were clearly African in origin. The emphasis on sinfulness and fear of damnation that were core themes of white Evangelicalism played a lesser role among blacks. For them, religion was more an affirmation of the joy of life than a rejection of worldly pleasures and temptations.

Slave sermons and religious songs spoke directly to the plight of a people in bondage and implicitly asserted their right to be free. The most popular of all biblical subjects was the deliverance of the children of Israel from slavery in Egypt. Many sermons and songs refer to the crossing of Jordan and the arrival in the Promised Land. Other songs invoke the liberation theme in different ways. One recalls that Jesus had "set poor sinners free."

Most of the songs of freedom and deliverance can be interpreted as referring exclusively to religious salvation and the afterlife—and this was undoubtedly how slaves hoped their masters would understand them. But the slaves did not forget that God had once freed a people from slavery in this life and punished their masters. The Bible thus gave African Americans the hope that they, as a people, would repeat the experience of the Israelites and be delivered from bondage. During the Civil War, observers noted that freed slaves seemed to regard their emancipation as something that had been preordained, and some were inclined to view Lincoln as the reincarnation of Moses.

Besides being the basis for a deep-rooted hope for eventual freedom, religion also helped the slaves endure bondage without losing their sense of inner worth. Religious slaves sometimes regarded themselves as superior to their owners and believed that all whites were damned because of their unjust treatment of blacks.

More important, slave religion gave African Americans a chance to create and control a world of their own. Preachers, elders, and other leaders of slave congregations could acquire status within their own community that had not been conferred by whites. Although religion seldom inspired slaves to open rebellion, it must be regarded as a prime source of resistance to the dehumanizing effects of enslavement. It helped create a sense of community, solidarity, and self-esteem among slaves by giving them something of their own that they found infinitely precious.

Resistance and Rebellion

Open rebellion, the bearing of arms against the oppressors by organized groups of slaves, was the most dramatic and clear-cut form of slave resistance. In the period between 1800 and 1831, a number of slaves participated in revolts that showed their willingness to risk their lives in a desperate bid for liberation. In 1800, a Virginia slave named Gabriel Prosser mobilized a large band of his fellows to march on Richmond, but whites suppressed the uprising without any loss of white life. In 1811, another band of rebellious slaves was stopped as it moved on New Orleans brandishing guns, waving flags, and beating drums. In 1822, whites in Charleston, South Carolina, uncovered an extensive and well-planned conspiracy, organized by a free black man named Denmark Vesey, to arm the slave population and take possession of the city.

As we have already seen, the bloodiest and most terrifying of all slave revolts was the Nat Turner insurrection of 1831. Although it was the last slave rebellion of this kind during the pre–Civil War period, armed resistance had not ended. In Florida, hundreds of black fugitives fought in the Second Seminole War (1835–1842) alongside the Indians who had given them a haven. Many of the blacks eventually accompanied their Indian allies to the trans-Mississippi West.

Only a tiny fraction of all slaves ever took part in organized acts of violent resistance against white power. Most realized that the odds against a successful revolt were very high, and bitter experience had shown them that the usual outcome was death to the rebels. As a consequence, therefore, they devised safer or more ingenious ways to resist white dominance.

Thousands of slaves showed their discontent and desire for freedom by running away. Although most fugitives never got beyond the neighborhood of the plantation, many escapees remained free for years by hiding in swamps or other remote areas, and a fraction made it to freedom in the North or Mexico. Some fugitives stowed away aboard ships; others traveled overland for hundreds of miles. One resourceful slave even had himself packed in a box and shipped to the North. Some escaped with the help of the **Underground Railroad,** an informal network of sympathetic free blacks (and a few whites) who helped fugitives make their way North. For the majority of slaves, however, flight was not a real option. Either they lived too deep in the South to have any chance of reaching free soil, or they were reluctant to leave family and friends behind. As a result the typical fugitive was a young, unmarried male from the upper South.

Underground Railroad A network of safe houses organized by abolitionists (usually free blacks) to aid slaves in their attempts to escape slavery in the North or Canada.

Slaves who did not revolt or run away often expressed discontent by engaging in indirect or passive resistance. Many slaves worked slowly and inefficiently, not because they were naturally lazy (as whites supposed) but as a gesture of protest. Others withheld labor by feigning illness or injury, stole provisions, and committed acts of sabotage such as breaking tools, mistreating livestock, and setting barns on fire. The ultimate act of clandestine resistance was poisoning the master's food.

The basic attitude behind such actions was revealed in the folktales that slaves passed down from generation to generation. The famous Brer Rabbit stories showed how a small, apparently defenseless animal could overcome a bigger and stronger one through cunning and deceit. Such tales served as an allegory for the black view of the master-slave relationship. Other stories—which were not told in front of whites—openly portrayed the slave as a clever trickster outwitting the master.

Free Blacks in the Old South

In the South, free blacks occupied an increasingly precarious position in the antebellum society. White Southerners' fears of free blacks inciting slave revolts, and their reaction to attacks by abolitionists, led slaveholders after 1830 increasingly to defend slavery as a positive good rather than a necessary evil. Southerners articulated this defense of slavery in terms of race, emphasizing a dual image of the black person: under the "domesticating" influence of a white master, the slave was a child, a happy Sambo; outside of this influence, he was a savage beast. As whites strove to convince themselves and Northerners that blacks were happy in slavery, they more frequently portrayed free blacks as savages who needed to be reined in. Free blacks were required to carry papers proving their free status, and their movements were strictly limited. Blacks were excluded from several occupations, prohibited from holding meetings or forming organizations, and often forced into a state of economic dependency barely distinguishable from slavery.

■ *Henry "Box" Brown emerges from the crate in which he escaped from slavery in Richmond, Virginia, to freedom in Philadelphia.* ■

Although beset by special problems of their own, most free blacks identified with the suffering of the slaves. Many of them had once been slaves themselves or were the children of slaves. Often they had close relatives who were still in bondage. Furthermore, they knew that as long as slavery existed, their own rights were likely to be denied, and even their freedom was at risk. Kidnapping or fraudulent seizure by slave-catchers was always a possibility.

Because of the elaborate system of control and surveillance, free blacks in the South were in a relatively weak position to work against slavery. Most free blacks found that survival depended on creating the impression of loyalty to the planter regime. In some parts of the lower South, groups of relatively privileged free blacks, mostly of racially mixed origin, were sometimes persuaded that it was to their advantage to preserve the status quo. As skilled artisans and small-business owners dependent on white favors and patronage, they had little incentive to risk everything by taking the side of the slaves. In southern Louisiana, there was even a small group of mulatto planters who lived in luxury, supported by the labor of other African Americans.

However, although some free blacks were able to create niches of relative freedom, their position in southern society became increasingly precarious in the late antebellum period. Beginning in the 1830s, Southern whites sought to draw the line between free and unfree more firmly as a line between black and white. Free blacks were an anomaly in this system; increasingly, the Southern answer was to exclude, degrade, and even enslave those free people of color who remained within their borders. Just before the outbreak of the Civil War, a campaign developed in some southern states to carry the pattern of repression and discrimination to its logical conclusion: several state legislatures proposed laws giving free people of color the choice of emigrating from the state or being enslaved.

WHITE SOCIETY IN THE ANTEBELLUM SOUTH

Those who know the Old South only from modern novels, films, and television programs are likely to envision a land filled with majestic plantations, courtly gentlemen, elegant ladies, and faithful retainers. It is easy to conclude from such images that the typical white Southerner was an aristocrat who belonged to a family that owned large numbers of slaves. Certainly the great houses existed and some wealthy slaveholders did maintain an aristocratic lifestyle. But this was the world of only a small percentage of slaveowners and a minuscule portion of the total white population. The number of large planters who had the means to build great houses and entertain lavishly, those who owned at least fifty slaves, comprised less than 1 percent of all whites.

Most Southern whites were nonslaveholding yeoman farmers. Yet even those who owned no slaves grew to depend on slavery in other ways, whether economically, because they hired slaves, or psychologically, because having a degraded class of blacks below them made them feel better about their own place in society. However, the class divisions between slaveholders and nonslaveholders did contribute to the political rifts that became increasingly apparent on the eve of the Civil War.

The Planters' World

The great planters, although few in number, had a weighty influence on southern life. They set the tone and values for much of the rest of society. Although many of them were too busy tending to their plantations to become openly involved in politics, wealthy planters held more than their share of high offices and often exerted a decisive influence on public policy. Within those regions of the South in which plantation agriculture predominated, they were a ruling class in every sense of the term.

Contrary to legend, most of the great planters of the pre–Civil War period were self-made rather than descendants of the old colonial gentry. Some were ambitious young men who married planters' daughters. Others started as lawyers and used their fees and connections to acquire plantations.

As the Cotton Kingdom spread westward, the men who became the largest slaveholders were even less likely to have genteel backgrounds. A large proportion of them began as hard-driving businessmen who built up capital from commerce, land speculation, banking, and even slave trading. They then used their profits to buy plantations. The highly competitive, boom-or-bust economy of the Southwest put a greater premium on sharp dealing and business skills than on genealogy. To be successful, a planter had to be not only a good plantation manager, but also a shrewd entrepreneur who kept a careful eye on the market, the prices of slaves and land, and the extent of his indebtedness. Hence few planters could be men of leisure.

Likewise, the responsibility of running an extended household that produced much of its own food and clothing kept most plantation mistresses from being the idle ladies of legend—few Southern women fit the stereotype of the Southern belle sipping tea on the veranda. Not only were plantation mistresses a tiny minority of the women who lived and worked in the slave states before the Civil War, but even those who were part of the planter elite rarely led lives of leisure.

A small number of the richest and most secure plantation families did aspire to live in the manner of a traditional landed aristocracy, with big houses, elegant carriages, fancy-dress balls, and excessive numbers of house servants. Dueling, despite efforts to repress it, remained the standard way to settle "affairs of honor" among gentlemen. Another sign of gentility was the tendency of planters' sons to avoid "trade" as a primary or secondary career in favor of law or the military. Planters' daughters were trained from girlhood to play the piano, speak French, dress in the latest fashions, and sparkle in the drawing room or on the dance floor. The aristocratic style originated among the older gentry of the seaboard slave states, but by the 1840s and 1850s it had spread southwest as a second generation of wealthy planters began to displace the rough-hewn pioneers of the Cotton Kingdom.

Planters, Racism, and Paternalism

No assessment of the planters' outlook or worldview can be made without considering their relations with their slaves. Planters owned more than half of all the slaves in the South and set standards for treatment and management. Most planters liked to think of themselves as benevolent masters and they often referred to their slaves as members of an extended patriarchal family. According to the ideology of paternalism, blacks were a race of perpetual children requiring care and supervision by superior whites. Paternalism went hand in hand with racism, as slaveholders justified slavery by the supposed mental and moral inferiority of Africans. Paternalistic rhetoric increased greatly after abolitionists began to charge that most slaveholders were sadistic monsters.

There was, nevertheless, an element of truth in the planters' claim that their slaves were relatively well treated. Food, clothing, and shelter usually were sufficient to sustain life and labor at above the bare subsistence level; family life was encouraged and to some extent flourished; and average life expectancy, birthrate, and natural growth in population were only slightly below the average for southern whites. Certainly North American slaves of the pre–Civil War period enjoyed a higher standard of living than those in other New World slave societies, where slave populations usually failed to reproduce themselves.

But relatively good physical conditions for slaves does not demonstrate that planters put ethical considerations ahead of self-interest. The ban on the transatlantic slave trade in 1808 was effective enough to make the domestic reproduction of the slave force an economic necessity if the system was to be perpetuated. While some historians have argued that paternalism was part of a social system that was organized like a family hierarchy rather than a brutal, profit-making arrangement, there was no inconsistency between planters' paternalism and capitalism. Slaves were valuable property and the main tools of production for a booming economy, and it was in the interest of masters to see that their property remained in good enough condition to work hard and produce large numbers of children.

The testimony of slaves themselves and of some independent white observers suggests that masters of large plantations generally did not have close and intimate relationships with the mass of field slaves. The kind of affection and concern associated with a father figure appears to have been limited mainly to relationships with a few favored house servants or other elite slaves, such as drivers and highly skilled artisans. The field hands on large estates dealt mostly with overseers who were hired or fired because of their ability to meet production quotas.

When they were being most realistic, planters conceded that the ultimate basis of their authority was force and intimidation, rather than the natural obedience resulting due to a loving parent. Devices for inspiring fear included whipping—a common practice on most plantations—and the threat of sale away from family and friends. Planters and overseers maintained order by swift punishment for any infraction of the rules or even for a surly attitude.

In spite of economic considerations, some masters inevitably yielded to the temptations of power or to their bad tempers and tortured or killed their slaves. Others raped slave women. Slaves had little legal protection against such abuse because their testimony was not accepted in court. Human nature being what it is, such a situation was bound to result in atrocities. As Harriet Beecher Stowe acknowledged in 1852 in *Uncle Tom's Cabin,* her celebrated antislavery novel, most slaveholders were not as sadistic and brutish as Simon Legree, but there was something terribly wrong with an institution that gave one human being nearly absolute power over another.

Small Slaveholders

As we have seen, 88 percent of all slaveholders in 1860 owned fewer than twenty slaves and thus were not planters in the usual sense of the term. Of these, the great majority had fewer than ten. Many were simply farmers who used one or two slave families to ease the burden of their own labor. Life on these small slaveholding farms was relatively spartan. Masters lived in log cabins or small frame cottages, and slaves lived in lofts or sheds that were not usually up to plantation housing standards.

For better or worse, relations between owners and their slaves were more intimate than on larger estates. Unlike planters, these farmers often worked in the fields alongside their slaves and sometimes ate at the same table or slept under the same roof. But such closeness did not necessarily result in better treatment. Both the best and the worst of slavery could be found on these farms, depending on the character and disposition of the master. Given a choice, most slaves preferred to live on

A Look at the Past
Slave Clothing

Slaves typically received a yearly clothing allotment of one complete outfit and a pair of shoes. Slaves sometimes received cast-off clothing or lengths of decent fabric to make the year's new outfit, but generally they were given the cheapest fabric on the market, osnaburg, a coarse factory-woven cloth. While northern factories spun cotton and wove it into osnaburg for the southern market, men and women throughout New England earned extra money making brogans for slaves. Coarsely put together with soles pegged on rather than sewn, brogans were cheap and quick to make. ✱ How did slaves' clothing reinforce their position? What do northern fabric and shoes made especially for the slave market suggest about connections between slavery and the northern economy?

plantations because they offered the sociability, culture, and kinship of the slave quarters, as well as better prospects for adequate food, clothing, and shelter.

Yeoman Farmers

yeoman Southern small land-holders who owned no slaves and who lived primarily in the foothills of the Appalachian and Ozark mountains. These farmers were self-reliant and grew mixed crops, although they usually did not produce a substantial amount to be sold on the market.

Just below the small slaveholders on the social scale was a substantial class of **yeoman** farmers. Contrary to another myth about the Old South, most of these people did not fit the image of the degraded, shiftless, "poor white." The majority of the nonslaveholding rural population were proud, self-reliant farmers whose way of life did not differ markedly from that of family farmers in the Midwest during the early stages of settlement.

The yeomen were mostly concentrated in the back country where slaves and plantations were rarely seen. The foothills or interior valleys of the Appalachians and the Ozarks were unsuitable for plantation agriculture but offered reasonably good soils for mixed farming, and long stretches of "piney barrens" along the Gulf Coast were suitable for raising livestock. Slaveless farmers concentrated in these regions, giving rise to the "white counties" that complicated southern politics.

Yeoman women, much more than their wealthy plantation counterparts, participated in every dimension of household labor. They worked in the garden, made clothing and handicrafts, and even labored in the fields when it was necessary. Women in the most dire economic circumstances even worked for wages in small businesses or on nearby farms. They raised much larger families than their wealthier neighbors because having many children supplied a valuable labor pool for the family farm.

The lack of transportation facilities, more than some failure of energy or character, limited the prosperity of the yeomen. A large part of their effort was devoted to growing subsistence crops, mainly corn. Their principle source of cash was livestock, especially hogs. But since the livestock was generally allowed to forage in the woods rather than being fattened on grain, it was of poor quality and did not bring high prices or big profits to raisers.

Although they did not benefit directly from the peculiar institution, most yeomen and other nonslaveholders tolerated slavery and were fiercely opposed to abolitionism in any form. Many abolitionists could not understand the reasons for their position, for undoubtedly the yeoman were hurt economically by the existence of slavery and a planter class. Most yeomen were staunch Jacksonians who resented aristocratic pretensions and feared concentrations of power and wealth in the hands of the few. On issues involving representation, banking, and internal improvements, yeomen sometimes voted against the planters. Why, then, did they fail to respond to antislavery appeals that called on them to strike at the real source of planter power and privilege?

One reason was that some nonslaveholders hoped to get ahead in the world, and in the South this meant acquiring slaves of their own. Just enough of the more prosperous yeomen broke into the slaveholding classes to make this dream seem believable. Planters, anxious to ensure the loyalty of nonslaveholders, strenuously encouraged the notion that every white man was a potential master.

Even if they did not aspire to own slaves, white farmers often viewed black servitude as providing a guarantee of their own liberty and independence. Although they had no natural love of planters and slavery, they believed that abolition would lead to disaster. In part, their anxieties were economic; freed slaves would compete with them for land or jobs. But their racism went deeper than this. Emancipation was unthinkable because it would remove the pride and status that automatically went along with a white skin in this acutely race-conscious society. Slavery, despite its drawbacks, served to keep blacks "in their place" and to make all whites, however poor and uneducated they might be, feel that they were free and equal members of a master race.

A Closed Mind and a Closed Society

Despite the tacit assent of most nonslaveholders, the dominant class never lost its fear that lower-class whites would turn against slavery. They felt threatened from two sides: from the slave quarters where a new Nat Turner might be gathering his forces, and from the back country where yeomen and poor whites might heed the call of abolitionists and rise up against planter domination. Beginning in the 1830s, the ruling element tightened their grip on southern society and culture.

Before the 1830s, open discussion of the rights or wrongs of slavery had been possible in many parts of the South. Apologists commonly described the institution as "a necessary evil" and in the upper South there was significant support for the **American Colonization Society**'s program of gradual emancipation accompanied by deportation of the freedmen. By the end of 1832, however, all talk about emancipation had ended in the South. The argument that slavery was a positive good, rather than an evil slated for gradual elimination, won the day.

The positive good defense of slavery was an answer to the abolitionist charge that the institution was inherently sinful. The message was carried in a host of books, pamphlets, and newspaper editorials published between the 1830s and the Civil War. Who, historians have asked, was it meant to persuade? Partly, the argument was aimed at the North. But Southerners themselves were a prime target. In popularized forms, the message was used to arouse racial anxieties that tended to neutralize antislavery sentiment among the lower classes.

The proslavery argument was based on three main propositions. The first and foremost was that enslavement was the natural and proper status for people of African descent. Blacks, it was alleged, were innately inferior to whites and suited only for slavery. Biased scientific and historical evidence was presented to support this claim. Second, slavery was held to be sanctioned by the Bible and Christianity—a position made necessary by the abolitionist appeal to Christian ethics. Third, efforts were made to show that slavery was consistent with the humanitarian spirit of the nineteenth century. The plantation was seen as a sort of asylum providing guidance and care for a race that could not look after itself.

By the 1850s, the proslavery argument had gone beyond mere apology for the South and its peculiar institution and featured an ingenious attack on the free-labor system of the North. According to Virginian George Fitzhugh, the master-slave relationship was more humane than the one prevailing between employers and wage laborers in the North. Slaves had security against unemployment and a guarantee of care in old age, whereas free workers might face destitution and even starvation at any time. Fitzhugh believed that slave societies were more orderly, just, and peaceful than free societies.

In addition to arguing against the abolitionists, proslavery Southerners attempted to seal off their region from antislavery ideas and influences. Whites who were bold enough to criticize slavery publicly were mobbed or persecuted. One of the last and bravest of the southern abolitionists, Cassius M. Clay of Kentucky, armed himself with a brace of pistols when he gave speeches. Clergymen who questioned the morality of slavery were driven from their pulpits, and northern travelers suspected of being abolitionist agents were tarred and feathered. When abolitionists tried to send their literature through the mails during the 1830s, it was seized in southern post offices and publicly burned.

Such flagrant denials of free speech and civil liberties were inspired in part by fears that nonslaveholding whites and slaves would get subversive ideas. Hinton R. Helper's 1857 book *The Impending Crisis of the South*, an appeal to nonslaveholders to resist the planter regime, was suppressed with particular vigor. But the deepest fear was that slaves would hear the abolitionist talk or read antislavery literature and be inspired to rebel. Consequently, new laws were passed making it a crime to teach slaves to read and write. Free blacks, thought to be possible instigators of slave

American Colonization Society Founded in 1817, this organization hoped to provide a mechanism by which slavery could be gradually eliminated. The society advocated the relocation of free blacks (followed by freed slaves) to the African colony of Monrovia, present-day Liberia.

revolt, were denied basic civil liberties and were the object of growing surveillance and harassment.

All these efforts at thought control and internal security did not allay planters' fears of abolitionist subversion, lower-class white dissent, and, above all, slave revolt. The persistent barrage of proslavery propaganda and the course of national events in the 1850s created a mood of panic and desperation. By this time, an increasing number of Southerners had become convinced that safety from abolitionism and its associated terrors required a formal withdrawal from the Union—secession.

SLAVERY AND THE SOUTHERN ECONOMY

Despite the internal divisions of Southern society, white Southerners from all regions and classes came to perceive their interests tied up with slavery. Southern society transformed itself according to the needs of the slave system because slavery was the cornerstone of the Southern economy. For the most part, the expansion of slavery—the number of slaves in the South more than tripled between 1810 and 1860 to nearly 4 million—can be attributed to the rise of King Cotton. The cotton-growing areas of the South were becoming more and more dependent on slavery, at the same time that agriculture in the upper South was actually moving away from the institution. Yet slavery continued to remain important to the economy of the upper South, through the slave trade. To understand Southern thought and behavior, it is necessary to bear in mind this major regional difference between a slave plantation society and a farming and slave-trading region.

The Internal Slave Trade

Tobacco, the original plantation crop of the colonial period, continued to be the principal slave-cultivated commodity of the upper tier of southern states during the pre–Civil War era. But markets were often depressed, and profitable tobacco cultivation was hard to sustain for very long in one place because the crop rapidly depleted the soil. During the lengthy depression of the tobacco market that lasted from the 1820s to the 1850s, tobacco farmers in Virginia and Maryland experimented with fertilizer use, crop rotation, and diversified farming, all of which increased the need for capital but reduced the demand for labor.

As slave prices rose (because of high demand in the lower South) and demand for slaves in the upper South fell, the "internal" slave trade took off. Increasingly, the most profitable business for slaveholders in Virginia, Kentucky, Maryland, and the Carolinas was selling "surplus" slaves from the upper South to regions of the lower South, where staple crop production was more profitable. This interstate slave trade sent an estimated six to seven hundred thousand slaves in a southwesterly direction between 1815 and 1860. Historian Michael Tadman estimates that the chances of a slave child in the Upper South in the 1820s to be "sold South" by 1860 was as high as 30 percent. Such sales were wrenching, not only splitting families, but making it especially unlikely that the slaves sold would ever see friends or family again.

Some economic historians have concluded that the most important crop produced in the tobacco kingdom was not the "stinking weed" but human beings cultivated for the auction block. Respectable planters did not like to think of themselves as raising slaves for market, but few would refuse to sell some of their "people" if they needed money to get out of debt or make expensive improvements. For the region as a whole, the slave trade provided a crucial source of capital in a period of transition and innovation. Nevertheless, the fact that slave labor was declining in importance in the upper South meant the peculiar institution had a weaker hold on public loyalty there than in the cotton states. Diversification of agriculture was accompanied by a more rapid rate of urban and industrial development than was occurring elsewhere in the South. As a result, Virginians, Marylanders, and Kentuckians were seriously divided on whether their ultimate future lay with the Deep South's plantation economy or with the industrializing free-labor system that was flourishing just north of their borders.

The Rise of the Cotton Kingdom

The warmer climate and good soils of the lower tier of southern states made it possible to raise crops more naturally suited than tobacco or cereals to the plantation form of agriculture and the heavy use of slave labor, including rice and long-staple cotton along the coast of South Carolina and Georgia, and sugar in lower Louisiana. But cultivation of these crops was limited by natural conditions to peripheral, semitropical areas. It was the rise of short-staple cotton as the South's major crop that strengthened the hold of slavery and the plantation on the southern economy.

Short-staple cotton differed from the long-staple variety in two important ways: its bolls contained seeds that were much more difficult to extract by hand, and it could be grown almost anywhere south of Virginia and Kentucky—the main requirement was a guarantee of two hundred frost-free days. The invention of the **cotton gin** in 1793 ended the seed extraction problem and made short-staple cotton the South's major crop. Unlike rice and sugar, cotton could be grown on small farms as well as on plantations. But large planters enjoyed certain advantages that made them the main producers. Only relatively large operators could afford their own gins or possessed the capital to acquire the fertile bottomlands that brought the highest yields. They also had lower transportation costs because they were able to monopolize land along rivers and streams that were the South's natural arteries of transportation.

The first major cotton-producing regions were inland areas of Georgia and South Carolina but the center of production shifted rapidly westward during the nineteenth century, first to Alabama and Mississippi and then to Arkansas, northwest Louisiana, and east Texas. The rise in total production that accompanied this geographic expansion was phenomenal. In 1792, the South's output of cotton was about 13,000 bales; in 1840, it was 1.35 million; and in 1860, production peaked at 4.8 million bales. Most of the cotton went to supply the booming textile industry of Great Britain.

"Cotton is king!" proclaimed a southern orator in the 1850s, and he was right. By that time, three-quarters of the world's supply of cotton came from the American South, and this single commodity accounted for more than half the total dollar value of American exports. Cotton growing and the network of commercial and industrial enterprises that marketed and processed the crop constituted the most important economic interest in the United States on the eve of the Civil War. Since slavery and cotton seemed inextricably linked, it appeared obvious to many Southerners that their peculiar institution was the keystone of national wealth and economic progress.

Despite its overall success, however, the rise of the Cotton Kingdom did not bring a uniform or steady prosperity to the lower South. Many planters worked the land until it was exhausted and then took their slaves westward to richer soils, leaving depressed and ravaged areas in their wake. Fluctuations in markets and prices also ruined many planters. Widespread depressions, including a wave of bankruptcies, followed the boom periods of 1815–1819, 1832–1837, and 1849–1860. But during the eleven years of rising output and high prices preceding the Civil War, the planters gradually forgot their earlier troubles and began to imagine they were immune to future economic disasters.

cotton gin Invented by Eli Whitney in 1793, this device for separating the seeds from the fibers of short-staple cotton enabled a slave to clean fifty times more cotton as by hand, which reduced production costs and gave new life to slavery in the South.

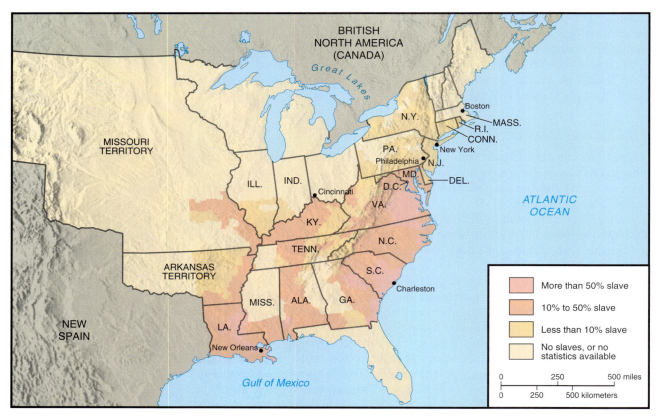

BRITISH
NORTH AMERICA
(CANADA)

SLAVE CONCENTRATION, 1820 *In 1820, most slaves lived in the eastern seaboard states of Virginia and South Carolina and in Louisiana on the Gulf of Mexico.* ■

Despite the insecurities associated with cotton production, most of the time the crop represented the Old South's best chance for profitable investment. Prudent planters who had not borrowed too heavily during flush times could survive periods of depression by cutting costs, making their plantations self-sufficient. For those with worn-out land, two options existed: they could sell their land and move west, or they could sell their slaves to raise capital for fertilization, crop rotation, and other improvements that could help them survive where they were. Hence planters had little incentive to seek alternatives to slavery, the plantation, and dependence on a single cash crop. From a purely economic point of view, they had every reason to defend slavery and to insist on their right to expand it.

Slavery and Industrialization

As the sectional quarrel with the North intensified, Southerners became increasingly alarmed by their region's lack of economic self-sufficiency. Dependence on the North for capital, marketing facilities, and manufactured goods was seen as evidence of a dangerous subservience to "external" economic interests. During the 1850s, Southern nationalists such as J. D. B. De Bow, editor of the influential *De Bow's Review,* called for the South to develop its own industries, commerce, and shipping. But such pleas for a diversified economy went unanswered. Men with capital were doing too well in plantation agriculture to risk their money in other ventures.

In the 1840s and 1850s, a debate raged among white capitalists over whether the South should use free whites or enslaved blacks as the labor supply for industry. Some leaders defended a white labor policy, arguing that factory work would provide new economic opportunities for a degraded class of poor whites. But other ad-

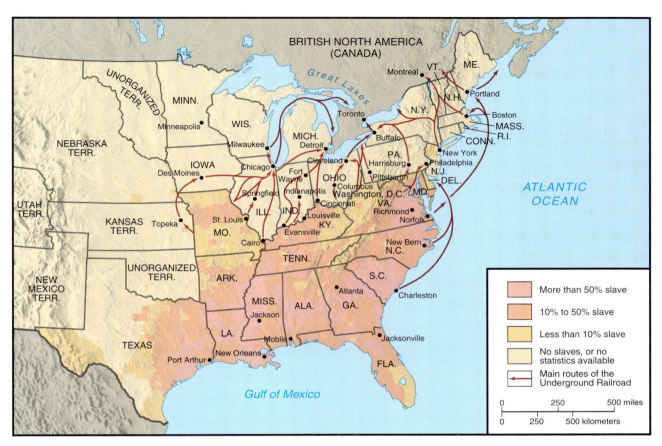

SLAVE CONCENTRATION, 1860   *In 1860, slavery had extended throughout the southern states, with the greatest concentrations of slaves in the states of the Deep South. There were also sizable slave populations in the new states of Missouri, Arkansas, Texas, and Florida.* ■

vocates of industrialization feared that the growth of a free working class would lead to social conflict among whites and preferred using slaves for all supervised manual labor. In practice, some factories employed slaves, others white workers, and a few even experimented with integrated workforces. As well as can be determined, mills that hired or purchased slave labor were just as profitable and efficient as those paying wages to whites. It is clear, however, that the union of slavery and cotton that was central to the South's prosperity impeded industrialization and left the region dependent on one-crop agriculture and on the North for capital and marketing.

The "Profitability" Issue

Some Southerners were making money, and a great deal of it, using slave labor to raise cotton. But did slavery yield a good return for the great majority of slaveholders who were not large planters? Did it provide the basis for general prosperity and a relatively high standard of living for the southern population in general, or at least for the two-thirds of it who were white and free? In short, was slavery profitable?

For many years historians believed that slave-based agriculture generally was not very lucrative. Planters' account books seemed to show at best a modest return on investment. In the 1850s, the price of slaves rose at a faster rate than the price of cotton, allegedly squeezing many operators. Some historians even concluded that

■ *A row of steamboats in New Orleans await bales of cotton for shipment. By 1860, production of "king" cotton in the south peaked at 4.8 million bales.* ■

slavery was a dying institution by the time of the Civil War. Profitability, they argued, depended on access to new and fertile land suitable for plantation agriculture, and virtually all such land within the limits of the United States had already been taken up by 1860. Hence slavery had allegedly reached its natural limits of expansion and was on the verge of becoming so unprofitable that it would fall of its own weight in the near future.

A more recent interpretation, based on modern economic theory, holds that slavery was in fact still an economically sound institution in 1860 and showed no signs of imminent decline. During the 1850s, planters usually could expect an annual return of 8 to 10 percent on capital invested. This yield was roughly equivalent to the best that could then be obtained from the most lucrative sectors of northern industry and commerce. Furthermore, it is no longer clear that plantation agriculture had reached its natural limits of expansion by 1860. Production in Texas had not yet peaked, and the construction of railroads and levees was opening up new areas for cotton growing elsewhere in the South. Those who argue that slavery was profitable and had an expansive future have made a strong and convincing case.

But the larger question remains: What sort of economic development did a slave plantation system foster? What portion of the southern population benefited from the system? Did it promote efficiency and progressive change? Economists Robert Fogel and Stanley Engerman have argued that the plantation was an internally efficient enterprise with good managers and industrious, well-motivated workers. Other economic historians have attributed the profitability almost exclusively to favorable market conditions.

Other evidence suggests that only the large plantations were profitable. Because of various factors—lack of credit, high transportation costs, and a greater vulnerability to market fluctuations—owners of smaller and nonslaveholding plantations had to devote a larger share of their acreage to subsistence crops. This kept their standard of living lower than that of most northern farmers. Slaves received sufficient food, clothing, and shelter for their subsistence and to make them strong enough to work, but their living standard was below that of the poorest free people in the United States.

The South's economic development was skewed in favor of a single route to wealth, open only to white men with access to capital. The concentration of capital and business energies on cotton production foreclosed the kind of diversified industrial and commercial growth that would have provided wider opportunities. Thus, in comparison to the industrializing North, the South was an underdeveloped region in which much of the population had little incentive to work hard. A lack of public education for whites and the denial of even minimal literacy to slaves represented a critical failure to develop human resources. The South's economy was probably condemned so long as it was based on slavery.

Chronology

1793	Eli Whitney invents the cotton gin
1800	Gabriel Prosser leads abortive slave rebellion in Virginia
1811	Slaves revolt in Point Coupée section of Louisiana
1822	Denmark Vesey conspiracy uncovered in Charleston, South Carolina
1829	David Walker publishes *Appeal* calling for slave insurrection
1830	First National Negro Convention meets
1831	Slaves under Nat Turner rebel in Virginia, killing almost sixty whites
1832	Virginia legislature votes against gradual emancipation
1835–1842	Blacks fight alongside Indians in the Second Seminole War
1837	Panic of 1837 is followed by major depression of the cotton market
1849	Cotton prices rise, and a sustained boom commences
1852	Harriet Beecher Stowe's antislavery novel *Uncle Tom's Cabin* is published and becomes a best-seller
1857	Hinton R. Helper attacks slavery on economic grounds in *The Impending Crisis of the South;* the book is suppressed in the southern states
1860	Cotton prices and production reach all-time peak

CONCLUSION: WORLDS IN CONFLICT

If slaves lived to some extent in a separate and distinctive world of their own, so did planters, less affluent whites, and even free blacks. The Old South was thus a deeply divided society—a kaleidoscope of groups divided by class, race, culture, and geography. What held it together and provided some measure of unity were a booming plantation economy and a web of customary relationships and loyalties that could obscure the underlying cleavages and antagonisms. The fractured and fragile nature of this society would soon become apparent when it was subjected to the pressures of civil war.

KEY TERMS

Old South, p. 205

African Methodist Episcopal (AME) Church, p. 208

Underground Railroad, p. 210

yeoman, p. 214

American Colonization Society, p. 215

cotton gin, p. 217

RECOMMENDED READING

Major works that take a broad view of slavery are Kenneth M. Stampp, *The Peculiar Institution: Slavery in the Antebellum South* (1956), which stresses its coercive features; John W. Blassingame, *The Slave Community: Plantation Life in the Antebellum South* (1972), which focuses on slave culture and psychology; and Eugene D. Genovese, *Roll, Jordan, Roll: The World the Slaves Made* (1974), which probes the paternalistic character of the institution and the way in which slaves made a world for themselves within its bounds. An insightful interpretation of an-

tebellum southern society is James Oakes, *Slavery and Freedom: An Interpretation of the Old South* (1990). For an overview of the history of slavery, see Peter Kolchin, *American Slavery, 1619–1877* (1993).

On the economics of slavery, see Gavin Wright, *The Political Economy of the Cotton South: Households, Markets, and Wealth in the Nineteenth Century* (1978). On women in the Old South, see Laura F. Edwards, *Scarlett Doesn't Live Here Anymore: Southern Women in the Civil War Era* (2000) and Deborah Gray White, *Ar'n't I a Woman: Female Slaves in* the Plantation South (1985). On the slave trade, see two excellent studies: Michael Tadman, *Speculators and Slaves: Masters, Traders, and Slaves in the Old South* (1989) and Walter Johnson, *Soul by Soul: Life Inside the Antebellum Slave Market* (1999). For the history of the slave family, see Herbert Gutman, *The Black Family in Slavery and Freedom, 1750–1925* (1976); Brenda Stevenson, *Life in Black and White: Family and Community in the Slave South* (1996); and Marie Jenkins Schwartz, *Born in Bondage: Growing Up Enslaved in the Antebellum South* (2000). For Southern law and slavery, see Thomas D. Morris, *Southern Slavery and the Law, 1619–1860* (1996) and Ariela J. Gross, *Double*

Character: Slavery and Mastery in the Antebellum Southern Courtroom (2000).

Black resistance to slavery is described in Vincent Harding, *There Is a River: The Black Struggle for Freedom in America* (1981). Slave culture is examined in Albert J. Raboteau, *Slave Religion: The "Invisible Institution" in the Antebellum South* (1978); Lawrence W. Levine, *Black Culture and Consciousness: Afro-American Folk Thought from Slavery to Freedom* (1977); Sterling Stuckey, *Slave Culture: Nationalist Theory and the Foundations of Black America* (1987); and Sharla M. Fett, *Healing, Health, and Power on Southern Slave Plantations* (2002).

SUGGESTED WEB SITES

"Been Here So Long": Selections from the WPA American Slave Narratives
newdeal.feri.org/asn/index.htm
Slave narratives are some of the more interesting primary sources about slavery.

Exploring Amistad
amistad.mysticseaport.org/main/welcome.html
Mystic Seaport runs this site that includes extensive collections of historical resources relating to the revolt and subsequent trial of enslaved Africans.

Africans in America: America's Journey Through Slavery
www.pbs.org/wgbh/aia/home.html
This PBS site contains images and documents recounting slavery in America.

Amistad Trials (1839–1840)
www.law.umkc.edu/faculty/projects/ftrials/amistad/AMISTD.HTM
Images, chronology, court and official documents comprise this site by Dr. Doug Linder at University of Missouri–Kansas City Law School.

Slave Narratives
docsouth.unc.edu/neh/neh.html
This site presents the telling narratives of several slaves housed at the Documents of the American South collection and the University of North Carolina.

Colonization: The African-American Mosaic
www.loc.gov/exhibits/african/afam002.html
This site contains images and text relating to the colonization movement to return African Americans to Africa.

Images of African Americans from the Nineteenth Century
digital.nypl.org/schomburg/images_aa19/
The New York Public Library–Schomburg Center for Research in Black Culture site contains numerous visuals.

Images of African American Slavery and Freedom
www.loc.gov/rr/print/list/082_slave.html
This site contains numerous photographs and other images of slaves and free blacks from the Library of Congress.

St. Louis Circuit Court Historical Records Project
stlcourtrecords.wustl.edu/resources.php
This site contains links to full-text reproductions of slaves' freedom suits in Missouri, including the Dred Scott case, and many other African American history links.

Women of Southern Households

Harriet Jacobs, born enslaved in North Carolina in 1813, became a slave in James and Maria Norcom's household in 1825. James began to "whisper foul words" in Harriet's ears when she was a young teenager. Harriet had no one to whom she could turn, except for her free black grandmother, who lived in the town. Although her grandmother had been a slave, Harriet's master "dreaded her scorching rebukes" and furthermore "he did not wish to have his villainy made public." For a time, this wish to "keep up some outward show of decency" protected Harriet.

Harriet Jacobs's grandmother was an unusual woman, who had worked extra for years to buy her children's freedom, only to be cheated out of her earnings at the end. Like most free black women, Harriet's grandmother was the unmarried head of her own household, separated long ago from the father of her children. Running their own households gave some free black women a measure of autonomy, but also left them with little support in the daily struggle against poverty and racism.

Maria Norcom, as the wife of a prominent doctor and large plantation owner, lived a life very different from Harriet's or her grandmother's. Yet it was not the life of carefree luxury sometimes portrayed in movies and books about the Old South. Compared to poorer women in the South, Maria had more access to education and periods of recreation and relaxation. But as a lady of the upper class, she was expected to master strict rules of womanhood that demanded moral purity and virtue. She also had to learn the personal and managerial skills necessary to oversee a household staffed by slaves.

Most southern white women worked hard to keep households and families together, and they all lived within a social system that denied them legal rights by placing them under the domination of husbands and fathers. James Norcom's behavior, while it certainly violated his vows of marriage, was not egregious enough to have won Maria a divorce under the laws of North Carolina.

Whether they were rich or poor, free or enslaved, women were, to a large degree, defined by their relationship to the head of the household, nearly always a white man. Although there were expectations that husbands would protect and care for their wives, women had little recourse against husbands who departed from those expectations. For example, Marion S. D. Converse, a woman from a prominent South Carolina family, dreaded her abusive second husband, Augustus. Through years of beatings and jealous tirades, Marion was unable to escape the bonds of marriage because Augustus's deplorable conduct fell short of legal grounds for divorce in South Carolina (only abandonment or impotence). Yet Marion Converse was able to gain aid and protection from her prominent family, who shielded her from the worst consequences of an abusive marriage.

When Maria Norcom discovered her husband's overtures toward Harriet, she was distraught and took Harriet to sleep in her own room. Yet as Harriet later described it, Maria "pitied herself as a martyr; but she was incapable of feeling for the condition of shame and misery in which her unfortunate, helpless slave was placed." Harriet often woke to find Maria bending over her, and came to fear for her safety around this "jealous mistress." Harriet Jacobs's and Maria Norcom's stories illustrate that planters ruled their wives as well as their slaves. All southern women were embedded in a social system that gave authority over their lives and choices to men. Despite this commonality, few women were able to reach across the divides of race and class to recognize these similarities. Tormented by jealousy and humiliation, Maria came to blame the slave rather than her husband for their intimacy, imagining that Harriet herself had seduced him.

Harriet managed to elude her master's advances, in part due to Maria's vigilance. Yet faced with harsh choices, she bore two children by another white man in the hope that he would offer her some protection. This worked for a time, but in the end, only escape saved Harriet from James Norcom. Enslaved women such as Harriet Jacobs were the most vulnerable of Southern women. They were subject to a level of violence and sexual assault that was unknown to other women in the South; and when they were victims of violence they lacked even the limited legal defenses that were open to poor white women. Because black women were considered unable to give or withhold consent, it was not a crime to rape a black woman. And had Harriet fought back physically against her master's advances, she risked criminal prosecution and even death. When the slave Celia killed the master who had been raping her for years, her court-appointed lawyer argued that she should not be criminally liable, based on a Georgia statute allowing women to use force to defend their "honor" against a rapist. The court, however, decreed that black women were not women within the meaning of the statute. Celia had no honor that the law recognized. She was thus convicted of murder, sentenced to death, and hanged.

Excluding black women from the laws of rape also reinforced common images of black women as either

■ This 1836 engraving from an anti-slavery novel depicts a plantation mistress scolding a slave woman while the master looks on. Though white women were also subjugated to the authority of white men in southern society, the divide of race prevented plantation ladies and slaves from finding potential solidarity as women. ■

sexually aggressive Jezebels or sexless, nurturing mammies. The first stereotype justified the sexual exploitation of slave women and the second fed the slaveowners' fantasy that their slaves loved and cared for them. Harriet Jacobs found herself in such a difficult position because she wanted to be neither a Jezebel nor a mammy. Of course, neither of these images corresponded to the realities and hardships of slave life. Enslaved women were often assigned backbreaking labor that paid little attention to common distinctions about so-called women's work. They were expected to do all of the normal tasks assigned to women—sewing, washing, child care—as well as work a full day in the fields. Despite these brutal conditions, slave women organized communities and households, and tried to protect themselves against the worst excesses of the slave system. Harriet and her grandmother were involved in a complicated network of extended kin, and invested a great deal of energy in protecting brothers and sons from sale "up the river."

Harriet eventually escaped from the Norcoms in 1835, hiding in her grandmother's attic for seven years while she tried to induce Norcom to sell her children to their father, the attorney Samuel Tredwell Sawyer.

Sawyer did eventually purchase the children, but did not emancipate them as he had promised; instead, he sent his daughter to Brooklyn, New York, to work as a house servant for his cousin, and kept his son as a slave at home. Although Harriet was eventually able to escape the bonds of slavery and join the battle to abolish it, it was a long time before she succeeded in being reunited with her children. Her book, *Incidents in The Life of A Slave Girl, The Autobiography of Linda Brent,* was published in 1861, with the help of abolitionist novelist Lydia Maria Child. For many years, critics dismissed the narrative as either a work of fiction or the product of Child's own pen, but historians today have laid those charges to rest, recognizing Harriet Jacobs's important contribution to the struggle against slavery and to American literature.

We know much less about what happened to Maria Norcom, who neither kept a diary nor wrote her own story. All that we know is that she continued in her unhappy marriage to James Norcom. Her daughter Mary Matilda, when she came of age, pursued and attempted to reclaim Harriet as her slave under the Fugitive Slave Act. In order to thwart this effort, Harriet allowed an abolitionist friend to buy her and set her free.

In slaveholding households like that of the Norcoms, all the women, whether white or black, free or enslaved, were subject to the will of the master of the household. Most Southern women depended on white men legally and socially, giving them little recourse against men like James Norcom, who burst the bounds of decency. Despite their shared submission to James, an impassable gulf separated Harriet and Maria, and its name was race. After the Civil War, Southern women, white and black, reorganized their households in a changed society, but it would still be another century before they began to bridge that gulf.

Questions for Discussion

* What did Harriet Jacobs and Maria Norcom have in common, if anything, and how did their experiences differ based on race?
* Were there any limits on the power, or constraints on the behavior, of slaveholding white men such as James Norcom?
* Would a law making it a crime to rape a slave have made a difference in Southern society? Why or why not?

Chapter 12

The Pursuit of Perfection

Redeeming the Middle Class

In the winter of 1830–1831, a wave of religious revival swept the northern states. For six months in Rochester, New York, Presbyterian evangelist Charles G. Finney preached almost daily, emphasizing that every man or woman had the power to choose Christ and a godly life. Finney broke with his church's traditional belief that it was God's inscrutable will that decided who would be saved when he preached that "sinners ought to be made to feel that they have something to do, and that something is to repent. That is something that no other being can do for them, neither God nor man, and something they can do and do now." He converted hundreds, and he urged them in turn to convert relatives, neighbors, and employees. If enough people enlisted in the evangelical crusade, Finney proclaimed, the millennium would be achieved within months.

Finney's call for religious and moral renewal fell on fertile ground in Rochester. The leading families in the bustling boomtown were divided into quarreling factions, and workingmen were breaking free from the control that their employers had previously exerted over their daily lives. More vigorous standards of proper behavior and religious conformity unified Rochester's elite and increased its ability to control the rest of the community. Evangelical Protestantism provided the middle class with a stronger sense of identity and purpose.

But the war on sin was not always so unifying. Among those converted in Rochester and elsewhere were religious and moral reformers inspired to take the logical step from individual to societal reformation. They demanded that all social and political institutions measure up to the standards of Christian perfection. They proceeded to attack such collective "sins" as liquor traffic, war, slavery, and even government. Religiously inspired reformism cut two ways. It brought a measure of order and cultural unity to previously divided and troubled communities such as Rochester. But it also inspired a variety of more radical movements or experiments that threatened to undermine established institutions and principles. One of these—abolitionism—would trigger political upheaval and ultimately civil war.

THE RISE OF EVANGELICALISM

American Protestantism was in a state of constant ferment during the early nineteenth century. The separation of church and state was now complete. Dissenting groups, such as the Baptists and Methodists, welcomed full religious freedom because it offered a better chance to win new converts. But all pious Protestants were concerned about the spread of "infidelity"—a term they applied to Catholics, freethinkers, Unitarians, Mormons, and anyone else who was not an evangelical

Christian. But they faced opposition to their effort to make the nation officially Protestant.

As deism—the belief in a God who expressed himself through natural laws accessible to human reason—declined in popularity in the early to mid-nineteenth century, Catholic immigration increased, and the spread of popery became the main focus of evangelical concern. Both Catholics and Unitarians (who quietly carried forward the rationalistic traditions of the eighteenth century) resented and resisted the evangelicals' efforts to convert them to "the Christianity of the heart." Most of those who accepted Christ as their personal savior in revival meetings previously had been indifferent to religion rather than adhering to an alternative set of beliefs.

Revivalism provided the best way to extend religious values and build up church membership. The Great Awakening of the mid-eighteenth century had shown the wonders that evangelists could accomplish, and the new revivalists repeated this success by increasing the proportion of the population that belonged to Protestant churches, forming voluntary organizations, and mobilizing the faithful into associations to spread the gospel and reform American morals.

Although both the evangelical reformers and the new democratic politicians sought popular favor and assumed that individuals were free agents capable of self-direction and self-improvement, the leaders differed in important respects. Jacksonians idealized common folk pretty much as they found them and saw no danger to the community if individuals pursued their worldly interests. Evangelical reformers, by contrast, believed that the common people needed to be redeemed and uplifted. They did not trust a democracy of unbelievers and sinners. The republic would be safe, they insisted, only if a right-minded minority preached, taught, and agitated until the mass of ordinary citizens was reborn into a higher life.

The Second Great Awakening: The Frontier Phase

Second Great Awakening A series of evangelical Protestant revivals that swept over America in the early nineteenth century.

The **Second Great Awakening** began in earnest on the southern frontier around the turn of the century. Highly emotional camp meetings, organized usually by Methodists or Baptists, became a regular feature of religious life in the South and lower Midwest. On the frontier, the camp meeting met social as well as religious needs. In the sparsely settled southern back country, for many people the only way to get baptized, be married, or have a communal religious experience was to attend a camp meeting.

Rowdies and scoffers also attended. Mostly they drank whiskey, caroused, and fornicated on the fringes of the small city of tents and wagons. But sometimes they, too, fell into emotional fits and were converted. Evangelists loved to tell stories of such conversions or near conversions.

The camp meetings obviously provided an emotional outlet for rural people whose everyday lives were often lonely and tedious. But they could also promote a sense of community and social discipline. Conversion at a campaign meeting could be a rite of passage, signifying that a young man or woman had outgrown wild or antisocial behavior and was now ready to become a respectable member of the community. But for the most part, frontier revivalism remained highly individualistic. It strengthened personal piety and morality but did not stimulate organized benevolence or social reform.

In the southern states, Baptists and Presbyterians eventually deemphasized camp meetings in favor of "protracted meetings" in local churches, which featured guest preachers holding forth day after day for up to two weeks. Southern evangelical churches grew rapidly in membership and influence during the first half of the nineteenth century and became the focus of community life in rural areas. Although they fostered societies to improve morals, they generally shied away from social reform. The conservatism of a slaveholding society discouraged radical efforts to change the world.

■ *Lithograph depicting a camp meeting. Religious revival meetings on the frontier attracted hundreds of people who camped for days to listen to the preacher and to share with their neighbors in a communal religious experience. Notice that the men and women are seated in separate sections.* ■

The Second Great Awakening in the North

Reformist tendencies were more evident in the distinctive kind of revivalism that originated in New England and western New York. The northern evangelists were mostly Congregationalists and Presbyterians, strongly influenced by the traditions of New England Puritanism. Their revivals, although somewhat less extravagant and emotional than those on the frontier, found fertile soil in small to medium-sized towns and cities. The northern brand of evangelism resulted in the formation of societies devoted to the redemption of the human race in general and American society in particular.

The reform movement began in New England as an effort to defend Calvinism against the liberal views of religion fostered by the Enlightenment. The Reverend Timothy Dwight, who became president of Yale College in 1795, and other like minds were alarmed by the growing tendency to view the Deity as the benevolent master architect of a rational universe rather than as an all-powerful and mysterious God. Some Congregationalist clergy reached the point of denying the doctrine of the Trinity, proclaiming themselves "Unitarians." Horrified when the Unitarians won control of the Harvard Divinity School, Dwight battled this liberal tendency by reaffirming the old Calvinist belief that man was sinful and depraved. But the harshness and pessimism of orthodox Calvinist doctrine, with its stress on original sin and predestination, had limited appeal in a republic committed to human freedom and progress.

Dwight himself made some concessions to the spirit of the age by agreeing that human beings had a limited control over their spiritual destiny. But a younger generation of Congregational ministers reshaped New England Puritanism to increase its appeal to people who shared the prevailing optimism about human capabilities.

The main theologian of early-nineteenth-century neo-Calvinism was Nathaniel Taylor, a disciple of Dwight. Taylor softened the doctrine of predestination and contended that every individual was a free agent who had the ability to overcome a natural inclination to sin. This reconciliation of original sin with free agency enabled the neo-Calvinists to compete with the revival denominations that preached that sinners had the ability to choose salvation.

The first great practitioner of the new evangelical Calvinism was Lyman Beecher, another of Dwight's pupils. In the period just before and after the War of 1812, Beecher helped promote a series of revivals in the Congregational churches of New England. Preaching his own homespun version of free agency, he induced thousands of churchgoers to acknowledge their sinfulness and surrender to God.

During the late 1820s, Beecher was forced to confront the new and more radical form of revivalism being practiced in western New York by Charles G. Finney. Upstate New York was a seedbed for religious enthusiasm. A majority of its population were transplanted New Englanders who had left behind their close-knit village communities and ancestral churches but not their Puritan consciences. Troubled by rapid economic changes and social dislocations, they were ripe for the assurances of a new faith and a sense of moral direction.

Although he worked within the Congregational and Presbyterian churches, Finney departed radically from traditional Calvinist doctrines. In his hands, the doctrine of free agency became unqualified free will. Indifferent to theological issues, Finney appealed strictly to emotion or the heart rather than to doctrine or reason. He eventually adopted the extreme view that it was possible for redeemed Christians to be totally free of sin—to be as perfect as their Father in Heaven.

Beginning in 1823, Finney conducted a series of highly successful revivals in the towns and cities of western New York. Even more controversial than his free-wheeling approach to theology were the means he used to win converts. Finney sought instantaneous conversions through a variety of new methods including protracted meetings lasting all night or several days in a row. He achieved dramatic results. Sometimes listeners fell to the floor in fits of excitement and immediately sought God's grace.

Beecher and the eastern evangelicals were disturbed by Finney's new methods and by the hysteria that they produced. The preachers were also upset because he violated long-standing Christian tradition by allowing women to pray aloud in church. But it soon became clear that Finney was not merely stirring people to temporary peaks of excitement; he was also leaving strong and active churches behind him, and eastern opposition gradually weakened.

From Revivalism to Reform

Northern revivalists inspired a great movement for social reform. Converts were organized into voluntary associations that sought to stamp out sin and social evil and win the world for Christ. Most of the converts of northern revivalism were middle-class citizens already active in the lives of their communities. They were seeking to adjust to the bustling world of the market revolution in ways that would not violate their traditional moral and social values. Given the generally optimistic and forward-looking attitudes of such Americans, it is understandable that a wave of conversions would fuel hopes for the salvation of the nation and the world.

In New England, Beecher and his evangelical associates were behind the establishment of a great network of missionary and benevolent societies. Foreign missionaries spread the gospel to remote parts of the world, and organizations such as the American Bible Society distributed Bibles in areas of the West where there was a scarcity of churches and clergymen. Missionaries even reached out to the many poor people in American cities.

Past and Present

Evangelical Religion in Politics

Despite America's constitutional separation of church and state, religiously motivated voters and reformers have played vital roles in American politics from its earliest beginnings to the present day. However, the antebellum era stands out as a period during which evangelical religion was especially important in triggering major political reform movements, and some commentators have argued that religion has not been so central to politics again until the contemporary era.

Millions of Protestant Americans participated in religious revivals in the mid-nineteenth century. Evangelical religion was the dominant form of religious life in both North and South, and it was also a major force in public life. Evangelical reformers in the antebellum North sought to make society more perfect through the Sunday school movement, the temperance movement, prison and school reform movements, and the abolitionist movement. Despite the separation of church and state, epitomized by the decline of state-sponsored religious education, religious figures and religious doctrines were at the center of politics at mid-nineteenth century.

Because early nineteenth-century evangelicals believed that the Second Coming of Christ would come only after a period of struggle with evil on Earth, they strived to prepare for Christ's return by making the world a better place. They were optimistic that both individuals and the nation could be perfected through their efforts; this "aiming at being perfect," as Charles Finney urged, is known as *perfectionism*. By contrast, twentieth-century fundamentalist movements believed that the Second Coming would precede the millennium, and were less optimistic about the possibilities for achieving reform.

Pre–Civil War evangelicals saw Catholic immigration as a "threatening darkness of hell." They worried that German and Irish Catholics, who immigrated in large numbers in the 1840s and 1850s, brought lax morality, strong drink, and the Church establishment in their wake. In the 1840s, while the evangelicals mostly became Whigs, the Catholic immigrants overwhelmingly allied themselves with the Democratic party.

By contrast, the more recent resurgence of evangelical engagement with politics that has been labeled the "New Christian Right" sprang up in the early 1980s—epitomized by organizations such as the Moral Majority—mostly a conservative force of reaction against great changes in American society. The fundamentalist Moral Majority crystallized around the issues of opposition to abortion and gay rights, as well as the promotion of school prayer and vouchers for private schools. While some commentators have attributed this evangelical resurgence to a new Great Awakening, the evidence suggests that evangelical religion has been consistently strong since the turn of the twentieth century. What is new in the past quarter-century is evangelical engagement with politics.

Unlike the reformers of the Second Great Awakening, the new evangelicals in politics are allied with traditionalist Catholics rather than opposed to them. In particular, religiously committed evangelicals and Catholics join together in opposition to abortion. Religiously committed voters of all denominations are more conservative than less committed Christians and Jews, and their religion contributes significantly to their conservative positions on sexual and cultural issues.

Today, religious rhetoric and religious actors continue to be important players in national and local politics. From efforts to introduce the teaching of "intelligent design" as an alternative to evolution in schools to the anti-abortion movement, evangelical Christians play a significant role in the dominant Republican party coalition in the first decade of the twenty-first century. Unlike earlier evangelical reformers, they are motivated less by millennial perfectionism than by alarm at the growing diversity and secularization of American society, and they have joined with other religious conservatives in their political campaigns.

Evangelicals formed moral reform societies as well as missions. Some of these aimed at curbing irreligious activity on the Sabbath; others sought to stamp out dueling, gambling, and prostitution. Crusaders attempted to redeem the prostitutes as well as to curtail the activities of their patrons. Others believed that the cause of virtue would be better served by suppressing public discussion and investigation of sexual vices.

Beecher was especially influential in the temperance crusade, the most successful of the reform movements. The **temperance movement** was directed at a real social evil, more serious in many ways than the drug problem of today. Since the Revolution, whiskey had become the most popular American beverage. It was cheaper than milk or beer and safer than water (which was often contaminated). Per capita annual consumption of distilled beverages in the 1820s was almost triple what it is today, and alcoholism had reached epidemic proportions.

temperance movement
Temperance—moderation or abstention in the use of alcoholic beverages—attracted many advocates in the early nineteenth century. Their crusade against alcohol became a powerful social and political force.

STEP 5.
The summit attained.
Jolly companions
A confirmed drunkard.

STEP 4.
Drunk
and
riotous.

STEP 6.
Poverty
and
Disease.

STEP 3.
A glass
too
much.

STEP 7.
Forsaken
by
Friends

STEP 2.
A glass to
keep the
cold out.

STEP 8.
Desperation
and
crime.

STEP 1.
A glass
With
a friend.

STEP 9.
Death
by
suicide.

THE DRUNKARD'S PROGRESS.

■ *Temperance propaganda warned that the drinker who began with "a glass with a friend" would inevitably follow the direct path to poverty, despair, and death.* ■

The temperance reformers viewed indulgence in alcohol as a threat to public morality. Drunkenness was seen as a loss of self-control and moral responsibility that spawned crime, vice, and disorder. Above all, it threatened the family. The main target of temperance propaganda was the husband and father who abused, neglected, or abandoned his wife and children because he was a slave to the bottle. The drinking habits of the poor and laboring classes also aroused great concern, for the "respectable" and propertied elements lived in fear that lower-class mobs, crazed with drink, would attack private property.

Many of the evangelical reformers regarded intemperance as the greatest single obstacle to the achievement of a republic of God-fearing, self-disciplined citizens. In 1826, a group of clergymen organized the American Temperance Society to educate Americans about the evils of hard liquor. The society sent out lecturers, issued a flood of literature, and sponsored essay contests.

The campaign was enormously effective. Although it may be doubted whether large numbers of confirmed drunkards were actually cured, the movement did succeed in altering the drinking habits of middle-class Americans by making temperance a mark of respectability. Per capita consumption of hard liquor declined more than 50 percent during the 1830s.

Cooperating missionary and reform societies—collectively known as the "benevolent empire"—were a major force in American culture by the early 1830s. A new ethic of self-control and self-discipline was being instilled in the middle class that equipped individuals to confront a new world of economic growth and social mobility without losing their cultural and moral bearings.

DOMESTICITY AND CHANGES IN THE AMERICAN FAMILY

The evangelical culture of the 1820s and 1830s influenced the family as an institution and inspired new conceptions of its role in American society. For many parents, child rearing was viewed as essential preparation for the self-disciplined Christian life. Women—regarded as particularly susceptible to religious and moral influences—were increasingly confined to the domestic circle but assumed a greater importance within it.

Marriage for Love

In the early nineteenth century, a new ideal of marriage for love arose among the American middle class. Many nineteenth-century Americans placed new value on ties of affection among family members, especially a married couple joined by romantic love. Parents now exercised even less control over their children's selection of mates than they had in the colonial period. The desire to protect family property and maintain social status remained strong, but mutual affection was now considered essential to a proper union.

Correspondence between spouses began to reflect this new "companionate" ideal. In the main, eighteenth-century letters had been formal and distant in tone. The husband often assumed a patriarchal role, even using such salutations as "my dear child" and rarely confessing that he missed his wife or craved her company. Letters from women to their husbands were highly deferential and did not usually give advice or express disapproval.

By the early nineteenth century, first names, pet names, and terms of endearment such as "honey" or "darling" were increasingly used by both sexes, and absent husbands frequently confessed they felt lost without their mates. In their replies, wives assumed a more egalitarian tone and offered counsel on a wide range of subjects.

The change in middle- and upper-class marriage should not be exaggerated or romanticized. In law, and in cases of conflict between spouses, the husband remained the unchallenged head of the household. True independence or equality for women was impossible at a time when men held exclusive legal authority over a couple's property and children. Divorce was difficult for everyone, but the double standard made it easier for husbands than wives to dissolve a marriage on grounds of adultery. Letters also reveal the strains spouses felt between their ideals of mutual love and the reality of very different gender roles and life paths—husbands away from home for long periods pursuing financial gain as "self-made men," while women stayed at home in the domestic sphere.

The Cult of Domesticity

The notion that women belonged in the home while the public sphere belonged to men has been called the ideology of "separate spheres." In particular, the view that women had a special role to play in the domestic sphere as guardians of virtue and spiritual heads of the home has been described as the **Cult of Domesticity** or the Cult of True Womanhood. In the view of most men, woman's place was in the home and on a pedestal. The ideal wife was a model of piety and virtue who exerted a wholesome moral and religious influence over members of the coarser sex.

Cult of Domesticity Term used by historians to describe the dominant gender role for white women in the antebellum period. The ideology of domesticity stressed the virtue of women as guardians of the home, which was considered their proper sphere.

The sociological reality behind the Cult of True Womanhood was a growing division between the working lives of middle class men and women. In the eighteenth century and earlier, most economic activity had been centered in the home and nearby, and husbands and wives often worked together in a common enterprise. By early in the mid-nineteenth century, this way of life was limited mainly to rural areas. In towns and cities, the rise of factories and countinghouses severed the home from the workplace. Men went forth every morning to their places of labor, leaving their wives at home to tend the house and the children. The Cult of Domesticity made a virtue of the fact that men were solely responsible for running the affairs of the world and building up the economy.

A new concept of gender roles justified and glorified this pattern. The doctrine of "separate spheres"—set forth in novels, advice literature, and the new ladies' magazines—sentimentalized the woman who kept a spotless house, nurtured her children, and offered her husband a refuge from the heartless world of commerce and industry. From a modern point of view, it is easy to condemn the Cult of Domesticity as a rationalization for male dominance. Yet the new norm of confinement to the home did not necessarily imply that women were inferior. By the standards of evangelical culture, women in the domestic sphere could be viewed as superior to men since women were in a good position to cultivate the "feminine" virtues of love and self-sacrifice and thus act as official guardians of religious and moral values.

Furthermore, many women used domestic ideology to fashion a role for themselves in the public sphere. The evangelical movement encouraged women's role as the keepers of moral virtue. The revivals not only gave women a role in converting men but presented as the main object of worship a Christ with stereotypical feminine characteristics. A nurturing, loving, merciful savior, mediating between a stern father and his erring children, provided the model for woman's new role as spiritual head of the home. Membership in evangelical church-based associations inspired and prepared women for new roles as civilizers of men and guardians of domestic culture and morality. Female reform societies taught women the strict ethical code they were to instill in other family members; organized mothers' groups gave instruction in how to build character and encourage piety in children.

While many working-class women read about and aspired to the ideal of true womanhood, domestic ideology only affected the daily lives of relatively affluent women. Working-class wives were not usually employed outside the home during this period, but they labored long and hard within the household, often taking in washing or piecework to supplement a meager family income. Their endless domestic drudgery made a sham of the notion that women had the time and energy for the "higher things in life." Life was especially hard for African American women. Most of those who were "free Negroes" rather than slaves did not have husbands who made enough to support them, and they were obliged to serve in white households or work long hours at home doing other people's washing and sewing.

In urban areas, unmarried working-class women often lived on their own and toiled as household servants, in the sweatshops of the garment industry, or in factories. Barely able to support themselves and at the mercy of male sexual predators, they were in no position to identify with the middle-class ideal of elevated, protected womanhood. For some of them, the relatively well-paid life of the prostitute seemed to offer an attractive alternative to a life of loneliness and privation.

For middle-class women whose husbands earned a good income, however, freedom from industrial or farm labor offered tangible benefits. They now had the leisure to read extensively the new literature directed primarily at housewives, to participate in female-dominated charitable activities, and to cultivate deep and lasting friendships with other women. The result was a distinctively feminine subculture emphasizing sisterhood or "sorority." This growing sense of solidarity with other women often bridged economic and social gaps as demonstrated when

A Look at the Past

Gothic Revival Cottage

Sentimentality and romanticism strengthened their hold on American culture after 1820. At the same time, the Cult of Domesticity arose, which promoted family life as critical to a person's moral regeneration. Evangelism and a wide variety of reform movements swept the nation as well. Middle-class Americans engaged enthusiastically in these social and cultural developments, spending money or hours buying or making materials that revealed their participation. New houses provided clean, neat spaces—and more of them—for families to pursue their interests together. Styles such as the Gothic Revival embodied the romantic and spiritual sentiments of the age. Gothic Revival presented home as more than a haven; home became a spiritual sanctuary. ✱ What does this house resemble? If homes became sanctuaries, what role did women play in creating and maintaining those sanctuaries?

upper- and middle-class women organized societies for the relief and rehabilitation of poor or "fallen" women.

For some women, the domestic ideal even sanctioned ladylike efforts to extend their sphere until it conquered the masculine world outside the home. This domestic feminism was reflected in women's involvement in crusades to stamp out such masculine sins as intemperance, gambling, and sexual vice. In the benevolent societies and reform movements of the Jacksonian era, women handled money, organized meetings and public appeals, made contracts, and sometimes even gave orders to male subordinates—activities they usually could not perform in their own households. The desire to extend the feminine sphere was also the motivating force behind the campaign to make schoolteaching a woman's occupation.

Women attempted to make the world a better place by properly rearing their children, who were captive pupils for the mother's instructions. Since women were considered particularly well qualified to transmit piety and morality to future citizens of the republic, the Cult of Domesticity exalted motherhood and encouraged a new concern with childhood as the time of life when "character" was formed.

The Discovery of Childhood

The nineteenth century has been called the "century of the child." More than before, childhood was seen as a distinct stage of life requiring the special and sustained attention of parents at least until the age of thirteen or fourteen. The middle-class family now became child-centered, which meant that the care, nurturing, and rearing of children was viewed as the family's prime function.

New customs and fashions heralded the "discovery" of childhood. Books aimed specifically at juveniles or providing expert advice to parents on child rearing began

A Look at the Past

Manufactured Toy

Manufactured toys, such as this pull toy, became common during the early nineteenth century and suggest dramatic changes in family life and consumer behavior. Before toys were manufactured in the United States, most parents or children themselves had to make toys or games from available materials, or if they were wealthy enough, they might purchase toys imported from Europe. The availability of cheap manufactured goods made of wood, cast iron, and tin gave parents the opportunity to lavish attention on their children, without the toil. ✳ What does the emergence of a toy manufacturing industry reveal about attitudes toward children?

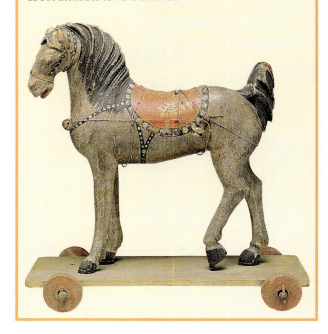

to roll off the presses. The ideal family described in the advice manuals and sentimental literature was bound together by affection rather than authority. Firm discipline remained at the core of "family government," but there was a change in the preferred method of enforcing good behavior. Corporal punishment declined, partially displaced by shaming or withholding of affection. The intended result of punishment was often described as "self-government," and to achieve it parents used guilt, rather than fear, as their main source of leverage.

Some shared realities of childhood cut across class and ethnic lines. For example, there was a high rate of mortality for infants and young children throughout the nineteenth century. Even wealthy families could expect to lose before the age of five one child out of five or six. But class and region made a big difference to children's lives. Farm children tended livestock, milked cows, churned butter, scrubbed laundry, harvested crops, and hauled water; working-class urban children did "outwork" in textiles, worked in street markets, and scavenged.

One important explanation for the growing focus on childhood is the smaller size of families. If nineteenth-century families had remained as large as those of earlier times, it would have been impossible to lavish so much care and attention on individual offspring. Between 1800 and 1850, the average family size declined about 25 percent, beginning a long-range trend lasting to the present day.

The practice of various forms of birth control undoubtedly contributed to this demographic revolution. Ancestors of the modern condom and diaphragm were openly advertised and sold during the pre–Civil War period, but it is likely that most couples controlled family size by practicing the withdrawal method or limiting the frequency of intercourse. Abortion was also surprisingly common and was on the rise.

Parents seemed to understand that having fewer children meant that they could provide their offspring with a better start in life. Such attitudes were appropriate to a society that was beginning to shift from agriculture to commerce and industry.

INSTITUTIONAL REFORM

The family could not carry the whole burden of socializing and reforming individuals. Children needed schooling as well as parental nurture. Some adults, too, seemed to require special kinds of attention and treatment. Seeking to extend the advantages of "family government" beyond the domestic circle, reformers worked to establish or improve public institutions that were designed to shape individual character and instill a capacity for self-discipline.

The Extension of Education

The period from 1820 to 1850 saw an enormous expansion of free public schools. The new resolve to put more children in school for longer periods reflected many of the same values that exalted the child-centered family. It was believed that formal training at a character-building institution would prepare children to make a living and bear the burdens of republican citizenship when they became adults. Purely intellectual training at school was seen as less important than moral indoctrination.

Besides being an extension of the family, the school could also serve as a substitute for it. Educational reformers were alarmed at the masses of poor and immigrant children who allegedly lacked a proper home environment. The safety of the republic depended on schools to make up for this disadvantage.

Before the 1820s, schooling in the United States was a haphazard affair. The wealthy sent their children to private schools, and some of the poor sent their children to charity or "pauper" schools that were usually financed in part by state or local governments. Between the 1820s and the 1850s, the movement for publicly supported common schools made great headway in the North and had limited success in parts of the South. In theory, the common school was an egalitarian institution providing a free basic education for children of all backgrounds.

The agitation for expanded public education began in the 1820s and early 1830s as a central demand of the workingmen's movements in eastern cities. These artisans and tradespeople viewed free schools open to all as a way of countering the growing gap between rich and poor. Middle-class reformers soon seized the initiative, shaped educational reform toward the goal of social discipline, and provided the momentum needed for legislative success.

The most influential spokesman for the common school movement was Horace Mann of Massachusetts. As a lawyer and a member of the state legislature, Mann worked tirelessly for the establishment of a state board of education and adequate tax support for local schools. His philosophy of education was based on the premise that children were clay in the hands of teachers and school officials and could be molded to a state of perfection. Like the advocates of child rearing through moral influence rather than physical force, he discouraged corporal punishment except as a last resort.

Against those who argued that school taxes violated the rights of property, Mann countered that private property was actually held in trust for the good of the community. Education, he stressed, saved children from drifting into lives of poverty and vice and prepared them to become good, law-abiding citizens. Mann's conception of public education as a means of social discipline converted the middle and upper classes to his cause.

In practice, the new or improved public schools often alienated working-class pupils and their families rather than reforming them. Compulsory attendance laws deprived poor families of needed wage earners without guaranteeing new occupational opportunities for those with an elementary education. Furthermore, Catholic immigrants complained quite correctly that Mann and his disciples were trying to impose a uniform Protestant culture on the pupils.

In addition to the "three Rs" ("reading, 'riting, and 'rithmetic"), the essence of what was being taught in the public schools of the mid-nineteenth century was the "Protestant ethic"—industry, punctuality, sobriety, and frugality. These were the virtues stressed in the famous *McGuffey's Eclectic Readers,* which first appeared in 1836. Such moral indoctrination helped produce generations of Americans with personalities and beliefs adapted to the needs of an industrialized society. If the system did not encourage thinking for oneself, it did prepare people who could easily adjust to the regular routines of the factory or the office.

Fortunately, however, education was not limited to the schools or devoted exclusively to children. Every city and almost every town or village had a lyceum, debating society, or mechanic's institute where adults of all social classes could broaden their intellectual horizons. Young Abe Lincoln, for example, sharpened his intellect and honed his debating skills as a member of such an institute in New Salem, Illinois, in the early 1830s. Unlike the public schools, the lyceums and debating societies fostered independent thought and the spread of new ideas.

■ *Dorothea Dix (1802–1887). Her efforts on behalf of the mentally ill led to the building of more than thirty institutions in the United States and the reform and restaffing—with well-trained personnel—of existing hospitals. She died in Trenton, New Jersey, in 1887, in a hospital that she had founded.* ■

Discovering the Asylum

Some segments of the population were obviously beyond the reach of family government and character training provided in homes and schools. In the 1820s and 1830s, reformers became acutely aware of the dangers to society posed by an apparently increasing number of criminals, lunatics, and paupers. Their answer was to establish special institutions to provide a controlled environment in which the inmates could be reformed and rehabilitated.

In earlier times, the existence of paupers, lawbreakers, and insane persons was viewed as the consequence of divine judgment or original sin. For the most part, these people were dealt with in ways that did not isolate them from local communities. But dealing with deviants in a neighborly way broke down as economic development and urbanization made communities less cohesive. At the same time, reformers were concluding that all defects of mind and character were correctable—that the insane could be cured, criminals reformed, and paupers taught to pull themselves out of destitution. The result was the discovery of the asylum.

The 1820s and 1830s saw the emergence of state-supported prisons, insane asylums, and poorhouses. New York and Pennsylvania led the way in prison reform. In theory, prisons and asylums substituted for the family. The custodians were intended to act as parents by providing moral advice and training. In practice, these institutions were far different from the affectionate families idealized by the Cult of Domesticity. Their most prominent feature was the imposition of a rigid daily routine. The early superintendents and wardens believed that the enforcement of an inflexible and demanding set of rules and procedures would encourage self-discipline.

In retrospect, it is clear that the prisons, asylums, and poorhouses did not achieve the aims of their founders. A combination of naive theories and poor performance doomed these institutions to a custodial rather than a reformatory role. Public support was inadequate to meet the needs of the growing inmate population, and the personnel of these places of confinement lacked the training needed to help their charges. The result was overcrowding and the use of brutality to keep order.

But conditions would have been even worse without the efforts of a remarkable woman, Dorothea Dix, one of the most effective of all the pre–Civil War reformers. As a direct result of her skill in publicizing the inhumane treatment prevailing in prisons, almshouses, and insane asylums, fifteen states built new hospitals and improved supervision of penitentiaries and other institutional facilities.

REFORM TURNS RADICAL

During the 1830s, internal dissension split the great reform movement spawned by the Second Great Awakening. Efforts to promote evangelical piety, improve personal and public morality, and shape character through familial or institutional discipline continued and even flourished. But bolder spirits went beyond such goals and set their sights on the total liberation and perfection of the individual.

Divisions in the Benevolent Empire

Early-nineteenth-century reformers were generally committed to changing existing attitudes and practices gradually in ways that would not invite conflict or disrupt the fabric of society. But by the mid-1830s, a new mood of impatience and perfectionism surfaced within the benevolent societies. The Temperance Society, for example, split between radicals who insisted on a total commitment to "cold water" and moderates who were willing to overlook moderate wine and beer drinking. The same sort of division arose in the American Peace Society between those insisting on absolute pacifism and those willing to sanction "defensive wars."

The new perfectionism realized its most dramatic and important success within the antislavery movement. Before the 1830s, many of the people who expressed religious and moral concern over slavery were affiliated with the **American Colonization Society,** a benevolent organization founded in 1817. Most colonizationists admitted that slavery was an evil, but they believed it should be eliminated only gradually and with the cooperation of slaveholders. Reflecting the power of racial prejudice, they proposed to transport freed blacks to Africa as a way of relieving southern fears that a race war would erupt if slaves were simply released from bondage and allowed to remain in America. In 1821, the society established a colony in West Africa, named it Liberia, and settled several thousand American blacks there over the next decade.

Colonization proved to be grossly inadequate as a step toward the elimination of slavery. Slaveholders rarely cooperated with the movement, and free blacks rejected the whole process. Black opposition to colonization helped persuade William Lloyd Garrison and other white abolitionists to repudiate the Colonization Society and support immediate emancipation without emigration.

Garrison launched a new and more radical antislavery movement in 1831 when he began to publish a journal called *The Liberator* in Boston. Garrison's rhetoric was as severe as his proposals were radical. As he wrote in the first issue of *The Liberator,* "I will be as harsh as the truth and as uncompromising as justice. . . . I will not retreat a single inch—AND I WILL BE HEARD."

■ *In the inaugural issue of his antislavery weekly,* The Liberator, *William Lloyd Garrison announced that he was launching a militant battle against the evil and sin of slavery. The stirring words that appeared in that first issue are repeated on* The Liberator's *banner.* ■

American Colonization Society Founded in 1817, this organization hoped to provide a mechanism by which slavery could be gradually eliminated. The society advocated the relocation of free blacks (followed by freed slaves) to the African colony of Monrovia, present-day Liberia.

The Abolitionist Enterprise

The abolitionist movement, like the temperance crusade, was a direct outgrowth of the Second Great Awakening. Many leading abolitionists had undergone conversion experiences in the 1820s and were already committed to a life of Christian activism before they dedicated themselves to freeing the slaves. Several were ministers or divinity students seeking a mission in life that would fulfill their spiritual and professional ambitions.

The career of Theodore Dwight Weld exemplified the connection between revivalism and abolitionism. Influenced strongly by Charles G. Finney, Weld underwent a conversion experience in 1826. He then became an itinerant lecturer for various reform causes. By the early 1830s, his attention was focused on the moral issue raised by the institution of slavery. After a brief flirtation with the colonization movement, he became a convert to abolitionism. Traveling throughout Ohio, where he and his associates founded Oberlin College as a center for abolitionist activity, he used the tried-and-true methods of the revival—fervent preaching, protracted meetings, the call for individuals to come forth and announce their redemption—in the cause of the antislavery movement. As a result of these efforts, northern Ohio and western New York became hotbeds of abolitionist sentiment.

Antislavery orators and organizers tended to have their greatest success in the smaller towns of the upper North. The typical convert came from an upwardly mobile family engaged in small business, the skilled trades, or market farming. In the cities, abolitionists were more likely to encounter fierce and effective opposition. Indeed, Garrison was once almost lynched in Boston.

Abolitionists who thought of taking their message to the fringes of the South had reason to pause, given the fate of the antislavery editor Elijah Lovejoy. In 1837, while attempting to defend himself and his printing press from a mob in Alton, Illinois, just across the Mississippi River from slaveholding Missouri, Lovejoy was shot and killed.

Racism was a major cause of antiabolitionist violence in the North. Rumors that abolitionists advocated or practiced interracial marriage could easily excite an urban crowd to destructive acts. Working-class whites tended to fear that economic and social competition with blacks would increase if abolitionists succeeded in freeing the slaves and making them citizens. But a striking feature of many of the mobs was that they were dominated by "gentlemen of property and standing." Upstanding citizens resorted to violence, it would appear, because abolitionism effectively threatened their conservative notions of social order and hierarchy.

By the end of the 1830s, the abolitionist movement was under great stress. Besides the burden of external repression, there was dissension within the movement. Becoming an abolitionist required an exacting conscience and unwillingness to compromise on matters of principle. These character traits also made it difficult for abolitionists to work together and maintain a united front against their opponents.

During the late 1830s, Garrison, the most visible spokesman for the cause, began to adopt positions that other abolitionists found extreme and divisive. He attacked government, clergy, and churches for refusing to take a strong antislavery stand, and he refused to work with any person or organization that did not fully support his crusade.

The positions alienated members of the Anti-Slavery Society who continued to hope that organized religion and the existing political system could be influenced or even taken over by abolitionists. But it was Garrison's stand on women's rights that led to an open break at the national convention of 1840. Many of his followers separated from Garrison and his organization when the Boston editor engineered the election of a female abolitionist to the executive committee of the Anti-Slavery Society.

Liberty party America's first antislavery political party, formed in 1840.

The schism weakened Garrison's influence within the movement. When he later repudiated the U.S. Constitution as a proslavery document and called for northern secession from the Union, few antislavery people in the Middle Atlantic or midwestern states went along. Outside of New England, most abolitionists operated *within* churches and the political system. The **Liberty party,** organized in 1840, was their first attempt to enter the electoral arena under their own banner; it signaled a new effort to turn antislavery sentiment into political power.

Black Abolitionists

From the beginning, the abolitionist movement depended heavily on the support of the northern free black community. Most of the early subscribers to Garrison's *Liberator* were African Americans. Black orators, especially escaped slaves such as Frederick Douglass, made northern audiences aware of the realities of bondage. But relations between white and black abolitionists were often tense and uneasy. Blacks protested that they did not have their fair share of leadership positions or influence over policy. Eventually a black antislavery movement emerged that was largely independent of the white-led crusade. The Negro Convention movement, which sponsored national meetings of black leaders beginning in 1830, provided an important forum for independent black expression.

Black newspapers, such as *Freedom's Journal,* first published in 1827, and the *North Star,* founded by Douglass in 1847, gave black writers a chance to preach their gospel of liberation to black readers. African American authors also produced a stream of books and pamphlets attacking slavery, refuting racism, and advocating various forms of resistance. One of the most influential publications was David Walker's *Appeal . . . to the Colored Citizens of the World,* which appeared in 1829. Walker denounced slavery in the most vigorous language possible and called for a black revolt against white tyranny.

Free blacks in the North did more than make verbal protests against racial injustice. They were also the main conductors on the fabled Underground Railroad that opened a path for fugitives from slavery. Courageous ex-slaves such as Harriet Tubman and Josiah Henson made regular forays into the slave states to lead other blacks to freedom, and many of the "stations" along the way were run by free blacks. In northern towns and cities, free blacks organized "vigilance committees" to protect fugitives and thwart the slave-catchers. Groups of blacks even used force to rescue recaptured fugitives from the authorities.

Historians have debated the question of whether the abolitionist movement of the 1830s and early 1840s was a success or a failure. It failed to convert a majority of Americans to its position on the evil of slavery. And in the South, it provoked a more militant and uncompromising defense of slavery. The belief that peaceful agitation, or what abolitionists called "moral suasion," would convert slaveholders and their northern sympathizers to abolition was obviously unrealistic.

But in another sense the crusade was successful. It brought the slavery issue to the forefront of public consciousness and convinced a substantial and growing segment of the northern population that the South's peculiar institution was morally wrong and potentially dangerous to the American way of life. The politicians who later mobilized the North against the expansion of slavery into the territories drew their strength from the reservoir of antislavery attitudes and sentiment created by the abolitionists.

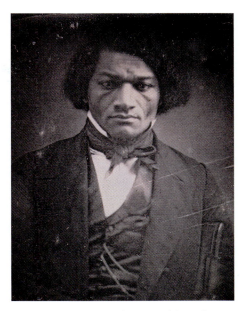

■ *Frederick Douglass, who escaped from slavery in 1838, became one of the most effective voices in the crusade against slavery.* ■

From Abolitionism to Women's Rights

Abolitionism also served as a catalyst for the women's rights movement. From the beginning, women were active participants in the abolitionist crusade. Some antislavery women defied conventional ideas of their proper sphere by becoming public speakers and demanding an equal role in the leadership of antislavery societies. The most famous of these were the Grimké sisters, Sarah and Angelina, who attracted enormous attention because they were the rebellious daughters of a South Carolina slaveholder.

The battle to participate equally in the antislavery crusade made a number of female abolitionists acutely aware of male dominance and oppression. For them, the same principles that justified the liberation of the slaves also applied to the emancipation of women from all restrictions on their rights as citizens. However, not all of the antislavery men agreed with the idea of equal rights for women.

Wounded by male reluctance to extend the cause of emancipation to include women, Lucretia Mott and Elizabeth Cady Stanton organized a new and independent movement for women's rights. The high point of their campaign was the famous 1848 **Seneca Falls Convention** in upstate New York. In their Declaration of Sentiments, the delegates condemned the treatment of women by men and demanded the right to vote and to control their own property, person, and children. Rejecting the cult of domesticity and its doctrine of separate spheres, these women and their male supporters launched the modern movement for gender equality.

Seneca Falls Convention The first women's rights convention, held in 1848 in Seneca Falls, New York, and co-sponsored by women's rights reformers Elizabeth Cady Stanton and Lucretia Mott. Delegates at the convention drafted the "Declaration of Sentiments," patterned on the Declaration of Independence, but which declared that "all men and women are created equal."

Radical Ideas and Experiments

Hopes for individual or social perfection were not limited to reformers inspired by evangelicalism. Between the 1820s and 1850s, a great variety of schemes for human redemption came from persons who had rejected orthodox Protestantism. Some were freethinkers carrying on the traditions of the Enlightenment, but most were individuals seeking new paths to spiritual or religious fulfillment. A movement that achieved remarkable success or notoriety was spiritualism—the belief that one could communicate with the dead. These philosophical and religious radicals attacked established institutions, proscribed new modes of living, and founded utopian communities where they could put their ideas into practice.

A radical movement of foreign origin that gained a toehold in Jacksonian America was utopian socialism. In 1825–1826, the British manufacturer and reformer Robert Owen founded a community based on common and equal ownership of property at New Harmony, Indiana. About the same time, Owen's associate, Frances Wright, gathered a group of slaves at Nashoba, Tennessee, and set them to work earning their freedom in an atmosphere of "rational cooperation." The rapid demise of both model communities suggests that utopian socialism did not easily take root in American soil.

But the impulse survived. In the 1840s, a number of Americans became interested in the ideas of the French utopian theorist Charles Fourier, who called for cooperative communities in which everyone did a fair share of the work and tasks were assigned to natural abilities of the members. Between 1842 and 1852, about thirty Fourierist "phalanxes" were established in the northeastern and midwestern states. Like the Owenite communities, the Fourierist phalanxes were short-lived, surviving for an average of only two years.

Two of the most successful and long-lived manifestations of pre–Civil War **utopianism** were the Shakers and the Oneida community. The **Shakers**—officially known as the Millennial Church or the United Society of Believers—began as a religious movement in England. In 1774, a Shaker leader, Mother Ann Lee, brought the group's radical beliefs to the United States. Lee believed herself to be the feminine

utopianism Between the 1830s and 1850s, hopes for societal perfection—utopia—were widespread among evangelical Christians as well as secular humanists.

Shakers A religious group, formally known as the United Society of Believers, that advocated strict celibacy, gender equality, and communal ownership.

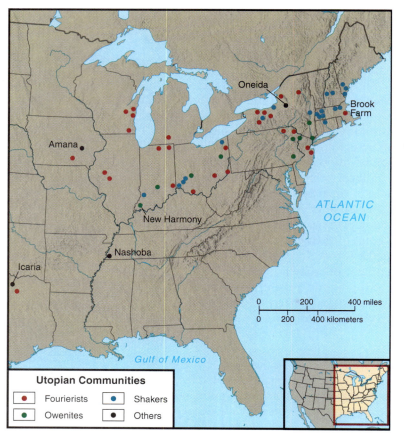

UTOPIAN COMMUNITIES BEFORE THE CIVIL WAR *The search for new paths to spiritual or religious fulfillment attracted many to utopian communitarian societies. By far the largest of these societies during the period before the Civil War was the Shakers, who by the 1830s had established twenty settlements in seven states with a combined membership of approximately six thousand. Their rule of celibacy meant that Shaker communities gained members through adoption and conversion, rather than by natural reproduction.* ∎

Utopian Communities

● Fourierists   ● Shakers
● Owenites   ● Others

Chronology

1801	Massive revival is held at Cane Ridge, Kentucky
1826	American Temperance Society is organized
1830–1831	Charles G. Finney evangelizes Rochester, New York
1831	William Lloyd Garrison publishes the first issue of *The Liberator*
1833	Abolitionists found the American Anti-Slavery Society
1836	American Temperance Society splits into factions
1836–1837	Theodore Weld advocates abolition in Ohio and upstate New York
1837	Massachusetts establishes a state board of education ■ Abolitionist editor Elijah Lovejoy is killed by a proslavery mob
1840	American Anti-Slavery Society splits over women's rights and other issues
1841	Transcendentalists organize a model community at Brook Farm
1848	Feminists gather at Seneca Falls, New York, and found the women's rights movement
1854	Thoreau's *Walden* is published

incarnation of Christ and advocated a new theology based squarely on the principle of sexual equality. The Shakers, named for their expressions of religious fervor through vigorous dancelike movements, believed in communal ownership and strict celibacy. They lived simply and minimized their contact with the outside world because they expected Christ's Second Coming to occur momentarily. The **Oneida community** was established in 1848 at Oneida, New York, and was inspired by an unorthodox brand of Christian perfectionism. Its founder, John Humphrey Noyes, believed the Second Coming of Christ had already occurred; hence human beings were no longer obliged to follow the moral rules that their previously fallen state had required. At Oneida, traditional marriage was outlawed, and a carefully regulated form of "free love" was put into practice.

It was a literary and philosophical movement known as **transcendentalism** that inspired the era's most memorable experiments in thinking and living on a higher plane. The main idea was that the individual could transcend material reality and ordinary understanding, attaining through a higher form of reason, or intuition, a oneness with the universe as a whole and with the spiritual forces that lay behind it. Transcendentalism was the major American version of the romantic and idealist thought that emerged in the early nineteenth century. Throughout the Western world, romanticism was challenging the rationalism and materialism of the Enlightenment in the name of exalted feeling and cosmic spirituality. Most American transcendentalists were dissatisfied with rationalistic religions but were unable to embrace evangelical Christianity because of intellectual resistance to its doctrines. Instead they sought inspiration from a philosophical and literary idealism of German origin. Their prophet was Ralph Waldo Emerson, a brilliant essayist and lecturer who preached that each individual could commune directly with a benign spiritual force that animated nature and the universe—he called it the "oversoul."

Emerson was an advocate of self-reliance and avoided all involvement in organized movements or associations. But in the vicinity of Emerson's home in Concord, Massachusetts, a group of like-minded seekers of truth and spiritual fulfillment gathered during the 1830s and 1840s. One group of transcendentalists, led by the Reverend George Ripley, rejected Emerson's radical individualism and founded a cooperative community at **Brook Farm,** near Roxbury, Massachusetts, in

Oneida community Founded in 1848 in Oneida, New York, this Christian utopian community earned notoriety for institutionalizing a form of "free love."

transcendentalism An American version of the romantic and idealist thought that emerged in Europe in the early nineteenth century, this literary and philosophical movement held that individuals could rise above material reality and ordinary understanding.

Brook Farm This transcendentalist commune, founded in Massachusetts in 1841, attracted many leading creative figures during its brief existence.

1841. For the next four years, they worked the land in common, conducted an excellent school on the principle that spontaneity rather than discipline was the key to education, and allowed ample time for conversation, meditation, communion with nature, and artistic activity of all kinds. The Brook Farm experiment ended in 1849.

Another experiment in transcendental living adhered more closely to the individualistic spirit of the movement. Between 1845 and 1847, Henry David Thoreau, a young disciple of Emerson, lived by himself in the woods along the shore of Walden Pond and carefully recorded his thoughts and impressions. In a sense, he pushed the ideal of "self-culture" to its logical outcome—a utopia of one. The result was *Walden* (published in 1854), one of the greatest achievements in American literature.

CONCLUSION: COUNTERPOINT ON REFORM

One great American writer observed at close quarters the perfectionist ferment of the age but held himself aloof, suggesting in his novels and tales that pursuit of the ideal led to a distorted sense of human nature and possibilities. Nathaniel Hawthorne's sense of human frailty and sinfulness made him skeptical about the lofty claims of transcendentalism and utopianism. He satirized transcendentalism as unworldly and overoptimistic and lampooned life in such cooperative communities as Brook Farm. His greatest novels, *The Scarlet Letter* (1850) and *The House of Seven Gables* (1851), imaginatively probed people's futile efforts to escape sin and evil. The world was imperfect, he suggested, and one simply had to accept that reality.

To be sure, the dreams of perfectionist reformers promised more than they could possibly deliver. Revivals could not make all men like Christ, temperance could not solve all social problems, abolitionist agitation could not bring a peaceful end to slavery, and transcendentalism could not fully emancipate people from the limitations and frustrations of daily life. But the reformers could argue that Hawthorne's skepticism and fatalism was a prescription for doing nothing in the face of intolerable evils. If the reform impulse was long on inspirational rhetoric but somewhat short on durable, practical achievements, it did challenge Americans to improve their country.

KEY TERMS

Second Great Awakening, p. 226

temperance movement, p. 229

Cult of Domesticity, p. 231

American Colonization Society, p. 237

Liberty party, p. 238

Seneca Falls Convention, p. 239

utopianism, p. 240

Shakers, p. 240

Oneida community, p. 241

transcendentalism, p. 241

Brook Farm, p. 241

RECOMMENDED READING

Ronald G. Walters, *American Reformers, 1815–1860,* rev. ed. (1997) and Steven Mintz, *Moralists and Modernizers: America's pre–Civil War Reformers* (1995), provide good overviews of Pre–Civil War reform activities. A particularly useful collection of documents on reform movements and other aspects of antebellum culture is David Brion Davis, *Antebellum American Culture: An Interpretive Anthology* (1979). Lori D. Ginzberg, *Women and the Work of Benevolence: Morality, Politics and Class in the Nineteenth*

Century United States (1990), and Bruce Dorsey, *Reforming Men and Women: Gender in the Antebellum City* (2002), relate reform politics to gender and class politics.

A general survey of the religious ferment of this period is Nathan O. Hatch, *The Democratization of American Christianity* (1989). Paul E. Johnson, *A Shopkeeper's Millennium: Society and Revivals in Rochester, New York, 1815–1837* (1978), incisively describes the impact of the revival on a single community. The connection between religion and reform is described in Robert H. Abzug, *Cosmos Crumbling: American Reform and the Religious Imagination* (1994).

Sara Evans, *Born for Liberty: A History of Women in America* (1997), provides an excellent synthesis of women's history. On the rise of the domestic ideology, see Nancy F. Cott, *The Bonds of Womanhood: "Woman's Sphere" in New England, 1780–1835* (1977). The condition of working-class women is incisively treated in Christine Stansell, *City of Women: Sex and Class in New York, 1789–1860* (1986). For an excellent legal history of marriage and divorce, see Hendrick Hartog, *Man and Wife in America: A History* (2000).

David J. Rothman, *The Discovery of the Asylum: Social Order and Disorder in the New Republic* (1971), provides a penetrating analysis of the movement for institutional reform. For good surveys of abolitionism, see James Brewer Stewart, *Holy Warriors: The Abolitionists and American Slavery* (1976) and Paul Goodman, *Of One Blood: Abolitionism and Racial Equality* (1998). Patrick Rael, *Black Identity and Black Protest in the Antebellum North* (2002), is an excellent treatment of black abolitionists. On transcendentalism, see Charles Capper and Conrad E. Wright, *Transient and Permanent: The Transcendentalist Movement and Its Contexts* (1999).

SUGGESTED WEB SITES

America's First Look into the Camera: Daguerreotype Portraits and Views, 1839–1862
memory.loc.gov/ammem/daghtml/daghome.html
The Library of Congress's daguerreotype collection consists of more than 650 photographs dating from 1839 to 1864. Portraits, architectural views, and some street scenes make up most of the collection.

1830s Clothing
www.connerprairie.org/historyonline/clothing.html
See how clothing worn in the Early Republic was quite different from what people wear today.

Votes for Women: Selections from the National American Woman Suffrage Association Collection, 1848–1921
memory.loc.gov/ammem/naw/nawshome.html
This Library of Congress site contains 167 books, pamphlets, and other artifacts documenting the suffrage campaign.

History of Women's Suffrage
www.rochester.edu/SBA/history.html
This site includes a chronology, important texts relating to woman suffrage, and biographical information about Susan B. Anthony and Elizabeth Cady Stanton.

By Popular Demand: "Votes for Women" Suffrage Pictures, 1850–1920
memory.loc.gov/ammem/vfwhtml/vfwhome.html
Portraits, suffrage parades, picketing suffragists, an antisuffrage display, and cartoons commenting on the movement make up this Library of Congress site.

Women in America, 1820 to 1842
xroads.virginia.edu/~HYPER/DETOC/FEM/home.htm
This University of Virginia site takes a look at women in antebellum America.

Godey's Lady's Book On-line
www.history.rochester.edu/godeys/
Here is on-line text of this interesting nineteenth-century journal.

Influence of Prominent Abolitionists
www.loc.gov/exhibits/african/afam006.html
An exhibit site from the Library of Congress, with pictures and text that discusses some of the key African American abolitionists and their efforts to end slavery.

Chapter *13*

An Age of Expansionism

The Spirit of Young America

In the 1840s and early 1850s, politicians, writers, and entrepreneurs frequently proclaimed themselves champions of **Young America.** One of the first to use the phrase was the famous author and lecturer Ralph Waldo Emerson, who told an audience of merchants and manufacturers in 1844 that the nation was entering a new era of commercial development, technological progress, and territorial expansion. Emerson suggested that a progressive new generation—the "Young Americans"— would lead this surge of physical development. More than a slogan and less than an organized movement, Young America stood for a positive attitude toward the market economy and industrial growth, a more aggressive and belligerent foreign policy, and a celebration of America's unique strengths and virtues.

Young Americans favored enlarging the national market by acquiring new territory. They called for the annexation of Texas, asserted an American claim to all of Oregon, and urged the appropriation of vast new territories from Mexico. They also celebrated the technological advances that would knit this new empire together, especially the telegraph and the railroad.

Young American attitudes found cultural and intellectual expression as well as economic and political beliefs. In 1845, a Washington journal hailed the election of the 49-year-old James K. Polk, at that time the youngest man to have been elected president, as a sign that youth would "dare to take antiquity by the beard, and tear the cloak from hoary-headed hypocrisy. Too young to be corrupt . . . it is Young America, awakened to a sense of her own intellectual greatness by her soaring spirit. It stands in strength, the voice of the majority." During the Polk administration, Young American writers and critics—mostly based in New York City—called for a new and distinctive national literature, free of subservience to European themes or models and expressive of the democratic spirit. Their organ was the *Literary World*, founded in 1847, and its ideals influenced two of the greatest writers that nation has produced: Walt Whitman and Herman Melville.

Whitman captured much of the exuberance, optimism, and expansion of Young America. He celebrated a nation whose limits were circumscribed only by the imagination. In *Moby-Dick*, Herman Melville produced a novel sufficiently original in form and conception to more than fulfill the demand of Young Americans for "a New Literature to fit the New Man in the New Age." But he was too deep a thinker not to see the perils that underlay the soaring ambition and aggressiveness of the new age. In the character of Ahab, the whaling captain who brings destruction of himself and his ship by his relentless pursuit of the white whale, Melville symbolized—among other things—the dangers facing a nation that was overreaching itself by indulging its pride and exalted sense of destiny with too little concern for the moral and practical consequences.

The Young American ideal—the idea of a young country led by young men into new paths of prosperity and greatness—appealed to many people and found support across political party lines. But the attitude came to be identified primarily with young Democrats who wanted to move their party away from its traditional fear of the expansion of commerce and industry. Unlike old-line Jeffersonians and Jacksonians, Young Americans had no qualms about the market economy and the speculative, materialistic spirit it called forth.

Before 1848, the Young American impulse focused mainly on the great expanse of western lands that lay just beyond the nation's borders. After the Mexican-American War, when territorial gains extended the nation's boundaries from the Atlantic to the Pacific, attention shifted to internal development. New discoveries of gold in the nation's western territories fostered economic growth, technological advances spurred industrialization, and increased immigration brought more people to populate the lands newly acquired—by agreement or by force.

Young America In the 1840s and early 1850s, many public figures, especially younger members of the Democratic party, used this term to describe a movement that advocated territorial expansion and industrial growth in the name of patriotism.

MOVEMENT TO THE FAR WEST

In the 1830s and 1840s, the westward movement of population left the valley of the Mississippi behind and penetrated the Far West all the way to the Pacific. Pioneers pursued fertile land and economic opportunities beyond the existing boundaries of the United States and thus helped set the stage for the annexations and international crises of the 1840s. Some went for material gain, others for adventure; a significant minority sought freedom from religious persecution. They carried American attitudes and loyalties with them into regions that were already occupied or at least claimed by Mexico or Great Britain. Whether they realized it or not, these pioneers were the vanguard of American expansionism.

Borderlands of the 1830s

Territorial ambition lured Americans northward as well as westward, and for a time it seemed that Canada might be a new frontier for expansionism. Conflicts over the border between America and British North America led periodically to calls for diplomatic or military action to wrest the northern half of the continent from the English. During the 1830s, tensions were particularly high as Americans and Canadians wrestled over the exact location of the border between Maine and New Brunswick. Finally, in 1842, Secretary of State Daniel Webster concluded an agreement with the British government, represented by Lord Ashburton. The **Webster-Ashburton Treaty** gave more than half of the disputed territory to the United States and established a definite northeastern boundary with Canada.

Webster-Ashburton Treaty This 1842 agreement with Britain resolved the boundary dispute between Maine and New Brunswick, Canada, setting the northeastern U.S. border.

On the other side of the continent, the United States and Britain both laid claim to Oregon, a vast area that lay between the Rockies and the Pacific from the 42nd parallel (the northern boundary of California) to the latitude of 54°40′ (the southern boundary of Alaska). Although in 1818 the two nations had agreed to joint occupation, the Americans had strengthened their claim by acquiring Spain's rights to the Pacific Northwest in the Adams-Onís Treaty (see Chapter 9), and the British had gained effective control of the northern portion of the Oregon Country. Blocking an equitable division was the reluctance of both sides to surrender access to the Columbia River basin and the adjacent territory extending north to the 49th parallel (which later became the northern border of the state of Washington).

The Oregon Country was scarcely populated before 1840, but the same could not be said of the Mexican borderlands that lay directly west of Jacksonian America. By 1827, Mexican settlements in present-day New Mexico contained about 44,000

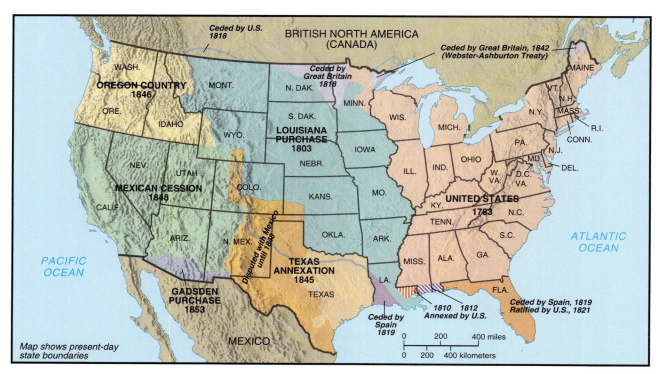

TERRITORIAL EXPANSION BY THE MID-NINETEENTH CENTURY   *Fervent nationalists identified the growth of America through territorial expansion as the divinely ordained "manifest destiny" of a chosen people.* ■

people. To save the province from economic stagnation, the Mexican authorities decided in 1822 to encourage trade between Santa Fe, the capital of New Mexico, and the United States. They succeeded in stimulating commercial prosperity, but they also whetted expansionist appetites on the Anglo side of the border.

California in the 1820s and 1830s was a more colorful, turbulent, and fragile northward expansion of Mexican civilization. Much less populous than New Mexico—there were only about four thousand Hispanic inhabitants in 1827—California was a land of huge estates and enormous herds of cattle. At the beginning of the 1830s, most of the land and the wealth of the province was controlled by the chain of twenty-one mission stations of the Catholic Church that stretched from San Diego to San Francisco.

In 1833, the Mexican government confiscated the church's lands and released the Indians from semislavery, but this in fact made their plight even worse. Rather than giving the land to the thirty thousand Christian Indians in California, the government awarded immense tracts to Mexican citizens. During the fifteen years that they held sway, the *rancheros,* as the large landowners were called, captured the fancy and aroused the envy of Anglo traders and visitors to California through their flamboyant lifestyle, superb horsemanship, and taste for violent and dangerous sports.

The Easterners who conveyed to the rest of the nation a romantic image of this sun-baked land of beautiful scenery and señoritas were mostly merchants and sailors involved in the oceanic trade between Boston and California ports. By the mid-1830s, several Yankee merchants had taken up permanent residence in towns such as Monterey and San Diego to conduct the California end of the business. The reports that they sent back about the Golden West sparked great interest in eastern business circles.

The Texas Revolution

At the same time as some Americans were trading with California, others were taking possession of Texas. In the early 1820s, Mexican officials encouraged settlers from the United States to settle in Texas. Newly independent Mexico granted Stephen F. Austin, son of a onetime Spanish citizen, a huge piece of land in hopes he would help attract and settle new colonists from the United States. Some fifteen other Anglo-American *empresarios* received land grants in the 1820s. In 1823, three hundred families from the United States were settled on the Austin grant, and within a year, the colony's population had swelled to 2021. The offer of fertile and inexpensive land attracted many American immigrants.

Friction soon developed between the Mexican government and the American colonists over such issues as the status of slavery and the Catholic Church. In 1829, Mexico formally freed all slaves under its jurisdiction, but the Texans simply ignored the decree. Mexican law also required that immigrants accept the Catholic faith, but this regulation also became a dead letter. The abuses of Mexican law grew, along with the size of the American population in Texas, and in 1830, the Mexican legislature prohibited further American immigration and importation of slaves to Texas.

But enforcement of the new law was feeble, and the flow of settlers, slaves, and smuggled goods continued virtually unabated. A long-standing complaint of the Texans was the failure of the Mexican constitution to grant them local self-government. In 1832, Texans showed their displeasure with Mexican rule by rioting in protest against the arrest of several Americans by the commander of the Galveston garrison.

Stephen Austin went to Mexico City in 1833 to present the Texans' grievances and seek concessions from the central government. He succeeded in having the ban against American immigration lifted but failed to win agreement for self-government. Then, as he was about to return to Texas, Austin was arrested and imprisoned for more than a year for writing a letter recommending that Texans set up a state government without Mexico City's consent.

In 1835, some Texans revolted against Mexico. The insurrectionists claimed that they were fighting for freedom against a long experience of oppression. Actually, Mexican rule had not been harsh, although it was inefficient and often corrupt. Furthermore, the Texans' devotion to "liberty" did not prevent them from defending slavery against Mexico's attempt to abolish it. Texans had done pretty much what they pleased, despite laws to the contrary and angry rumblings from south of the Rio Grande.

A more plausible justification for revolution was the Texans' fear of the future under the latest regime to be established in Mexico City. In 1834, General Antonio López de Santa Anna made himself dictator of Mexico and abolished the federal system of government. When news of these developments reached Texas late in the year, they were accompanied by rumors of the impending disfranchisement and even expulsion of American immigrants. Influenced by the rumors, the rebels tended to ascribe sinister motives to Santa Anna's new policy of enforcing tariff regulation by military force.

When he learned that the Texans were resisting customs collections, Santa Anna sent reinforcements. By October 1835, the two sides were engaged in a war. The first phase of the fighting ended when Stephen Austin laid siege to San Antonio with a force of five hundred men and after six weeks forced its surrender, thereby capturing most of the Mexican troops then in Texas.

The Republic of Texas

While early fighting was going on, delegates from the American communities met in convention and after some hesitation voted overwhelmingly to declare their independence on March 2, 1836. A constitution, based closely on that of the United

States, was adopted for the new Republic of Texas, and a temporary government was installed to carry on the military struggle.

Although the ensuing conflict was largely one of Americans against Mexicans, some Texas Mexicans, or *Tejanos,* joined the fray on the side of the Anglo rebels. They too wanted to be free from Santa Anna's heavy-handed rule, although after the rebellion many of them became victims of anti-Mexican prejudice.

Alamo In 1835, Americans living in the Mexican state of Texas fomented a revolution. Mexico lost the conflict, but not before its troops defeated and killed a group of American rebels at this former Spanish mission in San Antonio.

Within days after Texas declared itself a republic, rebels and Mexican troops in San Antonio fought the famous battle of the **Alamo.** Myths about the battle have magnified the Anglo rebels' valor at the Mexicans' expense. It is true that 187 rebels fought off a far larger Mexican force, capitulating only after more than a week of battling. It is not true, however, that all of the rebels fought to the death—apparently eight men were captured and then executed. Nevertheless, their stand was brave, and their deaths gave the insurrection new inspiration.

A few days later, another Texas detachment was surrounded and captured in an open plain near the San Antonio River and was marched to the town of Goliad, where all 350 of its members were summarily executed. The "Goliad massacre" provoked the Texas rebels to even more desperate resistance.

The main Texas army, under General Sam Houston, moved quickly to avenge these early defeats. On April 21, 1836, Houston led his force of seven hundred men in a daring assault on Santa Anna's encampment near the San Jacinto River. Within fifteen minutes, the battle was over, the Mexican force defeated, and Santa Anna captured. The Mexican leader was marched to Velasco, where he was forced to sign treaties recognizing the independence of Texas and its claim to territory all the way to the Rio Grande.

Sam Houston, the hero of San Jacinto, became the first president of the Texas republic. He sought annexation to the United States, but Andrew Jackson and others believed that domestic politics, the sectional issue of the expansion of slavery, and the possibility of a war with Mexico made such an action untenable. Congress and the Jackson administration, however, did formally recognize Texas sovereignty, and during the following decade of independence, the population of the "Lone Star Republic" soared from 30,000 to 142,000.

Trails of Trade and Settlement

After New Mexico opened its trade to American merchants in 1822, a thriving commerce developed along the trail that ran from Independence, Missouri, to Santa Fe. To protect themselves from the hostile Indians whose territory they had to cross, the traders traveled in large caravans. The federal government assisted them by providing troops when necessary and by appropriating money to purchase rights of passage from various tribes. Even so, the trip across the Cimarron Desert and the southern Rockies was often hazardous. But profits from the exchange of textiles and other manufactured goods for furs, mules, and precious metals were substantial enough to make the risk worth taking.

Relations between the United States and Mexico soured following the Texas revolution, and this had a devastating effect on the Santa Fe trade. Much of the ill feeling was caused by the Texans' blundering efforts to get a piece of the Santa Fe action. After several clashes with the Texans, the Mexican government in 1842 passed a new tariff banning the importation of many of the goods sold by American merchants and prohibiting the export of gold and silver.

The famous Oregon Trail was the great overland route that brought the wagon trains of American migrants to the West Coast during the 1840s. The journey took about six months; most parties departed in May, hoping to arrive in November before the great snows hit the last mountain barriers. After small groups had made their way to both Oregon and California in 1841 and 1842, a mass migration—mostly to Oregon—began in 1843. These migrants were quick to demand the extension of full American sovereignty over the Oregon Country.

WESTERN TRAILS *Among the greatest hazards faced by those migrating to the West was the rough and unfamiliar terrain over which their wagon trains traveled.* ∎

The Mormon Trek

Among the settlers moving west were members, known as Mormons, of the most successful religious denomination founded exclusively on American soil, the Church of Jesus Christ of Latter-day Saints. The background of the Mormon trek was a history of persecution in the eastern states. Joseph Smith of Palmyra, New York, the founder of Mormonism, revealed in 1830 that he had received over many years a series of revelations that called upon him to establish Christ's pure church on earth. As the prophet of this faith, he published the *Book of Mormon,* a new scripture that he claimed to have discovered and translated with the aid of an angel. It was the record of a community of pious Jews who left the Holy Land six centuries before the birth of Christ and sailed to the American continent. After his crucifixion and resurrection, Christ appeared to this community and proclaimed the Gospel. Four hundred years later, a fratricidal war annihilated the believing Christians but not all of the descendents of the original Jewish migrants. Mormons held that the survivors had contributed to the ancestry of the American Indians. This prophecy foretold the restoration of a purer Christianity that had once thrived on American soil. Smith and his followers were determined to establish a western Zion where they could practice their faith unmolested and carry out their special mission to convert the Native Americans.

In the 1830s, the Mormons established communities in Ohio and Missouri, but the former went bankrupt in the Panic of 1837 and the latter was the target of angry mobs and vigilante violence. In 1839, the Mormons found a temporary haven at Nauvoo, Illinois. But Smith soon reported new revelations that engendered dissension among his followers and hostility from neighboring "gentiles." Most controversial was his authorization of polygamy. In 1844, Smith was killed by a mob while being held in jail in Carthage, Illinois.

Smith's death confirmed the growing conviction of the Mormon leadership that they needed to move farther west to establish their Zion in the wilderness. In

■ *Carl Christian Anton Christensen,* Handcart, *ca. 1840. Instead of buying wagons and oxen, some groups of Mormon colonists made their trek to Deseret on foot, hauling their possessions in handcarts and working together as families to move their heavy loads.* ■

late 1845, Smith's successor, Brigham Young, decided to send a party of fifteen hundred men to assess the chances of maintaining a colony in the vicinity of the Great Salt Lake. In 1847, Young himself arrived in Utah and sent back word to the faithful that he had found the promised land.

The Mormon community that Young established in Utah is one of the great success stories of western settlement. In contrast to the extreme individualism and disorder that characterized the mining camps and other new communities, the state of Deseret (the name the Mormons originally applied to Utah) was a model of discipline and cooperation. Because of its communitarian form of social organization, its centralized government, and the religious dedication of its inhabitants, this frontier society was able to expand settlement in a planned and efficient way and develop a system of irrigation that "made the desert bloom."

After Utah came under American sovereignty in 1848, Deseret fought to maintain its autonomy and its custom of polygamy against the efforts of the federal government to extend American law and set up the usual type of territorial administration. In 1857, the Mormons and the federal government almost came to blows until President James Buchanan decided to use diplomacy rather than force.

MANIFEST DESTINY AND THE MEXICAN-AMERICAN WAR

Manifest Destiny Coined in 1845, this term referred to a doctrine in support of territorial expansion based on the beliefs that population growth demanded territorial expansion, that God supported American expansion, and that national expansion equaled the expansion of freedom.

The rush of settlers beyond the nation's borders in the 1830s and 1840s inspired politicians and propagandists to call for annexation of the areas that the migrants were occupying. Some went further and proclaimed that it was the **Manifest Destiny** of the United States to expand until it had absorbed all of North America, including Canada and Mexico. Such ambitions—and the policies they inspired— led to a major diplomatic confrontation with Great Britain and a war with Mexico.

Tyler and Texas

President John Tyler initiated the politics of Manifest Destiny. He was vice president when William Henry Harrison died in office in 1841 after serving scarcely a month. Tyler was a states' rights, proslavery Virginian who had been picked as Harrison's running mate to broaden the appeal of the Whig ticket. Profoundly out of sympathy with the mainstream of his own party, he soon broke with the Whigs in Congress, who had united behind the latest version of Henry Clay's American System. Despite the fact that he lacked a base in either of the major parties, Tyler hoped to be elected president in his own right in 1844. To accomplish this difficult feat, he needed a new issue around which he could build a following that would cut across established party lines.

In 1843, Tyler decided to put the full weight of his administration behind the annexation of Texas. He anticipated that this would be a popular move, especially in the slaveholding South, and would give him a solid base of support for the 1844 election.

To achieve his objective, Tyler enlisted the support of John C. Calhoun, the leading political defender of slavery and state sovereignty. Success or failure in the effort would constitute a decisive test of whether the North was willing to give the southern states a fair share of national power and adequate assurances for the future of their way of life. If antislavery sentiment succeeded in blocking the acquisition of Texas, the Southerners would at least know where they stood and begin to "calculate the value of the union."

To prepare the public for annexation, the Tyler administration launched a propaganda campaign in the summer of 1843. Rumors were circulated that the British were preparing to guarantee Texas independence and make a loan to that financially troubled republic in return for the abolition of slavery. Although the reports were groundless, the stories were believed and used to give urgency to the annexation cause.

The strategy of linking annexation explicitly to the interests of the South and slavery backfired politically. Northern antislavery Whigs charged that the whole scheme was a proslavery plot meant to advance the interest of one section of the nation against the other—an allegation that has more substance than most historians have been willing to acknowledge. Consequently, the Senate rejected the treaty of annexation by a decisive vote in June 1844.

The Triumph of Polk and Annexation

Tyler's initiative made the future of Texas the central issue in the 1844 campaign. But party lines held firm, and the president himself was unable to capitalize on it. Tyler tried to run as an independent, but his failure to gain significant support eventually forced him to withdraw from the race.

If the Democratic party convention had been held in 1843, as originally scheduled, ex-President Martin Van Buren would have won the nomination easily. But the convention was postponed until May 1844, and in the meantime the annexation question came to the fore. Van Buren persisted in the view he had held as president—that incorporation of Texas would arouse sectional strife and destroy the unity of the Democratic party. In an effort to keep the issue out of the campaign, Van Buren struck a gentleman's agreement with Henry Clay, the overwhelming favorite for the Whig nomination, that both of them would publicly oppose immediate annexation.

Van Buren's letter opposing annexation appeared just before the Democratic convention, and it cost him the nomination. Angry southern delegates invoked the rule requiring approval by a two-thirds vote. After several ballots, a dark horse candidate, James K. Polk of Tennessee, emerged triumphant. Polk, a protégé of

Andrew Jackson, had been speaker of the House of Representatives and governor of Tennessee.

An avowed expansionist, Polk ran on a platform calling for the simultaneous annexation of Texas and assertion of American claims to all of Oregon. He identified himself and his party with the popular cause of turning the United States into a continental nation, an aspiration that attracted support in the North as well as in the South. The Whig nominee, Henry Clay, was basically antiexpansionist, but his sense of the growing popularity of Texas annexation among southern Whigs caused him to waffle on the issue during the campaign. This vacillation cost Clay the support of a small but crucial group of northern antislavery Whigs, who defected to the abolitionist Liberty party.

Polk won the fall election by a relatively narrow popular margin. His triumph in the electoral college was secured by victories in New York and Michigan, where the Liberty party candidate, James G. Birney, had taken away enough votes from Clay to affect the outcome. Although the election was hardly a clear mandate for expansionism, the Democrats claimed that the people were behind their aggressive campaign to extend the borders of the United States.

After the election, Congress reconvened to consider the annexation of Texas. The mood had changed as a result of Polk's victory, and leading Democratic senators were now willing to support Tyler's scheme for annexation by joint resolution of Congress. As a result, annexation was approved a few days before Polk took office.

The Doctrine of Manifest Destiny

The expansionist mood that accompanied Polk's election and the annexation of Texas was given a name and a rationale in the summer of 1845. John L. O'Sullivan, a proponent of the Young America movement and an influential editor, charged that foreign governments were conspiring to block the annexation of Texas in an effort to thwart "the fulfillment of our manifest destiny to overspread the continent allotted by providence for the free development of our yearly multiplying millions."

Besides coining the phrase "manifest destiny," O'Sullivan pointed to the three main ideas that lay behind it. One was that God was on the side of American expansionism. A second idea, implied in the phrase "free development," was that the spread of American rule meant the extension of democratic institutions. O'Sullivan's third premise was that population growth required the outlet that territorial acquisitions would provide. Behind this notion lurked the fear that growing numbers would lead to diminished opportunities and European-type socioeconomic class divisions if the restless and the ambitious were not given new lands to settle and exploit.

In its most extreme form, Manifest Destiny meant that the United States would someday occupy the entire North American continent; nothing less would appease its land-hungry population. The only question in the minds of fervent expansionists and Young Americans was whether the United States would acquire its vast new domain through a gradual, peaceful process of settler infiltration or through active diplomacy backed by force and the threat of war. The decision was up to President Polk.

Polk and the Oregon Question

In 1845 and 1846, the United States came closer to armed conflict with Great Britain than at any time since the War of 1812. The willingness of some Americans to go to war over Oregon was expressed in the Democratic rallying cry, "Fifty-four forty or fight!" Polk fed this expansionist fever by laying claim in his inaugural address to all of the Oregon Country. Privately, however, he was willing to accept the 49th parallel. What made the situation so tense was that Polk was dedicated to an aggressive diplomacy of bluff and bluster.

In July 1845, Polk authorized Secretary of State James Buchanan to reply to the latest British request for terms by offering a boundary along the 49th parallel. The offer did not meet the British demand for all of Vancouver Island and free navigation of the Columbia River, and the British ambassador rejected the proposal out of hand. The rebuff infuriated Polk, who later called on Congress to terminate the agreement providing for joint occupation of the Pacific Northwest. Congress complied in April 1846.

Since abrogation of the joint agreement implied that the United States would attempt to extend its jurisdiction north to 54°40', the British government decided to take the diplomatic initiative in an effort to avert war while at the same time dispatching warships to the Western Hemisphere in case conciliation failed. Their new proposal accepted the 49th parallel as the border, gave Britain all of Vancouver Island, and provided for British navigation rights on the Columbia River. The Senate recommended that the treaty be accepted with the single change that British rights to navigate the Columbia be made temporary. It was ratified in that form on June 15.

NORTHWEST BOUNDARY DISPUTE *President Polk's policy of bluff and bluster nearly involved the United States in a war with Great Britain over the disputed boundary in Oregon.* ■

Polk was prompted to settle the Oregon question because he now had a war with Mexico on his hands. His reckless diplomacy had brought the nation within an eyelash of being involved in two wars at the same time. American policymakers obtained what they wanted from the Oregon treaty, the splendid natural deep-water harbor of Puget Sound. However, by agreeing to a compromise on Oregon, Polk alienated expansionist advocates in the Old Northwest who had supported his earlier call for "all of Oregon."

For many Northerners, the promise of new acquisitions of the Pacific Northwest was the only thing that made annexation of Texas palatable. They hoped that new free states could be created to counterbalance the admission of slaveholding Texas to the Union. As this prospect receded, the charge of antislavery defenders that Texas annexation was a southern plot drew more support; to Northerners, Polk began to look more and more like a president concerned mainly with furthering the interests of his native region.

War with Mexico

While the United States was avoiding a war with Great Britain, it was getting into one with Mexico. Although they had recognized Texas independence in 1845, the Mexicans rejected the Lone Star Republic's unjustified claim to the unsettled territory between the Nueces River and the Rio Grande. When the United States annexed Texas and assumed its claim to the disputed area, Mexico broke off diplomatic relations and prepared for armed conflict.

Polk responded by placing troops in Louisiana on the alert and by dispatching emissary John Slidell to Mexico City. Polk hoped Slidell could resolve the boundary dispute and could persuade the Mexicans to sell New Mexico and California. Slidell's mission failed. In January 1846, Polk ordered General Zachary Taylor,

■ *This 1846 cartoon, titled "This Is the House That Polk Built," shows President Polk sitting forlornly in a house of cards representing the delicately balanced issues facing him.* ■

Mexican-American War
Conflict (1846–1848) between the United States and Mexico after the U.S. annexation of Texas, which Mexico still considered its own. As victor, the United States acquired vast new territories from Mexico.

Treaty of Guadalupe Hidalgo
Signed in 1848, this treaty ended the Mexican-American War. Mexico relinquished its claims to Texas and ceded an additional 500,000 square miles to the United States for $15 million.

commander of American forces in the Southwest, to advance well beyond the Nueces and proceed toward the Rio Grande, thus encroaching upon Mexican territory. By April, Taylor had taken up a position near Matamoros on the Rio Grande. On April 24, sixteen hundred Mexican troops crossed the river from the south and the following day attacked a small American detachment. After learning of the incident, Taylor sent word to the president: "Hostilities may now be considered as commenced."

This news was neither unexpected nor unwelcome. Polk was in fact already preparing his war message to Congress when he learned of the fighting on the Rio Grande. A short and decisive war, he had concluded, would force the cession of California and New Mexico to the United States. Thus shortly after Congress declared war on May 13, American forces under Colonel Stephen Kearny captured Santa Fe and took possession of New Mexico. Kearny's troops then set off for California, where Anglo settlers and a so-called exploration expedition led by Captain John C. Frémont, aided by U.S. naval vessels, had revolted against Mexican rule. With the help of Kearny's forces, the Americans wrested control of California from Mexico.

The **Mexican-American War** lasted much longer than expected because the Mexicans refused to make peace despite a succession of military defeats. In the first major campaign of the conflict, Taylor followed up his victory in two battles fought north of the Rio Grande by crossing the river, taking Matamoros, and marching on Monterrey. In September, he captured the important northern city.

But Taylor's controversial decision to allow the Mexican garrison to go free and his unwillingness or inability to advance farther into Mexico angered Polk and led him to adopt a new strategy for winning the war and a new commander to implement it. General Winfield Scott was ordered to prepare an amphibious attack on Veracruz with the aim of placing an American army within striking distance of Mexico City itself. Taylor was left to hold his position in northern Mexico, where in February 1847 he defeated a sizable Mexican army at Buena Vista. Taylor was hailed afterward as a national hero and conceivable presidential material.

The decisive Veracruz campaign was slow to develop because of the massive and careful preparations required. But in March 1847, the main American army, now under General Scott, finally landed near that crucial port city and laid siege to it. Veracruz fell after eighteen days, and then Scott began his advance on Mexico City. In the most important single battle of the war, Scott met forces under General Santa Anna at Cerro Gordo on April 17 and 18. In a well-commanded attack, Scott's forces defeated the Mexican army and opened the road to Mexico City. By August, American troops were drawn up in front of the Mexican capital. After a temporary armistice, Scott ordered the massive assault that captured the city on September 14.

Settlement of the Mexican-American War

Accompanying Scott's army was a diplomat, Nicholas P. Trist, who was authorized to negotiate a peace treaty whenever the Mexicans decided they had had enough. Despite a sequence of American victories, however, no Mexican leader was willing to invite the wrath of an intensely proud and nationalistic citizenry by agreeing to the kinds of terms Polk wanted to impose. By November, Polk was so irked by the delay that he ordered Trist to return to Washington.

Trist, to his credit, ignored Polk's instructions and continued to negotiate. On February 2, 1848, he signed a treaty that gained all the concessions he had been commissioned to obtain. The **Treaty of Guadalupe Hidalgo** ceded New Mexico and

California to the United States for $15 million, established the Rio Grande as the border between Texas and Mexico, and promised that the United States government would assume the substantial claims of American citizens against Mexico. The Senate approved the treaty on March 10.

As a result of the Mexican-American War, the United States gained half a million square miles of territory, including the present states of California, Utah, New Mexico, and Arizona and parts of Colorado and Wyoming. In 1853, a dispute over the southern boundary of the cession was resolved by the Gadsden Purchase, whereby the United States acquired the southernmost parts of present-day Arizona and New Mexico. But one intriguing question remains: Why, given the expansionist spirit of the age, did the United States not take *all* of Mexico, as many Americans desired?

Racism and anticolonialism help account for the decision. It was one thing to acquire thinly populated areas that could be settled by "Anglo-Saxon" pioneers; it was something else again to incorporate a large population that was mainly of mixed Spanish and Indian origin. These "mongrels," charged racist opponents of the "All Mexico" movement, could never be fit citizens of a self-governing republic. They would have to be ruled in the way that the British governed India, and the possession of colonial dependencies was contrary to American ideals and traditions.

THE MEXICAN-AMERICAN WAR   *The Mexican-American War added half a million square miles of territory to the United States, but the cost was high: $100 million and 13,000 lives.* ■

The people actually making policy had more mundane and practical reasons for being satisfied with what was obtained at Guadalupe Hidalgo. What they had really wanted all along were the great California harbors of San Francisco and San Diego. From these ports, Americans could trade directly with the Orient and dominate the commerce of the Pacific. Once acquisition of California had been assured, policymakers had little incentive to press for more Mexican territory.

The war with Mexico divided the American public and provoked political dissension. A majority of the Whig party opposed the war in principle, arguing (correctly) that the United States had no valid claims to the area south of the Nueces. Whig congressmen voted for military appropriations while the conflict was going on, but they constantly criticized the president for starting it. More ominous was the charge from antislavery Northerners of both parties that the real purpose of the war was to spread the institution of slavery and increase the political power of the southern states. While battles were being fought in Mexico, Congress was debating a proposal to prohibit slavery in any territories that might be acquired from Mexico. A bitter sectional quarrel over the status of slavery in new areas was a major legacy of the Mexican-American War.

The domestic controversies aroused by the war and the propaganda of Manifest Destiny revealed the limits of mid-nineteenth-century American expansionism and put a damper on additional efforts to extend the nation's boundaries. Concerns about slavery and race blocked further southern expansion, and the desire to remain at peace with Great Britain prevented northern expansion. After 1848, Americans concentrated on populating and developing the vast territory already acquired.

INTERNAL EXPANSIONISM

The expansionists of the 1840s saw a clear link between acquisition of new territory and other forms of material growth and development. In 1844, Samuel F. B. Morse perfected and demonstrated his electric telegraph. Simultaneously, the railroad was becoming increasingly important as a means of moving people and goods over great distances. Improvements in manufacturing and agricultural methods led to an upsurge in the volume and range of internal trade, and the beginnings of mass immigration were providing human resources for the exploitation of new areas and economic opportunities.

The discovery of gold in California in 1848 encouraged thousands of emigrants to move to the West Coast. The gold they unearthed spurred the national economy, and the rapid growth of population centers on the Pacific Coast inspired projects for transcontinental telegraph lines and railroad tracks.

When the spirit of Manifest Destiny and the thirst for acquiring new territory waned after the Mexican-American War, the expansionist impulse turned inward. The technological advances and population increase of the 1840s continued during the 1850s. The result was an acceleration of economic growth, a substantial increase in industrialization and urbanization, and the emergence of a new American working class.

The Triumph of the Railroad

More than anything else, the rise of the railroad transformed the American economy during the 1840s and 1850s. The technology for steam locomotives came from England, and in 1830 and 1831, two American railroads began commercial operation. Although the lines were practical and profitable, canals proved to be strong competitors, especially for the freight business. Passengers might prefer the speed of trains, but the lower unit cost of freight on the canal boats prevented most shippers from changing their habits. Furthermore, states such as New York and

Pennsylvania that had invested heavily in canals resisted chartering a competitive form of transportation.

During the 1840s, rails extended beyond the northeastern and Middle Atlantic states, and mileage increased more than threefold, reaching a total of more than 9,000 miles by 1850. Expansion was even greater in the following decade, and by 1860, all the states east of the Mississippi had rail service. In addition, throughout the 1840s and 1850s, railroads cut deeply into the freight business of the canals and succeeded in driving many of them out of business.

The development of railroads had an enormous effect on the economy as a whole. Although the burgeoning demand for iron rails was initially met mainly by importation from England, that demand eventually spurred development of the domestic iron industry. Since railroads required an enormous outlay of capital, their promoters pioneered new methods for financing business enterprise. Railroad companies sold stock to the general public and helped set the pattern for the separation of ownership and control that characterizes the modern corporation.

But the gathering and control of private capital did not fully meet the needs of the early railroad barons. State and local governments, convinced that railroads were the key to their future prosperity, loaned the railroads money, bought their stock, and actively supported their development. Despite the dominant laissez-faire policy (which meant that the government should keep its hands off the economy), the federal government became involved by surveying the routes of projected lines and providing land grants. Thus a precedent was set for the massive land grants of the post–Civil War era.

The Industrial Revolution Takes Off

While railroads were initiating a revolution in transportation, American industry was entering a new phase of rapid and sustained growth. The factory mode of production, which had originated before 1840 in the cotton mills of New England (see Chapter 9), was extended to a variety of other products. Between 1830 and 1860, wool and iron production, shoemaking, and the firearms, clock, and sewing machine industries all moved toward the factory system.

The essential features of the factory mode of production were the gathering of a supervised workforce in a single place, the payment of cash wages to workers, the use of interchangeable parts, and manufacturing by "continuous process." Within a factory setting, standardized parts, manufactured separately and in bulk, could be efficiently and rapidly assembled into a final product by an ordered sequence of continuously repeated operations. Mass production, which involved the division of labor into a series of relatively simple and repetitive tasks, contrasted sharply with the traditional craft mode of production, in which a single worker produced the entire product out of raw materials.

New technology played an important role in the transition to mass production. Just as power looms and spinning machinery had made textile mills possible, the development of new and more reliable machines or industrial techniques revolutionized other industries. Elias Howe's invention of the sewing machine and Charles Goodyear's discovery of the process for vulcanizing rubber opened the way for the mass production of a wide range of consumer items.

Perhaps the greatest triumph of American technology during the mid-nineteenth century was the development of the world's most sophisticated and reliable machine tools. Such advances as the invention of the extraordinarily accurate measuring device known as the vernier caliper in 1851 and the first production of turret lathes in 1854 were signs of a special American aptitude for the kind of precision toolmaking that was essential to efficient industrialization.

Progress in industrial technology and organization did not mean that the United States had become an industrial society by 1860. Agriculture retained first

THE AGE OF PRACTICAL INVENTION

Year*	Inventor	Contribution	Importance/Description
1787	John Fitch	Steamboat	First successful American steamboat
1793	Eli Whitney	Cotton gin	Simplified process of separating fiber from seeds; helped make cotton a profitable staple of southern agriculture
1798	Eli Whitney	Jig for guiding tools	Facilitated manufacture of interchangeable parts
1802	Oliver Evans	Steam engine	First American steam engine; led to manufacture of high-pressure engines used throughout eastern United States
1813	Richard B. Chenaworth	Cast-iron plow	First iron plow to be made in three separate pieces, thus making possible replacement of parts
1830	Peter Cooper	Railroad locomotive	First steam locomotive built in America
1831	Cyrus McCormick	Reaper	Mechanized harvesting; early model could cut six acres of grain a day
1836	Samuel Colt	Revolver	First successful repeating pistol
1837	John Deere	Steel plow	Steel surface kept soil from sticking; farming thus made easier on rich prairies of Midwest
1839	Charles Goodyear	Vulcanization of rubber	Made rubber much more useful by preventing it from sticking and melting in hot weather
1842	Crawford W. Long	First administered ether in surgery	Reduced pain and risk of shock in surgery during operations
1844	Samuel F. B. Morse	Telegraph	Made long-distance communication almost instantaneous
1846	Elias Howe	Sewing machine	First practical machine for automatic sewing
1846	Norbert Rillieux	Vacuum evaporator	Improved method of removing water from sugar cane; revolutionized sugar industry and was later applied to many other products
1847	Richard M. Hoe	Rotary printing press	Printed an entire sheet in one motion; vastly speeded up printing process
1851	William Kelly	"Air-boiling process"	Improved method of converting iron into steel (usually known as Bessemer process because English inventor Bessemer had more advantageous patent and financial arrangements)
1853	Elisha G. Otis	Passenger elevator	Improved movement in buildings; when later electrified, stimulated development of skyscrapers
1859	Edwin L. Drake	First American oil well	Initiated oil industry in the United States
1859	George M. Pullman	Pullman passenger car	First railroad sleeping car suitable for long-distance travel

*Dates refer to patent or first successful use.
Source: From *Freedom and Crisis: An American History,* 3rd ed., by Allen Weinstein and Frank Otto Gatell. Copyright © 1974, 1978, 1981 by Random House, Inc. Reprinted by permission of Random House, Inc.

place both as a source of livelihood for individuals and as a contributor to the gross national product. But farming itself, at least in the North, was undergoing a technological revolution of its own. John Deere's steel plow enabled midwestern farmers to cultivate the tough prairie soils that had resisted cast-iron implements, and Cyrus McCormick's mechanical reaper offered an enormous saving in the labor required for harvesting grain.

A dynamic interaction between advances in transportation, industry, and agriculture gave great strength and resiliency to the economy of the northern states during the 1850s. Railroads offered western farmers better access to eastern markets. After Chicago and New York were linked by rail in 1853, the flow of most midwestern farm commodities shifted from the north-south direction based on riverborne traffic that had still predominated in the 1830s and 1840s to an east-west pattern.

The mechanization of agriculture did more than lead to more efficient and profitable commercial farming; it also provided an additional impetus to industrialization, and its laborsaving features released manpower for other economic activities. The growth of industry and the modernization of agriculture can thus be seen as mutually reinforcing aspects of a single process of economic growth.

Mass Immigration Begins

The original incentive to mechanize northern industry and agriculture came in part from a shortage of cheap labor. Compared with the industrializing nations of Europe, the United States of the early nineteenth century was a labor-scarce economy. Since it was difficult to attract able-bodied men to work for low wages in factories or on farms, women and children were used extensively in the early textile mills, and commercial farmers had to rely heavily on the labor of their family members. Although laborsaving machinery eased the problem, by the 1840s and 1850s industrialization had reached a point where it needed far more unskilled workers. The growth of industrial work opportunities helped attract a multitude of European immigrants between 1840 and 1860.

Between 1820 and 1840, an estimated 700,000 immigrants arrived in the United States. During the 1840s, the substantial flow suddenly became a flood. No less than 4.2 million newcomers crossed the Atlantic between 1840 and 1860. This was the greatest influx in proportion to total population—then about 20 million—that the nation has ever experienced. The largest sources of the new mass immigration were Ireland and Germany.

The massive transatlantic movement had many causes; some people were "pushed" out of their homes, while others were "pulled" toward America. The great potato blight, which brought famine to a population that subsisted on this single crop, accounted for much of the emigration from Ireland. Escape to America was made possible by the low fares then prevailing on sailing ships bound from England to North America. Ships involved in the timber trade carried their bulky cargoes from Boston or Halifax to Liverpool. As an alternative to returning to America partly in ballast, they packed Irish immigrants into their holds.

The location of the ports involved in the lumber trade meant that most Irish arrived in Canada or New England. Immobilized by poverty and a lack of skills required for pioneering in the West, most of them remained in the Northeast. Forced to subsist as low-paid menial laborers and crowded into festering urban slums, they were looked down on by most native-born Americans.

The million or so Germans who also came in the late 1840s and early 1850s were somewhat more fortunate. Most of them were also peasants, but they fled hard times rather than outright catastrophe. Unlike the Irish, they often escaped with a small amount of capital with which to make a fresh start in the New World. Many German immigrants were artisans and sought to ply their trades in cities such as New York, St. Louis, Cincinnati, and Milwaukee. But a large portion of those with peasant backgrounds went back to the land. Many became successful midwestern farmers, and they generally encountered less prejudice and discrimination than the Irish.

A Look at the Past

Steel Plow

In 1837, John Deere invented a plow with a smooth steel blade and successfully tested it on a farm in Illinois. Earlier plows had a blade made of cast iron. Deere's plow quickly became popular with pioneer farmers in the Midwest as an essential tool in cultivating the land. ✴ Why do you think Deere's new plow was necessary in the midwestern prairie? Why wouldn't a cast iron plow used in the East work equally well?

What attracted most of the Irish, German, and other European immigrants to America was the promise of economic opportunity. Although a minority chose the United States because they admired its democratic political system, most immigrants were more interested in the chance to make a decent living than in voting or running for office. During times of prosperity and high demand for labor, America proved a powerful magnet to discontented Europeans.

Yet the arrival of large numbers of immigrants worsened the already serious problems of America's rapidly growing cities. The old "walking city" in which rich and poor lived in close proximity near the center of town was changing to a more segregated environment. The advent of railroads and horse-drawn streetcars enabled the affluent to move to the first American suburbs, while areas nearer commercial and industrial centers became the congested settlements of newcomers from Europe. Emerging slums, such as the notorious Five Points district in New York City, were characterized by overcrowding, poverty, disease, and crime. Recognizing that these conditions created potential dangers for the entire urban population, middle-class reformers worked for the professionalization of police forces, introduction of sanitary water and sewage disposal systems, and upgrading of housing standards. They made some progress in these endeavors in the period before the Civil War, but the lot of the urban poor, mainly immigrants, was not dramatically improved. For most of them, urban life remained unsafe, unhealthy, and unpleasant.

The New Working Class

A majority of the immigrants ended up as wage workers in factories, mines, and construction camps or as casual day laborers doing the many unskilled tasks required by urban and commercial growth. By providing a vast pool of cheap labor, they fueled and accelerated the Industrial Revolution.

In the established industries and older mill towns of the Northeast, immigrants added to, or in some cases displaced, the native-born workers who had predominated in the 1830s and 1840s. In the textile mills especially, native female labor was replaced by foreign male workers. Irish males, employers found, were willing to perform tasks that native-born men had generally regarded as women's work.

The trend reveals much about the changing character of the American working class. In the 1830s, most male workers were artisans, while unskilled factory work was still largely the province of women and children. Both groups were predominantly of American stock. In the 1840s, the proportion of men engaged in factory work increased, although the workforce in the textile industry remained predominantly female. During that decade, working conditions in many mills deteriorated. Relations between management and labor became increasingly impersonal, and workers were pushed to increase their output. Workdays of twelve to fourteen hours were common.

The result was a new upsurge of labor militancy involving female as well as male factory workers. Workers' organizations petitioned state legislatures to pass laws limiting the workday to ten hours. Some such laws were actually passed, but they turned out to be ineffective because employers could still require a prospective worker to sign a special contract agreeing to longer hours as a condition of employment.

The employment of immigrants in increasing numbers between the mid-1840s and the late 1850s made it more difficult to organize industrial workers. Impoverished fugitives from the Irish potato famine tended to have lower economic expectations and little experience with labor organizations. Consequently, the Irish immigrants were willing to work for less and were not so prone to protest bad working conditions or organize into unions.

But the new working class of former rural folk did not make the transition to industrial wage labor easily or without protesting in subtle and indirect ways. Tardiness, absenteeism, drunkenness, loafing on the job, and other forms of resis-

Chronology

1822	Santa Fe is opened to American traders
1823	Earliest American settlers arrive in Texas
1830	Mexico attempts to halt American migration to Texas
1831	American railroads begin commercial operation
1834	Cyrus McCormick patents the mechanical reaper
1835	Revolution breaks out in Texas
1836	Texas becomes an independent republic
1837	John Deere invents the steel plow
1841	President John Tyler is inaugurated
1842	Webster-Ashburton Treaty fixes the border between Maine and New Brunswick
1843	Mass migration to Oregon begins ■ Mexico closes the Santa Fe trade to Americans
1844	Samuel F. B. Morse demonstrates the electric telegraph ■ James K. Polk is elected president on platform of expansionism
1845	Mass immigration from Europe begins ■ United States annexes Texas ■ John L. O'Sullivan coins the slogan "manifest destiny"
1846	War with Mexico breaks out ■ United States and Great Britain resolve the diplomatic crisis over Oregon
1847	American conquest of California is completed ■ Mormons settle Utah ■ American forces under Zachary Taylor defeat Mexicans at Buena Vista ■ Winfield Scott's army captures Veracruz and defeats Mexicans at Cerro Gordo ■ Mexico City falls to American invaders
1848	Treaty of Guadalupe Hidalgo consigns California and New Mexico to the United States ■ Gold is discovered in California
1849	"Forty-niners" rush to California to dig for gold
1858	War is averted between Utah Mormons and United States forces

tance to factory discipline reflected deep hostility to the unaccustomed and seemingly unnatural routines of "continuous process" production. The adjustment to new styles and rhythms of work was painful and took time.

CONCLUSION: THE COSTS OF EXPANSION

By 1860, industrial expansion and immigration had created a working class of men and women who seemed destined for a life of low-paid wage labor. This reality stood in contrast to America's self-image as a land of opportunity and upward mobility. The ideal still had some validity in rapidly developing regions of the western states, but it was mostly myth when applied to the increasingly foreign-born industrial workers of the Northeast.

Both internal and external expansion had come at a heavy cost. Tensions associated with class and ethnic rivalries were only one part of the price of rapid economic development. The acquisition of new territories became politically divisive and would soon lead to a catastrophic sectional controversy. From the late 1840s to the Civil War, the United States was a divided society in more senses than one, and the need to control or resolve these conflicts presented politicians and statesmen with a monumental challenge.

KEY TERMS

Young America, p. 245

Webster-Ashburton Treaty, p. 245

Alamo, p. 248

Manifest Destiny, p. 250

Mexican-American War, p. 254

Treaty of Guadalupe Hidalgo, p. 254

RECOMMENDED READING

An older overview of expansion to the Pacific is Ray A. Billington, *The Far Western Frontier, 1830–1860* (1956). A more recent account is Richard Where, *"It's Your Misfortune and None of My Own": A New History of the American West* (1993). The impulse behind Manifest Destiny has been variously interpreted. Albert K. Weinberg's classic *Manifest Destiny: A Study of National Expansionism in American History* (1935) describes and stresses the ideological rationale as does Anders Stephenson, *Manifest Destiny: American Expansion and the Empire of Right* (1995). Frederick Merk, *Manifest Destiny and Mission in American History* (1963), analyzes public opinion and shows how divided it was on the question of territorial acquisitions. Norman A. Graebner, *Empire on the Pacific: A Study in American Continental Expansionism* (1956), highlights the desire for Pacific harbors as a motive for adding new territory. The most complete and authoritative account of the diplomatic side of expansionism in this period is David M. Pletcher, *The Diplomacy of Annexation: Texas, Oregon, and the Mexican War* (1973). Charles G. Sellers, *James K. Polk: Continentalist, 1843–1846* (1966), is the definitive work on Polk's election and the expansionist policies of his administration. A very good account of the Mexican-American War is John S. D. Eisenhower, *So Far from God: The U.S. War with Mexico* (1989). The experience of the people incorporated into the United States is described by F. Rudolfo Acuñas in *Occupied America: A History of Chicanos* (2000). On gold rushes, see Malcolm J. Rohrbough, *Days of Gold: The California Gold Rush and the*

American Nation (1997) and Elliott West, *The Contested Plains: Indians, Goldseekers, and the Rush to Colorado* (1998).

Economic developments of the 1840s and 1850s are well covered in George R. Taylor, *The Transportation Revolution, 1815–1960* (1952) and Albert Fishlow, *American Railroads and the Transformation of the Ante-Bellum Economy* (1965). For an overview of immigration in this period, see the early chapters of Roger Daniels, *Coming to America: Immigration and Ethnicity in American Life* (1990). On the Irish, see Kerby A. Miller, *Emigrants and Exiles: Ireland and the Irish Exodus to America* (1985). Oscar Handlin, *Boston Immigrants: A Study in Acculturation*, rev. ed. (1959), is a classic study of immigration to one city. On how the United States managed immigration, see Aristotle R. Zolberg, *A Nation by Design: Immigration Policy in the Fashioning of America* (2006). A standard work on the antebellum working class is Sean Wilentz, *Chants Democratic: New York City and the Rise of the American Working Class, 1788–1850* (1984); for the new approach to labor history that emphasizes working-class culture, see Herbert G. Gutman, *Work, Culture, and Society in Industrializing America* (1976). For the rich public life of antebellum cities, see Mary P. Ryan, *Civic Wars: Democracy and Public Life in the American City During the Nineteenth Century* (1997). A pathbreaking and insightful study of workers in the textile industry is Thomas Dublin, *Women at Work: The Transformation of Work and Community in Lowell, Massachusetts, 1826–1860* (1979).

SUGGESTED WEB SITES

Pioneering the Upper Midwest: Books from Michigan, Minnesota, and Wisconsin, ca. 1820–1910

memory.loc.gov/ammem/umhtml/umhome.html

This Library of Congress site looks at first-person accounts, biographies, promotional literature, local histories, ethnographic and antiquarian texts, colonial archival documents, and other works from the seventeenth to the early twentieth century. It covers many topics and issues that affected Americans in the settlement and development of the Upper Midwest.

The Mexican-American War Memorial Homepage

sunsite.dcaa.unam.mx/revistas/1847/

Images and text explain the causes, courses, and outcomes of the Mexican-American War.

On the Trail in Kansas

www.kancoll.org/galtrl.htm

This Kansas Collection site holds several good primary sources with images concerning the Oregon Trail and America's early movement westward.

Mountain Men and the Fur Trade

www.xmission.com/~drudy/amm.html

Private letters can speak volumes about the concerns and environment of the writers and recipients. Letters from early settlers west of the Mississippi River are offered on this site, along with other resources relating to explorers, trappers, and traders.

Hispanic America After 1848
A Case Study in Majority Rule

With the discovery of gold in 1848, more than one thousand Californians of Mexican ancestry joined the frenetic rush to the Sierras. Among them was Don Antonio Franco Coronel, a Los Angeles school teacher, who led a group of fellow *Californios* into the rich goldfields. Just months before the expedition, the United States and Mexico had concluded the Treaty of Guadalupe Hidalgo, which transformed Coronel and his companions from Mexicans to Americans. At the insistence of the Mexican government, the treaty stipulated that Mexicans living in the newly acquired territories would be granted "all the rights of citizens of the United States . . . according to the principles of the Constitution." Coronel's gold-seeking enterprise would put that promise to the test. While panning rivers and staking claims, Coronel's company came into competitive contact with large numbers of Yankee miners. The interactions between the two ethnic communities suggested that a rough road lay ahead for Hispanic Americans.

Upon arriving in gold country, Coronel and his men immediately hit pay dirt. In the first day alone, Coronel pulled 45 ounces of gold from the ground; within eight days, one of his associates had amassed a pile of gold weighing a staggering 52 pounds. The Californios seemed to have a head start in the race for gold. They understood the terrain, cooperated among themselves, and were familiar with the best mining techniques. Not surprisingly, their dramatic successes stirred the envy of their Anglo-American competitors. Although the Mexican-American War technically had made the Yankee and Hispanic miners compatriots, the ten-sions of gold fever exposed the shallowness of that new relationship.

After a year of relatively peaceful competition, Anglo miners began to express their resentments. Lumping Californios with all other "foreigners," they unleashed a barrage of physical and political attacks against their competitors. Lynch mobs, camp riots, and legal harassment were common forms of Yankee intimidation. Despite their entitlements to the rights of citizenship, the Californios were badgered and bullied into retreat. Fearing for his life, Coronel returned to Southern California, where Hispanics still outnumbered the newcomers. Earning prestige and prosperity in Los Angeles, Coronel went on to become mayor and state treasurer. But to the end of his life, he still painfully remembered his experience in Northern California, where his rights as a U.S. citizen were so easily disregarded by his fellow Americans.

Coronel's experiences exemplify two truths about the effect of U.S. expansion on the lives of Mexicans who suddenly found themselves in American territory. First, in areas where Anglo-American settlement grew rapidly—such as Northern California—the Hispanic community typically faced discrimination, intimidation, and a denial of the very civil rights that Guadalupe Hidalgo had supposedly guaranteed. Second, in areas where the Hispanic population remained a majority—such as Southern California—Spanish-speaking Americans were able to exercise the rights of republican citizenship, often wielding considerable political influence. Coronel had a taste of both experiences, going from intimidated miner to powerful politician. However, as Anglo settlers began to stream into Southern California, even that region ceased to be a safe haven for Hispanic rights.

By the mid-1840s Hispanics living in Texas, known as *Tejanos,* were outnumbered by Anglos at a ratio of twenty to one. True to the pattern described above, this decided minority faced intense prejudice. Among the most notable victims of this prejudice was Juan Sequin, a hero of the Texas War for Independence. Perhaps no Tejano family fell further or faster than that of Don Martin de Leon. The scion of an aristocratic family, de Leon had spearheaded Spanish efforts to colonize Texas and continued to organize settlements after Mexican independence. Establishing extensive cattle ranches, the de Leons enjoyed prominence and wealth on their holdings. As with most Tejanos, they fervently supported the struggle for Texan independence, fighting shoulder to shoulder with their Anglo neighbors. But when the war ended, the de Leon estate fell under siege from the surging wave of new settlers. Relying on the intricacies of Anglo-American law and the power of an electoral majority, the newcomers quickly encroached on de Leon's lands. With frightening rapidity, the family was reduced from its preeminent position to abject poverty.

The de Leons were not alone. A contemporary observed that many Anglo settlers worked "dark intrigues against the native families, whose only crime was that they owned large tracts of land and desirable property." Even after U.S. annexation of the Lone Star Republic, Hispanics continued to be pushed off their land. In 1856, a Texas newspaper reported, "The people of Matagorda county have held a meeting and ordered every Mexican to leave the county. To strangers this may seem

■ *Blessing of the Enrequita Mine,* 1860, by Alexander Edouart. Spaniards and Mexicans, men and women, surround the makeshift altar where the priest is saying the blessing to dedicate the Enrequita Mine in northern California. The idyllic scene does not hint at the violent and rough treatment Hispanic miners experienced during the California gold rush days. ■

wrong, but we hold it to be perfectly right and highly necessary." For many Mexican Americans, life on U.S. soil taught the cruelest lesson in white man's democracy.

Yet majority rule actually worked to the favor of Hispanics living in New Mexico, where they enjoyed numerical dominance. When U.S. troops entered Santa Fe in 1846, Albino Chacón, a prominent city judge, controlled his own future. Although he had been loyal to the Mexican government throughout the war, the U.S. Army offered him the opportunity to retain his judgeship. Given similar offers, other New Mexicans who had initially opposed the U.S. invasion accepted positions of prominence, such as Donanciano Vigil, who served as interim governor of the territory. But Chacón lived by a strict code of honor and could not switch loyalties so easily. Opting for exile, Chacón moved out of Santa Fe, left the practice of law, and took up

farming. Aside from such self-imposed changes, however, American rule actually had little impact on most New Mexicans' lives. Hispanics still formed the demographic and political backbone of the territory and often served their new nation with distinction. Chacón's own son, Rafael, served as a Union officer during the Civil War, winning acclaim in defending New Mexico against a Confederate invasion from Texas, and was eventually elected as territorial senator. Rafael's son studied law at Notre Dame and held several important positions in the Department of Justice. Majority status afforded New Mexican Hispanics opportunities in the American system that were denied their compatriots living in Anglo-dominated regions.

As settlement increased throughout the century, such Hispanic-controlled communities dwindled. The rise of the railroad acted as a funnel through which Anglo-Americans

poured into western territories, and remaining pockets of Hispanic dominance rapidly disappeared. Majoritarianism and racism combined to place Hispanics in a position subordinate to the Anglo newcomers. Throughout the region the story was sadly similar; as Hispanic Americans lost their majority status, they also lost many of their basic rights.

Questions for Discussion

* What advantages did those people of Mexican ancestry in California, Texas, and New Mexico derive from the American citizenship they acquired under the terms of the Treaty of Guadalupe Hidalgo in 1848?
* To what extent and in what ways were these advantages denied in subsequent years as a result of Anglo prejudice and discrimination?

Chapter 14

The Sectional Crisis

The Brooks-Sumner Brawl in Congress

On May 22, 1856, Representative Preston Brooks of South Carolina suddenly appeared on the floor of the Senate. He was looking for Charles Sumner, the antislavery senator from Massachusetts who had recently given a speech condemning the South for plotting to extend slavery to the Kansas Territory. When he found Sumner seated at his desk, Brooks proceeded to batter him over the head with a cane. Sumner made a desperate effort to rise, ripped his bolted desk from the floor, and then collapsed.

Sumner was so badly injured by the assault that he could not return to the Senate for three years. In parts of the North that were up in arms against the expansion of slavery, he was hailed as a martyr to the cause of "free soil." Brooks, denounced in the North as a bully, was lionized by his fellow Southerners and won re-election without opposition.

These contrasting reactions show how bitter sectional antagonism had become by 1856. Sumner spoke for the radical wing of the new Republican party, which was making a bid for national power by mobilizing the North against the alleged aggression of "the slave power." Southerners viewed the very existence of this party as an insult to their section of the country and a threat to its vital interests. Many Southerners believed that Sumner and his political friends were plotting against their way of life. By 1856, therefore, the sectional cleavage that would lead to the Civil War had already undermined the foundations of national unity.

The crisis of the mid-1850s came only a few years after the elaborate Compromise of 1850 had seemingly resolved the dispute over the future of slavery in the territories acquired as a result of the Mexican-American War. The renewed agitation over the extension of slavery was set in motion by the Kansas-Nebraska Act of 1854. This legislation revived the sectional conflict and led to the emergence of the Republican party. From that point on, a dramatic series of events heightened the mood of sectional confrontation and destroyed the prospects for a new compromise. The caning of Charles Sumner was one of these events, and violence on the Senate floor foreshadowed violence on the battlefield.

THE COMPROMISE OF 1850

During the late 1840s, the leaders of the two major national parties, each with substantial followings in both the North and the South, had a vested interest in resolving the sectional crisis. Furthermore, the less tangible features of sectionalism—emotion and ideology—were not yet as divisive as they would later become. Hence

Outline

The Compromise of 1850

Political Upheaval, 1852–1856

The House Divided, 1857–1860

Conclusion: Explaining the Crisis

WE AMERICANS
The Irish in Boston, 1845–1865

265

■ *After his constituents learned of Preston Brooks's caning of Senator Sumner, they sent Brooks a gold-handled cowhide whip to use on other antislavery advocates.* ■

a fragile compromise was achieved through a kind of give-and-take that would not be possible after the emergence of strong sectional parties in the mid-1850s.

The Problem of Slavery in the Mexican Cession

The Founders, who were generally opposed to slavery, had attempted to exclude the slavery issue from national politics as the price of uniting states committed to slavery and those in the process of abolishing it. The Constitution gave the federal government no definite authority to regulate or destroy the institution where it existed under state law. Thus it was easy to condemn slavery in principle but very difficult to develop a practical program to eliminate it without defying the Constitution.

Radical abolitionists viewed the problem clearly and resolved it by rejecting the law of the land in favor of a "higher law" prohibiting human bondage. But during the 1840s, the majority of Northerners showed that while they disliked slavery, they also detested abolitionism. They were inclined to view slavery as a backward institution and slaveholders as power-hungry aristocrats. But they regarded the Constitution as a binding contract between slave and free states and were likely to be prejudiced against blacks and reluctant to accept large numbers of them as free citizens. Consequently, they saw no legal or desirable way to bring about emancipation within the southern states.

However, the Constitution had not predetermined the status of slavery in *future* states. Congress had the right to require the abolition of slavery as the price of admission into the Union. An effort to use this power had led to the Missouri crisis of 1819–1820 (see Chapter 9). The resulting Missouri Compromise line was designed to decide future cases and maintain a rough parity between slave and free states. Slavery was thus allowed to expand with the westward movement of the cotton kingdom but was discouraged or prohibited above the line of 36°30′.

The tradition of providing both the free North and the slave South with opportunities for expansion and the creation of new states broke down when new territories were wrested from Mexico in the 1840s. Many Northerners were unwilling to see California and New Mexico as well as Texas admitted into the Union as slave states. Since it was generally assumed in the North that Congress had the power to prohibit slavery in new territories, a movement developed in Congress to do just that.

The Wilmot Proviso Launches the Free-Soil Movement

The Free-Soil crusade began in August 1846, only three months after the start of the Mexican War, when Congressman David Wilmot, a Pennsylvania Democrat, proposed an amendment to the military appropriations bill that would ban slavery in any territory that might be acquired from Mexico.

Wilmot spoke for a large number of northern Democrats who felt neglected and betrayed by the policies of the Polk administration. Reductions in tariff duties and Polk's veto of an internal improvement bill upset many Democrats. Still others felt betrayed because Polk had gone back on his pledge to obtain "all of Oregon" up to 54°40′ and had then proceeded to wage war to win all of Texas. This twist in the course of Manifest Destiny convinced northern expansionists that the South and its interests were dominating the party and the administration.

Nevertheless, the pioneer Free-Soilers had a genuine interest in the issue actually at hand—the question of who would control and settle the new territories.

Combining an appeal to racial prejudice with opposition to slavery as an institution, Wilmot demanded that the new territories be opened only for white people. He wanted to give the common folk of the North a fair chance by excluding unfair competition with slavery and blacks from territory obtained in the Mexican cession.

Northern Whigs backed the **Wilmot Proviso** because they shared the concern about the outcome of unregulated competition between slave and free labor in the territories. Many of the northern Whigs had opposed the annexation of Texas and the Mexican-American War. If expansion was inevitable, they were determined that it should not be used to increase the power of the slave states.

In the first House vote on the Wilmot Proviso, party lines crumbled and were replaced by a sharp sectional cleavage. After passing the House, the Proviso was blocked in the Senate by a combination of southern influence and Democratic loyalty to the administration. When the appropriation bill went back to the House without the Proviso, the administration's arm-twisting succeeded in changing enough northern Democratic votes to defeat the Proviso.

Wilmot Proviso In 1846, shortly after the outbreak of the Mexican-American War, Congressman David Wilmot of Pennsylvania introduced this controversial amendment stating that any lands won from Mexico would be closed to slavery.

Squatter Sovereignty and the Election of 1848

After a futile attempt was made to extend the Missouri Compromise line to the Pacific—a proposal that was unacceptable to Northerners because most of the Mexican cession lay south of the line—a new approach was devised that appealed especially to Democrats. Its main proponent was Senator Lewis Cass of Michigan, an aspirant for the party's presidential nomination. He wanted to leave the determination of the status of slavery in a territory to the actual settlers. From the beginning, this proposal contained an ambiguity that allowed it to be interpreted differently in the North and the South. For the northern Democrats, "squatter sovereignty"—or **popular sovereignty,** as it was later called—meant that settlers could vote slavery up or down at the first meeting of a territorial legislature. For the southern wing of the party, it meant that a decision would be made only at the time a convention drew up a constitution and applied for statehood. It was in the interest of national Democratic leaders to leave this ambiguity intact for as long as possible.

popular sovereignty The concept that the settlers of a newly organized territory have the right to decide (through voting) whether to accept slavery. Promoted as a solution to the slavery question, popular sovereignty became a fiasco in Kansas in the 1850s.

Congress failed to resolve the future of slavery in the Mexican cession in time for the election of 1848. The Democrats nominated Cass on a platform of squatter sovereignty. The Whigs evaded the question by running war hero General Zachary Taylor without a platform. Northern Whigs favoring restrictions on the expansion of slavery took heart from the general's promise not to veto any territorial legislation passed by Congress. Southern Whigs supported Taylor because the general was a southern slaveholder.

Northerners who strongly supported the Wilmot Proviso were attracted by a third party movement. The **Free-Soil party** nominated former President Van Buren to carry their banner. Support for the Free-Soilers came mostly from Democrats and Whigs who opposed either the extension of slavery into the territories or the growing influence of the South in national policies. The founding of the Free-Soil party was the first significant effort to create a broadly based sectional party addressing itself to voters' concerns about the extension of slavery.

Free-Soil party Organized in 1848, this third party proposed to exclude slavery from federal territories and nominated former President Martin Van Buren in the presidential election of that year. Most Free-Soilers eventually became Republicans.

After a noisy and confusing campaign, Taylor came out on top, winning a majority of the electoral votes in both the North and the South. The Free-Soilers failed to carry a single state but were strong enough to run second behind Taylor in New York, Massachusetts, and Vermont.

Taylor Takes Charge

Once in office, Taylor devised a bold plan to decide the fate of slavery in the Mexican cession. He tried to engineer the immediate admission of California and New Mexico to the Union as states, bypassing the territorial stage entirely and eliminating the whole question of the status of slavery in the federal domain. The proposal made practical sense in regard to California, which was filling up rapidly with settlers drawn there by the lust for gold. Under the administration's urging, Californians convened a constitutional convention and applied for admission to the Union as a free state. In underpopulated New Mexico, it proved impossible to get a statehood movement off the ground.

Instead of resolving the crisis, President Taylor's initiative only worsened it. Fearing that New Mexico as well as California would choose to be a free state, Southerners of both parties accused the president of trying to impose the Wilmot Proviso in a new form. The prospect that only free states would emerge from the entire Mexican cession inspired serious talk of secession.

In Congress, Senator John C. Calhoun of South Carolina saw a chance to achieve his long-standing goal of creating a southern voting bloc that would cut across regular party lines. He warmly greeted each new sign of southern discontent and sectional solidarity. In the fall and winter of 1849–1850, several southern states agreed to participate in a convention, to be held in Nashville in June, where grievances could be aired and demands made. For an increasing number of southern political leaders, the survival of the Union would depend on the North's response to southern demands.

Forging a Compromise

When it became clear that the president would not abandon or modify his plan to appease the South, independent efforts began in Congress to arrange a compromise. Hoping once again to play the role of "great pacificator," Senator Henry Clay of Kentucky offered a series of resolutions meant to restore sectional harmony. On the critical territorial question, his solution was to admit California as a free state and organize the rest of the Mexican cession with no explicit prohibition of slavery. He also sought to resolve a major boundary dispute between New Mexico and Texas by granting the disputed region to New Mexico while compensating Texas through federal assumption of its state debt. As a concession to the North on another issue—the existence of slavery in the District of Columbia—he recommended prohibiting the buying and selling of slaves in the nation's capital. Finally, he called for more vigorous enforcement of the Fugitive Slave Law.

Clay proposed the plan in February 1850, but it received a mixed reception. One obstacle was President Taylor's firm resistance to the proposal; another was the difficulty of getting congressmen to vote for it in the form of a single package or "omnibus bill." The logjam was broken in July by two crucial developments. President Taylor died and was succeeded by Millard Fillmore, who favored the compromise, and a decision was made to abandon the omnibus strategy for a series of measures that could be voted on separately. After the breakup of the omnibus bill, Democrats, led by Senator Stephen A. Douglas, replaced the original Whig sponsors as leaders of the compromise movement and maneuvered the separate provisions of the plan through Congress.

As finally approved, the **Compromise of 1850** differed somewhat from Clay's original proposals. The popular sovereignty principle was included in the bills organizing New Mexico and Utah as the price of Democratic support. In addition, half of the compensation to Texas for giving up its claims to New Mexico was paid directly to holders of Texas bonds.

Abolition of the slave trade in the District of Columbia and a new **Fugitive Slave Law** were also enacted. According to the provisions of the latter act, suspected fugitives were now denied a jury trial, the right to testify in their own behalf, and other minimal constitutional rights. As a result, there were no effective safeguards against false identification and the kidnapping of blacks who were legally free.

Compromise of 1850 This series of five congressional statutes temporarily calmed the sectional crisis. Among other things, the compromise made California a free state, ended the slave trade in the District of Columbia, and strengthened the Fugitive Slave Law.

Fugitive Slave Law Passed in 1850, this federal law made it easier for slaveowners to recapture runaway slaves; it also made it easier for kidnappers to take free blacks.

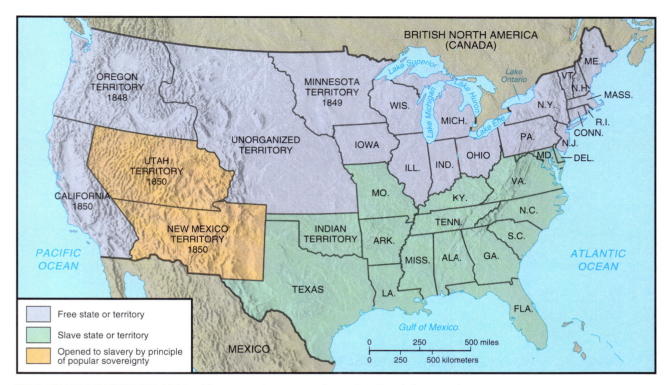

THE COMPROMISE OF 1850   *The compromise was actually a series of resolutions granting some concessions to abolitionists—admission of California as a free state, for example—and some to slaveholders, such as a stricter Fugitive Slave Law.* ■

The compromise passed because its key measures were supported by both northern Democrats and southern Whigs. No single bill was backed by a majority of the congressmen from both sections, and doubts persisted over the value or workability of a compromise that was really more like a cease-fire.

Yet the Compromise of 1850 did serve for a time as a basis for sectional peace. Southern moderates had carried the day, but southern nationalism remained strong. Southerners demanded strict northern adherence to the compromise, especially the Fugitive Slave Law, as the price for keeping threats of secession suppressed. In the North, the compromise received even greater support. The Fugitive Slave Law was unpopular in areas where abolitionism was particularly strong, and there were a few sensational rescues or attempted rescues of escaped slaves. But for the most part, the northern states adhered to the law during the next few years. When both the Democrats and the Whigs endorsed the compromise in their 1852 platforms, it appeared that sharp differences on the slavery issue had once again been banished from national politics.

POLITICAL UPHEAVAL, 1852–1856

The second party system—Democrats versus Whigs—survived the crisis over slavery in the Mexican cession, but in the long run, the Compromise of 1850 may have weakened it. Although both national parties had been careful during the 1840s not to take stands on the slavery issue that would alienate their supporters in either section of the country, they had in fact offered voters alternative ways of dealing with the question. Democrats had endorsed headlong territorial expansion with the promise of a fair division of the spoils between slave and free states. Whigs had generally opposed annexation of acquisitions that were likely to bring the slavery question to the fore and threaten sectional harmony. Each strategy could be presented to southern voters as a good way to protect slavery and to Northerners as a good way to contain it.

The consensus of 1852 meant that the parties had to find other issues on which to base their distinctive appeals. Their failure to do so encouraged voter apathy and disenchantment with the major parties. When the Democrats sought to revive the Manifest Destiny issue in 1854, they inadvertently reopened the explosive issue of slavery in the territories. By this time, the Whigs were too weak and divided to respond with a policy of their own, and a purely sectional Free-Soil party, the Republicans, gained prominence. The collapse of the second party system released sectional agitation from the earlier constraints imposed by the competition of strong national parties.

The Party System in Crisis

The presidential campaign of 1852 was singularly devoid of major issues. Both parties ignored the slavery question. Some Whigs tried to revive interest in nationalistic economic policies; but with business thriving under the Democratic program which limited government involvement in the economy, such proposals sounded empty and unnecessary.

Another tempting issue was immigration. Many Whigs were upset by the massive influx from Europe, partly because most of the new arrivals were Catholics and the Whig following was largely evangelical Protestant. In addition, immigrants voted overwhelmingly Democratic. The Whig leadership was divided on whether to compete for the immigrant vote or to seek restrictions on immigrant voting rights.

The Whigs nominated General Winfield Scott, of Mexican-American War fame, who supported the faction that resisted nativism and sought to broaden the appeal of the party. However, Scott and his supporters were unable to break the Democratic grip on the immigrant vote, and some nativist Whigs apparently sat out the election to protest their party's disregard of their cultural prejudice.

But the main cause for Scott's crushing defeat was the support he lost in the South when he allied himself with the northern antislavery wing of the party, led by Senator William Seward of New York. The Democratic candidate, Franklin Pierce of New Hampshire, was a colorless nonentity compared to his rival, but he easily swept the Deep South and edged out Scott in most of the free states. The outcome revealed that the Whig party was in deep trouble because it lacked a program that would appeal to voters in both sections of the country.

Despite their overwhelming victory in 1852, the Democrats also had reasons for anxiety about the loyalty of their supporters. Voter apathy was strong, and Democratic leaders were placed in the uncomfortable position of having to appeal to both northern Free-Soilers and southern slaveholders.

The Kansas-Nebraska Act Raises a Storm

In January 1854, Senator Stephen A. Douglas of Illinois proposed a bill to organize the territory west of Missouri and Iowa. Since this region fell within the area where slavery had been banned by the Missouri Compromise, Douglas hoped to head off southern opposition and keep the Democratic party united by disregarding the compromise line and setting up the territorial government in Kansas and Nebraska on the basis of popular sovereignty.

Douglas wanted to organize the region quickly because he was a strong supporter of the expansion of settlement and commerce. He hoped that a railroad would soon be built to the Pacific with Chicago or another midwestern city as its eastern terminus. A long controversy over the status of slavery in the Kansas-

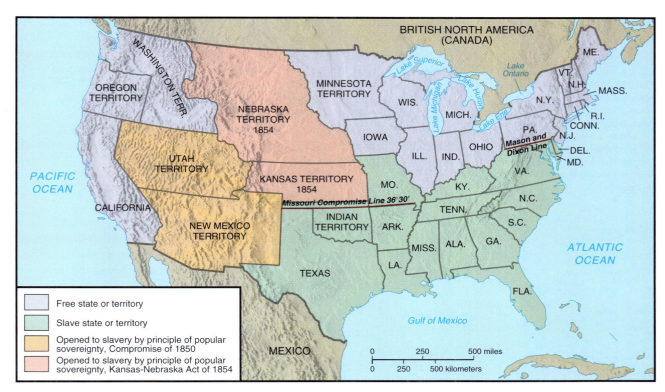

THE KANSAS-NEBRASKA ACT OF 1854   *The Kansas-Nebraska Act applied the principle of popular sovereignty to voters in the Kansas and Nebraska territories, allowing them to decide for themselves whether to permit slavery in their territories. The act repudiated the Missouri Compromise of 1820, which had prohibited slavery in the territory of the Louisiana Purchase north of 36°30′ latitude.* ■

Nebraska area would delay the building of a railroad through the territory. Moreover, by trying to revive the spirit of Manifest Destiny, he hoped to strengthen the Democratic party and enhance his chances of becoming president.

The price of southern support, Douglas soon discovered, was the addition of an amendment explicitly repealing the Missouri Compromise. He reluctantly agreed. Although the bill then made its way through Congress, it split the Democratic party. A manifesto of "independent Democrats" denounced the bill as "a gross violation of a sacred pledge." For many Northerners, the **Kansas-Nebraska Act** was an abomination because it appeared to permit slavery in an area where it had previously been prohibited. More than ever, Northerners were receptive to the theme that there was a conspiracy to extend slavery.

Douglas's bill had a catastrophic effect on the prospects for sectional harmony. It repudiated a compromise that many in the North regarded as binding. In defiance of the whole compromise tradition, it made a concession to the South on the issue of slavery extension without providing an equivalent concession to the North. From then on, northern sectionalists would be fighting to regain what they had lost, while Southerners would be battling just as furiously to maintain rights already conceded.

The act also destroyed what was left of the second party system. The already weakened Whig party disintegrated when its congressional representation split cleanly along sectional lines on the Kansas-Nebraska issue. The Democratic party survived, but northern desertions and southern gains resulting from recruitment of proslavery Whigs destroyed its sectional balance and placed the party under firm southern control.

Kansas-Nebraska Act This 1854 act repealed the Missouri Compromise, split the Louisiana Purchase into two territories, and allowed its settlers to accept or reject slavery by popular sovereignty. This act enflamed the slavery issue and led opponents to form the Republican party.

Finally, the furor over Kansas-Nebraska doomed the efforts of the Pierce administration to revive an expansionist foreign policy. Pierce and Secretary of State William Marcy were committed to acquiring Cuba from Spain. But Northerners interpreted the administration's plan, made public in a memorandum known as the **Ostend Manifesto,** as an attempt to create a "Caribbean slave empire." The resulting storm of protest forced Pierce and his cohorts to abandon their scheme. The only tangible result of the southern expansionist dream of the 1850s was the purchase for $10 million of a 30,000-square-mile slice of Mexican territory south of the Gila River (the Gadsden Purchase, 1853). This acquisition completed the contiguous continental United States as it is known today.

An Appeal to Nativism: The Know-Nothing Episode

The collapse of the Whigs created the opening for a new political party. The anti-Nebraska sentiment of 1854 suggested that such a party might be organized on the basis of northern opposition to the extension of slavery to the territories. Before such a prospect could be realized, however, an alternative emerged in the form of a major political movement based on hostility to immigrants. For a time, it appeared that the Whigs would be replaced by a nativist party rather than an antislavery one.

Massive immigration of Irish and Germans (see Chapter 13), most of whom were Catholic, led to increasing tensions between ethnic groups during the 1840s and early 1850s. Protestants were suspicious and distrustful of the Catholics, whom they viewed as bearers of an alien culture. Nativist agitators charged that immigrants were agents of a foreign despotism, based in Rome, that was bent on overthrowing the American republic.

Political nativism first emerged during the 1840s in the form of local "American" parties protesting immigrant influence in cities such as New York and Philadelphia. The organizations were often secretive, and one group instructed its members to answer questions about their organization with the reply, "I know nothing." The political objective of the **Know-Nothing party** was to extend the period of naturalization in order to undercut immigrant voting strength and to keep aliens in their place.

In 1854 and 1855, the nativist movement surfaced as a major political force, the American party. Most of the party's backing came from Whigs looking for a new home, but it also attracted some ex-Democrats. Know-Nothingism also appealed to native-born workers who feared competition from low-paid immigrants. Others supported the party simply as an alternative to the Democratic party. In the North, the Know-Nothing candidates generally opposed the Kansas-Nebraska Act and gained some of their support from voters anxious about the expansion of slavery.

The success of the new party was so dramatic that it was compared to a hurricane. In 1854 and 1855, Know-Nothings won control of a number of state governments, ranging from Massachusetts to Maryland to Texas. By late 1855, the Know-Nothings showed every sign of displacing the Whigs as the nation's second party.

Yet almost as rapidly as it had arisen, the Know-Nothing movement collapsed. Its demise in 1856 is one of the great mysteries of American political history. Admittedly, as a national party, it was unable to mend the deep sectional divisions over the question of slavery in the territories. Less clear is why Know-Nothings

■ *Know-Nothings often charged that immigrant voters were stealing American elections. In the cartoon above, German and Irish immigrants, represented by German beer and Irish whiskey, steal a ballot box.* ■

Past and Present

Nativism, a term historians use for movements and sentiments hostile to immigrants and immigration, has been a recurrent phenomenon in American history. Nativists glorify and defend what they take to be the traditional culture and interests of the "old stock" inhabitants of the nation. The first major outbreak of nativism occurred in response to the mass migration from northern Europe, mostly Ireland and Germany, from the 1830s through the 1850s. But nativist currents have since emerged in different ways even today.

Since virtually all of the Irish and many of the German immigrants of the mid-1800s were Catholics entering an overwhelmingly Protestant nation, it is not surprising that religious bigotry was a central theme of nativist propaganda at that time. Since white immigrants could become naturalized voters after five years, nativists feared that Catholic immigrants' alleged subservience to an authoritarian Church under a papal leader would prevent them from becoming independent, self-reliant citizens upon which the republic depended. Also, the fact that immigrants were often willing to work for lower wages than native-born workers fostered an economic resentment that sometimes led to violence. Nativists in this period did not propose ending or even limiting immigration from Europe. The Know-Nothing, or American, party, which emerged in the mid-1850s and enjoyed a brief but spectacular national success, simply proposed to extend the period of naturalization to twenty-one years. Nativist organization and political parties were most active in major eastern cities with large immigrant populations, especially New York and Philadelphia, both of which experienced anti-Catholic riots and saw the emergence in the 1840s of political parties vying for local office under the banner "American Republicans."

Late in the nineteenth century there was another surge of nativism, directed this time at the "new immigrants" from eastern and southern Europe, especially the Italians and Poles who were arriving in great numbers by the 1890s. Again, a combination of cultural anxiety and fear of competition for jobs fueled hostility to these immigrants. In addition, pseudoscientific racial theories posited that Mediterranean and Slavic newcomers were genetically inferior to Americans of northern European ancestry. Unlike the earlier nativist

movement this one had a major effect on immigration policy. It led to the discriminatory quota system that went into effect in the 1920s.

In our own time, nativist thought and activity has burgeoned once again in response to another new wave of immigration from Latin America and Asia. It has been the Latinos, especially illegal immigrants from Mexico, who have aroused the greatest concern. Part of this anxiety stemmed from fear that Latinos who persisted in speaking Spanish would threaten the dominance of English as the American language. Some also expressed fears that these immigrants were clustering together and refusing to assimilate into American society and culture (as earlier European newcomers were thought to have done).

A criticism directed specifically at illegal immigrants from Mexico was that they benefited from public services to which they were not entitled. In 1994, California voters approved Proposition 187, which attempted to deny most public benefits, including education, to illegal immigrants and their families. At first this new nativism was localized and sporadic, being strongest in California and other states bordering Mexico. But after a decade of relative indifference to the immigration issue, it burst back into prominence in 2006. How to deal with massive illegal immigration from Mexico and Central America became a major political issue—the focus of a national debate between those who wanted to force undocumented workers to go home and those who wanted to reduce the flow but also provide access to citizenship for those already in the United States.

In the past, efforts to control illegal immigration have been limited and ineffectual, partly because undocumented workers serve the economy as a source of low-wage labor, especially in agriculture and domestic service. It remains to be seen whether this need will be filled in the future by continued illegal immigration or by some kind of guest worker program to meet the economy's persistent demand for more unskilled workers than the native-born population can readily provide. America will remain the "nation of immigrants" it has always been, and some Americans will inevitably be uneasy about the ethnic diversity that results.

failed to become the major opposition party to the Democrats in the North. The most persuasive explanation is that their Free-Soil Republican rivals, who were seeking to build a party committed to the containment of slavery, had an issue with wider appeal.

Kansas and the Rise of the Republicans

The new **Republican party** was an outgrowth of the anti-Nebraska sentiment of 1854. The Republican name was first used in midwestern states to attract Free-Soil Democrats who refused to march under the Whig banner or support any candidate for high office who called himself a Whig.

nativism Term used by historians to describe attitudes, actions, and policies that favor native populations over immigrants.

Republican party Political party established following the enactment of the Kansas-Nebraska Act in 1854. Republicans were opposed to the extension of slavery into the western territories.

When the Know-Nothing party split over the Kansas-Nebraska issue in 1856, most of the northern nativists went over to the Republicans. Although Republicans were more concerned with "the slave power conspiracy" than any alleged "popish plot," nativists did not have to abandon their religious prejudices; the party had the distinct flavor of evangelical Protestantism. On the local level, Republicans sometimes supported causes that reflected an anti-immigrant or anti-Catholic bias, such as defense of Protestant Bible reading in schools and opposition to state aid for parochial education.

Unlike the Know-Nothings, the Republican party was led by seasoned professional politicians, men who had earlier been prominent Whigs or Democrats. Good organizers, they built up an effective party apparatus in an amazingly short time. By early 1856, the new party was well established throughout the North and was preparing to make a serious bid for the presidency.

Underlying the rapid growth of the Republican party was the strong and growing appeal of its position on slavery in the territories. Republicans viewed the unsettled West as a land of opportunities, a place to which the ambitious and hardworking could migrate in the hope of improving their social and economic position. But if slavery were permitted to expand, the rights of "free labor" would be denied. Republicans emphasized that slave labor was unfair competition and retarded the commercial and industrial development of a region. They envisioned a West that was free and white.

Although passage of the Kansas-Nebraska Act raised the territorial issues and gave birth to the Republican party, it was the turmoil associated with attempts to implement popular sovereignty in Kansas that kept the issue alive and enabled the Republicans to increase their following throughout the North. In Kansas, a bitter and violent contest for control of the territorial government was waged between transplanted New Englanders and Midwesterners, who were militantly Free-Soil, and slaveholding settlers from the neighboring state of Missouri. Joining the slaveholders were proslavery residents of Missouri who crossed over the border to vote illegally in territorial elections. In the first territorial election, slavery was wholeheartedly endorsed.

Settlers favoring free soil were already a majority of the actual residents of the territory when the fraudulently elected legislature denied them the right to agitate against slavery. To defend themselves and their convictions, they took up arms and established a rival territorial government under a constitution that outlawed slavery.

A small-scale civil war then broke out between the two regimes, culminating in May 1856 when proslavery adherents raided the free-state capital at Lawrence. Portrayed in Republican propaganda as the "sack of Lawrence," the incursion resulted in substantial property damage but no loss of life. In reprisal, antislavery zealot John Brown and several followers murdered five proslavery settlers in cold blood. During the next few months, a hit-and-run guerrilla war raged between free-state and slave-state factions.

The national Republican press had a field day with the events in Kansas, exaggerating the extent of the violence but correctly pointing out that the Pierce administration was favoring rule by a proslavery minority over a Free-Soil majority. Because the "sack of Lawrence" occurred at about the same time that Charles Sumner was assaulted on the Senate floor, the Republicans launched their 1856 campaign under the twin slogans, "Bleeding Kansas and Bleeding Sumner." The image of an evil and aggressive "slave power" South proved a potent device for arousing northern sympathies and winning votes.

Sectional Division in the Election of 1856

The Republican nominating convention displayed the strictly sectional nature of the new party. With no delegates from the Deep South in attendance, the

Republicans called for a congressional prohibition of slavery in all territories. The nominee was John C. Frémont, the western explorer who had helped win California during the Mexican War.

The Democratic party nominated James Buchanan of Pennsylvania, who had a long career in public service. Their platform endorsed popular sovereignty. The American party, a Know-Nothing remnant that survived mainly as the rallying point for anti-Democratic conservatives in the border states and parts of the South, chose ex-President Millard Fillmore as its standard-bearer and received the backing of northern Whigs who hoped to revive the tradition of sectional compromise.

The election was really two separate races—one in the North between Frémont and Buchanan and the other in the South between Fillmore and Buchanan. With strong southern support and victories in four crucial northern states, Buchanan won. But the Republicans did remarkably well for a party that was scarcely a year old. Frémont swept the upper North with substantial majorities and won a larger proportion of the northern popular vote than either of his opponents. Since the free states had a substantial majority in the electoral college, a future Republican candidate could attain the presidency simply by overcoming a narrow Democratic margin in the lower North.

In the South, the results of the election brought a momentary sense of relief tinged with anxiety about the future. For Southerners, the very existence of a sectional party committed to restricting the expansion of slavery constituted an insult to their way of life. They felt threatened. Only the continued success of a unified Democratic party under southern influence or control could maintain sectional balance and "southern rights."

THE HOUSE DIVIDED, 1857–1860

The sectional quarrel deepened and became virtually irreconcilable in the years between the elections of 1856 and 1860. A series of incidents provoked one side or the other, heightened the tension, and ultimately brought the crisis to a head. Behind the panicky reaction to public events lay a growing sense that the North and South were so different in culture and so opposed in basic interests that they could no longer coexist in the same nation.

Cultural Sectionalism

Signs of cultural and intellectual cleavage had appeared well before the triumph of sectional politics. As early as the mid-1840s, the slavery issue split the Baptist and Methodist churches into northern and southern wings. Instead of unifying Americans around a common Protestant faith, the churches became nurseries of sectional discord. Increasingly, northern preachers and congregations denounced slaveholding as a sin, while most southern church leaders rallied to a biblical defense of the peculiar institution and became influential apologists for the southern way of life. In both the North and the South, ministers turned political questions into moral issues, reducing the prospects for compromise.

American literature also became sectionalized during the 1840s and 1850s. Southern men of letters such as William Gilmore Simms and Edgar Allan Poe wrote proslavery polemics, and lesser writers penned novels that seemed to glorify southern civilization at the expense of northern society. In the North, prominent men of letters, including Ralph Waldo Emerson and Henry David Thoreau, expressed strong antislavery sentiments in prose and poetry.

Literary abolitionism reached a climax in 1852 when Harriet Beecher Stowe published *Uncle Tom's Cabin,* a novel that sold more than 300,000 copies in a single year and fixed in the northern mind the image of the slaveholder as the brutal

A Look at the Past

Poster for *Uncle Tom's Cabin*

Three hundred thousand Americans purchased *Uncle Tom's Cabin* in 1852, the year this poster appeared. While the poster might not have caused the sales, its design certainly appealed to middle-class readers. ✻ How does the scene depicted capture the ideal of domesticity? How does that ideal compare to the reality of slave life? Why would the scene appeal to middle-class Americans?

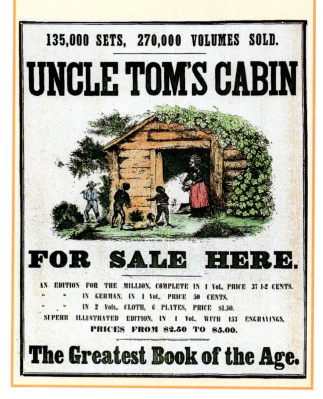

135,000 SETS, 270,000 VOLUMES SOLD.

UNCLE TOM'S CABIN

FOR SALE HERE.

AN EDITION FOR THE MILLION, COMPLETE IN 1 Vol. PRICE 37 1-2 CENTS.
"　"　IN GERMAN, IN 1 Vol., PRICE 50 CENTS.
"　"　IN 2 Vols., CLOTH, 6 PLATES, PRICE $1.50.
SUPERB ILLUSTRATED EDITION, IN 1 Vol., WITH 153 ENGRAVINGS.
PRICES FROM $2.50 TO $5.00.

The Greatest Book of the Age.

Simon Legree. Much of its emotional impact came from the book's portrayal of slavery as a threat to the family and the Cult of Domesticity. When the saintly Uncle Tom was sold away from his adoring wife and children, Northerners shuddered with horror and more than a few Southerners felt a painful twinge of conscience.

Southern defensiveness gradually hardened into cultural and economic nationalism. Southerners encouraged the use of proslavery textbooks, induced young men of the planter class to stay in the South for higher education, and sought to develop their own industry and commerce. Almost without exception, prominent southern educators and intellectuals of the late 1850s rallied behind the idea of an independent southern nation.

The Dred Scott Case

When James Buchanan was inaugurated on March 7, 1857, the dispute over the legal status of slavery in the territories was an open door through which sectional fears and hatreds could enter the political arena. Buchanan hoped to close that door by encouraging the Supreme Court to render a broad decision that would resolve the constitutional issue once and for all.

The Court was then about to render its decision in the case of *Dred Scott* v. *Sandford*. The case involved a Missouri slave who sued for his freedom on the grounds that he had lived for many years in an area where slavery had been outlawed by the Missouri Compromise. The Court, headed by Chief Justice Roger B. Taney, made several rulings in the case. First, it held that a slave was not a citizen and therefore had no right to sue in federal courts. Second, and more important for the general issue of slavery, the Court ruled that even if Scott had been a legitimate plaintiff, he would not have won his case. His residence in the Wisconsin Territory established no right to freedom because Congress had no power to prohibit slavery there. The Missouri Compromise was thus declared unconstitutional—and so, implicitly, was popular sovereignty, the main plank in the Republican platform.

In the North, especially among Republicans, the Court's verdict was viewed as the latest diabolical act of the "slave power conspiracy." Five of the six justices who voted in the majority, Northerners argued, were proslavery Southerners. Furthermore, the fact that Buchanan had played a role in the decision was widely known, and it was suspected that he had conspired with the justices in response to pressure from the prosouthern wing of the Democratic party.

Republicans denounced the decision as "a wicked and false judgment" and as "the greatest crime in the annals of the republic," but they stopped short of openly defying the Court's authority. Instead, they argued on narrow technical grounds that the decision as written was not binding on Congress and that a ban on slavery in the territories could still be enacted. The decision actually helped the Republicans build support because it lent credence to their claim that an aggressive slave power was dominating all branches of the federal government and attempting to use the Constitution to achieve its own ends.

The Lecompton Controversy

While the Dred Scott case was being decided, leaders of the proslavery faction in Kansas concluded that the time was ripe to draft a constitution and seek admission to the Union as a slave state. Since settlers with free-state views were now an overwhelming majority in the territory, the success of the plan required a rigged, gerrymandered election for convention delegates. When it became clear that the election was fixed, the free-staters boycotted it. The resulting constitution, drawn up at Lecompton, was certain to be rejected by Congress if a fairer election were not held.

To resolve the issue, supporters of the **Lecompton constitution** decided to permit a vote on the slavery provision alone, giving the electorate the narrow choice of allowing or forbidding the future importation of slaves. Since there was no way to vote for total abolition, the free-state majority again resorted to boycott, thus allowing ratification of a constitution that protected existing slave property and placed no restriction on importations. In a second referendum, proposed by the free-staters and boycotted by the proslavery forces, the Lecompton constitution was overwhelmingly rejected.

The Lecompton constitution was such an obvious perversion of popular sovereignty that Stephen Douglas spoke out against it. But the Buchanan administration tried to push it through Congress in early 1858. The resulting debate was bitter and sometimes violent. The bill to admit Kansas into the Union as a slave state passed the Senate but was defeated in the House.

The Lecompton controversy seriously aggravated the sectional quarrel and made it truly irreconcilable. The issue strengthened Republicans' belief that the Democratic party was dominated by Southerners, and at the same time it split the Democratic party between the followers of Douglas and the backers of Buchanan.

For Douglas, the affair was a disaster; it destroyed his hopes of uniting the Democratic party and defusing the slavery issue through the application of popular sovereignty. In practice, popular sovereignty was an invitation to civil war. Furthermore, the Dred Scott decision protected Southerners' rights to own human property in federal territories. For his stand against Lecompton, Douglas was denounced as a traitor in the South, and his hopes of being elected president were greatly diminished.

Lecompton constitution In 1857, a fraudulently elected group of pro-slavery delegates met in Lecompton, Kansas, and drafted a state constitution. After bitter debate, Congress narrowly denied Kansas' entry into the Union under this constitution.

Debating the Morality of Slavery

Douglas's more immediate problem was to win re-election to the Senate from Illinois in 1858. He faced surprisingly tough opposition from the Republican candidate, Abraham Lincoln, who set out to convince the voters that Douglas could not be relied on consistently to oppose the extension of slavery.

In the famous speech that opened his campaign, Lincoln tried to distance himself from his opponent by taking a more radical position. "'A house divided against itself cannot stand,'" he argued, paraphrasing a line from the Gospel of Mark. "I believe this government cannot endure, permanently half *slave* and half *free*." He then described the chain of events between the Kansas-Nebraska Act and the Dred Scott decision as evidence of a plot to extend slavery, and he tried to link Douglas to that proslavery conspiracy by pointing to his rival's unwillingness to take a stand on the morality of slavery. Lincoln demanded that slavery be considered a moral, and not simply a political, issue.

In the subsequent series of debates that focused national attention on the Illinois senatorial contest, Lincoln hammered away at the theme that Douglas was a covert defender of slavery because he was not a principled opponent of it. Douglas responded by accusing Lincoln of endangering the Union by his talk of putting slavery on the path to extinction. Lincoln denied that he was an abolitionist but readily admitted that he, like the Founders, opposed any extension of slavery.

In the debate at Freeport, Illinois, Lincoln questioned Douglas on how he could reconcile popular sovereignty with the Dred Scott decision. Douglas responded that slavery could not exist without supportive legislation to sustain it and that territorial legislatures could simply refrain from passing a slave code if they wanted to keep it out. Coupled with his anti-Lecompton stand, Douglas's "Freeport Doctrine" hardened southern opposition to his presidential ambitions.

Douglas's most effective debating point was to charge that Lincoln's moral opposition to slavery implied a belief in racial equality. Lincoln, facing an intensely racist electorate, vigorously denied this charge and affirmed his commitment to white supremacy. He would grant blacks the right to the fruits of their own labor while denying them the "privileges" of full citizenship. This was an inherently contradictory position, and Douglas made the most of it.

Although Republican candidates for the state legislature won a majority of the popular votes, the Democrats carried more counties and thus were able to send Douglas back to the Senate. Lincoln lost an office, but he won respect in Republican circles throughout the country. By stressing the moral dimension of the slavery question and undercutting any possibility of fusion between Republicans and Douglas Democrats, he had sharpened his party's ideological focus and had stiffened its backbone against any temptation to compromise the Free-Soil position.

The South's Crisis of Fear

After Kansas became a free territory instead of a slave state in August 1858, slavery in the territories became a symbolic issue rather than a practical and substantive one. The remaining unorganized areas in the Rockies and northern Great Plains were unlikely to attract slaveholding settlers. Nevertheless, Southerners continued to demand the "right" to take their slaves into territories, and Republicans persisted in denying it to them. Although they repeatedly promised not to interfere with slavery where it already existed, the Republicans did not gain the trust of the Southerners, who interpreted the Republicans' unyielding stand against the extension of slavery as a threat to southern rights and security.

A chain of events in late 1859 and early 1860 turned southern anxiety about northern attitudes and policies into a "crisis of fear." The first incident was John Brown's raid on Harpers Ferry, Virginia, in October 1859. Brown was a fervent abolitionist with the appearance of an Old Testament prophet. He believed he was God's chosen instrument "to purge this land with blood" and eradicate the sin of slaveholding. On October 16, he led a small band of men across the Potomac River from his base in Maryland and seized the federal arsenal and armory in Harpers Ferry.

Brown's aim was to commence a guerrilla war from havens in the Appalachians that would eventually extend to the plantation regions of the lower South. But the neighboring slaves did not rise up to join him, and his plan failed. In the fight with U.S. marines that followed, ten of Brown's men were killed or mortally wounded, along with seven of the townspeople and soldiers who opposed them.

The wounded Brown and his remaining followers were put on trial for treason against the state of Virginia. The subsequent investigation produced evidence that several prominent northern abolitionists had approved of Brown's plan and had raised money for his preparations. This revelation seemed to confirm southern fears that abolitionists were actively engaged in fomenting slave insurrection. Southerners were further stunned by the outpouring of sympathy and admiration for Brown in the North. His actual execution on December 2 completed Brown's elevation to the status of martyred saint of the antislavery cause.

Although Republican politicians were quick to denounce John Brown for his violent methods, Southerners interpreted the wave of northern sympathy as an expression of the majority opinion and the Republicans' "real" attitude. In the south-

■ *This painting,* The Last Moments of John Brown, *celebrates the passionate abolitionist as a hero and martyr to the antislavery cause. In his last speech to the court before his execution for conviction of murder, promoting slave insurrection, and treason, Brown proclaimed, "Now, if it is deemed necessary that I should forfeit my life for the furtherance of the ends of justice and mingle my blood further with the blood of my children and with the blood of millions in this slave country whose rights are disregarded by wicked, cruel, and unjust enactments—I say let it be done!"* ■

ern mind, abolitionists, Republicans, and Northerners were taking on one face. Within the South, the raid and its aftermath touched off a frenzy of fear. Southerners became increasingly vigilant for any sign of attack on their way of life, from without or from within.

Brown was scarcely in his grave when another set of events put southern nerves on edge. Next to abolitionist-abetted rebellions, the slaveholding South's greatest fear was that the nonslaveholding majority would turn against the master class and that the solidarity of southern whites would crumble. Hinton Rowan Helper's book *The Impending Crisis of the South,* which beseeched lower-class whites to resist planter dominance and abolish slavery in their own interest, was regarded by slaveholders as being even more seditious than *Uncle Tom's Cabin.* They feared the spread of "Helperism" among poor whites almost as much as the effect of "John Brownism" on the slaves.

The Republican candidate for speaker of the U.S. House of Representatives, John Sherman of Ohio, had endorsed Helper's book as a campaign document. Southern congressmen threatened secession if Sherman was elected, and feelings became so heated that some House members began to carry weapons on the floor of the chamber. A more moderate Republican was elected, and the impasse over the speakership was resolved, but the contest helped persuade Southerners that the Republicans were committed to stirring up class conflict among southern whites. The identification of Republicans with Helper's ideas may have been decisive in convincing many conservative planters that a Republican president in 1860 would be intolerable.

The Election of 1860

The Republicans, sniffing victory and generally unaware of the depth of southern feeling against them, met in Chicago on May 16 to nominate a presidential candidate. The initial front-runner, Senator William H. Seward of New York, proved unacceptable because of his reputation for radicalism and his long record of strong opposition to the nativist movement. Most delegates wanted a less controversial nominee who could win two or three of the northern states that had been in the Democratic column in 1856. Abraham Lincoln met their specifications: he was considered more moderate than Seward and had kept his personal distaste for Know-Nothingism to himself. In addition, his rise to prominence from humble beginnings embodied the Republican ideal of equal opportunity for all.

■ *In this cartoon from the 1860 election, candidates Lincoln and Douglas struggle for control of the country, while Breckinridge tears away the South. John Bell of the Constitutional Union party futilely attempts to repair the damage to the torn nation.* ■

The platform, like the nominee, was meant to broaden the party's appeal in the North. Although a commitment to halt the expansion of slavery remained, economic matters received more attention than they had in 1856. The platform called for a high protective tariff, free homesteads, and federal aid for internal improvements. The platform was cleverly designed to bring most ex-Whigs into the Republican camp while also accommodating enough renegade Democrats to give the party a solid majority in the northern states.

The Democrats failed to present a united front against this formidable challenge. When the party first met in the sweltering heat of Charleston in late April, Douglas was unable to win the nomination because of southern opposition. He did succeed in getting the convention to endorse popular sovereignty as its slavery platform, but the price was a walkout by southern delegates who favored a federal slave code for the territories.

Unable to agree on a nominee, the convention adjourned to reconvene in Baltimore in June. When the pro-Douglas force won most of the contested seats, another and more massive southern walkout took place. The result was a fracture of the Democratic party. The delegates who remained nominated Douglas, reaffirming their commitment to popular sovereignty; the southern bolters convened elsewhere to nominate John Breckinridge of Kentucky on a platform pledging federal protection of slavery in the territories.

By the time the campaign got under way, four parties were running presidential candidates. In addition to the Republicans, the Douglas Democrats, and the "Southern Rights" Democrats, a remnant of conservative Whigs and Know-Nothings nominated John Bell of Tennessee under the banner of the Constitutional Union party. Taking no explicit stand on slavery in the territories, Bell and his backers tried to represent the spirit of sectional compromise. In effect, the race became separate two-party contests in each section: in the North, the real choice was between Lincoln and Douglas, and in the South, the only candidates with a fighting chance were Breckinridge and Bell.

When the results came in, the Republicans had achieved a stunning victory. By gaining the electoral votes of all the free states except a fraction of New Jersey's, Lincoln won a decisive majority. The Republican strategy of seeking power by trying to win the majority section was brilliantly successful. Fewer than 40 percent of Americans who went to the polls actually voted for Lincoln, but his support in the North was so solid that he would have won in the electoral college even if all three opposing parties had been unified behind a single candidate.

Most Southerners saw the results of the election as a catastrophe. A candidate and a party with no support in their own section had won the presidency on a platform viewed as insulting to southern honor and hostile to vital southern interests. For the first time in history, southern interests were in no way represented in the White House. Rather than accept permanent minority status in American politics and face the threat to black slavery and white "liberty" that was bound to follow, the political leaders of the lower South launched a movement for immediate secession from the Union.

CONCLUSION: EXPLAINING THE CRISIS

Generations of historians have searched for the underlying causes of the crisis leading to the disruption of the Union but have failed to agree on an answer. Some have stressed the clash of economic interests between agrarian and industrializing nations. But this interpretation does not reflect the way people at the time expressed their concerns. The main issues in the sectional debates of the 1850s were whether slavery was right or wrong and whether it should be extended or contained. In the face of these issues, all economic considerations pale. Indeed, there was no necessity for the producers of raw materials to go to war with the people who marketed and processed them.

Another group of historians have blamed the crisis on "irresponsible" politicians and agitators on both sides of the debate. Public opinion, they argue, was whipped into a frenzy over issues that competent statesmen could have resolved. But this viewpoint has been sharply criticized for failing to acknowledge the depths of feeling that could be aroused by the slavery question and for underestimating the obstacles to a peaceful solution.

The dominant modern view is that the crisis was rooted in profound ideological differences over the morality and utility of slavery as an institution. Most

Chronology

1846	David Wilmot introduces a proviso banning slavery in the Mexican cession
1848	Free-Soil party is founded ■ Zachary Taylor (Whig) is elected president, defeating Lewis Cass (Democrat) and Martin Van Buren (Free-Soil)
1849	California seeks admission to the Union as a free state
1850	Congress debates sectional issues and enacts the Compromise of 1850
1852	Harriet Beecher Stowe publishes *Uncle Tom's Cabin* ■ Franklin Pierce (Democrat) is elected president by a large majority over Winfield Scott (Whig)
1854	Congress passes Kansas-Nebraska Act, repealing the Missouri Compromise ■ Republican party is founded in several northern states ■ Anti-Nebraska coalitions score victories in congressional elections in the North
1854–1855	Know-Nothing party achieves stunning successes in state politics
1854–1856	Free-state and slave-state forces struggle for control of Kansas Territory
1856	Preston Brooks assaults Charles Sumner on the Senate floor ■ James Buchanan (Democrat) wins the presidency despite a strong challenge in the North from John C. Frémont (Republican)
1857	Supreme Court decides the Dred Scott case legalizing slavery in all territories
1858	Congress refuses to admit Kansas to the Union under the proslavery Lecompton constitution ■ Lincoln and Douglas debate
1859	John Brown raids Harpers Ferry, is captured and executed
1859–1860	Fierce struggle takes place over election of a Republican as speaker of the House
1860	Republicans nominate Abraham Lincoln for the presidency ■ Democratic party splits into northern and southern factions with separate candidates and platforms ■ Lincoln wins the presidency over Douglas (northern Democrat), Breckinridge (southern Democrat), and Bell (Constitutional Unionist)

interpreters are now agreed that the conflict stemmed from the fact that the South was a slave society and was determined to stay that way, while the North was equally committed to a free-labor system. It is hard to imagine that secessionism would have developed if the South had followed the North's example and abolished slavery in the postrevolutionary period.

Nevertheless, the existence or nonexistence of slavery will not explain why the crisis came when it did and in the way that it did. Why did the conflict become "irreconcilable" in the 1850s and not earlier or later? Why did it take the form of a political struggle over the future of slavery in the territories? Adequate answers to both questions require an understanding of political developments that were not directly caused by tensions over slavery.

By the 1850s, the established Whig and Democratic parties were in trouble because they no longer offered the voters clear-cut alternatives on the economic issues that had been the bread and butter of politics during the heyday of the second party system. This situation created an opening for new parties and issues. The Republicans used the issue of slavery in the territories to build the first successful sectional party in American history. They called for "free soil" rather than freedom for blacks because abolitionism conflicted with the northern majority's commitment to white supremacy and its respect for the original constitutional compromise that established a hands-off policy toward slavery in the southern states.

If politicians seeking new ways to mobilize an apathetic electorate are seen as the main instigators of sectional crisis, the reason why certain appeals were more effective than others must still be explained. Why did the slavery extension issue arouse such strong feelings in the two sections during the 1850s? After all, the same issues had arisen earlier and had proved adjustable.

Ultimately, therefore, the crisis of the 1850s must be understood as social and cultural as well as political. Basic beliefs and values had diverged significantly in the North and the South between 1820 and the 1850s. In the free states, the rise of reform-minded evangelicalism had given a new sense of moral direction and purpose to a rising middle class adapting to the new market economy (see Chapter 12). At the same time, in much of the South, the slave plantation system prospered, and the notion that white liberty and equality depended on having enslaved blacks to do menial labor became more deeply entrenched.

When politicians appealed to sectionalism during the 1850s, therefore, they could evoke conflicting views of what constituted a good society. To most Northerners, the South—with its allegedly idle masters, degraded unfree workers, and shiftless poor whites—seemed in flagrant violation of the Protestant work ethic and the ideal of open competition. From the dominant southern point of view, the North was a land of hypocritical money-grubbers who denied the obvious fact that the dependent laboring classes—especially racially inferior ones—had to be kept under the kind of rigid control that only slavery could provide. Once these contrary views of the world had become the main themes of political discourse, sectional compromise was no longer possible.

Key Terms

Wilmot Proviso, p. 267
popular sovereignty, p. 267
Free-Soil party, p. 267
Compromise of 1850, p. 268

Fugitive Slave Law, p. 268
Kansas-Nebraska Act, p. 271
Ostend Manifesto, p. 272
Know-Nothing party, p. 272

nativism, p. 273
Republican party, p. 273
Lecompton constitution, p. 277

RECOMMENDED READING

The best general account of the politics of the section crisis is David M. Potter, *The Impending Crisis, 1848–1861* (1976). This well-written and authoritative work combines a vivid and detailed narrative of events with a shrewd and detailed interpretation of them. For a shorter overview, see Bruce C. Levine, *Half Slave and Half Free: The Roots of the Civil War* (1991). On the demise of the Whigs, see Michael F. Holt, *The Rise and Fall of the American Whig Party* (1999). The best treatment of the Know-Nothing movement is Tyler Anbinder, *Nativism and Slavery: The Northern Know-Nothings and the Politics of the 1850s* (1992). The most important studies of northern political sectionalism are Eric Foner, *Free Soil, Free Labor, Free Men: The Ideology of the Republican Party Before the Civil War* (1970), and William E. Gienapp, *The Origins of the Republican Party, 1852–1856*

(1987), on the Republican party generally; and Don E. Fehrenbacher, *Prelude to Greatness: Lincoln in the 1850s* (1962) on Lincoln's rise to prominence. On the climactic events of 1857, see Don E. Fehrenbacher, *The Dred Scott Case: Its Significance in American Law and Politics* (1978), and Kenneth M. Stampp, *America in 1857: A Nation on the Brink* (1990). On the constitutional context, see Don E. Fehrenbacher, *The Slaveholding Republic: An Account of the United States Government's Relations to Slavery* (2001). The sectional issue in politics is covered by Sean Wilentz, *The Rise of American Democracy: Jefferson to Lincoln* (2006). On the background of southern separatism, see William W. Freehling, *The Road to Disunion: Secessionists at Bay, 1776–1854* (1990), and William L. Barney, *The Road to Secession: A New Perspective on the Old South* (1972).

SUGGESTED WEB SITES

Secession Era Editorials Project
history.furman.edu/~benson/docs/
Furman University is digitizing editorials about the secession crisis and already includes scores of them on this site.

John Brown Trial Links
www.law.umkc.edu/faculty/projects/ftrials/Brown.html
This site provides a list of excellent links to information about the trial of John Brown.

Abraham Lincoln and Slavery
odur.let.rug.nl/~usa/H/1990/ch5_p6.htm
This site discusses Lincoln's views and actions concerning slavery, especially the Lincoln-Douglas debates.

Bleeding Kansas
www.Kancoll.org/galbks.htm
Contemporary and later accounts of America's rehearsal for the Civil War comprise this Kansas Collection site.

The Compromise of 1850 and the Fugitive Slave Act
www.pbs.org/wgbh/aia/part4/4p2951.html
From the series on Africans in America, an analysis of the Compromise of 1850 and of the effects of the Fugitive Slave Act on black Americans.

Words and Deeds in American History
lcweb2.loc.gov/ammem/mcchtml/corhome.html
A Library of Congress site containing links to Frederick Douglass, the Compromise of 1850, speeches by John C. Calhoun, Daniel Webster, and Henry Clay, and other topics from the Civil War era.

The Irish in Boston, 1845–1865

For the city of Boston, the period between 1845 and 1865 was an era of great change. Events half a world away rudely plucked more than fifty thousand Irish Catholic peasants from their homeland and transplanted them to a city that had hitherto been a homogeneous bastion of old-stock New England Puritanism. Some Bostonians viewed the mass of poor immigrants as an urban calamity. But the "invasion" was also a blessing, reinvigorating Boston with a substantial—and inimitable—Irish American contribution to its social, economic, and political life.

The Irish came to America because they had no other choice. By the early nineteenth century, large landowners on the "isle of wondrous beauty"—mainly of English descent—were masters over impoverished tenant farmers who had been forced by their wretched circumstances to live on a diet consisting mostly of potatoes. When a blight caused the potato crop to rot in the mid-1840s, Ireland entered a period known as the Great Hunger. During this "state of social decomposition" between 1845 and 1851, the only alternative to starvation for most Irish peasants was emigration. One million people emigrated and another million died of starvation or disease.

The immigrants disembarked at the large northeastern seaboard cities. Although the newcomers were of rural origins, they were too poor and sick to continue westward to America's rich agricultural regions; they settled where they were dropped. Boston's population nearly doubled, growing from 93,000 to 177,000 between 1840 and 1860. In part, the increase reflected the movement of a burgeoning native population from the country to the cities, but mainly it was the product of Ireland's Great Hunger.

Penniless and unskilled, the immigrants crowded into old buildings and warehouses that Boston's Yankees had abandoned—dark, unheated, unventilated, and unsanitary tenements. But as a social worker observed of the people living in Boston's Irish ghettos, "The Hibernian is first, last, and always a social being." In Ireland, poor tenant farmers had found comfort in lively conversation, sometimes made even more spirited by a convivial round of distilled refreshment, and nothing the immigrants found in Boston altered these customs. Talk came naturally to the Irish. They talked in the streets, in the shops, in the churches, in their homes—and in their saloons.

For men, by far the most popular locus of sociability was the corner saloon—where it was said a working man could not die of thirst. The Irish bar in Boston was devoid of frills. It featured wooden chairs, a long wooden bar with brass railings, card tables, sawdust-covered floors, and a philosophical bartender, who extended beer, whiskey, credit, and advice, in roughly equal doses. Irishmen sang, told stories, talked politics, or reminisced about the green fields and deep blue lakes of the Emerald Isle. In 1846, there were 850 liquor dealers in Boston, but by 1850 fully 1,500 saloons catered to the residents of the changing city.

Fortunately for Boston's capitalists and large-scale entrepreneurs, the most immediate need of the immigrants was employment—of any kind. At first the newcomers, who had been peasants in the "Ould Country," became street or yard laborers, but as it became apparent that the Irish were a potential pool of long-term proletarians—a large supply of workers who would remain in the least desirable jobs for low pay—capitalists responded by accelerating the Industrial Revolution in the Boston area. The number of industrial employees in Boston doubled in the decade of 1845–1855, and doubled again in the following decade. Moreover, Irish immigrants replaced much of the labor force from the early industrial era, especially in the textile mills of Boston's outlying suburbs. Irishmen were willing to work for lower wages than those paid to "mill girls," and were not so insistent on decent working conditions.

Although reluctant to work outside the home for wages, married Irish American women—who were usually raising a large family—often found themselves taking in lodgers, sewing at home for piece work rates on men's shirts and women's millinery, and doing other people's laundry. Their lot was frequently made more difficult by the long absences of their "railroading" husbands (Irishmen contracted out for months at a time to build and lay rails).

A large proportion of the Great Hunger immigrants from Ireland were unmarried women who, like their male counterparts, were desperate for employment. These Irishwomen relieved an acute shortage of domestics in New England. Few native-born American women would do household work for pay, not only because the job carried the stigma of servanthood, but also because New Englanders were not willing to pay good wages for what was sometimes a 24-hour responsibility. Many maids and cooks suffered from "shattered health." But for the single Irish American woman, the life of a domestic was often the best of a narrow range of alternatives. "Living in" removed her from much of the

■ Large numbers of Irish immigrants initially crowded into the disease-ridden slums and shanties of places such as Boston's Burgess Alley. This illustration of the deplorable living quarters of many of the city's immigrants is from the Report of the Committee on Internal Health on the Asiatic Cholera, issued in 1849. ■

squalor and disease of tenement life. She usually had two afternoons a week for her own pursuits, and sometimes had the opportunity to take jaunts to seaside resorts on Cape Code with her employers.

Few of the first generation of Boston Irish escaped from the ranks of unskilled or semi-skilled labor. The discriminatory attitudes of Yankee employers contributed significantly to the relative lack of mobility. (Many good jobs were advertised with the qualification that "no Irish need apply.") But occupational mobility was also inhibited to some extent by the tendency of the Irish immigrants to place group security above individual advancement. They used strong communal activities and neighborhood organizations to their advantage in politics and union-building; success in local political clubs and the labor movement meant that Irish politicians and labor leaders in Boston channeled several generations of Irish Americans into secure but dead-end municipal and industrial jobs.

Although they were slow to rise out of the working class, the Irish energized the economy of Boston and soon won for themselves respect and power. They were the first large immigrant group to test the notion of America as a great melting pot. More than 150,000 Irish Americans served in the Civil War, eager to demonstrate their loyalty to their adopted country. By 1865 the Irish, through their persistent efforts, their skill at local organization, and their willingness to be Boston's reliable working class, had found a permanent place in America's most venerable Puritan stronghold.

Questions for Discussion

* Why did so many Irish immigrants come to the United States in the mid-nineteenth century?
* How did many native-born Americans view these immigrants?
* What impact did immigrant workers have on the economy of cities such as Boston?

Chapter 15

Secession and the Civil War

The Emergence of Lincoln

President Abraham Lincoln was striking in appearance—at 6 feet 4 inches in height, he seemed even taller because of his disproportionately long legs and his habit of wearing a high silk "stovepipe" hat. His career prior to taking up residence in the White House in 1860 was less remarkable than his person, however. A look at his previous experience certainly provided no guarantee that he would one day tower over most of our other presidents in more than physical height.

Born to poor and illiterate parents on the Kentucky frontier in 1809, Lincoln received a few months of formal schooling in Indiana after the family moved there in 1816. But mostly he educated himself, reading and rereading a few treasured books by firelight. In 1831, when the family migrated to Illinois, he left home to make a living for himself. After failing as a merchant, he found a path to success in law and politics. Lincoln combined exceptional political and legal skills with a down-to-earth, humorous way of addressing jurors and voters. He became a leader of the Whig party in Illinois and one of the most sought-after of the lawyers who rode the central Illinois judicial circuit.

The high point of his political career as a Whig was one term in Congress (1847–1849), but he alienated much of his constituency by opposing the Mexican-American War and wisely chose not to run for re-election. In 1848, he campaigned vigorously and effectively for Zachary Taylor, but the new president failed to appoint Lincoln to a patronage job he coveted. Disappointed by his political fortunes, Lincoln concentrated on building his law practice.

The Kansas-Nebraska Act of 1854, with its advocacy of popular sovereignty, provided Lincoln with an opportunity to reconcile his driving ambition for political success with his personal convictions. Lincoln had long believed that slavery was an unjust institution that should be tolerated only to the extent that the Constitution and the tradition of sectional compromise required. Attacking Stephen Douglas's plan on popular sovereignty, Lincoln threw in his lot with the Republicans and assumed leadership of the new party in Illinois. He attracted national attention in his bid for Douglas's Senate seat in 1858 and happened to have the right qualifications when the Republicans chose a presidential nominee in 1860.

After Lincoln's election provoked southern secession and plunged the nation into the greatest crisis in its history, there was understandable skepticism about him in many quarters. After all, the onetime rail-splitter from Illinois had never been a governor, senator, cabinet officer, or high-ranking military officer. But some of his training as a prairie politician would prove extremely useful in the years ahead.

Another reason for Lincoln's effectiveness as a war leader was that he identified wholeheartedly with the northern cause and could inspire others to make sacrifices for it. In his view, the issue in the conflict was nothing less than the survival of the kind of political system that gave men like himself a chance for high office. For Lincoln, a government had to be strong enough to maintain its own existence and guarantee equality of opportunity.

The Civil War tested America's ability to preserve its democratic form of government in the face of domestic foes. It put on trial the very principle of democracy at a time when most European nations had rejected political liberalism and accepted the view that popular government would inevitably collapse into anarchy. As Lincoln put it in the Gettysburg Address, the only cause great enough to justify the enormous sacrifice of life on the battlefields was the struggle to preserve the democratic ideal, to ensure that "government of the people, by the people, and for the people, shall not perish from the earth."

As he prepared to take office in 1861, Abraham Lincoln could scarcely anticipate the challenges he would face. The immediate problem was how to respond to the secession of the Deep South. But secession was just an expression of the larger question: Did the authority of the federal government outweigh the power of the individual states? No less important were questions about slavery: Was it morally acceptable for one person to "own" another? Could the Union continue to exist half-slave and half-free?

The sectionalism that had already led to a number of violent incidents—bloody fighting in Kansas, John Brown's raid on Harpers Ferry, Brown's conviction on charges of treason against Virginia, and his eventual execution—continued to mount. Finally irreconcilable differences erupted into total war that left no part of society—North or South—untouched.

THE STORM GATHERS

Lincoln's election provoked the secession of seven states of the Deep South but did not lead immediately to armed conflict. Before the sectional quarrel turned from a cold war into a hot one, two things had to happen. A final effort to defuse the conflict by compromise and conciliation had to fail, and the North needed to develop a firm resolve to maintain the Union by military action. Both of these developments may seem inevitable today, but for most Americans living at the time, it was not clear until the guns blazed at Fort Sumter that the sectional crisis would have to be resolved on the battlefield.

The Deep South Secedes

South Carolina, which had long been in the forefront of southern rights and proslavery agitation, was the first state to leave the Union, on December 20, 1860. The constitutional theory behind secession was that the Union was a "compact" among sovereign states, each of which could withdraw from the Union by a vote of a convention similar to the one that had ratified the Constitution in the first place. The South Carolinians justified seceding at this time by charging that "a sectional party" had elected a president hostile to slavery.

In other states of the cotton kingdom, there was similar outrage at Lincoln's election but less certainty about how to respond to it. Some Southerners, labeled **cooperationists,** believed that the South should respond as a unit, after holding a southern convention. South Carolina's unilateral action, however, set a precedent.

When conventions in six other states of the Deep South met during January 1861, delegates favoring immediate secession were everywhere in the majority. By February 1, seven states had removed themselves from the Union: South Carolina, Alabama, Mississippi, Florida, Georgia, Louisiana, and Texas. In the upper South, however, calls for immediate secession were unsuccessful; majority opinion in

cooperationists In late 1860, southern secessionists debated two strategies: unilateral secession by each state or "cooperative" secession by the South as a whole. The cooperationists lost the debate.

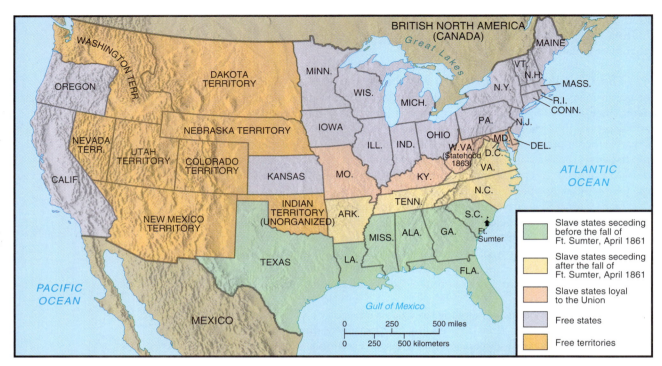

SECESSION *The fall of Fort Sumter was a watershed for the secessionist movement. With no room left for compromise, slave states of the Upper South chose to join the Confederacy.* ◼

Virginia, North Carolina, Tennessee, and Arkansas did not subscribe to the view that Lincoln's election was a sufficient reason for breaking up the Union.

Delegates from the Deep South met in Montgomery, Alabama, on February 4 to establish the Confederate States of America. Relatively moderate leaders dominated the proceedings and defeated or modified some of the pet schemes of a radical faction composed of extreme southern nationalists. Voted down were proposals to reopen the Atlantic slave trade, to count *all* slaves in determining congressional representation instead of three-fifths, and to prohibit the admission of free states to the new Confederacy.

The resulting provisional constitution was surprisingly similar to that of the United States. Most of the differences merely spelled out traditional southern interpretations of the federal charter. The central government was denied the authority to impose protective tariffs, subsidize internal improvements, or interfere with slavery in the states and was required to pass laws protecting slavery in the territories. As provisional president and vice president, the convention chose Jefferson Davis of Mississippi and Alexander Stephens of Georgia, men who had previously resisted secessionist agitation.

The moderation shown in Montgomery resulted in part from a desire to win support for the cause of secessionism in the reluctant states of the upper South. But it also revealed that proslavery reactionaries had never succeeded in getting a majority behind them. Most Southerners were staunchly proslavery but had been opposed to dissolving the Union and repudiating their traditional patriotic loyalties so long as there had been good reasons to believe that slavery was protected from northern interference.

The panic following Lincoln's election destroyed that sense of security. But it was clear from the actions of the Montgomery convention that the goal of the new converts to secessionism was not to establish a slaveholders' reactionary utopia. They only wished to recreate the Union that existed before the rise of the Republican party, and they opted for secession only when it seemed clear that separation was the only way to achieve their aim. Some optimists even predicted that all of the North except New England would eventually join the Confederacy.

Secession and the formation of the Confederacy thus amounted to a very conservative and defensive kind of "revolution." The only justification for southern independence on which a majority could agree was the need for greater security for slavery and the social relations that institution entailed.

The Failure of Compromise

While the Deep South was opting for independence, moderates in the North and the border slave states were trying to devise a compromise that would stem the secessionist tide before it could engulf the entire South. In Congress, Senator John Crittenden of Kentucky presented a plan that served as the focus for discussion. The proposed **Crittenden compromise** advocated extending the Missouri Compromise line to the Pacific to guarantee the protection of slavery in the southwestern territories. He also recommended a constitutional amendment that would forever prohibit the federal government from abolishing or regulating slavery in the states.

Initially, congressional Republicans showed some willingness to give ground and take these proposals seriously. However, Republican support quickly vanished when Lincoln sent word from Springfield that he was adamantly opposed to the extension of the compromise line. With Lincoln opposing the plan, Republicans voted against it in committee. When the senators and congressmen of the seceding states also voted against the plan, it was doomed to defeat.

Some historians have blamed Lincoln and the Republicans for causing unnecessary war by rejecting a compromise that would have appeased southern pride without providing any practical opportunity for the expansion of slavery. But it is quite possible that the secessionists, who wanted slavery protected in *all* territories, would not have been satisfied even if the Republicans had approved the plan.

Furthermore, Lincoln and his followers had what they considered very good reasons for not making territorial concessions. They mistakenly believed that secessionism reflected a minority opinion in the South and that a strong stand would win the support of southern Unionists and moderates. In addition, Lincoln took his stand on free soil seriously. He did not want to give slaveholders any chance to enlarge their domain.

Lincoln was also convinced that backing down in the face of secessionist threats would fatally undermine the democratic principle of majority rule. In his inaugural address of March 4, 1861, he recalled that during the winter, many "patriotic men" had urged him to accept a compromise that would "shift the ground" on which he had been elected. But to do so would have signified that a victorious presidential candidate "cannot be inaugurated till he betrays those who elected him by breaking his pledges, and surrendering to those who tried and failed to defeat him at the polls." Making such a concession would mean that "this government and all popular government is already at an end."

> **Crittenden compromise** Faced with the specter of secession and war, Congress tried and failed to resolve the sectional crisis in the months between Lincoln's election and inauguration. The leading proposal, introduced by Kentucky Senator John Crittenden, would have extended the Missouri Compromise line west to the Pacific.

And the War Came

By the time of Lincoln's inauguration, seven states had seceded, formed an independent republic, and seized most federal forts and other installations in the Deep South without firing a shot. Lincoln's predecessor, James Buchanan, rejected the right of secession but refused to use coercion to maintain federal authority. Many Northerners agreed with his stand.

The collapse of compromise efforts narrowed the choice to peaceful separation or war. By early March, the tide of public opinion was beginning to shift in favor of strong action to preserve the Union. Even in the business community, sentiment mounted in favor of a coercive policy.

In his inaugural address, Lincoln called for a cautious and limited use of force. He would defend federal forts and installations not yet in Confederate hands but would not attempt to recapture the ones already taken. He thus tried to shift the burden for beginning hostilities to the Confederacy. As Lincoln spoke, only four military installations within the seceded states were still held by United States forces. The most important and vulnerable of these installations was Fort Sumter, inside Charleston harbor. The Confederacy demanded the surrender of the garrison, and shortly after taking office, Lincoln was informed that Sumter could not hold out much longer without reinforcements and supplies.

After some initial indecision and opposition from his cabinet, Lincoln decided to reinforce the fort, and he so informed the governor of South Carolina on April 4. The Confederacy regarded the sending of provisions as a hostile act and began shelling the fort near dawn on April 12. After forty hours of bombardment, the commander of the Union forces surrendered, and the Confederate flag was raised over Fort Sumter. The South had won a victory but had also assumed responsibility for firing the first shot.

On April 15, Lincoln proclaimed that an insurrection existed in the Deep South and called on the militia of the loyal states to provide 75,000 troops for short-term service to put it down. Two days later, a Virginia convention voted to join the Confederacy. Within the next five weeks, Arkansas, Tennessee, and North Carolina followed suit. Lincoln's policy of coercion forced them to choose sides, and they opted to join the other slave states in the Confederacy.

■ *This contemporary Currier and Ives lithograph depicts the bombardment of Fort Sumter on April 12–13, 1861. The soldiers are firing from Fort Moultrie in Charleston Harbor, which the Union garrison had evacuated the previous December in order to strengthen Fort Sumter.* ■

In the North, the firing on Fort Sumter evoked strong feelings of patriotism and dedication to the Union. Like many other Northerners, Stephen Douglas, Lincoln's former political rival, pledged his full support for the crusade against secession and literally worked himself to death rallying midwestern Democrats behind the government. Everyone assumed that the war would be short and not very bloody. It remained to be seen whether Unionist fervor could be sustained through a long and costly struggle.

The entire Confederacy comprised only eleven of the fifteen states in which slavery was lawful. In the border slave states of Maryland, Delaware, Kentucky, and Missouri, a combination of local Unionism and federal intervention thwarted secession. By taking care to respect Kentucky's neutrality, using martial law ruthlessly in Maryland, and stationing regular troops in Missouri, Lincoln kept these crucial border states in the Union.

Hence the Civil War was not, strictly speaking, a struggle between slave and free states. More than anything else, conflicting views on the right of secession determined the ultimate division of states and the choices of individuals in areas where sentiment was divided. General Robert E. Lee, for example, was neither a defender of slavery nor a southern nationalist. But he followed Virginia out of the Union because he was the loyal son of a "sovereign state." Although concern about the future of slavery had driven the Deep South to secede in the first place, the war was seen less as a struggle over slavery than as a contest to determine whether the Union was indivisible.

ADJUSTING TO TOTAL WAR

The Civil War was a "total war" because the North could achieve its aim of restoring the Union only if the South was so thoroughly defeated that its separatist government was overthrown. It was a long war because the Confederacy put up "a hell of a fight" before it would agree to be put to death. A total war is a test of societies, economies, and political systems as well as a battle of wits between generals and military strategists.

Prospects, Plans, and Expectations

If the war was to be decided by sheer physical strength, the North had an enormous edge in population, industrial capacity, and railroad mileage. Nevertheless, the South also had some advantages. To achieve its aim of independence, the Confederacy needed only to defend its own territory successfully. The North, by contrast, had to invade and conquer the South. Consequently, the Confederacy faced a less serious supply problem, had a greater capacity to choose the time and place of combat, and could take advantage of familiar terrain and a sympathetic civilian population.

The nature of the war meant that southern leaders could define their cause as defense of their homeland against a Yankee invasion. It seemed doubtful in 1861 that Northerners would be willing to make an equal sacrifice for the relatively abstract principle that the Union was sacred and perpetual.

Confederate optimism on the eve of the war was also fed by more dubious calculations. It was widely assumed that Southerners, who were accustomed to riding and shooting, would make better soldiers than Yankees. When most of the large proportion of high-ranking officers in the U.S. Army who were of southern origin resigned to accept Confederate commands, Southerners confidently anticipated that their armies would be better led. Finally, Southerners assumed that if external help was needed, England and France would come to their aid because those nations depended on the importation of southern cotton.

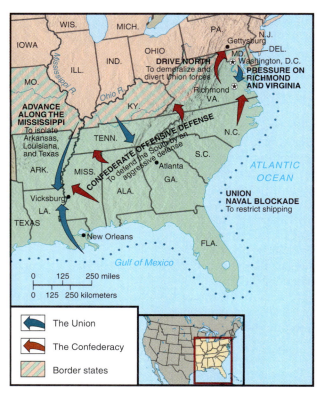

OVERVIEW OF CIVIL WAR STRATEGY *Confederate military leaders were convinced that the South could not be defended unless they took the initiative to determine where critical battles would be fought.* ■

anaconda policy A key point in the Union's war strategy was encircling the South as an anaconda squeezes its prey. This plan entailed a naval blockade and the capture of the Mississippi River corridor.

Both sides based their strategies on their advantages. The choice before President Davis, who assumed personal direction of the Confederate military effort, was whether to stay on the defensive or seek a sudden and dramatic victory by invading the North. He chose to wage an essentially defensive war in the hope that the North would soon tire of the blood and sacrifice and allow the Confederacy to go its own way.

Northern military planners had greater difficulty in working out a basic strategy, and it took a great deal of trial and error before there was a clear sense of what had to be done. Some optimists believed that the war could be won quickly and easily by sending an army to capture the Confederate capital of Richmond, scarcely 100 miles from Washington. The early battles in Virginia ended the casual optimism. Other Northerners favored a plan called the **anaconda policy.** Like a great boa constrictor, the North would squeeze the South into submission by blockading the southern coasts, seizing control of the Mississippi, and cutting off supplies of food and other essential commodities. This plan pointed to the West as the main focus of military operations.

Eventually, Lincoln decided on a two-front war. He would keep the pressure on Virginia while at the same time authorizing an advance down the Mississippi Valley. He also attached great importance to the coastal blockade and expected naval operations to seize the ports through which goods entered and left the Confederacy. His basic plan of applying pressure and probing for weaknesses at several points simultaneously was a good one because it took maximum advantage of the northern superiority in manpower and material. But it required better military leadership than the North possessed at the beginning of the war and took a painfully long time to put into effect.

Mobilizing the Home Fronts

The North and the South faced similar problems in trying to create the vast support systems needed by armies in the field. At the beginning of the conflict, both sides had more volunteers than could be armed and outfitted. But as hopes for a short and easy war faded, the pool of volunteers began to dry up. To resolve the problem, the Confederacy passed a conscription law in April 1862, and the Union edged toward a draft in July when Congress gave Lincoln the right to assign manpower quotas to each state and resort to conscription if they were not met.

To produce the materials of war, both governments relied mainly on private industry. In the North, especially, the system of contracting with private firms and individuals to support the army often resulted in corruption, inefficiency, and shoddy goods. But the North's economy was strong at the core, and by 1863, its factories and farms were producing more than enough to provision the troops without significantly lowering the living standards of the civilian population.

The southern economy was much less adaptable to the needs of total war. Dependent on the outside world for most of its manufactured goods before the war, the Union blockade forced the southern government to sponsor a crash program to produce its own war materials and to encourage private enterprise. Astonishingly, the Confederate Ordnance Bureau succeeded in producing or procuring sufficient armaments to keep southern armies well supplied throughout the conflict.

RESOURCES OF THE UNION AND THE CONFEDERACY, 1861

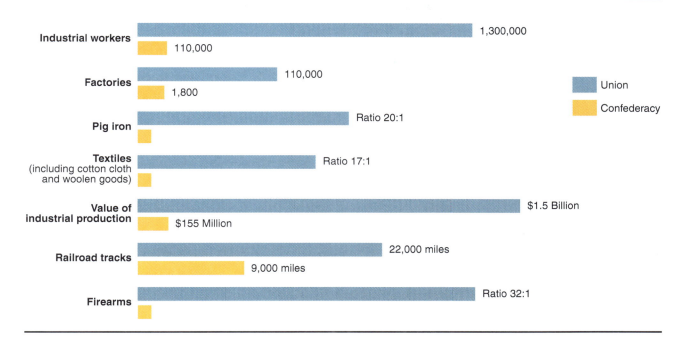

Industrial workers — Union 1,300,000; Confederacy 110,000
Factories — Union 110,000; Confederacy 1,800
Pig iron — Ratio 20:1
Textiles (including cotton cloth and woolen goods) — Ratio 17:1
Value of industrial production — Union $1.5 Billion; Confederacy $155 Million
Railroad tracks — Union 22,000 miles; Confederacy 9,000 miles
Firearms — Ratio 32:1

Legend: Union, Confederacy

Southern agriculture, however, failed to meet the challenge. Planters were reluctant to switch from cotton to foodstuffs, and the South's internal transportation system was inadequate. Its limited rail network was designed to link plantation regions to port cities rather than connect food-producing areas with centers of population. And when northern forces penetrated parts of the South, they created new gaps in the system. To supply the troops, the Confederate commissary resorted to impressment of agricultural produce, a policy so fiercely resisted by farmers and local politicians that it eventually had to be abandoned. By 1863, civilians in urban areas were rioting to protest food shortages.

Another challenge faced by both sides was how to finance an enormously costly struggle. Neither side was willing to resort to the heavy taxation that was needed to maintain fiscal integrity. Americans, it seems, were more willing to die for their government than to pay for it. Besides floating loans and selling bonds, both treasuries deliberately inflated the currency by printing large quantities of paper

A Look at the Past

Civil War Rations

Civil War soldiers depended on hardtack, a saltless hard biscuit, as a food staple. Quinine, a remedy for malaria, also represented an essential supply for soldiers. Together, these items testify to the hardships soldiers endured.

* If these were essential supplies, how common do you suppose were disease, hunger, and malnutrition?

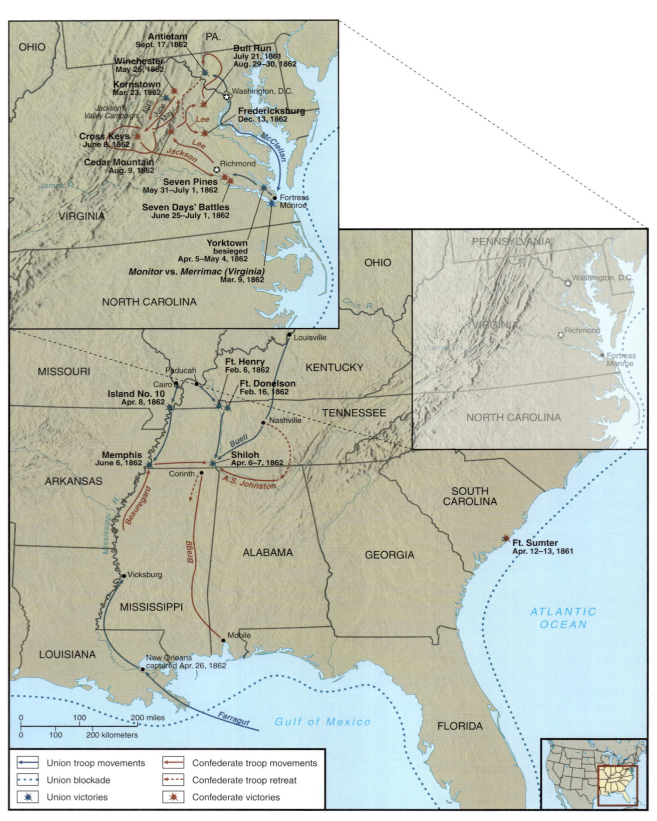

CIVIL WAR, 1861–1862 *Defeats on the battlefield forced a change in the Union's initial military campaign of capturing Richmond, the Confederate capital. The Union's targets in the West were the key cities of Vicksburg and New Orleans.* ∎

money that could not be redeemed in gold and silver. Runaway inflation was the inevitable result. But the problem was much less severe in the North because of the overall strength of its economy and the willingness of its citizens to buy bonds and pay taxes.

The Confederacy was hampered from the outset by a severe shortage of readily disposable wealth that could be tapped for public purposes. Land and cotton could not easily be turned into rifles and cannons, and the southern treasury had to accept payments "in kind." As a result, Confederate "assets" eventually consisted mainly of bales of cotton that were unexportable because of the blockade. As the Confederate government fell deeper and deeper into debt and printed more and more paper money, its rate of inflation soared out of sight.

Political Leadership: Northern Success and Southern Failure

Total war also forced political adjustment, and both the Union and the Confederacy had to face the question of how much democracy and individual freedom could be permitted when military success required an unprecedented exercise of governmental authority. Since both constitutions made the president commander in chief of the army and navy, Lincoln and Davis took actions that would have been regarded as arbitrary or even tyrannical in peacetime.

Lincoln was especially bold in assuming new executive powers. After the fighting started at Fort Sumter, he expanded the regular army and advanced public money to private individuals without authorization by Congress. On April 27, 1861, he declared martial law, which enabled the military to arrest and detain without trial civilians suspected of aiding the enemy, and he suspended the writ of habeas corpus in the area between Philadelphia and Washington. This latter action was deemed necessary because of mob attacks on Union troops passing through Baltimore. In September 1862, Lincoln extended this authority to all parts of the United States where "disloyal" elements were active. He argued that preservation of the Union justified such actions. In fact, most of the thousands of civilians arrested by military authorities were suspected deserters and draft dodgers, refugees, smugglers, or people who were simply found wandering in areas under military control.

For the most part, however, the Lincoln administration showed restraint and tolerated a broad spectrum of political dissent. "Politics as usual" persisted to a surprising degree. Anti-administration newspapers were allowed to criticize the president and his party almost at will, and opposition to Lincoln's programs was freely voiced in Congress.

Jefferson Davis proved a less effective war leader than Lincoln. He defined his powers as commander in chief narrowly and literally, which meant that he assumed personal direction of the armed forces but left policymaking for the mobilization and control of the civilian population primarily to the Confederate Congress. Unfortunately, Davis overestimated his capacities as a strategist and lacked the tact to handle field commanders who were as proud and testy as he was.

Davis's greatest failing, however, was his lack of initiative and leadership in dealing with the problems of the home front. He devoted little attention to a deteriorating economic situation that caused great hardship and sapped Confederate morale. In addition, although the South had a much more serious problem of internal division and disloyalty than the North, he chose to be extremely cautious in his use of martial law.

As the war dragged on, Davis's political and popular support eroded. He was opposed and obstructed by state governors who resisted conscription and other Confederate policies that violated the tradition of states' rights. The Confederate Congress and southern newspapers similarly criticized Davis's policies. His authority was further undermined because he did not even have an organized party behind him. As a result, it was difficult to mobilize the support required for hard decisions and controversial policies.

Early Campaigns and Battles

The war's first major battle was a disaster for northern arms. Against his better judgment, General Winfield Scott responded to the "On to Richmond" clamor and ordered poorly trained Union troops under General Irvin McDowell to advance against the Confederate forces gathered at Manassas Junction, Virginia. They attacked the enemy position near Bull Run Creek on July 21. Confederate forces held the line against the northern assault until reinforcements arrived and then counterattacked. The routed northern forces quickly broke ranks and fled toward Washington and safety. The humiliating defeat at Bull Run led to a shake-up of the northern high command. The man of the hour was George McClellan, who first replaced McDowell and then became general in chief when Scott was eased into retirement. A cautious disciplinarian, McClellan spent the fall and winter drilling his troops and whipping them into shape, much to the anxiety of a more and more impatient Lincoln.

Before McClellan moved, Union forces in the West won some important victories. In February 1862, a joint military-naval operation, commanded by General Ulysses S. Grant, captured Fort Henry on the Tennessee River and Fort Donelson on the Cumberland. The Confederate Army was forced to withdraw from Kentucky and middle Tennessee, amassing its western forces at Corinth, Mississippi. The Union Army slowly followed, but on April 6, the South launched a surprise attack. In the battle of Shiloh, one of the bloodiest of the war, only the timely arrival of reinforcements prevented the annihilation of Union troops backed up against the Tennessee River. After a second day of fierce fighting, the Confederates retreated to Corinth, leaving the enemy forces battered and exhausted.

Although the military effort to seize control of the Mississippi Valley was temporarily halted at Shiloh, the Union Navy soon contributed dramatically to the pursuit of that objective. On April 26, a fleet coming up from the Gulf captured the port of New Orleans. Besides securing the mouth of the Mississippi, the occupation of New Orleans climaxed a series of naval and amphibious operations around the edges of the Confederacy that provided strategically located bases for the northern blockade. The last serious challenge to the North's naval supremacy ended on March 9, 1862, when the Confederate ironclad vessel *Virginia* (originally the USS *Merrimack*) was driven back by the *Monitor,* an armored and turreted Union gunship.

Successes around the edges of the Confederacy did not relieve northern frustration at the inactivity or failure of Union forces on the eastern front. Finally, at Lincoln's insistence, McClellan started toward Richmond. He advanced his forces by water to the peninsula southeast of the Confederate capital and began his march toward Richmond in early April 1862. By late May, his forces had pushed to within 20 miles of the city. There he stopped, awaiting the additional troops that he expected Lincoln to send.

The reinforcements were not forthcoming because the president believed that they were needed to defend Washington. While McClellan was inching his way up the peninsula, a relatively small southern force under General Thomas J. "Stonewall" Jackson was on the rampage in the Shenandoah Valley. When it appeared by late May that Jackson might be poised to march east and attack the Union capital, Lincoln decided to withhold troops from McClellan.

If McClellan had moved more boldly and decisively, he probably could have captured Richmond with the forces he had. But a combination of faulty intelligence reports and his own natural caution led him to falter in the face of what he wrongly believed to be superior numbers. At the end of May, the Confederates under Joseph E. Johnston took the offensive when they discovered that McClellan's army was divided on either side of the Chickahominy River. In the battle of Seven Pines, McClellan was barely able to withstand the assault. During the battle, General Johnston was severely wounded; succeeding him in command of the Confederate Army of Northern Virginia was native Virginian and West Point graduate Robert E. Lee.

Toward the end of June, Lee began an all-out effort to expel McClellan from the outskirts of Richmond. In a series of battles that lasted seven days, the two armies clawed at each other indecisively. Nevertheless, McClellan decided to retreat down the peninsula to a more secure base. This backward step convinced Lincoln that the peninsula campaign was an exercise in futility.

On July 11, Lincoln appointed General Henry W. Halleck general in chief and through Halleck ordered McClellan to withdraw his army from the peninsula to join a force under General John Pope that was preparing to move on Richmond by an overland route. Before the ever-cautious McClellan could reach Pope, however, the Confederates attacked the overland army near Bull Run. In a battle superbly commanded by Lee, Pope was forced to retreat to Washington, where he was stripped of his command.

Lee proceeded to lead his exuberant troops on an invasion of Maryland, in the hope of isolating Washington from the rest of the North. McClellan caught up with him at Antietam, near Sharpsburg, and the bloodiest one-day battle of the war ensued. The result was a draw, but Lee was forced to fall back south of the Potomac. McClellan was slow in pursuit, and Lincoln blamed him for letting the enemy escape.

Convinced that McClellan was fatally infected with "the slows," Lincoln once again sought a more aggressive general and put Ambrose E. Burnside in command of the Army of the Potomac. Aggressive but rather dense, Burnside's limitations were disastrously revealed at the battle of Fredericksburg, Virginia, on December 13, 1862, when he launched a deadly charge against a Confederate uphill position. The range and accuracy of small arms fire made such a charge utter folly. Thus ended a year of bitter failure for the North on the eastern front.

The Diplomatic Struggle

The critical period of Civil War diplomacy was 1861–1862, when the South was making every effort to induce major foreign powers to recognize its independence and break the Union blockade. The hope that England and France could be persuaded to involve themselves in the war on the Confederate side stemmed from the fact that these nations depended on the South for three-quarters of their cotton supply.

■ *After Antietam, Lincoln visited McClellan's headquarters to urge the general to take action. McClellan is on the left facing the president.* ■

The Confederate commissioners sent to England and France in May 1861 succeeded in gaining recognition of southern "belligerency," which meant that the new government could claim some of the international rights of a nation at war, such as purchasing and outfitting privateers in neutral ports. As a result, Confederate raiders, built and armed in British shipyards, devastated northern shipping to such an extent that insurance costs eventually forced most of the American merchant marines off the high seas for the duration of the war.

In the fall of 1861, the Confederate government dispatched James M. Mason and John Slidell to be its permanent envoys to England and France, respectively, and instructed them to push for full recognition of the Confederacy. They took passage on the British steamer *Trent,* which was stopped and boarded in international waters by a United States warship. Mason and Slidell were taken into custody by the Union captain, causing a diplomatic crisis that nearly led to war between England and the United States. After several weeks of international tension, Lincoln and Secretary of State William H. Seward made the prudent decision to allow the Confederates to proceed to their destinations.

The envoys might as well have stayed home; they failed in their mission to obtain full recognition of the Confederacy from either England or France. The anticipated cotton shortage was slow to develop, for the bumper crop of 1860 had created a large surplus in British and French warehouses. For a time in the fall of 1862, the French ruler, Napoleon III, toyed with the idea of recognition, but he refused to act without British support. British leaders feared that recognition would lead to a war with the United States; the U.S. minister to Great Britain, Charles Francis Adams, knew well how to play on those fears. Only if the South won decisively on the battlefield would Britain be willing to risk the dangers of recognition and intervention.

The cotton famine finally hit in late 1862, causing massive unemployment in the British textile industry. But contrary to southern hopes, public opinion did not compel the government to abandon its neutrality and use force to break the Union blockade. Influential interest groups, which actually benefited from the famine, provided the crucial support for continuing a policy of nonintervention. Among these groups were owners of large cotton mills who had made bonanza profits on their existing stocks and were happy to see weaker competitors go under while they awaited new sources of supply. By early 1863, cotton from Egypt and India put the industry back on the track toward full production. Other obvious beneficiaries of nonintervention were manufacturers of wool and linen textiles, munitions makers who supplied both sides, and shipping interests that profited from the decline of American competition on the world's sea-lanes. Since the British economy as a whole gained more than it lost from neutrality, it is not surprising that there was little effective pressure for a change in policy.

By early 1863, when it was clear that "King Cotton diplomacy" had failed, the Confederacy broke off formal relations with Great Britain. For the European powers, the advantages of getting involved in the conflict were not worth the risk of a war with the United States. Independence for the South would have to be won on the battlefield.

FIGHT TO THE FINISH

The last two and one-half years of the struggle saw the implementation of more radical war measures. The most dramatic and important of these was the North's effort to follow through on Lincoln's decision to free the slaves and bring the black population into the war on the Union side. The tide of battle turned in the summer of 1863, but the South continued to resist valiantly for two more years until finally overcome by the sheer weight of the North's advantages in manpower and resources.

The Coming of Emancipation

At the beginning of the war, when the North still hoped for a quick and easy victory, only dedicated abolitionists favored turning the struggle for the Union into a crusade against slavery. But as it became clear how difficult it was going to be to suppress the "rebels," congressional and public sentiment developed for striking a fatal blow at the South's economic and social system by pressing for the freedom of its slaves. By this time, slaves were deserting their plantations in areas where the Union forces were close enough to offer a haven. In this way, they put pressure on the government to determine their status and, in effect, offered themselves as a source of manpower to the Union on the condition that they be made free.

Although Lincoln favored freedom for blacks as an ultimate goal, he was reluctant to commit his administration to a policy of immediate emancipation. In the fall of 1861 and again in the spring of 1862, he disallowed the orders of field commanders who sought to free slaves in areas occupied by their forces, thus angering the strongly antislavery Republicans known as "Radicals." Lincoln's caution stemmed from an effort to avoid alienating Unionist elements in the border slave states and from his own preference for a gradual, compensated form of emancipation.

Lincoln was also aware that one of the major obstacles to any program leading to emancipation was the strong racial prejudice of most whites in the North and the South. Pessimistic about the prospects of equality for blacks in the United States, Lincoln coupled a proposal for gradual emancipation with a plea for government subsidies to support the voluntary "colonization" of free blacks outside the United States, and he actively sought places that would accept them.

But the slaveholding states that remained loyal to the Union refused to endorse Lincoln's gradual plan, and the failure of Union arms in the spring and summer of 1862 increased the public clamor for striking directly at the South's peculiar institution. Responding to political pressure, on September 22, 1862, Lincoln issued his preliminary **Emancipation Proclamation.** Had he failed to act, he would have split the Republican party, most of whose members favored emancipation. The proclamation gave the Confederate states one hundred days to give up the struggle without losing their slaves.

When there was no response from the South and no enthusiasm in Congress for Lincoln's gradual, compensated plan, the president on January 1, 1863, declared that all slaves in those areas under Confederate control "shall be . . . thenceforward, and forever free." He justified the final proclamation as an act of "military necessity" sanctioned by the war powers of the president and authorized the enlistment of freed slaves in the Union army. The language and tone of the document had "all the grandeur of a bill of lading," and made it clear that blacks were being freed for reasons of state and not out of humanitarian conviction.

Despite its uninspiring origin and limited application—it did not extend to loyal slave states or occupied areas—the proclamation did enunciate the abolition of slavery as a war aim. It also accelerated the breakdown of slavery as a labor system. As word spread among the slaves that emancipation was now official policy, larger numbers of them were inspired to run off and seek the protection of approaching northern armies. Approximately one-quarter of the slave population gained freedom during the war under the terms of the Emancipation Proclamation and thus deprived the South of an important part of its agricultural workforce.

Emancipation Proclamation
On January 1, 1863, President Lincoln proclaimed that the slaves of the Confederacy were free. Since the South had not yet been defeated, the proclamation did not immediately free anyone, but it made emancipation an explicit war aim of the North.

African Americans and the War

Almost 200,000 African Americans, most of them newly freed slaves, eventually served in the Union armed forces and made a vital contribution to the North's victory. Without them it is doubtful the Union could have been preserved. Although they were enrolled in segregated units under white officers, initially paid less than their white counterparts, and used disproportionately for garrison duty or heavy labor behind the lines, "blacks in blue" fought heroically in several major battles during the last two years of the war.

Those freed during the war who did not serve in the military were often conscripted to serve as contract wage laborers on cotton plantations owned or leased by "loyal" white planters within the occupied areas of the Deep South. Abolitionists protested that the coercion used by military authorities to get blacks back into the cotton fields amounted to slavery in a new form, but those in power argued that the necessities of war and the northern economy required such "temporary" arrangements. To some extent, regimentation of the freedmen within the South was a way of assuring racially prejudiced Northerners that emancipation would not result in an influx of black refugees to their region of the country.

The heroic performance of African American troops and the easing of northern anxieties about massive black migration led to a deepening commitment to emancipation as a permanent and comprehensive policy. Realizing that his proclamation had a shaky constitutional foundation, Lincoln pressed for an amendment outlawing involuntary servitude. After supporting its inclusion as a central plank in the Republican platform of 1864, Lincoln used all his influence to win congressional approval for the new Thirteenth Amendment. The cause of freedom for blacks and the cause of the Union had at last become one and the same. Lincoln, despite his earlier hesitations and misgivings, had earned the right to go down in history as "the great emancipator."

The Tide Turns

By early 1863, the Confederate economy was in shambles, and its diplomacy had collapsed. The social order of the South was also showing signs of severe strain. Masters were losing control of their slaves, and nonslaveholding whites were becoming disillusioned with the hardships of a war that some of them described as a "rich man's war and a poor man's fight." Yet the North was slow to capitalize on the South's internal weaknesses; it had its own serious morale problems. The long series of defeats on the eastern front had engendered war weariness, and the new policies that "military necessity" forced the government to adopt encountered fierce opposition.

Although popular with Republicans, emancipation was viewed by most Democrats as a betrayal of northern war aims. Racism was a main ingredient in their opposition to freeing blacks. Especially in the Midwest, Democrats used the backlash against the proclamation to win political support. The Enrollment Act of March 1863, which provided for outright conscription, provoked a violent response from those unwilling to fight for the rights of blacks and too poor to buy exemption from the draft. A series of antidraft riots culminated in the bloodiest domestic disorder in American history, the New York riot of July 1863. A New York mob, composed mainly of Irish American laborers, burned the draft offices, the homes of leading Republicans, and an orphanage for black children. At least 120 people died before federal troops restored order. Besides racial prejudice, the draft riots also reflected working-class anger at the wartime privileges and prosperity of the middle and upper classes.

To fight dissension and "disloyalty," the government used its martial law authority to arrest the alleged ringleaders. Patriotic private organizations also issued a barrage of propaganda aimed at what they believed was a vast secret conspiracy to undermine the northern war effort. Historians disagree about the real extent of covert and illegal antiwar activity, but militant advocates of "peace at any price"— popularly known as **Copperheads**—were active in some areas, especially among the immigrant working classes of large cities and in southern Ohio, Indiana, and Illinois.

Copperheads Northern Democrats suspected of being indifferent or hostile to the Union cause in the Civil War.

■ *This 1890 lithograph by Kurz and Allison commemorates the 54th Massachusetts Colored Regiment charging Fort Wagner, South Carolina, in July 1863. The 54th was the first African American unit recruited during the war. Charles and Lewis Douglass, sons of Frederick Douglass, served with this regiment.* ■

The only effective way to overcome the disillusionment that fed the peace movement was to start winning battles and thus convince the northern public that victory was assured. But before this could happen, the North suffered one more humiliating defeat on the eastern front. In early May 1863, Union forces under General Joseph Hooker were routed at Chancellorsville, Virginia, by a much smaller Confederate army masterfully led by Robert E. Lee.

In the West, however, a major Union triumph was taking shape. For more than a year, General Grant had been trying to put his forces in position to capture Vicksburg, Mississippi, the almost inaccessible Confederate bastion that kept the North from controlling the Mississippi River. Finally, in late March 1863, he crossed the river north of the city and moved his forces to a point south of it, where he joined up with naval forces that had run the Confederate batteries mounted on Vicksburg's high bluffs. In one of the boldest campaigns of the war, Grant crossed the river, deliberately cutting himself off from his sources of supply, and marched into the interior of Mississippi. Living off the land and out of communication with an anxious and perplexed Lincoln, his troops won a series of victories and advanced on Vicksburg from the east. After unsuccessfully assaulting the city's defenses, Grant settled down for a siege on May 22.

In an effort to turn the tide of the war, President Davis approved Lee's plan for an all-out invasion of the Northeast. Although this plan provided no hope for relieving Vicksburg, it might lead to a dramatic victory that would more than compensate for the probable loss of the Mississippi stronghold. Lee's army crossed the Potomac in June and kept going until it reached Gettysburg, Pennsylvania. There Lee confronted a Union army that had taken up strong defensive positions on Cemetery Ridge and Culp's Hill.

Union troop movements		Confederate troop movements
Union blockade		Confederate troop retreat
Union victories		Confederate victories

CIVIL WAR, 1863–1865 *In the western theater of the war, Grant's victories at Port Gibson, Jackson, and Champion's Hill cleared the way for his siege of Vicksburg. In the east, after the hard-won Union victory at Gettysburg, the South never again invaded the north. In 1864 and 1865, Union armies gradually closed in on Lee's confederate forces in Virginia. Leaving Atlanta in flames, Sherman marched to the Georgia coast, took Savannah, then moved his troops north through the Carolinas. Grant's army, though suffering enormous losses, moved on toward Richmond, marching into the Confederate capital on April 3, 1865, and forcing surrender.* ■

On July 2, a series of Confederate attacks failed to dislodge General George Meade's troops from the high ground they occupied. The following day, Lee faced the choice of retreating to protect his lines of communication or launching a final, desperate assault. With more boldness than wisdom, he chose to make a direct attack on the strongest part of the Union line. The resulting charge on Cemetery Ridge was disastrous; advancing Confederate soldiers dropped like flies under the barrage of Union artillery and rifle fire.

Retreat was now inevitable, and Lee withdrew his battered troops to the Potomac, only to find that the river was at flood stage and could not be crossed for several days. For some reason, Meade failed to follow up his victory with a vigorous pursuit, and Lee was allowed to escape a trap that could have resulted in his annihilation. Vicksburg fell to Grant on July 4, the same day that Lee began his withdrawal, and Northerners rejoiced at the twin Independence Day victories. The Union had secured control of the Mississippi and had at last won a major battle in the East. But Lincoln's joy turned to frustration when he learned that his generals had missed the chance to capture Lee's army and bring a quick end to the war.

Last Stages of the Conflict

Later in 1863, the North finally gained control of the middle South, an area where indecisive fighting had been going on since the beginning of the conflict. The main Union target was Chattanooga, "gateway to the Southeast." In September, Union forces maneuvered the Confederates out of the city but were in turn eventually surrounded and besieged there by southern forces. After Grant arrived from Vicksburg to take command, the encirclement was broken by daring assaults on the Confederate positions on Lookout Mountain and Missionary Ridge. As a result of its success in the battle of Chattanooga, the North was poised for an invasion of Georgia.

Grant's victories in the West earned him promotion to general in chief of all the Union armies. After assuming that position in March 1864, he ordered a multipronged offensive to finish off the Confederacy. The main movements were a march on Richmond under his personal command and a thrust by the western armies, now led by General William T. Sherman, toward Atlanta and the heart of Georgia.

In May and early June, Grant and Lee fought a series of bloody battles in northern Virginia that tended to follow a set pattern. Lee would take up an entrenched position in the path of the invading force, and Grant would attack it, sustaining heavy losses but also inflicting casualties that the shrinking Confederate Army could ill afford. When his direct assault had failed, Grant would move to his left, hoping in vain to maneuver Lee into a less defensible position. After losing about sixty thousand men, Grant decided to change his tactics and moved his army to the south of Richmond. There he drew up before Petersburg, a rail center that linked Richmond to the rest of the Confederacy; after failing to take it by assault, he settled down for a siege.

The siege of Petersburg was a long, drawn-out affair, and the resulting stalemate caused northern morale to plummet during the summer of 1864. Lincoln was facing re-election, and his failure to end the war dimmed his prospects. Although nominated with ease in June, Lincoln confronted growing opposition within his own party, especially from Radicals who disagreed with his apparently lenient approach to the future restoration of seceded states to the Union.

The Democrats seemed in a good position to capitalize on Republican divisions and make a strong bid for the White House. Their platform appealed to war weariness by calling for a cease-fire followed by negotiations to reestablish the Union. The party's nominee, General George McClellan, announced that he would not be bound by the peace plank and would pursue the war. But he promised to end the conflict soon because he would not insist on emancipation as a condition for reconstruction. By late summer, Lincoln believed he would probably be defeated.

Northern military successes changed the political outlook. Sherman's invasion of Georgia went well. On September 2, Atlanta fell, and northern forces occupied the hub of the Deep South. The news unified the Republican party behind Lincoln. The election in November was almost an anticlimax; Lincoln won 212 of a possible 233 electoral votes and 55 percent of the popular vote. The Republican cause of "liberty and Union" was secure.

The concluding military operations revealed the futility of further southern resistance. Sherman marched almost unopposed through Georgia to the sea, destroying nearly everything of possible military or economic value in a corridor 300 miles long and 60 miles wide. The Confederate army that had opposed him at Atlanta moved northward into Tennessee, where it was defeated and almost destroyed by Union forces at Nashville in mid-December. Sherman captured Savannah on December 22. He then turned north and marched through the Carolinas, intending to join up with Grant at Petersburg.

While Sherman was bringing the war to the Carolinas, Grant finally ended the stalemate at Petersburg. When Lee's starving and exhausted army tried to break through the Union lines, Grant renewed his attack and forced the Confederates to abandon Petersburg and Richmond on April 2, 1865. A week later, Lee recognized that future fighting was pointless and surrendered his army at Appomattox Courthouse on April 9.

But the joy of the victorious North turned to sorrow and anger when actor John Wilkes Booth assassinated Abraham Lincoln at Ford's Theater in Washington on April 14. Although Booth had a few accomplices, popular theories that the assassination was the result of a vast conspiracy involving Confederate leaders or, according to another version, Radical Republicans, have never been substantiated and are extremely implausible. The man who had spoken at Gettysburg of the need to sacrifice for the Union cause had himself given "the last full measure of devotion." Four days after Lincoln's death, the only remaining Confederate force of any significance, the troops under Joseph E. Johnston, who had been opposing Sherman in North Carolina, laid down their arms. The Union was saved.

Effects of the War

The nation that emerged from four years of total war was not the same America that had split apart in 1861. More than 618,000 young men were in their graves, and the widows and sweethearts they left behind temporarily increased the proportion of unmarried women in the population. Some members of this generation of involuntary spinsters sought new opportunities for making a living or serving the community that went beyond the purely domestic roles previously prescribed for women. Some of the northern women who were prominent in wartime service organizations became leaders of postwar philanthropic and reform movements.

At enormous human and economic cost, the nation had emancipated four million African Americans from slavery, but it had not yet resolved that they should be equal citizens. At the time of Lincoln's assassination, most northern states still denied blacks equality under the law and the right to vote. Whether the North would extend more rights to southern freedmen than it had granted to "free Negroes" was an open question.

The impact of the war on white working people was also unclear. Those in the industrializing parts of the North had suffered and lost ground economically because prices had risen much faster than wages during the conflict. But Republican rhetoric stressing "equal opportunity" and the "dignity of labor" raised hopes that the crusade against slavery could be broadened into a movement to improve the lot of working people in general. Foreign-born workers had an additional reason to be optimistic: the fact that so many immigrants had fought and died for the Union cause had—for the moment—weakened nativist sentiment and encouraged ethnic tolerance.

What the war definitely decided was that the federal government was supreme over the states and had broad constitutional authority to act on matters affecting the "general welfare." The southern principle of state sovereignty and strict construction died at Appomattox; the United States was on its way to becoming a true nation-state with an effective central government. Although the states retained many powers and the Constitution placed limits on what the national government could do, the war ended all question about where ultimate authority rested.

A broadened definition of federal powers had its greatest impact in the realm of economic policy. During the war, Republican-dominated Congresses passed a rash of legislation designed to give stimulus and direction to the nation's economic development. Taking advantage of the absence of southern opposition, Republicans rejected the pre–Civil War tradition of laissez-faire and enacted a Whiggish program of active support for business and agriculture. In 1862, Congress passed a high protective tariff, approved a homestead act intended to encourage settlement of the West by providing free land to settlers, granted huge tracts of public land to railroad companies to support the building of a transcontinental railroad, and gave the states land for the establishment of agricultural colleges. The following year, Congress set up a national banking system. The notes that the national banks issued became the country's first standardized and reliable circulating paper currency.

The wartime achievements added up to a decisive shift in the relationship between the federal government and private enterprise. The Republicans took a limited government that did little more than seek to protect the marketplace from the threat of monopoly and changed it into an activist state that promoted and subsidized the efforts of the economically industrious and ambitious.

■ During the war, many women replaced skilled male workers in the manufacturing labor force. These women are filling cartridges in the U.S. Arsenal at Watertown, New York. ■

CASUALTIES OF WAR

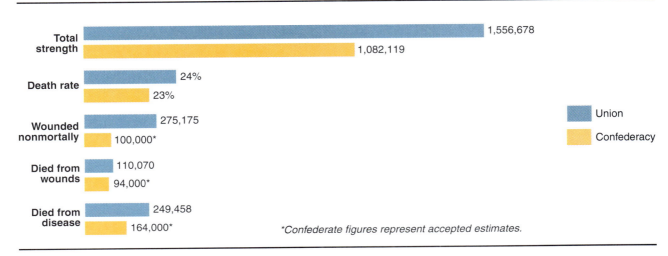

Total strength: 1,556,678 / 1,082,119
Death rate: 24% / 23%
Wounded nonmortally: 275,175 / 100,000*
Died from wounds: 110,070 / 94,000*
Died from disease: 249,458 / 164,000*

Union / Confederacy

*Confederate figures represent accepted estimates.

Chronology

1860	South Carolina secedes from the Union (December)
1861	Rest of Deep South secedes: Confederacy is founded (January–February) ■ Fort Sumter is fired on and surrenders to Confederate forces (April) ■ Upper South secedes (April–May) ■ South wins the first battle of Bull Run (July)
1862	Grant captures Forts Henry and Donelson (February) ■ Farragut captures New Orleans for the Union (April) ■ McClellan leads an unsuccessful campaign on the peninsula southeast of Richmond (March–July) ■ South wins the second battle of Bull Run (August) ■ McClellan stops Lee at Antietam (September) ■ Lincoln issues a preliminary Emancipation Proclamation (September) ■ Lee defeats a Union army at Fredericksburg (December)
1863	Lincoln issues the final Emancipation Proclamation (January) ■ Lee is victorious at Chancellorsville (May) ■ North gains major victories at Gettysburg and Vicksburg (July) ■ Grant defeats Confederate forces at Chattanooga (November)
1864	Grant and Lee battle in northern Virginia (May–June) ■ Atlanta falls to Sherman (September) ■ Lincoln is re-elected president, defeating McClellan (November) ■ Sherman marches through Georgia (November–December)
1865	Congress passes Thirteenth Amendment, abolishing slavery (January) ■ Grant captures Petersburg and Richmond ■ Lee surrenders at Appomattox (April) ■ Lincoln is assassinated by John Wilkes Booth (April) ■ Remaining Confederate forces surrender (April–May)

CONCLUSION: AN ORGANIZATIONAL REVOLUTION

The most pervasive effect of the war on northern society was to encourage an "organizational revolution." Aided by government policies, venturesome businessmen took advantage of the new national market created by military procurement to build larger firms that could operate across state lines; some of the huge corporate enterprises of the postwar era began to take shape. Philanthropists also developed more effective national associations. Both the men who served in the army and the men and women who supported them on the home front became accustomed to working in large, bureaucratic organizations of a kind that had scarcely existed before the war.

Ralph Waldo Emerson, the era's most prominent man of letters, noted that the conflict encouraged a dramatic shift in American thought about the relationship between the individual and society. Before the war, Emerson championed the individual who stood apart from institutions and organizations and sought fulfillment in an inner world of imagination and cosmic intuition. During the conflict, he began to exalt the claims of organization, government, and "civilization" over the endeavors of "the private man." In purging his philosophy of extreme individualism and hailing the need to accept social discipline and participate in organized, cooperative activity, Emerson epitomized the way the war affected American thought and patterns of behavior.

The North won the war mainly because it had shown a greater capacity than the South to organize, innovate, and modernize. Its victory meant that the nation as a whole would now be ready to embrace the conception of progress that the North had affirmed in its war effort—not only pursuing advances in science and technology but also bringing together and managing large numbers of men and women for economic and social goals. The Civil War was thus a catalyst for the great transformation of American society from an individualistic society of small producers into the more highly organized and "incorporated" America of the late nineteenth century.

KEY TERMS

cooperationists, p. 287

Crittenden compromise, p. 289

anaconda policy, p. 292

Emancipation Proclamation, p. 299

Copperheads, p. 300

RECOMMENDED READING

The best one-volume history of the Civil War is James M. McPherson, *Battle Cry of Freedom: The Civil War Era* (1988). Other valuable surveys of the war and its aftermath are J. G. Randall and David Herbert Donald, *The Civil War and Reconstruction,* 2nd ed. (1969), and James M. McPherson, *Ordeal by Fire: The Civil War and Reconstruction* (1981). An excellent shorter account is David Herbert Donald, *Liberty and Union* (1978). The Confederate experience is covered in Clement Eaton, *A History of the Southern Confederacy* (1954), and Emory M. Thomas, *The Confederate Nation, 1861–1865* (1979). Eaton stresses internal problems and weaknesses; Thomas highlights achievements under adversity. Gary W. Gallagher, *The Confederate War* (1997) argues, contrary to a common view, that the South lost the war simply because it was overpowered and not because of low morale or lack of a will to win. On the North's war effort, see Phillip Paludan, *A People's Contest: The Union and the Civil War, 1861–1865* (1988). The best one-volume introduction to the military side of the conflict is still Bruce Catton, *This Hallowed Ground: The Story of the Union Side of the Civil War* (1956).

Lincoln's career and wartime leadership are well treated in David Herbert Donald, *Lincoln* (1995). Another competent biography is Stephen B. Oates, *With Malice Toward None: The Life of Abraham Lincoln* (1977). For a shorter life of Lincoln, see William Gienapp, *Abraham Lincoln and Civil War America* (2002). A penetrating analysis of events immediately preceding the fighting is Kenneth M. Stampp, *And the War Came: The North and the Sectional Crisis* (1950). John Hope Franklin, *The Emancipation Proclamation* (1963), is a good short account of the North's decision to free the slaves. An incisive account of the transition from slavery to freedom is Barbara Jeanne Fields, *Slavery and Freedom on the Middle Ground: Maryland in the Nineteenth Century* (1985). The circumstances and activities of southern women during the war are covered in Drew Faust, *Mothers of Invention: Women of the Slaveholding States in the American Civil War* (1996) and in Laura F. Edwards, *Scarlett Doesn't Live Here Anymore: Southern Women in the Civil War Era* (2002). The experiences of northern women are described in Elizabeth D. Leonard, *Yankee Women: Gender Battles in the Civil War* (1994). Five leading historians offer conflicting interpretations in their attempts to explain the South's defeat in *Why the North Won the Civil War,* edited by David Donald (1960). A brilliant study of the writings of those who experienced the war is Edmund Wilson, *Patriotic Gore: Studies in the Literature of the American Civil War* (1962). On the intellectual impact of the war, see George M. Fredrickson, *The Inner Civil War: Northern Intellectuals and the Crisis of the Union,* 2nd ed. (1993).

SUGGESTED WEB SITES

The American Civil War Homepage
sunsite.utk.edu/civil-war/warweb.html
This site has a great collection of hypertext links to the most useful identified electronic files about the American Civil War.

The Valley of the Shadow: Living the Civil War in Pennsylvania and Virginia
jefferson.village.virginia.edu/vshadow/vshadow.html
This project tells the histories of two communities on either side of the Mason-Dixon line during the Civil War. It includes narrative and an electronic archive of sources.

Civil War @ Charleston
www.awod.com/gallery/probono/cwchas/cwlayout.html
This site covers the history of the Civil War in and around Charleston, South Carolina. See the left menu for historical topics.

Abraham Lincoln Association
www.alincolnassoc.com/
This site allows you to search digital versions of Lincoln's papers.

Crisis at Fort Sumter

www.tulane.edu/~sumter/

This well-crafted use of hypermedia with assignments or problems explains and explores the events in and around the start of the Civil War.

U.S. Civil War Center

www.cwc.lsu.edu/

This is a site whose mission is to "locate, index, and/or make available all appropriate private and public data regarding the Civil War and to promote the study of the Civil War from the perspectives of all professions, occupations, and academic disciplines."

The Papers of Jefferson Davis

jeffersondavis.rice.edu

This site tells about the collection of Jefferson Davis papers and includes a chronology of his life, a family genealogy, some key Davis documents on-line, and a collection of related links.

History of African Americans in the Civil War

www.itd.nps.gov/cwss/history/aa_history.htm

This National Park Service site explores the history of the United States Colored Troops.

Civil War Women

scriptorium.lib.duke.edu/collections/civil-war-women.html

This site includes original documents, links, and biographical information about several women and their lives during the Civil War.

Assassination of President Abraham Lincoln

memory.loc.gov/ammem/alhtml/alrintr.html

Part of the American Memory series with introduction, timeline, and gallery.

Selected Civil War Photographs

memory.loc.gov/ammem/cwphtml/cwphome.html

Library of Congress site with more than 1,000 photographs, many from Matthew Brady.

A Timeline of the Civil War

www.historyplace.com/civilwar/index.html

A complete timeline of the Civil War, well illustrated with photographs.

National Civil War Association

www.ncwa.org/index1.html

One of the many Civil War reenactment organizations in the United States.

Chapter 16

The Agony of Reconstruction

Robert Smalls and Black Politicians During Reconstruction

During the Reconstruction period immediately following the Civil War, African Americans struggled to become equal citizens of a democratic republic. They produced a number of remarkable leaders who showed that blacks were as capable as other Americans of voting, holding office, and legislating for a complex and rapidly changing society. Among these leaders was Robert Smalls of South Carolina. Although virtually forgotten by the time of his death in 1915, Smalls was perhaps the most famous and most widely respected southern black leader of the Civil War and Reconstruction era. His career reveals some of the main features of the African American experience during that crucial period.

Born a slave in 1839, Smalls had a white father whose identity has never been clearly established. But his white ancestry apparently gained him some advantages, and as a young man he was allowed to live and work independently, hiring his own time from a master who may have been his half-brother. Smalls worked as a sailor and trained himself to be a pilot in Charleston harbor. When the Union Navy blockaded Charleston in 1862, Smalls, who was then working on a Confederate steamship called the *Planter,* saw a chance to win his freedom in a particularly dramatic way. At three o'clock in the morning on May 13, 1862, when the white officers of the *Planter* were ashore, he took command of the vessel and its slave crew, sailed it out of the heavily fortified harbor, and surrendered it to the Union Navy. Smalls immediately became a hero to those antislavery Northerners who were seeking evidence that the slaves were willing and able to serve the Union. The *Planter* was turned into a Union transport, and Smalls was made its captain after being commissioned as an officer in the armed forces of the United States. During the remainder of the war, he rendered conspicuous and gallant service as captain and pilot of Union vessels off the coast of South Carolina.

Like a number of other African Americans who had fought valiantly for the Union, Smalls went on to a distinguished political career during Reconstruction, serving in the South Carolina constitutional convention, the state legislature, and several terms in the U.S. Congress. He was also a shrewd businessman and became the owner of extensive properties in Beaufort, South Carolina, and its vicinity. (His first purchase was the house of his former master, where he had spent his early years as a slave.) As the leading citizen of Beaufort during Reconstruction and for some years thereafter, he acted like many successful white Americans, acquiring both wealth and political power. The electoral organization he established resembled in some ways the well-oiled political machines being established in northern towns and cities. His was so effective that Smalls was able to control local government and

Outline

The President versus Congress

Reconstructing Southern Society

Retreat from Reconstruction

Reunion and the New South

Conclusion: The "Unfinished Revolution"

get himself elected to Congress even after the election of 1876 had placed the state under the control of white conservatives bent on depriving blacks of political power. Organized mob violence defeated him in 1878, but he bounced back to win a contested congressional election in 1880 by decision of Congress. He did not leave the House of Representatives for good until 1886, when he lost another contested election that had to be decided by Congress. It revealed the changing mood of the country that his white challenger was seated despite evidence of violence and intimidation against black voters.

In their efforts to defeat him, Smalls's white opponents frequently charged that he had a hand in the corruption that was allegedly rampant in South Carolina during Reconstruction. But careful historical investigation shows that he was, by the standards of the time, an honest and responsible public servant. In the South Carolina convention of 1868 and later in the state legislature, he was a conspicuous champion of free and compulsory public education. In Congress, he fought for the enactment and enforcement of federal civil rights laws. Not especially radical on social questions, he sometimes bent over backward to accommodate what he regarded as the legitimate interests and sensibilities of South Carolina whites. Like other middle-class black political leaders in Reconstruction-era South Carolina, he can perhaps be faulted in hindsight for not doing more to help poor blacks gain access to land of their own. But in 1875, he sponsored congressional legislation that opened for purchase at low prices the land in his own district that had been confiscated by the federal government during the war. As a result, blacks were able to buy most of it, and they soon owned three-fourths of the land in Beaufort and its vicinity.

Smalls spent the later years of his life as U.S. collector of customs for the port of Beaufort, a beneficiary of the patronage that the Republican party continued to provide for a few loyal southern blacks. But the loss of real political clout for Smalls and men like him was one of the tragic consequences of the failure of Reconstruction.

For a brief period of years, black politicians such as Robert Smalls exercised more power in the South than they would for another century. A series of political developments on the national and regional stage made Reconstruction "an unfinished revolution," promising but not delivering true equality for newly freed African Americans. National party politics, shifting priorities among Northern Republicans, and white Southerners' commitment to white supremacy, which was backed by legal restrictions as well as massive extra-legal violence against blacks, all combined to stifle the promise of Reconstruction. Yet the Reconstruction era also saw major transformations in American society in the wake of the Civil War—new ways of organizing labor and family life, new institutions within and outside of the government, and new ideologies regarding the role of institutions and government in social and economic life. Many of the changes begun during Reconstruction laid the groundwork for later revolutions in American life.

THE PRESIDENT VERSUS CONGRESS

The problem of how to reconstruct the Union in the wake of the South's military defeat was one of the most difficult challenges ever faced by American policymakers. The Constitution provided no firm guidelines, and once emancipation became a northern war aim, the problem was compounded by a new issue: How far should the federal government go to secure freedom and civil rights for four million former slaves?

The debate that evolved led to a major political crisis. Advocates of a minimal Reconstruction policy favored quick restoration of the Union with no protection for the freed slaves beyond the prohibition of slavery. Proponents of a more radical policy wanted readmission of the southern states to be dependent on guarantees that "loyal" men would replace the Confederate elite and that blacks would acquire some of the basic rights of American citizenship. The White House favored the minimal approach, while Congress came to endorse the more radical policy. The resulting struggle between Congress and the chief executive was the most serious clash between two branches of government in the nation's history.

Wartime Reconstruction

Tension between the president and Congress over how to reconstruct the Union began during the war. Although Lincoln did not set forth a final and comprehensive plan, he did indicate that he favored a lenient and conciliatory policy toward Southerners who would give up the struggle and repudiate slavery. In December 1863, he offered a full pardon to all Southerners (with the exception of certain classes of Confederate leaders) who would take an oath of allegiance to the Union and acknowledge the legality of emancipation. This **Ten Percent Plan** provided that once 10 percent or more of the voting population of any occupied state had taken the oath, they were authorized to set up a loyal government. By 1864, Louisiana and Arkansas had established fully functioning Unionist governments.

Lincoln's policy was meant to shorten the war by offering a moderate peace plan. It was also intended to further his emancipation policy by insisting that the new governments abolish slavery. When constitutional conventions operating under the 10 percent plan in Louisiana and Arkansas dutifully abolished slavery in 1864, emancipation came closer to being irreversible.

But Congress was unhappy with the president's reconstruction experiments and in 1864 refused to seat the Unionists elected to the House and Senate from Louisiana and Arkansas. A minority of congressional Republicans—the fiercely antislavery **Radical Republicans**—favored strong protection for black civil rights and provision for their franchisement as a precondition for the readmission of southern states. A larger group of moderates also opposed Lincoln's plan, but they did so primarily because they did not trust the repentant Confederates who would play a major role in the new governments.

Also disturbing Congress was a sense that the president was exceeding his authority by using executive powers to restore the Union. Lincoln operated on the theory that secession, being illegal, did not place the Confederate states outside the Union in a constitutional sense. Since individuals and not states had defied federal authority, the president could use his pardoning power to certify a loyal electorate, which could then function as the legitimate state government. The dominant view in Congress, however, was that the southern states had forfeited their place in the Union and that it was up to Congress to decide when and how they would be readmitted.

After refusing to recognize Lincoln's 10 percent governments, Congress passed a Reconstruction bill of its own in July 1864. Known as the **Wade-Davis Bill,** the legislation required that 50 percent of the voters take an oath of future loyalty before the restoration process could begin. Once this had occurred, those who could swear that they had never willingly supported the Confederacy could vote in an election for delegates to a constitutional convention. Lincoln exercised a pocket veto by refusing to sign the bill before Congress adjourned, angering many congressmen.

Congress and the president remained stalemated on the Reconstruction issue for the rest of the war. During his last months in office, however, Lincoln showed a willingness to compromise. But he died without clarifying his intentions, leaving historians to speculate on whether his quarrel with Congress would have escalated or been resolved. Given Lincoln's record of political flexibility, the best bet is that he would have come to terms with the majority of his party.

Ten Percent Plan
Reconstruction plan proposed by President Lincoln as a quick way to readmit the former Confederate states. It called for full pardon of all Southerners except Confederate leaders and readmission to the Union for any state after 10 percent of its voters in the 1860 election signed a loyalty oath and the state abolished slavery.

Radical Republicans The Radical Republicans in Congress, headed by Thaddeus Stevens and Charles Sumner, insisted on black suffrage and federal protection of civil rights of African Americans. They gained control of Reconstruction in 1867 and required the ratification of the Fourteenth Amendment as a condition of readmission for former Confederate states.

Wade-Davis Bill In 1864, Congress passed the Wade-Davis bill to counter Lincoln's Ten Percent Plan for Reconstruction. The bill required that a majority of a former Confederate state's white male population take a loyalty oath and guarantee equality for African Americans. President Lincoln pocket-vetoed the bill.

Andrew Johnson at the Helm

Andrew Johnson, the man suddenly made president by an assassin's bullet, attempted to put the Union back together on his own authority in 1865. But his policies eventually put him at odds with Congress and the Republican party and provoked a serious crisis in the system of checks and balances among the branches of the federal government.

Johnson's approach to Reconstruction was shaped by his background. Born in dire poverty in North Carolina, he migrated as a young man to eastern Tennessee, where he made his living as a tailor. Although poorly educated (he did not learn to write until adulthood), Johnson was an effective stump speaker who railed against the planter aristocracy. Entering politics as a Jacksonian Democrat, he became the political spokesman for Tennessee's nonslaveholding whites. He advanced from state legislator to congressman to governor and in 1857 was elected to the U.S. Senate.

When Tennessee seceded in 1861, Johnson was the only senator from a Confederate state who remained loyal to the Union and continued to serve in Washington. But his Unionism did not include antislavery sentiments or friendship for blacks. He wished that "every head of family in the United States had one slave to take the drudgery and menial service off his family."

During the war, while acting as military governor of Tennessee, Johnson implemented Lincoln's emancipation policy as a means of destroying the power of the hated planter class rather than as a recognition of black humanity. He was chosen as Lincoln's running mate in 1864 in order to strengthen the ticket. No one expected that this southern Democrat and fervent white supremacist would ever become president.

Some Radical Republicans initially welcomed Johnson's ascent to the nation's highest office. Like the Radicals themselves, he was loyal to the Union and believed that ex-Confederates should be treated severely. He seemed more likely than Lincoln to punish southern "traitors" and prevent them from regaining political influence. Only gradually did Johnson and the Republican majority in Congress drift apart.

The Reconstruction policy that Johnson initiated on May 29, 1865, created some uneasiness among the Radicals, but most other Republicans were willing to give it a chance. Johnson placed North Carolina and eventually other states under appointed provisional governors mainly chosen from among prominent southern politicians who had opposed the secession movement and had rendered no conspicuous service to the Confederacy. They were then responsible for calling constitutional conventions to elect "loyal" officeholders. Johnson's plan was specially designed to prevent his longtime adversaries, the planter class, from participating in the reconstruction of southern state governments.

Johnson urged the conventions to declare the ordinances of secession illegal, repudiate the Confederate debt, and ratify the **Thirteenth Amendment** abolishing slavery. After governments had been reestablished under constitutions meeting these conditions, the president assumed that the process of Reconstruction would be complete and that the ex-Confederate states would regain their full rights under the Constitution.

Many congressional Republicans were troubled by the work of the southern conventions, which balked at fully implementing Johnson's recommendations. Furthermore, in no state was even limited black suffrage approved. Johnson, however, seemed eager to give southern white majorities a free hand in determining the civil and political status of freed slaves.

Republican uneasiness turned to disillusionment and anger when the state legislatures elected under the new constitutions proceeded to pass **Black Codes** subjecting the former slaves to a variety of special regulations and restrictions on their

Thirteenth Amendment
Ratified in 1865, this amendment to the U.S. Constitution prohibited slavery and involuntary servitude.

Black Codes Laws passed by Southern states immediately after the Civil War in an effort to maintain the prewar social order. The codes attempted to tie freedmen to field work and prevent them from becoming equal to white Southerners.

freedom. Especially troubling were vagrancy and apprenticeship laws that forced blacks to work and denied them a choice of employers. To Radicals, the Black Codes looked suspiciously like slavery under a new guise.

The growing rift between the president and Congress came into the open in December when the House and Senate refused to seat the recently elected southern delegation. Instead of endorsing Johnson's work and recognizing the state governments he had called into being, Congress established a joint committee, chaired by William Pitt Fessenden of Maine, to review Reconstruction policy and set further conditions for readmission of the seceded states.

Congress Takes the Initiative

The struggle over how to reconstruct the Union ended with Congress doing the job all over again. The clash between Johnson and Congress was a matter of principle and could not be reconciled. Johnson's stubborn and prideful nature did not help his political cause. But the root of the problem was that he disagreed with the majority of Congress on what Reconstruction was supposed to accomplish. An heir of the Democratic states' rights tradition, he wanted to restore the prewar federal system as quickly as possible, except for the prohibition on slavery and secession.

Most Republicans wanted firm guarantees that the old southern ruling class would not regain regional power and national influence by devising new ways to subjugate blacks. They favored a Reconstruction policy that would give the federal government authority to limit the political role of ex-Confederates and provide some protection for black citizenship.

■ In this cartoon, President Andrew Johnson (left) and Thaddeus Stevens, the Radical Republican congressman from Pennsylvania, are depicted as train engineers in a deadlock on the tracks. Indeed, neither Johnson nor Stevens would give way on his plans for Reconstruction. ■

Except for a few extreme Radicals, Republican leaders were not convinced that blacks were inherently equal to whites. They were certain, however, that all citizens should have the same basic rights and opportunities. Principle coincided easily with political expediency; southern blacks were likely to be loyal to the Republican party that had emancipated them and thus increase that party's political power in the South.

The disagreement between the president and Congress became irreconcilable in early 1866 when Johnson vetoed two bills that had passed with overwhelming Republican support. The first bill extended the life of the **Freedmen's Bureau**—a temporary agency charged with providing former slaves with relief, legal help, and educational and employment assistance. The second, a civil rights bill, was intended to nullify the detested Black Codes and guarantee "equal benefit of all laws."

The vetoes shocked moderate Republicans, who had expected Johnson to accept the relatively modest measures. Congress promptly passed the Civil Rights Act over Johnson's veto, signifying that the president was now hopelessly at odds with most of the congressmen from what was supposed to be his own party.

Johnson soon revealed that he intended to abandon the Republicans and place himself at the head of a new conservative party uniting the small minority of Republicans who supported him with a reviving Democratic party that was rallying behind his Reconstruction policy. As the elections of 1866 neared, Johnson stepped up his criticism of Congress.

Freedman's Bureau Agency established by Congress in March 1865 to provide freedmen with shelter, food, and medical aid and to help them establish schools and find employment.

Fourteenth Amendment
Ratified in 1868, this amendment provided citizenship to the ex-slaves after the Civil War and constitutionally protected equal rights under the law for all citizens. Its provisions were used by Radical Republicans to enact a congressionally controlled Reconstruction policy in the former Confederate states.

Meanwhile, the Republican majority on Capitol Hill passed the **Fourteenth Amendment.** This, the most important of the constitutional amendments, gave the federal government responsibility for guaranteeing equal rights under the law to all Americans. The major section defined national citizenship for the first time as extending to "all persons born or naturalized in the United States." The states were prohibited from abridging the rights of American citizens and could neither "deprive any person of life, liberty, or property, without due process of law; nor deny to any person . . . equal protection of the laws." The amendment was sent to the states with an implied understanding that Southerners would be readmitted to Congress only if their states ratified it.

The congressional elections of 1866 served as a referendum on the Fourteenth Amendment. With the support of Johnson, all the southern states except Tennessee rejected the amendment. But bloody race riots in Memphis and New Orleans and maltreatment of blacks throughout the South made it painfully clear that southern state governments were failing abysmally to protect the "life, liberty, or property" of the ex-slaves.

Johnson further weakened his cause by taking the stump on behalf of candidates who supported his policies. His undignified speeches and his inflexibility enraged northern voters. The Republican majority in Congress increased to a solid two-thirds in both houses, and the radical wing of the party gained strength at the expense of moderates and conservatives.

Radical Reconstruction The Reconstruction Acts of 1867 divided the South into five military districts. They required the states to guarantee black male suffrage and to ratify the Fourteenth Amendment as a condition of their readmission to the Union.

Congressional Reconstruction Plan Enacted

Congress was now in a position to implement its own plan for Reconstruction. In 1867 and 1868, it passed a series of acts that reorganized the South on a new basis. Generally referred to as **Radical Reconstruction,** these measures actually repre-

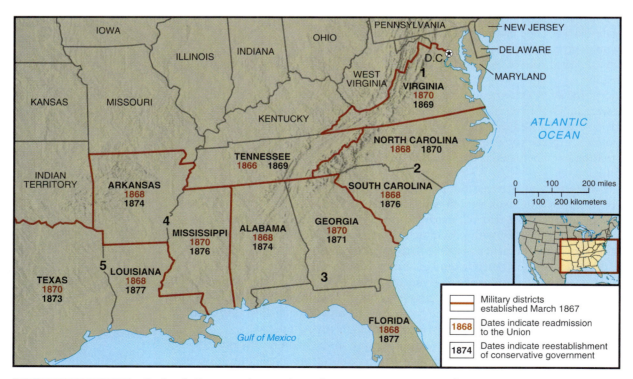

RECONSTRUCTION *During the Reconstruction era, the southern state governments passed through three phases: control by white ex-Confederates; domination by Republican legislators, both black and white; and, finally, the regain of control by conservative white Democrats.* ■

RECONSTRUCTION AMENDMENTS, 1865–1870

Amendment	Main Provisions	Congressional Passage (2/3 majority in each house required)	Ratification Process (3/4 of all states required, including ex-Confederate states)
13	Slavery prohibited in United States	January 1865	December 1865 (27 states, including 8 southern states)
14	National citizenship; State representation in Congress reduced proportionally to number of voters disfranchised; Former Confederates denied right to hold office; Confederate debt repudiated	June 1866	Rejected by 12 southern and border states, February 1867; Radicals make readmission of southern states hinge on ratification; ratified July 1868
15	Denial of franchise because of race, color, or past servitude explicitly prohibited	February 1869	Ratification required for readmission of Virginia, Texas, Mississippi, Georgia; ratified March 1870

sented a compromise between genuine Radicals and the more moderate elements within the party.

Consistent Radicals, such as Charles Sumner of Massachusetts and Thaddeus Stevens of Pennsylvania, wanted to reshape southern society before readmitting ex-Confederates to the Union. Their program required an extended period of military rule, confiscation and redistribution of large landholdings among freedmen, and federal aid for schools that would educate blacks for citizenship. But the majority of Republican congressmen found such a program unacceptable because it broke with American traditions of federalism and regard for property rights.

The First Reconstruction Act, passed over Johnson's veto on March 2, 1867, did place the South under military rule—but only for a short period. The act opened the way for the readmission of any state that framed and ratified a new constitution providing for black suffrage. Since blacks (but not ex-Confederates) were allowed to participate in this process, Republicans thought they had found a way to ensure that "loyal men" would dominate the new governments.

Radical Reconstruction was based on the dubious assumption that once blacks had the vote, they would have the power to protect themselves against the efforts of white supremacists to deny them their rights. The Reconstruction Acts thus signaled a retreat from the true Radical position that a sustained use of federal authority was needed to complete the transition from slavery to freedom and prevent the resurgence of the South's old ruling class.

Even so, congressional Reconstruction did have a radical aspect. It strongly endorsed black suffrage. The principle that even the poorest and most underprivileged should have access to the ballot box was bold and innovative. The problem was how to enforce it under conditions then existing in the postwar South.

The Impeachment Crisis

President Johnson was unalterably opposed to the congressional Reconstruction program, and he did everything within his power to prevent its full implementation. Congress responded by passing laws designed to limit presidential authority over Reconstruction matters. One of the measures was the Tenure of Office Act, requiring Senate approval for the removal of cabinet officers and other officials whose appointment had needed the consent of the Senate. Another measure sought to limit Johnson's authority to issue military orders.

Johnson objected vigorously to the restrictions on the grounds that they violated the constitutional doctrine of the separation of powers. Faced with Johnson's opposition, some congressmen began to call for his impeachment. When Johnson tried to discharge Secretary of War Edwin Stanton—the only Radical in his cabinet—the proimpeachment forces grew.

In January 1868, Johnson ordered General Grant to take over Stanton's job as head of the War Department. But Grant had his eye on the Republican presidential nomination and refused to defy Congress. Johnson then appointed General Lorenzo Thomas. Vexed by this apparent violation of the Tenure of Office Act, the House of Representatives voted overwhelmingly to impeach the president, and he was placed on trial before the Senate.

Johnson narrowly avoided conviction and removal from office when the impeachment effort fell one vote short of the necessary two-thirds. This outcome resulted in part from a skillful defense. Responding to the charge that Johnson had deliberately violated the Tenure of Office Act, the defense contended that the law did not apply to the removal of Stanton because he had been appointed by Lincoln.

The prosecution was more concerned that Johnson had abused the powers of his office in an effort to sabotage the congressional Reconstruction policy. Obstructing the will of the legislative branch, they claimed, was sufficient grounds for conviction. The Republicans who broke ranks to vote for acquittal feared that removal of a president for essentially political reasons would threaten the constitutional balance of powers and open the way to legislative supremacy over the executive. In addition, more conservative Republicans opposed the man who, as president pro tem of the Senate, would have succeeded Johnson, Ohio Senator Benjamin Wade.

The impeachment episode helped create an impression in the public mind that the Radicals were ready to turn the Constitution to their own use to gain their objectives. But the evidence of congressional ruthlessness and illegality is not as strong as most historians used to think. Modern legal scholars have found merit in the Radicals' claim that their actions did not violate the Constitution.

The failed conviction effort was an embarrassment to congressional Republicans, but the episode did ensure that Reconstruction in the South would proceed as the majority in Congress intended. During the trial, Johnson helped influence the verdict by pledging to enforce the Reconstruction Acts, and he held to this promise during his remaining months in office.

RECONSTRUCTING SOUTHERN SOCIETY

The Civil War left the South devastated, demoralized, and destitute. Slavery was dead, but what this meant for future relationships between whites and blacks was still in doubt. Most whites were determined to restrict the freedmen's rights, and many blacks were just as set on achieving real independence. For blacks, the acquisition of land, education, and the vote seemed the best means of achieving their goal. The thousands of Northerners who went south after the war for economic or humanitarian reasons hoped to extend Yankee "civilization" to what they viewed as a barbarous region. For most of them, this reformation required the aid of the freedmen.

The struggle of these groups to achieve their conflicting goals bred chaos, violence, and instability. It was not the ideal setting for an experiment in interracial democracy. When the federal government's support of reform faltered, the forces of reaction and white supremacy were unleashed.

Reorganizing Land and Labor

The Civil War scarred the southern landscape and wrecked its economy. Many plantations were ruined, and several major cities, including Atlanta and Richmond, were gutted by fire. Most factories were dismantled or destroyed, and long stretches of railroad were torn up.

Nor was there adequate investment capital for rebuilding. The substantial wealth represented by Confederate currency and bonds had melted away, and emancipation of the slaves had divested the propertied classes of their most valuable and productive assets. According to some estimates, the South's per capita wealth in 1865 was only about half what it had been in 1860.

Recovery could not even begin until a new labor system replaced slavery. The lack of capital hindered the rebuilding of plantations, and most Americans assumed that southern prosperity would depend on plantation-grown cotton. In addition, southern whites believed that blacks would work only under compulsion, and freedmen resisted labor conditions that recalled slavery.

Blacks strongly preferred to be small independent farmers rather than plantation laborers. For a time, they had reason to hope that the federal government would support their ambitions. Some 40-acre land grants were given by federal authorities to freedmen. By July 1865, forty thousand black farmers were at work on 300,000 acres of what they thought would be their own land.

But for most of them, the dream of "40 acres and a mule" was not to be realized. Neither President Johnson nor most congressmen favored a program of land confiscation and redistribution. Consequently, the vast majority of blacks in physical possession of small farms failed to acquire title and were left with little or no prospect of becoming landowners.

Despite their poverty and landlessness, ex-slaves were reluctant to settle down and commit themselves to wage labor for their former masters. Many took to the road, hoping to find something better. Some were still expecting grants of land, but others were simply trying to increase their bargaining power. As the end of 1865 drew nearer, many freedmen had still not signed up for the coming season; anxious planters feared that they were plotting to seize the land by force. Within a few weeks, however, most of the holdouts signed for the best terms they could get. The most common form of agricultural employment in 1866 was contract labor. Under this system, workers committed themselves for a year in return for fixed wages. Although blacks occasionally received help from the Freedmen's Bureau, more often than not they were worked hard and paid little, and the contracts normally protected the employers more than the employees.

Growing up alongside the contract system and eventually displacing it was the alternative capital-labor relationship of **sharecropping**—the right to work a small piece of land independently in return for a fixed share of the crop produced on it, usually one-half. A shortage of labor gave the freedmen enough leverage to force this arrangement on planters who were unwilling, but many landowners found it advantageous because it did not require much capital and forced the tenant to share the risks of crop failure or a fall in cotton prices.

Blacks initially viewed sharecropping as a step up from wage labor in the direction of landownership. But during the 1870s, this form of tenancy evolved into a new kind of servitude. Croppers had to live on credit until their cotton was sold, and planters or merchants seized the chance to "provision" them at high prices and exorbitant rates of interest. Soon croppers discovered that debts multiplied faster than profits. Furthermore, various methods were eventually devised to bind indebted tenants to a single landlord for extended periods, although some economic historians argue that considerable movement was still possible.

sharecropping After the Civil War, the southern states adopted a sharecropping system as a compromise between former slaves, who wanted land of their own, and former slave owners, who needed labor. The landowners provided land, tools, and seed to a farming family, who in turn provided labor. The resulting crop was divided between them, with the farmers receiving a "share" of one-third to one-half of the crop.

Black Codes: A New Name for Slavery?

While landless African Americans in the countryside were being reduced to economic dependence, those in towns and cities found themselves living in an increasingly segregated society. The Black Codes of 1865 attempted to require separation of the races in public places and facilities; when most of the codes were overturned by federal authorities as violations of the Civil Rights Act of 1866, the same end was

■ *The Civil War brought emancipation to slaves, but the sharecropping system kept many of them economically bound to their employers. At the end of a year the sharecropper tenants might owe most—or all—of what they had made to their landlord. Here, a sharecropping family poses in front of their cabin. Ex-slaves often built their living quarters near woods in order to have a ready supply of fuel for heating and cooking. The cabin's chimney lists away from the house so that it can be easily pushed away from the living quarters should it catch fire.* ■

often achieved through private initiative and community pressure. Blacks found it almost impossible to gain admittance to most hotels, restaurants, and other privately owned establishments catering to whites. Although separate black, or "Jim Crow," cars were not yet the rule on railroads, African Americans were often denied first-class accommodations. After 1868, black-supported Republican governments passed civil rights acts requiring equal access to public facilities, but little effort was made to enforce the legislation.

The Black Codes had other onerous provisions meant to control African Americans and return them to quasi-slavery. Most codes even made black unemployment a crime, which meant blacks had to make long-term contracts with white employers or be arrested for vagrancy. Others limited the rights of African Americans to own property or engage in occupations other than those of servant or laborer. The codes were set aside by the actions of Congress, the military, and the Freedmen's Bureau, but vagrancy laws remained in force across the South.

Furthermore, private violence and discrimination against blacks continued on a massive scale unchecked by state authorities. Hundreds, perhaps thousands, of blacks were murdered by whites in 1865–1866, and few of the perpetrators were brought to justice. The imposition of military rule in 1867 was designed in part to protect former slaves from such violence and intimidation, but the task was beyond the capacity of the few thousand troops stationed in the South. When new constitutions were approved and states readmitted to the Union under the congressional plan in 1868, the problem became more severe. White opponents of Radical Reconstruction adopted systematic terrorism and organized mob violence to keep blacks away from the polls.

The freed slaves tried to defend themselves by organizing their own militia groups for protection and to assert their political rights. However, the militia groups were not powerful enough to overcome the growing power of the anti-Republican forces. As the military presence was progressively reduced, the new Republican regimes were left to fight a losing battle against armed white supremacists.

Republican Rule in the South

Hastily organized in 1867, the southern Republican party dominated the constitution-making of 1868 and the regimes that came out of it. The party was an attempted coalition of three social groups: businessmen seeking aid for economic development, poor white farmers, and blacks. Although all three groups had different goals, their opposition to the old planter ruling class appeared to give them a basis for unity.

To be sure, the coalition faced difficulties even within its own ranks. Small farmers of the yeoman class had a bred-in-the-bone resistance to black equality. Conservative businessmen questioned costly measures for the elevation or relief of the lower classes of either race. In some states, astute Democratic politicians exploited the divisions by appealing to disaffected white Republicans.

But during the relatively brief period when they were in power in the South, the Republicans chalked up some notable achievements. They established (on paper at least) the South's first adequate system of public education, democratized state and local government, and appropriated funds for an enormous expansion of public services and welfare responsibilities.

Important though it was, social and political reform took second place to the major effort that Republicans made to foster economic development and restore southern prosperity by subsidizing the construction of railroads and other internal improvements. Although it addressed the region's real economic needs and was initially very popular, the policy of aiding railroads turned out disastrously. Extravagance, corruption, and the determination of routes based on political rather than sound economic considerations meant an increasing burden of public debt and taxation; the policy did not produce the promised payoff of reliable, cheap transportation. Subsidized railroads frequently went bankrupt, leaving the taxpayers holding the bag. When the Panic of 1873 brought many southern state governments to the verge of bankruptcy and railroad building came to an end, it was clear that the Republicans' "gospel of prosperity" through state aid to private enterprise had failed miserably. Their political opponents, most of whom had originally favored these policies, now saw an opportunity to make gains by charging that Republicans had ruined the southern economy.

These activities were often accompanied by inefficiency, waste, and corruption. State debts and tax burdens rose enormously, mainly because governments had undertaken heavy new responsibilities but partly as a result of waste and graft. In short, the Radical regimes brought needed reforms to the South, but they were not always model governments.

Southern corruption, however, was not exceptional, nor was it a special result of the extension of suffrage to uneducated blacks, as critics of Radical Reconstruction have claimed. It was part of a national pattern during an era when private interests considered buying government favors a part of the cost of doing business, and many politicians expected to profit by obliging them.

Blacks bore only a limited responsibility for the dishonesty of the Radical governments because they never controlled a state government and held few major offices. The biggest grafters were opportunistic whites; some of the most notorious were **carpetbaggers**—recent arrivals from the North—but others were native Southerners. Some black legislators went with the tide and accepted "loans" from those railroad lobbyists who would pay most for their votes, but the same men could usually be depended on to vote the will of their constituents on civil rights or educational issues. Although blacks who served or supported corrupt and wasteful regimes did so because they had no viable alternative, opponents of Radical Reconstruction were able to capitalize on racial prejudice and persuade many Americans that "good government" was synonymous with white supremacy. Contrary to myth, the small number of blacks elected to state or national office during Reconstruction demonstrated on the average more integrity and competence than their white counterparts. Most were fairly well educated, having been free Negroes or unusually privileged slaves before the war. Many battled tirelessly to promote the interests of their race.

carpetbaggers Thi applied to Northern to the South after order to aid in t the South or t ern econom claim that ried ever bag.

Claiming Public and Private Rights

As important as party politics to the changing political culture Reconstruction South were the ways that freed slaves claimed rights for th They did so not only in negotiations with employers and in public m convention halls, but also through the institutions they created, and important, the households they formed.

■ *On either side of Frederick Douglass on this poster are two African American heroes of the Reconstruction era. Senator Blanche K. Bruce of Mississippi, on the left, was the first African American to be elected to a full term in the U.S. Senate. Senator Hiram R. Revels, also representing Mississippi, was elected to the Senate in 1870 to fill the seat previously occupied by Confederate President Jefferson Davis.* ■

As one black corporal in the Union Army told an audience of ex-slaves, "The Marriage covenant is at the foundation of all our rights. In slavery we could not have *legalized* marriage: *now* we have it . . . and we shall be established as a people." Through marriage, African Americans claimed citizenship. Freedmen hoped that marriage would allow them to take on not only political rights, but the right to control the labor of wives and children.

While they were in effect in 1865–1866, many states' Black Codes included apprenticeship provisions, providing for freed children to be apprenticed by courts to some white person (with preference given to former masters) if their parents were paupers, unemployed, of "bad character," or even simply if it were found to be "better for the habits and comfort of a child." Ex-slaves struggled to win their children back from what often amounted to re-enslavement for arbitrary reasons. Freed people challenged the apprenticeship system in county courts, and through the Freedmen's Bureau.

While many former slaves lined up eagerly to formalize their marriages, many also retained their own definitions of marriage. Perhaps as many as 50 percent of ex-slaves chose not to marry legally, and whites criticized them heavily for it. African American leaders worried about this refusal to follow white norms. Yet many poor blacks continued to recognize as husband and wife people who cared for and supported one another without benefit of legal sanction. The new legal system punished couples who deviated from the legal norm through laws against bastardy, adultery, and fornication. Furthermore, the Freedmen's Bureau made the marriage of freedpeople a priority so that husbands, rather than the federal government, would be legally responsible for families' support.

Some ex-slaves used the courts to assert rights against white people as well as other blacks, suing over domestic violence, child support, assault, and debt. Freedwomen sued their husbands for desertion and alimony, in order to enlist the

Freedman's Bureau to help them claim property from men. Other ex-slaves mobilized kin networks and other community resources to make claims on property and family.

Immediately after the war, freed people flocked to create institutions that had been denied to them under slavery: churches, fraternal and benevolent associations, political organizations, and schools. Many joined all-black denominations such as the African Methodist Episcopal church, which provided freedom from white dominance and a more congenial style of worship. Black women formed all-black chapters of organizations such as the Women's Christian Temperance Union, and their own women's clubs to oppose lynching and work for "uplift" in the black community.

A top priority for most ex-slaves was the opportunity to educate their children; the first schools for freed people were all-black institutions established by the Freedmen's Bureau and various northern missionary societies. At the time, having been denied all education during the antebellum period, most blacks viewed separate schooling as an opportunity rather than as a form of discrimination. However, these schools were precursors to the segregated public school systems first instituted by Republican governments. Only in city schools of New Orleans and at the University of South Carolina were there serious attempts during Reconstruction to bring white and black students together in the same classrooms.

In a variety of ways, African American men and women during Reconstruction claimed freedom in the "private" realm as well as the public sphere, by claiming rights to their own families and building their own institutions. They did so in the face of the vigorous efforts of their former masters as well as the new government agencies to control their private lives and shape their new identities as husbands, wives, and citizens.

RETREAT FROM RECONSTRUCTION

The era of Reconstruction began coming to an end almost before it started. Although it was only a scant three years from the end of the Civil War, the impeachment crisis of 1868 represented the high point of popular interest in Reconstruction issues. That year, Ulysses S. Grant was elected president. Many historians blame Grant for the corruption of his administration and for the inconsistency and failure of his southern policy. He had neither the vision nor the sense of duty to tackle the difficult challenges the nation faced. From 1868 on, political issues other than southern Reconstruction moved to the forefront of national politics, and the plight of African Americans in the South receded in white consciousness.

Rise of the Money Question

In the years immediately following the Civil War, the question of how to manage the nation's currency and, more specifically, what to do about "greenbacks"—paper money issued during the war—competed with Reconstruction and corruption issues for public attention. Defenders of "sound" money, mostly financial interests in the East, wanted the greenbacks withdrawn from circulation and Civil War debts redeemed in specie payments (silver and gold). Opponents of this hard-money policy and the resulting deflation of the currency were mainly credit-hungry Westerners and expansionist-minded manufacturers, known as **greenbackers,** who wanted to keep greenbacks in circulation. Both political parties had hard- and easy-money factions, preventing the money question from becoming a heated presidential election issue in 1868 and 1872.

But the Panic of 1873, which brought much of the economy to its knees, led to agitation to inflate the currency by issuing more paper money. Debt-ridden farmers, who would be the backbone of the greenback movement for years to come, now

greenbackers Members of the National Greenback Party, founded in 1874, who wanted to keep wartime paper money (greenbacks) in circulation. They believed that a floating currency, not tied to either gold or silver, would provide relief to debtors and impoverished farmers by increasing the money supply.

joined the easy-money clamor for the first time. Responding to the money and credit crunch, Congress moved in 1874 to authorize a modest issue of new greenbacks, but Grant vetoed the bill. In 1875, Congress enacted the Specie Resumption Act, which provided for a gradual reduction of greenbacks leading to full resumption of specie payment by 1879. The act was interpreted as deflationary, and farmers and workers, who were already suffering from deflation, reacted with dismay and anger.

The Democratic party could not capitalize adequately on these sentiments because of the influence of its own hard-money faction, and in 1876, an independent Greenback party entered the national political arena. Greenbackers kept the money issue alive through the next decade.

Final Efforts of Reconstruction

Fifteenth Amendment Ratified in 1870, this amendment prohibited the denial or abridgment of the right to vote by the federal government or state governments on the basis of race, color, or prior condition as a slave. It was intended to guarantee African Americans the right to vote in the South.

The Republican effort to make equal rights for blacks the law of the land culminated in the **Fifteenth Amendment,** ratified in 1870, which prohibited any state from denying a male citizen the right to vote because of race, color, or previous condition of servitude. Much to the displeasure of advocates of women's rights, however, the amendment made no provision for woman suffrage. And states could still limit male suffrage by imposing literacy tests, property qualifications, or poll taxes allegedly applying to all racial groups; such devices would eventually be used to strip southern blacks of the right to vote. But the makers of the amendment did not foresee this result.

The Grant administration was charged with enforcing the amendment and protecting black voting rights in the reconstructed states. Since survival of the Republican regimes depended on black support, political partisanship dictated federal action, even though the North's emotional and ideological commitment to black citizenship was waning.

Ku Klux Klan A secret terrorist society first organized in Tennessee in 1866. The original Klan's goals were to disfranchise African Americans, stop Reconstruction, and restore the prewar social order of the South. The Ku Klux Klan reformed after World War II to promote white supremacy in the wake of the "Second Reconstruction."

Between 1868 and 1872, the main threat to southern Republican regimes came from the **Ku Klux Klan** and other secret societies bent on restoring white supremacy by intimidating blacks who sought to exercise their political rights. A grassroots vigilante movement rather than a centralized conspiracy, the Klan thrived on local initiative and gained support from whites of all social classes. Its secrecy, decentralization, popular support, and utter ruthlessness made it very difficult to suppress. Blacks who voted ran the risk of being verbally intimidated, whipped, or even murdered.

The methods were first used effectively in the presidential election of 1868. Terrorism by white supremacists cost Grant the electoral votes of Louisiana and Georgia. In Louisiana, political violence claimed hundreds of lives, and in Arkansas, more than two hundred Republicans were assassinated. Thereafter, Klan terrorism was directed mainly at Republican state governments. Insurrections broke out in Arkansas, Tennessee, North Carolina, and parts of South Carolina. In Tennessee, North Carolina, and Georgia, Klan activities helped undermine Republican control, thus allowing the Democrats to come to power in all those states by 1870.

Force Acts Congress attacked the Ku Klux Klan with three Enforcement or "Force" Acts in 1870–1871. Designed to protect black voters in the South, these laws placed state elections under federal jurisdiction and imposed fines and imprisonment on those guilty of interfering with any citizen exercising his right to vote.

Faced with the violent overthrow of the southern Republican party, Congress and the Grant administration were forced to act. A series of laws passed in 1870 and 1871 sought to enforce the Fifteenth Amendment by providing federal protection for black suffrage and authorizing use of the army against the Klan. Although the **Force Acts,** also known as the Ku Klux Klan Acts, did not totally destroy the Klan, the enforcement effort was vigorous enough to put a damper on hooded terrorism and ensure relatively fair and peaceful elections in 1872.

A heavy black turnout in the elections enabled the Republicans to hold on to power in most states of the Deep South, despite efforts of the Democratic-Conservative opposition to woo Republicans by taking moderate positions on racial and economic issues. This setback prompted the Democratic-Conservatives

A Look at the Past

Cartoon "Worse Than Slavery"

Political cartoonist Thomas Nast offered his commentary on and critique of contemporary events through his cartoons in *Harper's Weekly,* a popular magazine that had a circulation of more than 100,000 readers. This Nast cartoon, "Worse Than Slavery," appeared in the magazine on October 24, 1874. Carefully examine the individuals and items depicted in the cartoon. Note that the phrase near the top of the drawing, "This is a white man's government," is a quotation from the 1868 Democratic Party platform. ✱ According to the cartoon, what conditions or events are "worse than slavery"? What view of Reconstruction policy does the cartoonist appear to be expressing?

to make a significant change in their strategy and ideology. No longer did they try to take votes away from the Republicans by proclaiming support for black suffrage and government aid to business. Instead, they began to appeal openly to white supremacy and to the traditional Democratic agrarian hostility to governmental promotion of economic development. Consequently, they were able to bring back to the polls a portion of the white electorate, mostly small farmers, who had not been turning out because they were alienated by the leadership's apparent concessions to Yankee ideas.

The new and more effective electoral strategy dovetailed with a resurgence of violence meant to reduce Republican—especially black Republican—voting. The new reign of terror differed from the previous Klan episode; its agents no longer wore masks but acted quite openly. They were effective because the northern public was increasingly disenchanted with federal intervention on behalf of what were widely viewed as corrupt and tottering Republican regimes. Grant used force in the South for the last time in 1874. When an unofficial militia in Mississippi instigated a series of bloody race riots prior to the state elections in 1875, Grant refused the governor's request for federal troops. As a result, intimidation kept black voters away from the polls.

By 1876, Republicans held on to only three southern states—South Carolina, Louisiana, and Florida. Partly because of Grant's hesitant and inconsistent use of presidential power but mainly because the northern electorate would no longer tolerate military action to sustain Republican governments and black voting rights, Radical Reconstruction was falling into total eclipse.

Spoilsmen versus Reformers

One reason Grant found it increasingly difficult to take strong action to protect southern Republicans was the charge by reformers that his administration was propping up bad governments in the South for personal and partisan advantage. In some cases, the charges held a measure of truth.

The Republican party in the Grant era was rapidly losing the idealism and high purpose associated with the crusade against slavery. By the beginning of the 1870s, men who had been the conscience of the party had been replaced by a new breed of Republicans, such as Senator Roscoe Conkling of New York, whom historians have dubbed "spoilsmen" or "politicos." More often than not, Grant sided with the spoilsmen of his party.

During Grant's first administration, an aura of scandal surrounded the White House but did not directly implicate the president. In 1869, the financial buccaneer Jay Gould enlisted the aid of a brother-in-law of Grant's to further a fantastic scheme to corner the gold market. Gould failed in the attempt, but he did manage to come away with a huge profit.

Grant's first-term vice president, Schuyler Colfax of Indiana, was directly involved in the notorious Crédit Mobilier scandal. Crédit Mobilier was a construction company that actually served as a fraudulent device for siphoning off profits that should have gone to the stockholders of the Union Pacific Railroad, which was the beneficiary of massive federal land grants. To forestall government inquiry into this arrangement, Crédit Mobilier stock was distributed to influential congressmen. The whole business came to light just before the campaign of 1872.

Republicans who could not tolerate such corruption or had other grievances against the administration broke with Grant in 1872 and formed a third party committed to "honest government" and "reconciliation" between the North and the South. The Liberal Republicans, led initially by such high-minded reformers as Senator Carl Schurz of Missouri, endorsed reform of the civil service to curb the corruption-breeding patronage system and advocated strict laissez-faire economic policies, which meant low tariffs, an end to government subsidies for railroads, and hard money.

The Liberal Republicans' national convention nominated Horace Greeley, editor of the respected *New York Tribune* newspaper. This was a curious and divisive choice, seeing that Greeley was at odds with the founder of the movement on the tariff question and indifferent to civil service reform. The Democrats also endorsed Greeley, mainly because he vowed to end Radical Reconstruction. Greeley, however, did not attract support and was soundly defeated by Grant.

Grant's second administration bore out the reformers' worst suspicions about corruption in high places. In 1875, the public learned that federal revenue officials had conspired with distillers to defraud the government of millions of dollars in liquor taxes. Grant's private secretary, Orville E. Babcock, was indicted as a member of the "Whiskey Ring" and was saved from conviction only by the president's personal intercession. The next year, Grant's secretary of war, William W. Belknap, was impeached by the House after an investigation revealed that he had taken bribes for the sale of Indian trading posts. He avoided a Senate conviction by leaving office before the trial.

There is no evidence that Grant profited personally from any of the misdeeds of his subordinates. Yet he is not entirely without blame for the corruption of his administration. He failed to take action against the malefactors, and even after their guilt had been clearly established, he tried to shield them from justice. Ulysses S. Grant was the only president between Jackson and Wilson to serve two full and consecutive terms. But unlike other chief executives so favored by the electorate, Grant is commonly regarded as a failure. Although the problems he faced would have challenged any president, the shame of Grant's administration was that he made loyalty to old friends a higher priority than civil rights or sound economic principles.

REUNION AND THE NEW SOUTH

The end of Radical Reconstruction in 1877 opened the way to a reconciliation of North and South. But the costs of reunion were high for less privileged groups in the South. The civil and political rights of blacks, left unprotected, were stripped away by white supremacist regimes. Lower-class whites saw their interests sacrificed to those of capitalists and landlords. Despite the rhetoric hailing a prosperous "New South," the region remained poor and open to exploitation by northern business interests.

The Compromise of 1877

The election of 1876 pitted Rutherford B. Hayes of Ohio, an honest Republican governor, against Governor Samuel J. Tilden of New York, a Democratic reformer. Honest government was apparently the electorate's highest priority. When the returns came in, Tilden had clearly won the popular vote and seemed likely to win a narrow victory in the electoral college. But the result was placed in doubt when the returns from the three southern states still controlled by the Republicans were contested. If Hayes were to be awarded these three states, plus one contested electoral vote in Oregon, Republican strategists realized, he would triumph in the electoral college by a single vote.

The outcome of the election remained undecided for months. To resolve the impasse, Congress appointed a special electoral commission of fifteen members to determine who would receive the votes of the disputed states. The commission split along party lines and voted 8 to 7 to award Hayes the disputed states. But this decision still had to be ratified, and in the House there was strong Democratic opposition.

To ensure Hayes's election, Republican leaders negotiated secretly with conservative southern Democrats, some of whom seemed willing to abandon their opposition if the last troops were withdrawn and "home rule" was restored to the South. Vague pledges of federal support for southern railroads and internal improvements were made, and Hayes assured southern negotiators that he had every intention of ending Reconstruction. Eventually, an informal bargain, dubbed the **Compromise of 1877,** was struck. Precisely what was agreed to and by whom remains a matter of dispute, but one thing at least was understood by both sides: Hayes would be president, and southern Republicans would be abandoned to their fate.

Compromise of 1877 The Compromise of 1877 was struck during the contested presidential election of 1876. In the compromise, Democrats accepted the election of Rutherford B. Hayes (Republican) in exchange for the withdrawal of federal troops from the South and the ending of Reconstruction.

With southern Democratic acquiescence, the main opposition was overcome, and Hayes took the oath of office. He immediately ordered the army not to resist a Democratic takeover in South Carolina and Louisiana. Thus fell the last of the Radical governments.

"Redeeming" a New South

The men who came to power after the ending of Radical Reconstruction in one southern state after another are usually referred to as the **Redeemers.** They had differing backgrounds and previous loyalties. Some were members of the Old South's ruling planter class who had warmly supported secession and now sought to reestablish the old order with as few changes as possible. Others, of middle-class origin or outlook, favored commercial and industrial interests over agrarian groups and called for a New South, committed to diversified economic development. A third group consisted of professional politicians bending with the prevailing winds.

Rather than supporters of any single ideology or program, these leaders can perhaps best be understood as power brokers mediating among the dominant interest groups of the South in ways that served their own political advantage. In many ways, the "rings" that they established on the state and county levels were analogous to the political machines developing at the same time in northern cities.

They did, however, agree on and endorse two basic principles: laissez-faire and white supremacy. Laissez-faire, the notion that government should be limited and neutral in its economic activities, could unite planters, frustrated at seeing direct state support going to businessmen, and capitalist promoters, who had come to realize that low taxes and freedom from government regulation were even more advantageous than state subsidies. It soon became clear that the Redeemers responded only to privileged and entrenched interest groups, especially landlords, merchants, and industrialists, and offered little or nothing to tenants, small farmers, and working people. As industrialization began to gather steam in the 1880s, Democratic regimes became increasingly accommodating to manufacturing interests and hospitable to agents of northern capital who were gaining control of the South's transportation system and its extractive industries.

White supremacy was the principal rallying cry that brought the Redeemers to power in the first place. Once in office, they found that they could stay there by charging that opponents of ruling Democratic cliques were trying to divide the "white man's party" and open the way for a return to "black domination." Appeals to racism could also deflect attention away from the economic grievances of groups without political clout.

The new governments were more economical than those of Reconstruction, mainly because they cut back drastically on appropriations for schools and other needed public services. But they were scarcely more honest. Embezzlement of public funds and bribery of public officials continued to an alarming extent.

The Redeemer regimes of the late 1870s and 1880s badly neglected the interests of small white farmers.

Redeemers Redeemers were a loose coalition of prewar Democrats, Confederate Army veterans, and Southern Whigs who took over southern state governments in the 1870s, supposedly "redeeming" them from the corruption of Reconstruction. They shared a commitment to white supremacy and laissez-faire economics.

■ *Perhaps no event better expresses the cruel and barbaric nature of the racism and white supremacy that swept the South after Reconstruction than lynching. Although lynchings were not confined to the South, most occurred there, and African American men were the most frequent victims. Here, two men lean out of a barn window above a black man who is about to be hanged. Others below prepare to set on fire the pile of hay at the victim's feet. Lynchings were often public events, drawing huge crowds to watch the victim's agonizing death.* ■

SUPREME COURT DECISIONS AFFECTING BLACK CIVIL RIGHTS, 1875–1900

Case	Effects of Court's Decisions
Hall v. *DeCuir* (1878)	Struck down Louisiana law prohibiting racial discrimination by "common carriers" (railroads, steamboats, buses). Declared the law a "burden" on interstate commerce, over which states had no authority.
United States v. *Harris* (1882)	Declared federal laws to punish crimes such as murder and assault unconstitutional. Declared such crimes to be the sole concern of local government. Ignored the frequent racial motivation behind such crimes in the South.
Civil Rights Cases (1883)	Struck down Civil Rights Act of 1875. Declared that Congress may not legislate on civil rights unless a state passes a discriminatory law. Declared the Fourteenth Amendment silent on racial discrimination by private citizens.
Plessy v. *Ferguson* (1896)	Upheld Louisiana statute requiring "separate but equal" accommodations on railroads. Declared that segregation is *not* necessarily discrimination.
Williams v. *Mississippi* (1898)	Upheld state law requiring a literacy test to qualify for voting. Refused to find any implication of racial discrimination in the law, although it permitted illiterate whites to vote if they "understood" the Constitution. Using such laws, southern states rapidly disfranchised blacks.

Whites, as well as blacks, were suffering from the notorious crop lien system, which gave the local merchants who advanced credit at high rates of interest during the growing season the right to take possession of the harvested crop on terms that buried farmers deeper and deeper in debt. As a result, increasing numbers of whites lost title to their homesteads and were reduced to tenancy.

The Rise of Jim Crow

African Americans bore the greatest hardships imposed by the new order. From 1876 through the first decade of the twentieth century, Southern states imposed a series of restrictions on black civil rights known as **Jim Crow laws.** While segregation and disfranchisement began as informal arrangements, they culminated in a legal regime of separation and exclusion that took firm hold in the 1890s.

Jim Crow laws Laws enacted by states to segregate the population. They became widespread in the South after Reconstruction.

The rise of Jim Crow in the political arena was especially bitter for Southern blacks who realized that only political power could ensure other rights. The Redeemers had promised, as part of the understanding that led to the end of federal intervention in 1877, to respect the rights of blacks as set forth in the Fourteenth and Fifteenth Amendments. But when blacks tried to vote Republican in the "redeemed" states, they encountered renewed violence and intimidation. Blacks who withstood the threat of losing their jobs or being evicted from tenant farms if they voted for Republicans were visited at night and literally whipped into line. The message was clear: Vote Democratic, or vote not at all.

Furthermore, white Democrats now controlled the electoral machinery and were able to manipulate the black vote by stuffing ballot boxes, discarding unwanted votes, or reporting fraudulent totals. Some states also imposed complicated new voting requirements to discourage black participation. Full-scale disfranchisement did not occur until literacy tests and other legalized obstacles to voting were imposed in the period from 1890 to 1910, but by that time, less formal and comprehensive methods had already made a mockery of the Fifteenth Amendment.

Nevertheless, blacks continued to vote freely in some localities until the 1890s; a few districts, like the one Robert Smalls represented, even elected black Republicans to Congress during the immediate post-Reconstruction period. The last of these, Representative George H. White of North Carolina, served until 1901.

The dark night of racism that fell on the South after Reconstruction seemed to unleash all the baser impulses of human nature. Between 1889 and 1899, an average of 187 blacks were lynched every year for alleged offenses against white supremacy.

Chronology

1863	Lincoln sets forth his 10 percent Reconstruction plan
1864	Wade-Davis Bill passes Congress, is pocket-vetoed by Lincoln
1865	Johnson moves to reconstruct the South on his own initiative ■ Congress refuses to seat representatives and senators elected from states reestablished under the presidential plan
1866	Congress passes the Fourteenth Amendment ■ Republicans increase their congressional majority in the fall elections
1867	First Reconstruction Act is passed over Johnson's veto
1868	Johnson is impeached, avoids conviction by one vote ■ Grant wins the presidential election, defeating Horatio Seymour
1869	Congress passes the Fifteenth Amendment, granting blacks the right to vote
1870–1871	Congress passes the Force Acts to protect black voting rights in the South
1872	Grant is re-elected president, defeating Horace Greeley, candidate of the Liberal Republicans and Democrats
1873	Financial panic plunges the nation into a depression
1875	Congress passes the Specie Resumption Act ■ "Whiskey Ring" scandal is exposed
1876–1877	Disputed presidential election is resolved in favor of Republican Hayes over Democrat Tilden
1877	"Compromise of 1877" results in an end to military intervention in the South and the fall of the last Radical governments

Those convicted of petty crimes against property were often little better off; many were condemned to be leased out to private contractors whose brutality rivaled that of the most sadistic slaveholders. The convict-lease system enabled entrepreneurs, such as mine owners and extractors of forest products, to rent prisoners from the state and treat them as they saw fit. Unlike slaveowners, they suffered no loss when a forced laborer died from overwork. Finally, the dignity of blacks was cruelly affronted by the wave of segregation laws passed around the turn of the century, to some extent a white reaction to the refusal of many blacks to submit to voluntary segregation of railroads, streetcars, and other public facilities.

The North and the federal government did little or nothing to stem the tide of racial oppression in the South. A series of Supreme Court decisions between 1878 and 1898 gutted the Reconstruction amendments and the legislation passed to enforce them, leaving blacks virtually defenseless against political and social discrimination.

CONCLUSION: THE "UNFINISHED REVOLUTION"

By the late 1880s, the wounds of the Civil War were healing, and white Americans were seized by the spirit of sectional reconciliation. "Reunion" was becoming a cultural as well as political reality. But whites could come back together only because Northerners had tacitly agreed to give Southerners a free hand in their efforts to reduce blacks to a new form of servitude. The "outraged, heart-broken, bruised, and bleeding" African Americans of the South paid the heaviest price for sectional reunion. Reconstruction remained, in the words of historian Eric Foner, an "unfinished revolution." It would be another century before African Americans rose up once more to demand full civil and political rights.

KEY TERMS

Ten Percent Plan, p. 311

Radical Republicans, p. 311

Wade-Davis Bill, p. 311

Thirteenth Amendment, p. 312

Black Codes, p. 312

Freedman's Bureau, p. 313

Fourteenth Amendment, p. 314

Radical Reconstruction, p. 314

sharecropping, p. 317

carpetbaggers, p. 319

greenbackers, p. 321

Fifteenth Amendment, p. 322

Ku Klux Klan, p. 322

Force Acts, p. 322

Compromise of 1877, p. 325

Redeemers, p. 326

Jim Crow laws, p. 327

RECOMMENDED READING

The best one-volume account of Reconstruction is Eric Foner, *Reconstruction: America's Unfinished Revolution* (1988). Two excellent short surveys are Kenneth M. Stampp, *The Era of Reconstruction, 1865–1877* (1965), and John Hope Franklin, *Reconstruction: After the Civil War* (1961). Both were early efforts to synthesize modern "revisionist" interpretations. W. E. B. DuBois, *Black Reconstruction in America, 1860–1880* (1935), remains brilliant and provocative. On the politics of Reconstruction, see Stephen David Kantrowitz, *Ben Tillman and the Reconstruction of White Supremacy* (2001), Laura F. Edwards, *Gendered Strife and Confusion: The Political Culture of Reconstruction* (1997), J. Morgan Kousser and James M. McPherson, eds., *Region, Race, and Reconstruction: Essays in Honor of C. Vann Woodward* (1982), and Eric Foner, *Nothing But Freedom: Emancipation and Its Legacy* (1983).

Leon F. Litwack, *Been in the Storm So Long: The Aftermath of Slavery* (1979), provides a moving portrayal of the black experience of emancipation. On changing society and family life during Reconstruction, see Noralee Frankel, *Freedom's Women: Black Women and Families in Reconstruction Era Mississippi* (1999), Dylan Penningroth, *Claiming Kin and Property: African American Life Before and After Emancipation* (2003), and Amy Dru Stanley, *From Bondage to Contract: Wage Labor, Marriage, and the Market in the Age of Slave Emancipation* (1998). On what freedom meant in economic terms, see Gerald David Jaynes, *Branches Without Roots: Genesis of the Black Working Class in the American South, 1862–1882* (1986). A work that focuses on ex-slaves' attempts to create their own economic order is Julie Saville, *The Work of Reconstruction: Free Slave to Wage Laborer in South Carolina, 1860–1870* (1994). The best overview of the postwar southern economy is Gavin Wright, *Old South, New South* (1986). On the end of Reconstruction, see David W. Blight, *Race and Reunion: The Civil War in American Memory* (2000). On the character of the post-Reconstruction South, see the classic work by C. Vann Woodward, *Origins of the New South, 1877–1913* (1951) and Edward Ayers, *The Promise of the New South* (1992).

SUGGESTED WEB SITES

Diary and Letters of Rutherford B. Hayes
www.ohiohistory.org/onlinedoc/hayes/index.cfm
The Rutherford B. Hayes Presidential Center in Fremont, Ohio, maintains this searchable database of Hayes's writings.

Images of African Americans from the Nineteenth Century
digital.nypl.org/schomburg/images_aa19/
The New York Public Library–Schomburg Center for Research in Black Culture site contains numerous visuals.

Freedmen and Southern Society Project (University of Maryland, College Park)
www.inform.umd.edu/ARHU/Depts/History/Freedman/home.html
This site contains a chronology and sample documents from several print collections or primary sources about emancipation and freedom in the 1860s.

Andrew Johnson
www.whitehouse.gov/WH/glimpse/presidents/html/aj17.html
White House history of Johnson.

Ulysses S. Grant
www.whitehouse.gov/WH/glimpse/presidents/html/ug18.html
White House history of Grant.

History of the Suffrage Movement
www.rochester.edu/SBA
This site includes a chronology, important texts relating to woman suffrage, and biographical information about Susan B. Anthony and Elizabeth Cady Stanton.

Appendix

The Declaration of Independence

The Articles of Confederation

The Constitution of the United States of America

Amendments to the Constitution

Presidential Elections

Presidents and Vice Presidents

For additional reference material, go to
www.ablongman.com/americanhistory
The on-line appendix includes the following:

THE DECLARATION OF INDEPENDENCE

In Congress, July 4, 1776

The Unanimous Declaration of the Thirteen United States of America,

When, in the course of human events, it becomes necessary for one people to dissolve the political bonds which have connected them with another, and to assume, among the powers of the earth, the separate and equal station to which the laws of nature and of nature's God entitle them, a decent respect to the opinions of mankind requires that they should declare the causes which impel them to the separation.

We hold these truths to be self-evident: That all men are created equal; that they are endowed by their Creator with certain unalienable rights; that among these are life, liberty, and the pursuit of happiness; that, to secure these rights, governments are instituted among men, deriving their just powers from the consent of the governed; that whenever any form of government becomes destructive of these ends, it is the right of the people to alter or to abolish it, and to institute new government, laying its foundation on such principles, and organizing its powers in such form, as to them shall seem most likely to effect their safety and happiness. Prudence, indeed, will dictate that governments long established should not be changed for light and transient causes; and accordingly all experience hath shown that mankind are more disposed to suffer, while evils are sufferable, than to right themselves by abolishing the forms to which they are accustomed. But when a long train of abuses and usurpations, pursuing invariably the same object, evinces a design to reduce them under absolute despotism, it is their right, it is their duty, to throw off such government, and to provide new guards for their future security. Such has been the patient sufferance of these colonies; and such is now the necessity which constrains them to alter their former systems of government. The history of the present King of Great Britain is a history of repeated injuries and usurpations, all having in direct object the establishment of an absolute tyranny over these states. To prove this, let facts be submitted to a candid world.

He has refused his assent to laws, the most wholesome and necessary for the public good.

He has forbidden his governors to pass laws of immediate and pressing importance, unless suspended in their operation till his assent should be obtained; and, when so suspended, he has utterly neglected to attend to them.

He has refused to pass other laws for the accommodation of large districts of people, unless those people would relinquish the right of representation in the legislature, a right inestimable to them, and formidable to tyrants only.

He has called together legislative bodies at places unusual, uncomfortable, and distant from the depository of their public records, for the sole purpose of fatiguing them into compliance with his measures.

He has dissolved representative houses repeatedly, for opposing, with manly firmness, his invasions on the rights of the people.

He has refused for a long time, after such dissolutions, to cause others to be elected; whereby the legislative powers, incapable of annihilation, have returned to the people at large for their exercise; the state remaining, in the mean time, exposed to all the dangers of invasions from without and convulsions within.

He has endeavored to prevent the population of these states; for that purpose obstructing the laws for naturalization of foreigners; refusing to pass others to encourage their migration hither, and raising the conditions of new appropriations of lands.

He has obstructed the administration of justice, by refusing his assent to laws for establishing judiciary powers.

He has made judges dependent on his will alone, for the tenure of their offices, and the amount and payment of their salaries.

He has erected a multitude of new offices, and sent hither swarms of officers to harass our people and eat out their substance.

He has kept among us, in times of peace, standing armies, without the consent of our legislatures.

He has affected to render the military independent of, and superior to, the civil power.

He has combined with others to subject us to a jurisdiction foreign to our constitution, and unacknowledged by our laws, giving his assent to their acts of pretended legislation:

For quartering large bodies of armed troops among us;

For protecting them, by a mock trial, from punishment for any murder which they should commit on the inhabitants of these states;

For cutting off our trade with all parts of the world;

For imposing taxes on us without our consent;

For depriving us, in many cases, of the benefits of trial by jury;

For transporting us beyond seas, to be tried for pretended offenses;

For abolishing the free system of English laws in a neighboring province, establishing therein an arbitrary government, and enlarging its boundaries, so as to render it at once an example and fit instrument for introducing the same absolute rule into these colonies;

For taking away our charters, abolishing our most valuable laws, and altering fundamentally the forms of our governments;

For suspending our own legislatures, and declaring themselves invested with power to legislate for us in all cases whatsoever.

He has abdicated government here, by declaring us out of his protection and waging war against us.

He has plundered our seas, ravaged our coasts, burned our towns, and destroyed the lives of our people.

He is at this time transporting large armies of foreign mercenaries to complete the works of death, desolation, and tyranny already begun with circumstances of cruelty and perfidy scarcely paralleled in the most barbarous ages, and totally unworthy the head of a civilized nation.

He has constrained our fellow-citizens, taken captive on the high seas, to bear arms against their country, to become the executioners of their friends and brethren, or to fall themselves by their hands.

He has excited domestic insurrection among us, and has endeavored to bring on the inhabitants of our frontiers the merciless Indian savages, whose known rule of warfare is an undistinguished destruction of all ages, sexes, and conditions.

In every stage of these oppressions we have petitioned for redress in the most humble terms; our repeated petitions have been answered only by repeated injury. A prince, whose character is thus marked by every act which may define a tyrant, is unfit to be the ruler of a free people.

Nor have we been wanting in our attentions to our British brethren. We have warned them, from time to time, of attempts by their legislature to extend an unwarrantable jurisdiction over us. We have reminded them of the circumstances of our emigration and settlement here. We have appealed to their native justice and magnanimity; and we have conjured them, by the ties of our common kindred, to disavow these usurpations, which would inevitably interrupt our connections and correspondence. They, too, have been deaf to the voice of justice and of consanguinity. We must, therefore, acquiesce in the necessity which denounces our separation, and hold them, as we hold the rest of mankind, enemies in war, in peace friends.

We, therefore, the representatives of the United States of America, in General Congress assembled, appealing to the Supreme Judge of the world for the rectitude of our intentions, do, in the name and by the authority of the good people of these colonies, solemnly publish and declare, that these United Colonies are, and of right ought to be, FREE AND INDEPENDENT STATES; that they are absolved from all allegiance to the British crown, and that all political connection between them and the state of Great Britain is, and ought to be, totally dissolved; and that, as free and independent states, they have full power to levy war, conclude peace, contract alliances, establish commerce, and do all other acts and things which independent states may of right do. And for the support of this declaration, with a firm reliance on the protection of Divine Providence, we mutually pledge to each other our lives, our fortunes, and our sacred honor.

John Hancock

Button Gwinnett	Francis Lightfoot Lee	Jno. Witherspoon
Lyman Hall	Carter Braxton	Fras. Hopkinson
Geo. Walton	Robt. Morris	John Hart
Wm. Hooper	Benjamin Rush	Abra. Clark
Joseph Hewes	Benja. Franklin	Josiah Bartlett
John Penn	John Morton	Wm. Whipple
Edward Rutledge	Geo. Clymer	Saml. Adams
Thos. Heyward, Junr.	Jas. Smith	John Adams
Thomas Lynch, Junr.	Geo. Taylor	Robt. Treat Paine
Arthur Middleton	James Wilson	Elbridge Gerry
Samuel Chase	Geo. Ross	Step. Hopkins
Wm. Paca	Caesar Rodney	William Ellery
Thos. Stone	Geo. Read	Roger Sherman
Charles Carroll of Carrollton	Tho. M'kean	Sam'el Huntington
George Wythe	Wm. Floyd	Wm. Williams
Richard Henry Lee	Phil. Livingston	Oliver Wolcott
Th. Jefferson	Frans. Lewis	Matthew Thornton
Benj. Harrison	Lewis Morris	
Thos. Nelson, Jr.	Richd. Stockton	

THE ARTICLES OF CONFEDERATION

Between the States of New Hampshire, Massachusetts Bay, Rhode Island and Providence Plantations, Connecticut, New York, New Jersey, Pennsylvania, Delaware, Maryland, Virginia, North Carolina, South Carolina, Georgia

ARTICLE 1

The stile of this confederacy shall be "The United States of America."

ARTICLE 2

Each State retains its sovereignty, freedom and independence, and every power, jurisdiction, and right, which is not by this confederation expressly delegated to the United States, in Congress assembled.

ARTICLE 3

The said states hereby severally enter into a firm league of friendship with each other for their common defence, the security of their liberties and their mutual and general welfare; binding themselves to assist each other against all force offered to, or attacks made upon them, or any of them, on account of religion, sovereignty, trade, or any other pretence whatever.

ARTICLE 4

The better to secure and perpetuate mutual friendship and intercourse among the people of the different states in this union, the free inhabitants of each of these states, paupers, vagabonds, and fugitives from justice excepted, shall be entitled to all privileges and immunities of free citizens in the several states; and the people of each State shall have free ingress and regress to and from any other State, and shall enjoy therein all the privileges of trade and commerce, subject to the same duties, impositions, and restrictions, as the inhabitants thereof respectively; provided, that such restrictions shall not extend so far as to prevent the removal of property, imported into any State, to any other State of which the owner is an inhabitant; provided also, that no imposition, duties, or restriction, shall be laid by any State on the property of the United States, or either of them.

If any person guilty of, or charged with treason, felony, or other high misdemeanor in any State, shall flee from justice and be found in any of the United States, he shall, upon demand of the governor or executive power of the State from which he fled, be delivered up and removed to the State having jurisdiction of his offence.

Full faith and credit shall be given in each of these states to the records, acts, and judicial proceedings of the courts and magistrates of every other State.

ARTICLE 5

For the more convenient management of the general interests of the United States, delegates shall be annually appointed, in such manner as the legislature of each State shall direct, to meet in Congress, on the 1st Monday in November in every year, with a power reserved to each State to recall its delegates, or any of them, at any time within the year, and to send others in their stead for the remainder of the year.

No State shall be represented in Congress by less than two, nor by more than seven members; and no person shall be capable of being a delegate for more than three years in any term of six years; nor shall any person, being a delegate, be capable of holding any office under the United States, for which he, or any other for his benefit, receives any salary, fees, or emolument of any kind.

Each State shall maintain its own delegates in a meeting of the states, and while they act as members of the committee of the states.

In determining questions in the United States, in Congress assembled, each State shall have one vote.

Freedom of speech and debate in Congress shall not be impeached or questioned in any court or place out of Congress: and the members of Congress shall be protected in their persons from arrests and imprisonments, during the time of their going to and from, and attendance on Congress, except for treason, felony, or breach of the peace.

ARTICLE 6

No State, without the consent of the United States, in Congress assembled, shall send any embassy to, or receive any embassy from, or enter into any conference, agreement, alliance, or treaty with any king, prince, or state; nor shall any person, holding any office of profit or trust under the United States, or any of them, accept of any present, emolument, office or title, of any kind whatever, from any king, prince, or foreign state; nor shall the United States, in Congress assembled, or any of them, grant any title of nobility.

No two or more states shall enter into any treaty, confederation, or alliance, whatever, between them, without the consent of the United States, in Congress assembled, specifying accurately the purposes for which the same is to be entered into, and how long it shall continue.

No State shall lay any imposts or duties which may interfere with any stipulations in treaties entered into by the United States, in Congress assembled, with any king, prince, or state, in pursuance of any treaties already proposed by Congress to the courts of France and Spain.

No vessels of war shall be kept up in time of peace by any State, except such number only as shall be deemed necessary by the United States, in Congress assembled, for the defence of such State or its trade; nor shall any body of forces be kept up by any State, in time of peace, except such number only as, in the judgment of the United States, in Congress assembled, shall be deemed requisite to garrison the forts necessary for the defence of such State; but every State shall always keep up a well regulated and disciplined militia, sufficiently armed and accoutred, and shall provide, and constantly have ready for use, in public stores, a due number of field pieces and tents, and a proper quantity of arms, ammunition and camp equipage.

No State shall engage in any war without the consent of the United States, in Congress assembled, unless such State be actually invaded by enemies, or shall have received certain advice of a resolution being formed by some nation of Indians to invade such State, and the danger is so imminent as not to admit of a delay till the United States, in Congress assembled, can be consulted; nor shall any State grant commissions to any ships or vessels of war, nor letters of marque or reprisal, except it be after a declaration of war by the United States, in Congress assembled, and then only against the kingdom or state, and the subjects thereof, against which war has been so declared, and under such regulations as shall be established by the United States, in Congress assembled, unless such States be infested by pirates, in which case vessels of war may be fitted out for that occasion, and kept so long as the danger shall continue, or until the United States, in Congress assembled, shall determine otherwise.

ARTICLE 7

When land forces are raised by any State for the common defence, all officers of or under the rank of colonel, shall be appointed by the legislature of each State respectively, by whom such forces shall be raised, or in such manner as such State shall direct; and all vacancies shall be filled up by the State which first made the appointment.

ARTICLE 8

All charges of war and all other expences, that shall be incurred for the common defence or general welfare, and allowed by the United States, in Congress assembled, shall be defrayed out of a common treasury, which shall be supplied by the several states, in proportion to the value of all land within each State, granted to or surveyed for any person, as such land and the buildings and improvements thereon shall be estimated according to such mode as the United States, in Congress assembled, shall, from time to time, direct and appoint.

The taxes for paying that proportion shall be laid and levied by the authority and direction of the legislatures of the several states, within the time agreed upon by the United States, in Congress assembled.

ARTICLE 9

The United States, in Congress assembled, shall have the sole and exclusive right and power of determining on peace and war, except in the cases mentioned in the 6th article; of sending and receiving ambassadors; entering into treaties and alliances, provided that no treaty of commerce shall be made, whereby the legislative power of the respective states shall be restrained from imposing such imposts and duties on foreigners as their own people are subjected to, or from prohibiting the exportation or importation of any species of goods or commodities whatsoever; of establishing rules for

deciding, in all cases, what captures on land or water shall be legal, and in what manner prizes, taken by land or naval forces in the service of the United States, shall be divided or appropriated; of granting letters of marque and reprisal in times of peace; appointing courts for the trial of piracies and felonies committed on the high seas, and establishing courts for receiving and determining, finally, appeals in all cases of captures; provided, that no member of Congress shall be appointed a judge of any of the said courts.

The United States, in Congress assembled, shall also be the last resort on appeal in all disputes and differences now subsisting, or that hereafter may arise between two or more states concerning boundary, jurisdiction or any other cause whatever; which authority shall always be exercised in the manner following: whenever the legislative or executive authority, or lawful agent of any State, in controversy with another, shall present a petition to Congress, stating the matter in question, and praying for a hearing, notice thereof shall be given, by order of Congress, to the legislative or executive authority of the other State in controversy, and a day assigned for the appearance of the parties by their lawful agents, who shall then be directed to appoint, by joint consent, commissioners or judges to constitute a court for hearing and determining the matter in question; but, if they cannot agree, Congress shall name three persons out of each of the United States, and from the list of such persons each party shall alternately strike out one, in the petitioners beginning, until the number shall be reduced to thirteen; and from that number not less than seven, nor more than nine names, as Congress shall direct, shall, in the presence of Congress, be drawn out by lot; and the persons whose names shall be drawn, or any five of them, shall be commissioners or judges to hear and finally determine the controversy, so always as a major part of the judges who shall hear the cause shall agree in the determination; and if either party shall neglect to attend at the day appointed, without shewing reasons which Congress shall judge sufficient, or, being present, shall refuse to strike, the Congress shall proceed to nominate three persons out of each State, and the secretary of Congress shall strike in behalf of such party absent or refusing; and the judgment and sentence of the court to be appointed, in the manner before prescribed, shall be final and conclusive; and if any of the parties shall refuse to submit to the authority of such court, or to appear or defend their claim or cause, the court shall nevertheless proceed to pronounce sentence or judgment, which shall, in like manner, be final and decisive, the judgment or sentence and other proceedings being, in either case, transmitted to Congress, and lodged among the acts of Congress for the security of the parties concerned: provided, that every commissioner, before he sits in judgment, shall take an oath, to be administered by one of the judges of the supreme or superior court of the State where the cause shall be tried, "well and truly to hear and determine the matter in question, according to the best of his judgment, without favour, affection, or hope of reward": provided, also, that no State shall be deprived of territory for the benefit of the United States.

All controversies concerning the private right of soil, claimed under different grants of two or more states, whose jurisdictions, as they may respect such lands and the states which passed such grants, are adjusted, the said grants, or either of them, being at the same time claimed to have originated antecedent to such settlement of jurisdiction, shall, on the petition of either party to the Congress of the United States, be finally determined, as near as may be, in the same manner as is before prescribed for deciding disputes respecting territorial jurisdiction between different states.

The United States, in Congress assembled, shall also have the sole and exclusive right and power of regulating the alloy and value of coin struck by their own authority, or by that of the respective states; fixing the standard of weights and measures throughout the United States; regulating the trade and managing all affairs with the Indians not members of any of the states; provided that the legislative right of any State within its own limits be not infringed or violated; establishing and regulating post offices from one State to another throughout all the United States, and exacting such postage on the papers passing through the same as may be requisite to defray the expences of the said office; appointing all officers of the land forces in the service of the United States, excepting regimental officers; appointing all the officers of the naval forces, and commissioning all officers whatever in the service of the United States; making rules for the government and regulation of the said land and naval forces, and directing their operations.

The United States, in Congress assembled, shall have authority to appoint a committee to sit in the recess of Congress, to be denominated "a Committee of the States," and to consist of one delegate from each State, and to appoint such other committees and civil officers as may be necessary for managing the general affairs of the United States, under their direction; to appoint one of their number to preside; provided that no person be allowed to serve in the office of president more than one year in any term of three years; to ascertain the necessary sums of money to be raised for the service of the United States, and to appropriate and apply the same for defraying the public expences; to borrow money or emit bills on the credit of the United States, transmitting, every half year, to the respective states, an account of the sums of money so borrowed or emitted; to build and equip a navy; to agree upon the number of land forces, and to make requisitions from each State for its quota, in proportion to the number of white inhabitants in such State; which requisitions shall be binding; and, thereupon, the legislature of each State shall appoint the regimental officers, raise the men, and cloathe, arm, and equip them in a soldier-like manner, at the expence of the United States; and the officers and men so cloathed, armed, and equipped, shall march to the place appointed and within the time agreed on by the United States, in Congress assembled; but if the United States, in Congress assembled, shall, on consideration of circumstances, judge proper that any State should not raise men, or should raise a smaller number than its quota, and that any other State should raise a greater number of men than the quota thereof, such extra number shall be raised, officered, cloathed, armed, and equipped in the same manner as the quota of such State, unless the legislature of such State shall judge that such extra number cannot be safely spared out of the same, in which case they shall raise, officer, cloathe, arm, and equip as many of such extra number as they judge can be safely spared. And the officers and men so cloathed, armed, and equipped, shall march to the place appointed and within the time agreed on by the United States, in Congress assembled.

The United States, in Congress assembled, shall never engage in a war, nor grant letters of marque and reprisal in time of peace, nor enter into any treaties or alliances, nor coin money, nor regulate the value thereof, nor ascertain the sums and expences necessary for the defence and welfare of the United States, or any of them: nor emit bills, nor borrow money on the credit of the United States, nor appropriate money, nor agree upon the number of vessels of war to be built or purchased, or the number of land or sea forces to be raised, nor appoint a commander in chief of the army or navy, unless nine states assent to the same; nor shall a question on any other point, except for adjourning from day to day, be determined, unless by the votes of a majority of the United States, in Congress assembled.

The Congress of the United States shall have power to adjourn to any time within the year, and to any place within the United States, so that no period of adjournment be for a longer duration than the space of six months, and shall publish the journal of their proceedings monthly, except such parts thereof, relating to treaties, alliances or military operations, as, in their judgment, require secrecy; and the yeas and nays of the delegates of each State on any question shall be entered on the journal, when it is desired by any delegate; and the delegates of a State, or any of them, at his, or their request, shall be furnished with a transcript of the said journal, except such parts as are above excepted, to lay before the legislatures of the several states.

ARTICLE 10

The committee of the states, or any nine of them, shall be authorized to execute, in the recess of Congress, such of the powers of Congress as the United States, in Congress assembled, by the consent of nine states, shall, from time to time, think expedient to vest them with; provided, that no power be delegated to the said committee for the exercise of which, by the articles of confederation, the voice of nine states, in the Congress of the United States assembled, is requisite.

ARTICLE 11

Canada acceding to this confederation, and joining in the measures of the United States, shall be admitted into and entitled to all the advantages of this union; but no other colony shall be admitted into the same, unless such admission be agreed to by nine states.

ARTICLE 12

All bills of credit emitted, monies borrowed and debts contracted by, or under the authority of Congress before the assembling of the United States, in pursuance of the present confederation, shall be deemed and considered as a charge against the United States, for payment and satisfaction whereof the said United States and the public faith are hereby solemnly pledged.

ARTICLE 13

Every State shall abide by the determinations of the United States, in Congress assembled, on all questions which, by this confederation, are submitted to them. And the articles of this confederation shall be inviolably observed by every State, and the union shall be perpetual; nor shall any alteration at any time hereafter be made in any of them, unless such alteration be agreed to in a Congress of the United States, and be afterwards confirmed by the legislatures of every State.

These articles shall be proposed to the legislatures of all the United States, to be considered, and if approved of by them, they are advised to authorize their delegates to ratify the same in the Congress of the United States; which being done, the same shall become conclusive.

THE CONSTITUTION OF THE UNITED STATES OF AMERICA

PREAMBLE

We the People of the United States, in Order to form a more perfect Union, establish Justice, insure domestic Tranquility, provide for the common defence, promote the general Welfare, and secure the Blessings of Liberty to ourselves and our Posterity, do ordain and establish this Constitution for the United States of America.

ARTICLE I

Section 1

All legislative Powers herein granted shall be vested in a Congress of the United States, which shall consist of a Senate and House of Representatives.

Section 2

The House of Representatives shall be composed of Members chosen every second Year by the People of the several States, and the Electors in each State shall have the Qualifications requisite for Electors of the most numerous Branch of the State Legislature.

No Person shall be a Representative who shall not have attained to the Age of twenty five Years, and been seven Years a Citizen of the United States, and who shall not, when elected, be an inhabitant of that State in which he shall be chosen.

Representatives and direct Taxes shall be apportioned among the several States which may be included within this Union, according to their respective Numbers, *which shall be determined by adding to the whole Number of free Persons, including those bound to Service for a Term of Years, and excluding Indians not taxed, three fifths of all other Persons.** The actual Enumeration shall be made within three Years after the first Meeting of the Congress of the United States, and within every subsequent Term of ten Years, in such Manner as they shall by Law direct. The Number of Representatives shall not exceed one for every thirty Thousand, but each State shall have at Least one Representative; *and until such enumeration shall be made, the State of New Hampshire shall be entitled to chuse three, Massachusetts eight, Rhode-Island and Providence Plantations one, Connecticut five, New York six, New Jersey four, Pennsylvania eight, Delaware one, Maryland six, Virginia ten, North Carolina five, South Carolina five, and Georgia three.*

When vacancies happen in the Representation from any State, the Executive Authority thereof shall issue Writs of Election to fill such Vacancies.

The House of Representatives shall chuse their Speaker and other Officers; and shall have the sole Power of Impeachment.

Section 3

The Senate of the United States shall be composed of two Senators from each State, *chosen by the Legislature thereof,* for six Years; and each Senator shall have one Vote.

Immediately after they shall be assembled in Consequence of the first Election, they shall be divided as equally as may be into three Classes. The Seats of the Senators of the first Class shall be vacated at the Expiration of the second Year, of the second Class at the Expiration of the fourth Year, and of the third Class at the Expiration of the sixth Year so that one third may be chosen every second Year; and if Vacancies happen by Resignation, or otherwise, during the Recess of the Legislature of any state, the Executive thereof may make temporary Appointments until the next Meeting of the Legislature, which shall then fill such Vacancies.

No Person shall be a Senator who shall not have attained to the Age of thirty Years, and been nine Years a Citizen of the United States, and who shall not, when elected, be an Inhabitant of that State for which he shall be chosen.

The Vice President of the United States shall be President of the Senate, but shall have no Vote, unless they be equally divided.

The Senate shall chuse their other Officers, and also a President *pro tempore,* in the Absence of the Vice President, or when he shall exercise the Office of President of the United States.

The Senate shall have the sole Power to try all Impeachments. When sitting for that Purpose, they shall be on Oath or Affirmation. When the President of the United States is tried the Chief Justice shall preside: And no Person shall be convicted without the Concurrence of two thirds of the Members present.

Judgment in Cases of Impeachment shall not extend further than to removal from Office, and disqualification to hold and enjoy any Office of honor, Trust or Profit under the United States: but the Party convicted shall nevertheless be liable and subject to Indictment, Trial, Judgment and Punishment, according to Law.

Section 4

The Times, Places and Manner of holding Elections for Senators and Representatives, shall be prescribed in each State by the Legislature thereof; but the Congress may at any time by Law make or alter such Regulations, except as to the Places of chusing Senators.

The Congress shall assemble at least once in every Year, *and such Meeting shall be on the first Monday in December, unless they shall by Law appoint a different Day.*

---

*Passages no longer in effect are printed in italic type.

Section 5

Each House shall be the Judge of the Elections, Returns and Qualifications of its own Members, and a Majority of each shall constitute a Quorum to do Business; but a smaller Number may adjourn from day to day, and may be authorized to compel the Attendance of absent Members, in such Manner, and under such Penalties as each House may provide.

Each House may determine the Rules of its Proceedings, punish its Members for disorderly Behaviour, and, with the Concurrence of two thirds, expel a Member.

Each House shall keep a Journal of its Proceedings, and from time to time publish the same, excepting such Parts as may in their Judgment require Secrecy; and the Yeas and Nays of the Members of either House on any question shall, at the Desire of one fifth of those Present, be entered on the Journal.

Neither House, during the Session of Congress, shall, without the Consent of the other, adjourn for more than three days, nor to any other Place than that in which the two Houses shall be sitting.

Section 6

The Senators and Representatives shall receive a Compensation for their Services, to be ascertained by Law, and paid out of the Treasury of the United States. They shall in all Cases, except Treason, Felony and Breach of the Peace, be privileged from Arrest during their Attendance at the Session of their respective Houses, and in going to and returning from the same; and for any Speech or Debate in either House, they shall not be questioned in any other Place.

No Senator or Representative shall, during the Time for which he was elected, be appointed to any civil Office under the Authority of the United States, which shall have been created, or the Emoluments whereof shall have been encreased during such time, and no Person holding any Office under the United States, shall be a Member of either House during his Continuance in Office.

Section 7

All Bills for raising Revenue shall originate in the House of Representatives; but the Senate may propose or concur with Amendments as on other Bills.

Every Bill which shall have passed the House of Representatives and the Senate, shall, before it become a Law, be presented to the President of the United States; If he approve he shall sign it, but if not he shall return it, with his Objections to the House in which it shall have originated, who shall enter the Objections at large on their Journal, and proceed to reconsider it. If after such Reconsideration two thirds of that House shall agree to pass the Bill, it shall be sent, together with the Objections, to the other House, by which it shall likewise be reconsidered, and if approved by two thirds of that House, it shall become a Law. But in all such Cases the Votes of both Houses shall be determined by yeas and Nays, and the Names of the Persons voting for and against the Bill shall be entered on the Journal of each House respectively. If any Bill shall not be returned by the President within ten Days (Sundays excepted) after it shall have been presented to him, the Same shall be a Law, in like Manner as if he had signed it, unless the Congress by their Adjournment prevent its Return, in which Case it shall not be a Law.

Every Order, Resolution, or Vote to which the Concurrence of the Senate and House of Representatives may be necessary (except on a question of Adjournment) shall be presented to the President of the United States; and before the Same shall take Effect, shall be approved by him, or being disapproved by him, shall be repassed by two thirds of the Senate and House of Representatives, according to the Rules and Limitations prescribed in the Case of a Bill.

Section 8

The Congress shall have Power To lay and collect Taxes, Duties, Imposts and Excises, to pay the Debts and provide for the common Defence and general Welfare of the United States; but all Duties, Imposts and Excises shall be uniform throughout the United States;

To borrow Money on the credit of the United States;

To regulate Commerce with foreign Nations, and among the several States, and with the Indian Tribes;

To establish an uniform Rule of Naturalization, and uniform Laws on the subject of Bankruptcies throughout the United States;

To coin Money, regulate the Value thereof, and of foreign Coin, and fix the Standard of Weights and Measures;

To provide for the Punishment of counterfeiting the Securities and current Coin of the United States;

To establish Post Offices and post Roads;

To promote the Progress of Science and useful Arts, by securing for limited Times to Authors and Inventors the exclusive Right to their respective Writings and Discoveries;

To constitute Tribunals inferior to the supreme Court;

To define and punish Piracies and Felonies committed on the high Seas, and Offences against the Law of Nations;

To declare War, grant Letters of Marque and Reprisal, and make Rules concerning Captures on Land and Water;

To raise and support Armies, but no Appropriation of Money to that Use shall be for a longer Term than two Years;

To provide and maintain a Navy;

To make Rules for the Government and Regulation of the land and naval Forces;

To provide for calling forth the Militia to execute the Laws of the Union, suppress Insurrections and repel Invasions;

To provide for organizing, arming, and disciplining, the Militia, and for governing such Part of them as may be employed in the Service of the United States, reserving to the States respectively, the Appointment of the Officers, and the Authority of training the Militia according to the discipline prescribed by Congress;

To exercise exclusive Legislation in all Cases whatsoever, over such District (not exceeding ten Miles square) as may, by Cession of particular States, and the Acceptance of Congress, become the Seat of the Government of the United States, and to exercise like Authority over all Places purchased by the Consent of the Legislature of the State in which the Same shall be, for the Erection of Forts, Magazines, Arsenals, dock-Yards, and other needful Buildings;—And

To make all Laws which shall be necessary and proper for carrying into Execution the foregoing Powers, and all other Powers vested by this Constitution in the Government of the United States, or in any Department of Officer thereof.

Section 9

The Migration or Importation of such Persons as any of the States now existing shall think proper to admit, shall not be prohibited by the Congress prior to the Year one thousand eight hundred and eight, but a Tax or duty may be imposed on such Importation, not exceeding ten dollars for each Person.

The Privilege of the Writ of Habeas Corpus shall not be suspended, unless when in Cases of Rebellion or Invasion the public Safety may require it.

No Bill of Attainder or ex post facto Law shall be passed.

No Capitation, or other direct, Tax shall be laid, unless in Proportion to the Census or Enumeration herein before directed to be taken.

No Tax or Duty shall be laid on Articles exported from any State.

No Preference shall be given by any Regulation of Commerce or Revenue to the Ports of one State over those of another: nor shall Vessels bound to, or from, one State, be obliged to enter, clear, or pay Duties in another.

No Money shall be drawn from the Treasury, but in Consequence of Appropriations made by Law; and a regular Statement and Account of the Receipts and Expenditures of all public Money shall be published from time to time.

No Title of Nobility shall be granted by the United States: And no Person holding any Office of Profit or Trust under them, shall, without the Consent of the Congress, accept of any present, Emolument, Office, or Title, of any kind whatever, from any King, Prince, or foreign State.

Section 10

No State shall enter into any Treaty, Alliance, or Confederation; grant Letters of Marque and Reprisal; coin Money; emit Bills of Credit; make any Thing but gold and silver Coin a Tender in Payment of Debts; pass any Bill of Attainder, ex post facto Law, or Law impairing the obligation of Contracts, or grant any Title of Nobility.

No State shall, without the Consent of the Congress, lay any Imposts or Duties on Imports or Exports, except what may be absolutely necessary for executing its inspection Laws: and the net Produce of all Duties and Imposts, laid by any State on Imports or Exports, shall be for the Use of the Treasury of the United States; and all such Laws shall be subject to the Revision and Controul of the Congress.

No State shall, without the Consent of Congress, lay any Duty of Tonnage, keep Troops, or Ships of War in time of Peace, enter into any Agreement or Compact with another State, or with a foreign Power, or engage in War, unless actually invaded, or in such imminent Danger as will not admit of delay.

ARTICLE II

Section 1

The executive Power shall be vested in a President of the United States of America. He shall hold his Office during the Term of four Years, and, together with the Vice President, chosen for the same Term, be elected, as follows:

Each State shall appoint, in such Manner as the Legislature thereof may direct, a Number of Electors, equal to the whole Number of Senators and Representatives to which the State may be entitled in the Congress: but no Senator or Representative, or Person holding an Office of Trust or Profit under the United States, shall be appointed an Elector.

The Electors shall meet in their respective States, and vote by Ballot for two Persons, of whom one at least shall not be an Inhabitant of the same State with themselves. And they shall make a List of all the Persons voted for, and of the Number of Votes for each; which List they shall sign and certify, and transmit sealed to the Seat of the Government of the United States, directed to the President of the Senate. The President of the Senate shall, in the Presence of the Senate and House of Representatives, open all the Certificates, and the Votes shall then be counted. The Person having the greatest Number of Votes shall be the President, if such Number be a Majority of the whole number of Electors appointed; and if there be more than one who have such Majority, and have an equal Number of Votes, then the House of Representatives shall immediately chuse by Ballot one of them for President; and if no Person have a Majority, then from the five highest on the List the said House shall in like Manner chuse the President. But in chusing the President, the Votes shall be taken by States, the Representation from each State having one Vote; A quorum for this Purpose shall consist of a Member or Members from two thirds of the States, and a Majority of all the States shall be necessary to a Choice. In every Case, after the Choice of the President, the Person having the greatest Number of Votes of the Electors shall be the Vice President. But if there should remain two or more who have equal Votes, the Senate shall chuse from them by Ballot the Vice President.

The Congress may determine the time of chusing the Electors, and the Day on which they shall give their Votes; which Day shall be the same throughout the United States.

No person except a natural born Citizen, *or a Citizen of the United States, at the time of the Adoption of this Constitution,* shall be eligible to the Office of President; neither shall any Person be eligible to that Office who shall not have attained to the Age of thirty five Years, and been fourteen Years a Resident within the United States.

In Case of the Removal of the President from Office, or of his Death, Resignation, or Inability to discharge the Powers and Duties of the said Office, the Same shall devolve on the Vice President, and the Congress may by Law provide for the Case of Removal, Death, Resignation or Inability, both of the President and Vice President, declaring what Officer shall then act as President, and such Officer shall act accordingly, until the Disability be removed, or a President shall be elected.

The President shall, at stated Times, receive for his Services, a Compensation, which shall neither be increased nor diminished during the Period for which he shall have been elected, and he shall not receive within that period any other Emolument from the United States, or any of them.

Before he enter on the Execution of his Office, he shall take the following Oath or Affirmation:—"I do solemnly swear (or affirm) that I will faithfully execute the Office of

President of the United States, and will to the best of my Ability, preserve, protect and defend the Constitution of the United States."

Section 2

The President shall be Commander in Chief of the Army and Navy of the United States, and of the Militia of the several States, when called into the actual Service of the United States; he may require the Opinion, in writing, of the principal Officer in each of the executive Departments, upon any Subject relating to the Duties of their respective Offices, and he shall have Power to grant Reprieves and Pardons for Offences against the United States, except in Cases of Impeachment.

He shall have Power, by and with the Advice and Consent of the Senate, to make Treaties, provided two thirds of the Senators present concur; and he shall nominate, and by and with the Advice and Consent of the Senate, shall appoint Ambassadors, other public Ministers and Consuls, Judges of the supreme Court, and all other Officers of the United States, whose Appointments are not herein otherwise provided for, and which shall be established by Law: but the Congress may by Law vest the Appointment of such inferior Officers, as they think proper in the President alone, in the Courts of Law, or in the Heads of Departments.

The President shall have Power to fill up all Vacancies that may happen during the Recess of the Senate, by granting Commissions which shall expire at the End of their next Session.

Section 3

He shall from time to time give to the Congress Information of the State of the Union, and recommend to their Consideration such Measures as he shall judge necessary and expedient; he may, on extraordinary Occasions, convene both Houses, or either of them, and in Case of disagreement between them, with Respect to the Time of Adjournment, he may adjourn them to such Time as he shall think proper; he shall receive Ambassadors and other public Ministers; he shall take Care that the Laws be faithfully executed, and shall Commission all the officers of the United States.

Section 4

The President, Vice President and all civil Officers of the United States, shall be removed from Office on Impeachment for, and Conviction of, Treason, Bribery or other high Crimes and Misdemeanors.

ARTICLE III

Section 1

The judicial Power of the United States, shall be vested in one supreme Court, and in such inferior Courts as the Congress may from time to time ordain and establish. The Judges, both of the supreme and inferior Courts, shall hold their offices during good Behaviour, and shall, at stated Times, receive for their Services, a Compensation, which shall not be diminished during their Continuance in Office.

Section 2

The judicial Power shall extend to all Cases, in Law and Equity, arising under this Constitution, the Laws of the United States, and Treaties made, or which shall be made, under their Authority;—to all Cases affecting Ambassadors, other public Ministers and Consuls;—to all Cases of admiralty and maritime Jurisdiction;—to Controversies to which the United States shall be a Party;—to Controversies between two or more States;—*between a State and Citizens of another State;*—between Citizens of different States;—between Citizens of the same State claiming Lands under Grants of different States, and between a State, or the Citizens thereof, and foreign States, Citizens or Subjects.

In all Cases affecting Ambassadors, other public Ministers and Consuls, and those in which a State shall be Party, the supreme Court shall have original Jurisdiction. In all the other Cases before mentioned, the supreme Court shall have appellate Jurisdiction, both as to Law and Fact, with such Exceptions, and under such Regulations as the Congress shall make.

The Trial of all Crimes, except in Cases of Impeachment, shall be by Jury; and such Trial shall be held in the State where the said Crimes shall have been committed, but when not committed within any State, the Trial shall be at such Place or Places as the Congress may by Law have directed.

Section 3

Treason against the United States, shall consist only in levying War against them, or in adhering to their Enemies, giving them Aid and Comfort. No person shall be convicted of Treason unless on the Testimony of two Witnesses to the same overt Act, or on Confession in open Court.

The Congress shall have Power to declare the Punishment of Treason, but no Attainder of Treason shall work Corruption of Blood, or Forfeiture except during the Life of the Person attainted.

ARTICLE IV

Section 1

Full Faith and Credit shall be given in each State to the public Acts, Records, and judicial Proceedings of every other State. And the Congress may by general Laws prescribe the Manner in which such Acts, Records and Proceedings shall be proved, and the Effect thereof.

Section 2

The Citizens of each State shall be entitled to all Privileges and Immunities of Citizens in the several States.

A Person charged in any State with Treason, Felony, or other Crime, who shall flee from Justice, and be found in another State, shall on Demand of the executive Authority of the State from which he fled, be delivered up, to be removed to the State having Jurisdiction of the Crime.

No Person held to Service or Labour in one State, under the Laws thereof, escaping into another, shall, in Consequence of any Law or Regulation therein, be discharged from such Service or Labour, but shall be delivered up on Claim of the Party to whom such Service or Labour may be due.

Section 3

New States may be admitted by the Congress into this Union; but no new State shall be formed or erected within the Jurisdiction of any other State; nor any State be formed by the Junction of two or more States, or Parts of States, without the Consent of the Legislatures of the States concerned as well as of the Congress.

The Congress shall have Power to dispose of and make all needful Rules and Regulations respecting the Territory or other Property belonging to the United States; and nothing in this Constitution shall be so construed as to Prejudice any Claims of the United States, or of any particular States.

Section 4

The United States shall guarantee to every State in this Union a Republican Form of Government, and shall protect each of them against Invasion; and on Application of the Legislature, or of the Executive (when the Legislature cannot be convened) against domestic violence.

ARTICLE V

The Congress, whenever two thirds of both Houses shall deem it necessary, shall propose Amendments to this Constitution, or, on the Application of the Legislatures of two thirds of the several States, shall call a Convention for proposing Amendments, which, in either Case, shall be valid to all Intents and Purposes, as Part of this Constitution, when ratified by the Legislatures of three fourths of the several States, or by Conventions in three fourths thereof, as the one or the other Mode of Ratification may be proposed by the Congress; Provided *that no Amendment which may be made prior to the Year One thousand eight hundred and eight shall in any Manner affect the first and fourth Clauses in the Ninth Section of the first Article;* and that no State, without its Consent, shall be deprived of its equal Suffrage in the Senate.

ARTICLE VI

All Debts contracted and Engagements entered into, before the Adoption of this Constitution, shall be as valid against the United States under this Constitution, as under the Confederation.

This Constitution, and Laws of the United States which shall be made in Pursuance thereof; and all Treaties made, or which shall be made, under the Authority of the United States, shall be the supreme Law of the Land; and the Judges in every State shall be bound thereby, any Thing in the Constitution or Laws of any State to the Contrary notwithstanding.

The Senators and Representatives before mentioned, and the Members of the several State Legislatures, and all executive and Judcial Officers, both of the United States and of the several States, shall be bound by Oath or Affirmation, to support this Constitution; but no religious Test shall ever be required as a Qualification to any Office of public Trust under the United States.

ARTICLE VII

The Ratification of the Conventions of nine States, shall be sufficient for the Establishment of this Constitution between the States so ratifying the Same.

Done in Convention by the Unanimous Consent of the States present the Seventeenth Day of September in the Year of our Lord one thousand seven hundred and Eighty seven and of the Independence of the United States of America the Twelfth* IN WITNESS whereof We have hereunto subscribed our Names,

George Washington
President and Deputy from Virginia

Delaware
George Read
Gunning Bedford, Jr.
John Dickinson
Richard Bassett
Jacob Broom

Maryland
James McHenry
Daniel of St. Thomas Jenifer
Daniel Carroll

Virginia
John Blair
James Madison, Jr.

North Carolina
William Blount
Richard Dobbs Spraight
Hugh Williamson

South Carolina
John Rutledge
Charles Cotesworth Pinckney
Charles Pinckney
Pierce Butler

Georgia
William Few
Abraham Baldwin

New Hampshire
John Langdon
Nicholas Gilman

Massachusetts
Nathaniel Gorham
Rufus King

Connecticut
William Samuel Johnson
Roger Sherman

New York
Alexander Hamilton

New Jersey
William Livingston
David Brearley
William Paterson
Jonathan Dayton

Pennsylvania
Benjamin Franklin
Thomas Mifflin
Robert Morris
George Clymer
Thomas FitzSimons
Jared Ingersoll
James Wilson
Gouverneur Morris

*The Constitution was submitted on September 17, 1787, by the Constitutional Convention, was ratified by the Convention of several states at various dates up to May 29, 1790, and became effective on March 4, 1789.

AMENDMENTS TO THE CONSTITUTION

AMENDMENT I

Congress shall make no law respecting an establishment of religion, or prohibiting the free exercise thereof; or abridging the freedom of speech, or of the press; or the right of the people peaceably to assemble, and to petition the Government for a redress of grievances.

AMENDMENT II

A well regulated Militia being necessary to the security of a free State, the right of the people to keep and bear Arms, shall not be infringed.

AMENDMENT III

No Soldier shall, in time of peace be quartered in any house, without the consent of the Owner, nor in time of war, but in a manner to be prescribed by law.

AMENDMENT IV

The right of the people to be secure in their persons, houses, papers, and effects, against unreasonable searches and seizures, shall not be violated, and no Warrants shall issue, but upon probable cause, supported by Oath or affirmation, and particularly describing the place to be searched, and the persons or things to be seized.

AMENDMENT V

No person shall be held to answer for a capital, or otherwise infamous crime, unless on a presentment or indictment of a Grand Jury, except in cases arising in the land or naval forces, or in the Militia, when in actual service in time of War or public danger; nor shall any person be subject for the same offense to be twice put in jeopardy of life or limb; nor shall be compelled in any criminal case to be a witness against himself, nor be deprived of life, liberty, or property, without due process of law; nor shall private property be taken for public use, without just compensation.

AMENDMENT VI

In all criminal prosecutions, the accused shall enjoy the right to a speedy and public trial, by an impartial jury of the State and district wherein the crime shall have been committed, which district shall have been previously ascertained by law, and to be informed of the nature and cause of the accusation; to be confronted with the witnesses against him; to have compulsory process for obtaining witnesses in his favor, and to have the Assistance of Counsel for his defence.

AMENDMENT VII

In Suits at common law, where the value in controversy shall exceed twenty dollars, the right of trial by jury shall be preserved, and no fact tried by a jury, shall be otherwise re-examined in any Court of the United States, than according to the rules of the common law.

AMENDMENT VIII

Excessive bail shall not be required, nor excessive fines imposed, nor cruel and unusual punishments inflicted.

AMENDMENT IX

The enumeration in the Constitution, of certain rights, shall not be construed to deny or disparage others retained by the people.

AMENDMENT X*

The powers not delegated to the United States by the Constitution, nor prohibited by it to the States, are reserved to the States respectively, or to the people.

AMENDMENT XI
[ADOPTED 1798]

The Judicial power of the United States shall not be construed to extend to any suit in law or equity, commenced or prosecuted against one of the United States by Citizens of another State, or by Citizens or Subjects of any Foreign State.

AMENDMENT XII
[ADOPTED 1804]

The Electors shall meet in their respective states, and vote by ballot for President and Vice President, one of whom, at least, shall not be an inhabitant of the same state with themselves; they shall name in their ballots the person voted for as President, and in distinct ballots the person voted for as Vice President, and they shall make distinct lists of all persons voted for as President, and of all persons voted for as Vice President, and of the number of votes for each, which lists they shall sign and certify, and transmit sealed to the seat of the government of the United States, directed to the President of the Senate;—The President of the Senate shall, in the presence of the Senate and House of Representatives, open all the certificates and the votes shall then be counted;—The person having the greatest number of votes for President, shall be the President, if such number be a majority of the whole number of Electors appointed; and if no person have such majority, then from the persons having the highest numbers not exceeding three on the list of those voted for as President, the House of Representatives shall choose immediately, by ballot, the President. But in choosing the President, the votes shall be taken by states, the representation from each state having one vote; a quorum for this purpose shall consist of a member or members from two-thirds of the states, and a majority of all the states shall be necessary to a choice. And if the House of

---

*The first ten amendments (the Bill of Rights) were ratified and their adoption was certified on December 15, 1791.

Representatives shall not choose a President whenever the right of choice shall devolve upon them, before *the fourth day of March* next following, then the Vice President shall act as President, as in the case of the death or other constitutional disability of the President.—The person having the greatest number of votes as Vice President, shall be the Vice President, if such number be a majority of the whole number of Electors appointed, and if no person have a majority, then from the two highest numbers on the list, the Senate shall choose the Vice President; a quorum for the purpose shall consist of two-thirds of the whole number of Senators, and a majority of the whole number shall be necessary to a choice. But no person constitutionally ineligible to the office of President shall be eligible to that of Vice President of the United States.

AMENDMENT XIII
[ADOPTED 1865]
Section 1

Neither slavery nor involuntary servitude, except as a punishment for crime whereof the party shall have been duly convicted, shall exist within the United States, or any place subject to their jurisdiction.

Section 2

Congress shall have power to enforce this article by appropriate legislation.

AMENDMENT XIV
[ADOPTED 1868]
Section 1

All persons born or naturalized in the United States, and subject to the jurisdiction thereof, are citizens of the United States and of the State wherein they reside. No State shall make or enforce any law which shall abridge the privileges or immunities of citizens of the United States; nor shall any State deprive any person of life, liberty, or property, without due process of law; nor deny to any person within its jurisdiction the equal protection of the laws.

Section 2

Representatives shall be apportioned among the several States according to their respective numbers, counting the whole number of persons in each State, excluding Indians not taxed. But when the right to vote at any election for the choice of electors for President and Vice President of the United States, Representatives in Congress, the Executive and Judicial officers of a State, or the members of the Legislature thereof, is denied to any of the male inhabitants of such State, being twenty-one years of age, and citizens of the United States, or in any way abridged, except for participation in rebellion, or other crime, the basis of representation therein shall be reduced in the proportion which the number of such male citizens shall bear to the whole number of male citizens twenty-one years of age in such State.

Section 3

No person shall be a Senator or Representative in Congress, or elector of President and Vice President, or hold any office, civil or military, under the United States, or under any State, who, having previously taken an oath, as a member of Congress, or as an officer of the United States, or as a member of any State legislature, or as an executive or judicial officer of any State, to support the Constitution of the United States, shall have engaged in insurrection or rebellion against the same, or given aid or comfort to the enemies thereof. But Congress may by a vote of two-thirds of each House, remove such disability.

Section 4

The validity of the public debt of the United States, authorized by law, including debts incurred for payment of pensions and bounties for services in suppressing insurrection or rebellion, shall not be questioned. But neither the United States nor any State shall assume or pay any debt or obligation incurred in aid of insurrection or rebellion against the United States, or any claim for the loss or emancipation of any slave; but all such debts, obligations and claims shall be held illegal and void.

Section 5

The Congress shall have power to enforce, by appropriate legislation, the provisions of this article.

AMENDMENT XV
[ADOPTED 1870]
Section 1

The right of citizens of the United States to vote shall not be denied or abridged by the United States or by any State on account of race, color, or previous condition of servitude.

Section 2

The Congress shall have power to enforce this article by appropriate legislation.

AMENDMENT XVI
[ADOPTED 1913]

The Congress shall have power to lay and collect taxes on incomes, from whatever source derived, without apportionment among the several States, and without regard to any census or enumeration.

AMENDMENT XVII
[ADOPTED 1913]

The Senate of the United States shall be composed of two Senators from each State, elected by the people thereof, for six years; and each Senator shall have one vote. The electors in each State shall have the qualifications requisite for electors of the most numerous branch of the State legislatures.

When vacancies happen in the representation of any State in the Senate, the executive authority of such State shall issue writs of election to fill such vacancies: *Provided,* That the legislature of any State may empower the executive thereof to make temporary appointments until the people fill the vacancies by election as the legislature may direct.

This amendment shall not be so construed as to affect the election or term of any Senator chosen before it becomes valid as part of the Constitution.

AMENDMENT XVIII
[ADOPTED 1919, REPEALED 1933]

Section 1

After one year from the ratification of this article the manufacture, sale, or transportation of intoxicating liquors within, the importation thereof into, or the exportation thereof from the United States and all territory subject to the jurisdiction thereof for beverage purposes is hereby prohibited.

Section 2

The Congress and the several States shall have concurrent power to enforce this article by appropriate legislation.

Section 3

This article shall be inoperative unless it shall have been ratified as an amendment to the Constitution by the legislatures of the several States, as provided in the Constitution, within seven years from the date of the submission hereof to the States by the Congress.

AMENDMENT XIX
[ADOPTED 1920]

The right of citizens of the United States to vote shall not be denied or abridged by the United States or by any State on account of sex.

Congress shall have power to enforce this article by appropriate legislation.

AMENDMENT XX
[ADOPTED 1933]

Section 1

The terms of the President and Vice President shall end at noon on the 20th day of January, and the terms of Senators and Representatives at noon on the 3d day of January, of the years in which such terms would have ended if this article had not been ratified and the terms of their successors shall then begin.

Section 2

The Congress shall assemble at least once in every year, and such meeting shall begin at noon on the 3d day of January, unless they shall by law appoint a different day.

Section 3

If, at the time fixed for the beginning of the term of the President, the President elect shall have died, the Vice President elect shall become President. If a President shall not have been chosen before the time fixed for the beginning of his term, or if the President elect shall have failed to qualify, then the Vice President elect shall act as President until a President shall have qualified; and the Congress may by law provide for the case wherein neither a President elect nor a Vice President elect shall have qualified, declaring

who shall then act as President, or the manner in which one who is to act shall be selected, and such person shall act accordingly until a President or Vice President shall have qualified.

Section 4

The Congress may by law provide for the case of the death of any of the persons from whom the House of Representatives may choose a President whenever the right of choice shall have devolved upon them, and for the case of the death of any of the persons from whom the Senate may choose a Vice President whenever the right of choice shall have devolved upon them.

Section 5

Sections 1 and 2 shall take effect on the 15th day of October following the ratification of this article.

Section 6

This article shall be inoperative unless it shall have been ratified as an amendment to the Constitution by the legislatures of three fourths of the several States within seven years from the date of its submission.

AMENDMENT XXI
[ADOPTED 1933]

Section 1

The eighteenth article of amendment to the Constitution of the United States is hereby repealed.

Section 2

The transportation or importation into any State, Territory, or possession of the United States for delivery or use therein of intoxicating liquors in violation of the laws thereof, is hereby prohibited.

Section 3

This article shall be inoperative unless it shall have been ratified as an amendment to the Constitution by conventions in the several States, as provided in the Constitution, within seven years from the date of the submission hereof to the States by the Congress.

AMENDMENT XXII
[ADOPTED 1951]

Section 1

No person shall be elected to the office of the President more than twice, and no person who has held the office of President, or acted as President, for more than two years of a term to which some other person was elected President shall be elected to the office of the President more than once. But this Article shall not apply to any person holding the office of President when this Article was proposed by the Congress, and shall not prevent any person who may be holding the office of President, or acting as President, during the term within which this Article becomes operative from holding the office of President or acting as President during the remainder of such term.

Section 2

This article shall be inoperative unless it shall have been ratified as an amendment to the Constitution by the legislatures of three-fourths of the several States within seven years from the date of its submission to the States by the Congress.

AMENDMENT XXIII

[ADOPTED 1961]

Section 1

The District constituting the seat of Government of the United States shall appoint in such manner as the Congress shall direct:

A number of electors of President and Vice President equal to the whole number of Senators and Representatives in Congress to which the District would be entitled if it were a State, but in no event more than the least populous State; they shall be in addition to those appointed by the States, but they shall be considered, for the purposes of the election of President and Vice President, to be electors appointed by a State; and they shall meet in the District and perform such duties as provided by the twelfth article of amendment.

Section 2

The Congress shall have power to enforce this article by appropriate legislation.

AMENDMENT XXIV

[ADOPTED 1964]

Section 1

The right of citizens of the United States to vote in any primary or other election for President or Vice President, for electors for President or Vice President, or for Senator or Representative in Congress, shall not be denied or abridged by the United States or any state by reason of failure to pay any poll tax or other tax.

Section 2

The Congress shall have the power to enforce this article by appropriate legislation.

AMENDMENT XXV

[ADOPTED 1967]

Section 1

In case of the removal of the President from office or his death or resignation, the Vice President shall become President.

Section 2

Whenever there is a vacancy in the office of the Vice President, the President shall nominate a Vice President who shall take the office upon confirmation by a majority vote of both houses of Congress.

Section 3

Whenever the President transmits to the President pro tempore of the Senate and the Speaker of the House of Representatives his written declaration that he is unable to discharge the powers and duties of his office, and until he transmits to them a written declaration to the contrary, such powers and duties shall be discharged by the Vice President as Acting President.

Section 4

Whenever the Vice President and a majority of either the principal officers of the executive departments or of such other body as Congress may by law provide, transmit to the President pro tempore of the Senate and the Speaker of the House of Representatives their written declaration that the President is unable to discharge the powers and duties of his office, the Vice President shall immediately assume the powers and duties of the office as Acting President.

Thereafter, when the President transmits to the President pro tempore of the Senate and the Speaker of the House of Representatives his written declaration that no inability exists, he shall resume the powers and duties of his office unless the Vice President and a majority of either the principal officers of the executive department or of such other body as Congress may by law provide, transmit within four days to the President pro tempore of the Senate and the Speaker of the House of Representatives their written declaration that the President is unable to discharge the powers and duties of his office. Thereupon Congress shall decide the issue, assembling within 48 hours for that purpose if not in session. If the Congress, within 21 days after receipt of the latter written declaration, or, if Congress is not in session, within 21 days after Congress is required to assemble, determines by two-thirds vote of both houses that the President is unable to discharge the powers and duties of his office, the Vice President shall continue to discharge the same as Acting President; otherwise, the President shall resume the powers and duties of his office.

AMENDMENT XXVI

[ADOPTED 1971]

Section 1

The right of citizens of the United States, who are 18 years of age or older, to vote shall not be denied or abridged by the United States or any state on account of age.

Section 2

The Congress shall have the power to enforce this article by appropriate legislation.

AMENDMENT XXVII

[ADOPTED 1992]

No law, varying the compensation for the services of the Senators and Representatives shall take effect, until an election of Representatives shall have intervened.

PRESIDENTIAL ELECTIONS

Year	Candidates	Parties	Popular Vote	Electoral Vote	Voter Participation
1789	**George Washington**		*	69	
	John Adams			34	
	Others			35	
1792	**George Washington**		*	132	
	John Adams			77	
	George Clinton			50	
	Others			5	
1796	**John Adams**	Federalist	*	71	
	Thomas Jefferson	Democratic-Republican		68	
	Thomas Pinckney	Federalist		59	
	Aaron Burr	Dem.-Rep.		30	
	Others			48	
1800	**Thomas Jefferson**	Dem.-Rep.	*	73	
	Aaron Burr	Dem.-Rep.		73	
	John Adams	Federalist		65	
	C. C. Pinckney	Federalist		64	
	John Jay	Federalist		1	
1804	**Thomas Jefferson**	Dem.-Rep.	*	162	
	C. C. Pinckney	Federalist		14	
1808	**James Madison**	Dem.-Rep.	*	122	
	C. C. Pinckney	Federalist		47	
	George Clinton	Dem.-Rep.		6	
1812	**James Madison**	Dem.-Rep.	*	128	
	De Witt Clinton	Federalist		89	
1816	**James Monroe**	Dem.-Rep.	*	183	
	Rufus King	Federalist		34	
1820	**James Monroe**	Dem.-Rep.	*	231	
	John Quincy Adams	Dem.-Rep.		1	
1824	**John Quincy Adams**	Dem.-Rep.	108,740 (30.5%)	84	26.9%
	Andrew Jackson	Dem.-Rep.	153,544 (43.1%)	99	
	William H. Crawford	Dem.-Rep.	46,618 (13.1%)	41	
	Henry Clay	Dem.-Rep.	47,136 (13.2%)	37	
1828	**Andrew Jackson**	Democratic	647,286 (56.0%)	178	57.6%
	John Quincy Adams	National Republican	508,064 (44.0%)	83	

*Electors selected by state legislatures.

Year	Candidates	Parties	Popular Vote	Electoral Vote	Voter Participation
1832	**Andrew Jackson**	Democratic	**688,242 (54.2%)**	219	55.4%
	Henry Clay	National Republican	473,462 (37.4%)	49	
	John Floyd	Independent		11	
	William Wirt	Anti-Mason	101,051 (7.8%)	7	
1836	**Martin Van Buren**	Democratic	**762,198 (50.8%)**	170	57.8%
	William Henry Harrison	Whig	549,508 (36.6%)	73	
	Hugh L. White	Whig	145,342 (9.7%)	26	
	Daniel Webster	Whig	41,287 (2.7%)	14	
	W. P. Magnum	Independent		11	
1840	**William Henry Harrison**	**Whig**	**1,274,624 (53.1%)**	234	80.2%
	Martin Van Buren	Democratic	1,127,781 (46.9%)	60	
	J. G. Birney	Liberty	7069	—	
1844	**James K. Polk**	Democratic	**1,338,464 (49.6%)**	170	78.9%
	Henry Clay	Whig	1,300,097 (48.1%)	105	
	J. G. Birney	Liberty	62,300 (2.3%)	—	
1848	**Zachary Taylor**	**Whig**	**1,360,967 (47.4%)**	163	72.7%
	Lewis Cass	Democratic	1,222,342 (42.5%)	127	
	Martin Van Buren	Free-Soil	291,263 (10.1%)	—	
1852	**Franklin Pierce**	Democratic	**1,601,117 (50.9%)**	254	69.6%
	Winfield Scott	Whig	1,385,453 (44.1%)	42	
	John P. Hale	Free-Soil	155,825 (5.0%)	—	
1856	**James Buchanan**	Democratic	**1,832,955 (45.3%)**	174	78.9%
	John C. Frémont	Republican	1,339,932 (33.1%)	114	
	Millard Fillmore	American	871,731 (21.6%)	8	
1860	**Abraham Lincoln**	Republican	**1,865,593 (39.8%)**	180	81.2%
	Stephen A. Douglas	Democratic	1,382,713 (29.5%)	12	
	John C. Breckinridge	Democratic	848,356 (18.1%)	72	
	John Bell	Union	592,906 (12.6%)	39	
1864	**Abraham Lincoln**	Republican	**2,213,655 (55.0%)**	212*	73.8%
	George B. McClellan	Democratic	1,805,237 (45.0%)	21	
1868	**Ulysses S. Grant**	Republican	**3,012,833 (52.7%)**	214	78.1%
	Horatio Seymour	Democratic	2,703,249 (47.3%)	80	
1872	**Ulysses S. Grant**	Republican	**3,597,132 (55.6%)**	286	71.3%
	Horace Greeley	Dem.; Liberal Republican	2,834,125 (43.9%)	66[†]	
1876	**Rutherford B. Hayes[‡]**	Republican	**4,036,298 (48.0%)**	185	81.8%
	Samuel J. Tilden	Democratic	4,300,590 (51.0%)	184	
1880	**James A. Garfield**	Republican	**4,454,416 (48.5%)**	214	79.4%
	Winfield S. Hancock	Democratic	4,444,952 (48.1%)	155	

*Eleven secessionist states did not participate.
[†]Greeley died before the electoral college met. His electoral votes were divided among the four minor candidates.
[‡]Contested result settled by special election.

Year	Candidates	Parties	Popular Vote	Electoral Vote	Voter Participation
1884	**Grover Cleveland**	**Democratic**	**4,874,986 (48.5%)**	**219**	77.5%
	James G. Blaine	Republican	4,851,981 (48.2%)	182	
1888	**Benjamin Harrison**	**Republican**	**5,439,853 (47.9%)**	**233**	79.3%
	Grover Cleveland	Democratic	5,540,309 (48.6%)	168	
1892	**Grover Cleveland**	**Democratic**	**5,556,918 (46.1%)**	**277**	74.7%
	Benjamin Harrison	Republican	5,176,108 (43.0%)	145	
	James B. Weaver	People's	1,029,329 (8.5%)	22	
1896	**William McKinley**	**Republican**	**7,104,779 (51.1%)**	**271**	79.3%
	William Jennings Bryan	Democratic People's	6,502,925 (47.7%)	176	
1900	**William McKinley**	**Republican**	**7,207,923 (51.7%)**	**292**	73.2%
	William Jennings Bryan	Dem.-Populist	6,358,133 (45.5%)	155	
1904	**Theodore Roosevelt**	**Republican**	**7,623,486 (57.9%)**	**336**	65.2%
	Alton B. Parker	Democratic	5,077,911 (37.6%)	140	
	Eugene V. Debs	Socialist	402,400 (3.0%)	—	
1908	**William H. Taft**	**Republican**	**7,678,908 (51.6%)**	**321**	65.4%
	William Jennings Bryan	Democratic	6,409,104 (43.1%)	162	
	Eugene V. Debs	Socialist	402,820 (2.8%)	—	
1912	**Woodrow Wilson**	**Democratic**	**6,293,454 (41.9%)**	**435**	58.8%
	Theodore Roosevelt	Progressive	4,119,538 (27.4%)	88	
	William H. Taft	Republican	3,484,980 (23.2%)	8	
	Eugene V. Debs	Socialist	900,672 (6.0%)	—	
1916	**Woodrow Wilson**	**Democratic**	**9,129,606 (49.4%)**	**277**	61.6%
	Charles E. Hughes	Republican	8,538,221 (46.2%)	254	
	A. L. Benson	Socialist	585,113 (3.2%)	—	
1920	**Warren G. Harding**	**Republican**	**16,152,200 (60.4%)**	**404**	49.2%
	James M. Cox	Democratic	9,147,353 (34.2%)	127	
	Eugene V. Debs	Socialist	917,799 (3.4%)	—	
1924	**Calvin Coolidge**	**Republican**	**15,725,016 (54.0%)**	**382**	48.9%
	John W. Davis	Democratic	8,386,503 (28.8%)	136	
	Robert M. La Follette	Progressive	4,822,856 (16.6%)	13	
1928	**Herbert Hoover**	**Republican**	**21,391,381 (58.2%)**	**444**	56.9%
	Alfred E. Smith	Democratic	15,016,443 (40.9%)	87	
	Norman Thomas	Socialist	267,835 (0.7%)	—	
1932	**Franklin D. Roosevelt**	**Democratic**	**22,821,857 (57.4%)**	**472**	56.9%
	Herbert Hoover	Republican	15,761,841 (39.7%)	59	
	Norman Thomas	Socialist	884,781 (2.2%)	—	
1936	**Franklin D. Roosevelt**	**Democratic**	**27,751,597 (60.8%)**	**523**	61.0%
	Alfred M. Landon	Republican	16,679,583 (36.5%)	8	
	William Lemke	Union	882,479 (1.9%)	—	
1940	**Franklin D. Roosevelt**	**Democratic**	**27,244,160 (54.8%)**	**449**	62.5%
	Wendell L. Willkie	Republican	22,305,198 (44.8%)	82	
1944	**Franklin D. Roosevelt**	**Democratic**	**25,602,504 (53.5%)**	**432**	55.9%
	Thomas E. Dewey	Republican	22,006,285 (46.0%)	99	

Year	Candidates	Parties	Popular Vote	Electoral Vote	Voter Participation
1948	**Harry S Truman**	Democratic	**24,105,695 (49.5%)**	**304**	**53.0%**
	Thomas E. Dewey	Republican	21,969,170 (45.1%)	189	
	J. Strom Thurmond	State-Rights Democratic	1,169,021 (2.4%)	38	
	Henry A. Wallace	Progressive	1,157,326 (2.4%)	—	
1952	**Dwight D. Eisenhower**	Republican	**33,778,963 (55.1%)**	**442**	**63.3%**
	Adlai E. Stevenson	Democratic	27,314,992 (44.4%)	89	
1956	**Dwight D. Eisenhower**	Republican	**35,575,420 (57.6%)**	**457**	**60.6%**
	Adlai E. Stevenson	Democratic	26,033,066 (42.1%)	73	
	Other	—	—	1	
1960	**John F. Kennedy**	Democratic	**34,227,096 (49.9%)**	**303**	**62.8%**
	Richard M. Nixon	Republican	34,108,546 (49.6%)	219	
	Other	—	—	15	
1964	**Lyndon B. Johnson**	Democratic	**43,126,506 (61.1%)**	**486**	**61.7%**
	Barry M. Goldwater	Republican	27,176,799 (38.5%)	52	
1968	**Richard M. Nixon**	Republican	**31,770,237 (43.4%)**	**301**	**60.6%**
	Hubert H. Humphrey	Democratic	31,270,533 (42.7%)	191	
	George Wallace	American Indep.	9,906,141 (13.5%)	46	
1972	**Richard M. Nixon**	Republican	**46,740,323 (60.7%)**	**520**	**55.2%**
	George S. McGovern	Democratic	28,901,598 (37.5%)	17	
	Other	—	—	1	
1976	**Jimmy Carter**	Democratic	**40,828,587 (50.0%)**	**297**	**53.5%**
	Gerald R. Ford	Republican	39,147,613 (47.9%)	241	
	Other	—	1,575,459 (2.1%)	—	
1980	**Ronald Reagan**	Republican	**43,901,812 (50.7%)**	**489**	**52.6%**
	Jimmy Carter	Democratic	35,483,820 (41.0%)	49	
	John B. Anderson	Independent	5,719,437 (6.6%)	—	
	Ed Clark	Libertarian	921,188 (1.1%)	—	
1984	**Ronald Reagan**	Republican	**54,455,075 (59.0%)**	**525**	**53.3%**
	Walter Mondale	Democratic	37,577,185 (41.0%)	13	
1988	**George H. W. Bush**	Republican	**48,886,097 (53.4%)**	**426**	**57.4%**
	Michael S. Dukakis	Democratic	41,809,074 (45.6%)	111	
1992	**William J. Clinton**	Democratic	**44,908,254 (43%)**	**370**	**55.0%**
	George H. W. Bush	Republican	39,102,343 (37.5%)	168	
	H. Ross Perot	Independent	19,741,065 (18.9%)	—	
1996	**William J. Clinton**	Democratic	**45,590,703 (50%)**	**379**	**48.8%**
	Robert Dole	Republican	37,816,307 (41%)	159	
	Ross Perot	Reform	7,866,284	—	
2000	**George W. Bush**	Republican	**50,456,167 (47.88%)**	**271**	**51.2%**
	Al Gore	Democratic	50,996,064 (48.39%)	266*	
	Ralph Nader	Green	2,864,810 (2.72%)	—	
	Other		834,774 (less than 1%)	—	
2004	**George W. Bush**	Republican	**60,934,251 (51.0%)**	**286**	**50.0%**
	John F. Kerry	Democratic	57,765,291 (48.0%)	252	
	Ralph Nader	Independent	405,933 (less than 1%)	—	

*One District of Columbia Gore elector abstained.

Presidents and Vice Presidents

	President	Vice President	Term
1.	George Washington	John Adams	1789–1793
	George Washington	John Adams	1793–1797
2.	John Adams	Thomas Jefferson	1797–1801
3.	Thomas Jefferson	Aaron Burr	1801–1805
	Thomas Jefferson	George Clinton	1805–1809
4.	James Madison	George Clinton (d. 1812)	1809–1813
	James Madison	Elbridge Gerry (d. 1814)	1813–1817
5.	James Monroe	Daniel Tompkins	1817–1821
	James Monroe	Daniel Tompkins	1821–1825
6.	John Quincy Adams	John C. Calhoun	1825–1829
7.	Andrew Jackson	John C. Calhoun	1829–1833
	Andrew Jackson	Martin Van Buren	1833–1837
8.	Martin Van Buren	Richard M. Johnson	1837–1841
9.	William H. Harrison (d. 1841)	John Tyler	1841
10.	John Tyler	—	1841–1845
11.	James K. Polk	George M. Dallas	1845–1849
12.	Zachary Taylor (d. 1850)	Millard Fillmore	1849–1850
13.	Millard Fillmore	—	1850–1853
14.	Franklin Pierce	William R. King (d. 1853)	1853–1857
15.	James Buchanan	John C. Breckinridge	1857–1861
16.	Abraham Lincoln	Hannibal Hamlin	1861–1865
	Abraham Lincoln (d. 1865)	Andrew Johnson	1865
17.	Andrew Johnson	—	1865–1869
18.	Ulysses S. Grant	Schuyler Colfax	1869–1873
	Ulysses S. Grant	Henry Wilson (d. 1875)	1873–1877
19.	Rutherford B. Hayes	William A. Wheeler	1877–1881
20.	James A. Garfield (d. 1881)	Chester A. Arthur	1881
21.	Chester A. Arthur	—	1881–1885
22.	Grover Cleveland	Thomas A. Hendricks (d. 1885)	1885–1889
23.	Benjamin Harrison	Levi P. Morton	1889–1893
24.	Grover Cleveland	Adlai E. Stevenson	1893–1897
25.	William McKinley	Garret A. Hobart (d. 1899)	1897–1901
	William McKinley (d. 1901)	Theodore Roosevelt	1901
26.	Theodore Roosevelt	—	1901–1905
	Theodore Roosevelt	Charles Fairbanks	1905–1909
27.	William H. Taft	James S. Sherman (d. 1912)	1909–1913
28.	Woodrow Wilson	Thomas R. Marshall	1913–1917
	Woodrow Wilson	Thomas R. Marshall	1917–1921
29.	Warren G. Harding (d. 1923)	Calvin Coolidge	1921–1923

	President	Vice President	Term
30.	Calvin Coolidge	—	1923–1925
	Calvin Coolidge	Charles G. Dawes	1925–1929
31.	Herbert Hoover	Charles Curtis	1929–1933
32.	Franklin D. Roosevelt	John N. Garner	1933–1937
	Franklin D. Roosevelt	John N. Garner	1937–1941
	Franklin D. Roosevelt	Henry A. Wallace	1941–1945
	Franklin D. Roosevelt (d. 1945)	Harry S Truman	1945
33.	Harry S Truman	—	1945–1949
	Harry S Truman	Alben W. Barkley	1949–1953
34.	Dwight D. Eisenhower	Richard M. Nixon	1953–1957
	Dwight D. Eisenhower	Richard M. Nixon	1957–1961
35.	John F. Kennedy (d. 1963)	Lyndon B. Johnson	1961–1963
36.	Lyndon B. Johnson	—	1963–1965
	Lyndon B. Johnson	Hubert H. Humphrey	1965–1969
37.	Richard M. Nixon	Spiro T. Agnew	1969–1973
	Richard M. Nixon (resigned 1974)	Gerald R. Ford	1973–1974
38.	Gerald R. Ford	Nelson A. Rockefeller	1974–1977
39.	Jimmy Carter	Walter F. Mondale	1977–1981
40.	Ronald Reagan	George H.W. Bush	1981–1985
	Ronald Reagan	George H.W. Bush	1985–1989
41.	George H.W. Bush	J. Danforth Quayle	1989–1993
42.	William J. Clinton	Albert Gore, Jr.	1993–1997
	William J. Clinton	Albert Gore, Jr.	1997–2001
43.	George W. Bush	Richard Cheney	2001–2005
	George W. Bush	Richard Cheney	2005–

Credits

CHAPTER 1

3 Courtesy of the National Museum of the American Indian, Smithsonian Institution. Photo by Carmelo Guagagno.; **7** The Granger Collection, New York; **9B** Clement N'Taye/AP/Wide World Photo; **9T** Werner Forman/Art Resource, NY; **14** © North Wind Picture Archives; **18** © Courtesy of the Trustees of The British Museum

CHAPTER 2

25 Association for the Preservation of Virginia Antiquities; **26** The Granger Collection, New York; **31** © Paul Skilling; **35** The Library Company of Philadelphia

CHAPTER 3

43 New York Public Library, Astor, Lenox and Tilden Foundations/Art Resource; **45L** Worcester Art Museum, Worcester, Massachusetts, Sarah C. Garver Fund; **45R** Worcester Art Museum, Worcester, Massachusetts, Gift of Mr. and Mrs. Albert Rice; **47** The Maryland Historical Society; **49** Abby Aldrich Rockefeller Folk Art Museum, The Colonial Williamsburg Foundation, Williamsburg, VA; **53** © Shelburne Museum, Shelburne, VT

CHAPTER 4

59 Pennsylvania German Painted Box by Elmer G. Anderson. Index of American Design, © 2005 Board of trustees, National Gallery of Art, Washington, DC; **62** © Richard Cummins/Corbis; **65** Courtesy of Westover; **68** The National Portrait Gallery, London; **74** Courtesy of the Trustees of the British Library; **80** Scott Mickievicz

CHAPTER 5

83 Courtesy of the John Carter Brown Library at Brown University; **86** Stamp Act Repeal'd, English, 1766. Cream colored earthenware, lead glazed and hand painted. Photograph by Mark Sexton. Peabody Essex Museum; **88** The Library of Congress; **89** Courtesy, American Antiquarian Society; **95** The Historical Society of Pennsylvania/Atwater Kent Museum

CHAPTER 6

107 The Library Company of Philadelphia; **113L** Smithsonian Institution; **113R** Smithsonian Institution; **118** *Liberty Displaying the Arts and Sciences,* by Samuel Jennings. The Library Company of Philadelphia

CHAPTER 7

127 From the Collections of the Henry Ford Museum and Greenfield Village; **133** The Ohio Historical Society; **137** Courtesy Lilly Library, Indiana University, Bloomington, Ind.; **139** The Library of Congress; **140** *Mourning Picture for George Washington,* Ink on Paper, Thomas Clarke, prob.1801. Collection of Old Sturbridge Village, 20.8.6.; **145** National Museum of American History, Smithsonian Institution

CHAPTER 8

152 Peabody Museum of Archaeology and Ethnology, Harvard University; **156** Abby Aldrich Rockefeller Folk Art Museum, The Colonial Williamsburg Foundation, Williamsburg, VA; **157** Collection of The New-York Historical Society. Negative number 7278; **161** Collection of Davenport West, Jr.

CHAPTER 9

168 Courtesy of The Newberry Library, Chicago; **170** The Library of Congress; **173** The Granger Collection, New York; **174** © John Eastcott/ YVA Momatiuk/Photo Researchers, Inc.; **176** American Textile History Museum, Lowell, MA

CHAPTER 10

187 *General Andrew Jackson,* 1845, oil on canvas, 97-$\frac{1}{4}$ × 61-$\frac{1}{2}$ inches. In the collection of the Corcoran Gallery of Art, Gift of William Wilson Corcoran; **188** *Rustic Dance After a Sleigh Ride* by William Sidney Mount, 1830, oil on canvas, 22-$\frac{1}{8}$ × 27-$\frac{1}{8}$ inches. Museum of Fine Arts, Boston, Bequest of Martha C. Karolik for the M. and M. Karolik Collection of American Paintings, 1815-1865, 48.458. Reproduced with Permission; **190** *The Union,* 1836. Courtesy, New York Public Library/ Art Resource; **196** Collection of the New-York Historical Society. Negative number 42459; **199** Collection of David J. and Janice L. Frent; **200** The Saint Louis Art Museum

CHAPTER 11

206 The New-York Historical Society; **208** North Carolina Museum of Art, Raleigh, purchased with funds from the state of North Carolina; **210** The Library of Congress; **213** The Museum of the Confederacy, Richmond, Virginia. Photography by Katherine Wetzel; **220** The Library of Congress; **224** Fair Street Pictures

CHAPTER 12

227 Chicago Historical Society; **230** Fruitlands Museums, Harvard, Massachusetts; **233** © Susan Oristaglio/Esto Photographics, Inc.; **234** Photo by Mark Sexton Photograph Courtesy Peabody Essex Museum.; **236** Bettmann/Corbis; **237** Massachusetts Historical Society; **239** National Portrait Gallery, Smithsonian Institution/Art Resource, NY

CHAPTER 13

250 Handcart Pioneers by CCA Christensen. © by Intellectual Reserve, Inc. Courtesy of Museum of Church History and Art. Used by Permission; **254** © Bettmann/Corbis; **259** National Museum of American History

CHAPTER 14

266 New York Public Library, Astor, Lenox and Tilden Foundations; **272** New York Public Library, Astor, Lenox and Tilden Foundation; **276** From the Bella C. Landaur Collection of Business and Advertising Art. Collection of The New-York Historical Society.; **279** *Detail from The Last Moments of John Brown.* The Metropolitan Museum of Art, Gift of Mr. and Mrs. Carl Stoeckel, 1897. (97.5)Photograph © 1982 The Metropolitan Museum of Art; **280** The Library of Congress; **285** Blessing of the Enrequita Mine by Alexander Edouart, 1860. Bancroft Library, University of California, Berkeley

CHAPTER 15

290 The Library of Congress; **293L** National Museum of American History, Smithsonian Institution; **293R** The Museum of the Confederacy, Richmond, Va. Photography by Katherine Wetzel; **297** The Library of Congress; **301** The Library of Congress; **305** Harper's Weekly

CHAPTER 16

313 The Library of Congress; **318** Collection of the New-York Historical Society; **320** © Bettmann/Corbis; **323** Fair Street Pictures; **326** © Corbis

ON PAGE CREDITS

49R Pocomtuck Valley Memorial Association Library, Deerfield, Massachusetts

Index

Key terms and the text page on which the term is defined are highlighted in boldface type.

A

Abenaki Indians, 4

Abolition and abolitionism, 229; anti-Constitutionalism in, 266; black, 238–239; critique of, 239; evangelicalism and, 225; Jacksonian democracy and, 190; literary, 275–276; Nat Turner rebellion and, 204; revivalism and, 237–238; South and, 215–216; women's rights and, 238, 239; yeoman farmers and, 214. *See also* Antislavery movement

Abortion: in 19th century, 234

Accommodation: by Five Civilized Tribes, 168

Act of Supremacy (England), 16

Adams, Abigail, 106

Adams, Charles Francis, 298

Adams, John, 91; Alien and Sedition Acts and, 138; death of, 163; election of 1800 and, 140–142; at First Continental Congress, 90; Jeffersonians and, 146; Massachusetts constitution and, 108; midnight judicial appointments of, 153; peace with France and, 139–140; Philadelphia Convention and, 116; presidency of, 136–140; on president's title, 125; republican government and, 104; Treaty of Paris (1783) and, 100

Adams, John Quincy: administration of, 191; election of 1824 and, 190–191; election of 1828 and, 191–192; Monroe Doctrine and, 182; as secretary of state, 166, 178, 181–182

Adams, Samuel, 88–89, 90, 104

Adams-Onís Treaty (1818), **166**, 245

Adaptation: creative, 2

Adena people, 3

Affluence. *See* Wealth

Africa: European compounds in, 9 (illus.); influences on slave religion, 208, 209; Liberia colony in, 237; slave trade from, 48; triangular trade with, 66. *See also* West Africa

African Americans: as abolitionists, 238–239, 239 (illus.); African customs of, 50 (illus.); antidraft riots and, 300; Black Codes and, 312–313, 317–318; in British army, 94; census of 1790 and, 144, 145; Civil War and, 299–300, 301 (illus.), 304, 309; contract labor system and, 317; convict-lease system and, 328; emancipation and, 299; Fifteenth Amendment and, 322; hotel culture and, 184; identity of, 49; institutions of, 320; Jim Crow laws and, 327; Ku Klux Klan and, 322; lynchings of, 326 (illus.), 327; marriage and, 320; in New South, 327–328; in political office, 319, 327; population of, 146, 147; during Reconstruction, 309–310; religion of, 208–209; after Revolution, 105–106; in Second Seminole War, 169; as Seminole Negroes (estelusti), 168, 169; sharecropping and, 317; violence against, 323–324; voting and, 327; women and, 231. *See also* Freedpeople; Slaves and slavery

African Methodist Episcopal (AME) Church, 106, **208,** 321

African slaves. *See* Slaves and slavery

Agricultural colleges, 305

Agricultural fair, 148

Agricultural Revolution, 3

Agriculture: Anasazi, 3; during Civil War, 292, 293; commercial, 174–175; contract labor system in, 317; crop lien system of, 327; of Indians, 168; labor for, 177; mechanization of, 258–259; in New England, 44; in 19th century, 148; plantation, 211, 218, 220; river transportation and, 172; sharecropping in, 317; slavery and, 205, 206, 219–220; in South, 216–218; tariffs and, 177; western, 170; workforce for, 257–258. *See also* Farms and farming; Planters and plantations

Air-boiling process, 258 (illus.)

Aix-la-Chapelle, Treaty of, 72

Alabama: Indian removal and, 193; secession of, 287

Alamo, battle of, **248**

Albany: as Fort Orange, 33

Albany Congress, 73–74

Albany Plan, 74

Albany Regency, 191

Albemarle region, 36

Alcohol and alcoholism: consumption of, 229, 230; Indians and, 8

Alexander I (Russia), 181

Algiers, 8, 152

Algonquian Indians: death rates of, 8; fishing by, 18 (illus.)

Algonquian-speaking peoples, 4–5

Alien and Sedition Acts (1798), **138**–139, 149

Alien Enemies Law, 138

Alien Law (1798), 138

Allen, Richard, 106, 208

Alliance(s): with France, 96–97; Washington's warning against, 136

Alliance, Treaty of, 96

"All Mexico" movement, 255

Alphabet: Cherokee, 168, 168 (illus.)

Alton, Illinois: antiabolitionist violence in, 237–238

Amendments: Bill of Rights and, 122. *See also* specific amendments

American: meaning of term, 79–80

American Bible Society, 228

American Board of Customs Commissioners, 86

American Colonization Society, 215, 237

American Crisis (Paine), 95

American Indians. *See* Native Americans

American party, 272, 275. *See also* Know-Nothing party

American Peace Society, 237

"American plan": in hotels, 184

"American Republicans": nativists as, 273

American Revolution, 92 (map), 93–97; Continental Army in, 94; final campaign in, 97; Loyalists after, 98–99; opening battles of, 90; peace settlement after, 99–100; as world conflict, 96–97

American system (Clay), **177,** 191, 199, 251

American Temperance Society, 230

Americas: Columbus in, 11; Europeans in, 6–8; naming of, 11; Spanish colonization in, 12–14

Amherst, Jeffrey, 74, 75

Amity and Commerce, Treaty of, 96

Anaconda policy, 292

Anasazi culture, 3

Andros, Edmund, 54

Anglican Church. *See* Church of England (Anglican Church)

Anglicization: of colonial culture, 52, 79–80

state, 149, 153; Virginia Plan of, 116–117; War of 1812 and, 159

Magazines: in Jacksonian era, 186

Magistrates: in Massachusetts Bay, 30–31

Maine, 33; boundary of, 245, 246 (map); statehood for, 179

Mainland colonies: English, 37. *See also* Colonies and colonization

Majority rule principle: Hispanics and, 263–264; southern secession and, 289

Malaria, 46

Management: in mills, 260

Mandan Indians, 152 (illus.)

Manifest Destiny, 246 (map), **250,** 270, 271; controversies over, 256; doctrine of, 252; Mexican-American War and, 250–256; politics of, 251

Mann, Horace, 235

Manufacturing: continuous process, 257, 261; in early 19th century, 149; in 1815, 175; factory system and, 176; Hamilton on, 130–131; "putting-out" system of, 175–176; shift of capital to, 176; of toys, 234 (illus.)

Maps: of colonial frontiers, 57

Marbury, William, 153

Marbury v. *Madison,* **153**

Marcy, William, 272

Marian exiles: in England, 16

Marines (U.S.): at Harpers Ferry, 278

Market(s): for agricultural goods, 170; mercantilism and, 50

Market economy: commerce and banking in, 175; commercial agriculture in, 174–175; industrialization and, 175–177; Marshall Court and, 181; wealth gap and, 190; Whigs and, 201; Young America movement and, 244, 245

Marketing: agriculture and, 174, 175

Maroon communities, 168

Marquette, Jacques, 14

Marriage: in antebellum era, 223; in Chesapeake, 46; freedmen and, 320; among Indians, 7; for love, 231; in New England, 42–43; slaves and, 207, 208 (illus.)

Marshall, John, 137, 154; Burr and, 155; as chief justice, 141, 153, 180–181; implied powers doctrine of, 180–181

Martha's Vineyard, 33

Martial law: during Civil War, 295

Mary I (Tudor, England), 16

Mary II (England), 54

Maryland: Civil War in, 297; colony of, 27–28; families in, 45–47; Glorious Revolution in, 55; martial law in, 291; Pennsylvania and, 35–36

Mason, George: Bill of Rights and, 121; at Philadelphia Convention, 116, 119

Mason, James M., 298

Massachusetts: church in, 31 (illus.); in Dominion of New England, 53; restructuring of, 89; royal charter for, 54

Massachusetts Bay Colony, 29, 30–32; colonies created from, 32; Glorious Revolution in, 53–54; Hutchinson in, 31–32; sumptuary laws in, 44; Williams in, 31; witchcraft and, 54

Massachusetts Bay Company: annulment of charter, 53; charter for, 29

Massachusetts House of Representatives: circular letter by, 87

Massasoit, 29

Mass democracy: election of 1828 and, 191

Mass production, 257

Master-slave relationship, 212–213, 215

Matamoros, battle at, 254

Material culture: in colonies, 52

Mather, Cotton, 54, 55

Mather, Increase, 54

Matrifocal slave families: slavery and, 207

Matrilineal kinship system: of Cherokee, 168

Mayan peoples, 4

Mayflower (ship), 28

Mayflower Compact, 28

Mayr, Christian, 208 (illus.)

Maysville Road, 194

McCarthy, Joseph R.: politics of fear and, 73

McClellan, George: in Civil War, 296, 297, 297 (illus.); election of 1864 and, 303

McCormick, Cyrus, 258, 258 (illus.)

McCulloch v. *Maryland,* **180**

McDowell, Irvin, 296

McGuffey's Eclectic Readers, 235

McHenry, Fort, 160

Meade, George, 303

Measles, 6, 8

Mechanic's institutes, 235

Mechanization: in textile industry, 176

Melodramas, 187

Melting pot image, 285

Melville, Herman, 188, 244

Memphis: race riots in, 314

Men: Cult of Domesticity and, 232; as indentured servants, 46; Jacksonian era clothing for, 187 (illus.)

Menéndez de Avilés, Pedro, 62

Mentally ill: reform and, 236 (illus.)

Mercantilism, 50

Mercenaries: German, 91

Mercer, William, 95 (illus.)

Merchant marine, 148

Merchants: wealth of, 148, 149

Merino sheep, 174 (illus.)

Merrimack (ship), 296

Mestizos, 13, 62

Metacomet (King Philip, Wampanoag), 53, 53 (illus.)

Methodists, 225, 226

Mexican-American War, 245, 253–**254,** 255 (map), 286; Guadalupe Hidalgo Treaty and, 254–256; political dissension caused by, 256

Mexican cession, 246 (map), 255–256; Compromise of 1850 and, 268–269, 269 (map); Missouri Compromise and, 267; slavery in, 265, 266

Mexicans and Mexican Americans: after Mexican-American War, 263–264

Mexico: Americans in Texas and, 247–248; Aztecs in, 4; Cortés in, 12; illegal immigrants from, 273; recognition of, 181; Santa Fe trade and, 248; Texas Revolution and, 247; U.S. expansionism and, 244, 245–246; wealth in, 12

Mexico City: siege of, 254

Micco (Seminole chief), 169

Michilimackinac, 159

Middle class: blacks in Reconstruction-era, 310; children in, 233–234; revivalism and, 225, 228; Whigs and, 197; women in, 232–233

Middle Colonies: blacks in, 49; cultural diversity in, 32–36; in 1685, 33 (map)

Middle ground, 61

Middle West: Second Great Awakening in, 226

Midnight appointments: by Adams, John, 141, 153

Migrants and migration: to Carolina, 37; from England, 22; on frontier, 170–171; by Mormons, 249–250, 249 (map); to North America, 2; by Puritans, 29–30; from Spain to New World, 13; after War of 1812, 166; to West, 104; along western trails, 248, 249 (map). *See also* Immigrants and immigration

Milan Decree (1807), 156

Military: British, 71. *See also* Armed forces; specific battles and wars

Military academy: at West Point, 150

Military districts: in Reconstruction South, 314 (map), 315, 318

Militia: blacks in, 105; in Civil War, 290; of freedmen, 318; Jefferson and, 150; in Lexington, 90; during War of 1812, 159

Miller, Lewis, 156 (illus.)

Mill girls: labor militancy of, 176

Mines and mining: Mexican Americans and, 263

Minorca, 62

Minorities, 79

"Minutemen," 90

Missions and missionaries: revivalism and, 228; Spanish, 12–13, 62, 62 (illus.)

O

P

Popular sovereignty, 185, **267,** 268, 277, 286; in arts, 188; *Dred Scott* case and, 278; in Kansas, 274; Kansas-Nebraska Act and, 271 (map)

Popular vote: presidential electors chosen by, 189

Population: in agriculture, 148; beyond Appalachians (1810 and 1840), 169; black, 48; of Boston, 284; census of 1790 and, 144–145; in Chesapeake, 46; in cities, 148; colonial, 58–59, 63; in early 19th century, 147; of immigrants, 259; of Louisiana Territory, 152; of New England, 42; of New Jersey, 34; of slaves, 216; of Spanish to Americas, 13; after Texas independence, 248; of Virginia, 26. *See also* Immigrants and immigration

Port cities: cotton exported from, 175; on Ohio River, 147

Port Gibson: battle at, 302 (map)

Portolá, Gaspar de, 62

Port Royal region, 36

Port towns, 63–64

Portugal: Africa and, 9; exploration by, 11; Treaty of Tordesillas and, 12

Positive good defense: of slavery, 206, 210, 215

Potato blight: in Ireland, 259, 263

Poverty: in cities, 260. *See also* Poor people

Power (political): under Articles of Confederation, 109; of blacks, 309–310; colonial factions and, 52–55; of people, 108; virtue and, 84; Washington and, 126

Power loom, 176, 176 (illus.)

Powhatan Indians, 4

Predestination doctrine, 227, 228

Preemption rights, 170

Prejudice: in Old South, 205; against *Tejanos,* 248. *See also* Discrimination

Presbyterians, 59, 226, 227, 228

Prescott, Samuel, 90

Presidency: national parties and, 191; "Virginia dynasty" of, 178

President: electors for, 189; selection of, 117; title of, 125; Washington as, 126–127. *See also* Executive; specific presidents

Presidential pardons: for Confederates, 311

Presidential powers. *See* Executive power

Presidential Reconstruction, 312–313

Presidios: Spanish, 62

Princeton: battle of, 95 (illus.)

Princeton University, 68

Principall Navigations, Voyages, and Discoveries of the English Nation, The (Hakluyt), 19–20

Printing: colonial, 91; rotary press, 258 (illus.); technological revolution in, 187

Printing press, 11

Prisons, 236; reform movement in, 229

Privateers: French, 136; in War of 1812, 160

Private schools, 235. *See also* Education; Schools

Proclamation of 1763, 84

Production: craft mode of, 257; factory form of, 175, 176, 257; mass, 257; standardization in, 176; technology and, 66

Professions: during Jacksonian era, 186

Profitability: of slavery, 219–220

Progress, 103

Prohibitory Act (1775), 91

Propaganda: political, 135; politics of fear and, 73; proslavery, 216; for Texas annexation, 251

Property qualifications: for voting, 322

Property rights, 180

Property taxes: for public education, 235

Proposition 187 (California), 273

Proprietors: in Carolina, 36; in Pennsylvania, 35

Proslavery argument, 215

Prosser, Gabriel, 209

Prostitution: revivalism and, 229; working class women and, 231

Protective tariffs: Hamilton on, 130; nullification crisis and, 194–195. *See also* Tariff(s)

Protest(s): popular colonial, 85–86; by slaves, 49

Protestant Association, 55

Protestant ethic: in public schools, 235

Protestant Reformation, 15–16, 29

Protestants and Protestantism: English colonization and, 15; evangelicalism and, 67–68, 225–228; of German settlers, 59; Mary I (England) and, 16; tensions with Catholics, 55

Protracted meetings, 226

Providence, 31

Provisional council: in Pennsylvania, 35

Public education: expansion of, 235; in New England, 43; in South, 319. *See also* Education; Schools

Public facilities: equal access laws and, 318

Public opinion, 125–126, 281

Public policies: after War of 1812, 177

Public services: in South, 319

Pueblos, 3

Puget Sound, 253

Pullman, George M., 258 (illus.)

Pullman car, 258 (illus.)

Punishment: of slaves, 213. *See also* Crime and criminals

Puritans, 29–31; families of, 42; on Long Island, 33; in New England, 22; revivalism and, 227–228; society of, 42–44. *See also* New England

Put-in-Bay: battle at, 160

Putting-out system, 175–176

Q

Quakers, 33 (map), **34**–36, 103

Quasi-War, 136–137, 138

Quebec, 71, 72 (map), 74; British conquest of, 75; Champlain at, 14 (illus.)

Quebec Act (1774), 89–90

Queen Anne's War, 71, 75

Quetzalcoatl, 12

Quinine: for Civil War soldiers, 293 (illus.)

Quotas: for immigration, 273

R

"Rabble-rousers": Jacksonians as, 189

Race and racism: annexation of Mexico and, 255; antiabolitionist violence and, 238; antidraft riots and, 300; in British America, 47–49; congressional representation and, 144; emancipation and, 299; Hispanics and, 263–264; mulattos and, 49; in New South, 326, 327–328; in Old South, 205; paternalism of planters and, 212–213; yeoman farmers and, 214

Race riots: in Memphis, 314; in New Orleans, 314; in South (1875), 324

Racial theories: nativism and, 273

Radical Reconstruction, 314–315, 318, 319, 325

Radical Republicans, 303, 304, **311,** 316; Black Codes and, 313; emancipation and, 299; presidential Reconstruction and, 312; Reconstruction and, 311, 314–315

Radicals and radicalism: of labor, 190; reform movements and, 236–242

Raiders (ships): Confederate, 298

Railroads: canals and, 173; in Civil War, 293; growth of, 256–257; Irish immigrants and, 284; land grants to, 305; Pullman car for, 258 (illus.); segregation and, 318; slaves and, 206; in South, 319; steam locomotive for, 256, 258 (illus.); suburbs and, 260; transcontinental, 270–271, 305

Ralegh, Walter: Roanoke and, 18–19; second colony of, 19

Rancheros: in California, 246

PRESENT DAY WORLD

| | 1 | 2 | | | 6 | 7 |

ARCTIC OCEAN

80°

GREENLAND

Beaufort Sea

Baffin Bay

ALASKA (U.S.)

C A N A D A

ICELAND

60°

Bering Sea

Gulf of Alaska

Hudson Bay

Labrador Sea

40°

UNITED STATES

ATLANTIC OCEAN

MOROCCO

SEE CARIBBEAN INSET

Hawaiian Islands (U.S.)

MEXICO

Gulf of Mexico

BELIZE

WESTERN SAHARA

20°

CAPE VERDE

MAURITANIA

BURK. FASO

GUATEMALA

EL SALVADOR

Caribbean Sea

SENEGAL

THE GAMBIA

GUINEA-BISSAU

MALI

GUINEA

PACIFIC OCEAN

COLOMBIA

FRENCH GUIANA (FR.)

SIERRA LEONE

LIBERIA

CÔTE D'IVOIRE

Galapagos Islands (EQ.)

ECUADOR

SURINAME

GHANA

0°

KIRIBATI

SÃO TOMÉ & PRÍNCIPE

TOKELAU

PERU

B R A Z I L

SAMOA

AM. SAMOA

COOK ISLANDS

FRENCH POLYNESIA

TONGA

20°

BOLIVIA

PARAGUAY

ATLANTIC OCEAN

CHILE

URUGUAY

ARGENTINA

40°

Falkland Islands (U.K.)

South Georgia (U.K.)

0   1500   3000 mi

0   1500   3000 km

Weddell Sea

A N T A R C T I C A

Caribbean Inset

80°   70°   60°

UNITED STATES

BAHAMAS

0   300   600 mi

0   300   600 km

ATLANTIC OCEAN

CUBA

Turks & Caicos Is. (U.K.)

Cayman Is. (U.K.)

HAITI

DOMINICAN REPUBLIC

PUERTO RICO (U.S.)

Virgin Is.(U.S.)

ANTIGUA & BARBUDA

20°

JAMAICA

ST. KITTS AND NEVIS

GUADALOUPE

HONDURAS

Caribbean Sea

DOMINICA

MARTINIQUE

ST. LUCIA

NICARAGUA

ST. VINCENT AND THE GRENADINES

BARBADOS

CURACAO

GRENADA

TRINIDAD AND TOBAGO

COSTA RICA

PANAMA

COLOMBIA

VENEZUELA

GUYANA

10°

| | 1 | 2 | 3 | 4 | 5 | 6 | 7 |